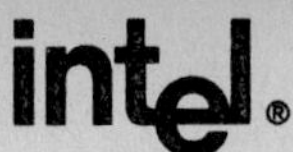

U.S. and CANADA LITERATURE ORDER FORM

NAME: ______________________

COMPANY: ______________________

ADDRESS: ______________________

CITY: ______________ STATE: ________ ZIP: ________

COUNTRY: ______________________

PHONE NO.: ( ) ______________________

ORDER NO.	TITLE	QTY.		PRICE		TOTAL
			×		=	
			×		=	
			×		=	
			×		=	
			×		=	
			×		=	
			×		=	
			×		=	
			×		=	
			×		=	

Subtotal ________

Must Add Your Local Sales Tax ________

Include postage:
Must add 15% of Subtotal to cover U.S. and Canada postage. (20% all other.) → Postage ________

Total ________

Pay by check, money order, or include company purchase order with this form ($200 minimum). We also accept VISA, MasterCard or American Express. Make payment to Intel Literature Sales. Allow 2-3 weeks for delivery.

☐ VISA ☐ MasterCard ☐ American Express Expiration Date ______________

Account No. ______________________

Signature ______________________

Mail To: Intel Literature Sales
P.O. Box 7641
Mt. Prospect, IL 60056-7641

International Customers outside the U.S. and Canada should use the International order form on the next page or contact their local Sales Office or Distributor.

For phone orders in the U.S. and Canada, call Toll Free: (800) 548-4725 or FAX to (708) 296-3699. Please print clearly in ink to expedite your order.

Prices good until 12/31/94.
Source HB

LOFUS1/100693

INTERNATIONAL LITERATURE ORDER FORM

NAME: ______________________________

COMPANY: ______________________________

ADDRESS: ______________________________

CITY: ______________ STATE: ________ ZIP: ________

COUNTRY: ______________________________

PHONE NO.: ( ) ______________________________

ORDER NO.	TITLE	QTY.		PRICE		TOTAL
			×		=	
			×		=	
			×		=	
			×		=	
			×		=	
			×		=	
			×		=	
			×		=	
			×		=	
			×		=	

Subtotal ________

Must Add Your Local Sales Tax ________

Total ________

PAYMENT

Cheques should be made payable to your ***local*** Intel Sales Office (see inside back cover).

Other forms of payment may be available in your country. Please contact the Literature Coordinator at your ***local*** Intel Sales Office for details.

The completed form should be marked to the attention of the LITERATURE COORDINATOR and returned to your ***local*** Intel Sales Office.

LOFINT1/100693

intel®

EMBEDDED MICROPROCESSORS

1994

Additional copies of this document or other Intel literature may be obtained from:

Intel Corporation
Literature Sales
P.O. Box 7641
Mt. Prospect, IL 60056-7641

or call 1-800-879-4683

LGCPY1/100693

DATA SHEET DESIGNATIONS

Intel uses various data sheet markings to designate each phase of the document as it relates to the product. The marking appears in the upper, right-hand corner of the data sheet. The following is the definition of these markings:

Data Sheet Marking	Description
Product Preview	Contains information on products in the design phase of development. Do not finalize a design with this information. Revised information will be published when the product becomes available.
Advanced Information	Contains information on products being sampled or in the initial production phase of development.*
Preliminary	Contains preliminary information on new products in production.*
No Marking	Contains information on products in full production.*

*Specifications within these data sheets are subject to change without notice. Verify with your local Intel sales office that you have the latest data sheet before finalizing a design.

MCS® 80/85 Microprocessor Family 1

80186/80188 Family 2

376 Embedded Processors 3

Embedded Intel386™ Processors 4

Table of Contents

Alphanumeric Index x

MCS® 80/85 MICROPROCESSOR FAMILY

Chapter 1

MCS® 80/85 MICROPROCESSOR DATA SHEETS

8080A/8080A-1/8080A-2 8-Bit N-Channel Microprocessor 1-1

8085AH/8085AH-2/8085AH-1 8-Bit HMOS Microprocessors 1-11

8155H/8156H/8155H-2/8156H-2 2048-Bit Static HMOS RAM with I/O Ports and Timer 1-31

8185/8185-2 1024 x 8-Bit Static RAM for MCS®-85 1-45

8224 Clock Generator and Driver for 8080A CPU 1-50

8228 System Controller and Bus Driver for 8080A CPU 1-55

8755A 16,384-Bit EPROM with I/O 1-59

80186/80188 FAMILY

Chapter 2

80186/188/C186/C188/L186/L188 DATA SHEETS

80186/80188 High Integration 16-Bit Microprocessors 2-1

80C186XL/80C188XL 16-Bit High-Integration Embedded Processors 2-34

80C186EA/80C188EA and 80L186EA/80L188EA 16-Bit High-Integration Embedded Processors 2-82

80C186EB/80C188EB and 80L186EB/80L188EB 16-Bit High-Integration Embedded Processors 2-132

80C186EC/80C188EC and 80L186EC/80L188EC 16-Bit High-Integration Embedded Processors 2-186

80C187 80-Bit Math Coprocessor 2-239

80186/188/C186/C188 APPLICATION NOTE (1994 ADDITION)

AP-477 Low Voltage Embedded Design 2-269

For additional Application Note information, reference the 1993/1994 Embedded Applications Handbook (Document Order Number: 270648)

80186/80188 Development Tools information is now available in the Development Tools Handbook (Document Order Number: 272326)

376 EMBEDDED PROCESSORS

Chapter 3

376 PROCESSOR AND PERIPHERALS DATA SHEETS

376 High Performance 32-Bit Embedded Processor 3-1

Intel387 SX Math CoProcessor 3-96

82355 Bus Master Interface Controller (BMIC) 3-97

82370 Integrated System Peripheral 3-98

82596DX and 82596SX High-Performance 32-Bit Local Area Network Coprocessor 3-99

376 PROCESSOR DEVELOPMENT TOOLS

Intel386 and Intel486 Family Development Support 3-100

TRANS 186-376 Assembly Code Translator 3-108

EMBEDDED Intel386™ PROCESSORS

Chapter 4

Intel386™ PROCESSOR DATA SHEETS

Intel386 CX Embedded Microprocessor 4-1

Intel386 EX Embedded Microprocessor 4-20

Static Intel386 SX Embedded Microprocessor 4-47

Alphanumeric Index

376 High Performance 32-Bit Embedded Processor 3-1
80186/80188 High Integration 16-Bit Microprocessors 2-1
8080A/8080A-1/8080A-2 8-Bit N-Channel Microprocessor 1-1
8085AH/8085AH-2/8085AH-1 8-Bit HMOS Microprocessors 1-11
80C186EA/80C188EA and 80L186EA/80L188EA 16-Bit High-Integration Embedded Processors 2-82
80C186EB/80C188EB and 80L186EB/80L188EB 16-Bit High-Integration Embedded Processors 2-132
80C186EC/80C188EC and 80L186EC/80L188EC 16-Bit High-Integration Embedded Processors 2-186
80C186XL/80C188XL 16-Bit High-Integration Embedded Processors 2-34
80C187 80-Bit Math Coprocessor 2-239
8155H/8156H/8155H-2/8156H-2 2048-Bit Static HMOS RAM with I/O Ports and Timer 1-31
8185/8185-2 1024 x 8-Bit Static RAM for MCS®-85 1-45
8224 Clock Generator and Driver for 8080A CPU 1-50
8228 System Controller and Bus Driver for 8080A CPU 1-55
82355 Bus Master Interface Controller (BMIC) 3-97
82370 Integrated System Peripheral 3-98
82596DX and 82596SX High-Performance 32-Bit Local Area Network Coprocessor 3-99
8755A 16,384-Bit EPROM with I/O 1-59
AP-477 Low Voltage Embedded Design 2-269
Intel386 and Intel486 Family Development Support 3-100
Intel386 CX Embedded Microprocessor 4-1
Intel386 EX Embedded Microprocessor 4-20
Intel387 SX Math CoProcessor 3-96
Static Intel386 SX Embedded Microprocessor 4-47
TRANS 186-376 Assembly Code Translator 3-108

MCS® 80/85 Microprocessor Family

1

1

intel®

8080A/8080A-1/8080A-2
8-BIT N-CHANNEL MICROPROCESSOR

- **TTL Drive Capability**
- **2 μs (−1:1.3 μs, −2:1.5 μs) Instruction Cycle**
- **Powerful Problem Solving Instruction Set**
- **6 General Purpose Registers and an Accumulator**
- **16-Bit Program Counter for Directly Addressing up to 64K Bytes of Memory**
- **16-Bit Stack Pointer and Stack Manipulation Instructions for Rapid Switching of the Program Environment**
- **Decimal, Binary, and Double Precision Arithmetic**
- **Ability to Provide Priority Vectored Interrupts**
- **512 Directly Addressed I/O Ports**
- **Available in EXPRESS — Standard Temperature Range**
- **Available in 40-Lead Cerdip and Plastic Packages**
  (See Packaging Spec. Order #231369)

1

The Intel 8080A is a complete 8-bit parallel central processing unit (CPU). It is fabricated on a single LSI chip using Intel's n-channel silicon gate MOS process. This offers the user a high performance solution to control and processing applications.

The 8080A contains 6 8-bit general purpose working registers and an accumulator. The 6 general purpose registers may be addressed individually or in pairs providing both single and double precision operators. Arithmetic and logical instructions set or reset 4 testable flags. A fifth flag provides decimal arithmetic operation.

The 8080A has an external stack feature wherein any portion of memory may be used as a last in/first out stack to store/retrieve the contents of the accumulator, flags, program counter, and all of the 6 general purpose registers. The 16-bit stack pointer controls the addressing of this external stack. This stack gives the 8080A the ability to easily handle multiple level priority interrupts by rapidly storing and restoring processor status. It also provides almost unlimited subroutine nesting.

This microprocessor has been designed to simplify systems design. Separate 16-line address and 8-line bidirectional data busses are used to facilitate easy interface to memory and I/O. Signals to control the interface to memory and I/O are provided directly by the 8080A. Ultimate control of the address and data busses resides with the HOLD signal. It provides the ability to suspend processor operation and force the address and data busses into a high impedance state. This permits OR-tying these busses with other controlling devices for (DMA) direct memory access or multi-processor operation.

NOTE:
The 8080A is functionally and electrically compatible with the Intel 8080.

November 1986
Order Number: 231453-001

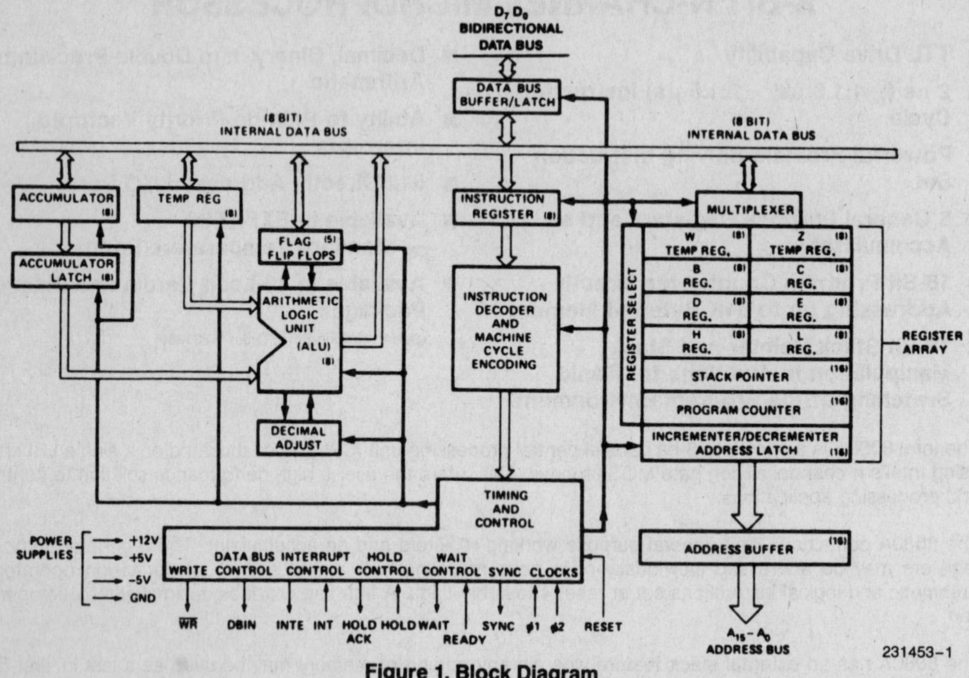

Figure 1. Block Diagram

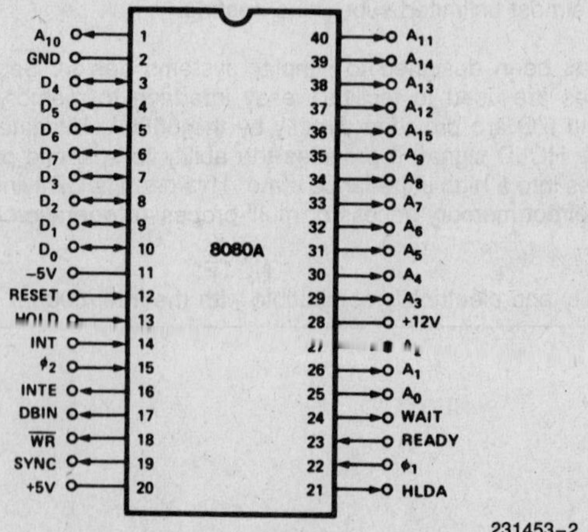

Figure 2. Pin Configuration

Table 1. Pin Description

Symbol	Type	Name and Function
A_{15}–A_0	O	**ADDRESS BUS:** The address bus provides the address to memory (up to 64K 8-bit words) or denotes the I/O device number for up to 256 input and 256 output devices. A_0 is the least significant address bit.
D_7–D_0	I/O	**DATA BUS:** The data bus provides bi-directional communication between the CPU, memory, and I/O devices for instructions and data transfers. Also, during the first clock cycle of each machine cycle, the 8080A outputs a status word on the data bus that describes the current machine cycle. D_0 is the least significant bit.
SYNC	O	**SYNCHRONIZING SIGNAL:** The SYNC pin provides a signal to indicate the beginning of each machine cycle.
DBIN	O	**DATA BUS IN:** The DBIN signal indicates to external circuits that the data bus is in the input mode. This signal should be used to enable the gating of data onto the 8080A data bus from memory or I/O.
READY	I	**READY:** The READY signal indicates to the 8080A that valid memory or input data is available on the 8080A data bus. This signal is used to synchronize the CPU with slower memory or I/O devices. If after sending an address out the 8080A does not receive a READY input, the 8080A will enter a WAIT state for as long as the READY line is low. READY can also be used to single step the CPU.
WAIT	O	**WAIT:** The WAIT signal acknowledges that the CPU is in a WAIT state.
$\overline{WR}$	O	**WRITE:** The $\overline{WR}$ signal is used for memory WRITE or I/O output control. The data on the data bus is stable while the $\overline{WR}$ signal is active low ($\overline{WR} = 0$).
HOLD	I	**HOLD:** The HOLD signal requests the CPU to enter the HOLD state. The HOLD state allows an external device to gain control of the 8080A address and data bus as soon as the 8080A has completed its use of these busses for the current machine cycle. It is recognized under the following conditions: • the CPU is in the HALT state. • the CPU is in the T2 or TW state and the READY signal is active. As a result of entering the HOLD state the CPU ADDRESS BUS (A_{15}–A_0) and DATA BUS (D_7–D_0) will be in their high impedance state. The CPU acknowledges its state with the HOLD ACKNOWLEDGE (HLDA) pin.
HLDA	O	**HOLD ACKNOWLEDGE:** The HLDA signal appears in response to the HOLD signal and indicates that the data and address bus will go to the high impedance state. The HLDA signal begins at: • T3 for READ memory or input. • The Clock Period following T3 for WRITE memory or OUTPUT operation. In either case, the HLDA signal appears after the rising edge of ϕ_2.
INTE	O	**INTERRUPT ENABLE:** Indicates the content of the internal interrupt enable flip/flop. This flip/flop may be set or reset by the Enable and Disable Interrupt instructions and inhibits interrupts from being accepted by the CPU when it is reset. It is automatically reset (disabling further interrupts) at time T1 of the instruction fetch cycle (M1) when an interrupt is accepted and is also reset by the RESET signal.
INT	I	**INTERRUPT REQUEST:** The CPU recognizes an interrupt request on this line at the end of the current instruction or while halted. If the CPU is in the HOLD state or if the Interrupt Enable flip/flop is reset it will not honor the request.
RESET[1]	I	**RESET:** While the RESET signal is activated, the content of the program counter is cleared. After RESET, the program will start at location 0 in memory. The INTE and HLDA flip/flops are also reset. Note that the flags, accumulator, stack pointer, and registers are not cleared.
V_{SS}		**GROUND:** Reference.
V_{DD}		**POWER:** $+12 \pm 5\%$ V.
V_{CC}		**POWER:** $+5 \pm 5\%$ V.
V_{BB}		**POWER:** $-5 \pm 5\%$ V.
ϕ_1, ϕ_2		**CLOCK PHASES:** 2 externally supplied clock phases. (non TTL compatible)

NOTE:
1. The RESET signal must be active for a minimum of 3 clock cycles.

ABSOLUTE MAXIMUM RATINGS*

Temperature Under Bias ....0°C to +70°C
Storage Temperature ....−65°C to +150°C
All Input or Output Voltages
with Respect to V_{BB} ....−0.3V to +20V
V_{CC}, V_{DD} and V_{SS}
with Respect to V_{BB} ....−0.3V to +20V
Power Dissipation...........................1.5W

NOTICE: This is a production data sheet. The specifications are subject to change without notice.

**WARNING: Stressing the device beyond the "Absolute Maximum Ratings" may cause permanent damage. These are stress ratings only. Operation beyond the "Operating Conditions" is not recommended and extended exposure beyond the "Operating Conditions" may affect device reliability.*

D.C. CHARACTERISTICS

T_A = 0°C to 70°C, V_{DD} = +12V ±5%, V_{CC} = +5V ±5%, V_{BB} = −5V ±5%, V_{SS} = 0V; unless otherwise noted

Symbol	Parameter	Min	Typ	Max	Unit	Test Condition
V_{ILC}	Clock Input Low Voltage	V_{SS} − 1		V_{SS} + 0.8	V	
V_{IHC}	Clock Input High Voltage	9.0		V_{DD} + 1	V	
V_{IL}	Input Low Voltage	V_{SS} − 1		V_{SS} + 0.8	V	
V_{IH}	Input High Voltage	3.3		V_{CC} + 1	V	
V_{OL}	Output Low Voltage			0.45	V	I_{OL} = 1.9 mA on All Outputs,
V_{OH}	Output High Voltage	3.7			V	I_{OH} = −150 μA.
$I_{DD (AV)}$	Avg. Power Supply Current (V_{DD})		40	70	mA	Operation
$I_{CC (AV)}$	Avg. Power Supply Current (V_{CC})		60	80	mA	
$I_{BB (AV)}$	Avg. Power Supply Current (V_{BB})		0.01	1	mA	T_{CY} = 0.48 μs
I_{IL}	Input Leakage			±10	μA	$V_{SS} \leq V_{IN} \leq V_{CC}$
I_{CL}	Clock Leakage			±10	μA	$V_{SS} \leq V_{CLOCK} \leq V_{DD}$
I_{DL}	Data Bus Leakage in Input Mode			−100 −2.0	μA mA	$V_{SS} \leq V_{IN} \leq V_{SS} + 0.8V$ $V_{SS} + 0.8V \leq V_{IN} \leq V_{CC}$
I_{FL}	Address and Data Bus Leakage During HOLD			+10 −100	μA	$V_{ADDR/DATA} = V_{CC}$ $V_{ADDR/DATA} = V_{SS} + 0.45V$

CAPACITANCE

T_A = 25°C, V_{CC} = V_{DD} = V_{SS} = 0V, V_{BB} = −5V

Symbol	Parameter	Typ	Max	Unit	Test Condition
C_ϕ	Clock Capacitance	17	25	pF	f_c = 1 MHz
C_{IN}	Input Capacitance	6	10	pF	Unmeasured Pins
C_{OUT}	Output Capacitance	10	20	pF	Returned to V_{SS}

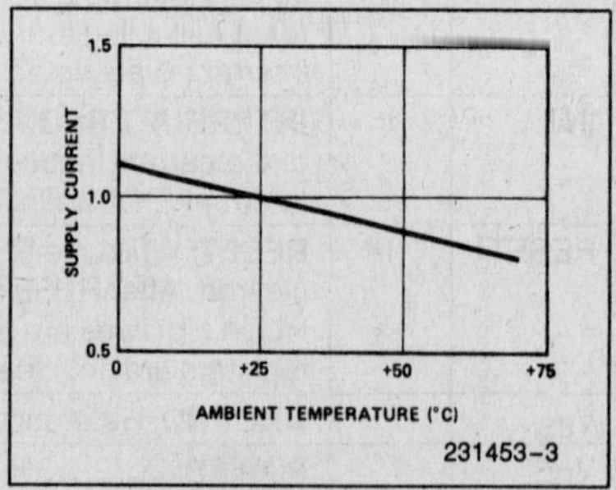

Typical Supply Current vs Temperature, Normalized
ΔI Supply/ΔT_A = −0.45%/°C

A.C. CHARACTERISTICS (8080A) T_A = 0°C to 70°C, V_{DD} = +12V ±5%, V_{CC} = +5V ±5%, V_{BB} = −5V ±5%, V_{SS} = 0V; unless otherwise noted

Symbol	Parameter	Min	Max	−1 Min	−1 Max	−2 Min	−2 Max	Unit	Test Condition
t_{CY} (3)	Clock Period	0.48	2.0	0.32	2.0	0.38	2.0	μs	
t_r, t_f	Clock Rise and Fall Time	0	50	0	25	0	50	ns	
$t_{\phi 1}$	ϕ_1 Pulse Width	60		50		60		ns	
$t_{\phi 2}$	ϕ_2 Pulse Width	220		145		175		ns	
t_{D1}	Delay ϕ_1 to ϕ_2	0		0		0		ns	
t_{D2}	Delay ϕ_1 to ϕ_2	70		60		70		ns	
t_{D3}	Delay ϕ_1 to ϕ_2 Leading Edges	80		60		70	ns		
t_{DA}	Address Output Delay From ϕ_2		200		150		175	ns	C_L = 100 pF
t_{DD}	Data Output Delay From ϕ_2		200		180		200	ns	
t_{DC}	Signal Output Delay From ϕ_1 or ϕ_2 (SYNC, WR, WAIT, HLDA)		120		110		120	ns	C_L = 50 pF
t_{DF}	DBIN Delay From ϕ_2	25	140	25	130	25	140	ns	
t_{DI} (1)	Delay for Input Bus to Enter Input Mode		t_{DF}		t_{DF}		t_{DF}	ns	
t_{DS1}	Data Setup Time During ϕ_1 and DBIN	30		10		20		ns	
t_{DS2}	Data Setup Time to ϕ_2 During DBIN	150		120		130		ns	
t_{DH} (1)	Data Hold Time From ϕ_2 and DBIN	(1)		(1)		(1)		ns	
t_{IE}	INTE Output Delay From ϕ_2		200		200		200	ns	C_L = 50 pF
t_{RS}	READY Setup Time During ϕ_2	120		90		90		ns	
t_{HS}	HOLD Setup Time During ϕ_2	140		120		120		ns	
t_{IS}	INT Setup Time During ϕ_2	120		100		100		ns	
t_H	Hold Time From ϕ_2 (READY, INT, HOLD)	0		0		0		ns	
t_{FD}	Delay to Float During Hold (Address and Data Bus)		120		120		120	ns	
t_{AW}	Address Stable Prior to WR	(5)		(5)		(5)		ns	
t_{DW}	Output Data Stable Prior to WR	(6)		(6)		(6)		ns	
t_{WD}	Output Data Stable From WR	(7)		(7)		(7)		ns	
t_{WA}	Address Stable From WR	(7)		(7)		(7)		ns	
t_{HF}	HLDA to Float Delay	(8)		(8)		(8)		ns	
t_{WF}	WR to Float Delay	(9)		(9)		(9)		ns	
t_{AH}	Address Hold Time After DBIN During HLDA	−20		−20		−20		ns	

A.C. TESTING LOAD CIRCUIT

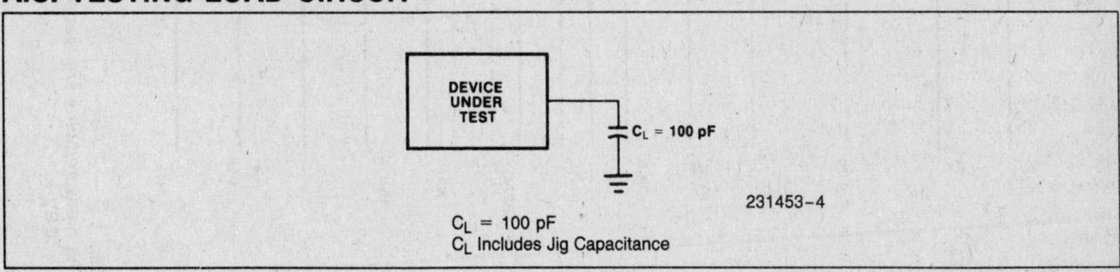

C_L = 100 pF
C_L Includes Jig Capacitance

WAVEFORMS

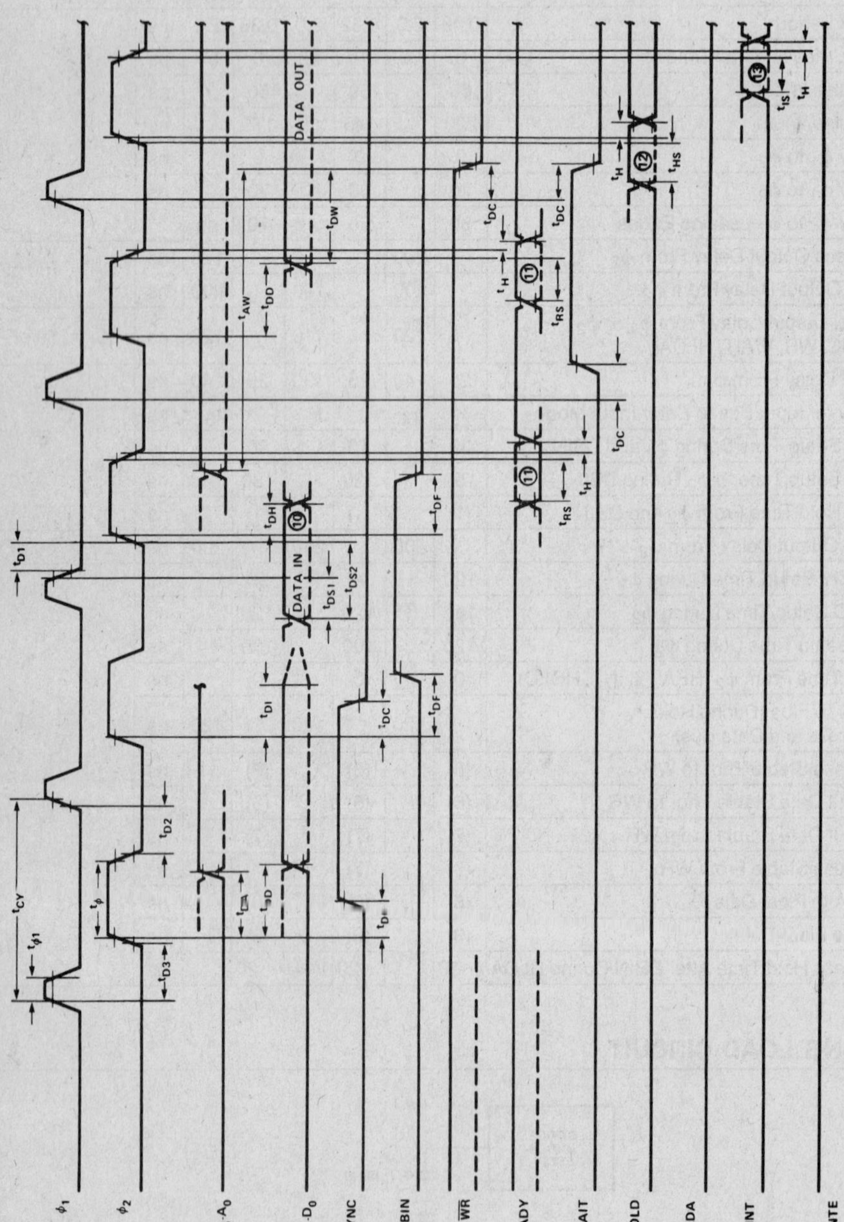

231453-5

NOTE:
Timing measurements are made at the following reference voltages: CLOCK "1" = 8.0V, "0" = 1.0V; INPUTS "1" = 3.3V, "0" = 0.8V; OUTPUTS "1" = 2.0V, "0" = 0.8V

WAVEFORMS (Continued)

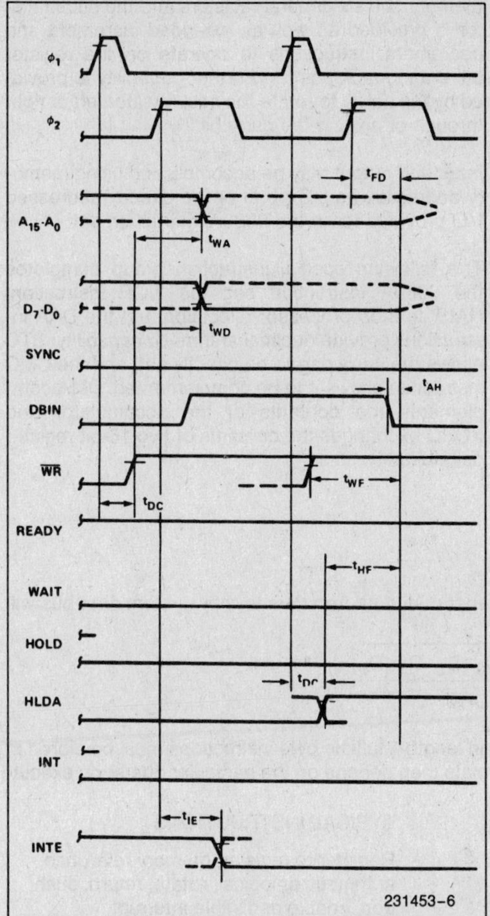

231453-6

Typical Δ Output Delay vs Δ Capacitance

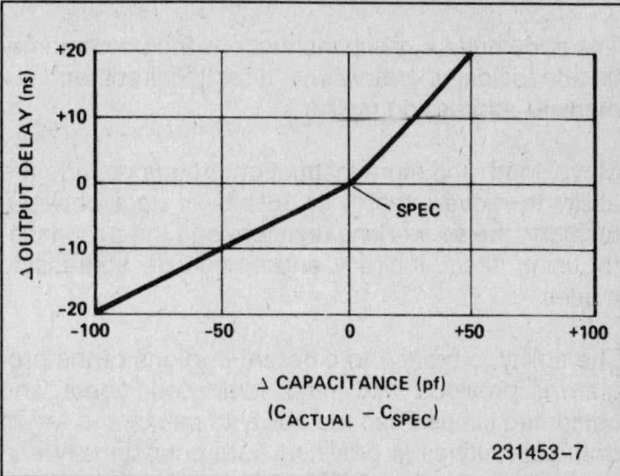

231453-7

NOTES:

(Parenthesis gives −1, −2 specifications, respectively.)

1. Data input should be enabled with DBIN status. No bus conflict can then occur and data hold time is assured.
t_{DH} = 50 ns or t_{DF}, whichever is less.
2. $t_{CY} = t_{D3} + t_{r\phi2} + t_{\phi2} + t_{f\phi2} + t_{D2} + t_{r\phi1} \geq$ 480 ns (−1:320 ns, − 2:380 ns).
3. The following are relevant when interfacing the 8080A to devices having V_{IH} = 3.3V:
   a) Maximum output rise time from 0.8V to 3.3V = 100 ns @ C_L = SPEC.
   b) Output delay when measured to 3.0V = SPEC +60 ns @ C_L = SPEC.
   c) If C_L = SPEC, add 0.6 ns/pF if $C_L > C_{SPEC}$, subtract 0.3 ns/pF (from modified delay) if $C_L < C_{SPEC}$.
4. $t_{AW} = 2\ t_{CY} - t_{D3} - t_{r\phi2}$ − 140 ns (−1:110 ns, − 2:130 ns).
5. $t_{DW} = t_{CY} - t_{D3} - t_{r\phi2}$ − 170 ns (−1:150 ns, − 2:170 ns).
6. If not HLDA, $t_{WD} = t_{WA} = t_{D3} + t_{r\phi2}$ + 10 ns. If HLDA, $t_{WD} = t_{WA} = t_{WF}$.
7. $t_{HF} = t_{D3} + t_{r\phi2}$ −50 ns.
8. $t_{WF} = t_{D3} + t_{r\phi2}$ − 10 ns.
9. Data in must be stable for this period during DBIN T_3. Both t_{DS1} and t_{DS2} must be satisfied.
10. Ready signal must be stable for this period during T_2 or T_W. (Must be externally synchronized.)
11. Hold signal must be stable for this period during T_2 or T_W when entering hold mode, and during T_3, T_4, T_5 and T_{WH} when in hold mode. (External synchronization is not required.)
12. Interrupt signal must be stable during this period of the last clock cycle of any instruction in order to be recognized on the following instruction. (External synchronization is not required.)
13. This timing diagram shows timing relationships only; it does not represent any specific machine cycle.

INSTRUCTION SET

The accumulator group instructions include arithmetic and logical operators with direct, indirect, and immediate addressing modes.

Move, load, and store instruction groups provide the ability to move either 8 or 16 bits of data between memory, the six working registers and the accumulator using direct, indirect, and immediate addressing modes.

The ability to branch to different portions of the program is provided with jump, jump conditional, and computed jumps. Also the ability to call to and return from subroutines is provided both conditionally and unconditionally. The RESTART (or single byte call instruction) is useful for interrupt vector operation.

Double precision operators such as stack manipulation and double add instructions extend both the arithmetic and interrupt handling capability of the 8080A. The ability to increment and decrement memory, the six general registers and the accumulator is provided as well as extended increment and decrement instructions to operate on the register pairs and stack pointer. Further capability is provided by the ability to rotate the accumulator left or right through or around the carry bit.

Input and output may be accomplished using memory addresses as I/O ports or the directly addressed I/O provided for in the 8080A instruction set.

The following special instruction group completes the 8080A instruction set: the NOP instruction, HALT to stop processor execution and the DAA instructions provide decimal arithmetic capability. STC allows the carry flag to be directly set, and the CMC instruction allows it to be complemented. CMA complements the contents of the accumulator and XCHG exchanges the contents of two 16-bit register pairs directly.

Data and Instruction Formats

Data in the 8080A is stored in the form of 8-bit binary integers. All data transfers to they system data bus will be in the same format.

D_7	D_6	D_5	D_4	D_3	D_2	D_1	D_0

DATA WORD

The program instructions may be one, two, or three bytes in length. Multiple byte instructions must be stored in successive words in program memory. The instruction formats then depend on the particular operation executed.

Format		TYPICAL INSTRUCTIONS
One Byte Instructions		
D_7 D_6 D_5 D_4 D_3 D_2 D_1 D_0	OP CODE	Register to register, memory reference, arithmetic or logical, rotate, return, push, pop, enable or disable Interrupt instructions
Two Byte Instructions		
D_7 D_6 D_5 D_4 D_3 D_2 D_1 D_0	OP CODE	Immediate mode or I/O instructions
D_7 D_6 D_5 D_4 D_3 D_2 D_1 D_0	OPERAND	
Three Byte Instructions		
D_7 D_6 D_5 D_4 D_3 D_2 D_1 D_0	OP CODE	Jump, call or direct load and store instructions
D_7 D_6 D_5 D_4 D_3 D_2 D_1 D_0	LOW ADDRESS OR OPERAND 1	
D_7 D_6 D_5 D_4 D_3 D_2 D_1 D_0	HIGH ADDRESS OR OPERAND 2	

For the 8080A a logic "1" is defined as a high level and a logic "0" is defined as a low level.

Table 2. Instruction Set Summary

Mnemonic*	Instruction Code (1) D_7 D_6 D_5 D_4 D_3 D_2 D_1 D_0	Operations Description	Clock Cycles (2)
MOVE, LOAD, AND STORE			
MOVr1,r2	0 1 D D D S S S	Move register to register	5
MOV M,r	0 1 1 1 0 S S S	Move register to memory	7
MOV r,M	0 1 D D D 1 1 0	Move memory to register	7
MVI r	0 0 D D D 1 1 0	Move immediate register	7
MVI M	0 0 1 1 0 1 1 0	Move immediate memory	10
LXI B	0 0 0 0 0 0 0 1	Load immediate register Pair B & C	10
LXI D	0 0 0 1 0 0 0 1	Load immediate register Pair D & E	10
LXI H	0 0 1 0 0 0 0 1	Load immediate register Pair H & L	10
STAX B	0 0 0 0 0 0 1 0	Store A indirect	7
STAX D	0 0 0 1 0 0 1 0	Store A indirect	7
LDAX B	0 0 0 0 1 0 1 0	Load A indirect	7
LDAX D	0 0 0 1 1 0 1 0	Load A indirect	7
STA	0 0 1 1 0 0 1 0	Store A direct	13
LDA	0 0 1 1 1 0 1 0	Load A direct	13
SHLD	0 0 1 0 0 0 1 0	Store H & L direct	16
LHLD	0 0 1 0 1 0 1 0	Load H & L direct	16
XCHG	1 1 1 0 1 0 1 1	Exchange D & E, H & L Registers	4
STACK OPS			
PUSH B	1 1 0 0 0 1 0 1	Push register Pair B & C on stack	11
PUSH D	1 1 0 1 0 1 0 1	Push register Pair D & E on stack	11
PUSH H	1 1 1 0 0 1 0 1	Push register Pair H & L on stack	11
PUSH PSW	1 1 1 1 0 1 0 1	Push A and Flags on stack	11
POP B	1 1 0 0 0 0 0 1	Pop register Pair B & C off stack	10
POP D	1 1 0 1 0 0 0 1	Pop register Pair D & E off stack	10
POP H	1 1 1 0 0 0 0 1	Pop register Pair H & L off stack	10
POP PSW	1 1 1 1 0 0 0 1	Pop A and Flags off stack	10
XTHL	1 1 1 0 0 0 1 1	Exchange top of stack, H & L	18
SPHL	1 1 1 1 1 0 0 1	H & L to stack pointer	5
LXI SP	0 0 1 1 0 0 0 1	Load immediate stack pointer	10
INX SP	0 0 1 1 0 0 1 1	Increment stack pointer	5
DCX SP	0 0 1 1 1 0 1 1	Decrement stack pointer	5
JUMP			
JMP	1 1 0 0 0 0 1 1	Jump unconditional	10
JC	1 1 0 1 1 0 1 0	Jump on carry	10
JNC	1 1 0 1 0 0 1 0	Jump on no carry	10
JZ	1 1 0 0 1 0 1 0	Jump on zero	10
JNZ	1 1 0 0 0 0 1 0	Jump on no zero	10
JP	1 1 1 1 0 0 1 0	Jump on positive	10
JM	1 1 1 1 1 0 1 0	Jump on minus	10
JPE	1 1 1 0 1 0 1 0	Jump on parity even	10
JPO	1 1 1 0 0 0 1 0	Jump on parity odd	10
PCHL	1 1 1 0 1 0 0 1	H & L to program counter	5
CALL			
CALL	1 1 0 0 1 1 0 1	Call unconditional	17
CC	1 1 0 1 1 1 0 0	Call on carry	11/17
CNC	1 1 0 1 0 1 0 0	Call on no carry	11/17
CZ	1 1 0 0 1 1 0 0	Call on zero	11/17
CNZ	1 1 0 0 0 1 0 0	Call on no zero	11/17
CP	1 1 1 1 0 1 0 0	Call on positive	11/17
CM	1 1 1 1 1 1 0 0	Call on minus	11/17
CPE	1 1 1 0 1 1 0 0	Call on parity even	11/17
CPO	1 1 1 0 0 1 0 0	Call on parity odd	11/17
RETURN			
RET	1 1 0 0 1 0 0 1	Return	10
RC	1 1 0 1 1 0 0 0	Return on carry	5/11
RNC	1 1 0 1 0 0 0 0	Return on no carry	5/11
RZ	1 1 0 0 1 0 0 0	Return on zero	5/11
RNZ	1 1 0 0 0 0 0 0	Return on no zero	5/11
RP	1 1 1 1 0 0 0 0	Return on positive	5/11
RM	1 1 1 1 1 0 0 0	Return on minus	5/11
RPE	1 1 1 0 0 0 0 0	Return on parity even	5/11
RPO	1 1 1 0 0 0 0 0	Return on parity odd	5/11
RESTART			
RST	1 1 A A A 1 1 1	Restart	11
INCREMENT AND DECREMENT			
INR r	0 0 D D D 1 0 0	Increment register	5
DCR r	0 0 D D D 1 0 1	Decrement register	5
INR M	0 0 1 1 0 1 0 0	Increment memory	10
DCR M	0 0 1 1 0 1 0 1	Decrement memory	10
INX B	0 0 0 0 0 0 1 1	Increment B & C registers	5
INX D	0 0 0 1 0 0 1 1	Increment D & E registers	5
INX H	0 0 1 0 0 0 1 1	Increment H & L registers	5
DCX B	0 0 0 0 1 0 1 1	Decrement B & C	5
DCX D	0 0 0 1 1 0 1 1	Decrement D & E	5
DCX H	0 0 1 0 1 0 1 1	Decrement H & L	5
ADD			
ADD r	1 0 0 0 0 S S S	Add register to A	4
ADC r	1 0 0 0 1 S S S	Add register to A with carry	4
ADD M	1 0 0 0 0 1 1 0	Add memory to A	7
ADC M	1 0 0 0 1 1 1 0	Add memory to A with carry	7
ADI	1 1 0 0 0 1 1 0	Add immediate to A	7
ACI	1 1 0 0 1 1 1 0	Add immediate to A with carry	7
DAD B	0 0 0 0 1 0 0 1	Add B & C to H & L	10
DAD D	0 0 0 1 1 0 0 1	Add D & E to H & L	10
DAD H	0 0 1 0 1 0 0 1	Add H & L to H & L	10
DAD SP	0 0 1 1 1 0 0 1	Add stack pointer to H & L	10

Table 2. Instruction Set Summary (Continued)

Mnemonic*	Instruction Code (1) D_7 D_6 D_5 D_4 D_3 D_2 D_1 D_0	Operations Description	Clock Cycles (2)
SUBTRACT			
SUB r	1 0 0 1 0 S S S	Subtract register from A	4
SBB r	1 0 0 1 1 S S S	Subtract register from A with borrow	4
SUB M	1 0 0 1 0 1 1 0	Subtract memory from A	7
SBB M	1 0 0 1 1 1 1 0	Subtract memory from A with borrow	7
SUI	1 1 0 1 0 1 1 0	Subtract immediate from A	7
SBI	1 1 0 1 1 1 1 0	Subtract immediate from A with borrow	7
LOGICAL			
ANA r	1 0 1 0 0 S S S	And register with A	4
XRA r	1 0 1 0 1 S S S	Exclusive or register with A	4
ORA r	1 0 1 1 0 S S S	Or register with A	4
CMP r	1 0 1 1 1 S S S	Compare register with A	4
ANA M	1 0 1 0 0 1 1 0	And memory with A	7
XRA M	1 0 1 0 1 1 1 0	Exclusive Or memory with A	7
ORA M	1 0 1 1 0 1 1 0	Or memory with A	7
CMP M	1 0 1 1 1 1 1 0	Compare memory with A	7
ANI	1 1 1 0 0 1 1 0	And immediate with A	7
XRI	1 1 1 0 1 1 1 0	Exclusive Or immediate with A	7
ORI	1 1 1 1 0 1 1 0	Or immediate with A	7
CPI	1 1 1 1 1 1 1 0	Compare immediate with A	7

Mnemonic*	Instruction Code (1) D_7 D_6 D_5 D_4 D_3 D_2 D_1 D_0	Operations Description	Clock Cycles (2)
ROTATE			
RLC	0 0 0 0 0 1 1 1	Rotate A left	4
RRC	0 0 0 0 1 1 1 1	Rotate A right	4
RAL	0 0 0 1 0 1 1 1	Rotate A left through carry	4
RAR	0 0 0 1 1 1 1 1	Rotate A right through carry	4
SPECIALS			
CMA	0 0 1 0 1 1 1 1	Complement A	4
STC	0 0 1 1 0 1 1 1	Set carry	4
CMC	0 0 1 1 1 1 1 1	Complement carry	4
DAA	0 0 1 0 0 1 1 1	Decimal adjust A	4
INPUT/OUTPUT			
IN	1 1 0 1 1 0 1 1	Input	10
OUT	1 1 0 1 0 0 1 1	Output	10
CONTROL			
EI	1 1 1 1 1 0 1 1	Enable Interrupts	4
DI	1 1 1 1 0 0 1 1	Disable Interrupt	4
NOP	0 0 0 0 0 0 0 0	No-operation	4
HLT	0 1 1 1 0 1 1 0	Halt	7

NOTES:
1. DDD or SSS: B = 000, C = 001, D = 010, E = 011, H = 100, L = 101, Memory = 110, A = 111.
2. Two possible cycle times (6/12) indicate instruction cycles dependent on condition flags.

8085AH/8085AH-2/8085AH-1
8-BIT HMOS MICROPROCESSORS

- **Single +5V Power Supply with 10% Voltage Margins**
- **3 MHz, 5 MHz and 6 MHz Selections Available**
- **20% Lower Power Consumption than 8085A for 3 MHz and 5 MHz**
- **1.3 μs Instruction Cycle (8085AH); 0.8 μs (8085AH-2); 0.67 μs (8085AH-1)**
- **100% Software Compatible with 8080A**
- **On-Chip Clock Generator (with External Crystal, LC or RC Network)**
- **On-Chip System Controller; Advanced Cycle Status Information Available for Large System Control**
- **Four Vectored Interrupt Inputs (One Is Non-Maskable) Plus an 8080A-Compatible Interrupt**
- **Serial In/Serial Out Port**
- **Decimal, Binary and Double Precision Arithmetic**
- **Direct Addressing Capability to 64K Bytes of Memory**
- **Available in 40-Lead Cerdip and Plastic Packages**
  (See Packaging Spec., Order #231369)

The Intel 8085AH is a complete 8-bit parallel Central Processing Unit (CPU) implemented in N-channel, depletion load, silicon gate technology (HMOS). Its instruction set is 100% software compatible with the 8080A microprocessor, and it is designed to improve the present 8080A's performance by higher system speed. Its high level of system integration allows a minimum system of three IC's [8085AH (CPU), 8156H (RAM/IO) and 8755A (EPROM/IO)] while maintaining total system expandability. The 8085AH-2 and 8085AH-1 are faster versions of the 8085AH.

The 8085AH incorporates all of the features that the 8224 (clock generator) and 8228 (system controller) provided for the 8080A, thereby offering a higher level of system integration.

The 8085AH uses a multiplexed data bus. The address is split between the 8-bit address bus and the 8-bit data bus. The on-chip address latches of 8155H/8156H/8755A memory products allow a direct interface with the 8085AH.

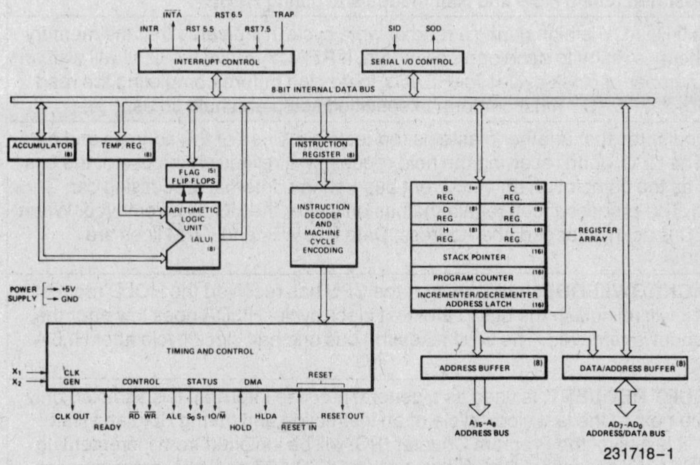

Figure 1. 8085AH CPU Functional Block Diagram

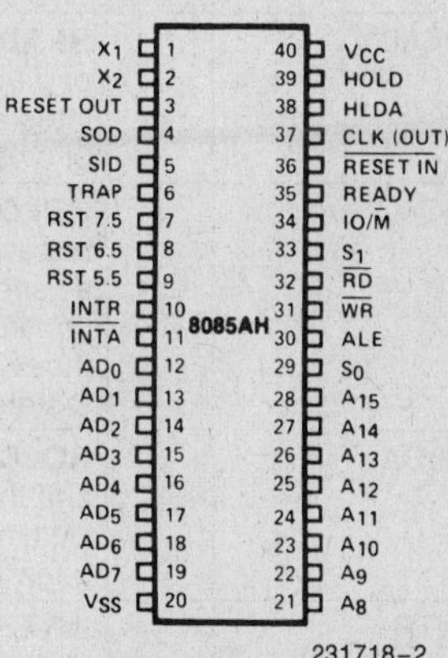

Figure 2. 8085AH Pin Configuration

September 1987
Order Number: 231718-001

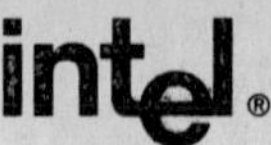

Table 1. Pin Description

Symbol	Type	Name and Function
A_8–A_{15}	O	**ADDRESS BUS:** The most significant 8 bits of memory address or the 8 bits of the I/O address, 3-stated during Hold and Halt modes and during RESET.
AD_{0-7}	I/O	**MULTIPLEXED ADDRESS/DATA BUS:** Lower 8 bits of the memory address (or I/O address) appear on the bus during the first clock cycle (T state) of a machine cycle. It then becomes the data bus during the second and third clock cycles.
ALE	O	**ADDRESS LATCH ENABLE:** It occurs during the first clock state of a machine cycle and enables the address to get latched into the on-chip latch of peripherals. The falling edge of ALE is set to guarantee setup and hold times for the address information. The falling edge of ALE can also be used to strobe the status information. ALE is never 3-stated.
S_0, S_1 and IO/$\overline{M}$	O	**MACHINE CYCLE STATUS:** **IO/$\overline{M}$ S_1 S_0 Status** 0 0 1 Memory write 0 1 0 Memory read 1 0 1 I/O write 1 1 0 I/O read 0 1 1 Opcode fetch 1 1 1 Interrupt Acknowledge * 0 0 Halt * X X Hold * X X Reset * = 3-state (high impedance) X = unspecified S_1 can be used as an advanced R/$\overline{W}$ status. IO/$\overline{M}$, S_0 and S_1 become valid at the beginning of a machine cycle and remain stable throughout the cycle. The falling edge of ALE may be used to latch the state of these lines.
$\overline{RD}$	O	**READ CONTROL:** A low level on $\overline{RD}$ indicates the selected memory or I/O device is to be read and that the Data Bus is available for the data transfer, 3-stated during Hold and Halt modes and during RESET.
$\overline{WR}$	O	**WROTE CONTROL:** A low level on $\overline{WR}$ indicates the data on the Data Bus is to be written into the selected memory or I/O location. Data is set up at the trailing edge of $\overline{WR}$. 3-stated during Hold and Halt modes and during RESET.
READY	I	**READY:** If READY is high during a read or write cycle, it indicates that the memory or peripheral is ready to send or receive data. If READY is low, the CPU will wait an integral number of clock cycles for READY to go high before completing the read or write cycle. READY must conform to specified setup and hold times.
HOLD	I	**HOLD:** Indicates that another master is requesting the use of the address and data buses. The CPU, upon receiving the hold request, will relinquish the use of the bus as soon as the completion of the current bus transfer. Internal processing can continue. The processor can regain the bus only after the HOLD is removed. When the HOLD is acknowledged, the Address, Data $\overline{RD}$, $\overline{WR}$, and IO/$\overline{M}$ lines are 3-stated.
HLDA	O	**HOLD ACKNOWLEDGE:** Indicates that the CPU has received the HOLD request and that it will relinquish the bus in the next clock cycle. HILDA goes low after the Hold request is removed. The CPU takes the bus one half clock cycle after HLDA goes low.
INTR	I	**INTERRUPT REQUEST:** Is used as a general purpose interrupt. It is sampled only during the next to the last clock cycle of an instruction and during Hold and Halt states. If it is active, the Program Counter (PC) will be inhibited from incrementing and an $\overline{INTA}$ will be issued. During this cycle a RESTART or CALL instruction can be inserted to jump to the interrupt service routine. The INTR is enabled and disabled by software. It is disabled by Reset and immediately after an interrupt is accepted.

1

Table 1. Pin Description (Continued)

Symbol	Type	Name and Function
$\overline{INTA}$	O	**INTERRUPT ACKNOWLEDGE:** Is used instead of (and has the same timing as) $\overline{RD}$ during the Instruction cycle after an INTR is accepted. It can be used to activate an 8259A Interrupt chip or some other interrupt port.
RST 5.5 RST 6.5 RST 7.5	I	**RESTART INTERRUPTS:** These three inputs have the same timing as INTR except they cause an internal RESTART to be automatically inserted. The priority of these interrupt is ordered as shown in Table 2. These interrupts have a higher priority than INTR. In addition, they may be individually masked out using the SIM instruction.
TRAP	I	**TRAP:** Trap interrupt is a non-maskable RESTART interrupt. It is recognized at the same time as INTR or RST 5.5–7.5. It is unaffected by any mask or Interrupt Enable. It has the highest priority of any interrupt. (See Table 2.)
$\overline{RESET\ IN}$	I	**RESET IN:** Sets the Program Counter to zero and resets the Interrupt Enable and HLDA flip-flops. The data and address buses and the control lines are 3-stated during RESET and because of the asynchronous nature of RESET, the processor's internal registers and flags may be altered by RESET with unpredictable results. $\overline{RESET\ IN}$ is a Schmitt-triggered input, allowing connection to an R-C network for power-on RESET delay (see Figure 3). Upon power-up, $\overline{RESET\ IN}$ must remain low for at least 10 ms after minimum V_{CC} has been reached. For proper reset operation after the power-up duration, $\overline{RESET\ IN}$ should be kept low a minimum of three clock periods. The CPU is held in the reset condition as long as $\overline{RESET\ IN}$ is applied.
RESET OUT	O	**RESET OUT:** Reset Out indicates CPU is being reset. Can be used as a system reset. The signal is synchronized to the processor clock and lasts an integral number of clock periods.
X_1, X_2	I	**X_1 and X_2:** Are connected to a crystal, LC, or RC network to drive the internal clock generator. X_1 can also be an external clock input from a logic gate. The input frequency is divided by 2 to give the processor's internal operating frequency.
CLK	O	**CLOCK:** Clock output for use as a system clock. The period of CLK is twice the X_1, X_2 input period.
SID	I	**SERIAL INPUT DATA LINE:** The data on this line is loaded into accumulator bit 7 whenever a RIM instruction is executed.
SOD	O	**SERIAL OUTPUT DATA LINE:** The output SOD is set or reset as specified by the SIM instruction.
V_{CC}		**POWER:** +5 volt supply.
V_{SS}		**GROUND:** Reference.

Table 2. Interrupt Priority, Restart Address and Sensitivity

Name	Priority	Address Branched to(1) When Interrupt Occurs	Type Trigger
TRAP	1	24H	Rising Edge AND High Level until Sampled
RST 7.5	2	3CH	Rising Edge (Latched)
RST 6.5	3	34H	High Level until Sampled
RST 5.5	4	2CH	High Level until Sampled
INTR	5	(Note 2)	High Level until Sampled

NOTES:
1. The processor pushes the PC on the stack before branching to the indicated address.
2. The address branched to depends on the instruction provided to the CPU when the interrupt is acknowledged.

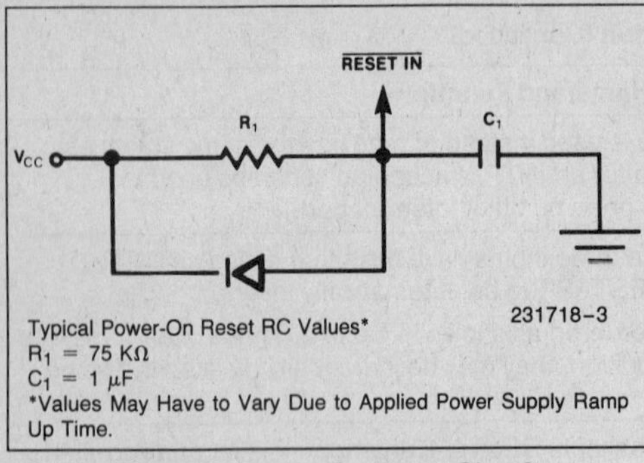

RESET IN
R1
C1
VCC
231718-3
Typical Power-On Reset RC Values*
R1 = 75 KΩ
C1 = 1 μF
*Values May Have to Vary Due to Applied Power Supply Ramp Up Time.

Figure 3. Power-On Reset Circuit

FUNCTIONAL DESCRIPTION

The 8085AH is a complete 8-bit parallel central processor. It is designed with N-channel, depletion load, silicon gate technology (HMOS), and requires a single +5V supply. Its basic clock speed is 3 MHz (8085AH), 5 MHz (8085AH-2), or 6 MHz (8085-AH-1), thus improving on the present 8080A's performance with higher system speed. Also it is designed to fit into a minimum system of three IC's: The CPU (8085AH), a RAM/IO (8156H), and an EPROM/IO chip (8755A).

The 8085AH has twelve addressable 8-bit registers. Four of them can function only as two 16-bit register pairs. Six others can be used interchangeably as 8-bit registers or as 16-bit register pairs. The 8085AH register set is as follows:

Mnemonic	Register	Contents
ACC or A	Accumulator	8 Bits
PC	Program Counter	16-Bit Address
BC, DE, HL	General-Purpose Registers; data pointer (HL)	8-Bits x 6 or 16 Bits x 3
SP	Stack Pointer	16-Bit Address
Flags or F	Flag Register	5 Flags (8-Bit Space)

The 8085AH uses a multiplexed Data Bus. The address is split between the higher 8-bit Address Bus and the lower 8-bit Address/Data Bus. During the first T state (clock cycle) of a machine cycle the low order address is sent out on the Address/Data bus. These lower 8 bits may be latched externally by the Address Latch Enable signal (ALE). During the rest of the machine cycle the data bus is used for memory or I/O data.

The 8085AH provides $\overline{RD}$, $\overline{WR}$, S_0, S_1, and IO/$\overline{M}$ signals for bus control. An Interrupt Acknowledge signal ($\overline{INTA}$) is also provided. HOLD and all Interrupts are synchronized with the processor's internal clock. The 8085AH also provides Serial Input Data (SID) and Serial Output Data (SOD) lines for simple serial interface.

In addition to these features, the 8085AH has three maskable, vector interrupt pins, one nonmaskable TRAP interrupt, and a bus vectored interrupt, INTR.

INTERRUPT AND SERIAL I/O

The 8085AH has 5 interrupt inputs: INTR, RST 5.5, RST 6.5, RST 7.5, and TRAP. INTR is identical in function to the 8080A INT. Each of the three RESTART inputs, 5.5, 6.5, and 7.5, has a programmable mask. TRAP is also a RESTART interrupt but it is nonmaskable.

The three maskable interrupt cause the internal execution of RESTART (saving the program counter in the stack and branching to the RESTART address) if the interrupts are enabled and if the interrupt mask is not set. The nonmaskable TRAP causes the internal execution of a RESTART vector independent of the state of the interrupt enable or masks. (See Table 2.)

There are two different types of inputs in the restart interrupts. RST 5.5 and RST 6.5 are *high level-sensitive* like INTR (and INT on the 8080) and are recognized with the same timing as INTR. RST 7.5 is *rising edge-sensitive.*

For RST 7.5, only a pulse is required to set an internal flip-flop which generates the internal interrupt request (a normally high level signal with a low going pulse is recommended for highest system noise immunity). The RST 7.5 request flip-flop remains set until the request is serviced. Then it is reset automatically. This flip-flop may also be reset by using the SIM instruction or by issuing a $\overline{\text{RESET IN}}$ to the 8085AH. The RST 7.5 internal flip-flop will be set by a pulse on the RST 7.5 pin even when the RST 7.5 interrupt is masked out.

The status of the three RST interrupt masks can only be affected by the SIM instruction and $\overline{\text{RESET IN}}$. (See SIM, Chapter 5 of the 8080/8085 User's Manual.)

The interrupts are arranged in a fixed priority that determines which interrupt is to be recognized if more than one is pending as follows: TRAP—highest priority, RST 7.5, RST 6.5, RST 5.5, INTR—lowest priority. This priority scheme does not take into account the priority of a routine that was started by a higher priority interrupt. RST 5.5 can interrupt an RST 7.5 routine if the interrupts are re-enabled before the end of the RST 7.5 routine.

The TRAP interrupt is useful for catastrophic events such as power failure or bus error. The TRAP input is recognized just as any other interrupt but has the

highest priority. It is not affected by any flag or mask. The TRAP input is both *edge and level sensitive.* The TRAP input must go high and remain high until it is acknowledged. It will not be recognized again until it goes low, then high again. This avoids any false triggering due to noise or logic glitches. Figure 4 illustrates the TRAP interrupt request circuitry within the 8085AH. Note that the servicing of any interrupt (TRAP, RST 7.5, RST 6.5, RST 5.5, INTR) disables all future interrupts (except TRAPs) until an EI instruction is executed.

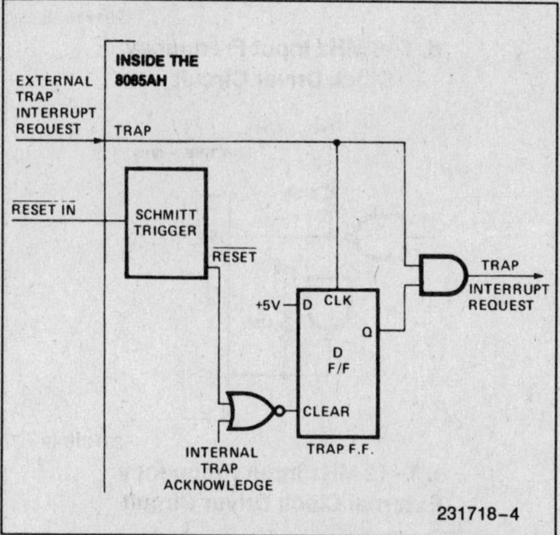

Figure 4. TRAP and RESET In Circuit

The TRAP interrupt is special in that it disables interrupts, but preserves the previous interrupt enable status. Performing the first RIM instruction following a TRAP interrupt allows you to determine whether interrupts were enabled or disabled prior to the TRAP. All subsequent RIM instructions provide current interrupt enable status. Performing a RIM instruction following INTR, or RST 5.5–7.5 will provide current Interrupt Enable status, revealing that interrupts are disabled. See the description of the RIM instruction in the 8080/8085 Family User's Manual.

The serial I/O system is also controlled by the RIM and SIM instruction. SID is read by RIM, and SIM sets the SOD data.

DRIVING THE X_1 AND X_2 INPUTS

You may drive the clock inputs of the 8085AH, 8085AH-2, or 8085AH-1 with a crystal, an LC tuned circuit, an RC network, or an external clock source. The crystal frequency must be at least 1 MHz, and must be twice the desired internal clock frequency; hence, the 8085AH is operated with a 6 MHz crystal (for 3 MHz clock), the 8085AH-2 operated with a 10 MHz crystal (for 5 MHz clock), and the 8085AH-1 can be operated with a 12 MHz crystal (for 6 MHz clock). If a crystal is used, it must have the following characteristics:

Parallel resonance at twice the clock frequency desired
C_L (load capacitance) $\leq$ 30 pF
C_S (Shunt capacitance) $\leq$ 7 pF
R_S (equivalent shunt resistance) $\leq 75\Omega$
Drive level: 10 mW
Frequency tolerance: $\pm$0.005% (suggested)

Note the use of the 20 pF capacitor between X_2 and ground. This capacitor is required with crystal frequencies below 4 MHz to assure oscillator startup at the correct frequency. A parallel-resonant LC citcuit may be used as the frequency-determining network for the 8085AH, providing that its frequency tolerance of approximately $\pm$10% is acceptable. The components are chosen from the formula:

$$f = \frac{1}{2\pi\sqrt{L(C_{ext} + C_{int})}}$$

To minimize variations in frequency, it is recommended that you choose a value for C_{ext} that is at least twice that of C_{int}, or 30 pF. The use of an LC circuit is not recommended for frequencies higher than approximately 5 MHz.

An RC circuit may be used as the frequency-determining network for the 8085AH if maintaining a precise clock frequency is of no importance. Variations in the on-chip timing generation can cause a wide variation in frequency when using the RC mode. Its advantage is its low component cost. The driving frequency generated by the circuit shown is approximately 3 MHz. It is not recommended that frequencies greatly higher or lower than this be attempted.

Figure 5 shows the recommended clock driver circuits. Note in d and e that pullup resistors are required to assure that the high level voltage of the input is at least 4V and maximum low level voltage of 0.8V.

For driving frequencies up to and including 6 MHz you may supply the driving signal to X_1 and leave X_2 open-circuited (Figure 5d). If the driving frequency is from 6 MHz to 12 MHz, stability of the clock generator will be improved by driving both X_1 and X_2 with a push-pull source (Figure 5e). To prevent self-oscillation of the 8085AH, be sure that X_2 is not coupled back to X_1 through the driving circuit.

1

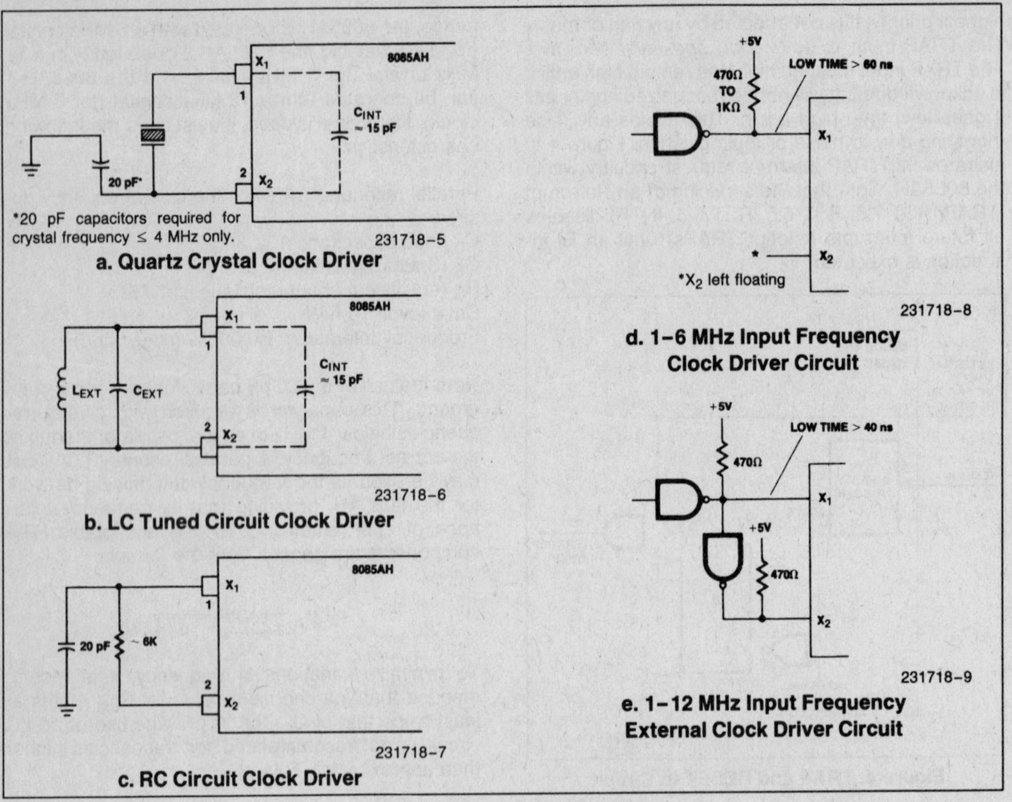

*20 pF capacitors required for crystal frequency ≤ 4 MHz only.

231718-5

a. Quartz Crystal Clock Driver

231718-6

b. LC Tuned Circuit Clock Driver

231718-7

c. RC Circuit Clock Driver

*X_2 left floating

231718-8

d. 1–6 MHz Input Frequency Clock Driver Circuit

231718-9

e. 1–12 MHz Input Frequency External Clock Driver Circuit

Figure 5. Clock Driver Circuits

GENERATING AN 8085AH WAIT STATE

If your system requirements are such that slow memories or peripheral devices are being used, the circuit shown in Figure 6 may be used to insert one WAIT state in each 8085AH machine cycle.

The D flip-flops should be chosen so that

- CLK is rising edge-triggered
- CLEAR is low-level active.

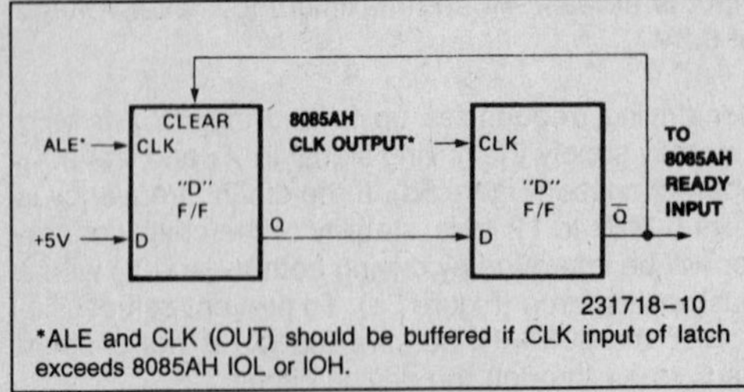

Figure 6. Generation of a Wait State for 8085AH CPU

As in the 8080, the READY line is used to extend the read and write pulse lengths so that the 8085AH can be used with slow memory. HOLD causes the CPU to relinquish the bus when it is through with it by floating the Address and Data Buses.

SYSTEM INTERFACE

The 8085AH family includes memory components, which are directly compatible to the 8085AH CPU. For example, a system consisting of the three chips, 8085AH, 8156H and 8755A will have the following features:

- 2K Bytes EPROM
- 256 Bytes RAM
- 1 Timer/Counter
- 4 8-bit I/O Ports
- 1 6-bit I/O Port
- 4 Interrupt Levels
- Serial In/Serial Out Ports

This minimum system, using the standard I/O technique is as shown in Figure 7.

In addition to the standard I/O, the memory mapped I/O offers an efficient I/O addressing technique. With this technique, an area of memory address space is assigned for I/O address, thereby, using the memory address for I/O manipulation. Figure 8 shows the system configuration of Memory Mapped I/O using 8085AH.

The 8085AH CPU can also interface with the standard memory that does *not* have the multiplexed address/data bus. It will require a simple 8-bit latch as shown in Figure 9.

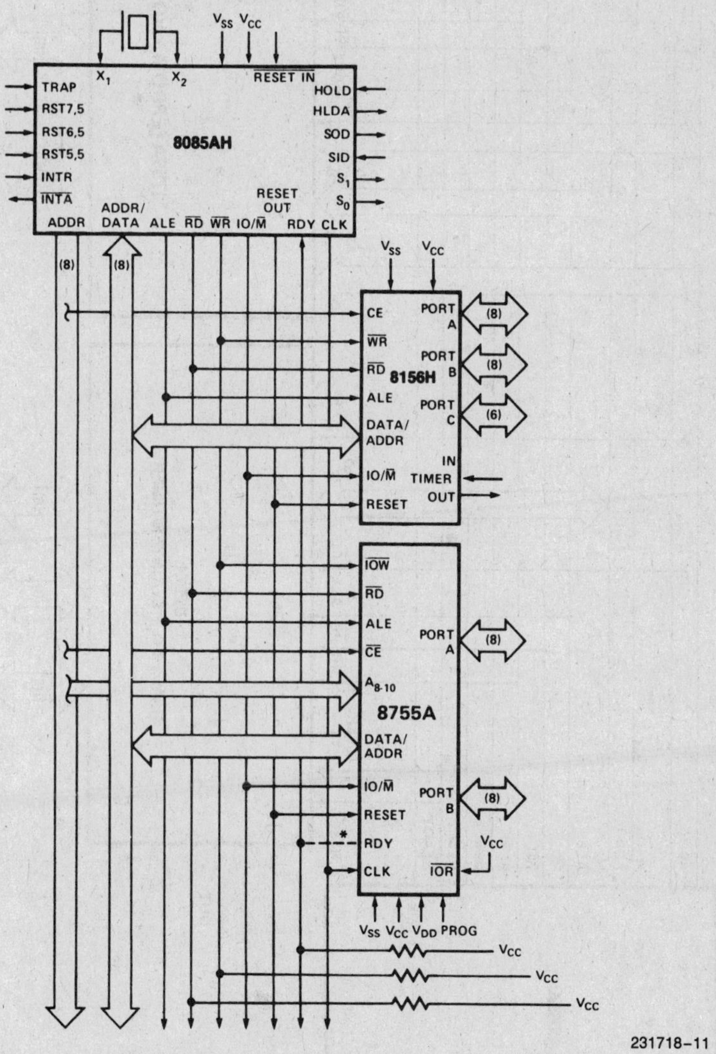

231718–11

***NOTE:**
Optional Connection

Figure 7. 8085AH Minimum System (Standard I/O Technique)

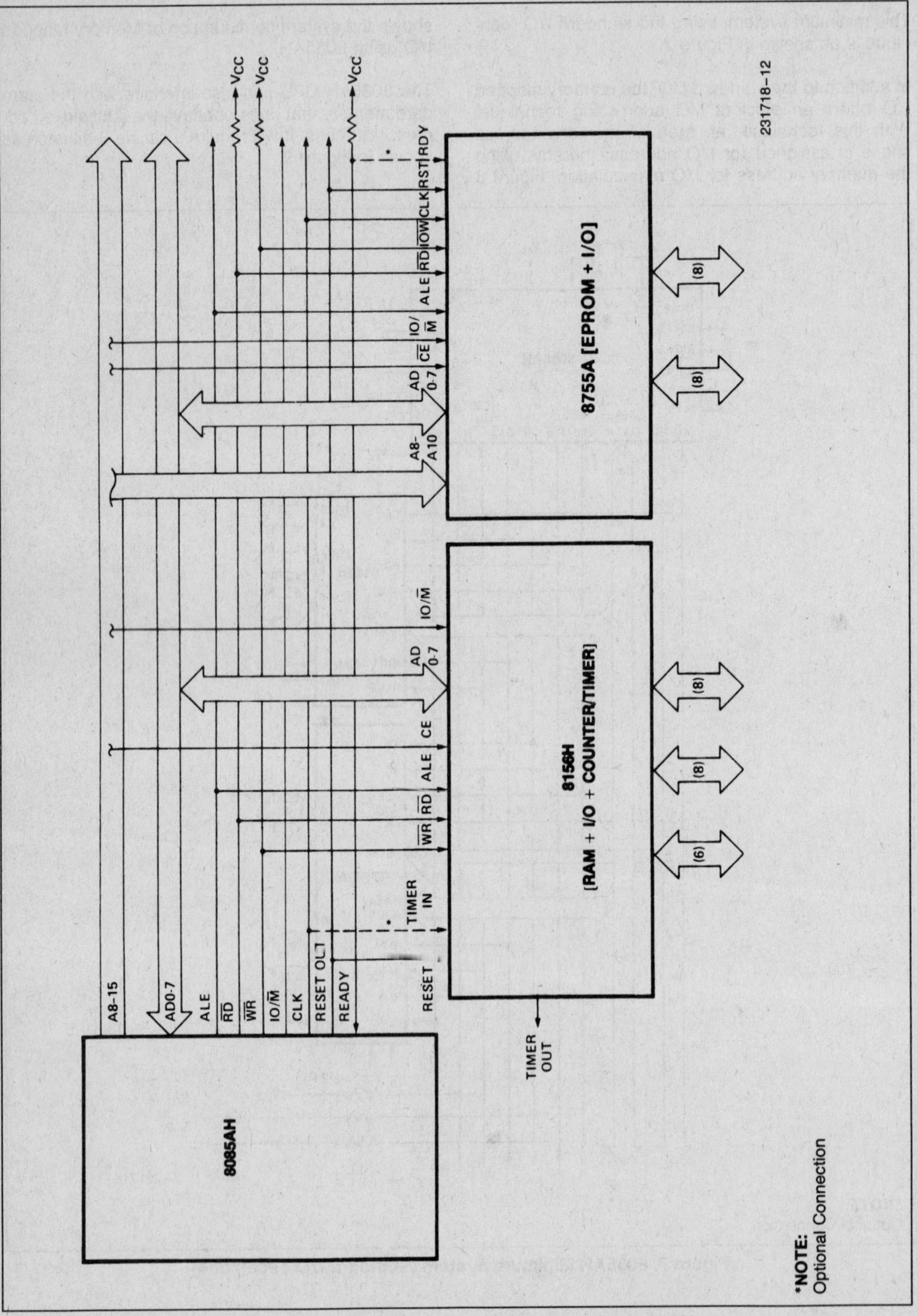

Figure 8. 8085 Minimum System (Memory Mapped I/O)

231718-13

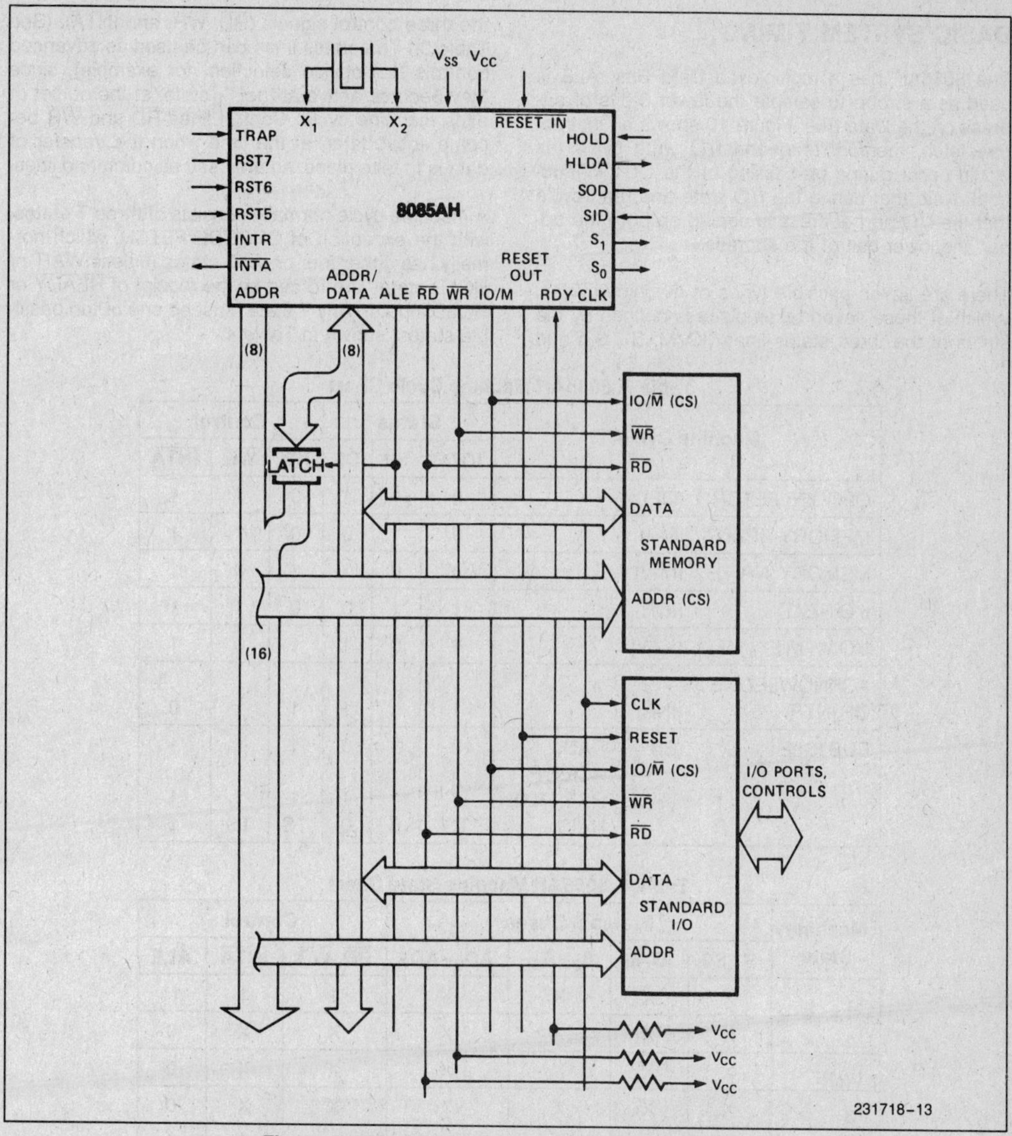

Figure 9. 8085 System (Using Standard Memories)

BASIC SYSTEM TIMING

The 8085AH has a multiplexed Data Bus. ALE is used as a strobe to sample the lower 8-bits of address on the Data Bus. Figure 10 shows an instruction fetch, memory read and I/O write cycle (as would occur during processing of the OUT instruction). Note that during the I/O write and read cycle that the I/O port address is copied on both the upper and lower half of the address.

There are seven possible types of machine cycles. Which of these seven takes place is defined by the status of the three status lines ($IO/\overline{M}$, S_1, S_0) and the three control signals ($\overline{RD}$, $\overline{WR}$, and $\overline{INTA}$). (See Table 3.) The status lines can be used as advanced controls (for device selection, for example), since they become active at the T_1 state, at the outset of each machine cycle. Control lines $\overline{RD}$ and $\overline{WR}$ become active later, at the time when the transfer of data is to take place, so are used as command lines.

A machine cycle normally consists of three T states, with the exception of OPCODE FETCH, which normally has either four or six T states (unless WAIT or HOLD states are forced by the receipt of $\overline{READY}$ or HOLD inputs). Any T state must be one of ten possible states, shown in Table 4.

Table 3. 8085AH Machine Cycle Chart

Machine Cycle			Status			Control		
			$IO/\overline{M}$	S1	S0	$\overline{RD}$	$\overline{WR}$	$\overline{INTA}$
OPCODE FETCH	(OF)		0	1	1	0	1	1
MEMORY READ	(MR)		0	1	0	0	1	1
MEMORY WRITE	(MW)		0	0	1	1	0	1
I/O READ	(IOR)		1	1	0	0	1	1
I/O WRITE	(IOW)		1	0	1	1	0	1
ACKNOWLEDGE OF INTR	(INA)		1	1	1	1	1	0
BUS IDLE	(BI):	DAD	0	1	0	1	1	1
		ACK.OF RST,TRAP	1	1	1	1	1	1
		HALT	TS	0	0	TS	TS	1

Table 4. 8085AH Machine State Chart

Machine State	Status & Buses				Control		
	S1,S0	$IO/\overline{M}$	A_8-A_{15}	AD_0-AD_7	$\overline{RD}$, $\overline{WR}$	$\overline{INTA}$	ALE
T_1	X	X	X	X	1	1	1*
T_2	X	X	X	X	X	X	0
T_{WAIT}	X	X	X	X	X	X	0
T_3	X	X	X	X	X	X	0
T_4	1	0†	X	TS	1	1	0
T_5	1	0†	X	TS	1	1	0
T_6	1	0†	X	TS	1	1	0
T_{RESET}	X	TS	TS	TS	TS	1	0
T_{HALT}	0	TS	TS	TS	TS	1	0
T_{HOLD}	X	TS	TS	TS	TS	1	0

0 = Logic "0" TS = High Impedance
1 = Logic "1" X = Unspecified
*ALE not generated during 2nd and 3rd machine cycles of DAD instruction.
†$IO/\overline{M}$ = 1 during T_4-T_6 of INA machine cycle.

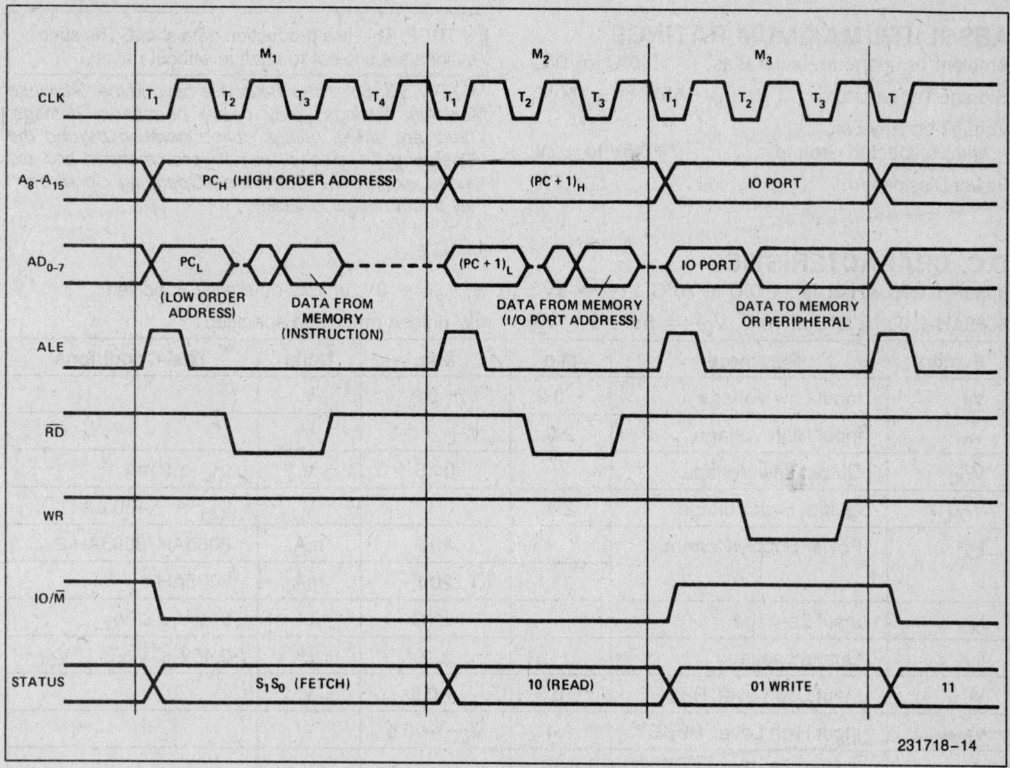

M1 M2 M3

CLK T1 T2 T3 T4 T1 T2 T3 T1 T2 T3 T

A8-A15 PCH (HIGH ORDER ADDRESS) (PC + 1)H IO PORT

AD0-7 PCL (PC + 1)L IO PORT

(LOW ORDER ADDRESS) DATA FROM MEMORY (INSTRUCTION) DATA FROM MEMORY (I/O PORT ADDRESS) DATA TO MEMORY OR PERIPHERAL

ALE

RD

WR

IO/M

STATUS S1S0 (FETCH) 10 (READ) 01 WRITE 11

231718–14

Figure 10. 8085AH Basic System Timing

1

ABSOLUTE MAXIMUM RATINGS*

Ambient Temperature under Bias ......0°C to 70°C
Storage Temperature ....−65°C to +150°C
Voltage on Any Pin
with Respect to Ground..........−0.5V to +7V
Power Dissipation..........................1.5W

NOTICE: This is a production data sheet. The specifications are subject to change without notice.

**WARNING: Stressing the device beyond the "Absolute Maximum Ratings" may cause permanent damage. These are stress ratings only. Operation beyond the "Operating Conditions" is not recommended and extended exposure beyond the "Operating Conditions" may affect device reliability.*

D.C. CHARACTERISTICS

8085AH, 8085AH-2: T_A = 0°C to 70°C, V_{CC} = 5V ±10%, V_{SS} = 0V; unless otherwise specified*
8085AH-1: T_A = 0°C to 70°C, V_{CC} = 5V ±5%, V_{SS} = 0V; unless otherwise specified*

Symbol	Parameter	Min	Max	Units	Test Conditions
V_{IL}	Input Low Voltage	−0.5	+0.8	V	
V_{IH}	Input High Voltage	2.0	V_{CC} +0.5	V	
V_{OL}	Output Low Voltage		0.45	V	I_{OL} = 2 mA
V_{OH}	Output High Voltage	2.4		V	I_{OH} = −400 μA
I_{CC}	Power Supply Current		135	mA	8085AH, 8085AH-2
			200	mA	8085AH-1
I_{IL}	Input Leakage		±10	μA	$0 \le V_{IN} \le V_{CC}$
I_{LO}	Output Leakage		±10	μA	$0.45V \le V_{OUT} \le V_{CC}$
V_{ILR}	Input Low Level, RESET	−0.5	+0.8	V	
V_{IHR}	Input High Level, RESET	2.4	V_{CC} + 0.5	V	
V_{HY}	Hysteresis, RESET	0.15		V	

A.C. CHARACTERISTICS

8085AH, 8085AH-2: T_A = 0°C to 70°C, V_{CC} = 5V ±10%, V_{SS} = 0V*
8085AH-1: T_A = 0°C to 70°C, V_{CC} = 5V ±5%, V_{SS} = 0V

Symbol	Parameter	8085AH (2)		8085AH-2 (2)		8085AH-1 (2)		Units
		Min	Max	Min	Max	Min	Max	
t_{CYC}	CLK Cycle Period	320	2000	200	2000	167	2000	ns
t_1	CLK Low Time (Standard CLK Loading)	80		40		20		ns
t_2	CLK High Time (Standard CLK Loading)	120		70		50		ns
t_r, t_f	CLK Rise and Fall Time		30		30		30	ns
t_{XKR}	X_1 Rising to CLK Rising	20	120	20	100	20	100	ns
t_{XKF}	X_1 Rising to CLK Falling	20	150	20	110	20	110	ns
t_{AC}	A_{8-15} Valid to Leading Edge of Control (1)	270		115		70		ns
t_{ACL}	A_{0-7} Valid to Leading Edge of Control	240		115		60		ns
t_{AD}	A_{0-15} Valid to Valid Data In		575		350		225	ns
t_{AFR}	Address Float after Leading Edge of $\overline{READ}$ ($\overline{INTA}$)		0		0		0	ns
t_{AL}	A_{8-15} Valid before Trailing Edge of ALE (1)	115		50		25		ns

***NOTE:**
For Extended Temperature EXPRESS use M8085AH Electricals Parameters.

A.C. CHARACTERISTICS (Continued)

Symbol	Parameter	8085AH (2)		8085AH-2 (2)		8085AH-1 (2)		Units
		Min	Max	Min	Max	Min	Max	
t_{ALL}	A_{0-7} Valid before Trailing Edge of ALE	90		50		25		ns
t_{ARY}	READY Valid from Address Valid		220		100		40	ns
t_{CA}	Address (A_{8-15}) Valid after Control	120		60		30		ns
t_{CC}	Width of Control Low ($\overline{RD}$, $\overline{WR}$, $\overline{INTA}$) Edge of ALE	400		230		150		ns
t_{CL}	Trailing Edge of Control to Leading Edge of ALE	50		25		0		ns
t_{DW}	Data Valid to Trialing Edge of $\overline{WRITE}$	420		230		140		ns
t_{HABE}	HLDA to Bus Enable		210		150		150	ns
t_{HABF}	Bus Float after HLDA		210		150		150	ns
t_{HACK}	HLDA Valid to Trailing Edge of CLK	110		40		0		ns
t_{HDH}	HOLD Hold Time	0		0		0		ns
t_{HDS}	HOLD Setup Time to Trailing Edge of CLK	170		120		120		ns
t_{INH}	INTR Hold Time	0		0		0		ns
t_{INS}	INTR, RST, and TRAP Setup Time to Falling Edge of CLK	160		150		150		ns
t_{LA}	Address Hold Time after ALE	100		50		20		ns
t_{LC}	Trailing Edge of ALE to Leading Edge of Control	130		60		25		ns
t_{LCK}	ALE Low During CLK High	100		50		15		ns
t_{LDR}	ALE to Valid Data during Read		460		270		175	ns
t_{LDW}	ALE to Valid Data during Write		200		140		110	ns
t_{LL}	ALE Width	140		80		50		ns
t_{LRY}	ALE to READY Stable		110		30		10	ns
t_{RAE}	Trailing Edge of $\overline{READ}$ to Re-Enabling of Address	150		90		50		ns
t_{RD}	$\overline{READ}$ (or $\overline{INTA}$) to Valid Data		300		150		75	ns
t_{RV}	Control Trailing Edge to Leading Edge of Next Control	400		220		160		ns
t_{RDH}	Data Hold Time after $\overline{READ}$ $\overline{INTA}$	0		0		0		ns
t_{RYH}	READY Hold Time	0		0		5		ns
t_{RYS}	READY Setup Time to Leading Edge of CLK	110		100		100		ns
t_{WD}	Data Valid after Trailing Edge of $\overline{WRITE}$	100		60		30		ns
t_{WDL}	LEADING Edge of $\overline{WRITE}$ to Data Valid		40		20		30	ns

NOTES:

1. A_8–A_{15} address Specs apply IO/$\overline{M}$, S_0, and S_1 except A_8–A_{15} are undefined during T_4–T_6 of OF cycle whereas IO/$\overline{M}$, S_0, and S_1 are stable.
2. *Test Conditions:* t_{CYC} = 320 ns (8085AH)/200 ns (8085AH-2);/167 ns (8085AH-1); C_L = 150 pF.
3. For all output timing where C ≠ 150 pF use the following correction factors:
   25 pF ≤ C_L < 150 pF: −0.10 ns/pF
   150 pF < C_L ≤ 300 pF: +0.30 ns/pF
4. Output timings are measured with purely capacitive load.
5. To calculate timing specifications at other values of t_{CYC} use Table 5.

A.C. TESTING INPUT, OUTPUT WAVEFORM

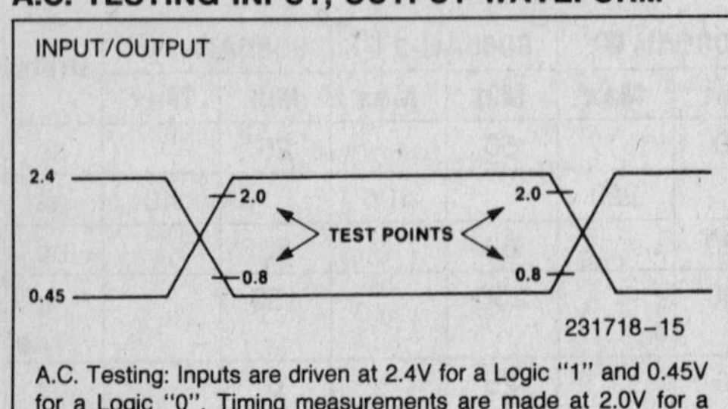

A.C. Testing: Inputs are driven at 2.4V for a Logic "1" and 0.45V for a Logic "0". Timing measurements are made at 2.0V for a Logic "1" and 0.8V for a Logic "0".

A.C. TESTING LOAD CIRCUIT

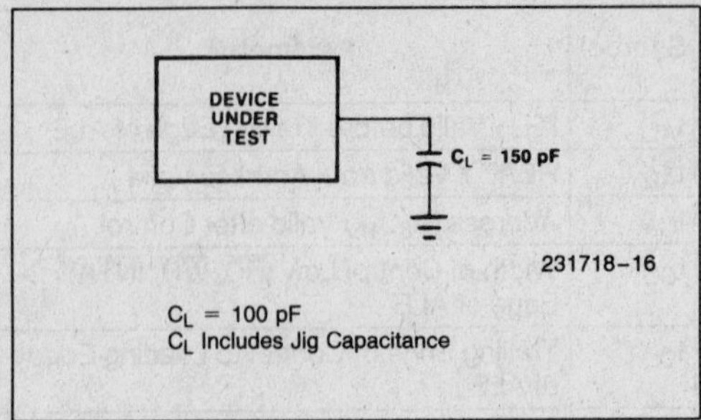

C_L = 100 pF
C_L Includes Jig Capacitance

Table 5. Bus Timing Specification as a T_{CYC} Dependent

Symbol	8085AH	8085AH-2	8085AH-1	
t_{AL}	(1/2)T − 45	(1/2)T − 50	(1/2)T − 58	Minimum
t_{LA}	(1/2)T − 60	(1/2)T − 50	(1/2)T − 63	Minimum
t_{LL}	(1/2)T − 20	(1/2)T − 20	(1/2)T − 33	Minimum
t_{LCK}	(1/2)T − 60	(1/2)T − 50	(1/2)T − 68	Minimum
t_{LC}	(1/2)T − 30	(1/2)T − 40	(1/2)T − 58	Minimum
t_{AD}	(5/2 + N)T − 225	(5/2 + N)T − 150	(5/2 + N)T − 192	Maximum
t_{RD}	(3/2 + N)T − 180	(3/2 + N)T − 150	(3/2 + N)T − 175	Maximum
t_{RAE}	(1/2)T − 10	(1/2)T − 10	(1/2)T − 33	Minimum
t_{CA}	(1/2)T − 40	(1/2)T − 40	(1/2)T − 53	Minimum
t_{DW}	(3/2 + N)T − 60	(3/2 + N)T − 70	(3/2 + N)T − 110	Minimum
t_{WD}	(1/2)T − 60	(1/2)T − 40	(1/2)T − 53	Minimum
t_{CC}	(3/2 + N)T − 80	(3/2 + N)T − 70	(3/2 + N)T − 100	Minimum
t_{CL}	(1/2)T − 110	(1/2)T − 75	(1/2)T − 83	Minimum
t_{ARY}	(3/2)T − 260	(3/2)T − 200	(3/2)T − 210	Maximum
t_{HACK}	(1/2)T − 50	(1/2)T − 60	(1/2)T − 83	Minimum
t_{HABF}	(1/2)T + 50	(1/2)T + 50	(1/2)T + 67	Maximum
t_{HABE}	(1/2)T + 50	(1/2)T + 50	(1/2)T + 67	Maximum
t_{AC}	(2/2)T − 50	(2/2)T − 85	(2/2)T − 97	Minimum
t_1	(1/2)T − 80	(1/2)T − 60	(1/2)T − 63	Minimum
t_2	(1/2)T − 40	(1/2)T − 30	(1/2)T − 33	Minimum
t_{RV}	(3/2)T − 80	(3/2)T − 80	(3/2)T − 90	Minimum
t_{LDR}	(4/2 + N)T − 180	(4/2)T − 130	(4/2)T − 159	Maximum

NOTE:
N is equal to the total WAIT states. T = t_{CYC}.

WAVEFORMS

CLOCK

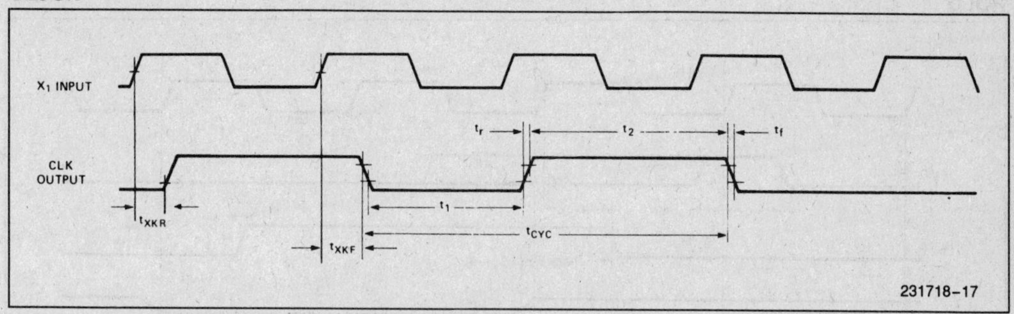

READ

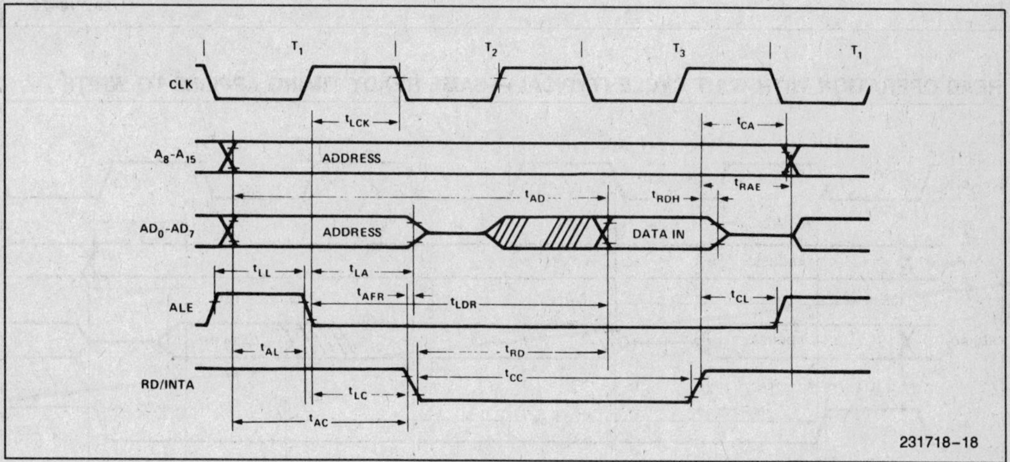

WRITE

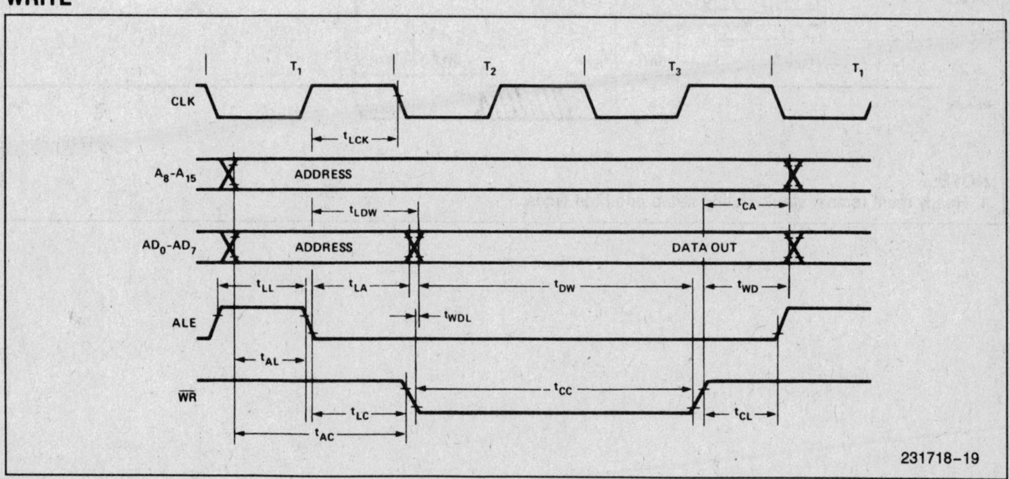

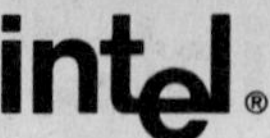

WAVEFORMS (Continued)

HOLD

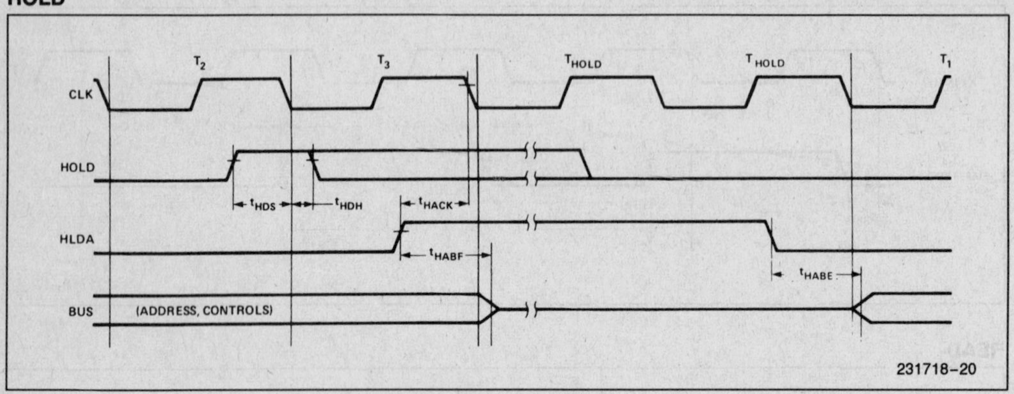

READ OPERATION WITH WAIT CYCLE (TYPICAL)—SAME READY TIMING APPLIES TO WRITE

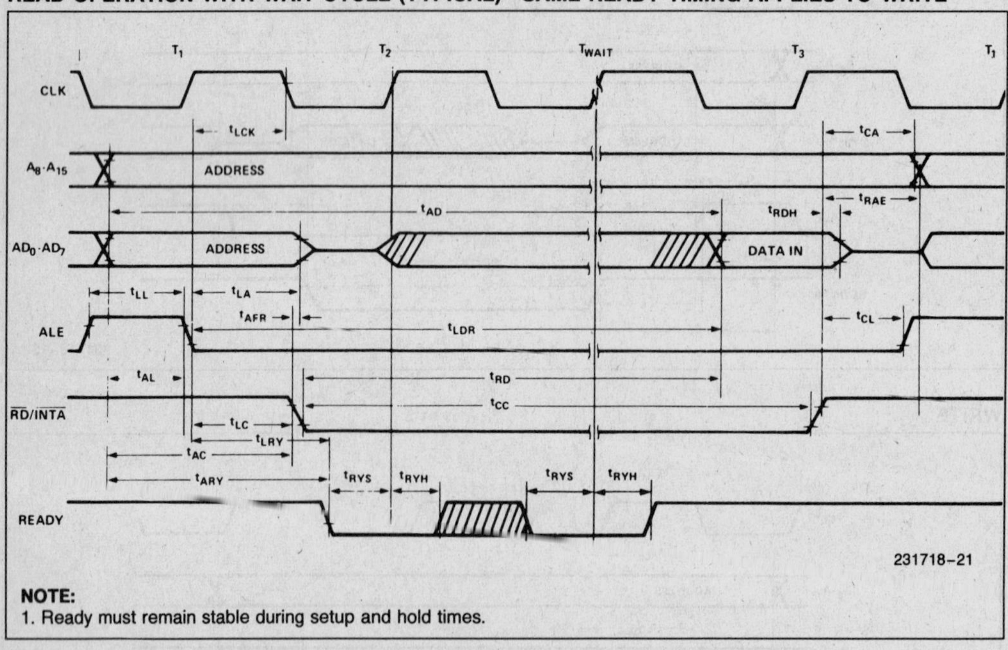

NOTE:
1. Ready must remain stable during setup and hold times.

WAVEFORMS (Continued)

INTERRUPT AND HOLD

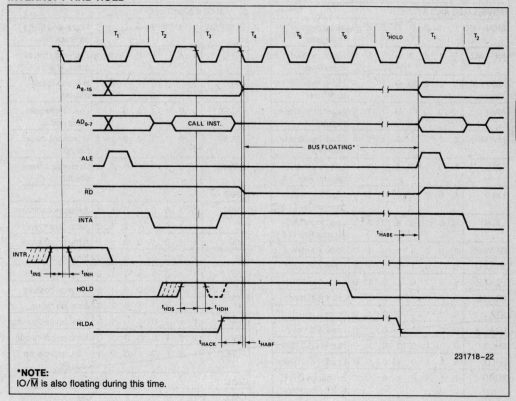

***NOTE:**
IO/$\overline{M}$ is also floating during this time.

Table 6. Instruction Set Summary

Mnemonic	Instruction Code								Operations Description
	D_7	D_6	D_5	D_4	D_3	D_2	D_1	D_0	
MOVE, LOAD AND STORE									
MOVr1 r2	0	1	D	D	D	S	S	S	Move register to register
MOV M.r	0	1	1	1	0	S	S	S	Move register to memory
MOV r.M	0	1	D	D	D	1	1	0	Move memory to register
MVI r	0	0	D	D	D	1	1	0	Move immediate register
MVI M	0	0	1	1	0	1	1	0	Move immediate memory
LXI B	0	0	0	0	0	0	0	1	Load immediate register Pair B & C
LXI D	0	0	0	1	0	0	0	1	Load immediate register Pair D & E
LXI H	0	0	1	0	0	0	0	1	Load immediate register Pair H & L
STAX B	0	0	0	0	0	0	1	0	Store A indirect
STAX D	0	0	0	1	0	0	1	0	Store A indirect
LDAX B	0	0	1	0	1	0	1	0	Load A indirect
LDAX D	0	0	0	1	1	0	1	0	Load A indirect
STA	0	0	1	1	0	0	1	0	Store A direct
LDA	0	0	1	1	1	0	1	0	Load A direct
SHLD	0	0	1	0	0	0	1	0	Store H & L direct
LHLD	0	0	1	0	1	0	1	0	Load H & L direct
XCHG	1	1	1	0	1	0	1	1	Exchange D & E, H & L Registers
STACK OPS									
PUSH B	1	1	0	0	0	1	0	1	Push register Pair B & C on stack
PUSH D	1	1	0	1	0	1	0	1	Push register Pair D & E on stack
PUSH H	1	1	1	0	0	1	0	1	Push register Pair H & L on stack
PUSH PSW	1	1	1	1	0	1	0	1	Push A and Flags on stack
POP B	1	1	0	0	0	0	0	1	Pop register Pair B & C off stack
POP D	1	1	0	1	0	0	0	1	Pop register Pair D & E off stack
POP H	1	1	1	0	0	0	0	1	Pop register Pair H & L off stack

Mnemonic	Instruction Code								Operations Description
	D_7	D_6	D_5	D_4	D_3	D_2	D_1	D_0	
STACK OPS (Continued)									
POP PSW	1	1	1	1	0	0	0	1	Pop A and Flags off stack
XTHL	1	1	1	0	0	0	1	1	Exchange top of stack, H & L
SPHL	1	1	1	1	1	0	0	1	H & L to stack pointer
LXI SP	0	0	1	1	0	0	0	1	Load immediate stack pointer
INX SP	0	0	1	1	0	0	1	1	Increment stack pointer
DCX SP	0	0	1	1	1	0	1	1	Decrement stack pointer
JUMP									
JMP	1	1	0	0	0	0	1	1	Jump unconditional
JC	1	1	0	1	1	0	1	0	Jump on carry
JNC	1	1	0	1	0	0	1	0	Jump on no carry
JZ	1	1	0	0	1	0	1	0	Jump on zero
JNZ	1	1	0	0	0	0	1	0	Jump on no zero
JP	1	1	1	1	0	0	1	0	Jump on positive
JM	1	1	1	1	1	0	1	0	Jump on minus
JPE	1	1	1	0	1	0	1	0	Jump on parity even
JPO	1	1	1	0	0	0	1	0	Jump on parity odd
PCHL	1	1	1	0	1	0	0	1	H & L to program counter
CALL									
CALL	1	1	0	0	1	1	0	1	Call unconditional
CC	1	1	0	1	1	1	0	0	Call on carry
CNC	1	1	0	1	0	1	0	0	Call on no carry
CZ	1	1	0	0	1	1	0	0	Call on zero
CNZ	1	1	0	0	0	1	0	0	Call on no zero
CP	1	1	1	1	0	1	0	0	Call on positive
CM	1	1	1	1	1	1	0	0	Call on minus
CPE	1	1	1	0	1	1	0	0	Call on parity even
CPO	1	1	1	0	0	1	0	0	Call on parity odd
RETURN									
RET	1	1	0	0	1	0	0	1	Return
RC	1	1	0	1	1	0	0	0	Return on carry
RNC	1	1	0	1	0	0	0	0	Return on no carry
RZ	1	1	0	0	1	0	0	0	Return on zero

Table 6. Instruction Set Summary (Continued)

Mnemonic	Instruction Code D_7	D_6	D_5	D_4	D_3	D_2	D_1	D_0	Operations Description
RETURN (Continued)									
RNZ	1	1	0	0	0	0	0	0	Return on no zero
RP	1	1	1	1	0	0	0	0	Return on positive
RM	1	1	1	1	1	0	0	0	Return on minus
RPE	1	1	1	0	1	0	0	0	Return on parity even
RPO	1	1	1	0	0	0	0	0	Return on parity odd
RESTART									
RST	1	1	A	A	A	1	1	1	Restart
INPUT/OUTPUT									
IN	1	1	0	1	1	0	1	1	Input
OUT	1	1	0	1	0	0	1	1	Output
INCREMENT AND DECREMENT									
INR r	0	0	D	D	D	1	0	0	Increment register
DCR r	0	0	D	D	D	1	0	1	Decrement register
INR M	0	0	1	1	0	1	0	0	Increment memory
DCR M	0	0	1	1	0	1	0	1	Decrement memory
INX B	0	0	0	0	0	0	1	1	Increment B & C registers
INX D	0	0	0	1	0	0	1	1	Increment D & E registers
INX H	0	0	1	0	0	0	1	1	Increment H & L registers
DCX B	0	0	0	0	1	0	1	1	Decrement B & C
DCX D	0	0	0	1	1	0	1	1	Decrement D & E
DCX H	0	0	1	0	1	0	1	1	Decrement H & L
ADD									
ADD r	1	0	0	0	0	S	S	S	Add register to A
ADC r	1	0	0	0	1	S	S	S	Add register to A with carry
ADD M	1	0	C	0	0	1	1	0	Add memory to A
ADC M	1	0	0	0	1	1	1	0	Add memory to A with carry
ADI	1	1	0	0	0	1	1	0	Add immediate to A
ACI	1	1	0	0	1	1	1	0	Add immediate to A with carry
DAD B	0	0	0	0	1	0	0	1	Add B & C to H & L

Mnemonic	Instruction Code D_7	D_6	D_5	D_4	D_3	D_2	D_1	D_0	Operations Description
ADD (Continued)									
DAD D	0	0	0	1	1	0	0	1	Add D & E to H & L
DAD H	0	0	1	0	1	0	0	1	Add H & L to H & L
DAD SP	0	0	1	1	1	0	0	1	Add stack pointer to H & L
SUBTRACT									
SUB r	1	0	0	1	0	S	S	S	Subtract register from A
SBB r	1	0	0	1	1	S	S	S	Subtract register from A with borrow
SUB M	1	0	0	1	0	1	1	0	Subtract memory from A
SBB M	1	0	0	1	1	1	1	0	Subtract memory from A with borrow
SUI	1	1	0	1	0	1	1	0	Subtract immediate from A
SBI	1	1	0	1	1	1	1	0	Subtract immediate from A with borrow
LOGICAL									
ANA r	1	0	1	0	0	S	S	S	And register with A
XRA r	1	0	1	0	1	S	S	S	Exclusive OR register with A
ORA r	1	0	1	1	0	S	S	S	OR register with A
CMP r	1	0	1	1	1	S	S	S	Compare register with A
ANA M	1	0	1	0	0	1	1	0	And memory with A
XRA M	1	0	1	0	1	1	1	0	Exclusive OR memory with A
ORA M	1	0	1	1	0	1	1	0	OR memory with A
CMP M	1	0	1	1	1	1	1	0	Compare memory with A
ANI	1	1	1	0	0	1	1	0	And immediate with A
XRI	1	1	1	0	1	1	1	0	Exclusive OR immediate with A
ORI	1	1	1	1	0	1	1	0	OR immediate with A
CPI	1	1	1	1	1	1	1	0	Compare immediate with A

Table 6. Instruction Set Summary (Continued)

Mnemonic	D_7	D_6	D_5	D_4	D_3	D_2	D_1	D_0	Operations Description
ROTATE									
RLC	0	0	0	0	0	1	1	1	Rotate A left
RRC	0	0	0	0	1	1	1	1	Rotate A right
RAL	0	0	0	1	0	1	1	1	Rotate A left through carry
RAR	0	0	0	1	1	1	1	1	Rotate A right through carry
SPECIALS									
CMA	0	0	1	0	1	1	1	1	Complement A
STC	0	0	1	1	0	1	1	1	Set carry
CMC	0	0	1	1	1	1	1	1	Complement carry
DAA	0	0	1	0	0	1	1	1	Decimal adjust A

Mnemonic	D_7	D_6	D_5	D_4	D_3	D_2	D_1	D_0	Operations Description
CONTROL									
EI	1	1	1	1	1	0	1	1	Enable Interrupts
DI	1	1	1	1	0	0	1	1	Disable Interrupt
NOP	0	0	0	0	0	0	0	0	No-operation
HLT	0	1	1	1	0	1	1	0	Halt
NEW 8085AH INSTRUCTIONS									
RIM	0	0	1	0	0	0	0	0	Read Interrupt Mask
SIM	0	0	1	1	0	0	0	0	Set Interrupt Mask

NOTES:
1. DDS or SSS: B 000, C 001, D 010, E011, H 100, L101, Memory 110, A 111.
2. Two possible cycle times (6/12) indicate instruction cycles dependent on condition flags.

8155H/8156H/8155H-2/8156H-2 2048-BIT STATIC HMOS RAM WITH I/O PORTS AND TIMER

- **Single +5V Power Supply with 10% Voltage Margins**
- **30% Lower Power Consumption than the 8155 and 8156**
- **256 Word x 8 Bits**
- **Completely Static Operation**
- **Internal Address Latch**
- **2 Programmable 8-Bit I/O Ports**
- **1 Programmable 6-Bit I/O Port**
- **Programmable 14-Bit Binary Counter/ Timer**
- **Compatible with 8085AH and 8088 CPU**
- **Multiplexed Address and Data Bus**
- **Available in EXPRESS**
  - **—Standard Temperature Range**
  - **—Extended Temperature Range**

1

The Intel 8155H and 8156H are RAM and I/O chips implemented in N-Channel, depletion load, silicon gate technology (HMOS), to be used in the 8085AH and 8088 microprocessor systems. The RAM portion is designed with 2048 static cells organized as 256 x 8. They have a maximum access time of 400 ns to permit use with no wait states in 8085AH CPU. The 8155H-2 and 8156H-2 have maximum access times of 330 ns for use with the 8085H-2 and the 5 MHz 8088 CPU.

The I/O portion consists of three general purpose I/O ports. One of the three ports can be programmed to be status pins, thus allowing the other two ports to operate in handshake mode.

A 14-bit programmable counter/timer is also included on chip to provide either a square wave or terminal count pulse for the CPU system depending on timer mode.

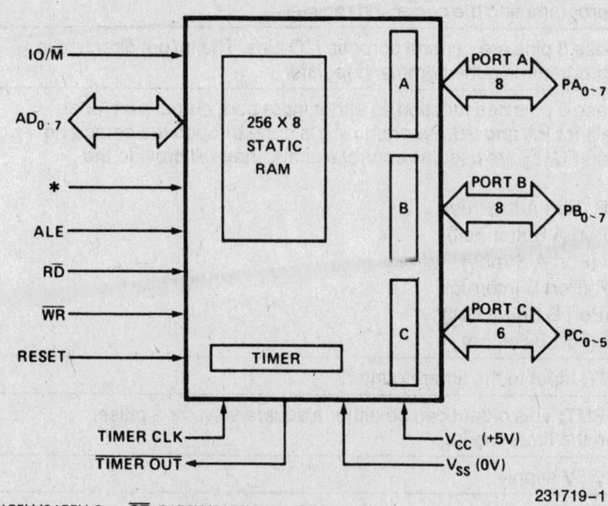

*8155H/8155H-2 = $\overline{CE}$, 8156H/8156H-2 = CE

Figure 1. Block Diagram

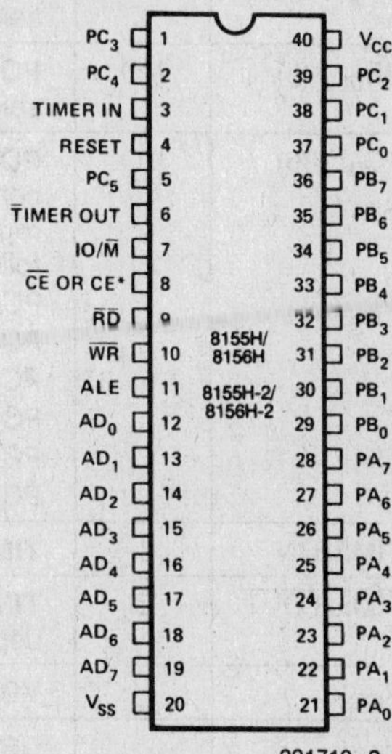

Figure 2. Pin Configuration

December 1986
Order Number: 231719-001

Table 1. Pin Description

Symbol	Type	Name and Function
RESET	I	**RESET:** Pulse provided by the 8085AH to initialize the system (connect to 8085AH RESET OUT). Input high on this line resets the chip and initializes the three I/O ports to input mode. The width of RESET pulse should typically be two 8085AH clock cycle times.
AD_{0-7}	I/O	**ADDRESS/DATA:** 3-state Address/Data lines that interface with the CPU lower 8-bit Address/Data Bus. The 8-bit address is latched into the address latch inside the 8155H/56H on the falling edge of ALE. The address can be either for the memory section or the I/O section depending on the $IO/\overline{M}$ input. The 8-bit data is either written into the chip or read from the chip, depending on the $\overline{WR}$ or $\overline{RD}$ input signal.
CE or $\overline{CE}$	I	**CHIP ENABLE:** On the 8155H, this pin is $\overline{CE}$ and is ACTIVE LOW. On the 8156H, this pin is CE and is ACTIVE HIGH.
$\overline{RD}$	I	**READ CONTROL:** Input low on this line with the Chip Enable active enables and AD_{0-7} buffers. If $IO/\overline{M}$ pin is low, the RAM content will be read out to the AD bus. Otherwise the content of the selected I/O port or command/status registers will be read to the AD bus.
$\overline{WR}$	I	**WRITE CONTROL:** Input low on this line with the Chip Enable active causes the data on the Address/Data bus to be written to the RAM or I/O ports and command/status register, depending on $IO/\overline{M}$.
ALE	I	**ADDRESS LATCH ENABLE:** This control signal latches both the address on the AD_{0-7} lines and the state of the Chip Enable and $IO/\overline{M}$ into the chip at the falling edge of ALE.
$IO/\overline{M}$	I	**I/O MEMORY:** Selects memory if low and I/O and command/status registers if high.
PA_{0-7} (8)	I/O	**PORT A:** These 8 pins are general purpose I/O pins. The in/out direction is selected by programming the command register.
PB_{0-7} (8)	I/O	**PORT B:** These 8 pins are general purpose I/O pins. The in/out direction is selected by programming the command register.
PC_{0-5} (6)	I/O	**PORT C:** These 6 pins can function as either input port, output port, or as control signals for PA and PB. Programming is done through the command register. When PC_{0-5} are used as control signals, they will provide the following: PC_0—A INTR (Port A Interrupt) PC_1—ABF (Port A Buffer Full) PC_2—$\overline{A\ STB}$ (Port A Strobe) PC_3—B INTR (Port B Interrupt) PC_4—B BF (Port B Buffer Full) PC_5—$\overline{B\ STB}$ (Port B Strobe)
TIMER IN	I	**TIMER INPUT:** Input to the timer-counter.
$\overline{TIMER\ OUT}$	O	**TIMER OUTPUT:** This output can be either a square wave or a pulse, depending on the timer mode.
V_{CC}		**VOLTAGE:** +5V supply.
V_{SS}		**GROUND:** Ground reference.

FUNCTIONAL DESCRIPTION

The 8155H/8156H contains the following:

- 2K Bit Static RAM organized as 256 x 8
- Two 8-bit I/O ports (PA & PB) and one 6-bit I/O port (PC)
- 14-bit timer-counter

The IO/$\overline{M}$ (IO/Memory Select) pin selects either the five registers (Command, Status, PA_{0-7}, PB_{0-7}, PC_{0-5}) or the memory (RAM) portion.

The 8-bit address on the Address/Data lines, Chip Enable input CE or $\overline{CE}$, and IO/$\overline{M}$ are all latched on-chip at the falling edge of ALE.

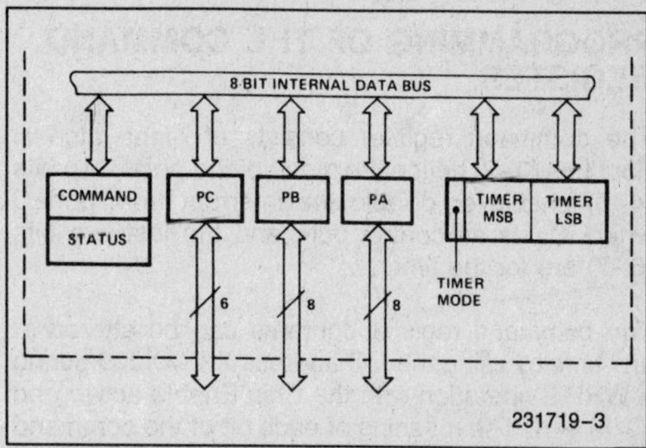

Figure 3. 8155H/8156H Internal Registers

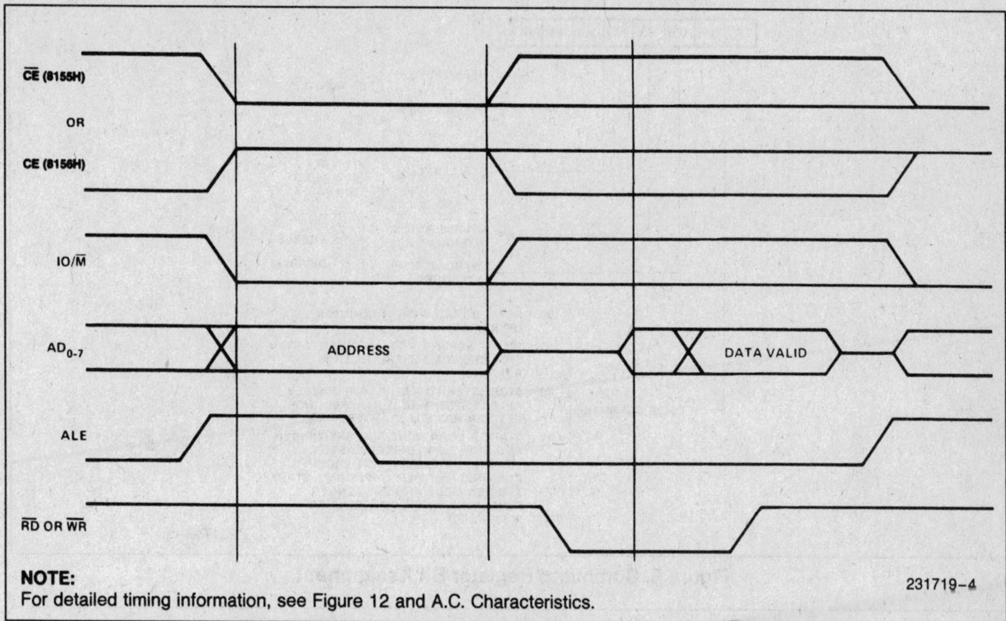

NOTE:
For detailed timing information, see Figure 12 and A.C. Characteristics.

Figure 4. 8155H/8156H On-Board Memory Read/Write Cycle

PROGRAMMING OF THE COMMAND REGISTER

The command register consists of eight latches. Four bits (0–3) define the mode of the ports, two bits (4–5) enable or disable the interrupt from port C when it acts as control port, and the last two bits (6–7) are for the timer.

The command register contents can be altered at any time by using the I/O address XXXXX000 during a WRITE operation with the Chip Enable active and $IO/\overline{M} = 1$. The meaning of each bit of the command byte is defined in Figure 5. The contents of the command register may never be read.

READING THE STATUS REGISTER

The status register consists of seven latches, one for each bit; six (0–5) for the status of the ports and one (6) for the status of the timer.

The status of the timer and the I/O section can be polled by reading the Status Register (Address XXXXX000). Status word format is shown in Figure 6. Note that you may never write to the status register since the command register shares the same I/O address and the command register is selected when a write to that address is issued.

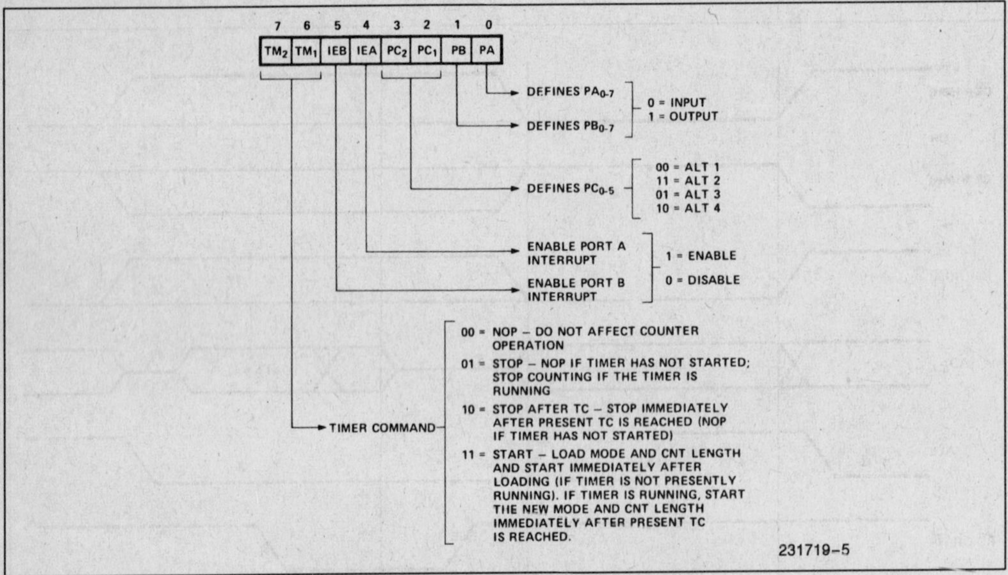

Figure 5. Command Register Bit Assignment

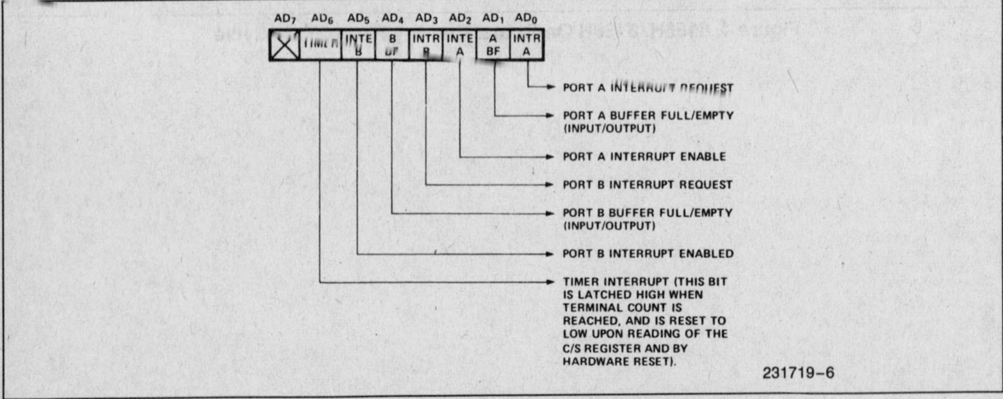

Figure 6. Status Register Bit Assignment

INPUT/OUTPUT SECTION

The I/O section of the 8155H/8156H consists of five registers: (see Figure 7.)

- **Command/Status Register (C/S)**—Both registers are assigned the address XXXXX000. The C/S address serves the dual purpose.
  When the C/S registers are selected during WRITE operation, a command is written into the command register. The contents of this register are *not* accessible through the pins.
  When the C/S (XXXXX000) is selected during a READ operation, the status information of the I/O ports and the timer becomes available on the AD_{0-7} lines.
- **PA Register**—This register can be programmed to be either input or output ports depending on the status of the contents of the C/S Register. Also depending on the command, this port can operate in either the basic mode or the strobed mode (see timing diagram). The I/O pins assigned in relation to this register are PA_{0-7}. The address of this register is XXXXX001.
- **PB Register**—This register functions the same as PA Register. The I/O pins assigned are PB_{0-7}. The address of this register is XXXXX010.
- **PC Register**—This register has the address XXXXX011 and contains only 6 bits. The 6 bits can be programmed to be either input ports, output ports or as control signals for PA and PB by properly programming the AD_2 and AD_3 bits of the C/S register.
  When PC_{0-5} is used as a control port, 3 bits are assigned for Port A and 3 for Port B. The first bit is an interrupt that the 8155H sends out. The second is an output signal indicating whether the buffer is full or empty, and the third is an input pin to accept a strobe for the strobed input mode. (See Table 2.)

When the 'C' port is programmed to either ALT3 or ALT4, the control signals for PA and PB are initialized as follows:

Control	Input Mode	Output Mode
BF	Low	Low
INTR	Low	High
STB	Input Control	Input Control

I/O Address†								Selection
A7	A6	A5	A4	A3	A2	A1	A0	
X	X	X	X	X	0	0	0	Interval Command/Status Register
X	X	X	X	X	0	0	1	General Purpose I/O Port A
X	X	X	X	X	0	1	0	General Purpose I/O Port B
X	X	X	X	X	0	1	1	Port C—General Purpose I/O or Control
X	X	X	X	X	1	0	0	Low-Order 8 bits of Timer Count
X	X	X	X	X	1	0	1	High 6 bits of Timer Count and 2 bits of Timer Mode

X: Don't Care.
†: I/O Address must be qualified by CE = 1 (8156H) or $\overline{CE}$ = 0 (8155H) and IO/$\overline{M}$ = 1 in order to select the appropriate register.

Figure 7. I/O Port and Timer Addressing Scheme

Figure 8 shows how I/O PORTS A and B are structured within the 8155H and 8156H:

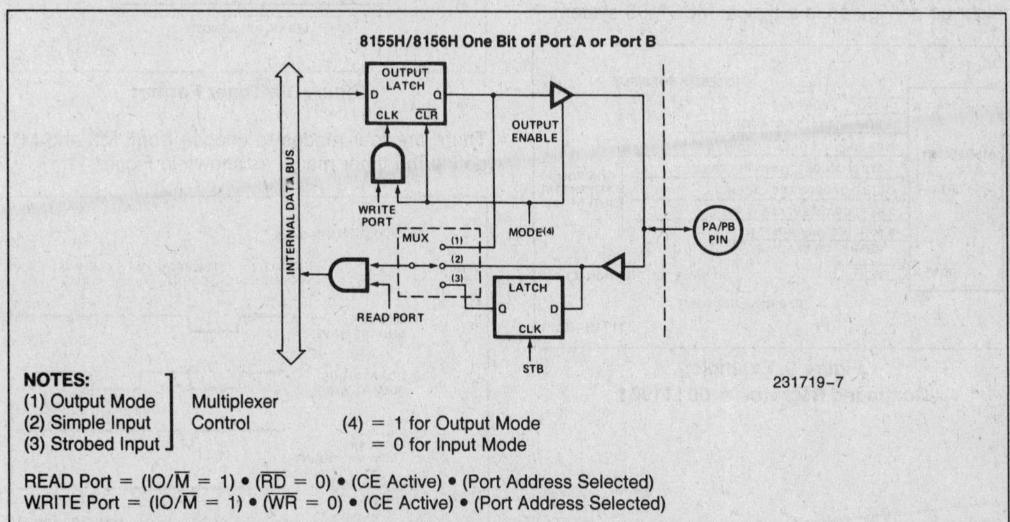

NOTES:
(1) Output Mode
(2) Simple Input
(3) Strobed Input
Multiplexer Control

(4) = 1 for Output Mode
= 0 for Input Mode

READ Port = (IO/$\overline{M}$ = 1) • ($\overline{RD}$ = 0) • (CE Active) • (Port Address Selected)
WRITE Port = (IO/$\overline{M}$ = 1) • ($\overline{WR}$ = 0) • (CE Active) • (Port Address Selected)

Figure 8. 8155H/8156H Port Functions

Table 2. Port Control Assignment

Pin	ALT 1	ALT 2	ALT 3	ALT 4
PC0	Input Port	Output Port	A INTR (Port A Interrupt)	A INTR (Port A Interrupt)
PC1	Input Port	Output Port	A BF (Port A Buffer Full)	A BF (Port A Buffer Full)
PC2	Input Port	Output Port	A $\overline{\text{STB}}$ (Port A Strobe)	A $\overline{\text{STB}}$ (Port A Strobe)
PC3	Input Port	Output Port	Output Port	B INTR (Port B Interrupt)
PC4	Input Port	Output Port	Output Port	B BF (Port B Buffer Full)
PC5	Input Port	Output Port	Output Port	B $\overline{\text{STB}}$ (Port B Strobe)

Note in the diagram that when the I/O ports are programmed to be output ports, the contents of the output ports can still be read by a READ operation when appropriately addressed.

The outputs of the 8155H/8156H are "glitch-free" meaning that you can write a "1" to a bit position that was previously "1" and the level at the output pin will not change.

Note also that the output latch is cleared when the port enters the input mode. The output latch cannot be loaded by writing to the port if the port is in the input mode. The result is that each time a port mode is changed from input to output, the output pin will go low. When the 8155H/56H is RESET, the output latches are all cleared and all 3 ports enter the input mode.

When in the ALT 1 or ALT 2 modes, the bits of PORT C are structured like the diagram above in the simple input or output mode, respectively.

Reading from an input port with nothing connected to the pins will provide unpredictable results.

Figure 9 shows how the 8155H/8156H I/O ports might be configured in a typical MCS®-85 system.

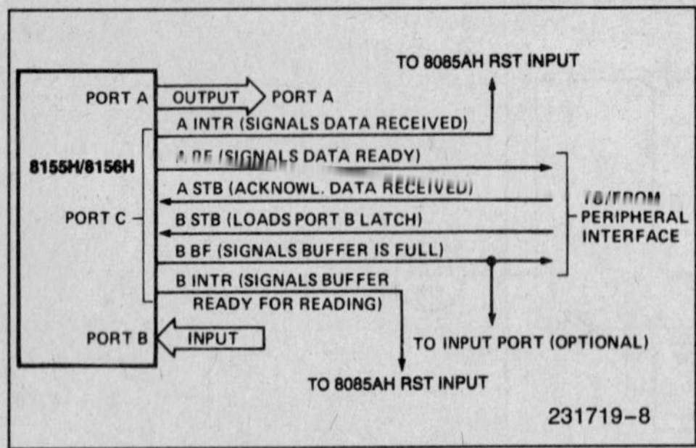

Figure 9. Example: Command Register = 00111001

TIMER SECTION

The time is a 14-bit down-counter that counts the TIMER IN pulses and provides either a square wave or pulse when terminal count (TC) is reached.

The timer has the I/O address XXXXX100 for the low order byte of the register and the I/O address XXXXX101 for the high order byte of the register. (See Figure 7.)

To program the timer, the COUNT LENGTH REG is loaded first, one byte at a time, by selecting the timer addresses. Bits 0–13 of the high order count register will specify the length of the next count and bits 14–15 of the high order register will specify the timer output mode (see Figure 10). The value loaded into the count length register can have any value from 2H through 3FFFH in Bits 0–13.

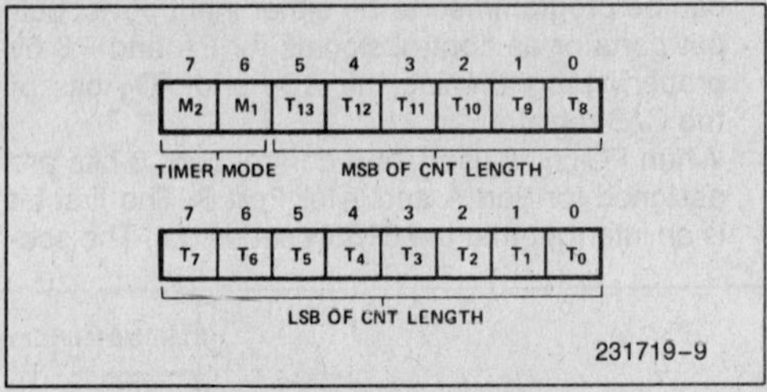

Figure 10. Timer Format

There are four modes to choose from: M2 and M1 define the timer mode, as shown in Figure 11.

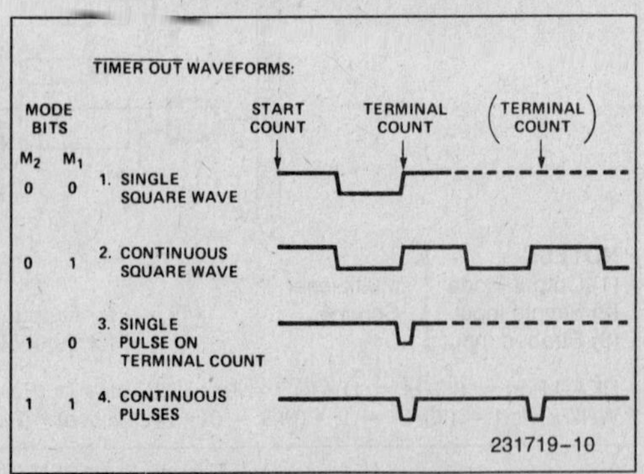

Figure 11. Timer Modes

Bits 6–7 (TM_2 and TM_1) of command register contents are used to start and stop the counter. There are four commands to choose from:

TM_2	TM_1	
0	0	NOP—Do not affect counter operation.
0	1	STOP—NOP if timer has not started; stop counting if the timer is running.
1	0	STOP AFTER TC—Stop immediately after present TC is reached (NOP if timer has not started)
1	1	START—Load mode and CNT length and start immediately after loading (if timer is not presently running). If timer is running, start the new mode and CNT length immediately after present TC is reached.

Note that while the counter is counting, you may load a new count and mode into the count length registers. Before the new count and mode will be used by the counter, you **must** issue a START command to the counter. This applies even though you may only want to change the count and use the previous mode.

In case of an odd-numbered count, the first half-cycle of the squarewave output, which is high, is one count longer than the second (low) half-cycle, as shown in Figure 12.

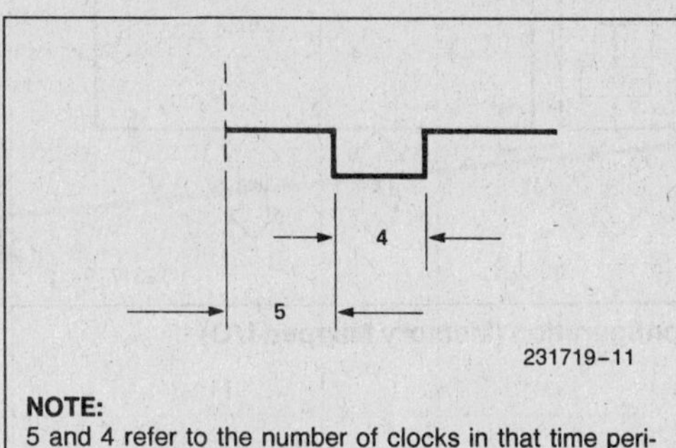

NOTE:
5 and 4 refer to the number of clocks in that time period.

Figure 12. Asymmetrical Square-Wave Output Resulting from Count of 9

The counter in the 8155H is not initialized to any particular mode or count when hardware RESET occurs, but RESET does *stop* the counting. Therefore, counting cannot begin following RESET until a START command is issued via the C/S register.

Please note that the timer circuit on the 8155H/8156H chip is designed to be a square-wave timer, not an event counter. To achieve this, it counts down by twos twice in completing one cycle. Thus, its registers do not contain values directly representing the number of TIMER IN pulses received. You cannot load an initial value of 1 into the count register and cause the timer to operate, as its terminal count value is 10 (binary) or 2 (decimal). (For the detection of single pulses, it is suggested that one of the hardware interrupt pins on the 8085AH be used.) After the timer has started counting down, the values residing in the count registers can be used to calculate the actual number of TIMER IN pulses required to complete the timer cycle if desired. To obtain the remaining count, perform the following operations in order:

1. Stop the count
2. Read in the 16-bit value from the count length registers
3. Reset the upper two mode bits
4. Reset the carry and rotate right one position all 16 bits through carry
5. If carry is set, add ½ of the full original count (½ full count—1 if full count is odd).

NOTE:

If you started with an odd count and you read the count length register before the third count pulse occurs, you will not be able to discern whether one or two counts has occurred. Regardless of this, the 8155H/56H always counts out the right number of pulses in generating the $\overline{\text{TIMER OUT}}$ waveforms.

1

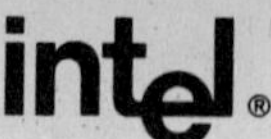

8085AH MINIMUM SYSTEM CONFIGURATION

Figure 13a shows a minimum system using three chips, containing:

- 256 Bytes RAM
- 2K Bytes EPROM
- 38 I/O Pins
- 1 Interval Timer
- 4 Interrupt Levels

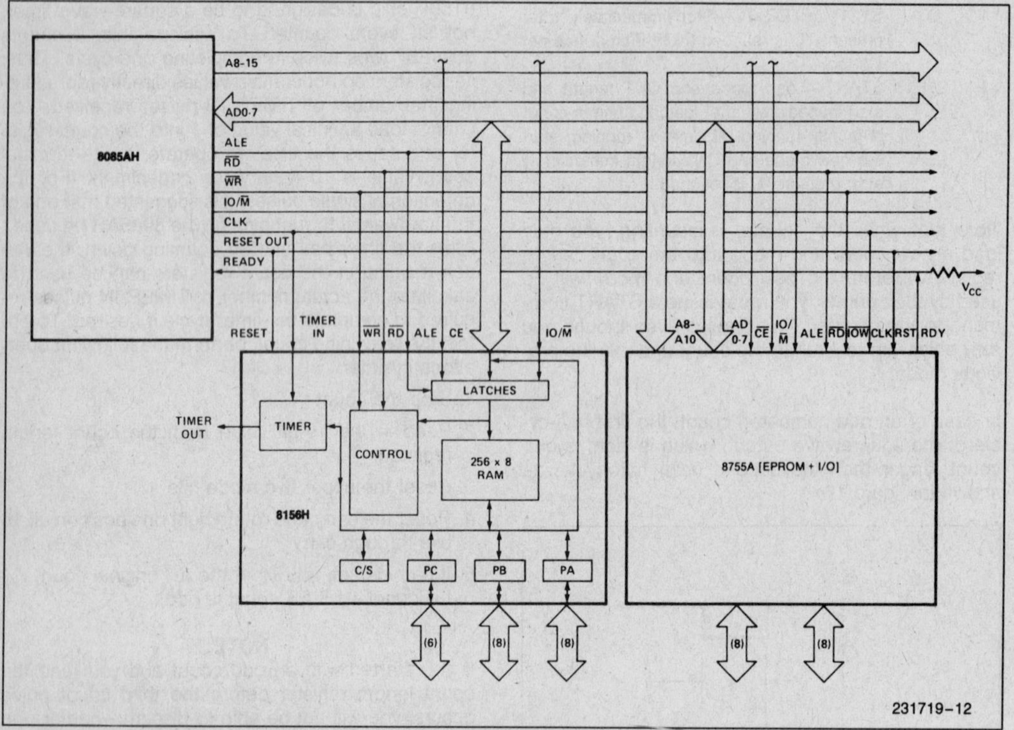

231719-12

Figure 13a. 8085AH Minimum System Configuration (Memory Mapped I/O)

8088 FIVE CHIP SYSTEM

Figure 13b shows a five chip system containing:

- 1.25K Bytes RAM
- 2K Bytes EPROM
- 38 I/O Pins
- 1 Interval Timer
- 2 Interrupt Levels

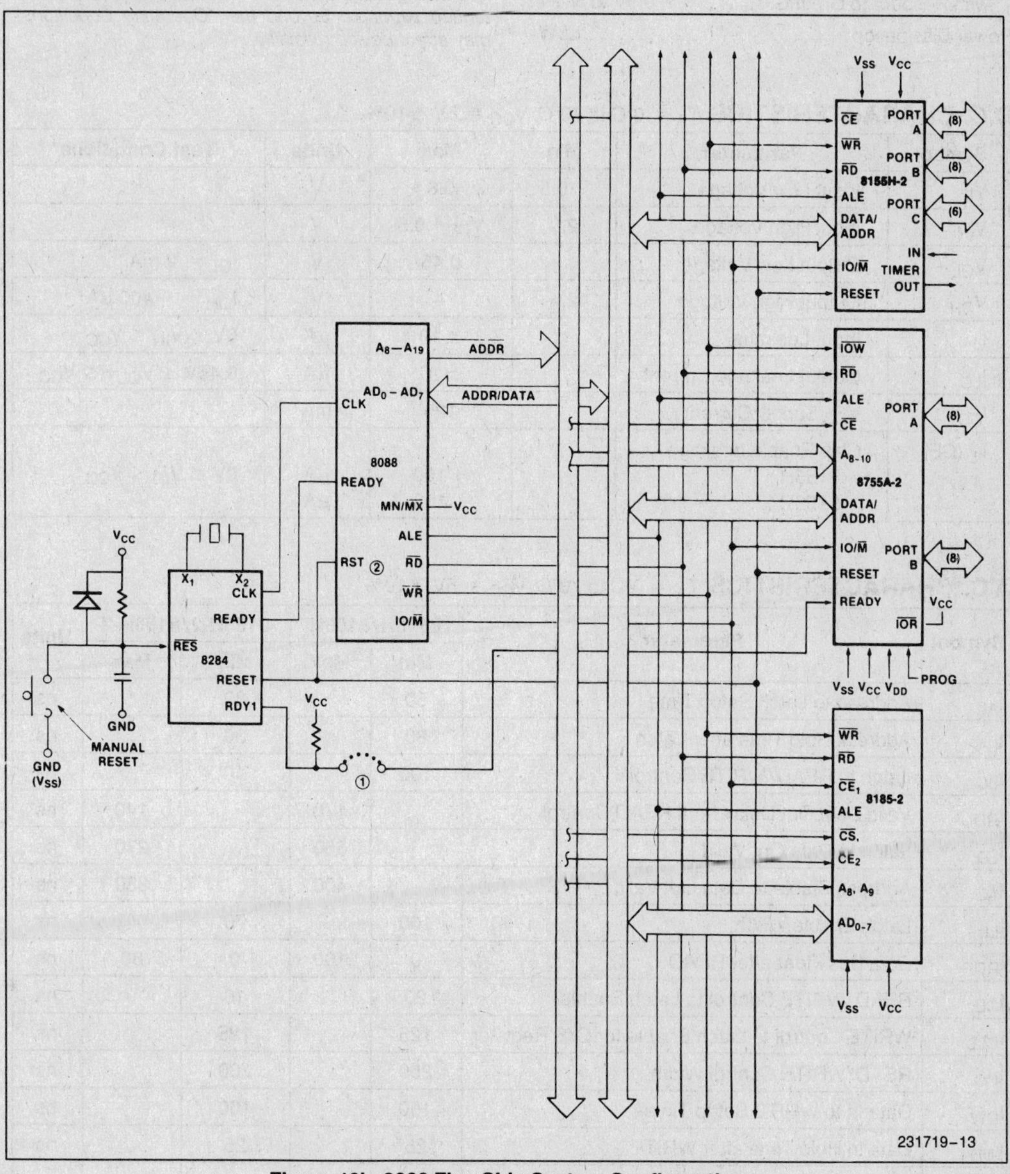

231719-13

Figure 13b. 8088 Five Chip System Configuration

ABSOLUTE MAXIMUM RATINGS*

Temperature Under Bias .... 0°C to +70°C
Storage Temperature .... −65°C to +150°C
Voltage on Any Pin
  with Respect to Ground.......... −0.5V to +7V
Power Dissipation.......................... 1.5W

NOTICE: This is a production data sheet. The specifications are subject to change without notice.

**WARNING: Stressing the device beyond the "Absolute Maximum Ratings" may cause permanent damage. These are stress ratings only. Operation beyond the "Operating Conditions" is not recommended and extended exposure beyond the "Operating Conditions" may affect device reliability.*

D.C. CHARACTERISTICS T_A = 0°C to 70°C, V_{CC} = 5V ±10%

Symbol	Parameter	Min	Max	Units	Test Conditions
V_{IL}	Input Low Voltage	−0.5	0.8	V	
V_{IH}	Input High Voltage	2.0	V_{CC}+0.5	V	
V_{OL}	Output Low Voltage		0.45	V	I_{OL} = 2 mA
V_{OH}	Output High Voltage	2.4		V	I_{OH} = −400 μA
I_{IL}	Input Leakage		±10	μA	0V ≤ V_{IN} ≤ V_{CC}
I_{LO}	Output Leakage Current		±10	μA	0.45V ≤ V_{OUT} ≤ V_{CC}
I_{CC}	V_{CC} Supply Current		125	mA	
I_{IL} (CE)	Chip Enable Leakage 8155H 8156H		 +100 −100	 μA μA	0V ≤ V_{IN} ≤ V_{CC}

A.C. CHARACTERISTICS T_A = 0°C to 70°C, V_{CC} = 5V ±10%

Symbol	Parameter	8155H/8156H		8155H-2/8156H-2		Units
		Min	Max	Min	Max	
t_{AL}	Address to Latch Setup Time	50		30		ns
t_{LA}	Address Hold Time after Latch	80		30		ns
t_{LC}	Latch to READ/WRITE Control	100		40		ns
t_{RD}	Valid Data Out Delay from READ Control		170		140	ns
t_{LD}	Latch to Data Out Valid		350		270	ns
t_{AD}	Address Stable to Data Out Valid		400		330	ns
t_{LL}	Latch Enable Width	100		70		ns
t_{RDF}	Data Bus Float after READ	0	100	0	80	ns
t_{CL}	READ/WRITE Control to Latch Enable	20		10		ns
t_{CLL}	WRITE Control to Latch Enable for C/S Register	125		125		ns
t_{CC}	READ/WRITE Control Width	250		200		ns
t_{DW}	Data In to WRITE Setup Time	150		100		ns
t_{WD}	Data In Hold Time after WRITE	25		25		ns
t_{RV}	Recovery Time between Controls	300		200		ns
t_{WP}	WRITE to Port Output		400		300	ns

A.C. CHARACTERISTICS $T_A = 0°C$ to $70°C$, $V_{CC} = 5V \pm 10\%$ (Continued)

Symbol	Parameter	8155H/8156H		8155H-2/8156H-2		Units
		Min	Max	Min	Max	
t_{PR}	Port Input Setup Time	70		50		ns
t_{RP}	Port Input Hold Time	50		10		ns
t_{SBF}	Strobe to Buffer Full		400		300	ns
t_{SS}	Strobe Width	200		150		ns
t_{RBE}	READ to Buffer Empty		400		300	ns
t_{SI}	Strobe to INTR On		400		300	ns
t_{RDI}	READ to INTR Off		400		300	ns
t_{PSS}	Port Setup Time to Strobe	50		0		ns
t_{PHS}	Port Hold Time After Strobe	120		100		ns
t_{SBE}	Strobe to Buffer Empty		400		300	ns
t_{WBF}	WRITE to Buffer Full		400		300	ns
t_{WI}	WRITE to INTR Off		400		300	ns
t_{TL}	TIMER-IN to $\overline{\text{TIMER-OUT}}$ Low		400		300	ns
t_{TH}	TIMER-IN to $\overline{\text{TIMER-OUT}}$ High		400		300	ns
t_{RDE}	Data Bus Enable from READ Control	10		10		ns
t_1	TIMER-IN Low Time	80		40		ns
t_2	TIMER-IN High Time	120		70		ns
t_{WT}	WRITE to TIMER-IN (for writes which start counting)	360		200		ns

A.C. TESTING INPUT, OUTPUT WAVEFORM

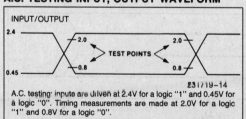

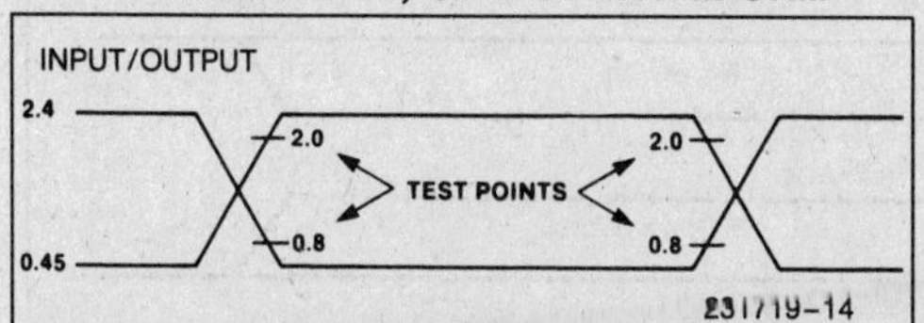

A.C. testing inputs are driven at 2.4V for a logic "1" and 0.45V for a logic "0". Timing measurements are made at 2.0V for a logic "1" and 0.8V for a logic "0".

A.C. TESTING LOAD CIRCUIT

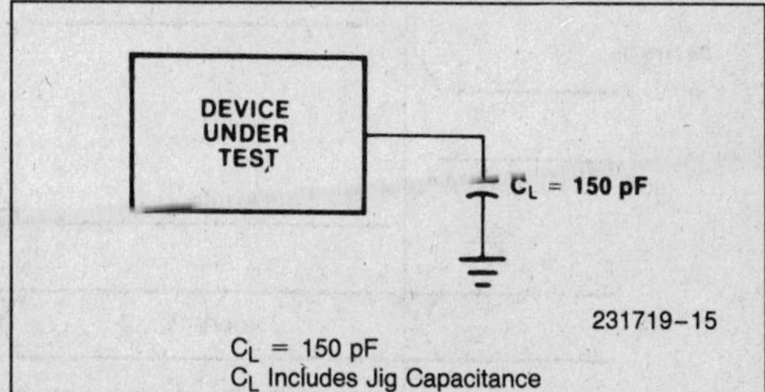

C_L = 150 pF
C_L Includes Jig Capacitance

WAVEFORMS

READ

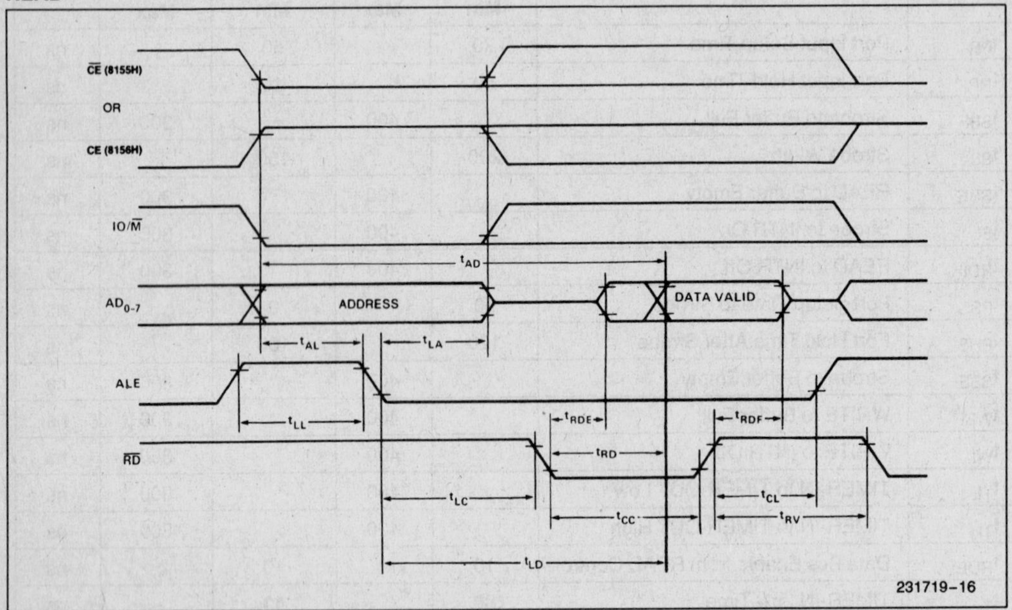

WRITE

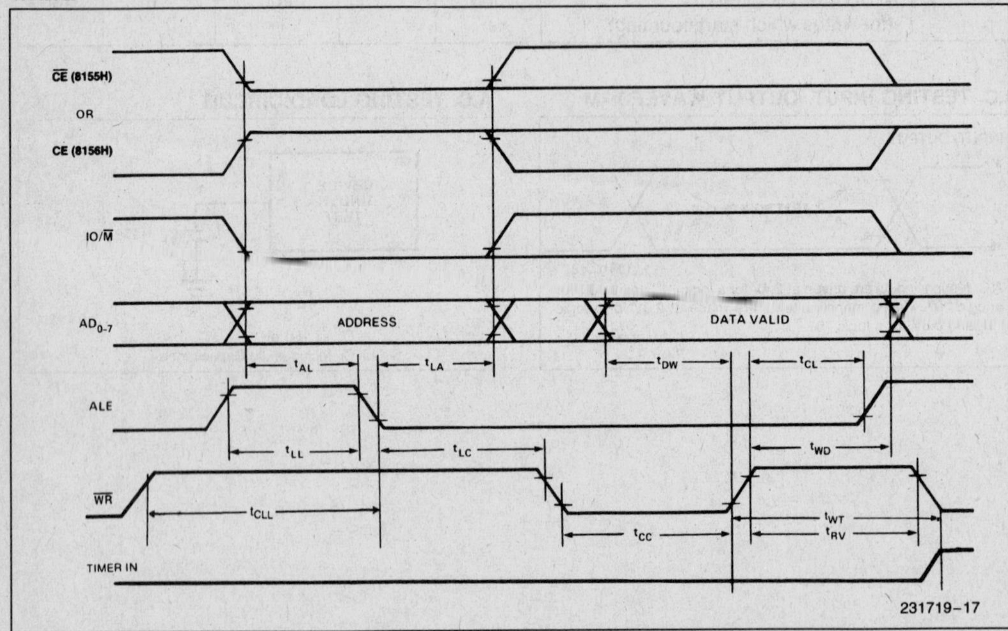

WAVEFORMS (Continued)

STROBED INPUT

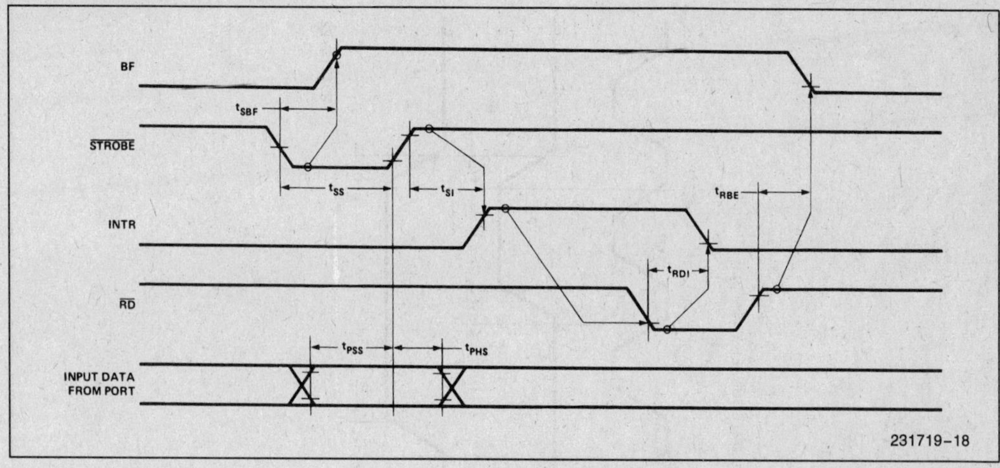

231719-18

STROBED OUTPUT

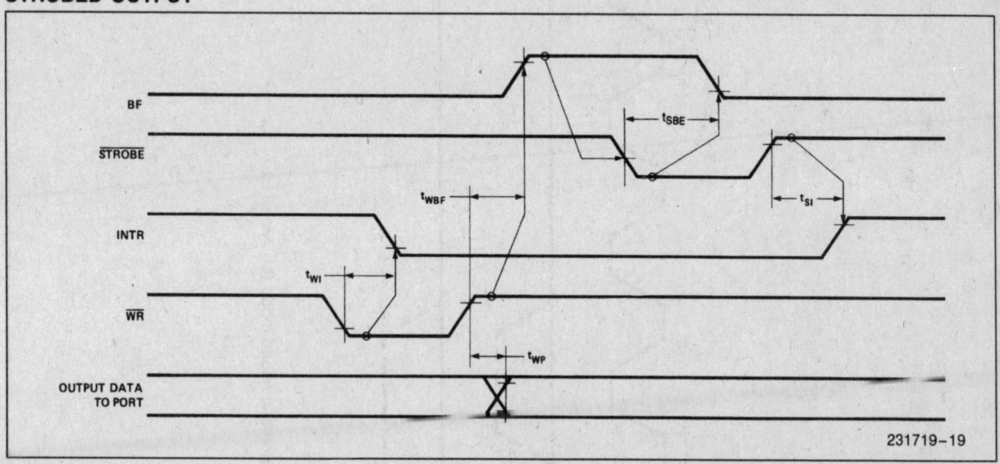

231719-19

BASIC INPUT

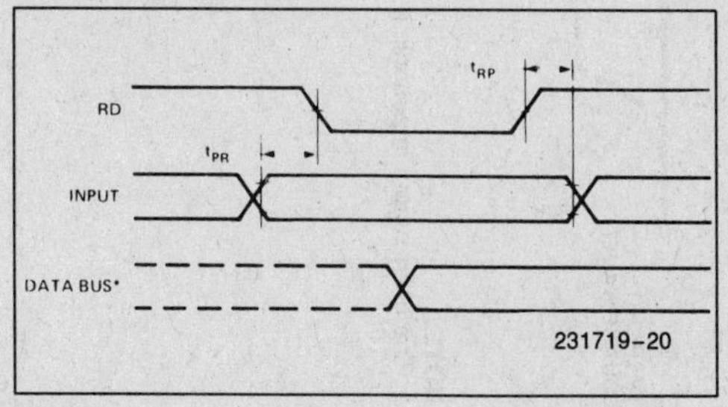

231719-20

BASIC OUTPUT

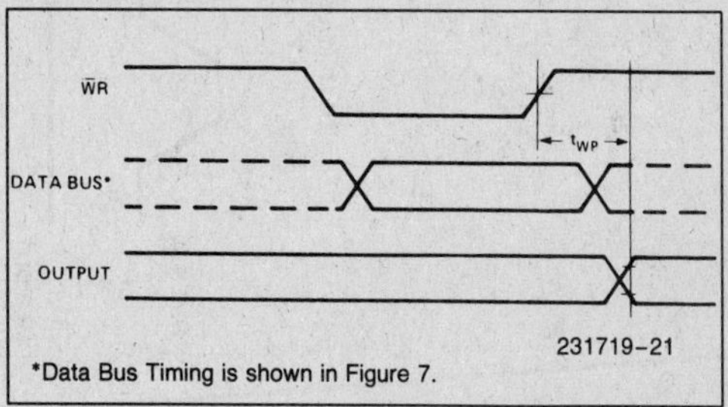

231719-21

*Data Bus Timing is shown in Figure 7.

WAVEFORMS (Continued)

TIMER OUTPUT COUNTDOWN FROM 5 TO 1

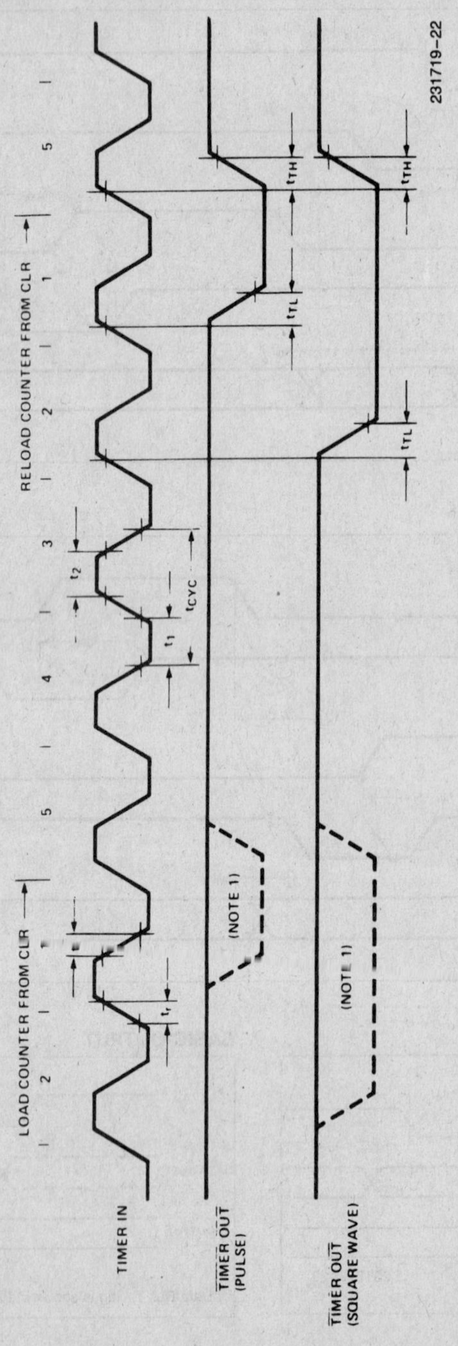

TIMER IN

TIMER OUT (PULSE)

TIMER OUT (SQUARE WAVE)

LOAD COUNTER FROM CLR

RELOAD COUNTER FROM CLR

(NOTE 1)

231719–22

NOTE:

1. The timer output is periodic if in an automatic reload mode (M_1 Mode bit = 1).

8185/8185-2 1024 x 8-BIT STATIC RAM FOR MCS®-85

- Multiplexed Address and Data Bus
- Directly Compatible with 8085AH and 8088 Microprocessors
- Low Operating Power Dissipation
- Low Standby Power Dissipation
- Single +5V Supply
- High Density 18-Pin Package

The Intel 8185 is an 8192-bit static random access memory (RAM) organized as 1024 words by 8-bits using N-channel Silicon-Gate MOS technology. The multiplexed address and data bus allows the 8185 to interface directly to the 8085AH and 8088 microprocessors to provide a maximum level of system integration.

The low standby power dissipation minimizes system power requirements when the 8185 is disabled.

The 8185-2 is a high-speed selected version of the 8185 that is compatible with the 5 MHz 8085AH-2 and the 5 MHz 8088.

1

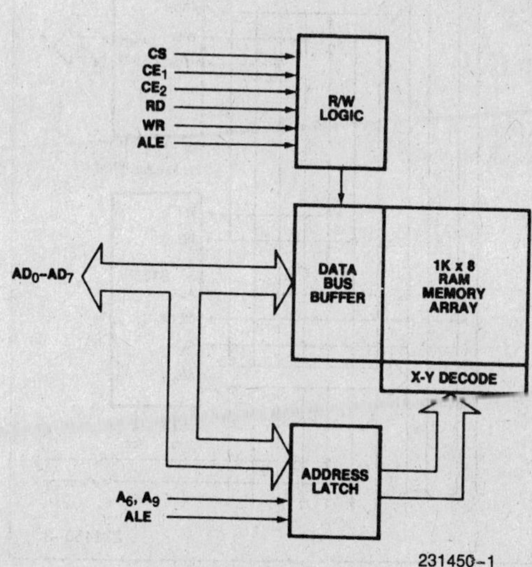

Figure 1. Block Diagram

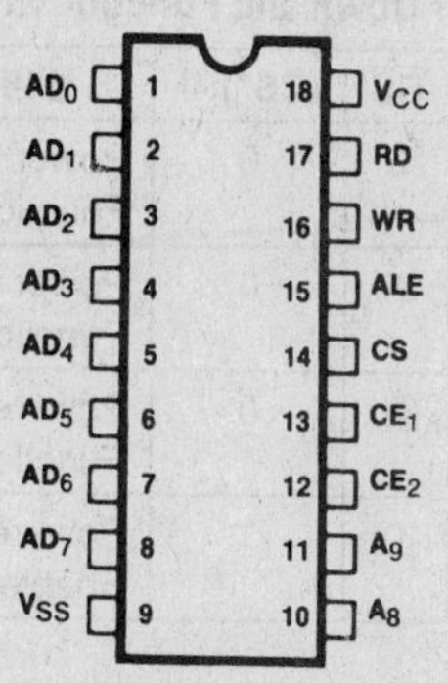

Figure 2. Pin Configuration

Pin Names

AD_0–AD_7	Address/Data Lines
A_8, A_9	Address Lines
CS	Chip Select
CE_1	Chip Enable (IO/M)
CE_2	Chip Enable
ALE	Address Latch Enable
WR	Write Enable

FUNCTIONAL DESCRIPTION

The 8185 has been designed to provide for direct interface to the multiplexed bus structure and bus timing of the 8085A microprocessor.

At the beginning of an 8185 memory access cycle, the 8-bit address on AD_{0-7}, A_8 and A_9, and the status of $\overline{CE}_1$ and CE_2 are all latched internally in the 8185 by the falling edge of ALE. If the latched status of both $\overline{CE}_1$ and CE_2 are active, the 8185 powers itself up, but no action occurs until the $\overline{CS}$ line goes low and the appropriate $\overline{RD}$ or $\overline{WR}$ control signal input is activated.

The $\overline{CS}$ input is not latched by the 8185 in order to allow the maximum amount of time for address decoding in selecting the 8185 chip. Maximum power consumption savings will occur, however, only when $\overline{CE}_1$ and CE_2 are activated selectively to power down the 8185 when it is not in use. A possible connection would be to wire the 8085A's IO/$\overline{M}$ line to the 8185's $\overline{CE}_1$ input, thereby keeping the 8185 powered down during I/O and interrupt cycles.

Table 1. Truth Table for Power Down and Function Enable

$\overline{CE}_1$	CE_2	$\overline{CS}$	$(CS^*)^{(2)}$	8185 Status
1	X	X	0	Power Down and Function Disable(1)
X	0	X	0	Power Down and Function Disable(1)
0	1	1	0	Powered Up and Function Disable(1)
0	1	0	1	Powered Up and Enabled

NOTES:
X = Don't Care.
1: Function Disable implies Data Bus in high impedance state and not writing.
2: $CS^* = (\overline{CE}_1 = 0) \times (CE_2 = 1) \times (\overline{CS} = 0)$.
$CS^* = 1$ signifies all chip enables and chip select active.

Table 2. Truth Table for Control and Data Bus Pin Status

(CS*)	$\overline{RD}$	$\overline{WR}$	AD_{0-7} During Data Portion of Cycle	8185 Function
0	X	X	Hi-Impedance	No Function
1	0	1	Data from Memory	Read
1	1	0	Data to Memory	Write
1	1	1	Hi-Impedance	Reading, but not Driving Data Bus

NOTE:
X = Don't Care.

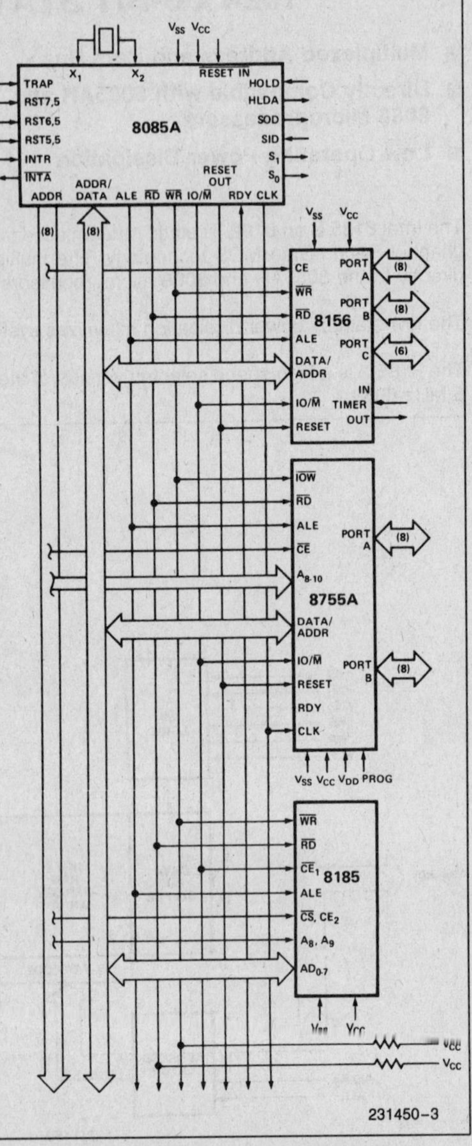

Figure 3. 8185 in an MCS®-85 System

4 Chips:
- 2K Bytes EPROM
- 1.25K Bytes RAM
- 38 I/O Lines
- 1 Counter/Timer
- 2 Serial I/O Lines
- 5 Interrupt Inputs

iAPX 88 FIVE CHIP SYSTEM:

- 1.25K Bytes RAM
- 2K Bytes EPROM
- 38 I/O Pins
- 1 Internal Timer
- 2 Interrupt Levels

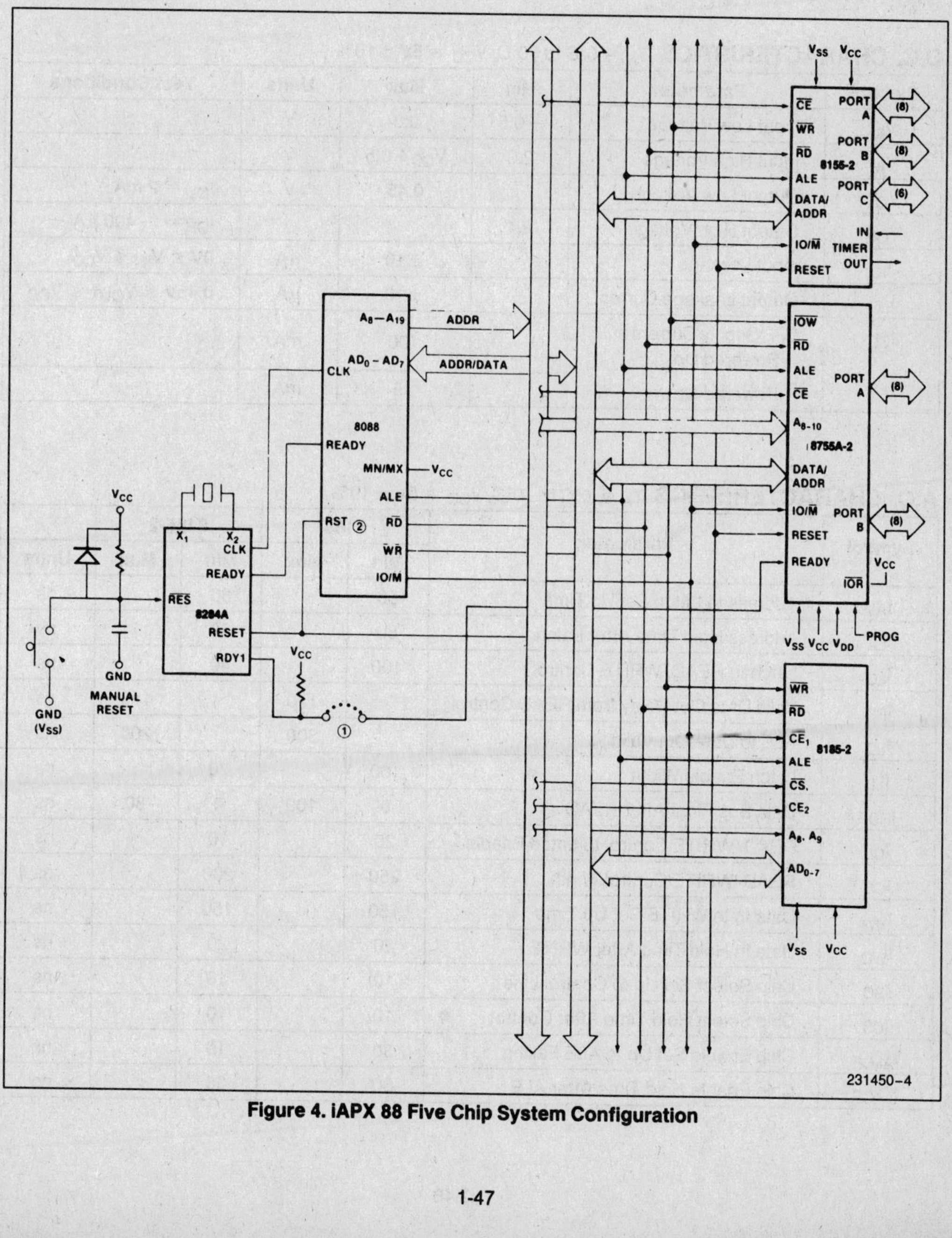

231450–4

Figure 4. iAPX 88 Five Chip System Configuration

ABSOLUTE MAXIMUM RATINGS*

Temperature Under Bias ....0°C to +70°C
Storage Temperature ....−65°C to +150°C
Voltage on Any Pin
with Respect to Ground..........−0.5V to +7V
Power Dissipation..........................1.5W

NOTICE: This is a production data sheet. The specifications are subject to change without notice.

**WARNING: Stressing the device beyond the "Absolute Maximum Ratings" may cause permanent damage. These are stress ratings only. Operation beyond the "Operating Conditions" is not recommended and extended exposure beyond the "Operating Conditions" may affect device reliability.*

D.C. CHARACTERISTICS $T_A = 0°C$ to $70°C$, $V_{CC} = 5V \pm 10\%$

Symbol	Parameter	Min	Max	Units	Test Conditions
V_{IL}	Input Low Voltage	−0.5	0.8	V	
V_{IH}	Input High Voltage	2.0	$V_{CC}+0.5$	V	
V_{OL}	Output Low Voltage		0.45	V	$I_{OL} = 2$ mA
V_{OH}	Output High Voltage	2.4			$I_{OH} = -400$ μA
I_{IL}	Input Leakage		±10	μA	$0V \le V_{IN} \le V_{CC}$
I_{LO}	Output Leakage Current		±10	μA	$0.45V \le V_{OUT} \le V_{CC}$
I_{CC}	V_{CC} Supply Current Powered Up		100	mA	
	Powered Down		35	mA	

A.C. CHARACTERISTICS $T_A = 0°C$ to $70°C$, $V_{CC} = 5V \pm 10\%$

Symbol	Parameter	8185		8185-2		Units
		Min	Max	Min	Max	
t_{AL}	Address to Latch Set Up Time	50		30		ns
t_{LA}	Address Hold Time After Latch	80		30		ns
t_{LC}	Latch to READ/WRITE Control	100		40		ns
t_{RD}	Valid Data Out Delay from READ Control		170		140	ns
t_{LD}	ALE to Data Out Valid		300		200	ns
t_{LL}	Latch Enable Width	100		70		ns
t_{RDF}	Data Bus Float After READ	0	100	0	80	ns
t_{CL}	READ/WRITE Control to Latch Enable	20		10		ns
t_{CC}	READ/WRITE Control Width	250		200		ns
t_{DW}	Data In to WRITE Set Up Time	150		150		ns
t_{WD}	Data In Hold Time After WRITE	20		20		ns
t_{SC}	Chip Select Set Up to Control Line	10		10		ns
t_{CS}	Chip Select Hold Time After Control	10		10		ns
t_{ALCE}	Chip Enable Set Up to ALE Falling	30		10		ns
t_{LACE}	Chip Enable Hold Time After ALE	50		30		ns

A.C. TESTING INPUT, OUTPUT WAVEFORM

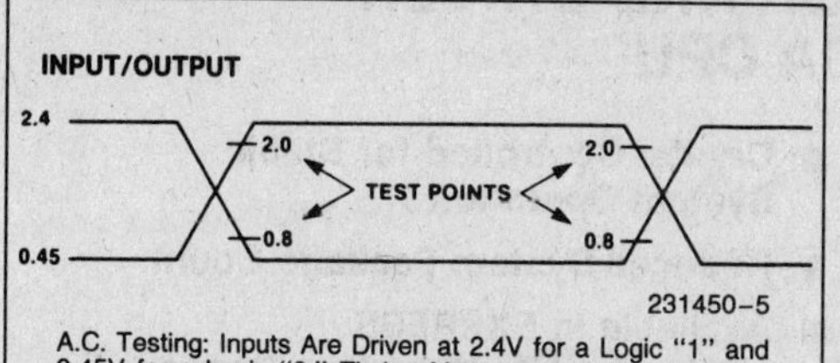

231450–5

A.C. Testing: Inputs Are Driven at 2.4V for a Logic "1" and 0.45V for a Logic "0." Timing Measurements Are Made at 2.0V for a Logic "1" and 0.8V for a Logic "0."

A.C. TESTING LOAD CIRCUIT

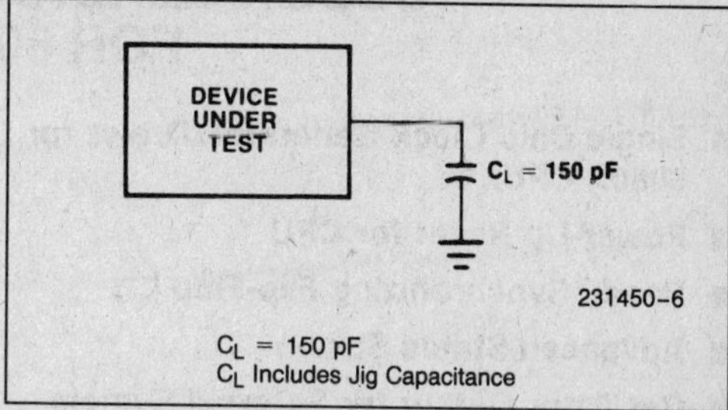

231450–6

C_L = 150 pF
C_L Includes Jig Capacitance

WAVEFORM

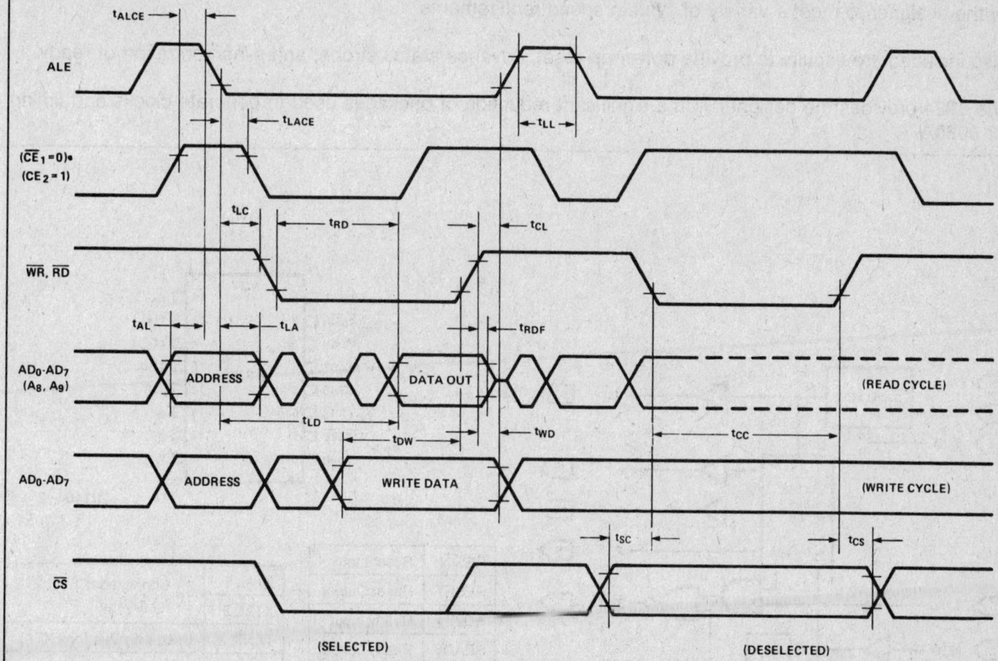

231450–7

8224 CLOCK GENERATOR AND DRIVER FOR 8080A CPU

- Single Chip Clock Generator/Driver for 8080A CPU
- Power-Up Reset for CPU
- Ready Synchronizing Flip-Flop
- Advanced Status Strobe
- Oscillator Output for External System Timing
- Crystal Controlled for Stable System Operation
- Reduces System Package Count
- Available in EXPRESS — Standard Temperature Range
- Available in 16-Lead Cerdip Package (See Packaging Spec, Order #231369)

The Intel 8224 is a single chip clock generator/driver for the 8080A CPU. It is controlled by a crystal, selected by the designer to meet a variety of system speed requirements.

Also included are circuits to provide power-up reset, advance status strobe, and synchronization of ready.

The 8224 provides the designer with a significant reduction of packages used to generate clocks and timing for 8080A.

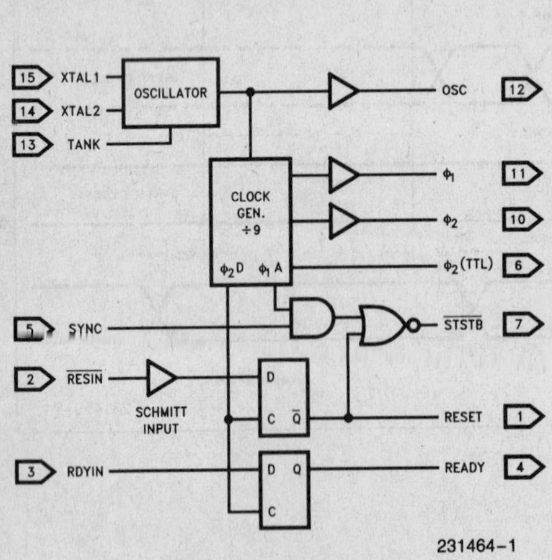

Figure 1. Block Diagram

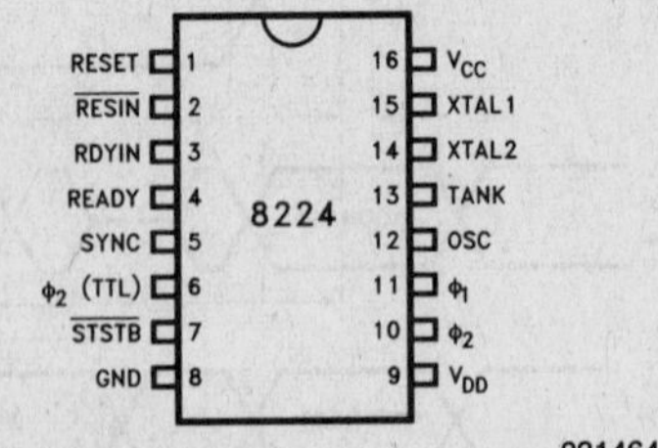

$\overline{RESIN}$	Reset Input
RESET	Reset Output
RDYIN	Ready Input
READY	Ready Output
SYNC	Sync Input
$\overline{STSTB}$	Status STB (Active Low)
ϕ_1	8080 Clocks
ϕ_2	

XTAL 1	Connections for Crystal
XTAL 2	
TANK	Used with Overtone XTAL
OSC	Oscillator Output
ϕ_2 (TTL)	ϕ_2 CLK (TTL Level)
V_{CC}	+5V
V_{DD}	+12V
GND	0V

Figure 2. Pin Configuration

November 1992
Order Number: 231464-001

ABSOLUTE MAXIMUM RATINGS*

Temperature Under Bias .... 0°C to +70°C
Storage Temperature .... −65°C to +150°C
Supply Voltage, V_{CC} .... −0.5V to +7V
Supply Voltage, V_{DD} .... −0.5V to +13.5V
Input Voltage .... −1.5V to +7V
Output Current .... 100 mA

NOTICE: This is a production data sheet. The specifications are subject to change without notice.

**WARNING: Stressing the device beyond the "Absolute Maximum Ratings" may cause permanent damage. These are stress ratings only. Operation beyond the "Operating Conditions" is not recommended and extended exposure beyond the "Operating Conditions" may affect device reliability.*

1

D.C. CHARACTERISTICS

T_A = 0°C to +70°C, V_{CC} = +5.0V ±5%, V_{DD} = +12V ±5%

Symbol	Parameter	Limits			Units	Test Conditions
		Min	Typ	Max		
I_F	Input Current Loading			−0.25	mA	V_F = 0.45V
I_R	Input Leakage Current			10	μA	V_R = 5.25V
V_C	Input Forward Clamp Voltage			1.0	V	I_C = −5 mA
V_{IL}	Input "Low" Voltage			0.8	V	V_{CC} = 5.0V
V_{IH}	Input "High" Voltage	2.6			V	Reset Input
		2.0			V	All Other Inputs
V_{IH}−V_{IL}	RESIN Input Hysteresis	0.25			V	V_{CC} = 5.0V
V_{OL}	Output "Low" Voltage			0.45	V	(ϕ_1, ϕ_2), Ready, Reset, $\overline{STSTB}$ I_{OL} = 2.5 mA
				0.45	V	All Other Outputs I_{OL} = 15 mA
V_{OH}	Output "High" Voltage ϕ_1, ϕ_2	9.4			V	I_{OH} = −100 μA
	READY, RESET	3.6			V	I_{OH} = −100 μA
	All Other Outputs	2.4			V	I_{OH} = −1 mA
I_{CC}	Power Supply Current			115	mA	
I_{DD}	Power Supply Current			12	mA	

NOTE:
1. For crystal frequencies of 18 MHz connect 510Ω resistors between the X1 input and ground as well as the X2 input and ground to prevent oscillation at harmonic frequencies.

Crystal Requirements

Tolerance: 0.005% at 0°C–70°C
Resonance: Series (Fundamental)*
Load Capacitance: 20 pF–35 pF
Equivalent Resistance: 75Ω–20Ω

Power Dissipation (Min): 4 mW

***NOTE:**
With tank circuit use 3rd overtone mode.

A.C. CHARACTERISTICS

Symbol	Parameter	Limits Min	Limits Typ	Limits Max	Units	Test Conditions
$t_{\phi 1}$	ϕ_1 Pulse Width	$\frac{2tcy}{9} - 20$ ns			ns	$C_L = 20$ pF to 50 pF
$t_{\phi 2}$	ϕ_2 Pulse Width	$\frac{5tcy}{9} - 35$ ns				
t_{D1}	ϕ_1 to ϕ_2 Delay	0				
t_{D2}	ϕ_2 to ϕ_1 Delay	$\frac{2tcy}{9} - 14$ ns				
t_{D3}	ϕ_1 to ϕ_2 Delay	$\frac{2tcy}{9}$		$\frac{2tcy}{9} + 20$ ns		
t_R	ϕ_1 and ϕ_2 Rise Time			20		
t_F	ϕ_1 and ϕ_2 Fall Time			20		
$t_{D\phi 2}$	ϕ_2 to ϕ_2 (TTL) Delay	−5		+15	ns	ϕ_2 TTL, CL = 30 $R_1 = 300\Omega$ $R_2 = 600\Omega$
t_{DSS}	ϕ_2 to $\overline{STSTB}$ Delay	$\frac{6tcy}{9} - 30$ ns		$\frac{6tcy}{9}$	ns	
t_{PW}	$\overline{STSTB}$ Pulse Width	$\frac{tcy}{9} - 15$ ns			ns	$\overline{STSTB}$, $C_L = 15$ pF $R_1 = 2K$ $R_2 = 4K$
t_{DRS}	RDYIN Setup Time to Status Strobe	$50 \text{ ns} - \frac{4tcy}{9}$				
t_{DRH}	RDYIN Hold Time after $\overline{STSTB}$	$\frac{4tcy}{9}$				
t_{DR}	RDYIN or RESIN to ϕ_2 Delay	$\frac{4tcy}{9} - 25$ ns			ns	Ready & Reset $C_L = 10$ pF $R_1 = 2K$ $R_2 = 4K$
t_{CLK}	CLK Period		$\frac{tcy}{9}$		ns	
f_{max}	Maximum Oscillating Frequency			27	MHz	
C_{in}	Input Capacitance			8	pF	$V_{CC} = +5.0V$ $V_{DD} = +12V$ $V_{BIAS} = 2.5V$ f = 1 MHz

NOTE:
These formulas are based on the internal workings of the part and intended for customer convenience. Actual testing of the part is done at $t_{cy} = 488.28$ ns.

A.C. CHARACTERISTICS (Continued)

For t_{CY} = 488.28 ns; T_A = 0°C to 70°C, V_{CC} = +5V ±5%, V_{DD} = +12V ±5%

Symbol	Parameter	Limits			Units	Test Conditions
		Min	Typ	Max		
$t_{\phi 1}$	ϕ_1 Pulse Width	89			ns	t_{CY} = 488.28 ns
$t_{\phi 2}$	ϕ_2 Pulse Width	236			ns	
t_{D1}	Delay ϕ_1 to ϕ_2	0			ns	
t_{D2}	Delay ϕ_2 to ϕ_1	95			ns	ϕ_1 & ϕ_2 Loaded to C_L = 20 pF to 50 pF
t_{D3}	Delay ϕ_1 to ϕ_2 Leading Edges	109		129	ns	
t_r	Output Rise Time			20	ns	
t_f	Output Fall Time			20	ns	
t_{DSS}	ϕ_2 to $\overline{STSTB}$ Delay	296		326	ns	
$t_{D\phi 2}$	ϕ_2 to ϕ_2 (TTL) Delay	−5		+15	ns	
t_{PW}	Status Strobe Pulse Width	40			ns	Ready & Reset Loaded to 2 mA/10 pF All measurements referenced to 1.5V unless specified otherwise.
t_{DRS}	RDYIN Setup Time to $\overline{STSTB}$	−167			ns	
t_{DRH}	RDYIN Hold Time after $\overline{STSTB}$	217			ns	
t_{DR}	READY or RESET to ϕ_2 Delay	192			ns	
f_{MAX}	Oscillator Frequency			18.432	MHz	

A.C. TESTING, INPUT, OUTPUT WAVEFORM

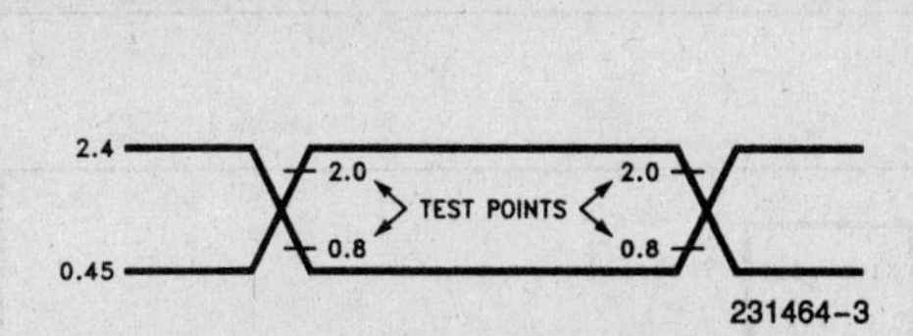

A.C. Testing: Inputs are driven at 2.4V for a logic "1" and 0.45V for a logic "0". Timing measurements are made at 2.0V for a logic "1" and 0.8V for a logic "0" (unless otherwise noted).

A.C. TESTING LOAD CIRCUIT

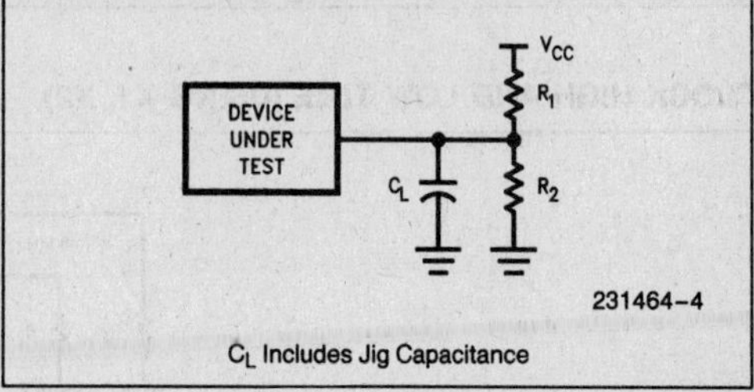

C_L Includes Jig Capacitance

WAVEFORMS

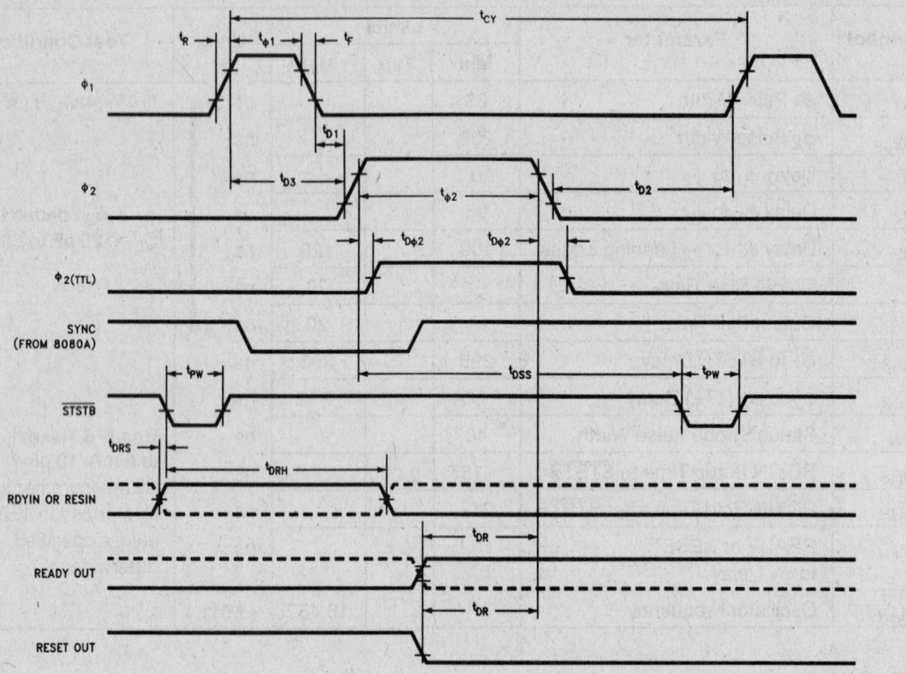

231464-5

VOLTAGE MEASUREMENT POINTS: ϕ_1, ϕ_2 Logic "0" = 1.0V, Logic "1" = 8.0V. All other signals measured at 1.5V.

CLOCK HIGH AND LOW TIME (USING X1, X2)

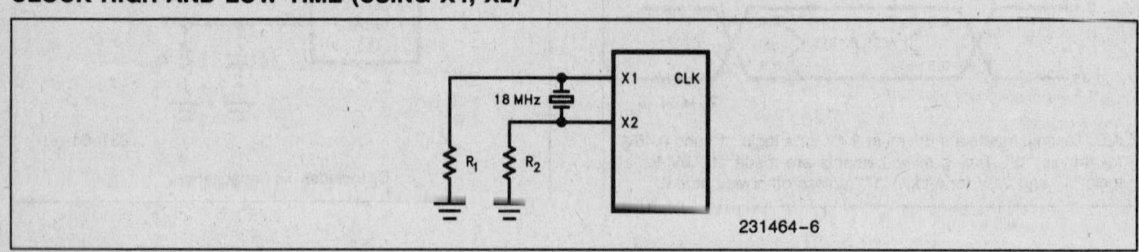

231464-6

8228
SYSTEM CONTROLLER AND BUS DRIVER FOR 8080A CPU

- **Single Chip System Control for MCS®-80 Systems**
- **Built-In Bidirectional Bus Driver for Data Bus Isolation**
- **Allows the Use of Multiple Byte Instructions (e.g. CALL) for Interrupt Acknowledge**
- **Reduces System Package Count**
- **User Selected Single Level Interrupt Vector (RST 7)**
- **Available in EXPRESS — Standard Temperature Range**
- **Available in 28-Lead Cerdip and Plastic Packages**
  (See Packaging Spec, Order #231369)

The Intel 8228 is a single chip system controller and bus driver for MCS®-80. It generates all signals required to directly interface MCS-80 family RAM, ROM, and I/O components.

A bidirectional bus driver is included to provide high system TTL fan-out. It also provides isolation of the 8080 data bus from memory and I/O. This allows for the optimization of control signals, enabling the systems designer to use slower memory and I/O. The isolation of the bus driver also provides for enhanced system noise immunity.

A user selected single level interrupt vector (RST 7) is provided to simplify real time, interrupt driven, small system requirements. The 8228 also generates the correct control signals to allow the use of multiple byte instructions (e.g., CALL) in response to an interrupt acknowledge by the 8080A. This feature permits large, interrupt driven systems to have an unlimited number of interrupt levels.

The 8228 is designed to support a wide variety of system bus structures and also reduce system package count for cost effective, reliable design of MCS-80 systems.

NOTE:
The specifications for the 3228 are identical with those for the 8228.

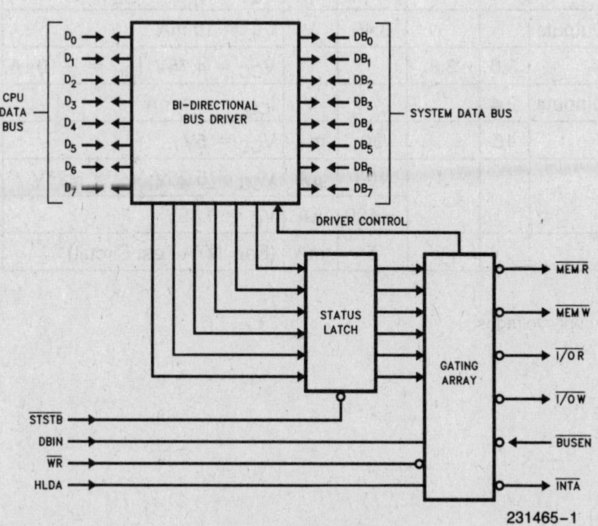

Figure 1. Block Diagram

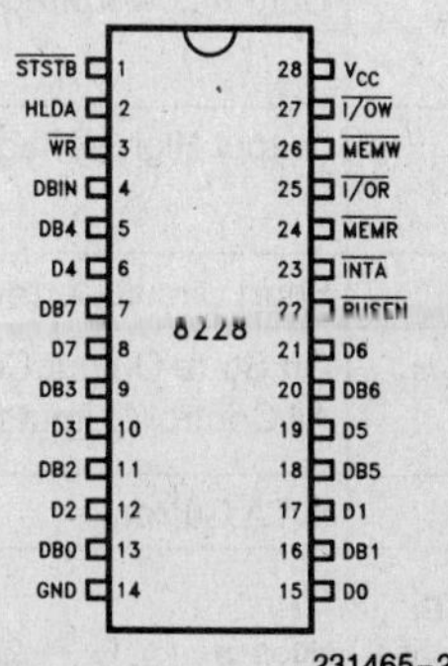

D7-DO	Data Bus (8080 Side)
DB7-DB0	Data Bus (System Side)
I/OR	I/O Read
I/OW	I/O Write
MEMR	Memory Read
MEMW	Memory Write
DBIN	DBIN (from 8080)

INTA	Interrupt Acknowledge
HLDA	HLDA (from 8080)
WR	WR (from 8080)
BUSEN	Bus Enable Input
STSTB	Status Strobe (from 8224)
V_{CC}	+5V
GND	0 Volts

Figure 2. Pin Configuration

ABSOLUTE MAXIMUM RATINGS*

Temperature Under Bias .... 0°C to +70°C
Storage Temperature .... −65°C to +150°C
Supply Voltage, V_{CC} .... −0.5V to +7V
Input Voltage .... −1.5 to +7V
Output Current .... 100 mA

NOTICE: This is a production data sheet. The specifications are subject to change without notice.

******WARNING: Stressing the device beyond the "Absolute Maximum Ratings" may cause permanent damage. These are stress ratings only. Operation beyond the "Operating Conditions" is not recommended and extended exposure beyond the "Operating Conditions" may affect device reliability.*

D.C. CHARACTERISTICS T_A = 0°C to +70°C, V_{CC} = 5V ±5%

Symbol	Parameter		Limits			Unit	Test Conditions
			Min	Typ(1)	Max		
V_C	Input Clamp Voltage, All Input			0.75	−1.0	V	V_{CC} = 4.75V; I_C = −5 mA
I_F	Input Load Current	$\overline{STSTB}$			500	μA	V_{CC} = 5.25V
		D_2 & D_6			750	μA	V_F = 0.45V
		D_0, D_1, D_4, D_5 & D_7			250	μA	
		All Other Inputs			250	μA	
I_R	Input Leakage Current	$\overline{STSTB}$			100	μA	V_{CC} = 5.25V
		DB_0–DB_7			20	μA	V_R = 5.25V
		All Other Inputs			100	μA	
V_{TH}	Input Threshold Voltage, All Inputs		0.8		2.0	V	V_{CC} = 5V
I_{CC}	Power Supply Current			140	190	mA	V_{CC} = 5.25V
V_{OL}	Output Low Voltage	D_0–D_7			0.45	V	V_{CC} = 4.75V; I_{OL} = 2 mA
		All Other Outputs			0.45	V	I_{OL} = 10 mA
V_{OH}	Output High Voltage	D_0–D_7	3.6	3.8		V	V_{CC} = 4.75V; I_{OH} = −10μA
		All Other Outputs	2.4			V	I_{OH} = −1 mA
I_{OS}	Short Circuit Current, All Outputs		15		90	mA	V_{CC} = 5V
$I_{O(off)}$	Off State Output Current All Control Outputs				100	μA	V_{CC} = 5.25V; V_O = 5.25V
					−100	μA	V_O = 0.45V
I_{INT}	INTA Current				5	mA	(See INTA Test Circuit)

NOTE:
1. Typical values are for T_A = 25°C and nominal supply voltages.

CAPACITANCE $V_{BIAS} = 2.5V$, $V_{CC} = 5.0V$, $T_A = 25°C$, f = 1 MHz

1. This parameter is periodically sampled and not 100% tested.

Symbol	Parameter	Limits			Unit
		Min	Typ(1)	Max	
C_{IN}	Input Capacitance		8	12	pF
C_{OUT}	Output Capacitance Control Signals		7	15	pF
I/O	I/O Capacitance (D or DB)		8	15	pF

A.C. CHARACTERISTICS $T_A = 0°C$ to $+70°C$, $V_{CC} = 5V \pm 5\%$

Symbol	Parameter	Limits		Unit	Conditions
		Min	Max		
t_{PW}	Width of Status Strobe	22		ns	
t_{SS}	Setup Time, Status Inputs D_0–D_7	8		ns	
t_{SH}	Hold Time, Status Inputs D_0–D_7	5		ns	
t_{DC}	Delay from $\overline{STSTB}$ to any Control Signal	20	60	ns	$C_L = 100$ pF
t_{RR}	Delay from DBIN to Control Outputs		30	ns	$C_L = 100$ pF
t_{RE}	Delay from DBIN to Enable/Disable 8080 Bus		45	ns	$C_L = 25$ pF
t_{RD}	Delay from System Bus to 8080 Bus during Read		30	ns	$C_L = 25$ pF
t_{WR}	Delay from $\overline{WR}$ to Control Outputs	5	45	ns	$C_L = 100$ pF
t_{WE}	Delay to Enable System Bus DB_0–DB_7 after $\overline{STSTB}$		30	ns	$C_L = 100$ pF
t_{WD}	Delay from 8080 Bus D_0–D_7 to System Bus DB_0–DB_7 during Write	5	40	ns	$C_L = 100$ pF
t_E	Delay from $\overline{\text{System Bus Enable}}$ to System Bus DB_0–DB_7		30	ns	$C_L = 100$ pF
t_{HD}	HLDA to Read Status Outputs		25	ns	
t_{DS}	Setup Time, System Bus Inputs to HLDA	10		ns	
t_{DH}	Hold Time, System Bus Inputs to HLDA	20		ns	$C_L = 100$ pF

A.C. TESTING LOAD CIRCUIT

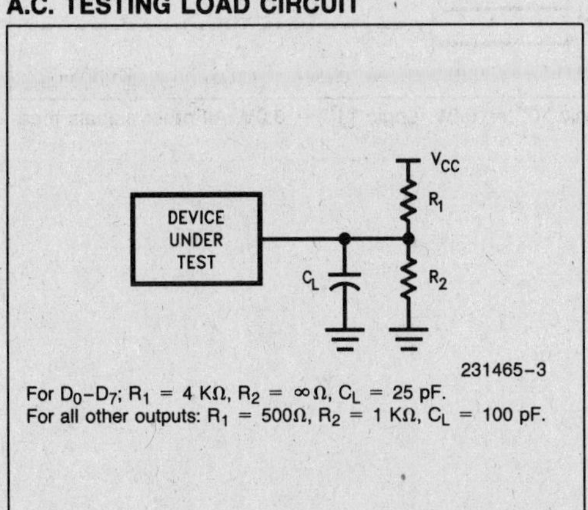

INTA Test Circuit (for RST 7)

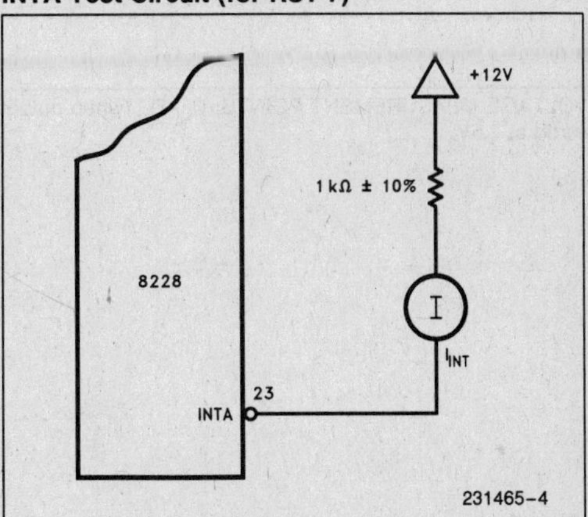

WAVEFORMS

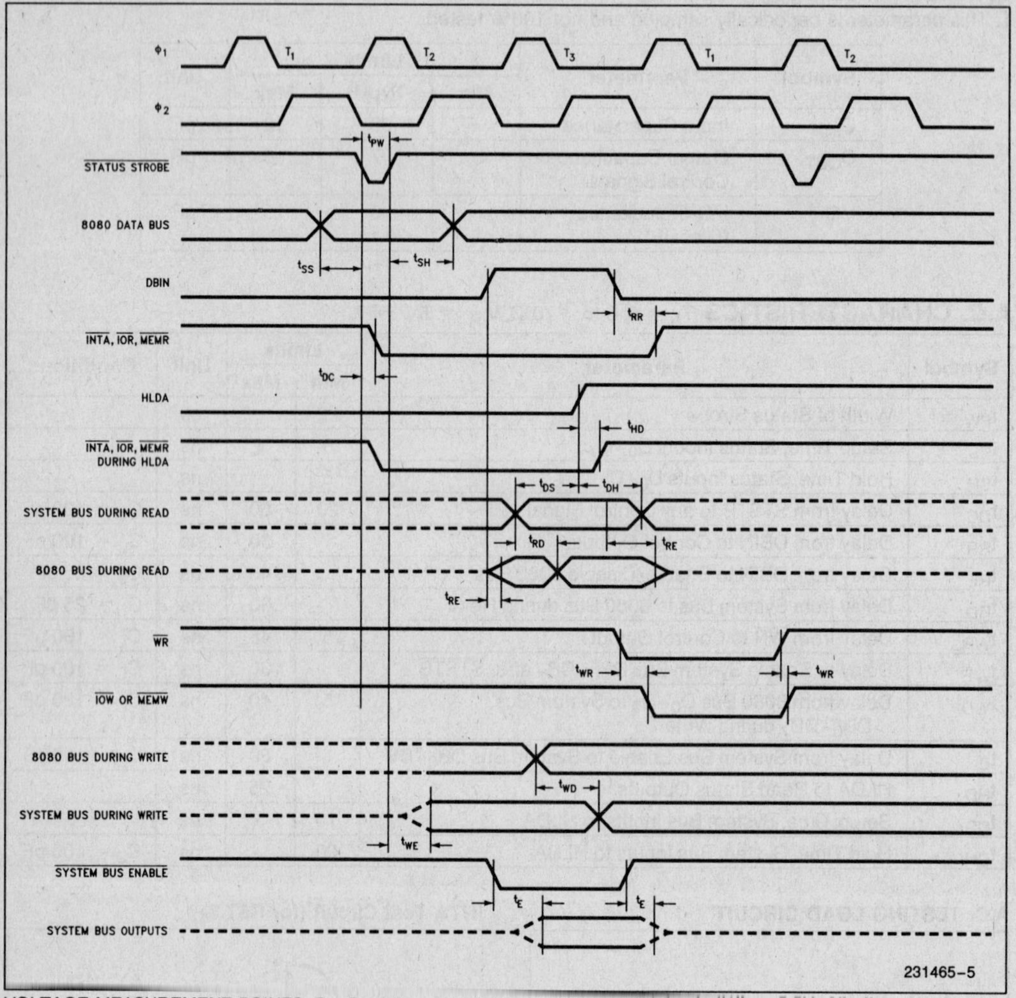

ϕ_1 T1 T2 T3 T1 T2

ϕ_2

t_{PW}

$\overline{\text{STATUS STROBE}}$

8080 DATA BUS

t_{SS} t_{SH}

DBIN

t_{RR}

$\overline{\text{INTA}}$, $\overline{\text{IOR}}$, $\overline{\text{MEMR}}$

t_{DC}

HLDA

t_{HD}

$\overline{\text{INTA}}$, $\overline{\text{IOR}}$, $\overline{\text{MEMR}}$ DURING HLDA

t_{DS} t_{DH}

SYSTEM BUS DURING READ

t_{RD} t_{RE}

8080 BUS DURING READ

t_{RE}

$\overline{\text{WR}}$

t_{WR} t_{WR}

$\overline{\text{IOW}}$ OR $\overline{\text{MEMW}}$

8080 BUS DURING WRITE

t_{WD}

SYSTEM BUS DURING WRITE

t_{WE}

$\overline{\text{SYSTEM BUS ENABLE}}$

t_E t_E

SYSTEM BUS OUTPUTS

231465–5

VOLTAGE MEASUREMENT POINTS: D_0–D_7 (when outputs) Logic "0" = 0.8V, Logic "1" = 3.0V. All other signals measured at 1.5V.

8755A
16,384-BIT EPROM WITH I/O

- 2048 Words x 8 Bits
- Single +5V Power Supply (V_{CC})
- Directly Compatible with 8085AH
- U.V. Erasable and Electrically Reprogrammable
- Internal Address Latch
- 2 General Purpose 8-Bit I/O Ports
- Each I/O Port Line Individually Programmable as Input or Output
- Multiplexed Address and Data Bus
- 40-Pin DIP
- Available in EXPRESS
  - Standard Temperature Range
  - Extended Temperature Range

1

The Intel 8755A is an erasable and electrically reprogrammable ROM (EPROM) and I/O chip to be used in the 8085AH microprocessor systems. The EPROM portion is organized as 2048 words by 8 bits. It has a maximum access time of 450 ns to permit use with no wait states in an 8085AH CPU.

The I/O portion consists of 2 general purpose I/O ports. Each I/O port has 8 port lines, and each I/O port line is individually programmable as input or output.

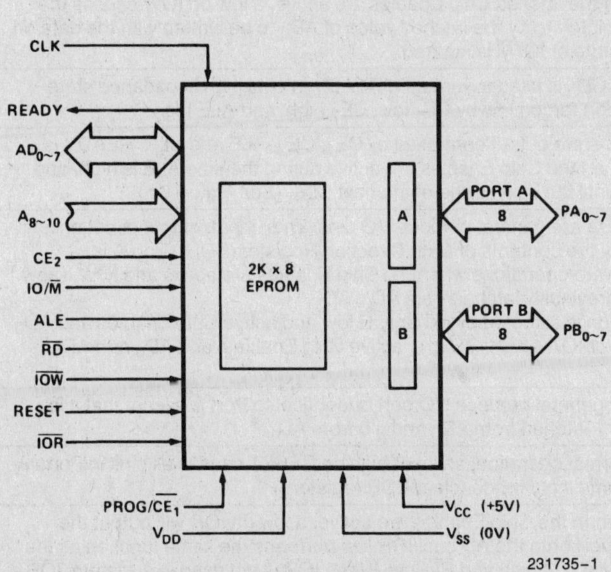

Figure 1. Block Diagram

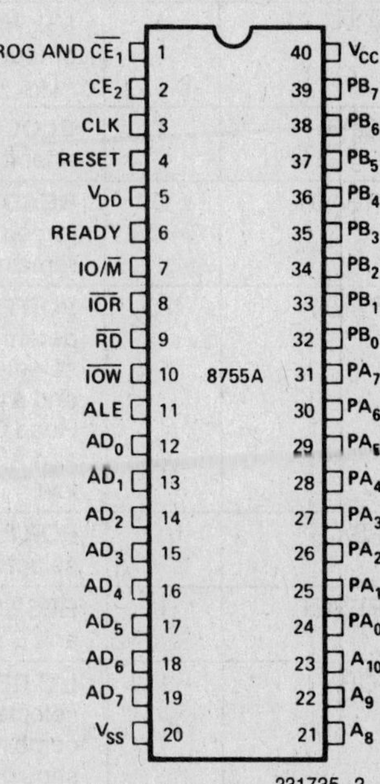

Figure 2. Pin Configuration

November 1986
Order Number: 231735-002

Table 1. Pin Description

Symbol	Type	Name and Function
ALE	I	**ADDRESS LATCH ENABLE:** When Address Latch Enable goes *high,* AD_{0-7}, $IO/\overline{M}$, A_{8-10}, CE_2, and $\overline{CE}_1$ enter the address latches. The signals, (AD, $IO/\overline{M}$, AD_{8-10}, CE_2, $\overline{CE}_1$) are latched in at the trailing edge of ALE.
AD_{0-7}	I	**BIDIRECTIONAL ADDRESS/DATA BUS:** The lower 8 bits of the PROM or I/O address are applied to the bus lines when ALE is high. During an I/O cycle, Port A or B is selected based on the latched value of AD_0. IF $\overline{RD}$ or $\overline{IOR}$ is low when the latched Chip Enables are active, the output buffers present data on the bus.
AD_{8-10}	I	**ADDRESS BUS:** These are the high order bits of the PROM address. They do not affect I/O operations.
PROG/$\overline{CE}_1$ CE_2	I	**CHIP ENABLE INPUTS:** $\overline{CE}_1$ is active low and CE_2 is active high. The 8755A can be accessed only when *both* Chip Enables are active at the time the ALE signal latches them up. If either Chip Enable input is not active, the AD_{0-7}, and READY ouputs will be in a high impedance state. $\overline{CE}_1$ is also used as a programming pin. (See section on programming.)
$IO/\overline{M}$	I	**I/O MEMORY:** If the latched $IO/\overline{M}$ is high when $\overline{RD}$ is low, the output data comes from an I/O port. If it is low the output data comes from the PROM.
$\overline{RD}$	I	**READ:** If the latched Chip Enables are active when $\overline{RD}$ goes low, the AD_{0-7} output buffers are enabled and output either the selected PROM location or I/O port. When both $\overline{RD}$ and $\overline{IOR}$ are high, the AD_{0-7} output buffers are 3-stated.
$\overline{IOW}$	I	**I/O WRITE:** If the latched Chip Enables are active, a low on $\overline{IOW}$ causes the output port pointed to by the latched value of AD_0 to be written with the data on AD_{0-7}. The state of $IO/\overline{M}$ is ignored.
CLK	I	**CLOCK:** The CLK is used to force the READY into its high impedance state after it has been forced low by $\overline{CE}_1$ low, CE_2 high, and ALE high.
READY	O	**READY** is a 3-state output controlled by $\overline{CE}_1$, CE_2, ALE and CLK. READY is forced low when the Chip Enables are active during the time ALE is high, and remains low until the rising edge of the next CLK. (See Figure 6c.)
PA_{0-7}	I/O	**PORT A:** These are general purpose I/O pins. Their input/output direction is determined by the contents of Data Direction Register (DDR). Port A is selected for write operations when the Chip Enables are active and $\overline{IOW}$ is low and a 0 was previously latched from AD_0, AD_1. Read Operation is selected by either $\overline{IOR}$ low and active Chip Enables and AD_0 and AD_1 low, *or* $IO/\overline{M}$ high, $\overline{RD}$ low, active Chip Enables, and AD_0 and AD_1 low.
PB_{0-7}	I/O	**PORT B:** The general purpose I/O port is identical to Port A except that it is selected by a 1 latched from AD_0 and a 0 from AD_1.
RESET	I	**RESET:** In normal operation, an input high on RESET causes all pins in Ports A and B to assume input mode (clear DDR register).
$\overline{IOR}$	I	**I/O READ:** When the Chip Enables are active, a low on $\overline{IOR}$ will output the selected I/O port onto the AD bus. $\overline{IOR}$ low performs the same function as the combination of $IO/\overline{M}$ high and $\overline{RD}$ low. When $\overline{IOR}$ is not used in a system, $\overline{IOR}$ should be tied to V_{CC} ("1").
V_{CC}		**POWER:** +5V supply.
V_{SS}		**GROUND:** Reference.
V_{DD}		**POWER SUPPLY:** V_{DD} is a programming voltage, and must be tied to V_{CC} when the 8755A is being read. For programming, a high voltage is supplied with V_{DD} = 25V, typical. (See section on programming.)

FUNCTIONAL DESCRIPTION

PROM Section

The 8755A contains an 8-bit address latch which allows it to interface directly to MCS®-48 and MCS®-85 processors without additional hardware.

The PROM section of the chip is addressed by the 11-bit address and the Chip Enables. The address, $\overline{CE_1}$ and CE_2 are latched into the address latches on the falling edge of ALE. If the latched Chip Enables are active and IO/$\overline{M}$ is low when $\overline{RD}$ goes low, the contents of the PROM location addressed by the latched address are put out on the AD_{0-7} lines (provided that V_{DD} is tied to V_{CC}).

I/O Section

The I/O section of the chip is addressed by the latched value of AD_{0-1}. Two 8-bit Data Direction Registers (DDR) in 8755A determine the input/output status of each pin in the corresponding ports. A "0" in a particular bit position of a DDR signifies that the corresponding I/O port bit is in the input mode. A "1" in a particular bit position signifies that the corresponding I/O port bit is in the output mode. In this manner the I/O ports of the 8755A are bit-by-bit programmable as inputs or outputs. The table summarizes port and DDR designation. DDR's cannot be read.

AD_1	AD_0	Selection
0	0	Port A
0	1	Port B
1	0	Port A Data Direction Register (DDR A)
1	1	Port B Data Direction Register (DDR B)

When $\overline{IOW}$ goes low and the Chip Enables are active, the data on the AD_{0-7} is written into I/O port selected by the latched value of AD_{0-1}. During this operation all I/O bits of the selected port are affected, regardless of their I/O mode and the state of IO/$\overline{M}$. The actual output level does not change until $\overline{IOW}$ returns high. (Glitch free output.)

A port can be read out when the latched Chip Enables are active and either $\overline{RD}$ goes low with IO/$\overline{M}$ high, or $\overline{IOR}$ goes low. Both input and output mode bits of a selected port will appear on lines AD_{0-7}.

To clarify the function of the I/O Ports and Data Direction Registers, the following diagram shows the configuration of one bit of PORT A and DDR A. The same logic applies to PORT B and DDR B.

8755A ONE BIT OF PORT A AND DDR A

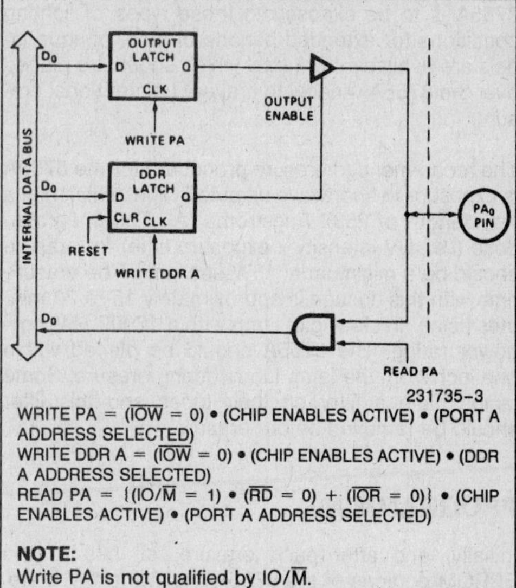

231735-3

WRITE PA = ($\overline{IOW}$ = 0) • (CHIP ENABLES ACTIVE) • (PORT A ADDRESS SELECTED)
WRITE DDR A = ($\overline{IOW}$ = 0) • (CHIP ENABLES ACTIVE) • (DDR A ADDRESS SELECTED)
READ PA = {(IO/$\overline{M}$ = 1) • ($\overline{RD}$ = 0) + ($\overline{IOR}$ = 0)} • (CHIP ENABLES ACTIVE) • (PORT A ADDRESS SELECTED)

NOTE:
Write PA is not qualified by IO/$\overline{M}$.

Note that hardware RESET or writing a zero to the DDR latch will cause the output latch's output buffer to be disabled, preventing the data in the Output Latch from being passed through to the pin. This is equivalent to putting the port in the input mode. Note also that the data can be written to the Output Latch even though the Output Buffer has been disabled. This enables a port to be initialized with a value prior to enabling the output.

The diagram also shows that the contents of PORT A and PORT B can be read even when the ports are configured as outputs.

ERASURE CHARACTERISTICS

The erasure characteristics of the 8755A are such that erasure begins to occur when exposed to light with wavelengths shorter than approximately 4000 Angstroms (Å). It should be noted that sunlight and certain types of fluorescent lamps have wavelengths in the 3000–4000Å range. Data show that constant exposure to room level fluorescent lighting could erase the typical 8755A in approximately 3 years while it would take approximately 1 week to cause erasure when exposed to direct sunlight. If the 8755A is to be exposed to these types of lighting conditions for extended periods of time, opaque labels are available from Intel which should be placed over the 8755A window to prevent unintentional erasure.

The recommended erasure procedure for the 8755A is exposure to shortwave ultraviolet light which has a wavelength of 2537 Angstroms (Å). The integrated dose (i.e., UV intensity x exposure time) for erasure should be a minimum of 15W-sec/cm^2. The erasure time with this dosage is approximately 15 to 20 minutes using an ultraviolet lamp with a 12000 μW/cm^2 power rating. The 8755A should be placed within one inch from the lamp tubes during erasure. Some lamps have a filter on their tubes and this filter should be removed before erasure.

PROGRAMMING

Initially, and after each erasure, all bits of the EPROM portions of the 8755A are in the "1" state. Information is introduced by selectively programming "0" into the desired bit locations. A programmed "0" can only be changed to a "1" by UV erasure.

The 8755A can be programmed on the Intel Universal Programmer (iUP), and iUPF8744A programming module.

The program mode itself consists of programming a single address at a time, giving a single 50 msec pulse for every address. Generally, it is desirable to have a verify cycle after a program cycle for the same address as shown in the attached timing diagram. **In the verify cycle (i.e., normal memory read cycle) 'V_{DD}' should be at +5V.**

SYSTEM APPLICATIONS

System Interface with 8085AH

A system using the 8755A can use either one of the two I/O Interface techniques:

- Standard I/O
- Memory Mapped I/O

If a standard I/O technique is used, the system can use the feature of both CE_2 and $\overline{CE_1}$. By using a combination of unused address lines A_{11-15} and the Chip Enable inputs, the 8085AH system can use up to 5 8755A's without requiring a CE decoder. See Figure 4.

If a memory mapped I/O approach is used the 8755A will be selected by the combination of both the Chip Enables and IO/$\overline{M}$ using AD_{8-15} address lines. See Figure 3.

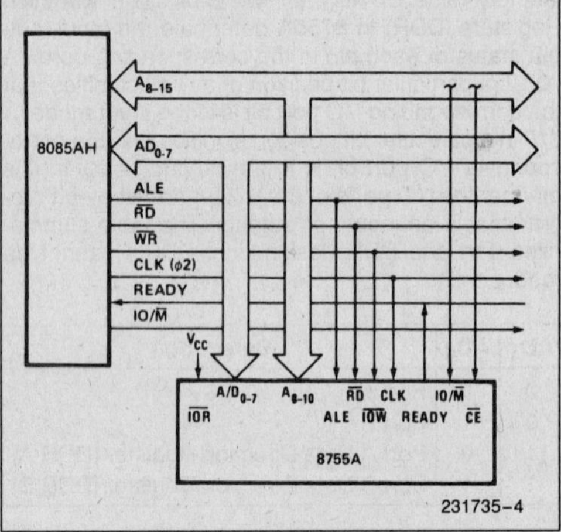

Figure 3. 8755A in 8085AH System (Memory-Mapped I/O)

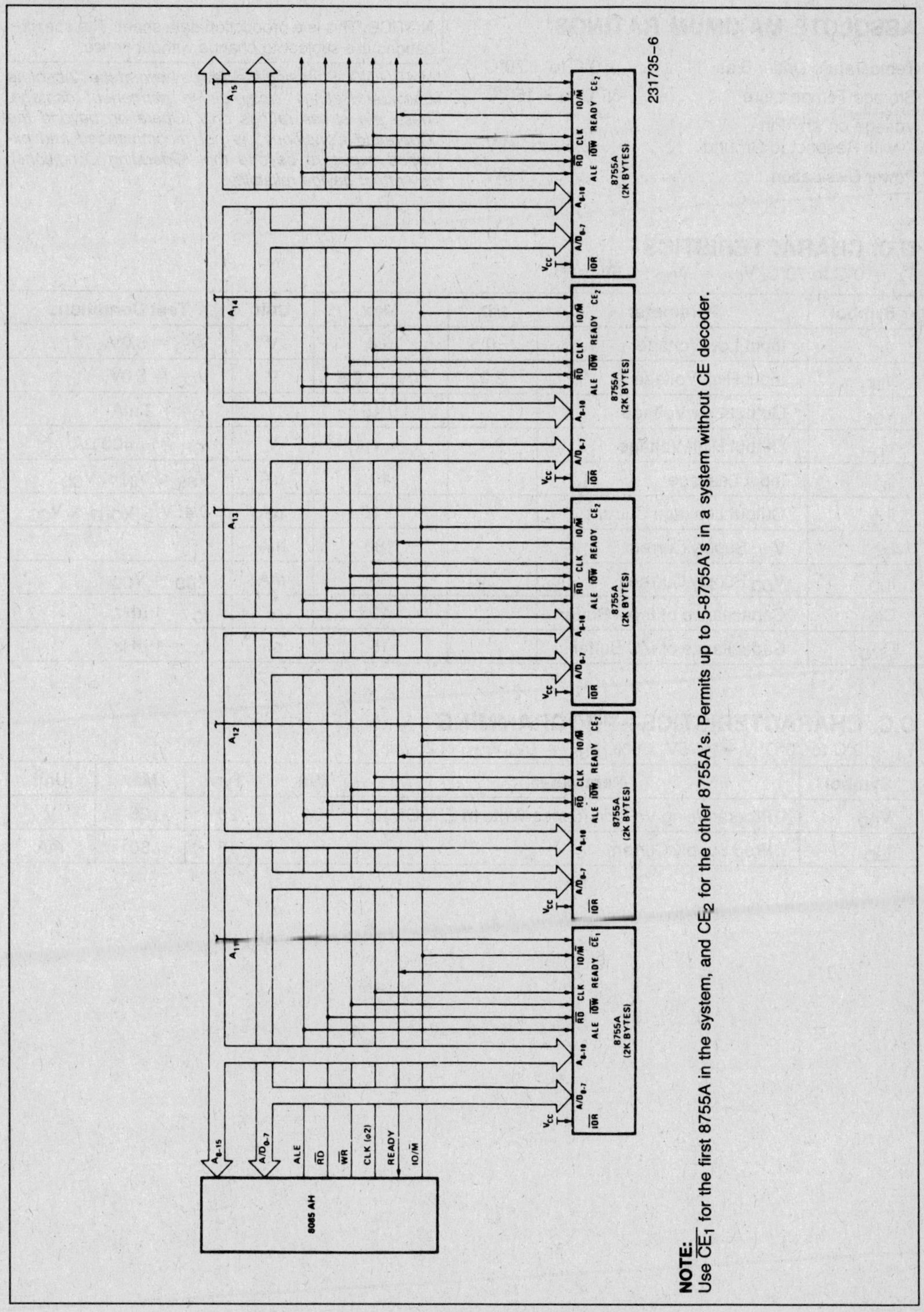
8085 AH
A_{8-15}
A/D_{0-7}
ALE
RD
WR
CLK (φ2)
READY
IO/M
A_{11}
A_{12}
A_{13}
A_{14}
A_{15}
8755A (2K BYTES)
231735-6
NOTE:
Use $\overline{CE_1}$ for the first 8755A in the system, and CE_2 for the other 8755A's. Permits up to 5-8755A's in a system without CE decoder.

Figure 4. 8755A in 8085AH System (Standard I/O)

ABSOLUTE MAXIMUM RATINGS*

Temperature Under Bias .... 0°C to +70°C
Storage Temperature .... −65°C to +150°C
Voltage on any Pin
with Respect to Ground .... −0.5V to +7V
Power Dissipation 1.5W

NOTICE: This is a production data sheet. The specifications are subject to change without notice.

**WARNING: Stressing the device beyond the "Absolute Maximum Ratings" may cause permanent damage. These are stress ratings only. Operation beyond the "Operating Conditions" is not recommended and extended exposure beyond the "Operating Conditions" may affect device reliability.*

D.C. CHARACTERISTICS

T_A = 0°C to 70°C, V_{CC} = V_{DD} = 5V ±5%

Symbol	Parameter	Min	Max	Unit	Test Conditions
V_{IL}	Input Low Voltage	−0.5	0.8	V	V_{CC} = 5.0V
V_{IH}	Input High Voltage	2.0	V_{CC} + 0.5	V	V_{CC} = 5.0V
V_{OL}	Output Low Voltage		0.45	V	I_{OL} = 2 mA
V_{OH}	Output High Voltage	2.4		V	I_{OH} = −400 μA
I_{IL}	Input Leakage		10	μA	$V_{SS} \leq V_{IN} \leq V_{CC}$
I_{LO}	Output Leakage Current		±10	μA	$0.45V \leq V_{OUT} \leq V_{CC}$
I_{CC}	V_{CC} Supply Current		180	mA	
I_{DD}	V_{DD} Supply Current		30	mA	V_{DD} = V_{CC}
C_{IN}	Capacitance of Input Buffer		10	pF	f_C = 1 μHz
$C_{I/O}$	Capacitance of I/O Buffer		15	pF	f_C = 1 μHz

D.C. CHARACTERISTICS—PROGRAMMING

T_A = 0°C to 70°C, V_{CC} = 5V ±5%, V_{SS} = 0V, V_{DD} = 25V ±1V

Symbol	Parameter	Min	Typ	Max	Unit
V_{DD}	Programming Voltage (during Write to EPROM)	24	25	26	V
I_{DD}	Prog Supply Current		15	30	mA

A.C. CHARACTERISTICS

T_A = 0°C to 70°C, V_{CC} = 5V ±5%

Symbol	Parameter	8755A		Unit
		Min	Max	
t_{CYC}	Clock Cycle Time	320		ns
T_1	CLK Pulse Width	80		ns
T_2	CLK Pulse Width	120		ns
t_f, t_r	CLK Rise and Fall Time		30	ns
t_{AL}	Address to Latch Set Up Time	50		ns
t_{LA}	Address Hold Time after Latch	80		ns
t_{LC}	Latch to READ/WRITE Control	100		ns
t_{RD}	Valid Data Out Delay from READ Control*		170	ns
t_{AD}	Address Stable to Data Out Valid**		450	ns
t_{LL}	Latch Enable Width	100		ns
t_{RDF}	Data Bus Float after READ	0	100	ns
t_{CL}	READ/WRITE Control to Latch Enable	20		ns
t_{CC}	READ/WRITE Control Width	250		ns
t_{DW}	Data in Write Set Up Time	150		ns
t_{WD}	Data in Hold Time after WRITE	30		ns
t_{WP}	WRITE to Port Output		400	ns
t_{PR}	Port Input Set Up Time	50		ns
t_{RP}	Port Input Hold Time to Control	50		ns
t_{RYH}	READY HOLD Time to Control	0	160	ns
t_{ARY}	ADDRESS (CE) to READY		160	ns
t_{RV}	Recovery Time between Controls	300		ns
t_{RDE}	READ Control to Data Bus Enable	10		ns

NOTES:

C_{LOAD} = 150 pF.

*Or T_{AD} − (T_{AL} + T_{LC}), whichever is greater.

**Defines ALE to Data Out Valid in conjunction with T_{AL}.

A.C. CHARACTERISTICS—PROGRAMMING

T_A = 0°C to 70°C, V_{CC} = 5V ±5%, V_{SS} = 0V, V_{DD} = 25V ±1V

Symbol	Parameter	Min	Typ	Max	Unit
t_{PS}	Data Setup Time	10			ns
t_{PD}	Data Hold Time	0			ns
t_S	Prog Pulse Setup Time	2			μs
t_H	Prog Pulse Hold Time	2			μs
t_{PR}	Prog Pulse Rise Time	0.01	2		μs
t_{PF}	Prog Pulse Fall Time	0.01	2		μs
t_{PRG}	Prog Pulse Width	45	50		ms

A.C. TESTING INPUT, OUTPUT WAVEFORM

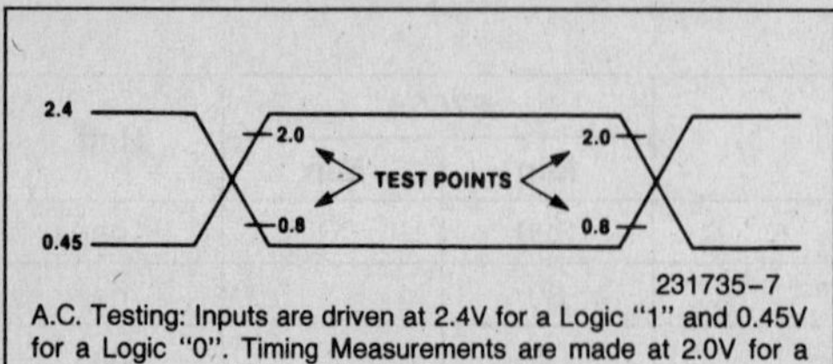

231735-7

A.C. Testing: Inputs are driven at 2.4V for a Logic "1" and 0.45V for a Logic "0". Timing Measurements are made at 2.0V for a Logic "1" and 0.8V for a Logic "0".

A.C. TESTING LOAD CIRCUIT

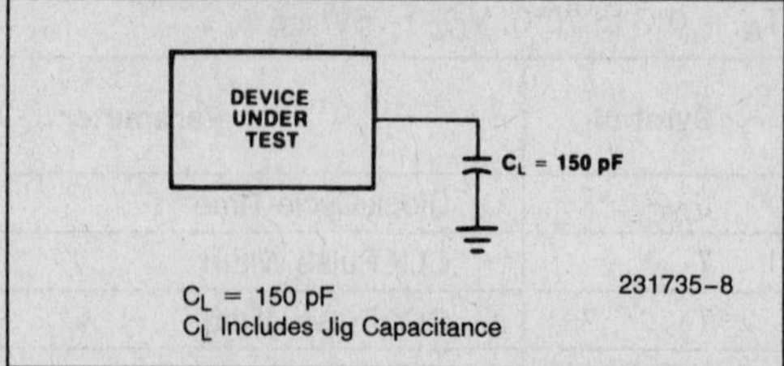

231735-8

C_L = 150 pF
C_L Includes Jig Capacitance

WAVEFORMS

CLOCK SPECIFICATION FOR 8755A

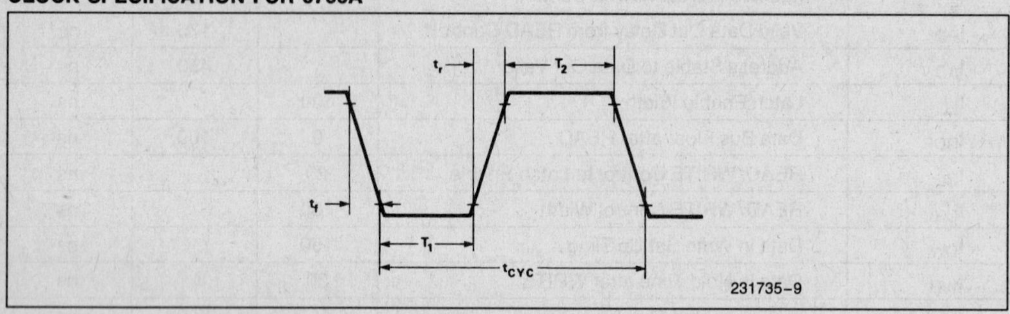

231735-9

PROM READ, I/O READ AND WRITE

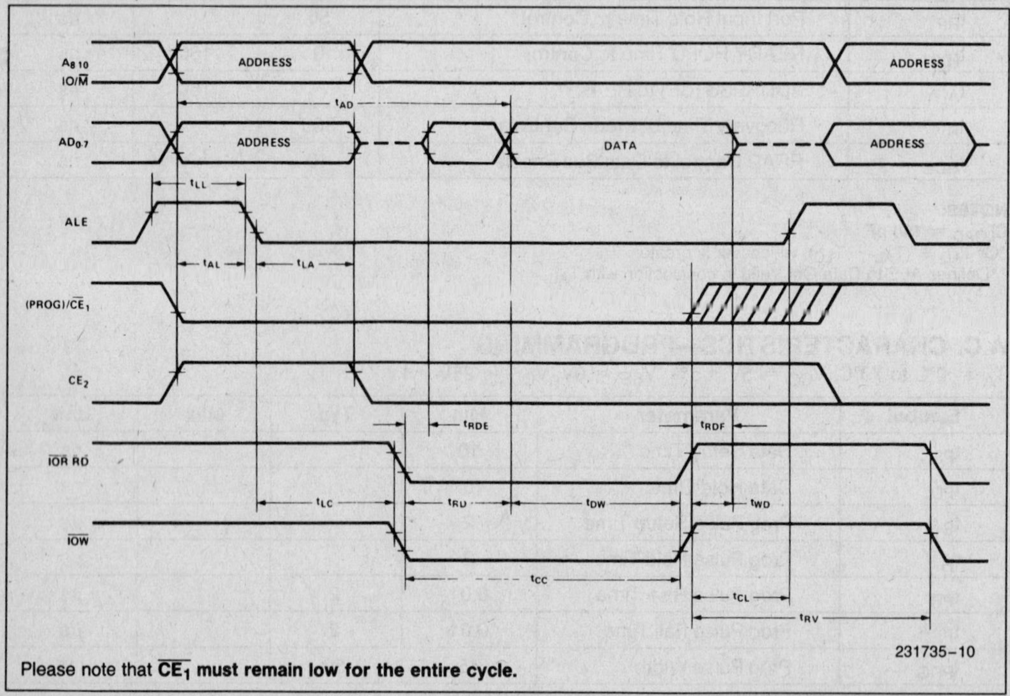

231735-10

Please note that $\overline{CE_1}$ **must remain low for the entire cycle.**

WAVEFORMS (Continued)

I/O PORT

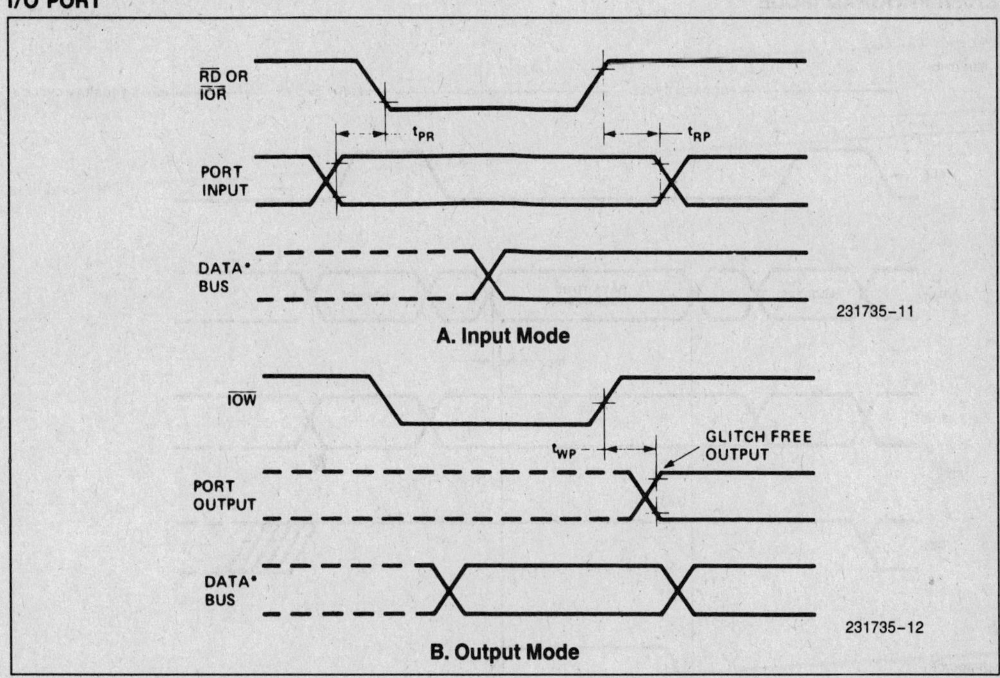

A. Input Mode

B. Output Mode

WAIT STATE (READY = 0)

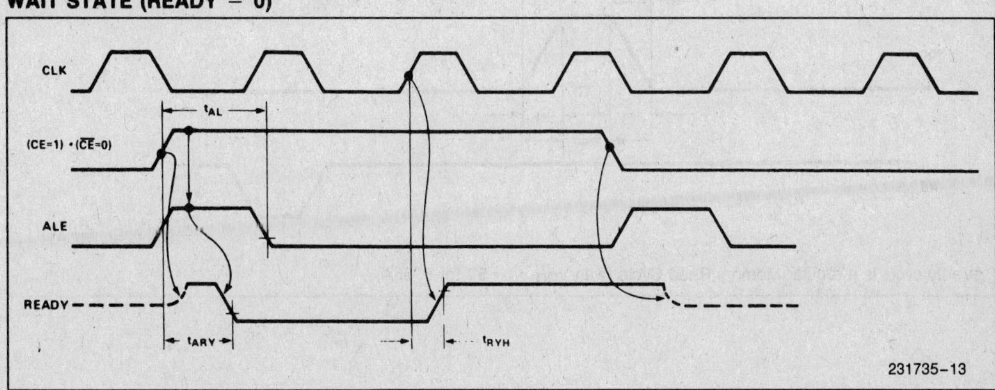

WAVEFORMS (Continued)

8755A PROGRAM MODE

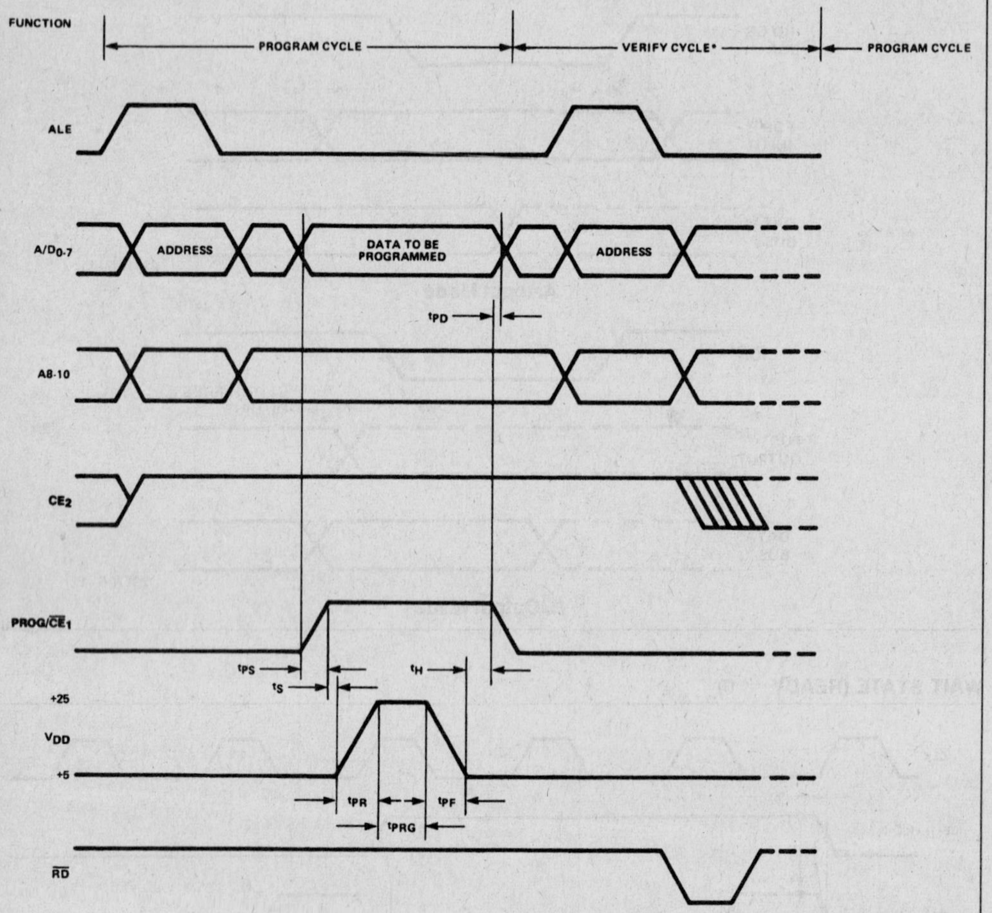

231735–14

*Verify cycle is a regular Memory Read Cycle (with V_{DD} = +5V for 8755A).

80186/80188 Family

2

80186/80188 HIGH-INTEGRATION 16-BIT MICROPROCESSORS

- Integrated Feature Set
  - Enhanced 8086-2 CPU
  - Clock Generator
  - 2 Independent DMA Channels
  - Programmable Interrupt Controller
  - 3 Programmable 16-bit Timers
  - Programmable Memory and Peripheral Chip-Select Logic
  - Programmable Wait State Generator
  - Local Bus Controller
- Available in 10 MHz and 8 MHz Versions
- High-Performance Processor
  - 4 Mbyte/Sec Bus Bandwidth Interface @ 8 MHz (80186)
  - 5 Mbyte/Sec Bus Bandwidth Interface @ 10 MHz (80186)
- Direct Addressing Capability to 1 Mbyte of Memory and 64 Kbyte I/O
- Completely Object Code Compatible with All Existing 8086, 8088 Software
  - 10 New Instruction Types
- Complete System Development Support
  - Development Software: ASM 86 Assembler, PL/M-86, C-86, and System Utilities
  - In-Circuit-Emulator
- Numerics Coprocessing Capability Through 8087 Interface
- Available in 68 Pin:
  - Plastic Leaded Chip Carrier (PLCC)
  - Ceramic Pin Grid Array (PGA)
  - Ceramic Leadless Chip Carrier (LCC)
- Available in EXPRESS
  - Standard Temperature with Burn-In
  - Extended Temperature Range (−40°C to +85°C)

2

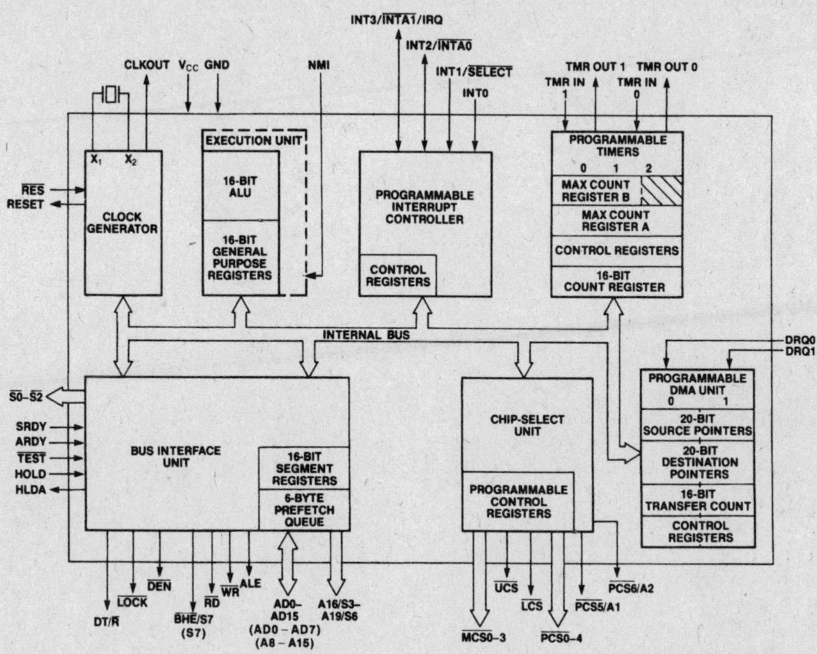

Figure 1. Block Diagram

November 1993
Order Number: 272430-001

80186/80188 High-Integration 16-Bit Microprocessors

CONTENTS

CONTENTS	PAGE
FUNCTIONAL DESCRIPTION	2-9
Introduction	2-9
CLOCK GENERATOR	2-9
Oscillator	2-9
Clock Generator	2-9
READY Synchronization	2-9
RESET Logic	2-9
LOCAL BUS CONTROLLER	2-9
Memory/Peripheral Control	2-10
Local Bus Arbitration	2-10
Local Bus Controller and Reset	2-10
PERIPHERAL ARCHITECTURE	2-10
Chip-Select/Ready Generation Logic	2-10
DMA Channels	2-11
Timers	2-11
Interrupt Controller	2-12
ABSOLUTE MAXIMUM RATINGS	2-15
D.C. CHARACTERISTICS	2-15
A.C. CHARACTERISTICS	2-16
EXPLANATION OF THE AC SYMBOLS	2-18
WAVEFORMS	2-19
EXPRESS	2-25
EXECUTION TIMINGS	2-26
INSTRUCTION SET SUMMARY	2-27
FOOTNOTES	2-32
REVISION HISTORY	2-33

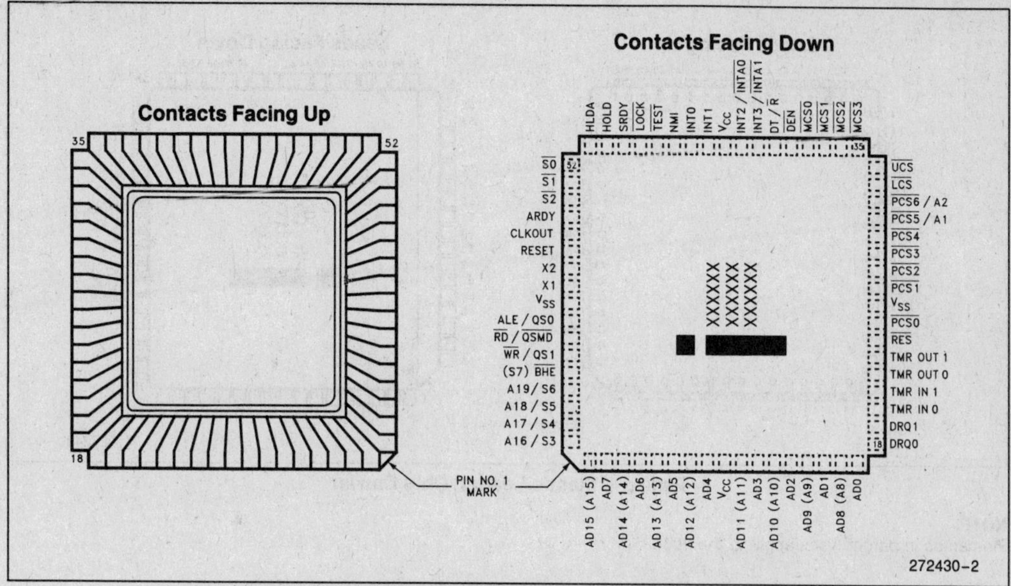

Figure 2. Ceramic Leadless Chip Carrier (JEDEC Type A)

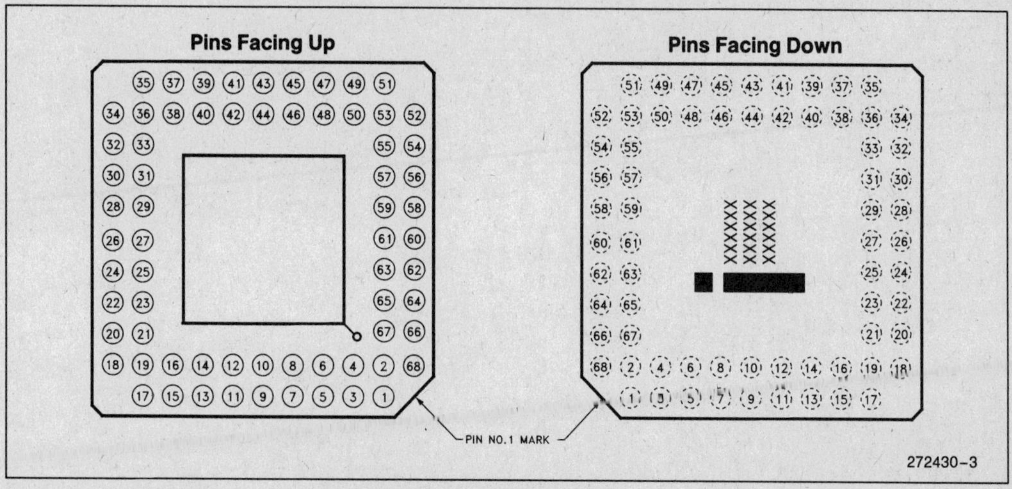

Figure 3. Ceramic Pin Grid Array

NOTE:
Pin names in parentheses apply to the 80188.

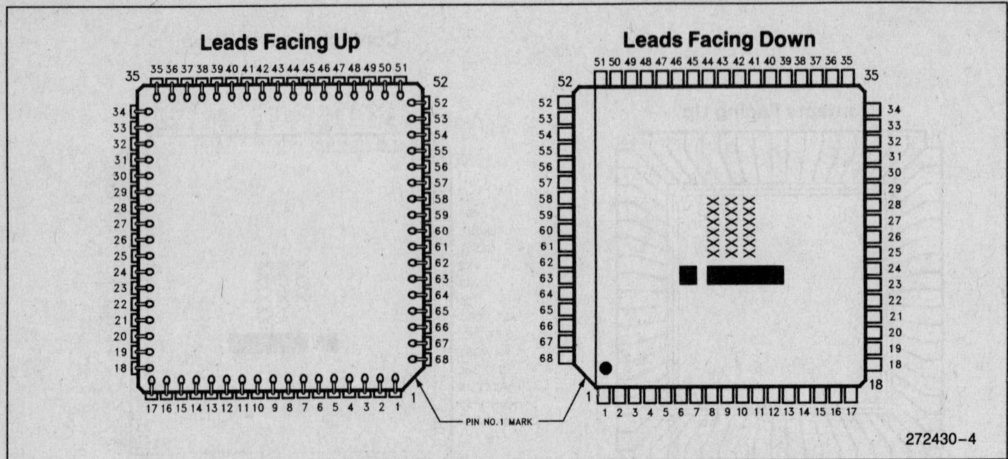

Figure 4. Plastic Leaded Chip Carrier

NOTE:
Pin names in parentheses apply to the 80188.

Table 1. Pin Descriptions

Symbol	Pin No.	Type	Name and Function
V_{CC}	9 43	I	**SYSTEM POWER:** +5 volt power supply.
V_{SS}	26 60	I	System Ground.
RESET	57	O	Reset Output indicates that the CPU is being reset, and can be used as a system reset. It is active HIGH, synchronized with the processor clock, and lasts an integer number of clock periods corresponding to the length of the $\overline{\text{RES}}$ signal.
X1 X2	59 58	I O	Crystal Inputs X1 and X2 provide external connections for a fundamental mode parallel resonant crystal for the internal oscillator. Instead of using a crystal, an external clock may be applied to X1 while minimizing stray capacitance on X2. The input or oscillator frequency is internally divided by two to generate the clock signal (CLKOUT).
CLKOUT	56	O	Clock Output provides the system with a 50% duty cycle waveform. All device pin timings are specified relative to CLKOUT.
$\overline{\text{RES}}$	24	I	An active $\overline{\text{RES}}$ causes the processor to immediately terminate its present activity, clear the internal logic, and enter a dormant state. This signal may be asynchronous to the processor clock. The processor begins fetching instructions approximately 6½ clock cycles after $\overline{\text{RES}}$ is returned HIGH. For proper initialization, V_{CC} must be within specifications and the clock signal must be stable for more than 4 clocks with $\overline{\text{RES}}$ held LOW. $\overline{\text{RES}}$ is internally synchronized. This input is provided with a Schmitt-trigger to facilitate power-on $\overline{\text{RES}}$ generation via an RC network.
$\overline{\text{TEST}}$	47	I/O	$\overline{\text{TEST}}$ is examined by the WAIT instruction. If the $\overline{\text{TEST}}$ input is HIGH when "WAIT" execution begins, instruction execution will suspend. $\overline{\text{TEST}}$ will be resampled until it goes LOW, at which time execution will resume. If interrupts are enabled while the processor is waiting for $\overline{\text{TEST}}$, interrupts will be serviced. During power-up, active $\overline{\text{RES}}$ is required to configure $\overline{\text{TEST}}$ as an input. This pin is synchronized internally.
TMR IN 0 TMR IN 1	20 21	I I	Timer Inputs are used either as clock or control signals, depending upon the programmed timer mode. These inputs are active HIGH (or LOW-to-HIGH transitions are counted) and internally synchronized.
TMR OUT 0 TMR OUT 1	22 23	O O	Timer outputs are used to provide single pulse or continous waveform generation, depending upon the timer mode selected.
DRQ0 DRQ1	18 19	I I	DMA Request is asserted HIGH by an external device when it is ready for DMA Channel 0 or 1 to perform a transfer. These signals are level-triggered and internally synchronized.
NMI	46	I	The Non-Maskable Interrupt input causes a Type 2 interrupt. An NMI transition from LOW to HIGH is latched and synchronized internally, and initiates the interrupt at the next instruction boundary. NMI must be asserted for at least one clock. The Non-Maskable Interrupt cannot be avoided by programming.
INT0 INT1/$\overline{\text{SELECT}}$ INT2/$\overline{\text{INTA0}}$ INT3/$\overline{\text{INTA1}}$/IRQ	45 44 42 41	I I I/O I/O	Maskable Interrupt Requests can be requested by activating one of these pins. When configured as inputs, these pins are active HIGH. Interrupt Requests are synchronized internally. INT2 and INT3 may be configured to provide active-LOW interrupt-acknowledge output signals. All interrupt inputs may be configured to be either edge- or level-triggered. To ensure recognition, all interrupt requests must remain active until the interrupt is acknowledged. When Slave Mode is selected, the function of these pins changes (see Interrupt Controller section of this data sheet).

NOTE:
Pin names in parentheses apply to the 80188.

2

Table 1. Pin Descriptions (Continued)

<table>
<tr><th>Symbol</th><th>Pin No.</th><th>Type</th><th>Name and Function</th></tr>
<tr><td>A19/S6
A18/S5
A17/S4
A16/S3</td><td>65
66
67
68</td><td>O
O
O
O</td><td>Address Bus Outputs (16–19) and Bus Cycle Status (3–6) indicate the four most significant address bits during T_1. These signals are active HIGH. During T_2, T_3, T_W, and T_4, the S6 pin is LOW to indicate a CPU-initiated bus cycle or HIGH to indicate a DMA-initiated bus cycle. During the same T-states, S3, S4, and S5 are always LOW. The status pins float during bus HOLD or RESET.</td></tr>
<tr><td>AD15 (A15)
AD14 (A14)
AD13 (A13)
AD12 (A12)
AD11 (A11)
AD10 (A10)
AD9 (A9)
AD8 (A8)
AD7
AD6
AD5
AD4
AD3
AD2
AD1
AD0</td><td>1
3
5
7
10
12
14
16
2
4
6
8
11
13
15
17</td><td>I/O
I/O
I/O
I/O
I/O
I/O
I/O
I/O
I/O
I/O
I/O
I/O
I/O
I/O
I/O
I/O</td><td>Address/Data Bus signals constitute the time multiplexed memory or I/O address (T_1) and data (T_2, T_3, T_W, and T_4) bus. The bus is active HIGH. A_0 is analogous to $\overline{BHE}$ for the lower byte of the data bus, pins D_7 through D_0. It is LOW during T_1 when a byte is to be transferred onto the lower portion of the bus in memory or I/O operations. $\overline{BHE}$ does not exist on the 80188, as the data bus is only 8 bits wide.</td></tr>
<tr><td>$\overline{BHE}$/S7
(S7)</td><td>64</td><td>O</td><td>During T_1 the Bus High Enable signal should be used to determine if data is to be enabled onto the most significant half of the data bus; pins D_{15}–D_8. $\overline{BHE}$ is LOW during T_1 for read, write, and interrupt acknowledge cycles when a byte is to be transferred on the higher half of the bus. The S_7 status information is available during T_2, T_3, and T_4. S_7 is logically equivalent to $\overline{BHE}$. $\overline{BHE}$/S7 floats during HOLD. On the 80188, S7 is high during normal operation.

<table><tr><th colspan="3">$\overline{BHE}$ and A0 Encodings (80186 Only)</th></tr><tr><th>$\overline{BHE}$ Value</th><th>A0 Value</th><th>Function</th></tr><tr><td>0</td><td>0</td><td>Word Transfer</td></tr><tr><td>0</td><td>1</td><td>Byte Transfer on upper half of data bus (D15–D8)</td></tr><tr><td>1</td><td>0</td><td>Byte Transfer on lower half of data bus (D_7–D_0)</td></tr><tr><td>1</td><td>1</td><td>Reserved</td></tr></table></td></tr>
<tr><td>ALE/QS0</td><td>61</td><td>O</td><td>Address Latch Enable/Queue Status 0 is provided by the processor to latch the address. ALE is active HIGH. Addresses are guaranteed to be valid on the trailing edge of ALE. The ALE rising edge is generated off the rising edge of the CLKOUT immediately preceding T_1 of the associated bus cycle, effectively one-half clock cycle earlier than in the 8086. The trailing edge is generated off the CLKOUT rising edge in T_1 as in the 8086. Note that ALE is never floated.</td></tr>
<tr><td>$\overline{WR}$/QS1</td><td>63</td><td>O</td><td>Write Strobe/Queue Status 1 indicates that the data on the bus is to be written into a memory or an I/O device. $\overline{WR}$ is active for T_2, T_3, and T_W of any write cycle. It is active LOW, and floats during HOLD. When the processor is in queue status mode, the ALE/QS0 and $\overline{WR}$/QS1 pins provide information about processor/instruction queue interaction.

<table><tr><th>QS1</th><th>QS0</th><th>Queue Operation</th></tr><tr><td>0</td><td>0</td><td>No queue operation</td></tr><tr><td>0</td><td>1</td><td>First opcode byte fetched from the queue</td></tr><tr><td>1</td><td>1</td><td>Subsequent byte fetched from the queue</td></tr><tr><td>1</td><td>0</td><td>Empty the queue</td></tr></table></td></tr>
</table>

NOTE:
Pin names in parentheses apply to the 80188.

Table 1. Pin Descriptions (Continued)

<table>
<tr><th>Symbol</th><th>Pin No.</th><th>Type</th><th>Name and Function</th></tr>
<tr><td>$\overline{RD}/\overline{QSMD}$</td><td>62</td><td>I/O</td><td>Read Strobe is an active LOW signal which indicates that the processor is performing a memory or I/O read cycle. It is guaranteed not to go LOW before the A/D bus is floated. An internal pull-up ensures that $\overline{RD}$ is HIGH during RESET. Following RESET the pin is sampled to determine whether the processor is to provide ALE, $\overline{RD}$, and $\overline{WR}$, or queue status information. To enable Queue Status Mode, $\overline{RD}$ must be connected to GND. $\overline{RD}$ will float during bus HOLD.</td></tr>
<tr><td>ARDY</td><td>55</td><td>I</td><td>Asynchronous Ready informs the processor that the addressed memory space or I/O device will complete a data transfer. The ARDY pin accepts a rising edge that is asynchronous to CLKOUT, and is active HIGH. The falling edge of ARDY must be synchronized to the processor clock. Connecting ARDY HIGH will always assert the ready condition to the CPU. If this line is unused, it should be tied LOW to yield control to the SRDY pin.</td></tr>
<tr><td>SRDY</td><td>49</td><td>I</td><td>Synchronous Ready informs the processor that the addressed memory space or I/O device will complete a data transfer. The SRDY pin accepts an active-HIGH input synchronized to CLKOUT. The use of SRDY allows a relaxed system timing over ARDY. This is accomplished by elimination of the one-half clock cycle required to internally synchronize the ARDY input signal. Connecting SRDY high will always assert the ready condition to the CPU. If this line is unused, it should be tied LOW to yield control to the ARDY pin.</td></tr>
<tr><td>$\overline{LOCK}$</td><td>48</td><td>O</td><td>$\overline{LOCK}$ output indicates that other system bus masters are not to gain control of the system bus while $\overline{LOCK}$ is active LOW. The $\overline{LOCK}$ signal is requested by the LOCK prefix instruction and is activated at the beginning of the first data cycle associated with the instruction following the LOCK prefix. It remains active until the completion of that instruction. No instruction prefetching will occur while $\overline{LOCK}$ is asserted. When executing more than one LOCK instruction, always make sure there are 6 bytes of code between the end of the first LOCK instruction and the start of the second LOCK instruction. $\overline{LOCK}$ is driven HIGH for one clock during RESET and then floated.</td></tr>
<tr><td>$\overline{S0}$
$\overline{S1}$
$\overline{S2}$</td><td>52
53
54</td><td>O
O
O</td><td>Bus cycle status $\overline{S0}-\overline{S2}$ are encoded to provide bus-transaction information:
<table>
<tr><th colspan="4">Bus Cycle Status Information</th></tr>
<tr><th>$\overline{S2}$</th><th>$\overline{S1}$</th><th>$\overline{S0}$</th><th>Bus Cycle Initiated</th></tr>
<tr><td>0</td><td>0</td><td>0</td><td>Interrupt Acknowledge</td></tr>
<tr><td>0</td><td>0</td><td>1</td><td>Read I/O</td></tr>
<tr><td>0</td><td>1</td><td>0</td><td>Write I/O</td></tr>
<tr><td>0</td><td>1</td><td>1</td><td>Halt</td></tr>
<tr><td>1</td><td>0</td><td>0</td><td>Instruction Fetch</td></tr>
<tr><td>1</td><td>0</td><td>1</td><td>Read Data from Memory</td></tr>
<tr><td>1</td><td>1</td><td>0</td><td>Write Data to Memory</td></tr>
<tr><td>1</td><td>1</td><td>1</td><td>Passive (no bus cycle)</td></tr>
</table>
The status pins float during HOLD.
$\overline{S2}$ may be used as a logical M/$\overline{IO}$ indicator, and $\overline{S1}$ as a DT/$\overline{R}$ indicator.</td></tr>
</table>

NOTE:
Pin names in parentheses apply to the 80188.

Table 1. Pin Descriptions (Continued)

Symbol	Pin No.	Type	Name and Function
HOLD HLDA	50 51	I O	HOLD indicates that another bus master is requesting the local bus. The HOLD input is active HIGH. HOLD may be asynchronous with respect to the processor clock. The processor will issue a HLDA (HIGH) in response to a HOLD request at the end of T_4 or T_i. Simultaneous with the issuance of HLDA, the processor will float the local bus and control lines. After HOLD is detected as being LOW, the processor will lower HLDA. When the processor needs to run another bus cycle, it will again drive the local bus and control lines.
$\overline{UCS}$	34	O	Upper Memory Chip Select is an active LOW output whenever a memory reference is made to the defined upper portion (1K–256K block) of memory. This line is not floated during bus HOLD. The address range activating $\overline{UCS}$ is software programmable.
$\overline{LCS}$	33	O	Lower Memory Chip Select is active LOW whenever a memory reference is made to the defined lower portion (1K–256K) of memory. This line is not floated during bus HOLD. The address range activating $\overline{LCS}$ is software programmable.
$\overline{MCS0}$ $\overline{MCS1}$ $\overline{MCS2}$ $\overline{MCS3}$	38 37 36 35	O O O O	Mid-Range Memory Chip Select signals are active LOW when a memory reference is made to the defined mid-range portion of memory (8K–512K). These lines are not floated during bus HOLD. The address ranges activating $\overline{MCS0}$–3 are software programmable.
$\overline{PCS0}$ $\overline{PCS1}$ $\overline{PCS2}$ $\overline{PCS3}$ $\overline{PCS4}$	25 27 28 29 30	O O O O O	Peripheral Chip Select signals 0–4 are active LOW when a reference is made to the defined peripheral area (64 Kbyte I/O space). These lines are not floated during bus HOLD. The address ranges activating $\overline{PCS0}$–4 are software programmable.
$\overline{PCS5}$/A1	31	O	Peripheral Chip Select 5 or Latched A1 may be programmed to provide a sixth peripheral chip select, or to provide an internally latched A1 signal. The address range activating $\overline{PCS5}$ is software-programmable. $\overline{PCS5}$/A1 does not float during bus HOLD. When programmed to provide latched A1, this pin will retain the previously latched value during HOLD.
$\overline{PCS6}$/A2	32	O	Peripheral Chip Select 6 or Latched A2 may be programmed to provide a seventh peripheral chip select, or to provide an internally latched A2 signal. The address range activating $\overline{PCS6}$ is software programmable. $\overline{PCS6}$/A2 does not float during bus HOLD. When programmed to provide latched A2, this pin will retain the previously latched value during HOLD.
DT/$\overline{R}$	40	O	Data Transmit/Receive controls the direction of data flow through an external data bus transceiver. When LOW, data is transferred to the processsor. When HIGH, the processor places write data on the data bus.
$\overline{DEN}$	39	O	Data Enable is provided as a data bus transceiver output enable. $\overline{DEN}$ is active LOW during each memory and I/O access. $\overline{DEN}$ is HIGH whenever DT/$\overline{R}$ changes state. During RESET, $\overline{DEN}$ is driven HIGH for one clock, then floated. $\overline{DEN}$ also floats during HOLD.

NOTE:
Pin names in parentheses apply to the 80188.

FUNCTIONAL DESCRIPTION

Introduction

The following Functional Description describes the base architecture of the 80186. The 80186 is a very high integration 16-bit microprocessor. It combines 15–20 of the most common microprocessor system components onto one chip while providing twice the performance of the standard 8086. The 80186 is object code compatible with the 8086/8088 microprocessors and adds 10 new instruction types to the 8086/8088 instruction set.

For more detailed information on the architecture, please refer to the 80C186XL/80C188XL User's Manual. The 80186 and the 80186XL devices are functionally and register compatible.

CLOCK GENERATOR

The processor provides an on-chip clock generator for both internal and external clock generation. The clock generator features a crystal oscillator, a divide-by-two counter, synchronous and asynchronous ready inputs, and reset circuitry.

Oscillator

The oscillator circuit is designed to be used with a parallel resonant fundamental mode crystal. This is used as the time base for the processor. The crystal frequency selected will be double the CPU clock frequency. Use of an LC or RC circuit is not recommended with this oscillator. If an external oscillator is used, it can be connected directly to the input pin X1 in lieu of a crystal. The output of the oscillator is not directly available outside the processor. The recommended crystal configuration is shown in Figure 5.

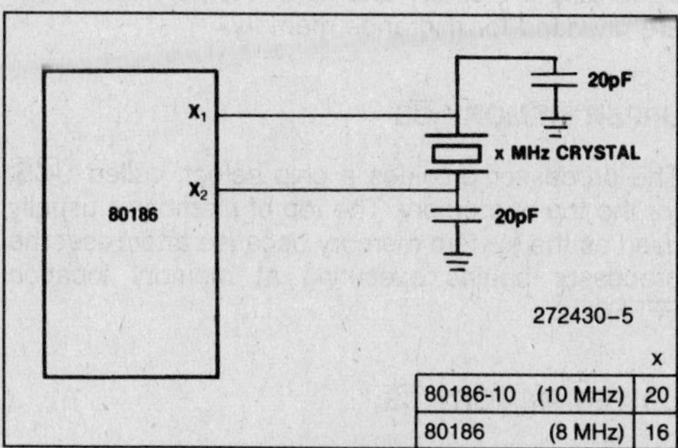

	x
80186-10 (10 MHz)	20
80186 (8 MHz)	16

Figure 5. Recommended Crystal Configuration

Intel recommends the following values for crystal selection parameters:

Temperature Range:	0 to 70°C
ESR (Equivalent Series Resistance):	30Ω max
C_0 (Shunt Capacitance of Crystal):	7.0 pf max
C_1 (Load Capacitance):	20 pf ± 2 pf
Drive Level:	1 mW max

Clock Generator

The clock generator provides the 50% duty cycle processor clock for the processor. It does this by dividing the oscillator output by 2 forming the symmetrical clock. If an external oscillator is used, the state of the clock generator will change on the falling edge of the oscillator signal. The CLKOUT pin provides the processor clock signal for use outside the device. This may be used to drive other system components. All timings are referenced to the output clock.

READY Synchronization

The processor provides both synchronous and asynchronous ready inputs. In addition, the processor, as part of the integrated chip-select logic, has the capability to program WAIT states for memory and peripheral blocks.

RESET Logic

The processor provides both a $\overline{\text{RES}}$ input pin and a synchronized RESET output pin for use with other system components. The $\overline{\text{RES}}$ input pin is provided with hysteresis in order to facilitate power-on Reset generation via an RC network. RESET output is guaranteed to remain active for at least five clocks given a $\overline{\text{RES}}$ input of at least six clocks.

LOCAL BUS CONTROLLER

The processor provides a local bus controller to generate the local bus control signals. In addition, it employs a HOLD/HLDA protocol for relinquishing the local bus to other bus masters. It also provides outputs that can be used to enable external buffers and to direct the flow of data on and off the local bus.

2

Memory/Peripheral Control

The processor provides ALE, $\overline{RD}$, and $\overline{WR}$ bus control signals. The $\overline{RD}$ and $\overline{WR}$ signals are used to strobe data from memory or I/O to the processor or to strobe data from the processor to memory or I/O. The ALE line provides a strobe to latch the address when it is valid. The local bus controller does not provide a memory/$\overline{I/O}$ signal. If this is required, use the $\overline{S2}$ signal (which will require external latching), make the memory and I/O spaces nonoverlapping, or use only the integrated chip-select circuitry.

Local Bus Arbitration

The processor uses a HOLD/HLDA system of local bus exchange. This provides an asynchronous bus exchange mechanism. This means multiple masters utilizing the same bus can operate at separate clock frequencies. The processor provides a single HOLD/HLDA pair through which all other bus masters may gain control of the local bus. External circuitry must arbitrate which external device will gain control of the bus when there is more than one alternate local bus master. When the processor relinquishes control of the local bus, it floats $\overline{DEN}$, $\overline{RD}$, $\overline{WR}$, $\overline{S0}$–$\overline{S2}$, $\overline{LOCK}$, AD0–AD15 (AD0–AD7), A16–A19 (A8–A19), $\overline{BHE}$ (S7), and DT/$\overline{R}$ to allow another master to drive these lines directly.

Local Bus Controller and Reset

During RESET the local bus controller will perform the following action:

- Drive $\overline{DEN}$, $\overline{RD}$, and $\overline{WR}$ HIGH for one clock cycle, then float.

  NOTE:
  $\overline{RD}$ is also provided with an internal pull-up device to prevent the processor from inadvertently entering Queue Status Mode during RESET.

- Drive $\overline{S0}$–$\overline{S2}$ to the inactive state (all HIGH) and then float.
- Drive $\overline{LOCK}$ HIGH and then float.
- Float AD0–15 (AD0–AD7), A16–19 (A8–A19), $\overline{BHE}$ (S7), DT/$\overline{R}$.
- Drive ALE LOW (ALE is never floated).
- Drive HLDA LOW.

PERIPHERAL ARCHITECTURE

All of the integrated peripherals are controlled by 16-bit registers contained within an internal 256-byte control block. The control block may be mapped into either memory or I/O space. Internal logic will recognize control block addresses and respond to bus cycles. During bus cycles to internal registers, the bus controller will signal the operation externally (i.e., the $\overline{RD}$, $\overline{WR}$, status, address, data, etc., lines will be driven as in a normal bus cycle), but D_{15-0} (D_{7-0}), SRDY, and ARDY will be ignored. The base address of the control block must be on an even 256-byte boundary (i.e., the lower 8 bits of the base address are all zeros).

The control block base address is programmed by a 16-bit relocation register contained within the control block at offset FEH from the base address of the control block. It provides the upper 12 bits of the base address of the control block.

In addition to providing relocation information for the control block, the relocation register contains bits which place the interrupt controller into Slave Mode, and cause the CPU to interrupt upon encountering ESC instructions.

Chip-Select/Ready Generation Logic

The processor contains logic which provides programmable chip-select generation for both memories and peripherals. In addition, it can be programmed to provide READY (or WAIT state) generation. It can also provide latched address bits A1 and A2. The chip-select lines are active for all memory and I/O cycles in their programmed areas, whether they be generated by the CPU or by the integrated DMA unit.

MEMORY CHIP SELECTS

The processor provides 6 memory chip select outputs for 3 address areas; upper memory, lower memory, and midrange memory. One each is provided for upper memory and lower memory, while four are provided for midrange memory.

UPPER MEMORY $\overline{CS}$

The processor provides a chip select, called $\overline{UCS}$, for the top of memory. The top of memory is usually used as the system memory because after reset the processor begins executing at memory location FFFF0H.

LOWER MEMORY $\overline{CS}$

The processor provides a chip select for low memory called $\overline{LCS}$. The bottom of memory contains the interrupt vector table, starting at location 00000H.

The lower limit of memory defined by this chip select is always 0H, while the upper limit is programmable. By programming the upper limit, the size of the memory block is defined.

MID-RANGE MEMORY $\overline{CS}$

The processor provides four $\overline{MCS}$ lines which are active within a user-locatable memory block. This block can be located within the 1-Mbyte memory address space exclusive of the areas defined by $\overline{UCS}$ and $\overline{LCS}$. Both the base address and size of this memory block are programmable.

PERIPHERAL CHIP SELECTS

The processor can generate chip selects for up to seven peripheral devices. These chip selects are active for seven contiguous blocks of 128 bytes above a programmable base address. The base address may be located in either memory or I/O space. Seven $\overline{CS}$ lines called $\overline{PCS0-6}$ are generated by the processor. $\overline{PCS5}$ and $\overline{PCS6}$ can also be programmed to provide latched address bits A1 and A2. If so programmed, they cannot be used as peripheral selects. These outputs can be connected directly to the A0 and A1 pins used for selecting internal registers of 8-bit peripheral chips.

READY GENERATION LOGIC

The processor can generate a READY signal internally for each of the memory or peripheral $\overline{CS}$ lines. The number of WAIT states to be inserted for each peripheral or memory is programmable to provide 0–3 wait states for all accesses to the area for which the chip select is active. In addition, the processor may be programmed to either ignore external READY for each chip-select range individually or to factor external READY with the integrated ready generator.

CHIP SELECT/READY LOGIC AND RESET

Upon RESET, the Chip-Select/Ready Logic will perform the following actions:

- All chip-select outputs will be driven HIGH.
- Upon leaving RESET, the $\overline{UCS}$ line will be programmed to provide chip selects to a 1K block with the accompanying READY control bits set at 011 to insert 3 wait states in conjunction with external READY (i.e., UMCS resets to FFFBH).
- No other chip select or READY control registers have any predefined values after RESET. They will not become active until the CPU accesses their control registers. Both the PACS and MPCS registers must be accessed before the $\overline{PCS}$ lines will become active.

DMA Channels

The DMA controller provides two independent DMA channels. Data transfers can occur between memory and I/O spaces (e.g., Memory to I/O) or within the same space (e.g., Memory to Memory or I/O to I/O). Data can be transferred either in bytes or in words (80186 only) to or from even or odd addresses. Each DMA channel maintains both a 20-bit source and destination pointer which can be optionally incremented or decremented after each data transfer (by one or two depending on byte or word transfers). Each data transfer consumes 2 bus cycles (a minimum of 8 clocks), one cycle to fetch data and the other to store data. This provides a maximum data transfer rate of 1.25 Mword/sec or 2.5 Mbytes/sec at 10 MHz (half of this rate for the 80188).

DMA CHANNELS AND RESET

Upon RESET, the DMA channels will perform the following actions:

- The Start/Stop bit for each channel will be reset to STOP.
- Any transfer in progress is aborted.

Timers

The processor provides three internal 16-bit programmable timers. Two of these are highly flexible and are connected to four external pins (2 per timer). They can be used to count external events, time external events, generate nonrepetitive waveforms, etc. The third timer is not connected to any external pins, and is useful for real-time coding and time delay applications. In addition, the third timer can be used as a prescaler to the other two, or as a DMA request source.

TIMERS AND RESET

Upon RESET, the Timers will perform the following actions:

- All EN (Enable) bits are reset preventing timer counting.
- For Timers 0 and 1, the RIU bits are reset to zero and the ALT bits are set to one. This results in the Timer Out pins going high.

Interrupt Controller

The processor can receive interrupts from a number of sources, both internal and external. The internal interrupt controller serves to merge these requests on a priority basis, for individual service by the CPU.

Internal interrupt sources (Timers and DMA channels) can be disabled by their own control registers or by mask bits within the interrupt controller. The interrupt controller has its own control register that sets the mode of operation for the controller.

INTERRUPT CONTROLLER AND RESET

Upon RESET, the interrupt controller will perform the following actions:

- All SFNM bits reset to 0, implying Fully Nested Mode.
- All PR bits in the various control registers set to 1. This places all sources at lowest priority (level 111).
- All LTM bits reset to 0, resulting in edge-sense mode.
- All Interrupt Service bits reset to 0.
- All Interrupt Request bits reset to 0.
- All MSK (Interrupt Mask) bits set to 1 (mask).
- All C (Cascade) bits reset to 0 (non-Cascade).
- All PRM (Priority Mask) bits set to 1, implying no levels masked.
- Initialized to Master Mode.

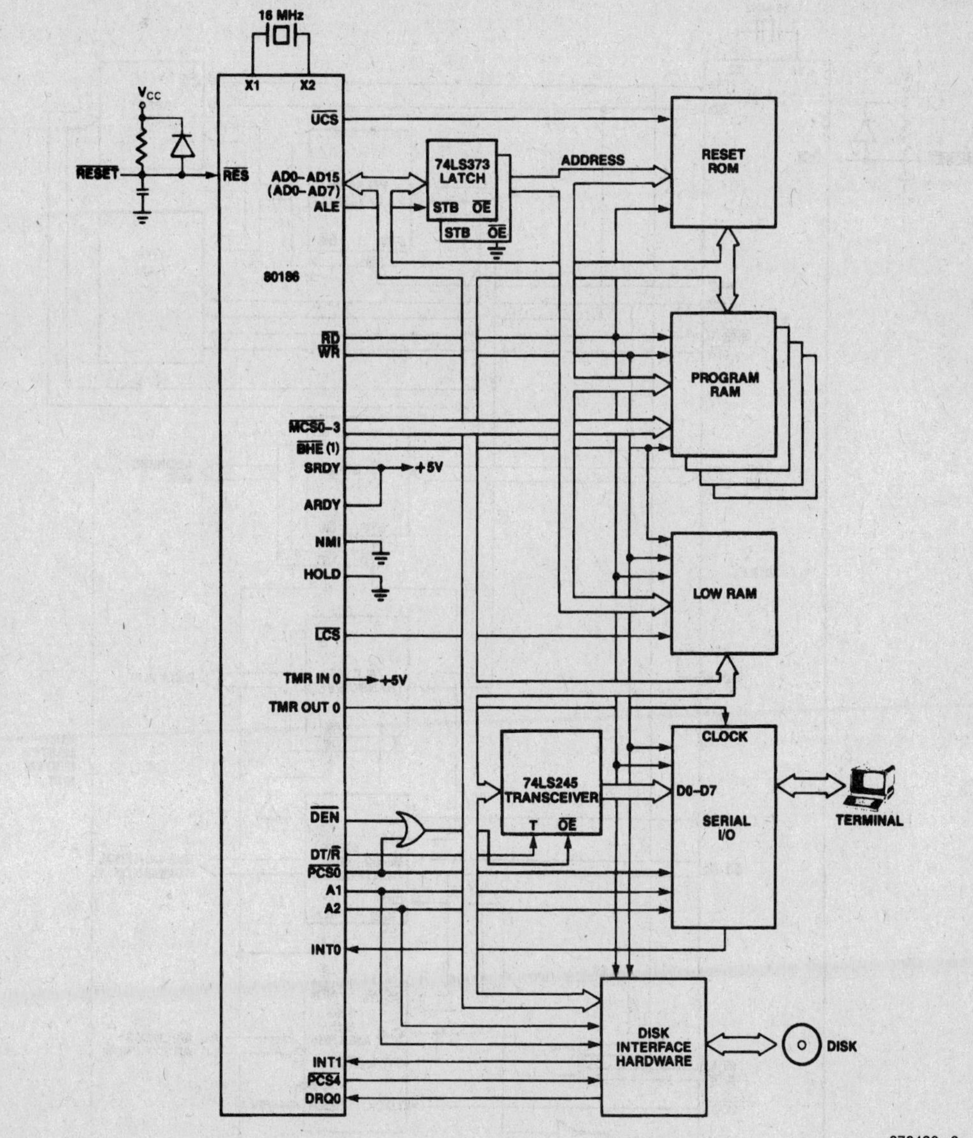

NOTE:
Pin names in parenthesis apply to 80188.
(1) BHE does not exist on the 80188, this is only required for a 16-bit data bus.

Figure 6. Typical 80186/80188 Computer

2

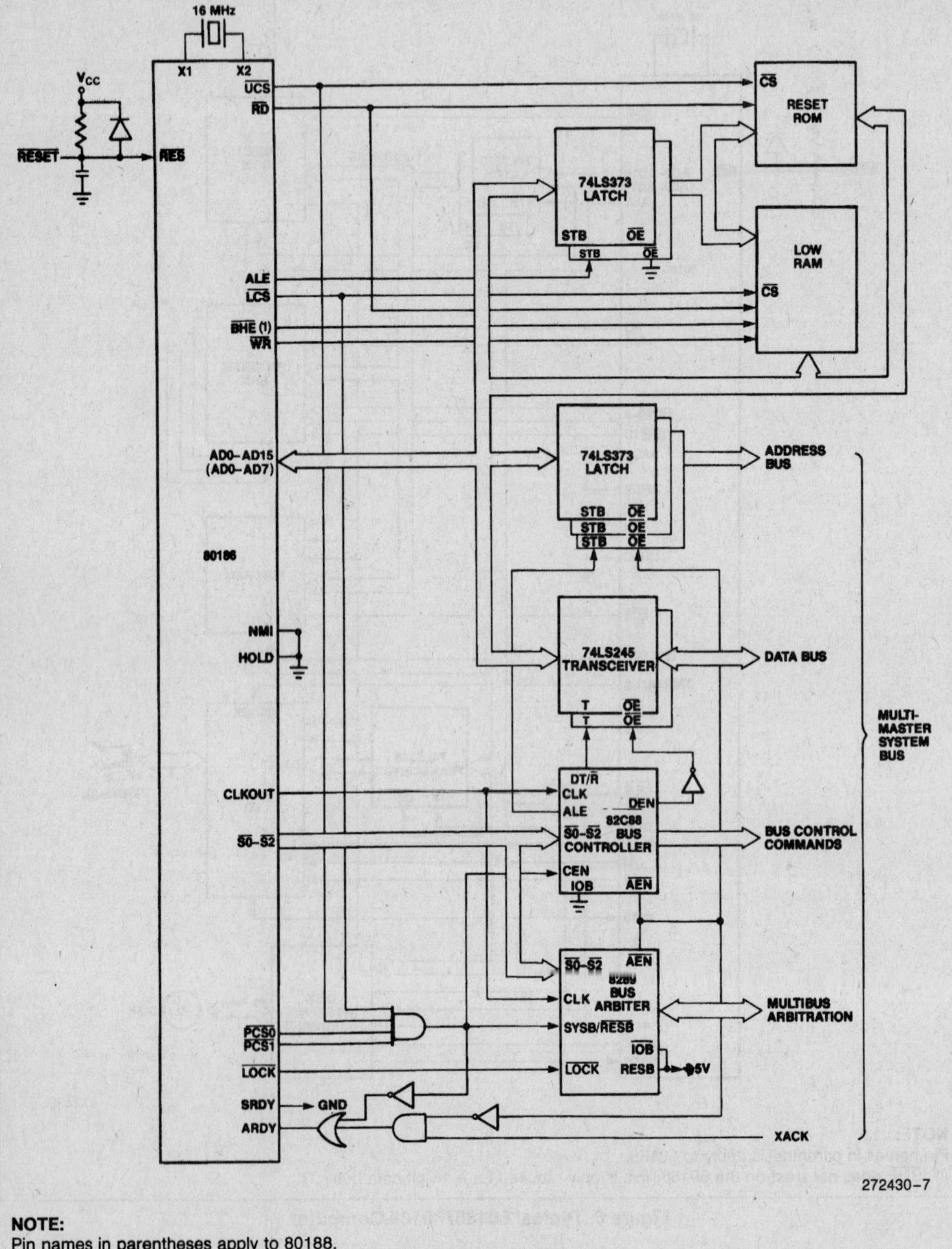

272430–7

NOTE:
Pin names in parentheses apply to 80188.
(1) $\overline{BHE}$ does not exist on the 80188, this is only required for a 16-bit data bus.

Figure 7. Typical 80186/80188 Multi-Master Bus Interface

ABSOLUTE MAXIMUM RATINGS*

Ambient Temperature under Bias ......0°C to 70°C
Storage Temperature ....−65°C to +150°C
Voltage on any Pin with
Respect to Ground..............−1.0V to +7V
Power Dissipation 3W

NOTICE: This is a production data sheet. The specifications are subject to change without notice.

**WARNING: Stressing the device beyond the "Absolute Maximum Ratings" may cause permanent damage. These are stress ratings only. Operation beyond the "Operating Conditions" is not recommended and extended exposure beyond the "Operating Conditions" may affect device reliability.*

D.C. CHARACTERISTICS (T_A = 0°C to +70°C, V_{CC} = 5V ±10%)

Applicable to 8 MHz and 10 MHz devices.

Symbol	Parameter	Min	Max	Units	Test Conditions
V_{IL}	Input Low Voltage	−0.5	+0.8	V	
V_{IH}	Input High Voltage (All except X1 and ($\overline{RES}$)	2.0	V_{CC} + 0.5	V	
V_{IH1}	Input High Voltage ($\overline{RES}$)	3.0	V_{CC} + 0.5	V	
V_{OL}	Output Low Voltage		0.45	V	I_a = 2.5 mA for $\overline{S0}$–$\overline{S2}$ I_a = 2.0 mA for all other Outputs
V_{OH}	Output High Voltage	2.4		V	I_{oa} = −400 μA
I_{CC}	Power Supply Current		600*	mA	T_A = −40°C
			550	mA	T_A = 0°C
			415	mA	T_A = +70°C
I_{LI}	Input Leakage Current		±10	μA	0V < V_{IN} < V_{CC}
I_{LO}	Output Leakage Current		±10	μA	0.45V < V_{OUT} < V_{CC}
V_{CLO}	Clock Output Low		0.6	V	I_a = 4.0 mA
V_{CHO}	Clock Output High	4.0		V	I_{oa} = −200 μA
V_{CLI}	Clock Input Low Voltage	−0.5	0.6	V	
V_{CHI}	Clock Input High Voltage	3.9	V_{CC} + 1.0	V	
C_{IN}	Input Capacitance		10	pF	
C_{IO}	I/O Capacitance		20	pF	

*For extended temperature parts only.

2

A.C. CHARACTERISTICS (T_A = 0°C to +70°C, V_{CC} = 5V ±10%)

Timing Requirements All Timings Measured At 1.5V Unless Otherwise Noted.

Symbol	Parameter	8 MHz		10 MHz		Units	Test Conditions
		Min	Max	Min	Max		
T_{DVCL}	Data in Setup (A/D)	20		15		ns	
T_{CLDX}	Data in Hold (A/D)	10		8		ns	
T_{ARYHCH}	Asynchronous Ready (ARDY) Active Setup Time(1)	20		15		ns	
T_{ARYLCL}	ARDY Inactive Setup Time	35		25		ns	
T_{CLARX}	ARDY Hold Time	15		15		ns	
T_{ARYCHL}	Asynchronous Ready Inactive Hold Time	15		15		ns	
T_{SRYCL}	Synchronous Ready (SRDY) Transition Setup Time(2)	20		20		ns	
T_{CLSRY}	SRDY Transition Hold Time(2)	15		15		ns	
T_{HVCL}	HOLD Setup(1)	25		20		ns	
T_{INVCH}	INTR, NMI, $\overline{TEST}$, TIM IN, Setup(1)	25		25		ns	
T_{INVCL}	DRQ0, DRQ1, Setup(1)	25		20		ns	

Master Interface Timing Responses

Symbol	Parameter	8 MHz Min	8 MHz Max	10 MHz Min	10 MHz Max	Units	Test Conditions
T_{CLAV}	Address Valid Delay	5	55	5	44	ns	C_L = 20 pF–200 pF all Outputs (Except T_{CLTMV}) @ 8 MHz and 10 MHz
T_{CLAX}	Address Hold	10		10		ns	
T_{CLAZ}	Address Float Delay	T_{CLAX}	35	T_{CLAX}	30	ns	
T_{CHCZ}	Command Lines Float Delay		45		40	ns	
T_{CHCV}	Command Lines Valid Delay (after Float)		55		45	ns	
T_{LHLL}	ALE Width	$T_{CLCL}-35$		$T_{CLCL}-30$		ns	
T_{CHLH}	ALE Active Delay		35		30	ns	
T_{CHLL}	ALE Inactive Delay		35		30	ns	
T_{LLAX}	Address Hold from ALE Inactive	$T_{CHCL}-25$		$T_{CHCL}-20$		ns	
T_{CLDV}	Data Valid Delay	10	44	10	40	ns	
T_{CLDOX}	Data Hold Time	10		10		ns	
T_{WHDX}	Data Hold after WR	$T_{CLCL}-40$		$T_{CLCL}-34$		ns	
T_{CVCTV}	Control Active Delay 1	5	50	5	40	ns	
T_{CHCTV}	Control Active Delay 2	10	55	10	44	ns	
T_{CVCTX}	Control Inactive Delay	5	55	5	44	ns	
T_{CVDEX}	$\overline{DEN}$ Inactive Delay (Non-Write Cycle)	10	70	10	56	ns	

1. To guarantee recognition at next clock.
2. To guarantee proper operation.

A.C. CHARACTERISTICS (T_A = 0°C to +70°C, V_{CC} = 5V ±10%) (Continued)

Master Interface Timing Responses (Continued)

Symbol	Parameter	8 MHz Min	8 MHz Max	10 MHz Min	10 MHz Max	Units	Test Conditions
T_{AZRL}	Address Float to $\overline{RD}$ Active	0		0		ns	
T_{CLRL}	$\overline{RD}$ Active Delay	10	70	10	56	ns	
T_{CLRH}	$\overline{RD}$ Inactive Delay	10	55	10	44	ns	
T_{RHAV}	$\overline{RD}$ Inactive to Address Active	$T_{CLCL}-40$		$T_{CLCL}-40$		ns	
T_{CLHAV}	HLDA Valid Delay	5	50	5	40	ns	
T_{RLRH}	$\overline{RD}$ Width	$2T_{CLCL}-50$		$2T_{CLCL}-46$		ns	
T_{WLWH}	$\overline{WR}$ Width	$2T_{CLCL}-40$		$2T_{CLCL}-34$		ns	
T_{AVLL}	Address Valid to ALE Low	$T_{CLCH}-25$		$T_{CLCH}-19$		ns	
T_{CHSV}	Status Active Delay	10	55	10	45	ns	
T_{CLSH}	Status Inactive Delay	10	65	10	50	ns	
T_{CLTMV}	Timer Output Delay		60		48	ns	100 pF max @ 8 & 10 MHz
T_{CLRO}	Reset Delay		60		48	ns	
T_{CHQSV}	Queue Status Delay		35		28	ns	
T_{CHDX}	Status Hold Time	10		10		ns	
T_{AVCH}	Address Valid to Clock High	10		10		ns	
T_{CLLV}	$\overline{LOCK}$ Valid/Invalid Delay	5	65	5	60	ns	

Chip-Select Timing Responses

Symbol	Parameter	8 MHz Min	8 MHz Max	10 MHz Min	10 MHz Max	Units	Test Conditions
T_{CLCSV}	Chip-Select Active Delay		66		45	ns	
T_{CXCSX}	Chip-Select Hold from Command Inactive	35		35		ns	
T_{CHCSX}	Chip-Select Inactive Delay	5	35	5	32	ns	

CLKIN Requirements

Symbol	Parameter	8 MHz Min	8 MHz Max	10 MHz Min	10 MHz Max	Units	Test Conditions
T_{CKIN}	CLKIN Period	62.5	250	50	250	ns	
T_{CKHL}	CLKIN Fall Time		10		10	ns	3.5 to 1.0V
T_{CKLH}	CLKIN Rise Time		10		10	ns	1.0 to 3.5V
T_{CLCK}	CLKIN Low Time	25		20		ns	1.5V
T_{CHCK}	CLKIN High Time	25		20		ns	1.5V

CLKOUT Timing (200 pF load)

Symbol	Parameter	8 MHz Min	8 MHz Max	10 MHz Min	10 MHz Max	Units	Test Conditions
T_{CICO}	CLKIN to CLKOUT Skew		50		25	ns	
T_{CLCL}	CLKOUT Period	125	500	100	500	ns	
T_{CLCH}	CLKOUT Low Time	$\frac{1}{2}T_{CLCL}-7.5$		$\frac{1}{2}T_{CLCL}-6.0$		ns	1.5V
T_{CHCL}	CLKOUT High Time	$\frac{1}{2}T_{CLCL}-7.5$		$\frac{1}{2}T_{CLCL}-6.0$		ns	1.5V
T_{CH1CH2}	CLKOUT Rise Time		15		12	ns	1.0 to 3.5V
T_{CL2CL1}	CLKOUT Fall Time		15		12	ns	3.5 to 1.0V

EXPLANATION OF THE AC SYMBOLS

Each timing symbol has from 5 to 7 characters. The first character is always a "T" (stands for time). The other characters, depending on their positions, stand for the name of a signal or the logical status of that signal. The following is a list of all the characters and what they stand for.

A: Address
ARY: Asynchronous Ready Input
C: Clock Output
CK: Clock Input
CS: Chip Select
CT: Control (DT/$\overline{R}$, $\overline{DEN}$, . . .)
D: Data Input
DE: $\overline{DEN}$
H: Logic Level High
IN: Input (DRQ0, TIM0, . . .)
L: Logic Level Low or ALE
O: Output
QS: Queue Status (QS1, QS2)
R: $\overline{RD}$ signal, RESET signal
S: Status ($\overline{S0}$, $\overline{S1}$, $\overline{S2}$)
SRY: Synchronous Ready Input
V: Valid
W: WR Signal
X: No Longer a Valid Logic Level
Z: Float

Examples:

T_{CLAV} — Time from Clock low to Address valid
T_{CHLH} — Time from Clock high to ALE high
T_{CLCSV} — Time from Clock low to Chip Select valid

WAVEFORMS

MAJOR CYCLE TIMING

V_{CH} T_1 T_2 T_3 T_W T_4
TCH1CH2 TCL2CL1 TCLCL
CLK OUT (NOTE 2)
V_{CL} TCHSV TCHCL TCLSH TCLCH
$\overline{S2}$–$\overline{S0}$
TCLAV TCLDV TCLAX TCHDX
$\overline{BHE}/S_7$ $(\overline{S_7})$, A_{19}/S_6–A_{16}/S_3 S7, A19–A16 S_7–S_3
TCLAV
(A15–A8) A15–A8 (FLOAT DURING INTA)
TLHLL TLLAX
ALE TAVLL
TCHLH TCHLL
TCLAV TCLDV TCLAX TCLDOX
WRITE CYCLE
AD15+0 AD_7–AD_0 ADDR. DATA OUT
TAVCH TLLAX TWHDX
TCVCTV TCVCTX
$\overline{DEN}$
$\overline{RD}$, $\overline{INTA}$, DT/$\overline{R}$=V_{OH}
TCVCTV TWLWH
$\overline{WR}$
TCVCTX
TCLDX
TCLAZ TDVCL
INTA CYCLE
AD15–0 (AD_7–AD_0) FLOAT POINTER FLOAT
TCHCTV TCHCTV
DT/$\overline{R}$
TCVCTV
$\overline{INTA}$ (NOTE 1)
$\overline{RD}$, $\overline{WR}$, =V_{OH}
TCVCTV TCVDEX
$\overline{DEN}$
SOFTWARE HALT-DT/$\overline{R}$=V_{OL}, $\overline{RD}$, $\overline{WR}$, $\overline{INTA}$, $\overline{DEN}$=V_{OH} INVALID ADDRESS
TCLAV TCHCSX
TCLCSV TCXCSX
$\overline{PCS}$, $\overline{MCS}$, $\overline{LCS}$, $\overline{UCS}$ (NOTE 3)

272430–8

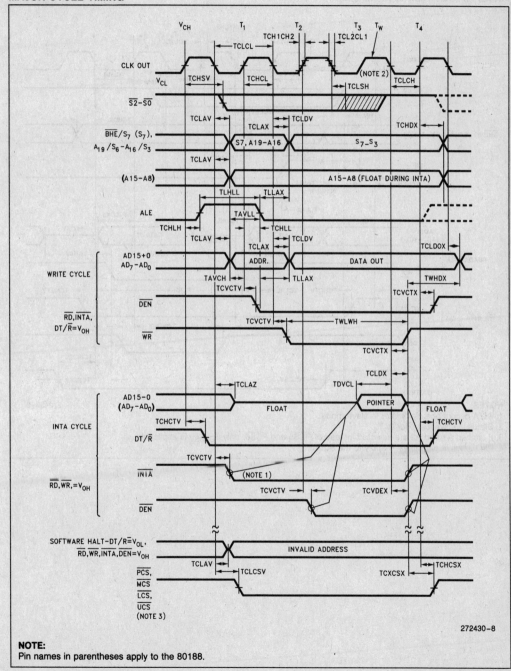

NOTE:
Pin names in parentheses apply to the 80188.

WAVEFORMS (Continued)

MAJOR CYCLE TIMING (Continued)

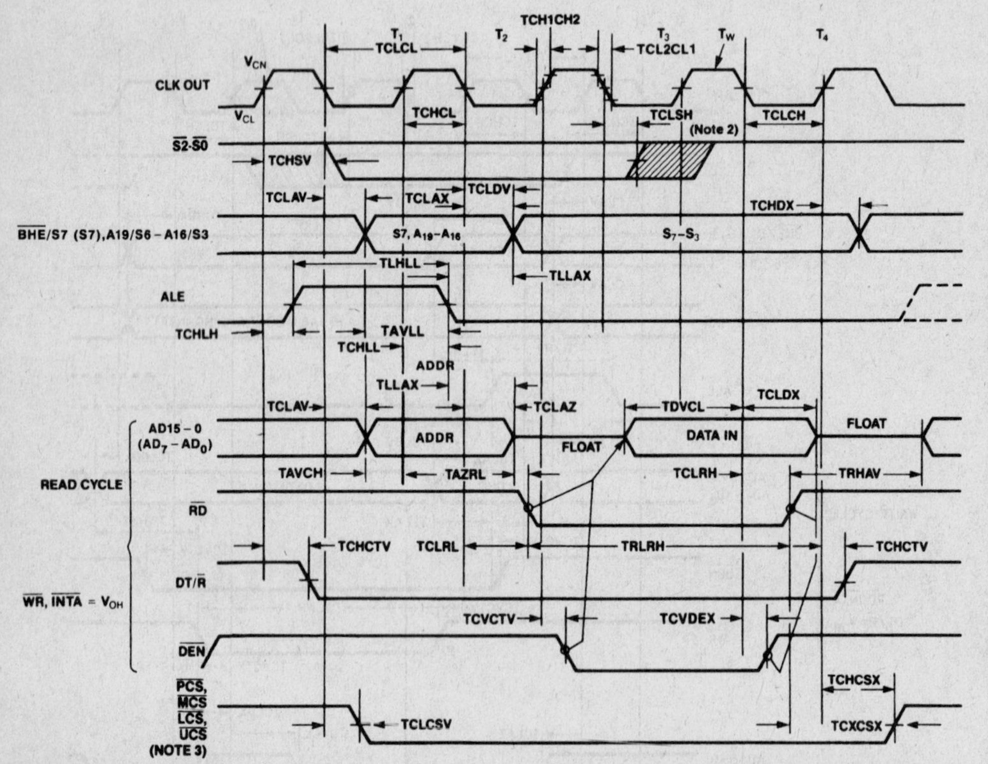

NOTES:

1. INTA occurs one clock later in slave mode.
2. Status inactive just prior to T_4.
3. If latched A1 and A2 are selected instead of $\overline{PCS5}$ and $\overline{PCS6}$, only T_{CLCSV} is applicable.
4. Pin names in parentheses apply to the 80188.

272430–9

WAVEFORMS (Continued)

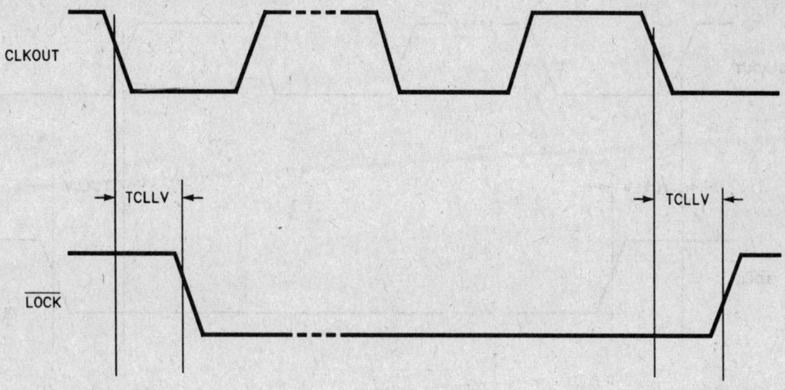

272430-10

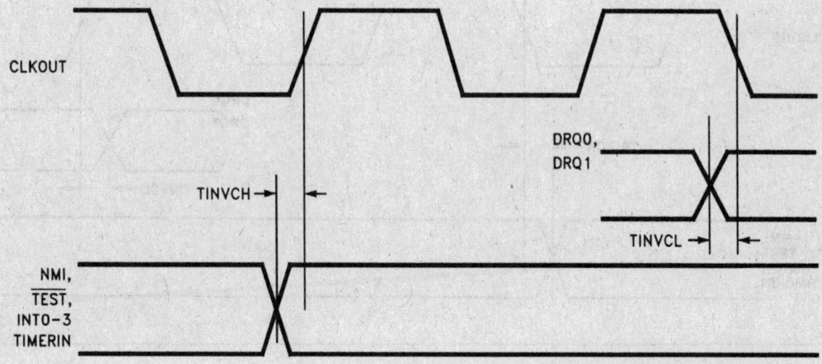

272430-11

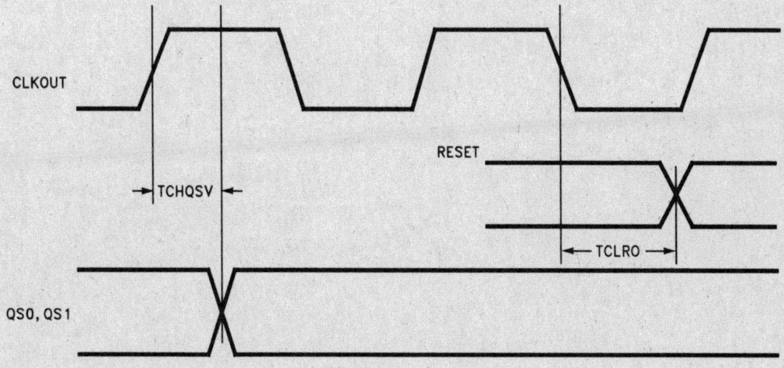

272430-12

2

WAVEFORMS (Continued)

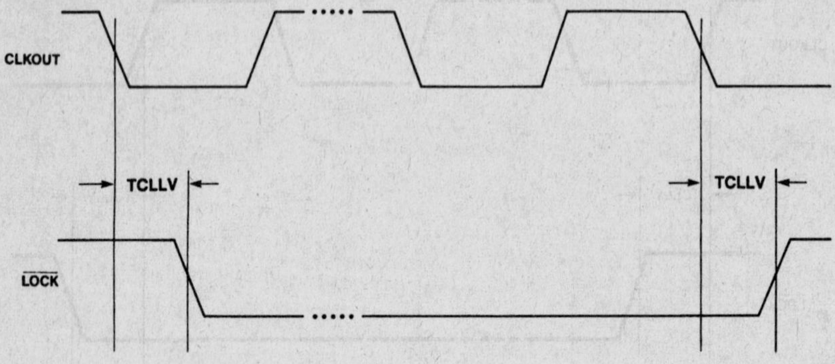

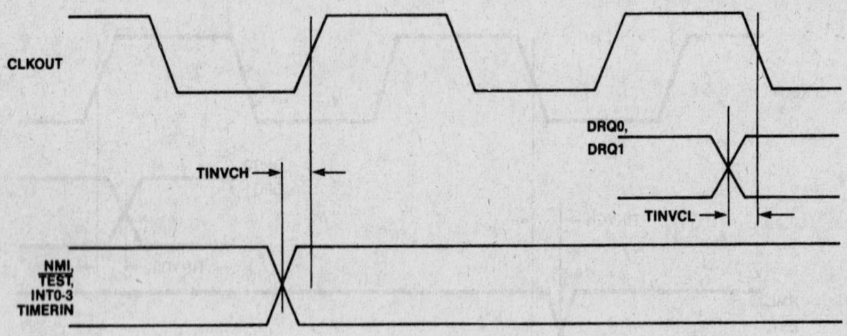

WAVEFORMS (Continued)

READY TIMING

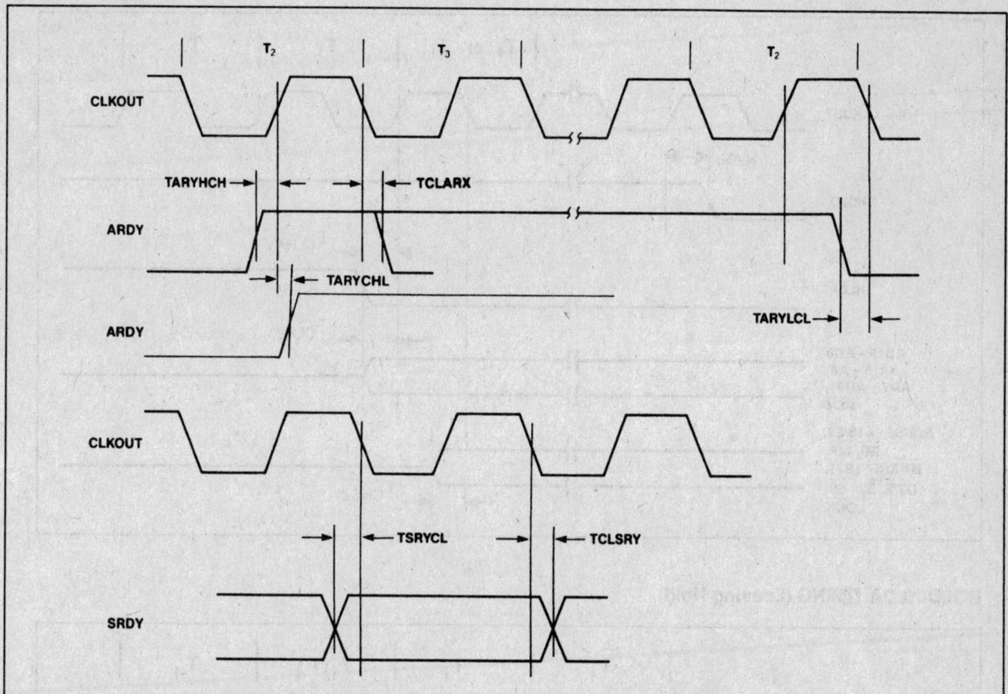

272430-15

WAVEFORMS (Continued)

HOLD/HLDA TIMING (Entering Hold)

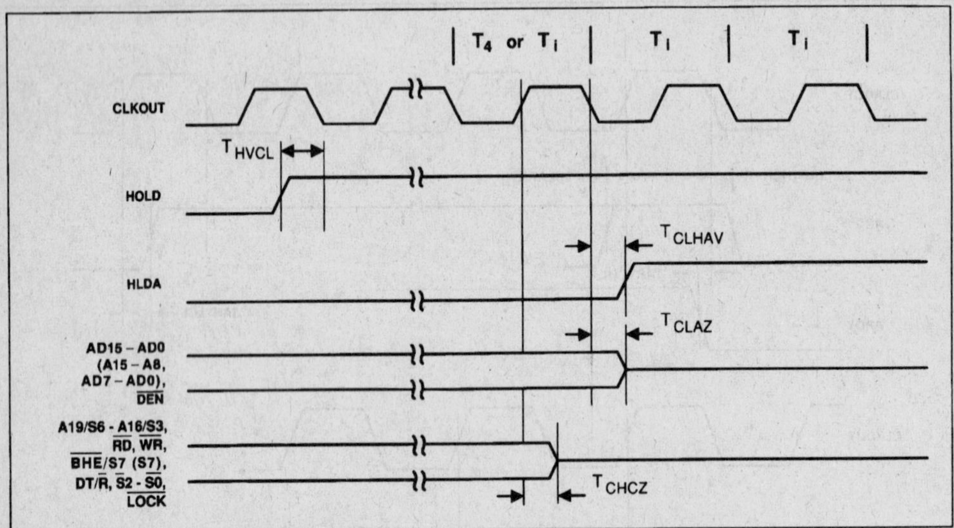

HOLD/HLDA TIMING (Leaving Hold)

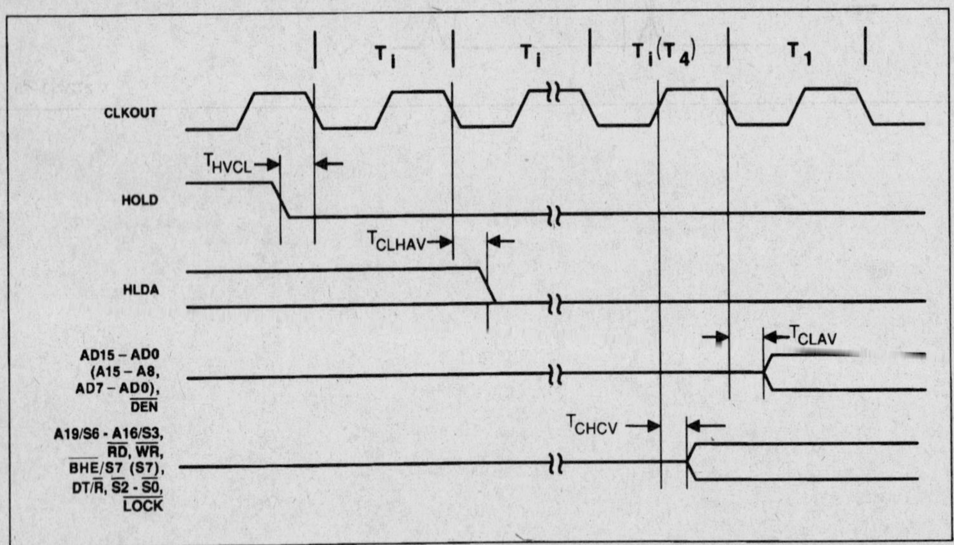

272430–16

NOTE:
Pin names in parentheses apply to the 80188.

WAVEFORMS (Continued)

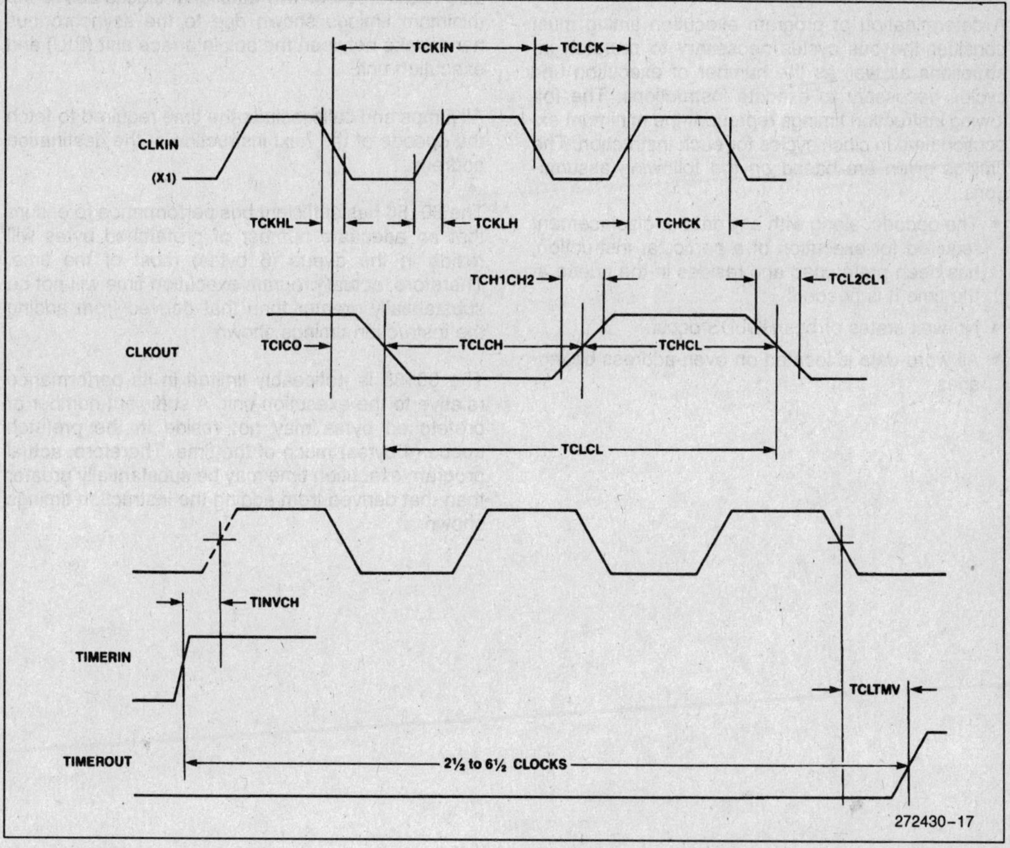

EXPRESS

The Intel EXPRESS system offers enhancements to the operational specifications of the microprocessor. EXPRESS products are designed to meet the needs of those applications whose operating requirements exceed commercial standards.

The EXPRESS program includes the commercial standard temperature range with burn-in and an extended temperature range without burn-in.

With the commercial standard temperature range operational characteristics are guaranteed over the temperature range of 0°C to +70°C. With the extended temperature range option, operational characteristics are guaranteed over the range of −40°C to +85°C.

The optional burn-in is dynamic, for a minimum time of 160 hours at +125°C with V_{CC} = 5.5V ±0.25V, following guidelines in MIL-STD-883, Method 1015.

Package types and EXPRESS versions are identified by a one- or two-letter prefix to the part number. The prefixes are listed in Table 2. All A.C. and D.C. specifications not mentioned in this section are the same for both commercial and EXPRESS parts.

Table 2. Prefix Identification

Prefix	Package Type	Temperature Range	Burn-In
A	PGA	Commercial	No
N	PLCC	Commercial	No
R	LCC	Commercial	No
TA	PGA	Extended	No
QA	PGA	Commercial	Yes
QR	LCC	Commercial	Yes

NOTE:
Not all package/temperature range/speed combinations are available.

EXECUTION TIMINGS

A determination of program execution timing must consider the bus cycles necessary to prefetch instructions as well as the number of execution unit cycles necessary to execute instructions. The following instruction timings represent the minimum execution time in clock cycles for each instruction. The timings given are based on the following assumptions:

- The opcode, along with any data or displacement required for execution of a particular instruction, has been prefetched and resides in the queue at the time it is needed.
- No wait states or bus HOLDS occur.
- All word-data is located on even-address boundaries.

All instructions which involve memory accesses can also require one or two additional clocks above the minimum timings shown due to the asynchronous handshake between the bus interface unit (BIU) and execution unit.

All jumps and calls include the time required to fetch the opcode of the next instruction at the destination address.

The 80186 has sufficient bus performance to ensure that an adequate number of prefetched bytes will reside in the queue (6 bytes) most of the time. Therefore, actual program execution time will not be substantially greater than that derived from adding the instruction timings shown.

The 80188 is noticeably limited in its performance relative to the execution unit. A sufficient number of prefetched bytes may not reside in the prefetch queue (4 bytes) much of the time. Therefore, actual program execution time may be substantially greater than that derived from adding the instruction timings shown.

INSTRUCTION SET SUMMARY

Function	Format				80186 Clock Cycles	80188 Clock Cycles	Comments
DATA TRANSFER							
MOV = Move:							
Register to Register/Memory	1000100w	mod reg r/m			2/12	2/12*	
Register/memory to register	1000101w	mod reg r/m			2/9	2/9*	
Immediate to register/memory	1100011w	mod 000 r/m	data	data if w=1	12/13	12/13	8/16-bit
Immediate to register	1011w reg	data	data if w=1		3/4	3/4	8/16-bit
Memory to accumulator	1010000w	addr-low	addr-high		8	8*	
Accumulator to memory	1010001w	addr-low	addr-high		9	9*	
Register/memory to segment register	10001110	mod 0 reg r/m			2/9	2/13	
Segment register to register/memory	10001100	mod 0 reg r/m			2/11	2/15	
PUSH = Push:							
Memory	11111111	mod 1 1 0 r/m			16	20	
Register	01010 reg				10	14	
Segment register	000reg110				9	13	
Immediate	011010s0	data	data if s=0		10	14	
PUSHA = Push All	01100000				36	68	
POP = Pop:							
Memory	10001111	mod 0 0 0 r/m			20	24	
Register	01011 reg				10	14	
Segment register	000reg111	(reg≠01)			8	12	
POPA = Pop All	01100001				51	83	
XCHG = Exchange:							
Register/memory with register	1000011w	mod reg r/m			4/17	4/17*	
Register with accumulator	10010 reg				3	3	
IN = Input from:							
Fixed port	1110010w	port			10	10*	
Variable port	1110110w				8	8*	
OUT = Output to:							
Fixed port	1110011w	port			9	9*	
Variable port	1110111w				7	7*	
XLAT = Translate byte to AL	11010111				11	15	
LEA = Load EA to register	10001101	mod reg r/m			6	6	
LDS = Load pointer to DS	11000101	mod reg r/m	(mod≠11)		18	26	
LES = Load pointer to ES	11000100	mod reg r/m	(mod≠11)		18	26	
LAHF = Load AH with flags	10011111				2	2	
SAHF = Store AH into flags	10011110				3	3	
PUSHF = Push flags	10011100				9	13	
POPF = Pop flags	10011101				8	12	

Shaded areas indicate instructions not available in 8086, 8088 microsystems.

NOTE:
*Clock cycles shown for byte transfers, for word operations, add 4 clock cycles for each memory transfer.

INSTRUCTION SET SUMMARY (Continued)

Function	Format				80186 Clock Cycles	80188 Clock Cycles	Comments
DATA TRANSFER (Continued)							
SEGMENT = Segment Override:							
CS	00101110				2	2	
SS	00110110				2	2	
DS	00111110				2	2	
ES	00100110				2	2	
ARITHMETIC							
ADD = Add:							
Reg/memory with register to either	000000dw	mod reg r/m			3/10	3/10*	
Immediate to register/memory	100000sw	mod 0 0 0 r/m	data	data if s w = 01	4/16	4/16*	
Immediate to accumulator	0000010w	data	data if w = 1		3/4	3/4	8/16-bit
ADC = Add with carry:							
Reg/memory with register to either	000100dw	mod reg r/m			3/10	3/10*	
Immediate to register/memory	100000sw	mod 0 1 0 r/m	data	data if s w = 01	4/16	4/16*	
Immediate to accumulator	0001010w	data	data if w = 1		3/4	3/4	8/16-bit
INC = Increment:							
Register/memory	1111111w	mod 0 0 0 r/m			3/15	3/15*	
Register	01000 reg				3	3	
SUB = Subtract:							
Reg/memory and register to either	001010dw	mod reg r/m			3/10	3/10*	
Immediate from register/memory	100000sw	mod 1 0 1 r/m	data	data if s w = 01	4/16	4/16*	
Immediate from accumulator	0010110w	data	data if w = 1		3/4	3/4	8/16-bit
SBB = Subtract with borrow:							
Reg/memory and register to either	000110dw	mod reg r/m			3/10	3/10*	
Immediate from register/memory	100000sw	mod 0 1 1 r/m	data	data if s w = 01	4/16	4/16*	
Immediate from accumulator	0001110w	data	data if w = 1		3/4	3/4	8/16-bit
DEC = Decrement							
Register/memory	1111111w	mod 0 0 1 r/m			3/15	3/15*	
Register	01001 reg				3	3	
CMP = Compare:							
Register/memory with register	0011101w	mod reg r/m			3/10	3/10*	
Register with register/memory	0011100w	mod reg r/m			3/10	3/10*	
Immediate with register/memory	100000sw	mod 1 1 1 r/m	data	data if s w = 01	3/10	3/10*	
Immediate with accumulator	0011110w	data	data if w = 1		3/4	3/4	8/16-bit
NEG = Change sign register/memory	1111011w	mod 0 1 1 r/m			3/10	3/10*	
AAA = ASCII adjust for add	00110111				8	8	
DAA = Decimal adjust for add	00100111				4	4	
AAS = ASCII adjust for subtract	00111111				7	7	
DAS = Decimal adjust for subtract	00101111				4	4	
MUL = Multiply (unsigned):	1111011w	mod 100 r/m					
Register-Byte					26–28	26–28	
Register-Word					35–37	35–37	
Memory-Byte					32–34	32–34	
Memory-Word					41–43	41–43*	

Shaded areas indicate instructions not available in 8086, 8088 microsystems.

NOTE:
*Clock cycles shown for byte transfers, for word operations, add 4 clock cycles for each memory transfer.

INSTRUCTION SET SUMMARY (Continued)

Function	Format				80186 Clock Cycles	80188 Clock Cycles	Comments
ARITHMETIC (Continued)							
IMUL = Integer multiply (signed):	1 1 1 1 0 1 1 w	mod 1 0 1 r/m					
Register-Byte					25–28	25–28	
Register-Word					34–37	34–37	
Memory-Byte					31–34	31–34	
Memory-Word					40–43	40–43*	
IMUL = Integer Immediate multiply (signed)	0 1 1 0 1 0 s 1	mod reg r/m	data	data if s=0	22–25/ 29–32	22–25/ 29–32	
DIV = Divide (unsigned):	1 1 1 1 0 1 1 w	mod 1 1 0 r/m					
Register-Byte					29	29	
Register-Word					38	38	
Memory-Byte					35	35	
Memory-Word					44	44*	
IDIV = Integer divide (signed):	1 1 1 1 0 1 1 w	mod 1 1 1 r/m					
Register-Byte					44–52	44–52	
Register-Word					53–61	53–61	
Memory-Byte					50–58	50–58	
Memory-Word					59–67	59–67*	
AAM = ASCII adjust for multiply	1 1 0 1 0 1 0 0	0 0 0 0 1 0 1 0			19	19	
AAD = ASCII adjust for divide	1 1 0 1 0 1 0 1	0 0 0 0 1 0 1 0			15	15	
CBW = Convert byte to word	1 0 0 1 1 0 0 0				2	2	
CWD = Convert word to double word	1 0 0 1 1 0 0 1				4	4	
LOGIC							
Shift/Rotate Instructions:							
Register/Memory by 1	1 1 0 1 0 0 0 w	mod TTT r/m			2/15	2/15	
Register/Memory by CL	1 1 0 1 0 0 1 w	mod TTT r/m			5+n/17+n	5+n/17+n	
Register/Memory by Count	1 1 0 0 0 0 0 w	mod TTT r/m	count		5+n/17+n	5+n/17+n	
		TTT Instruction					
		0 0 0 ROL					
		0 0 1 ROR					
		0 1 0 RCL					
		0 1 1 RCR					
		1 0 0 SHL/SAL					
		1 0 1 SHR					
		1 1 1 SAR					
AND = And:							
Reg/memory and register to either	0 0 1 0 0 0 d w	mod reg r/m			3/10	3/10*	
Immediate to register/memory	1 0 0 0 0 0 0 w	mod 1 0 0 r/m	data	data if w=1	4/16	4/16*	
Immediate to accumulator	0 0 1 0 0 1 0 w	data	data if w=1		3/4	3/4	8/16-bit
TEST = And function to flags, no result:							
Register/memory and register	1 0 0 0 0 1 0 w	mod reg r/m			3/10	3/10*	
Immediate data and register/memory	1 1 1 1 0 1 1 w	mod 0 0 0 r/m	data	data if w=1	4/10	4/10*	
Immediate data and accumulator	1 0 1 0 1 0 0 w	data	data if w=1		3/4	3/4	8/16-bit
OR = Or:							
Reg/memory and register to either	0 0 0 0 1 0 d w	mod reg r/m			3/10	3/10*	
Immediate to register/memory	1 0 0 0 0 0 0 w	mod 0 0 1 r/m	data	data if w=1	4/16	4/16*	
Immediate to accumulator	0 0 0 0 1 1 0 w	data	data if w=1		3/4	3/4	8/16-bit

Shaded areas indicate instructions not available in 8086, 8088 microsystems.

NOTE:
*Clock cycles shown for byte transfers, for word operations, add 4 clock cycles for each memory transfer.

INSTRUCTION SET SUMMARY (Continued)

Function	Format				80186 Clock Cycles	80188 Clock Cycles	Comments
LOGIC (Continued)							
XOR = Exclusive or:							
Reg/memory and register to either	001100dw	mod reg r/m			3/10	3/10*	
Immediate to register/memory	1000000w	mod 1 1 0 r/m	data	data if w = 1	4/16	4/16*	
Immediate to accumulator	0011010w	data	data if w = 1		3/4	3/4	8/16-bit
NOT = Invert register/memory	1111011w	mod 0 1 0 r/m			3/10	3/10*	
STRING MANIPULATION							
MOVS = Move byte/word	1010010w				14	14*	
CMPS = Compare byte/word	1010011w				22	22*	
SCAS = Scan byte/word	1010111w				15	15*	
LODS = Load byte/wd to AL/AX	1010110w				12	12*	
STOS = Store byte/wd from AL/AX	1010101w				10	10*	
INS = Input byte/wd from DX port	0110110w				14	14	
OUTS = Output byte/wd to DX port	0110111w				14	14	
Repeated by count in CX (REP/REPE/REPZ/REPNE/REPNZ)							
MOVS = Move string	11110010	1010010w			8+8n	8+8n*	
CMPS = Compare string	1111001z	1010011w			5+22n	5+22n*	
SCAS = Scan string	1111001z	1010111w			5+15n	5+15n*	
LODS = Load string	11110010	1010110w			6+11n	6+11n*	
STOS = Store string	11110010	1010101w			6+9n	6+9n*	
INS = Input string	11110010	0110110w			8+8n	8+8n*	
OUTS = Output string	11110010	0110111w			8+8n	8+8n*	
CONTROL TRANSFER							
CALL = Call:							
Direct within segment	11101000	disp-low	disp-high		15	19	
Register/memory indirect within segment	11111111	mod 0 1 0 r/m			13/19	17/27	
Direct intersegment	10011010	segment offset			23	31	
		segment selector					
Indirect intersegment	11111111	mod 0 1 1 r/m	(mod ≠ 11)		38	54	
JMP = Unconditional jump:							
Short/long	11101011	disp-low			14	14	
Direct within segment	11101001	disp-low	disp-high		14	14	
Register/memory indirect within segment	11111111	mod 1 0 0 r/m			11/17	11/21	
Direct intersegment	11101010	segment offset			14	14	
		segment selector					
Indirect intersegment	11111111	mod 1 0 1 r/m	(mod ≠ 11)		26	34	

Shaded areas indicate instructions not available in 8086, 8088 microsystems.

NOTE:
*Clock cycles shown for byte transfers, for word operations, add 4 clock cycles for each memory transfer.

INSTRUCTION SET SUMMARY (Continued)

Function	Format	80186 Clock Cycles	80188 Clock Cycles	Comments
CONTROL TRANSFER (Continued)				
RET = Return from CALL:				
Within segment	11000011	16	20	
Within seg adding immed to SP	11000010 | data-low | data-high	18	22	
Intersegment	11001011	22	30	
Intersegment adding immediate to SP	11001010 | data-low | data-high	25	33	
JE/JZ = Jump on equal/zero	01110100 | disp	4/13	4/13	JMP not taken/JMP taken
JL/JNGE = Jump on less/not greater or equal	01111100 | disp	4/13	4/13	
JLE/JNG = Jump on less or equal/not greater	01111110 | disp	4/13	4/13	
JB/JNAE = Jump on below/not above or equal	01110010 | disp	4/13	4/13	
JBE/JNA = Jump on below or equal/not above	01110110 | disp	4/13	4/13	
JP/JPE = Jump on parity/parity even	01111010 | disp	4/13	4/13	
JO = Jump on overflow	01110 000 | disp	4/13	4/13	
JS = Jump on sign	01111000 | disp	4/13	4/13	
JNE/JNZ = Jump on not equal/not zero	01110101 | disp	4/13	4/13	
JNL/JGE = Jump on not less/greater or equal	01111101 | disp	4/13	4/13	
JNLE/JG = Jump on not less or equal/greater	01111111 | disp	4/13	4/13	
JNB/JAE = Jump on not below/above or equal	01110011 | disp	4/13	4/13	
JNBE/JA = Jump on not below or equal/above	01110111 | disp	4/13	4/13	
JNP/JPO = Jump on not par/par odd	01111011 | disp	4/13	4/13	
JNO = Jump on not overflow	01110001 | disp	4/13	4/13	
JNS = Jump on not sign	01111001 | disp	4/13	4/13	
JCXZ = Jump on CX zero	11100011 | disp	5/15	5/15	
LOOP = Loop CX times	11100010 | disp	6/16	6/16	LOOP not taken/LOOP taken
LOOPZ/LOOPE = Loop while zero/equal	11100001 | disp	6/16	6/16	
LOOPNZ/LOOPNE = Loop while not zero/equal	11100000 | disp	6/16	6/16	
ENTER = Enter Procedure	11001000 | data-low | data-high | L			
L = 0		15	19	
L = 1		25	29	
L > 1		22 + 16(n − 1)	26 + 20(n − 1)	
LEAVE = Leave Procedure	11001001	8	8	
INT = Interrupt:				
Type specified	11001101 | type	47	47	
Type 3	11001100	45	45	if INT. taken/ if INT. not taken
INTO = Interrupt on overflow	11001110	48/4	48/4	
IRET = Interrupt return	11001111	28	28	
BOUND = Detect value out of range	01100010 | mod reg r/m	33–35	33–35	

Shaded areas indicate instructions not available in 8086, 8088 microsystems.

NOTE:
*Clock cycles shown for byte transfers, for word operations, add 4 clock cycles for each memory transfer.

INSTRUCTION SET SUMMARY (Continued)

Function	Format		80186 Clock Cycles	80188 Clock Cycles	Comments
PROCESSOR CONTROL					
CLC = Clear carry	11111000		2	2	
CMC = Complement carry	11110101		2	2	
STC = Set carry	11111001		2	2	
CLD = Clear direction	11111100		2	2	
STD = Set direction	11111101		2	2	
CLI = Clear interrupt	11111010		2	2	
STI = Set interrupt	11111011		2	2	
HLT = Halt	11110100		2	2	
WAIT = Wait	10011011		6	6	if $\overline{TEST}$ = 0
LOCK = Bus lock prefix	11110000		2	3	
ESC = Processor Extension Escape	11011TTT	mod LLL r/m	6	6	
	(TTT LLL are opcode to processor extension)				
NOP = No Operation	10010000		3	3	

Shaded areas indicate instructions not available in 8086, 8088 microsystems.

NOTE:
*Clock cycles shown for byte transfers, for word operations, add 4 clock cycles for each memory transfer.

FOOTNOTES

The Effective Address (EA) of the memory operand is computed according to the mod and r/m fields:

if mod = 11 then r/m is treated as REG field
if mod = 00 then DISP = 0*, disp-low and disp-high are absent
if mod = 01 then DISP = disp-low sign-extended to 16-bits, disp-high is absent
if mod = 10 then DISP = disp-high: disp-low
if r/m = 000 then EA = (BX) + (SI) + DISP
if r/m = 001 then EA = (BX) + (DI) + DISP
if r/m = 010 then EA = (BP) + (SI) + DISP
if r/m = 011 then EA = (BP) + (DI) + DISP
if r/m = 100 then EA = (SI) + DISP
if r/m = 101 then EA = (DI) + DISP
if r/m = 110 then EA = (BP) + DISP*
if r/m = 111 then EA = (BX) + DISP

DISP follows 2nd byte of instruction (before data if required)

*except if mod = 00 and r/m = 110 then EA = disp-high: disp-low.

EA calculation time is 4 clock cycles for all modes, and is included in the execution times given whenever appropriate.

Segment Override Prefix

0	0	1	reg	1	1	0

reg is assigned according to the following:

reg	Segment Register
00	ES
01	CS
10	SS
11	DS

REG is assigned according to the following table:

16-Bit (w = 1)	8-Bit (w = 0)
000 AX	000 AL
001 CX	001 CL
010 DX	010 DL
011 BX	011 BL
100 SP	100 AH
101 BP	101 CH
110 SI	110 DH
111 DI	111 BH

The physical addresses of all operands addressed by the BP register are computed using the SS segment register. The physical addresses of the destination operands of the string primitive operations (those addressed by the DI register) are computed using the ES segment, which may not be overridden.

REVISION HISTORY

This data sheet replaces the following data sheets:

210706-011 80188

210451-011 80186

2

PRELIMINARY

80C186XL/80C188XL
16-BIT HIGH-INTEGRATION EMBEDDED PROCESSORS

- **Low Power, Fully Static Versions of 80C186/80C188**
- **Operation Modes:**
  - **—Enhanced Mode**
    - **—DRAM Refresh Control Unit**
    - **—Power-Save Mode**
    - **—Direct Interface to 80C187 (80C186XL Only)**
  - **—Compatible Mode**
    - **—NMOS 80186/80188 Pin-for-Pin Replacement for Non-Numerics Applications**
- **Integrated Feature Set**
  - **—Static, Modular CPU**
  - **—Clock Generator**
  - **—2 Independent DMA Channels**
  - **—Programmable Interrupt Controller**
  - **—3 Programmable 16-Bit Timers**
  - **—Dynamic RAM Refresh Control Unit**
  - **—Programmable Memory and Peripheral Chip Select Logic**
  - **—Programmable Wait State Generator**
  - **—Local Bus Controller**
  - **—Power-Save Mode**
  - **—System-Level Testing Support (High Impedance Test Mode)**
- **Completely Object Code Compatible with Existing 8086/8088 Software and Has 10 Additional Instructions over 8086/8088**
- **Speed Versions Available**
  - **—20 MHz (80C186XL20/80C188XL20)**
  - **—12 MHz (80C186XL12/80C188XL12)**
- **Direct Addressing Capability to 1 MByte Memory and 64 Kbyte I/O**
- **Complete System Development Support**
  - **—ASM 86 Assembler, PL/M-86, iC-86 and System Utilities**
  - **—In-Circuit-Emulator**
- **Available in 68-Pin:**
  - **—Plastic Leaded Chip Carrier (PLCC)**
  - **—Ceramic Pin Grid Array (PGA)**
  - **—Ceramic Leadless Chip Carrier (JEDEC A Package)**
- **Available in 80-Pin:**
  - **—Quad Flat Pack (EIAJ)**
  - **—Shrink Quad Flat Pack (SGFP)**
- **Available in Extended Temperature Range (−40°C to +85°C)**

The Intel 80C186XL is a Modular Core re-implementation of the 80C186 Microprocessor. It offers higher speed and lower power consumption than the standard 80C186 but maintains 100% clock-for-clock functional compatibility. Packaging and pinout are also identical.

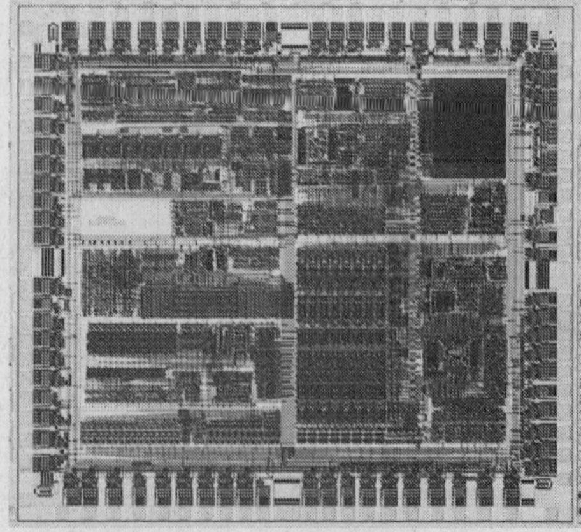

272431-1

80C186XL/80C188XL
16-Bit High-Integration Embedded Processors

CONTENTS

CONTENTS	PAGE
INTRODUCTION	2-37
80C186XL CORE ARCHITECTURE	2-37
80C186XL Clock Generator	2-37
Bus Interface Unit	2-38
80C186XL PERIPHERAL ARCHITECTURE	2-38
Chip-Select/Ready Generation Logic	2-38
DMA Unit	2-39
Timer/Counter Unit	2-39
Interrupt Control Unit	2-39
Enhanced Mode Operation	2-39
Queue-Status Mode	2-39
DRAM Refresh Control Unit	2-40
Power-Save Control	2-40
Interface for 80C187 Math Coprocessor (80C186XL Only)	2-40
ONCE Test Mode	2-40
PACKAGE INFORMATION	2-41
Pin Descriptions	2-41
80C186XL/80C188XL Pinout Diagrams	2-49
ELECTRICAL SPECIFICATIONS	2-55
Absolute Maximum Ratings	2-55
DC SPECIFICATIONS	2-55
Power Supply Current	2-56
AC SPECIFICATIONS	2-57
Major Cycle Timings (Read Cycle)	2-57
Major Cycle Timings (Write Cycle)	2-59
Major Cycle Timings (Interrupt Acknowledge Cycle)	2-60
Software Halt Cycle Timings	2-61
Clock Timings	2-62
Ready, Peripheral and Queue Status Timings	2-63
Reset and Hold/HLDA Timings	2-64
AC TIMING WAVEFORMS	2-69
AC CHARACTERISTICS	2-70
EXPLANATION OF THE AC SYMBOLS	2-72
DERATING CURVES	2-73
80C186XL/80C188XL EXPRESS	2-74
80C186XL/80C188XL EXECUTION TIMINGS	2-74
INSTRUCTION SET SUMMARY	2-75
REVISION HISTORY	2-81
ERRATA	2-81
PRODUCT IDENTIFICATION	2-81

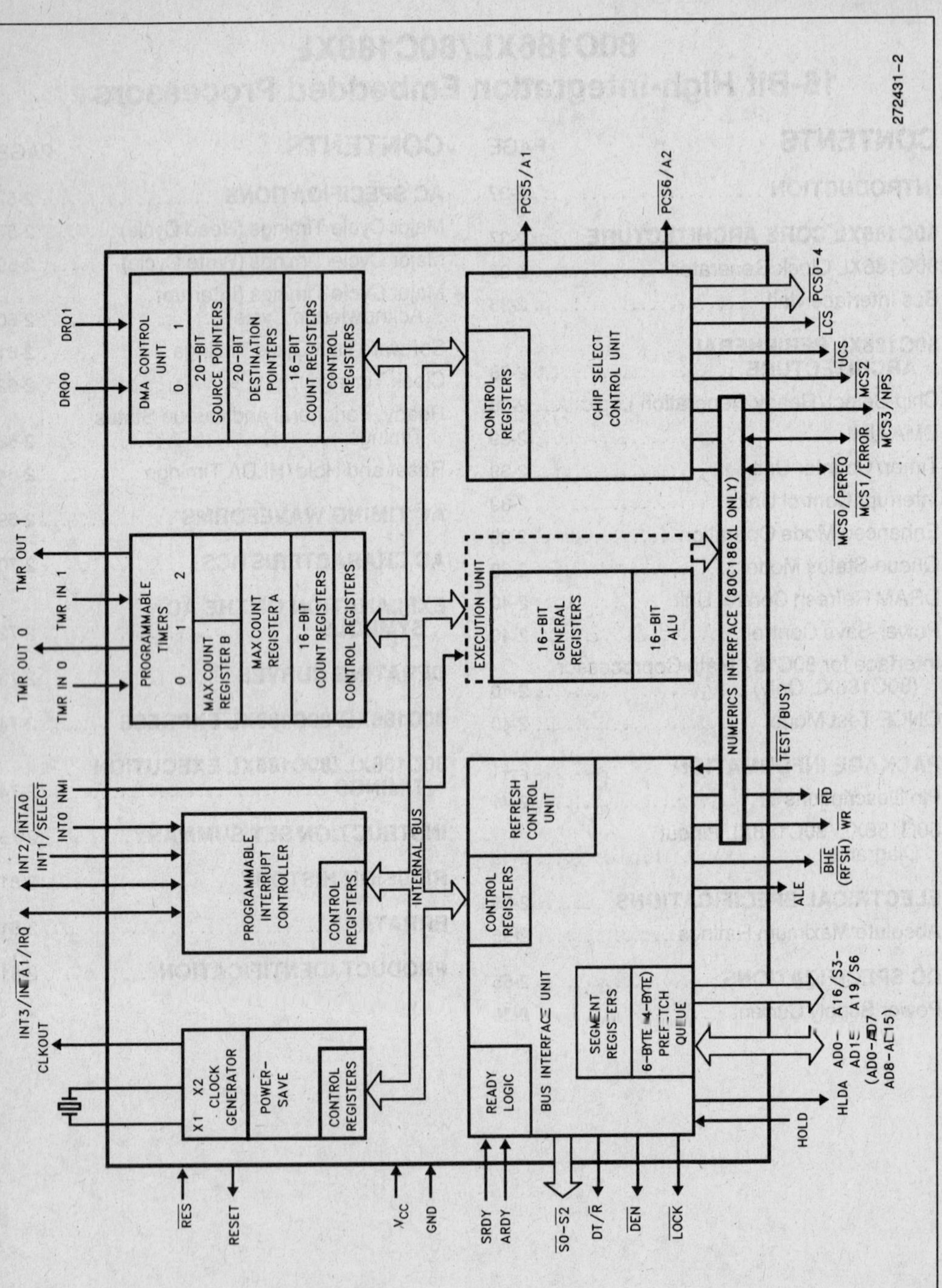

272431-2

NOTE:
Pin names in parentheses applies to 80C188XL.

Figure 1. 80C186XL/80C188XL Block Diagram

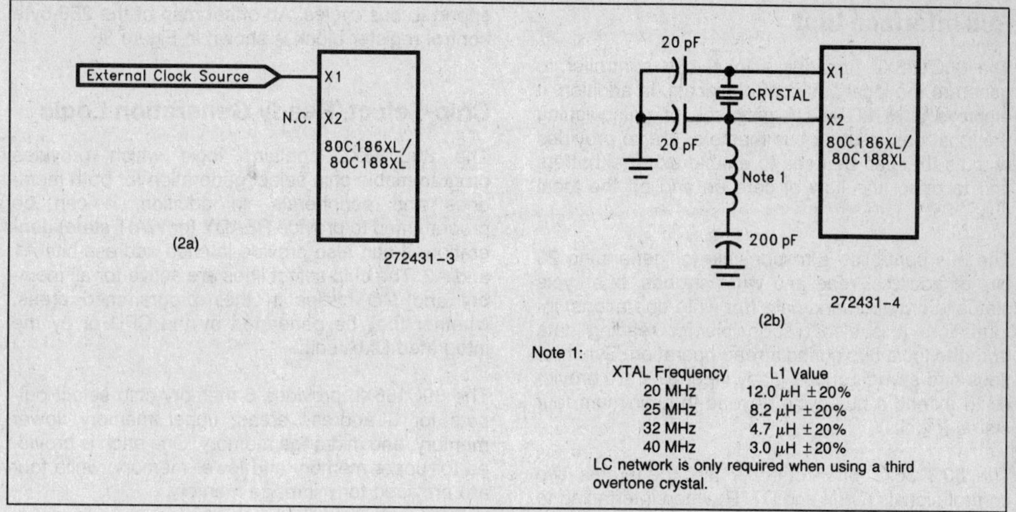

Figure 2. Oscillator Configurations (see text)

INTRODUCTION

Unless specifically noted, all references to the 80C186XL apply to the 80C188XL. References to pins that differ between the 80C186XL and the 80C188XL are given in parentheses.

The following Functional Description describes the base architecture of the 80C186XL. The 80C186XL is a very high integration 16-bit microprocessor. It combines 15–20 of the most common microprocessor system components onto one chip. The 80C186XL is object code compatible with the 8086/8088 microprocessors and adds 10 new instruction types to the 8086/8088 instruction set.

The 80C186XL has two major modes of operation, Compatible and Enhanced. In Compatible Mode the 80C186XL is completely compatible with NMOS 80186, with the exception of 8087 support. The Enhanced mode adds three new features to the system design. These are Power-Save control, Dynamic RAM refresh, and an asynchronous Numerics Coprocessor interface (80C186XL only).

80C186XL CORE ARCHITECTURE

80C186XL Clock Generator

The 80C186XL provides an on-chip clock generator for both internal and external clock generation. The clock generator features a crystal oscillator, a divide-by-two counter, synchronous and asynchronous ready inputs, and reset circuitry.

The 80C186XL oscillator circuit is designed to be used either with a parallel resonant fundamental or third-overtone mode crystal, depending upon the frequency range of the application. This is used as the time base for the 80C186XL.

The output of the oscillator is not directly available outside the 80C186XL. The recommended crystal configuration is shown in Figure 2b. When used in third-overtone mode, the tank circuit is recommended for stable operation. Alternately, the oscillator may be driven from an external source as shown in Figure 2a.

The crystal or clock frequency chosen must be twice the required processor operating frequency due to the internal divide by two counter. This counter is used to drive all internal phase clocks and the external CLKOUT signal. CLKOUT is a 50% duty cycle processor clock and can be used to drive other system components. All AC Timings are referenced to CLKOUT.

Intel recommends the following values for crystal selection parameters.

Temperature Range:	Application Specific
ESR (Equivalent Series Resistance):	60Ω max
C_0 (Shunt Capacitance of Crystal):	7.0 pF max
C_1 (Load Capacitance):	20 pF ±2 pF
Drive Level:	2 mW max

Bus Interface Unit

The 80C186XL provides a local bus controller to generate the local bus control signals. In addition, it employs a HOLD/HLDA protocol for relinquishing the local bus to other bus masters. It also provides outputs that can be used to enable external buffers and to direct the flow of data on and off the local bus.

The bus controller is responsible for generating 20 bits of address, read and write strobes, bus cycle status information and data (for write operations) information. It is also responsible for reading data from the local bus during a read operation. Synchronous and asynchronous ready input pins are provided to extend a bus cycle beyond the minimum four states (clocks).

The 80C186XL bus controller also generates two control signals ($\overline{DEN}$ and DT/$\overline{R}$) when interfacing to external transceiver chips. This capability allows the addition of transceivers for simple buffering of the multiplexed address/data bus.

During RESET the local bus controller will perform the following action:

- Drive $\overline{DEN}$, $\overline{RD}$ and $\overline{WR}$ HIGH for one clock cycle, then float them.
- Drive $\overline{S0}$–$\overline{S2}$ to the inactive state (all HIGH) and then float.
- Drive $\overline{LOCK}$ HIGH and then float.
- Float AD0–15 (AD0–8), A16–19 (A9–A19), $\overline{BHE}$ ($\overline{RFSH}$), DT/$\overline{R}$.
- Drive ALE LOW
- Drive HLDA LOW.

$\overline{RD}$/$\overline{QSMD}$, $\overline{UCS}$, $\overline{LCS}$, $\overline{MCS0}$/PEREQ, $\overline{MCS1}$/$\overline{ERROR}$ and $\overline{TEST}$/BUSY pins have internal pullup devices which are active while $\overline{RES}$ is applied. Excessive loading or grounding certain of these pins causes the 80C186XL to enter an alternative mode of operation:

- $\overline{RD}$/$\overline{QSMD}$ low results in Queue Status Mode.
- $\overline{UCS}$ and $\overline{LCS}$ low results in ONCE Mode.
- $\overline{TEST}$/BUSY low (and high later) results in Enhanced Mode.

80C186XL PERIPHERAL ARCHITECTURE

All the 80C186XL integrated peripherals are controlled by 16-bit registers contained within an internal 256-byte control block. The control block may be mapped into either memory or I/O space. Internal logic will recognize control block addresses and respond to bus cycles. An offset map of the 256-byte control register block is shown in Figure 3.

Chip-Select/Ready Generation Logic

The 80C186XL contains logic which provides programmable chip-select generation for both memories and peripherals. In addition, it can be programmed to provide READY (or WAIT state) generation. It can also provide latched address bits A1 and A2. The chip-select lines are active for all memory and I/O cycles in their programmed areas, whether they be generated by the CPU or by the integrated DMA unit.

The 80C186XL provides 6 memory chip select outputs for 3 address areas; upper memory, lower memory, and midrange memory. One each is provided for upper memory and lower memory, while four are provided for midrange memory.

Register	OFFSET
Relocation Register	FEH
DMA Descriptors Channel 1	DAH – D0H
DMA Descriptors Channel 0	CAH – C0H
Chip-Select Control Registers	A8H – A0H
Time 2 Control Registers	66H – 60H
Time 1 Control Registers	5EH – 58H
Time 0 Control Registers	56H – 50H
Interrupt Controller Registers	3EH – 20H

Figure 3. Internal Register Map

The 80C186XL provides a chip select, called $\overline{UCS}$, for the top of memory. The top of memory is usually used as the system memory because after reset the 80C186XL begins executing at memory location FFFF0H.

The 80C186XL provides a chip select for low memory called $\overline{LCS}$. The bottom of memory contains the interrupt vector table, starting at location 00000H.

The 80C186XL provides four $\overline{MCS}$ lines which are active within a user-locatable memory block. This block can be located within the 80C186XL 1 Mbyte memory address space exclusive of the areas defined by $\overline{UCS}$ and $\overline{LCS}$. Both the base address and size of this memory block are programmable.

The 80C186XL can generate chip selects for up to seven peripheral devices. These chip selects are active for seven contiguous blocks of 128 bytes above a programmable base address. The base address may be located in either memory or I/O space.

The 80C186XL can generate a READY signal internally for each of the memory or peripheral $\overline{CS}$ lines. The number of WAIT states to be inserted for each peripheral or memory is programmable to provide 0–3 wait states for all accesses to the area for which the chip select is active. In addition, the 80C186XL may be programmed to either ignore external READY for each chip-select range individually or to factor external READY with the integrated ready generator.

Upon RESET, the Chip-Select/Ready Logic will perform the following actions:

- All chip-select outputs will be driven HIGH.
- Upon leaving RESET, the $\overline{UCS}$ line will be programmed to provide chip selects to a 1K block with the accompanying READY control bits set at 011 to insert 3 wait states in conjunction with external READY (i.e., UMCS resets to FFFBH).
- No other chip select or READY control registers have any predefined values after RESET. They will not become active until the CPU accesses their control registers.

DMA Unit

The 80C186XL DMA controller provides two independent high-speed DMA channels. Data transfers can occur between memory and I/O spaces (e.g., Memory to I/O) or within the same space (e.g., Memory to Memory or I/O to I/O). Data can be transferred either in bytes (8 bits) or in words (16 bits) to or from even or odd addresses.

NOTE:
Only byte transfers are possible on the 80C188XL.

Each DMA channel maintains both a 20-bit source and destination pointer which can be optionally incremented or decremented after each data transfer (by one or two depending on byte or word transfers). Each data transfer consumes 2 bus cycles (a minimum of 8 clocks), one cycle to fetch data and the other to store data.

Timer/Counter Unit

The 80C186XL provides three internal 16-bit programmable timers. Two of these are highly flexible and are connected to four external pins (2 per timer). They can be used to count external events, time external events, generate nonrepetitive waveforms, etc. The third timer is not connected to any external pins, and is useful for real-time coding and time delay applications. In addition, the third timer can be used as a prescaler to the other two, or as a DMA request source.

Interrupt Control Unit

The 80C186XL can receive interrupts from a number of sources, both internal and external. The 80C186XL has 5 external and 2 internal interrupt sources (Timer/Couners and DMA). The internal interrupt controller serves to merge these requests on a priority basis, for individual service by the CPU.

Enhanced Mode Operation

In Compatible Mode the 80C186XL operates with all the features of the NMOS 80186, with the exception of 8087 support (i.e. no math coprocessing is possible in Compatible Mode). Queue-Status information is still available for design purposes other than 8087 support.

All the Enhanced Mode features are completely masked when in Compatible Mode. A write to any of the Enhanced Mode registers will have no effect, while a read will not return any valid data.

In Enhanced Mode, the 80C186XL will operate with Power-Save, DRAM refresh, and numerics coprocessor support (80C186XL only) in addition to all the Compatible Mode features.

If connected to a math coprocessor (80C186XL only), this mode will be invoked automatically. Without an NPX, this mode can be entered by tying the $\overline{RESET}$ output signal from the 80C186XL to the $\overline{TEST}$/BUSY input.

Queue-Status Mode

The queue-status mode is entered by strapping the $\overline{RD}$ pin low. $\overline{RD}$ is sampled at RESET and if LOW, the 80C186XL will reconfigure the ALE and $\overline{WR}$ pins to be QS0 and QS1 respectively. This mode is available on the 80C186XL in both Compatible and Enhanced Modes.

DRAM Refresh Control Unit

The Refresh Control Unit (RCU) automatically generates DRAM refresh bus cycles. The RCU operates only in Enhanced Mode. After a programmable period of time, the RCU generates a memory read request to the BIU. If the address generated during a refresh bus cycle is within the range of a properly programmed chip select, that chip select will be activated when the BIU executes the refresh bus cycle.

Power-Save Control

The 80C186XL, when in Enhanced Mode, can enter a power saving state by internally dividing the processor clock frequency by a programmable factor. This divided frequency is also available at the CLKOUT pin.

All internal logic, including the Refresh Control Unit and the timers, have their clocks slowed down by the division factor. To maintain a real time count or a fixed DRAM refresh rate, these peripherals must be re-programmed when entering and leaving the power-save mode.

Interface for 80C187 Math Coprocessor (80C186XL Only)

In Enhanced Mode, three of the mid-range memory chip selects are redefined according to Table 1 for use with the 80C187. The fourth chip select, MCS2 functions as in compatible mode, and may be programmed for activity with ready logic and wait states accordingly. As in Compatible Mode, MCS2 will function for one-fourth a programmed block size.

Table 1. MCS Assignments

Compatible Mode	Enhanced Mode	
MCS0	PEREQ	Processor Extension Request
MCS1	ERROR	NPX Error
MCS2	MCS2	Mid-Range Chip Select
MCS3	NPS	Numeric Processor Select

ONCE Test Mode

To facilitate testing and inspection of devices when fixed into a target system, the 80C186XL has a test mode available which allows all pins to be placed in a high-impedance state. ONCE stands for "ON Circuit Emulation". When placed in this mode, the 80C186XL will put all pins in the high-impedance state until RESET.

The ONCE mode is selected by tying the UCS and the LCS LOW during RESET. These pins are sampled on the low-to-high transition of the RES pin. The UCS and the LCS pins have weak internal pull-up resistors similar to the RD and TEST/BUSY pins to guarantee ONCE Mode is not entered inadvertently during normal operation. LCS and UCS must be held low at least one clock after RES goes high to guarantee entrance into ONCE Mode.

PACKAGE INFORMATION

This section describes the pin functions, pinout and thermal characteristics for the 80C186XL in the Quad Flat Pack (QFP), Plastic Leaded Chip Carrier (PLCC), Leadless Chip Carrier (LCC) and the Shrink Quad Flat Pack (SQFP). For complete package specifications and information, see the Intel Packaging Outlines and Dimensions Guide (Order Number: 231369).

Pin Descriptions

Each pin or logical set of pins is described in Table 3. There are four columns for each entry in the Pin Description Table. The following sections describe each column.

Column 1: Pin Name

In this column is a mnemonic that describes the pin function. Negation of the signal name (i.e., $\overline{\text{RESIN}}$) implies that the signal is active low.

Column 2: Pin Type

A pin may be either power (P), ground (G), input only (I), output only (O) or input/output (I/O). Please note that some pins have more than one function.

Column 3: Input Type (for I and I/O types only)

These are two different types of input pins on the 80C186XL: asynchronous and synchronous. **Asynchronous** pins require that setup and hold times be met only to *guarantee recognition.* **Synchronous** input pins require that the setup and hold times be met to *guarantee proper operation.* Stated simply, missing a setup or hold on an asynchronous pin will result in something minor (i.e., a timer count will be missed) whereas missing a setup or hold on a synchronous pin result in system failure (the system will "lock up").

An input pin may also be edge or level sensitive.

Column 4: Output States (for O and I/O types only)

The state of an output or I/O pin is dependent on the operating mode of the device. There are four modes of operation that are different from normal active mode: Bus Hold, Reset, Idle Mode, Powerdown Mode. This column describes the output pin state in each of these modes.

The legend for interpreting the information in the Pin Descriptions is shown in Table 2.

As an example, please refer to the table entry for AD7:0. The "I/O" signifies that the pins are bidirectional (i.e., have both an input and output function). The "S" indicates that, as an input the signal must be synchronized to CLKOUT for proper operation. The "H(Z)" indicates that these pins will float while the processor is in the Hold Acknowledge state. R(Z) indicates that these pins will float while $\overline{\text{RESIN}}$ is low.

All pins float while the processor is in the ONCE Mode (with the exception of X2).

2

Table 2. Pin Description Nomenclature

Symbol	Description
P	Power Pin (apply + V_{CC} voltage)
G	Ground (connect to V_{SS})
I	Input only pin
O	Output only pin
I/O	Input/Output pin
S(E)	Synchronous, edge sensitive
S(L)	Synchronous, level sensitive
A(E)	Asynchronous, edge sensitive
A(L)	Asynchronous, level sensitive
H(1)	Output driven to V_{CC} during bus hold
H(0)	Output driven to V_{SS} during bus hold
H(Z)	Output floats during bus hold
H(Q)	Output remains active during bus hold
H(X)	Output retains current state during bus hold
R(WH)	Output weakly held at V_{CC} during reset
R(1)	Output driven to V_{CC} during reset
R(0)	Output driven to V_{SS} during reset
R(Z)	Output floats during reset
R(Q)	Output remains active during reset
R(X)	Output retains current state during reset

Table 3. Pin Descriptions

Pin Name	Pin Type	Input Type	Output States	Pin Description
V_{CC}	P			System Power: +5 volt power supply.
V_{SS}	G			System Ground.
RESET	O		H(0) R(1)	RESET Output indicates that the CPU is being reset, and can be used as a system reset. It is active HIGH, synchronized with the processor clock, and lasts an integer number of clock periods corresponding to the length of the $\overline{RES}$ signal. Reset goes inactive 2 clockout periods after $\overline{RES}$ goes inactive. When tied to the $\overline{TEST}$/BUSY pin, RESET forces the processor into enhanced mode. RESET is not floated during bus hold.
X1	I	A(E)		Crystal Inputs X1 and X2 provide external connections for a fundamental mode or third overtone parallel resonant crystal for the internal oscillator. X1 can connect to an external clock instead of a crystal. In this case, minimize the capacitance on X2. The input or oscillator frequency is internally divided by two to generate the clock signal (CLKOUT).
X2	O		H(Q) R(Q)	
CLKOUT	O		H(Q) R(Q)	Clock Output provides the system with a 50% duty cycle waveform. All device pin timings are specified relative to CLKOUT. CLKOUT is active during reset and bus hold.
$\overline{RES}$	I	A(L)		An active $\overline{RES}$ causes the processor to immediately terminate its present activity, clear the internal logic, and enter a dormant state. This signal may be asynchronous to the clock. The processor begins fetching instructions approximately 6½ clock cycles after $\overline{RES}$ is returned HIGH. For proper initialization, V_{CC} must be within specifications and the clock signal must be stable for more than 4 clocks with $\overline{RES}$ held LOW. $\overline{RES}$ is internally synchronized. This input is provided with a Schmitt-trigger to facilitate power-on $\overline{RES}$ generation via an RC network.
$\overline{TEST}$/BUSY ($\overline{TEST}$)	I	A(E)		The $\overline{TEST}$ pin is sampled during and after reset to determine whether the processor is to enter Compatible or Enhanced Mode. Enhanced Mode requires $\overline{TEST}$ to be HIGH on the rising edge of $\overline{RES}$ and LOW four CLKOUT cycles later. Any other combination will place the processor in Compatible Mode. During power-up, active $\overline{RES}$ is required to configure $\overline{TEST}$/BUSY as an input. A weak internal pullup ensures a HIGH state when the input is not externally driven. $\overline{TEST}$—In Compatible Mode this pin is configured to operate as $\overline{TEST}$. This pin is examined by the WAIT instruction. If the $\overline{TEST}$ input is HIGH when WAIT execution begins, instruction execution will suspend. $\overline{TEST}$ will be resampled every five clocks until it goes LOW, at which time execution will resume. If interrupts are enabled while the processor is waiting for $\overline{TEST}$, interrupts will be serviced. BUSY (80C186XL Only)—In Enhanced Mode, this pin is configured to operate as BUSY. The BUSY input is used to notify the 80C186XL of Math Coprocessor activity. Floating point instructions executing in the 80C186XL sample the BUSY pin to determine when the Math Coprocessor is ready to accept a new command. BUSY is active HIGH.

NOTE:
Pin names in parentheses apply to the 80C188XL.

Table 3. Pin Descriptions (Continued)

Pin Name	Pin Type	Input Type	Output States	Pin Description
TMR IN 0 TMR IN 1	I	A(L) A(E)		Timer Inputs are used either as clock or control signals, depending upon the programmed timer mode. These inputs are active HIGH (or LOW-to-HIGH transitions are counted) and internally synchronized. Timer Inputs must be tied HIGH when not being used as clock or retrigger inputs.
TMR OUT 0 TMR OUT 1	O		H(Q) R(1)	Timer outputs are used to provide single pulse or continuous waveform generation, depending upon the timer mode selected. These outputs are not floated during a bus hold.
DRQ0 DRQ1	I	A(L)		DMA Request is asserted HIGH by an external device when it is ready for DMA Channel 0 or 1 to perform a transfer. These signals are level-triggered and internally synchronized.
NMI	I	A(E)		The Non-Maskable Interrupt input causes a Type 2 interrupt. An NMI transition from LOW to HIGH is latched and synchronized internally, and initiates the interrupt at the next instruction boundary. NMI must be asserted for at least one CLKOUT period. The Non-Maskable Interrupt cannot be avoided by programming.
INT0 INT1/$\overline{\text{SELECT}}$	I	A(E) A(L)		Maskable Interrupt Requests can be requested by activating one of these pins. When configured as inputs, these pins are active HIGH. Interrupt Requests are synchronized internally. INT2 and INT3 may be configured to provide active-LOW interrupt-acknowledge output signals. All interrupt inputs may be configured to be either edge- or level-triggered. To ensure recognition, all interrupt requests must remain active until the interrupt is acknowledged. When Slave Mode is selected, the function of these pins changes (see Interrupt Controller section of this data sheet).
INT2/$\overline{\text{INTA0}}$ INT3/$\overline{\text{INTA1}}$/IRQ	I/O	A(E) A(L)	H(1) R(Z)	
A19/S6 A18/S5 A17/S4 A16/S3 (A8–A15)	O		H(Z) R(Z)	Address Bus Outputs and Bus Cycle Status (3–6) indicate the four most significant address bits during T_1. These signals are active HIGH. During T_2, T_3, T_W and T_4, the S6 pin is LOW to indicate a CPU-initiated bus cycle or HIGH to indicate a DMA-initiated or refresh bus cycle. During the same T-states, S3, S4 and S5 are always LOW. On the 80C188XL, A15–A8 provide valid address information for the entire bus cycle.
AD0–AD15 (AD0–AD7)	I/O	S(L)	H(Z) R(Z)	Address/Data Bus signals constitute the time multiplexed memory or I/O address (T_1) and data (T_2, T_3, T_W and T_4) bus. The bus is active HIGH. For the 80C186XL, A_0 is analogous to $\overline{\text{BHE}}$ for the lower byte of the data bus, pins D_7 through D_0. It is LOW during T_1 when a byte is to be transferred onto the lower portion of the bus in memory or I/O operations.

NOTE:
Pin names in parentheses apply to the 80C188XL.

Table 3. Pin Descriptions (Continued)

Pin Name	Pin Type	Input Type	Output States	Pin Description
$\overline{\text{BHE}}$ ($\overline{\text{RFSH}}$)	O		H(Z) R(Z)	The $\overline{\text{BHE}}$ (Bus High Enable) signal is analogous to A0 in that it is used to enable data on to the most significant half of the data bus, pins D15–D8. $\overline{\text{BHE}}$ will be LOW during T_1 when the upper byte is transferred and will remain LOW through T_3 and T_W. $\overline{\text{BHE}}$ does not need to be latched. On the 80C188XL, $\overline{\text{RFSH}}$ is asserted LOW to indicate a refresh bus cycle. In Enhanced Mode, $\overline{\text{BHE}}$ ($\overline{\text{RFSH}}$) will also be used to signify DRAM refresh cycles. A refresh cycle is indicated by both $\overline{\text{BHE}}$ ($\overline{\text{RFSH}}$) and A0 being HIGH.

80C186XL $\overline{\text{BHE}}$ and A0 Encodings

$\overline{\text{BHE}}$ Value	A0 Value	Function
0	0	Word Transfer
0	1	Byte Transfer on upper half of data bus (D15–D8)
1	0	Byte Transfer on lower half of data bus (D_7–D_0)
1	1	Refresh

Pin Name	Pin Type	Input Type	Output States	Pin Description
ALE/QS0	O		H(0) R(0)	Address Latch Enable/Queue Status 0 is provided by the processor to latch the address. ALE is active HIGH, with addresses guaranteed valid on the trailing edge.
$\overline{\text{WR}}$/QS1	O		H(Z) R(Z)	Write Strobe/Queue Status 1 indicates that the data on the bus is to be written into a memory or an I/O device. It is active LOW. When the processor is in Queue Status Mode, the ALE/QS0 and $\overline{\text{WR}}$/QS1 pins provide information about processor/instruction queue interaction.

QS1	QS0	Queue Operation
0	0	No queue operation
0	1	First opcode byte fetched from the queue
1	1	Subsequent byte fetched from the queue
1	0	Empty the queue

Pin Name	Pin Type	Input Type	Output States	Pin Description
$\overline{\text{RD}}$/$\overline{\text{QSMD}}$	O		H(Z) R(1)	Read Strobe is an active LOW signal which indicates that the processor is performing a memory or I/O read cycle. It is guaranteed not to go LOW before the A/D bus is floated. An internal pull-up ensures that $\overline{\text{RD}}$/$\overline{\text{QSMD}}$ is HIGH during RESET. Following RESET the pin is sampled to determine whether the processor is to provide ALE, $\overline{\text{RD}}$, and $\overline{\text{WR}}$, or queue status information. To enable Queue Status Mode, $\overline{\text{RD}}$ must be connected to GND.
ARDY	I	A(L) S(L)		Asynchronous Ready informs the processor that the addressed memory space or I/O device will complete a data transfer. The ARDY pin accepts a rising edge that is asynchronous to CLKOUT and is active HIGH. The falling edge of ARDY must be synchronized to the processor clock. Connecting ARDY HIGH will always assert the ready condition to the CPU. If this line is unused, it should be tied LOW to yield control to the SRDY pin.

NOTE:
Pin names in parentheses apply to the 80C188XL.

2

Table 3. Pin Descriptions (Continued)

<table>
<tr><th>Pin Name</th><th>Pin Type</th><th>Input Type</th><th>Output States</th><th>Pin Description</th></tr>
<tr><td>SRDY</td><td>I</td><td>S(L)</td><td>—</td><td>Synchronous Ready informs the processor that the addressed memory space or I/O device will complete a data transfer. The SRDY pin accepts an active-HIGH input synchronized to CLKOUT. The use of SRDY allows a relaxed system timing over ARDY. This is accomplished by elimination of the one-half clock cycle required to internally synchonize the ARDY input signal. Connecting SRDY high will always assert the ready condition to the CPU. If this line is unused, it should be tied LOW to yield control to the ARDY pin.</td></tr>
<tr><td>$\overline{LOCK}$</td><td>O</td><td>—</td><td>H(Z)
R(Z)</td><td>$\overline{LOCK}$ output indicates that other system bus masters are not to gain control of the system bus. $\overline{LOCK}$ is active LOW. The $\overline{LOCK}$ signal is requested by the LOCK prefix instruction and is activated at the beginning of the first data cycle associated with the instruction immediately following the LOCK prefix. It remains active until the completion of that instruction. No instruction prefetching will occur while $\overline{LOCK}$ is asserted.</td></tr>
<tr><td>$\overline{S0}$
$\overline{S1}$
$\overline{S2}$</td><td>O</td><td>—</td><td>H(Z)
R(1)</td><td>Bus cycle status $\overline{S0}$–$\overline{S2}$ are encoded to provide bus-transaction information:
<table>
<tr><th colspan="4">Bus Cycle Status Information</th></tr>
<tr><th>$\overline{S2}$</th><th>$\overline{S1}$</th><th>$\overline{S0}$</th><th>Bus Cycle Initiated</th></tr>
<tr><td>0</td><td>0</td><td>0</td><td>Interrupt Acknowledge</td></tr>
<tr><td>0</td><td>0</td><td>1</td><td>Read I/O</td></tr>
<tr><td>0</td><td>1</td><td>0</td><td>Write I/O</td></tr>
<tr><td>0</td><td>1</td><td>1</td><td>Halt</td></tr>
<tr><td>1</td><td>0</td><td>0</td><td>Instruction Fetch</td></tr>
<tr><td>1</td><td>0</td><td>1</td><td>Read Data from Memory</td></tr>
<tr><td>1</td><td>1</td><td>0</td><td>Write Data to Memory</td></tr>
<tr><td>1</td><td>1</td><td>1</td><td>Passive (no bus cycle)</td></tr>
</table>
$\overline{S2}$ may be used as a logical M/$\overline{IO}$ indicator, and $\overline{S1}$ as a DT/$\overline{R}$ indicator.</td></tr>
<tr><td>HOLD</td><td>I</td><td>A(L)</td><td>—</td><td rowspan="2">HOLD indicates that another bus master is requesting the local bus. The HOLD input is active HIGH. The processor generates HLDA (HIGH) in response to a HOLD request. Simultaneous with the issuance of HLDA, the processor will float the local bus and control lines. After HOLD is detected as being LOW, the processor will lower HLDA. When the processor needs to run another bus cycle, it will again drive the local bus and control lines.

In Enhanced Mode, HLDA will go low when a DRAM refresh cycle is pending in the processor and an external bus master has control of the bus. It will be up to the external master to relinquish the bus by lowering HOLD so that the processor may execute the refresh cycle.</td></tr>
<tr><td>HLDA</td><td>O</td><td>—</td><td>H(1)
R(0)</td></tr>
</table>

NOTE:
Pin names in parentheses apply to the 80C188XL.

Table 3. Pin Descriptions (Continued)

Pin Name	Pin Type	Input Type	Output States	Pin Description
$\overline{\text{UCS}}$	I/O	A(L)	H(1) R(WH)	Upper Memory Chip Select is an active LOW output whenever a memory reference is made to the defined upper portion (1K–256K block) of memory. The address range activating $\overline{\text{UCS}}$ is software programmable. $\overline{\text{UCS}}$ and $\overline{\text{LCS}}$ are sampled upon the rising edge of $\overline{\text{RES}}$. If both pins are held low, the processor will enter ONCE Mode. In ONCE Mode all pins assume a high impedance state and remain so until a subsequent RESET. $\overline{\text{UCS}}$ has a weak internal pullup that is active during RESET to ensure that the processor does not enter ONCE Mode inadvertently.
$\overline{\text{LCS}}$	I/O	A(L)	H(1) R(WH)	Lower Memory Chip Select is active LOW whenever a memory reference is made to the defined lower portion (1K–256K) of memory. The address range activating $\overline{\text{LCS}}$ is software programmable. $\overline{\text{UCS}}$ and $\overline{\text{LCS}}$ are sampled upon the rising edge of $\overline{\text{RES}}$. If both pins are held low, the processor will enter ONCE Mode. In ONCE Mode all pins assume a high impedance state and remain so until a subsequent RESET. $\overline{\text{LCS}}$ has a weak internal pullup that is active only during RESET to ensure that the processor does not enter ONCE mode inadvertently.
$\overline{\text{MCS0}}$/PEREQ $\overline{\text{MCS1}}$/$\overline{\text{ERROR}}$	I/O	A(L)	H(1) R(WH)	Mid-Range Memory Chip Select signals are active LOW when a memory reference is made to the defined mid-range portion of memory (8K–512K). The address ranges activating $\overline{\text{MCS0–3}}$ are software programmable. On the 80C186XL, in Enhanced Mode, $\overline{\text{MCS0}}$ becomes a PEREQ input (Processor Extension Request). When connected to the Math Coprocessor, this input is used to signal the 80C186XL when to make numeric data transfers to and from the coprocessor. $\overline{\text{MCS3}}$ becomes $\overline{\text{NPS}}$ (Numeric Processor Select) which may only be activated by communication to the 80C187. $\overline{\text{MCS1}}$ becomes $\overline{\text{ERROR}}$ in Enhanced Mode and is used to signal numerics coprocessor errors.
$\overline{\text{MCS2}}$ $\overline{\text{MCS3}}$/$\overline{\text{NPS}}$	O		H(1) R(1)	
$\overline{\text{PCS0}}$ $\overline{\text{PCS1}}$ $\overline{\text{PCS2}}$ $\overline{\text{PCS3}}$ $\overline{\text{PCS4}}$	O		H(1) R(1)	Peripheral Chip Select signals 0–4 are active LOW when a reference is made to the defined peripheral area (64 Kbyte I/O or 1 MByte memory space). The address ranges activating $\overline{\text{PCS0–4}}$ are software programmable.
$\overline{\text{PCS5}}$/A1	O		H(1)/H(X) R(1)	Peripheral Chip Select 5 or Latched A1 may be programmed to provide a sixth peripheral chip select, or to provide an internally latched A1 signal. The address range activating $\overline{\text{PCS5}}$ is software-programmable. $\overline{\text{PCS5}}$/A1 does not float during bus HOLD. When programmed to provide latched A1, this pin will retain the previously latched value during HOLD.

NOTE:
Pin names in parentheses apply to the 80C188XL.

Table 3. Pin Descriptions (Continued)

Pin Name	Pin Type	Input Type	Output States	Pin Description
$\overline{PCS6}$/A2	O	—	H(1)/H(X) R(1)	Peripheral Chip Select 6 or Latched A2 may be programmed to provide a seventh peripheral chip select, or to provide an internally latched A2 signal. The address range activating $\overline{PCS6}$ is software-programmable. $\overline{PCS6}$/A2 does not float during bus HOLD. When programmed to provide latched A2, this pin will retain the previously latched value during HOLD.
DT/$\overline{R}$	O	—	H(Z) R(Z)	Data Transmit/Receive controls the direction of data flow through an external data bus transceiver. When LOW, data is transferred to the procesor. When HIGH the processor places write data on the data bus.
$\overline{DEN}$	O	—	H(Z) R(1,Z)	Data Enable is provided as a data bus transceiver output enable. $\overline{DEN}$ is active LOW during each memory and I/O access (including 80C187 access). $\overline{DEN}$ is HIGH whenever DT/$\overline{R}$ changes state. During RESET, $\overline{DEN}$ is driven HIGH for one clock, then floated.
N.C.	—	—	—	Not connected. To maintain compatibility with future products, do not connect to these pins.

NOTE:
Pin names in parentheses apply to the 80C188XL.

Ceramic Leadless Chip Carrier (JEDEC Type A)

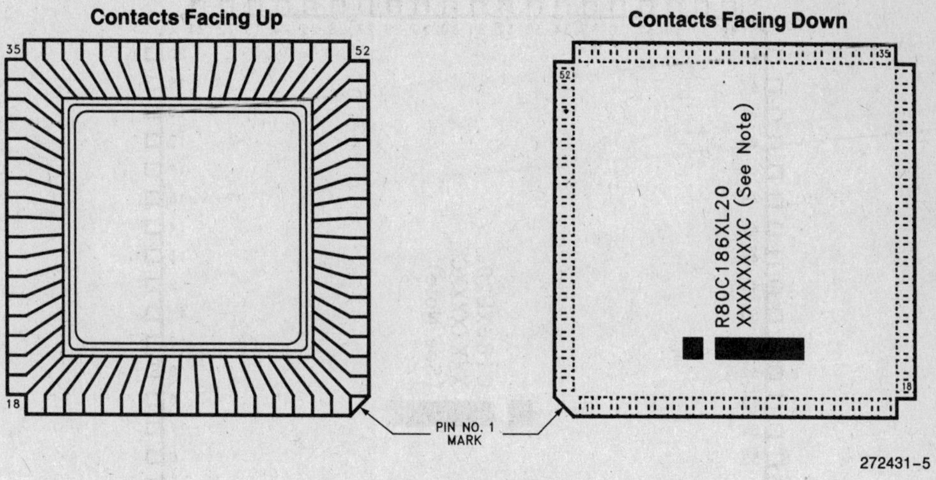

272431-5

Ceramic Pin Grid Array

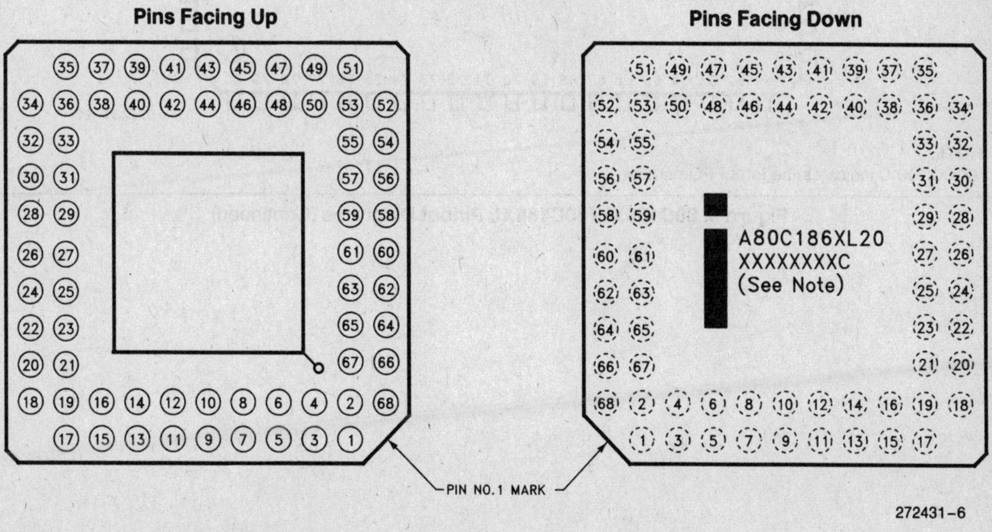

272431-6

NOTE:
XXXXXXXXC indicates the Intel FPO number.

Figure 4. 80C186XL/80C188XL Pinout Diagrams

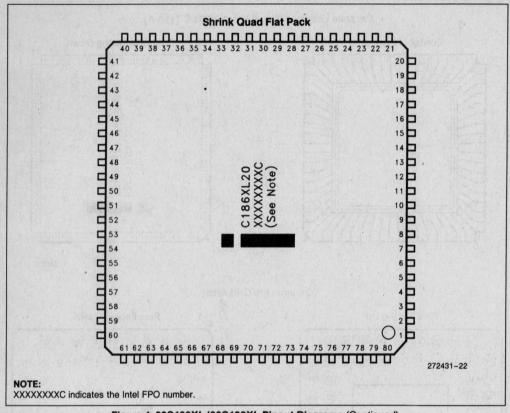

Shrink Quad Flat Pack

NOTE:
XXXXXXXXC indicates the Intel FPO number.

Figure 4. 80C186XL/80C188XL Pinout Diagrams (Continued)

Plastic Leaded Chip Carrier

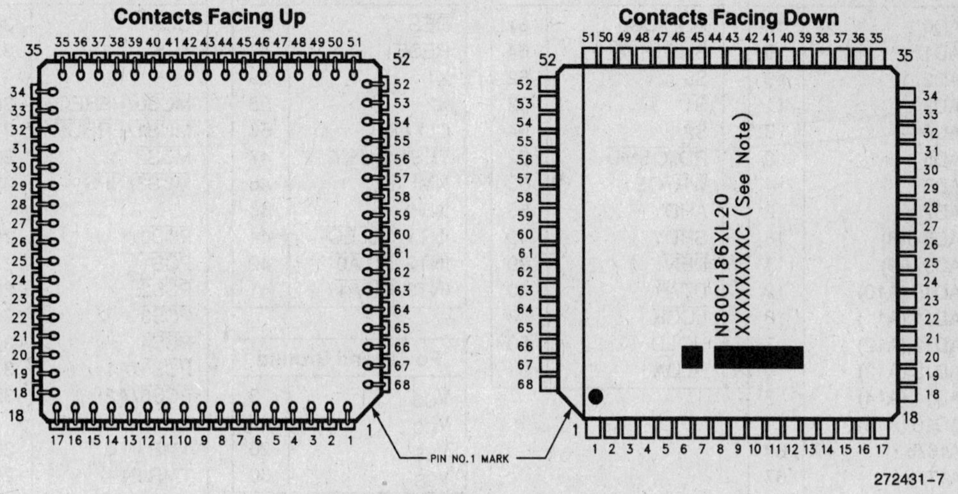

Contacts Facing Up

Contacts Facing Down

N80C186XL20
XXXXXXXXC (See Note)

PIN NO. 1 MARK

272431-7

80-Pin Quad Flat Pack (EIAJ)

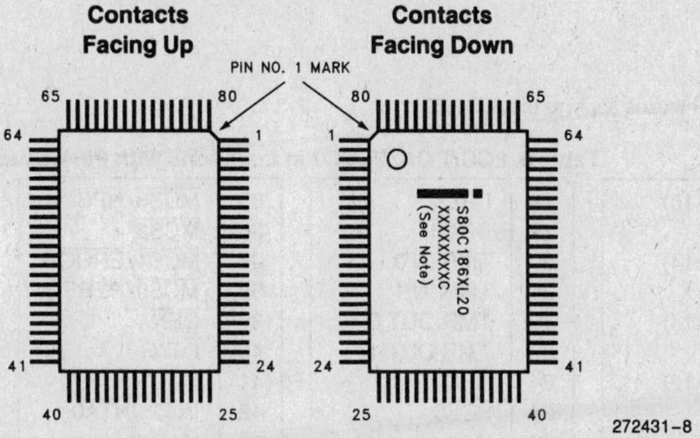

Contacts Facing Up

Contacts Facing Down

PIN NO. 1 MARK

S80C186XL20
XXXXXXXXC
(See Note)

272431-8

NOTE:
XXXXXXXXA indicates the Intel FPO number.

Figure 4. 80C186XL/80C288XL Pinout Diagrams (Continued)

Table 4. LCC/PLCC Pin Functions with Location

AD Bus	
AD0	17
AD1	15
AD2	13
AD3	11
AD4	8
AD5	6
AD6	4
AD7	2
AD8 (A8)	16
AD9 (A9)	14
AD10 (A10)	12
AD11 (A11)	10
AD12 (A12)	7
AD13 (A13)	5
AD14 (A14)	3
AD15 (A15)	1
A16/S3	68
A17/S4	67
A18/S5	66
A19/S6	65

Bus Control	
ALE/QS0	61
$\overline{BHE}$ ($\overline{RFSH}$)	64
$\overline{S0}$	52
$\overline{S1}$	53
$\overline{S2}$	54
$\overline{RD}$/$\overline{QSMD}$	62
$\overline{WR}$/QS1	63
ARDY	55
SRDY	49
$\overline{DEN}$	39
DT/$\overline{R}$	40
$\overline{LOCK}$	48
HOLD	50
HLDA	51

Processor Control	
$\overline{RES}$	24
RESET	57
X1	59
X2	58
CLKOUT	56
$\overline{TEST}$/BUSY	47
NMI	46
INT0	45
INT1/$\overline{SELECT}$	44
INT2/$\overline{INTA0}$	42
INT3/$\overline{INTA1}$	41

Power and Ground	
V_{CC}	9
V_{CC}	43
V_{SS}	26
V_{SS}	60

I/O	
$\overline{UCS}$	34
$\overline{LCS}$	33
$\overline{MCS0}$/PEREQ	38
$\overline{MCS1}$/ERROR	37
$\overline{MCS2}$	36
$\overline{MCS3}$/$\overline{NPS}$	35
$\overline{PCS0}$	25
$\overline{PCS1}$	27
$\overline{PCS2}$	28
$\overline{PCS3}$	29
$\overline{PCS4}$	30
$\overline{PCS5}$/A1	31
$\overline{PCS6}$/A2	32
TMR IN 0	20
TMR IN 1	21
TMR OUT 0	22
TMR OUT 1	23
DRQ0	18
DRQ1	19

NOTE:
Pin names in parentheses apply to the 80C188XL.

Table 5. LCC/PGA/PLCC Pin Locations with Pin Names

1	AD15 (A15)	18	DRQ0	35	$\overline{MCS3}$/$\overline{NPS}$	52	$\overline{S0}$
2	AD7	19	DRQ1	36	$\overline{MCS2}$	53	$\overline{S1}$
3	AD14 (A14)	20	TMR IN 0	37	$\overline{MCS1}$/ERROR	54	$\overline{S2}$
4	AD6	21	TMR IN 1	38	$\overline{MCS0}$/PEREQ	55	ARDY
5	AD13 (A13)	22	TMR OUT 0	39	$\overline{DEN}$	56	CLKOUT
6	AD5	23	TMR OUT 1	40	DT/$\overline{R}$	57	RESET
7	AD12 (A12)	24	$\overline{RES}$	41	INT3/$\overline{INTA1}$	58	X2
8	AD4	25	$\overline{PCS0}$	42	INT2/$\overline{INTA0}$	59	X1
9	V_{CC}	26	V_{SS}	43	V_{CC}	60	V_{SS}
10	AD11 (A11)	27	$\overline{PCS1}$	44	INT1/$\overline{SELECT}$	61	ALE/QS0
11	AD3	28	$\overline{PCS2}$	45	INT0	62	$\overline{RD}$/$\overline{QSMD}$
12	AD10 (A10)	29	$\overline{PCS3}$	46	NMI	63	$\overline{WR}$/QS1
13	AD2	30	$\overline{PCS4}$	47	$\overline{TEST}$/BUSY	64	$\overline{BHE}$ ($\overline{RFSH}$)
14	AD9 (A9)	31	$\overline{PCS5}$/A1	48	$\overline{LOCK}$	65	A19/S2
15	AD1	32	$\overline{PCS6}$/A2	49	SRDY	66	A18/S3
16	AD8 (A8)	33	$\overline{LCS}$	50	HOLD	67	A17/S4
17	AD0	34	$\overline{UCS}$	51	HLDA	68	A16/S3

NOTE:
Pin names in parentheses apply to the 80C188XL.

Table 6. QFP Pin Functions with Location

AD Bus	
AD0	64
AD1	66
AD2	68
AD3	70
AD4	74
AD5	76
AD6	78
AD7	80
AD8 (A8)	65
AD9 (A9)	67
AD10 (A10)	69
AD11 (A11)	71
AD12 (A12)	75
AD13 (A13)	77
AD14 (A14)	79
AD15 (A15)	1
A16/S3	3
A17/S4	4
A18/S5	5
A19/S6	6

Bus Control	
ALE/QS0	10
$\overline{BHE}$ ($\overline{RFSH}$)	7
$\overline{S0}$	23
$\overline{S1}$	22
$\overline{S2}$	21
$\overline{RD}/\overline{QSMD}$	9
$\overline{WR}$/QS1	8
ARDY	20
SRDY	27
$\overline{DEN}$	38
DT/$\overline{R}$	37
$\overline{LOCK}$	28
HOLD	26
HLDA	25

No Connection	
N.C.	2
N.C.	11
N.C.	14
N.C.	15
N.C.	24
N.C.	43
N.C.	44
N.C.	62
N.C.	63

Processor Control	
$\overline{RES}$	55
RESET	18
X1	16
X2	17
CLKOUT	19
$\overline{TEST}$/BUSY	29
NMI	30
INT0	31
INT1/$\overline{SELECT}$	32
INT2/$\overline{INTA0}$	35
INT3/$\overline{INTA1}$	36

Power and Ground	
V_{CC}	33
V_{CC}	34
V_{CC}	72
V_{CC}	73
V_{SS}	12
V_{SS}	13
V_{SS}	53

I/O	
$\overline{UCS}$	45
$\overline{LCS}$	46
$\overline{MCS0}$/PEREQ	39
$\overline{MCS1}/\overline{ERROR}$	40
$\overline{MCS2}$	41
$\overline{MCS3}/\overline{NPS}$	42
$\overline{PCS0}$	54
$\overline{PCS1}$	52
$\overline{PCS2}$	51
$\overline{PCS3}$	50
$\overline{PCS4}$	49
$\overline{PCS5}$/A1	48
$\overline{PCS6}$/A2	47
TMR IN 0	59
TMR IN 1	58
TMR OUT 0	57
TMR OUT 1	56
DRQ0	61
DRQ1	60

NOTE:
Pin names in parentheses apply to the 80C188XL.

Table 7. QFP Pin Locations with Pin Names

1	AD15 (A15)	21	$\overline{S2}$	41	$\overline{MCS2}$	61	DRQ0
2	N.C.	22	$\overline{S1}$	42	$\overline{MCS3}/\overline{NPS}$	62	N.C.
3	A16/S3	23	$\overline{S0}$	43	N.C.	63	N.C.
4	A17/S4	24	N.C.	44	N.C.	64	AD0
5	A18/S5	25	HLDA	45	$\overline{UCS}$	65	AD8 (A8)
6	A19/S6	26	HOLD	46	$\overline{LCS}$	66	AD1
7	$\overline{BHE}$/($\overline{RFSH}$)	27	SRDY	47	$\overline{PCS6}$/A2	67	AD9 (A9)
8	$\overline{WR}$/QS1	28	$\overline{LOCK}$	48	$\overline{PCS5}$/A1	68	AD2
9	$\overline{RD}/\overline{QSMD}$	29	$\overline{TEST}$/BUSY	49	$\overline{PCS4}$	69	AD10 (A10)
10	ALE/QS0	30	NMI	50	$\overline{PCS3}$	70	AD3
11	N.C.	31	INT0	51	$\overline{PCS2}$	71	AD11 (A11)
12	V_{CC}	32	INT1/$\overline{SELECT}$	52	$\overline{PCS1}$	72	V_{CC}
13	V_{CC}	33	V_{CC}	53	V_{CC}	73	V_{CC}
14	N.C.	34	V_{CC}	54	$\overline{PCS0}$	74	AD4
15	N.C.	35	INT2/$\overline{INTA0}$	55	$\overline{RES}$	75	AD12 (A12)
16	X1	36	INT3/$\overline{INTA1}$	56	TMR OUT 1	76	AD5
17	X2	37	DT/$\overline{R}$	57	TMR OUT 0	77	AD13 (A13)
18	RESET	38	$\overline{DEN}$	58	TMR IN 1	78	AD6
19	CLKOUT	39	$\overline{MCS0}$/PEREQ	59	TMR IN 0	79	AD14 (A14)
20	ARDY	40	$\overline{MCS1}/\overline{ERROR}$	60	DRQ1	80	AD7

NOTE:
Pin names in parentheses apply to the 80C188XL.

Table 8. SQFP Pin Functions with Location

AD Bus	
AD0	1
AD1	3
AD2	6
AD3	8
AD4	12
AD5	14
AD6	16
AD7	18
AD8 (A8)	2
AD9 (A9)	5
AD10 (A10)	7
AD11 (A11)	9
AD12 (A12)	13
AD13 (A13)	15
AD14 (A14)	17
AD15 (A15)	19
A16/S3	21
A17/S4	22
A18/S5	23
A19/S6	24

Bus Control	
ALE/QS0	29
$\overline{BHE}$ ($\overline{RFSH}$)	26
$\overline{S0}$	40
$\overline{S1}$	39
$\overline{S2}$	38
$\overline{RD}$/$\overline{QSMD}$	28
$\overline{WR}$/QS1	27
ARDY	37
SRDY	44
$\overline{DEN}$	56
DT/$\overline{R}$	54
$\overline{LOCK}$	45
HOLD	43
HLDA	42

No Connection	
N.C.	4
N.C.	25
N.C.	35
N.C.	55
N.C.	72

Processor Control	
$\overline{RES}$	73
RESET	34
X1	32
X2	33
CLKOUT	36
$\overline{TEST}$/BUSY	46
NMI	47
INT0	48
INT1/$\overline{SELECT}$	49
INT2/$\overline{INTA0}$	52
INT3/$\overline{INTA1}$	53

Power and Ground	
V_{CC}	10
V_{CC}	11
V_{CC}	20
V_{CC}	50
V_{CC}	51
V_{CC}	61
V_{SS}	30
V_{SS}	31
V_{SS}	41
V_{SS}	70
V_{SS}	80

I/O	
$\overline{UCS}$	62
$\overline{LCS}$	63
$\overline{MCS0}$/PEREQ	57
$\overline{MCS1}$/$\overline{ERROR}$	58
$\overline{MCS2}$	59
$\overline{MCS3}$/$\overline{NPS}$	60
$\overline{PCS0}$	71
$\overline{PCS1}$	69
$\overline{PCS2}$	68
$\overline{PCS3}$	67
$\overline{PCS4}$	66
$\overline{PCS5}$/A1	65
$\overline{PCS6}$/A2	64
TMR IN 0	77
TMR IN 1	76
TMR OUT 0	75
TMR OUT 1	74
DRQ0	79
DRQ1	78

NOTE:
Pin names in parentheses apply to the 80C188XL.

Table 9. SQFP Pin Locations with Pin Names

1	AD0	21	A16/S3	41	V_{SS}	61	V_{CC}
2	AD8 (A8)	22	A17/S4	42	HLDA	62	$\overline{UCS}$
3	AD1	23	A18/S5	43	HOLD	63	$\overline{LCS}$
4	N.C.	24	A19/S6	44	SRDY	64	$\overline{PCS6}$/A2
5	AD9 (A9)	25	N.C.	45	$\overline{LOCK}$	65	$\overline{PCS5}$/A1
6	AD2	26	$\overline{BHE}$ ($\overline{RFSH}$)	46	$\overline{TEST}$/BUSY	66	$\overline{PCS4}$
7	AD10 (A10)	27	$\overline{WR}$/QS1	47	NMI	67	$\overline{PCS3}$
8	AD3	28	$\overline{RD}$/$\overline{QSMD}$	48	INT0	68	$\overline{PCS2}$
9	AD11 (A11)	29	ALE/QS0	49	INT1/$\overline{SELECT}$	69	$\overline{PCS1}$
10	V_{CC}	30	V_{SS}	50	V_{CC}	70	V_{SS}
11	V_{CC}	31	V_{SS}	51	V_{CC}	71	$\overline{PCS0}$
12	AD4	32	X1	52	INT2/$\overline{INTA0}$	72	N.C.
13	AD12 (A12)	33	X2	53	INT3/$\overline{INTA1}$	73	$\overline{RES}$
14	AD5	34	RESET	54	DT/$\overline{R}$	74	TMR OUT 1
15	AD13 (A13)	35	N.C.	55	N.C.	75	TMR OUT 0
16	AD6	36	CLKOUT	56	$\overline{DEN}$	76	TMR IN 1
17	AD14 (A14)	37	ARDY	57	$\overline{MCS0}$/PEREQ	77	TMR IN 0
18	AD7	38	$\overline{S2}$	58	$\overline{MCS1}$/$\overline{ERROR}$	78	DRQ1
19	AD15 (A15)	39	$\overline{S1}$	59	$\overline{MCS2}$	79	DRQ0
20	V_{CC}	40	$\overline{S0}$	60	$\overline{MCS3}$/$\overline{NPS}$	80	V_{SS}

NOTE:
Pin names in parentheses apply to the 80C188XL.

ELECTRICAL SPECIFICATIONS

Absolute Maximum Ratings*

Ambient Temperature under Bias .... 0°C to +70°C

Storage Temperature .... −65°C to +150°C

Voltage on Any Pin with Respect to Ground .... −1.0V to +7.0V

Package Power Dissipation 1W

Not to exceed the maximum allowable die temperature based on thermal resistance of the package.

NOTICE: This data sheet contains preliminary information on new products in production. The specifications are subject to change without notice. Verify with your local Intel Sales office that you have the latest data sheet before finalizing a design.

**WARNING: Stressing the device beyond the "Absolute Maximum Ratings" may cause permanent damage. These are stress ratings only. Operation beyond the "Operating Conditions" is not recommended and extended exposure beyond the "Operating Conditions" may affect device reliability.*

NOTICE: The specifications are subject to change without notice.

DC SPECIFICATIONS T_A = 0°C to +70°C, V_{CC} = 5V ±10%

Symbol	Parameter	Min	Max	Units	Test Conditions
V_{IL}	Input Low Voltage (Except X1)	−0.5	0.2 V_{CC} − 0.3	V	
V_{IL1}	Clock Input Low Voltage (X1)	−0.5	0.6	V	
V_{IH}	Input High Voltage (All except X1 and $\overline{RES}$)	0.2 V_{CC} + 0.9	V_{CC} + 0.5	V	
V_{IH1}	Input High Voltage ($\overline{RES}$)	3.0	V_{CC} + 0.5	V	
V_{IH2}	Clock Input High Voltage (X1)	3.9	V_{CC} + 0.5	V	
V_{OL}	Output Low Voltage		0.45	V	I_{OL} = 2.5 mA (S0, 1, 2) I_{OL} = 2.0 mA (others)
V_{OH}	Output High Voltage	2.4	V_{CC}	V	I_{OH} = −2.4 mA @ 2.4V (4)
		V_{CC} − 0.5	V_{CC}	V	I_{OH} = −200 μA @ V_{CC} −0.5(4)
I_{CC}	Power Supply Current		100	mA	@ 20 MHz, 0°C V_{CC} = 5.5V(3)
			62.5	mA	@ 12 MHz, 0°C V_{CC} = 5.5V (3)
			100	μA	@ DC 0°C V_{CC} = 5.5V
I_{LI}	Input Leakage Current		±10	μA	@ 0.5 MHz, 0.45V ≤ V_{IN} ≤ V_{CC}
I_{LO}	Output Leakage Current		±10	μA	@ 0.5 MHz, 0.45V ≤ V_{OUT} ≤ V_{CC}(1)
V_{CLO}	Clock Output Low		0.45	V	I_{CLO} = 4.0 mA

DC SPECIFICATIONS (Continued) T_A = 0°C to +70°C, V_{CC} = 5V ±10%

Symbol	Parameter	Min	Max	Units	Test Conditions
V_{CHO}	Clock Output High	$V_{CC} - 0.5$		V	$I_{CHO} = -500\ \mu A$
C_{IN}	Input Capacitance		10	pF	@ 1 MHz(2)
C_{IO}	Output or I/O Capacitance		20	pF	@ 1 MHz(2)

NOTES:
1. Pins being floated during HOLD or by invoking the ONCE Mode.
2. Characterization conditions are a) Frequency = 1 MHz; b) Unmeasured pins at GND; c) V_{IN} at + 5.0V or 0.45V. This parameter is not tested.
3. Current is measured with the device in RESET with X1 and X2 driven and all other non-power pins open.
4. $\overline{RD}/\overline{QSMD}$, $\overline{UCS}$, $\overline{LCS}$, $\overline{MCS0}$/PEREQ, $\overline{MCS1}/\overline{ERROR}$ and $\overline{TEST}$/BUSY pins have internal pullup devices. Loading some of these pins above $I_{OH} = -200\ \mu A$ can cause the processor to go into alternative modes of operation. See the section on Local Bus Controller and Reset for details.

Power Supply Current

Current is linearly proportional to clock frequency and is measured with the device in RESET with X1 and X2 driven and all other non-power pins open.

Maximum current is given by I_{CC} = 5 mA × freq. (MHz) + I_{QL}.

I_{QL} is the quiescent leakage current when the clock is static. I_{QL} is typically less than 100 μA.

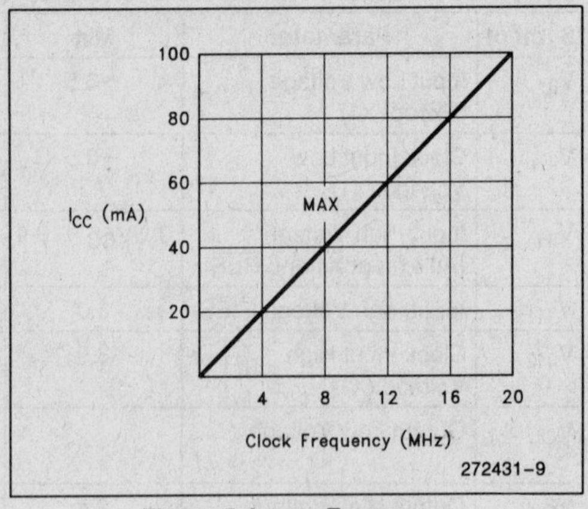

Figure 5. I_{CC} vs Frequency

AC SPECIFICATIONS

MAJOR CYCLE TIMINGS (READ CYCLE)

T_A = 0°C to +70°C, V_{CC} = 5V ±10%
All timings are measured at 1.5V and 50 pF loading on CLKOUT unless otherwise noted.
All output test conditions are with C_L = 50 pF.
For AC tests, input V_{IL} = 0.45V and V_{IH} = 2.4V except at X1 where V_{IH} = V_{CC} − 0.5V.

Symbol	Parameter	Values				Unit	Test Conditions
		80C186XL12		80C186XL20			
		Min	Max	Min	Max		
80C186XL GENERAL TIMING REQUIREMENTS (Listed More Than Once)							
T_{DVCL}	Data in Setup (A/D)	15		10		ns	
T_{CLDX}	Data in Hold (A/D)	3		3		ns	
80C186XL GENERAL TIMING RESPONSES (Listed More Than Once)							
T_{CHSV}	Status Active Delay	3	35	3	25	ns	
T_{CLSH}	Status Inactive Delay	3	35	3	25	ns	
T_{CLAV}	Address Valid Delay	3	36	3	27	ns	
T_{CLAX}	Address Hold	0		0		ns	
T_{CLDV}	Data Valid Delay	3	36	3	27	ns	
T_{CHDX}	Status Hold Time	10		10		ns	
T_{CHLH}	ALE Active Delay		25		20	ns	
T_{LHLL}	ALE Width	T_{CLCL} − 15		T_{CLCL} − 15		ns	
T_{CHLL}	ALE Inactive Delay		25		20	ns	
T_{AVLL}	Address Valid to ALE Low	T_{CLCH} − 15		T_{CLCH} − 10		ns	Equal Loading
T_{LLAX}	Address Hold from ALE Inactive	T_{CHCL} − 15		T_{CHCL} − 10		ns	Equal Loading
T_{AVCH}	Address Valid to Clock High	0		0		ns	
T_{CLAZ}	Address Float Delay	T_{CLAX}	25	T_{CLAX}	20	ns	
T_{CLCSV}	Chip-Select Active Delay	3	33	3	25	ns	
T_{CXCSX}	Chip-Select Hold from Command Inactive	T_{CLCH} − 10		T_{CLCH} − 10		ns	Equal Loading
T_{CHCSX}	Chip-Select Inactive Delay	3	30	3	20	ns	
T_{DXDL}	$\overline{DEN}$ Inactive to DT/$\overline{R}$ Low	0		0		ns	Equal Loading
T_{CVCTV}	Control Active Delay 1	3	37	3		ns	
T_{CVDEX}	$\overline{DEN}$ Inactive Delay	3	37	3		ns	
T_{CHCTV}	Control Active Delay 2	3	37	3		ns	
T_{CLLV}	$\overline{LOCK}$ Valid/Invalid Delay	3	37	3		ns	

2

AC SPECIFICATIONS (Continued)

MAJOR CYCLE TIMINGS (READ CYCLE) (Continued)
T_A = 0°C to +70°C, V_{CC} = 5V ±10%
All timings are measured at 1.5V and 50 pF loading on CLKOUT unless otherwise noted.
All output test conditions are with C_L = 50 pF.
For AC tests, input V_{IL} = 0.45V and V_{IH} = 2.4V except at X1 where V_{IH} = V_{CC} − 0.5V.

Symbol	Parameter	Values				Unit	Test Conditions
		80C186XL12		80C186XL20			
		Min	Max	Min	Max		
80C186XL TIMING RESPONSES (Read Cycle)							
T_{AZRL}	Address Float to $\overline{RD}$ Active	0		0		ns	
T_{CLRL}	$\overline{RD}$ Active Delay	3	37	3	27	ns	
T_{RLRH}	$\overline{RD}$ Pulse Width	$2T_{CLCL} - 25$		$2T_{CLCL} - 20$		ns	
T_{CLRH}	$\overline{RD}$ Inactive Delay	3	37	3	27	ns	
T_{RHLH}	$\overline{RD}$ Inactive to ALE High	$T_{CLCH} - 14$		$T_{CLCH} - 14$		ns	Equal Loading
T_{RHAV}	$\overline{RD}$ Inactive to Address Active	$T_{CLCL} - 15$		$T_{CLCL} - 15$		ns	Equal Loading

PRELIMINARY

AC SPECIFICATIONS (Continued)

MAJOR CYCLE TIMINGS (WRITE CYCLE)

T_A = 0°C to +70°C, V_{CC} = 5V ±10%
All timings are measured at 1.5V and 50 pF loading on CLKOUT unless otherwise noted.
All output test conditions are with C_L = 50 pF.
For AC tests, input V_{IL} = 0.45V and V_{IH} = 2.4V except at X1 where V_{IH} = V_{CC} − 0.5V.

Symbol	Parameter	Values				Unit	Test Conditions
		80C186XL12		80C186XL20			
		Min	Max	Min	Max		
80C186XL GENERAL TIMING RESPONSES (Listed More Than Once)							
T_{CHSV}	Status Active Delay	3	35	3	25	ns	
T_{CLSH}	Status Inactive Delay	3	35	3	25	ns	
T_{CLAV}	Address Valid Delay	3	36	3	27	ns	
T_{CLAX}	Address Hold	0		0		ns	
T_{CLDV}	Data Valid Delay	3	36	3	27	ns	
T_{CHDX}	Status Hold Time	10		10		ns	
T_{CHLH}	ALE Active Delay		25		20	ns	
T_{LHLL}	ALE Width	T_{CLCL} − 15		T_{CLCL} − 15		ns	
T_{CHLL}	ALE Inactive Delay		25		20	ns	
T_{AVLL}	Address Valid to ALE Low	T_{CLCH} − 15		T_{CLCH} − 10		ns	Equal Loading
T_{LLAX}	Address Hold from ALE Inactive	T_{CHCL} − 15		T_{CHCL} − 10		ns	Equal Loading
T_{AVCH}	Address Valid to Clock High	0		0		ns	
T_{CLDOX}	Data Hold Time	3		3		ns	
T_{CVCTV}	Control Active Delay 1	3	37	3	25	ns	
T_{CVCTX}	Control Inactive Delay	3	37	3	25	ns	
T_{CLCSV}	Chip-Select Active Delay	3	33	3	25	ns	
T_{CXCSX}	Chip-Select Hold from Command Inactive	T_{CLCH} − 10		T_{CLCH} − 10		ns	Equal Loading
T_{CHCSX}	Chip-Select Inactive Delay	3	30	3	20	ns	
T_{DXDL}	$\overline{DEN}$ Inactive to DT/$\overline{R}$ Low	0		0		ns	Equal Loading
T_{CLLV}	$\overline{LOCK}$ Valid/Invalid Delay	3	37	3	22	ns	
80C186XL TIMING RESPONSES (Write Cycle)							
T_{WLWH}	$\overline{WR}$ Pulse Width	$2T_{CLCL}$ − 25		$2T_{CLCL}$ − 20		ns	
T_{WHLH}	$\overline{WR}$ Inactive to ALE High	T_{CLCH} − 14		T_{CLCH} − 14		ns	Equal Loading
T_{WHDX}	Data Hold after $\overline{WR}$	T_{CLCL} − 20		T_{CLCL} − 15		ns	Equal Loading
T_{WHDEX}	$\overline{WR}$ Inactive to $\overline{DEN}$ Inactive	T_{CLCH} − 10		T_{CLCH} − 10		ns	Equal Loading

AC SPECIFICATIONS (Continued)

MAJOR CYCLE TIMINGS (INTERRUPT ACKNOWLEDGE CYCLE)

T_A = 0°C to +70°C, V_{CC} = 5V ±10%
All timings are measured at 1.5V and 50 pF loading on CLKOUT unless otherwise noted.
All output test conditions are with C_L = 50 pF.
For AC tests, input V_{IL} = 0.45V and V_{IH} = 2.4V except at X1 where V_{IH} = V_{CC} − 0.5V.

Symbol	Parameter	Values				Unit	Test Conditions
		80C186XL12		80C186XL20			
		Min	Max	Min	Max		
80C186XL GENERAL TIMING REQUIREMENTS (Listed More Than Once)							
T_{DVCL}	Data in Setup (A/D)	15		10		ns	
T_{CLDX}	Data in Hold (A/D)	3		3		ns	
80C186XL GENERAL TIMING RESPONSES (Listed More Than Once)							
T_{CHSV}	Status Active Delay	3	35	3	25	ns	
T_{CLSH}	Status Inactive Delay	3	35	3	25	ns	
T_{CLAV}	Address Valid Delay	3	36	3	27	ns	
T_{AVCH}	Address Valid to Clock High	0		0		ns	
T_{CLAX}	Address Hold	0		0		ns	
T_{CLDV}	Data Valid Delay	3	36	3	27	ns	
T_{CHDX}	Status Hold Time	10		10		ns	
T_{CHLH}	ALE Active Delay		25		20	ns	
T_{LHLL}	ALE Width	T_{CLCL} − 15		T_{CLCL} − 15		ns	
T_{CHLL}	ALE Inactive Delay		25		20	ns	
T_{AVLL}	Address Valid to ALE Low	T_{CLCH} − 15		T_{CLCH} − 10		ns	Equal Loading
T_{LLAX}	Address Hold to ALE Inactive	T_{CHCL} − 15		T_{CHCL} − 10		ns	Equal Loading
T_{CLAZ}	Address Float Delay	T_{CLAX}	25	T_{CLAX}	20	ns	
T_{CVCTV}	Control Active Delay 1	3	37	3	25	ns	
T_{CVCTX}	Control Inactive Delay	3	37	3	25	ns	
T_{DXDL}	$\overline{DEN}$ Inactive to DT/$\overline{R}$ Low	0		0		ns	Equal Loading
T_{CHCTV}	Control Active Delay 2	3	37	3	22	ns	
T_{CVDEX}	$\overline{DEN}$ Inactive Delay (Non-Write Cycles)	3	37	3	22	ns	
T_{CLLV}	$\overline{LOCK}$ Valid/Invalid Delay	3	37	3	22	ns	

AC SPECIFICATIONS (Continued)

SOFTWARE HALT CYCLE TIMINGS

T_A = 0°C to +70°C, V_{CC} = 5V ±10%
All timings are measured at 1.5V and 50 pF loading on CLKOUT unless otherwise noted.
All output test conditions are with C_L = 50 pF.
For AC tests, input V_{IL} = 0.45V and V_{IH} = 2.4V except at X1 where V_{IH} = V_{CC} − 0.5V.

Symbol	Parameter	Values				Unit	Test Conditions
		80C186XL12		80C186XL20			
		Min	Max	Min	Max		
80C186XL GENERAL TIMING REQUIREMENTS (Listed More Than Once)							
T_{CHSV}	Status Active Delay	3	35	3	25	ns	
T_{CLSH}	Status Inactive Delay	3	35	3	25	ns	
T_{CLAV}	Address Valid Delay	3	36	3	27	ns	
T_{CHLH}	ALE Active Delay		25		20	ns	
T_{LHLL}	ALE Width	T_{CLCL} − 15		T_{CLCL} − 15		ns	
T_{CHLL}	ALE Inactive Delay		25		20	ns	
T_{DXDL}	$\overline{DEN}$ Inactive to DT/$\overline{R}$ Low		0		0	ns	Equal Loading
T_{CHCTV}	Control Active Delay 2	3	37	3	22	ns	

AC SPECIFICATIONS (Continued)

CLOCK TIMINGS

T_A = 0°C to +70°C, V_{CC} = 5V ±10%
All timings are measured at 1.5V and 50 pF loading on CLKOUT unless otherwise noted.
All output test conditions are with C_L = 50 pF.
For AC tests, input V_{IL} = 0.45V and V_{IH} = 2.4V except at X1 where V_{IH} = V_{CC} − 0.5V.

Symbol	Parameter	Values				Unit	Test Conditions
		80C186XL12		80C186XL20			
		Min	Max	Min	Max		
80C186XL CLKIN REQUIREMENTS[(1)]							
T_{CKIN}	CLKIN Period	40	∞	25	∞	ns	
T_{CLCK}	CLKIN Low Time	16	∞	10	∞	ns	1.5V[(2)]
T_{CHCK}	CLKIN High Time	16	∞	10	∞	ns	1.5V[(2)]
T_{CKHL}	CLKIN Fall Time		5		5	ns	3.5 to 1.0V
T_{CKLH}	CLKIN Rise Time		5		5	ns	1.0 to 3.5V
80C186XL CLKOUT TIMING							
T_{CICO}	CLKIN to CLKOUT Skew		21		17	ns	
T_{CLCL}	CLKOUT Period	80	∞	50		ns	
T_{CLCH}	CLKOUT Low Time	0.5 T_{CLCL} − 5		0.5 T_{CLCL} − 5		ns	C_L = 100 pF[(3)]
T_{CHCL}	CLKOUT High Time	0.5 T_{CLCL} − 5		0.5 T_{CLCL} − 5		ns	C_L = 100 pF[(4)]
T_{CH1CH2}	CLKOUT Rise Time		10		8	ns	1.0 to 3.5V
T_{CL2CL1}	CLKOUT Fall Time		10		8	ns	3.5 to 1.0V

NOTES:
1. External clock applied to X1 and X2 not connected.
2. T_{CLCK} and T_{CHCK} (CLKIN Low and High times) should not have a duration less than 40% of T_{CKIN}.
3. Tested under worst case conditions: V_{CC} = 5.5V. T_A = 70°C.
4. Tested under worst case conditions: V_{CC} = 4.5V. T_A = 0°C.

AC SPECIFICATIONS (Continued)

READY, PERIPHERAL AND QUEUE STATUS TIMINGS

T_A = 0°C to +70°C, V_{CC} = 5V ±10%
All timings are measured at 1.5V and 50 pF loading on CLKOUT unless otherwise noted.
All output test conditions are with C_L = 50 pF.
For AC tests, input V_{IL} = 0.45V and V_{IH} = 2.4V except at X1 where V_{IH} = V_{CC} − 0.5V.

Symbol	Parameter	Values				Unit	Test Conditions
		80C186XL12		80C186XL20			
		Min	Max	Min	Max		
80C186XL READY AND PERIPHERAL TIMING REQUIREMENTS (Listed More Than Once)							
T_{SRYCL}	Synchronous Ready (SRDY) Transition Setup Time(1)	15		10		ns	
T_{CLSRY}	SRDY Transition Hold Time(1)	15		10		ns	
T_{ARYCH}	ARDY Resolution Transition Setup Time(2)	15		10		ns	
T_{CLARX}	ARDY Active Hold Time(1)	15		10		ns	
T_{ARYCHL}	ARDY Inactive Holding Time	15		10		ns	
T_{ARYLCL}	Asynchronous Ready (ARDY) Setup Time(1)	25		15		ns	
T_{INVCH}	INTx, NMI, $\overline{TEST}$/BUSY, TMR IN Setup Time(2)	15		10		ns	
T_{INVCL}	DRQ0, DRQ1 Setup Time(2)	15		10		ns	
80C186XL PERIPHERAL AND QUEUE STATUS TIMING RESPONSES							
T_{CLTMV}	Timer Output Delay		33		22	ns	
T_{CHQSV}	Queue Status Delay		32		27	ns	

NOTES:
1. To guarantee proper operation.
2. To guarantee recognition at clock edge.

2

AC SPECIFICATIONS (Continued)

RESET AND HOLD/HLDA TIMINGS

T_A = 0°C to +70°C, V_{CC} = 5V ±10%
All timings are measured at 1.5V and 50 pF loading on CLKOUT unless otherwise noted.
All output test conditions are with C_L = 50 pF.
For AC tests, input V_{IL} = 0.45V and V_{IH} = 2.4V except at X1 where V_{IH} = V_{CC} − 0.5V.

Symbol	Parameter	Values				Unit	Test Conditions
		80C186XL12		80C186XL20			
		Min	Max	Min	Max		
80C186XL RESET AND HOLD/HLDA TIMING REQUIREMENTS							
T_{RESIN}	$\overline{RES}$ Setup	15		15		ns	
T_{HVCL}	HOLD Setup(1)	15		10		ns	
80C186XL GENERAL TIMING RESPONSES (Listed More Than Once)							
T_{CLAZ}	Address Float Delay	T_{CLAX}	25	T_{CLAX}	20	ns	
T_{CLAV}	Address Valid Delay	3	36	3	22	ns	
80C186XL RESET AND HOLD/HLDA TIMING RESPONSES							
T_{CLRO}	Reset Delay		33		22	ns	
T_{CLHAV}	HLDA Valid Delay	3	33	3	22	ns	
T_{CHCZ}	Command Lines Float Delay		33		25	ns	
T_{CHCV}	Command Lines Valid Delay (after Float)		36		26	ns	

NOTE:
1. To guarantee recognition at next clock.

AC SPECIFICATIONS (Continued)

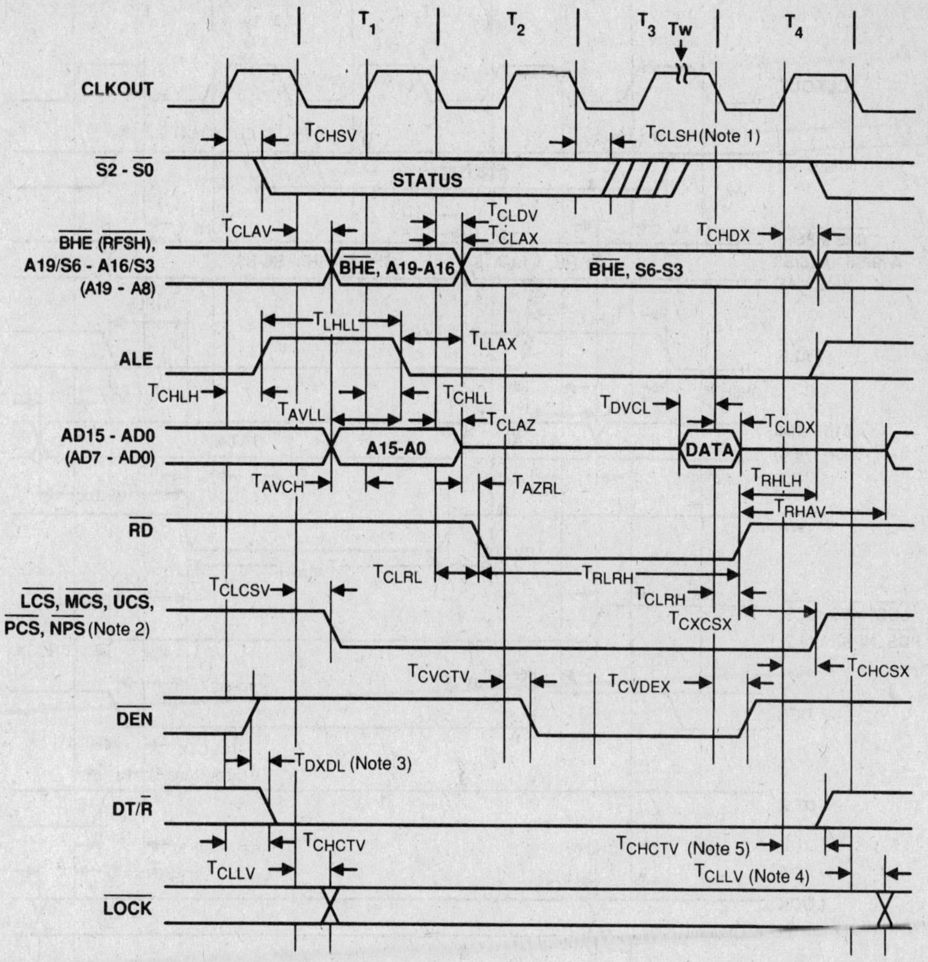

NOTES:

1. Status inactive in state preceding T_4.
2. If latched A_1 and A_2 are selected instead of $\overline{PCS5}$ and $\overline{PCS6}$, only T_{CLCSV} is applicable.
3. For write cycle followed by read cycle.
4. T_1 of next bus cycle.
5. Changes in T-state preceding next bus cycle if followed by write.

Pin names in parentheses apply to the 80C188XL.

Figure 6. Read Cycle Waveforms

AC SPECIFICATIONS (Continued)

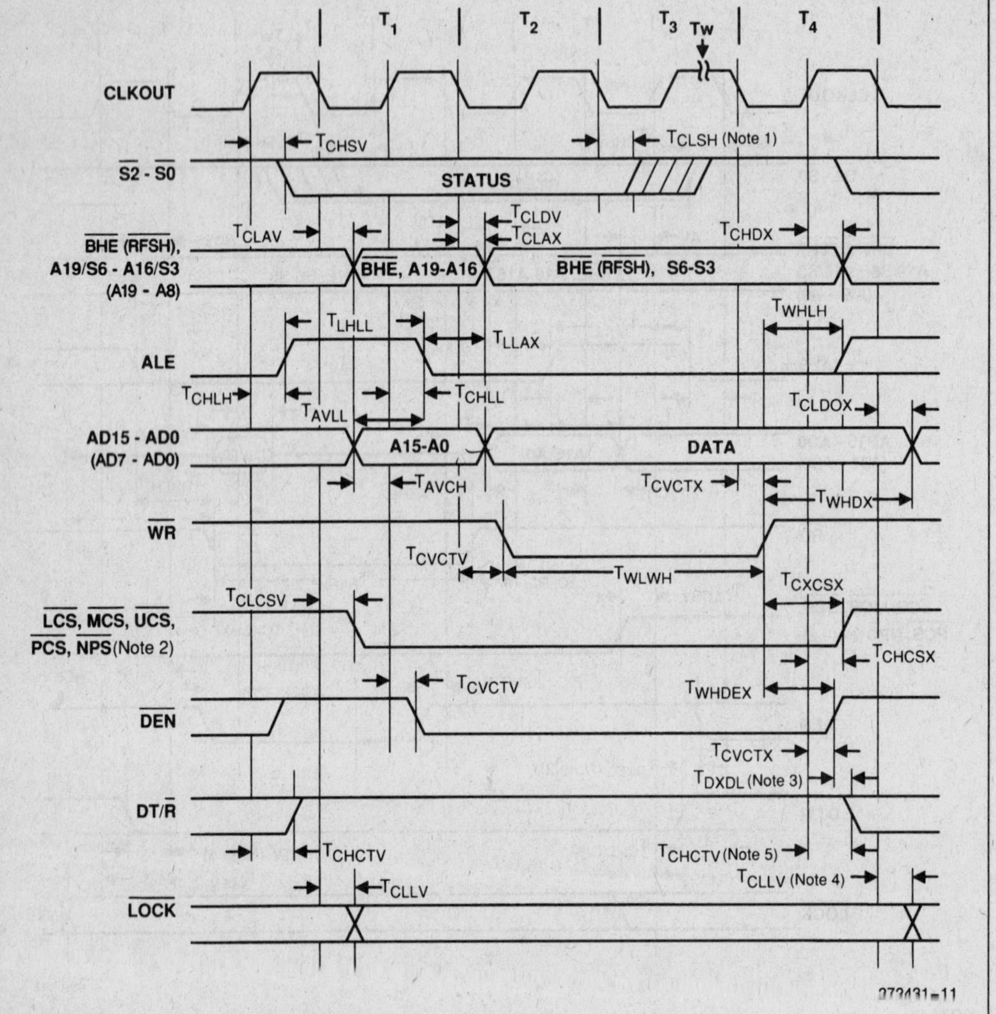

NOTES:

1. Status inactive in state preceding T_4.
2. If latched A_1 and A_2 are selected instead of $\overline{PCS5}$ and $\overline{PCS6}$, only T_{CLCSV} is applicable.
3. For write cycle followed by read cycle.
4. T_1 of next bus cycle.
5. Changes in T-state preceding next bus cycle if followed by read, INTA, or halt.

Pin names in parentheses apply to the 80C188XL.

Figure 7. Write Cycle Waveforms

AC SPECIFICATIONS (Continued)

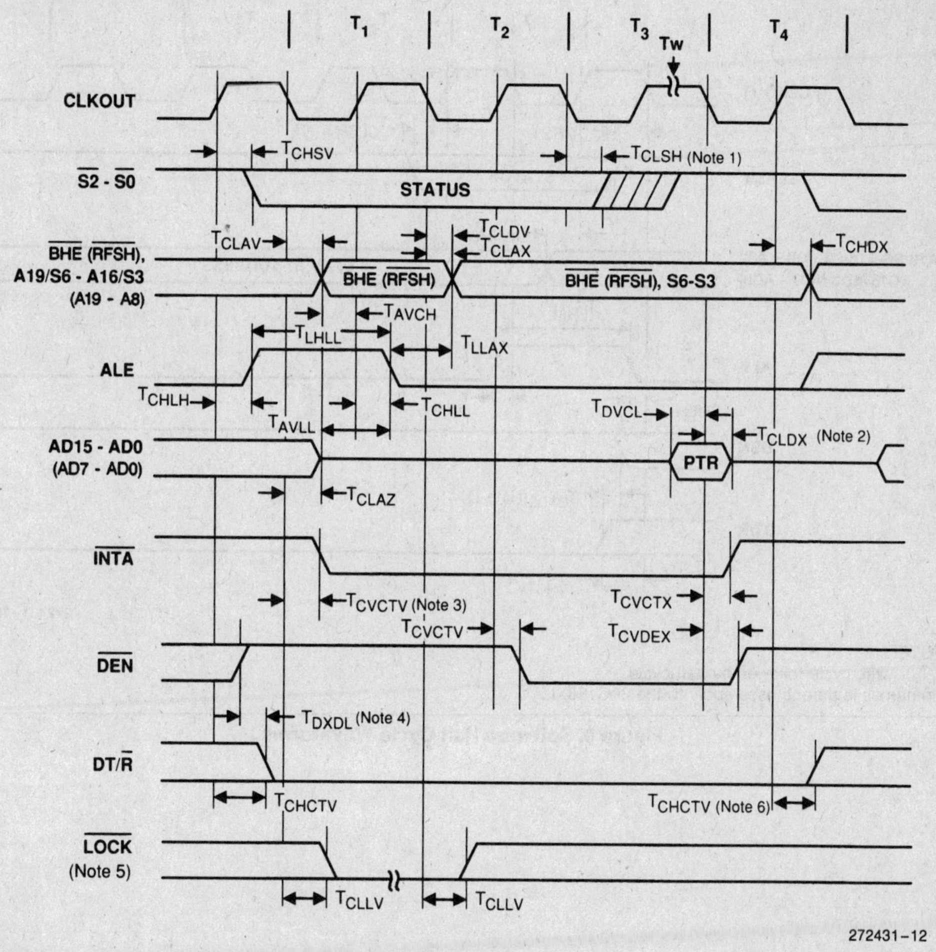

NOTES:
1. Status inactive in state preceding T_4.
2. The data hold time lasts only until $\overline{\text{INTA}}$ goes inactive, even if the $\overline{\text{INTA}}$ transition occurs prior to T_{CLDX} (min).
3. $\overline{\text{INTA}}$ occurs one clock later in Slave Mode.
4. For write cycle followed by interrupt acknowledge cycle.
5. $\overline{\text{LOCK}}$ is active upon T_1 of the first interrupt acknowledge cycle and inactive upon T_2 of the second interrupt acknowledge cycle.
6. Changes in T-state preceding next bus cycle if followed by write.

Pin names in parentheses apply to the 80C188XL.

Figure 8. Interrupt Acknowledge Cycle Waveforms

AC SPECIFICATIONS (Continued)

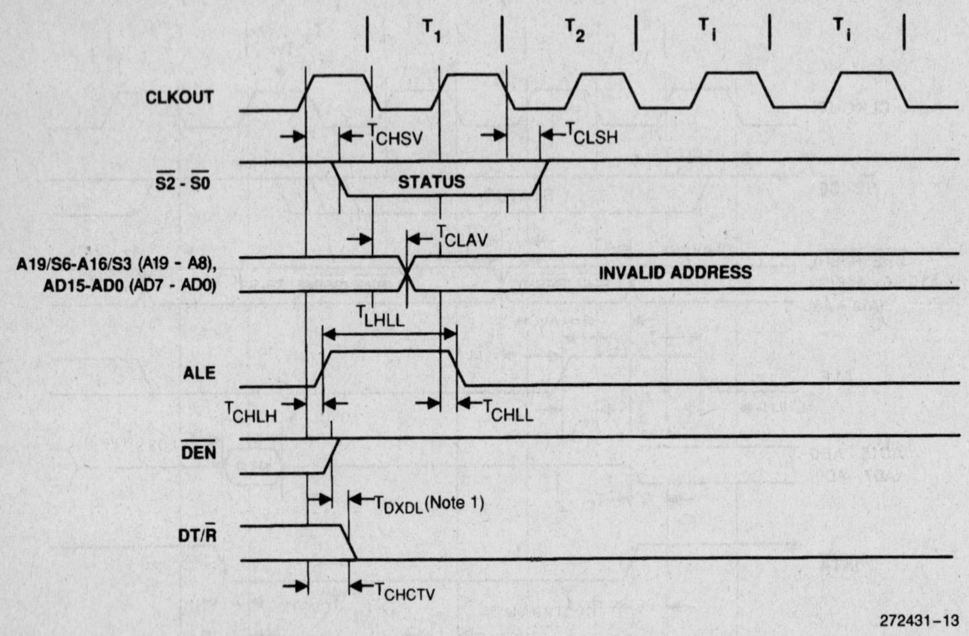

NOTE:
1. For write cycle followed by halt cycle.
Pin names in parentheses apply to the 80C188XL.

Figure 9. Software Halt Cycle Waveforms

WAVEFORMS

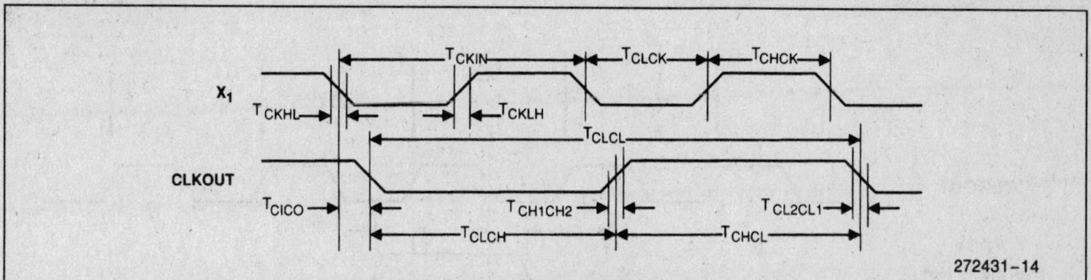

Figure 10. Clock Waveforms

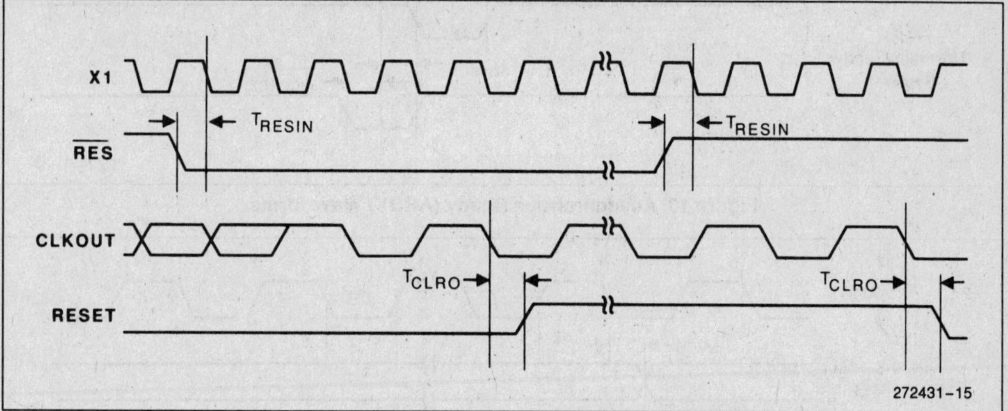

Figure 11. Reset Waveforms

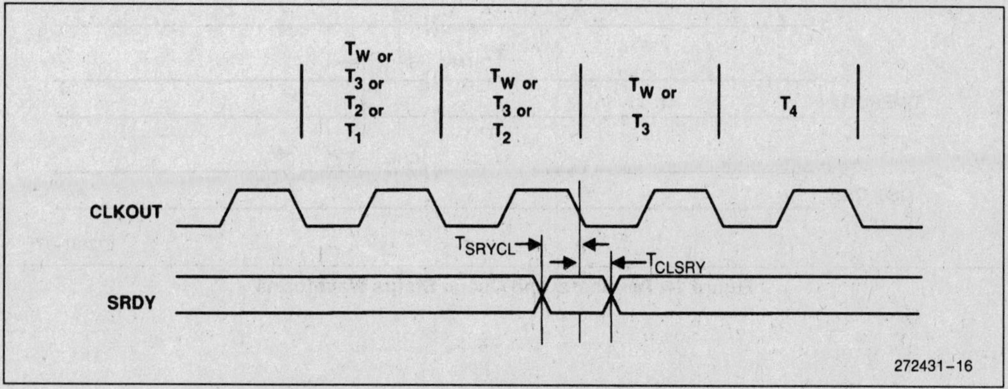

Figure 12. Synchronous Ready (SRDY) Waveforms

AC CHARACTERISTICS

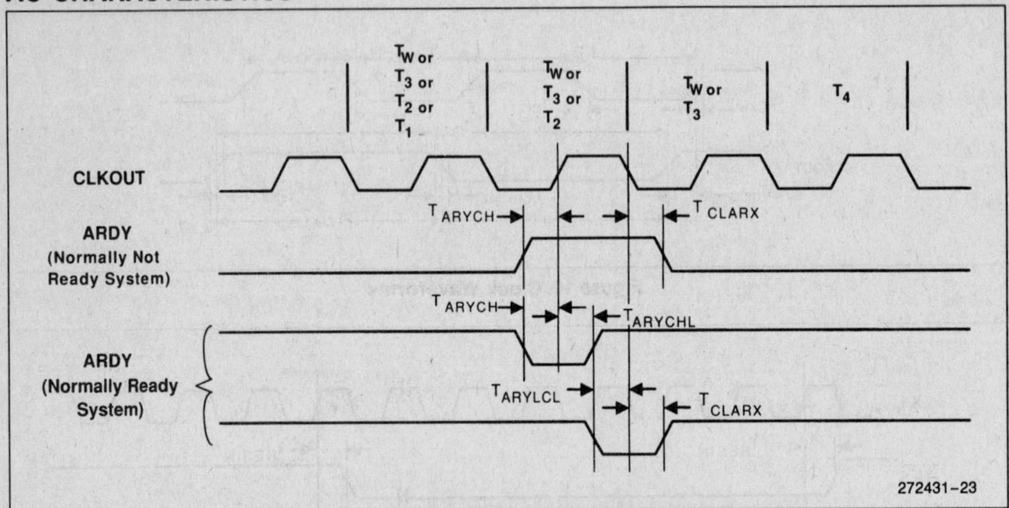

Figure 13. Asynchronous Ready (ARDY) Waveforms

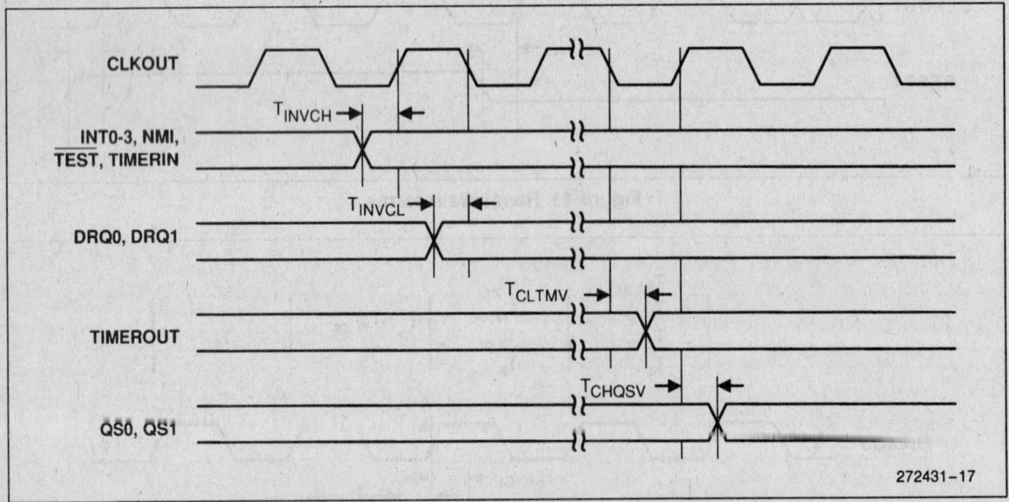

Figure 14. Peripheral and Queue Status Waveforms

AC CHARACTERISTICS (Continued)

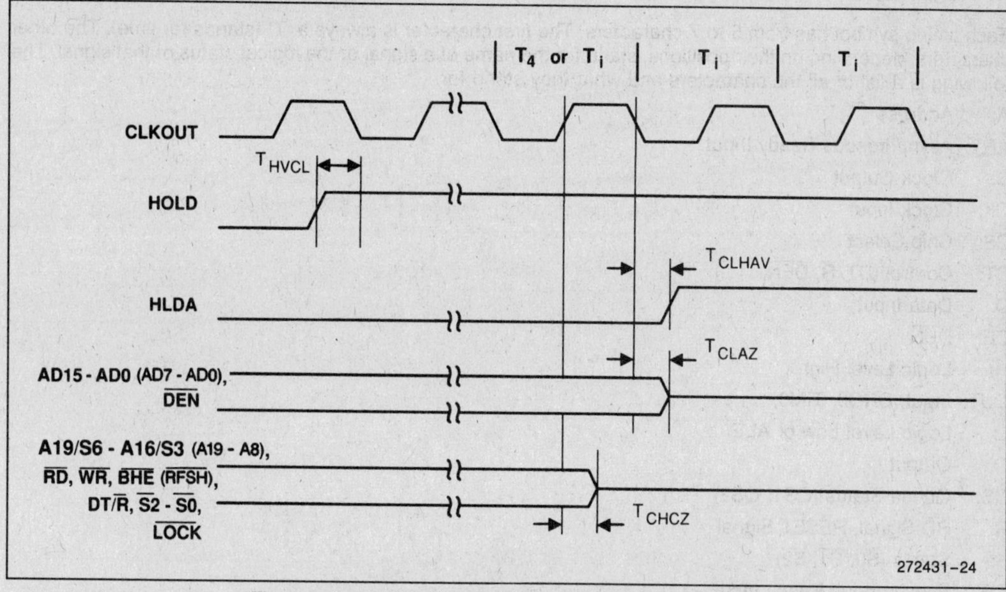

Figure 15. HOLDA/HLDA Waveforms (Entering Hold)

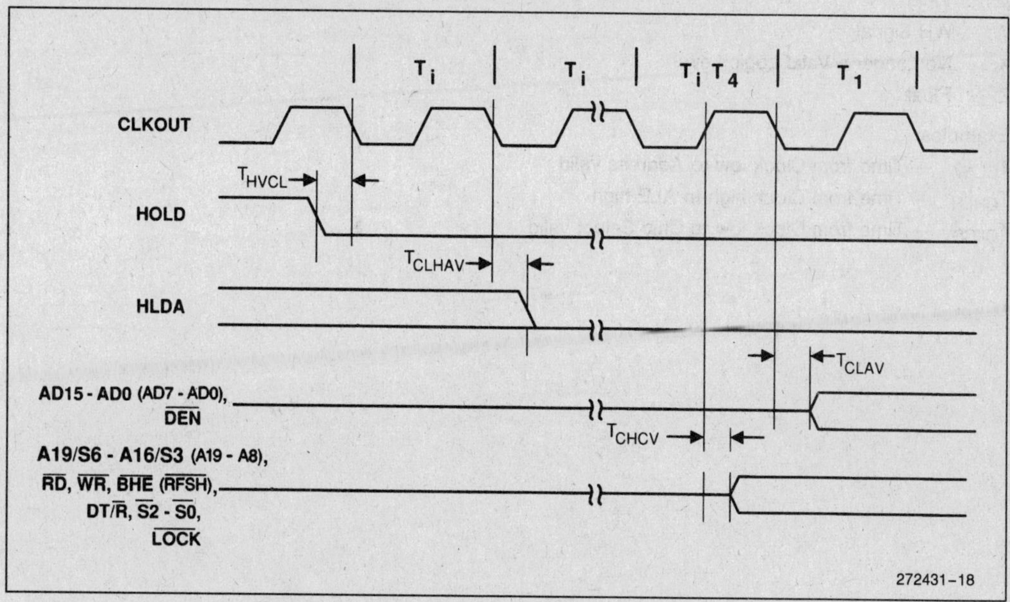

Figure 16. HOLD/HLDA Waveforms (Leaving Hold)

EXPLANATION OF THE AC SYMBOLS

Each timing symbol has from 5 to 7 characters. The first character is always a 'T' (stands for time). The other characters, depending on their positions, stand for the name of a signal or the logical status of that signal. The following is a list of all the characters and what they stand for.

A: Address
ARY: Asynchronous Ready Input
C: Clock Output
CK: Clock Input
CS: Chip Select
CT: Control (DT/$\overline{R}$, $\overline{DEN}$, . . .)
D: Data Input
DE: $\overline{DEN}$
H: Logic Level High
OUT: Input (DRQ0, TIM0, . . .)
L: Logic Level Low or ALE
O: Output
QS: Queue Status (QS1, QS2)
R: $\overline{RD}$ Signal, RESET Signal
S: Status ($\overline{S0}$, $\overline{S1}$, $\overline{S2}$)
SRY: Synchronous Ready Input
V: Valid
W: WR Signal
X: No Longer a Valid Logic Level
Z: Float

Examples:

T_{CLAV} — Time from Clock low to Address valid
T_{CHLH} — Time from Clock high to ALE high
T_{CLCSV} — Time from Clock low to Chip Select valid

DERATING CURVES

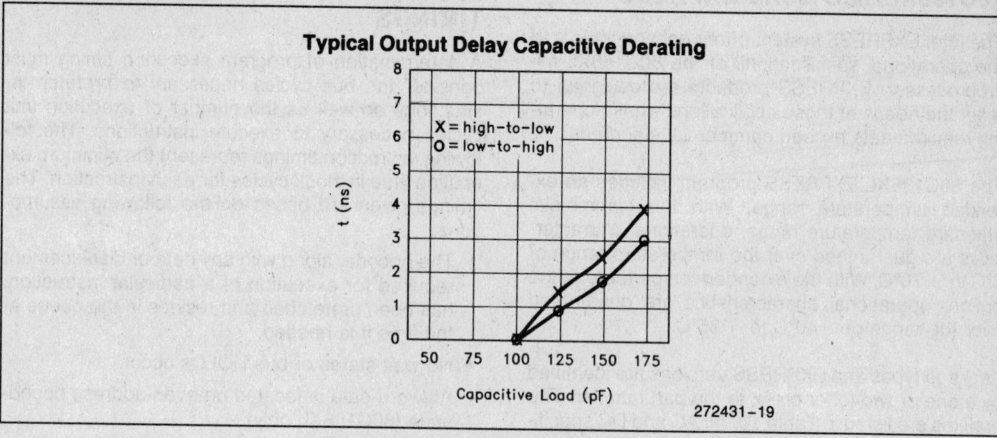

Figure 17. Capacitive Derating Curve

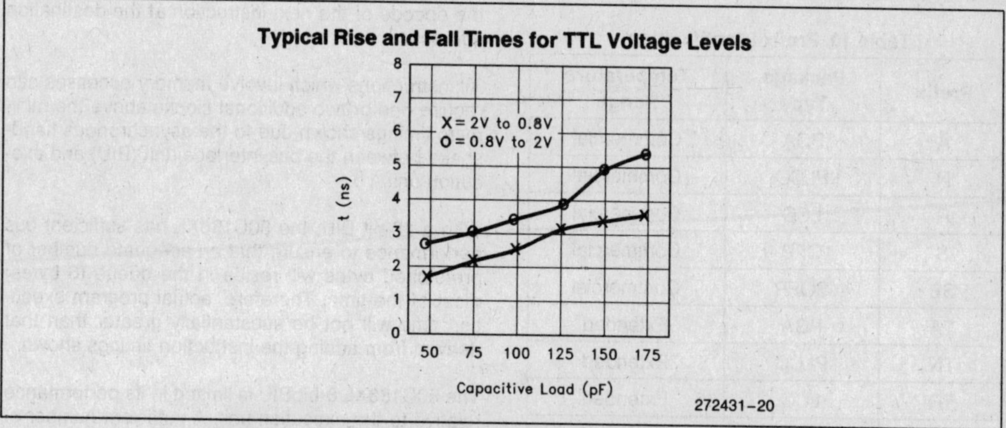

Figure 18. TTL Level Rise and Fall Times for Output Buffers

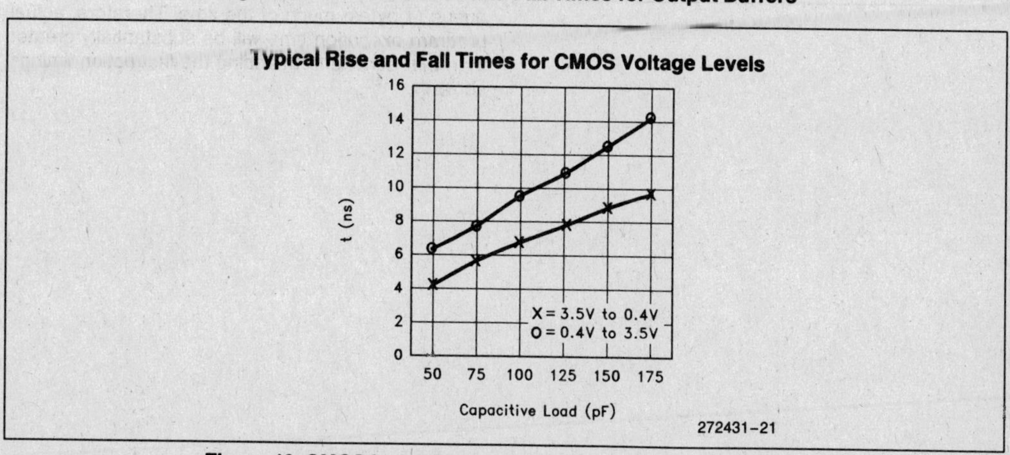

Figure 19. CMOS Level Rise and Fall Times for Output Buffers

80C186XL/80C188XL EXPRESS

The Intel EXPRESS system offers enhancements to the operational specifications of the 80C186XL microprocessor. EXPRESS products are designed to meet the needs of those applications whose operating requirements exceed commercial standards.

The 80C186XL EXPRESS program includes an extended temperature range. With the commercial standard temperature range, operational characteristics are guaranteed over the temperature range of 0°C to +70°C. With the extended temperature range option, operational characteristics are guaranteed over the range of −40°C to +85°C.

Package types and EXPRESS versions are identified by a one or two-letter prefix to the part number. The prefixes are listed in Table 10. All AC and DC specifications not mentioned in this section are the same for both commercial and EXPRESS parts.

Table 10. Prefix Identification

Prefix	Package Type	Temperature Range
A	PGA	Commercial
N	PLCC	Commercial
R	LCC	Commercial
S	QFP	Commercial
SB	SQFP	Commercial
TA	PGA	Extended
TN	PLCC	Extended
TR	LCC	Extended
TS	QFP	Extended

80C186XL/80C188XL EXECUTION TIMINGS

A determination of program execution timing must consider the bus cycles necessary to prefetch instructions as well as the number of execution unit cycles necessary to execute instructions. The following instruction timings represent the minimum execution time in clock cycles for each instruction. The timings given are based on the following assumptions:

- The opcode, along with any data or displacement required for execution of a particular instruction, has been prefetched and resides in the queue at the time it is needed.
- No wait states or bus HOLDs occur.
- All word-data is located on even-address boundaries (80C186XL only).

All jumps and calls include the time required to fetch the opcode of the next instruction at the destination address.

All instructions which involve memory accesses can require one or two additional clocks above the minimum timings shown due to the asynchronous handshake between the bus interface unit (BIU) and execution unit.

With a 16-bit BIU, the 80C186XL has sufficient bus performance to ensure that an adequate number of prefetched bytes will reside in the queue (6 bytes) most of the time. Therefore, actual program execution time will not be substantially greater than that derived from adding the instruction timings shown.

The 80C188XL 8-bit BIU is limited in its performance relative to the execution unit. A sufficient number of prefetched bytes may not reside in the prefetch queue (4 bytes) much of the time. Therefore, actual program execution time will be substantially greater than that derived from adding the instruction timings shown.

INSTRUCTION SET SUMMARY

Function	Format				80C186XL Clock Cycles	80C188XL Clock Cycles	Comments
DATA TRANSFER							
MOV = Move:							
Register to Register/Memory	1000100w	mod reg r/m			2/12	2/12*	
Register/memory to register	1000101w	mod reg r/m			2/9	2/9*	
Immediate to register/memory	1100011w	mod 000 r/m	data	data if w=1	12/13	12/13	8/16-bit
Immediate to register	1011w reg	data	data if w=1		3/4	3/4	8/16-bit
Memory to accumulator	1010000w	addr-low	addr-high		8	8*	
Accumulator to memory	1010001w	addr-low	addr-high		9	9*	
Register/memory to segment register	10001110	mod 0 reg r/m			2/9	2/13	
Segment register to register/memory	10001100	mod 0 reg r/m			2/11	2/15	
PUSH = Push:							
Memory	11111111	mod 1 1 0 r/m			16	20	
Register	01010 reg				10	14	
Segment register	000 reg 110				9	13	
Immediate	011010s0	data	data if s=0		10	14	
PUSHA = Push All	01100000				36	68	
POP = Pop:							
Memory	10001111	mod 0 0 0 r/m			20	24	
Register	01011 reg				10	14	
Segment register	000 reg 111	(reg≠01)			8	12	
POPA = Pop All	01100001				51	83	
XCHG = Exchange:							
Register/memory with register	1000011w	mod reg r/m			4/17	4/17*	
Register with accumulator	10010 reg				3	3	
IN = Input from:							
Fixed port	1110010w	port			10	10*	
Variable port	1110110w				0	8*	
OUT = Output to:							
Fixed port	1110011w	port			9	9*	
Variable port	1110111w				7	7*	
XLAT = Translate byte to AL	11010111				11	15	
LEA = Load EA to register	10001101	mod reg r/m			6	6	
LDS = Load pointer to DS	11000101	mod reg r/m	(mod≠11)		18	26	
LES = Load pointer to ES	11000100	mod reg r/m	(mod≠11)		18	26	
LAHF = Load AH with flags	10011111				2	2	
SAHF = Store AH into flags	10011110				3	3	
PUSHF = Push flags	10011100				9	13	
POPF = Pop flags	10011101				8	12	

Shaded areas indicate instructions not available in 8086/8088 microsystems.

NOTE:
*Clock cycles shown for byte transfers. For word operations, add 4 clock cycles for all memory transfers.

2

INSTRUCTION SET SUMMARY (Continued)

Function	Format				80C186XL Clock Cycles	80C188XL Clock Cycles	Comments
DATA TRANSFER (Continued)							
SEGMENT = Segment Override:							
CS	00101110				2	2	
SS	00110110				2	2	
DS	00111110				2	2	
ES	00100110				2	2	
ARITHMETIC							
ADD = Add:							
Reg/memory with register to either	000000dw	mod reg r/m			3/10	3/10*	
Immediate to register/memory	100000sw	mod 000 r/m	data	data if s w = 01	4/16	4/16*	
Immediate to accumulator	0000010w	data	data if w = 1		3/4	3/4	8/16-bit
ADC = Add with carry:							
Reg/memory with register to either	000100dw	mod reg r/m			3/10	3/10*	
Immediate to register/memory	100000sw	mod 010 r/m	data	data if s w = 01	4/16	4/16*	
Immediate to accumulator	0001010w	data	data if w = 1		3/4	3/4	8/16-bit
INC = Increment:							
Register/memory	1111111w	mod 000 r/m			3/15	3/15*	
Register	01000 reg				3	3	
SUB = Subtract:							
Reg/memory and register to either	001010dw	mod reg r/m			3/10	3/10*	
Immediate from register/memory	100000sw	mod 101 r/m	data	data if s w = 01	4/16	4/16*	
Immediate from accumulator	0010110w	data	data if w = 1		3/4	3/4	8/16-bit
SBB = Subtract with borrow:							
Reg/memory and register to either	000110dw	mod reg r/m			3/10	3/10*	
Immediate from register/memory	100000sw	mod 011 r/m	data	data if s w = 01	4/16	4/16*	
Immediate from accumulator	0001110w	data	data if w = 1		3/4	3/4*	8/16-bit
DEC = Decrement							
Register/memory	1111111w	mod 001 r/m			3/15	3/15*	
Register	01001 reg				3	3	
CMP = Compare:							
Register/memory with register	0011101w	mod reg r/m			3/10	3/10*	
Register with register/memory	0011100w	mod reg r/m			3/10	3/10*	
Immediate with register/memory	100000sw	mod 111 r/m	data	data if s w = 01	3/10	3/10*	
Immediate with accumulator	0011110w	data	data if w = 1		3/4	3/4	8/16-bit
NEG = Change sign register/memory	1111011w	mod 011 r/m			3/10	3/10*	
AAA = ASCII adjust for add	00110111				8	8	
DAA = Decimal adjust for add	00100111				4	4	
AAS = ASCII adjust for subtract	00111111				7	7	
DAS = Decimal adjust for subtract	00101111				4	4	
MUL = Multiply (unsigned):	1111011w	mod 100 r/m					
Register-Byte					26–28	26–28	
Register-Word					35–37	35–37	
Memory-Byte					32–34	32–34	
Memory-Word					41–43	41–43*	

Shaded areas indicate instructions not available in 8086/8088 microsystems.

NOTE:
*Clock cycles shown for byte transfers. For word operations, add 4 clock cycles for all memory transfers.

INSTRUCTION SET SUMMARY (Continued)

Function	Format				80C186XL Clock Cycles	80C188XL Clock Cycles	Comments
ARITHMETIC (Continued)							
IMUL = Integer multiply (signed):	1111011w	mod 101 r/m					
Register-Byte					25–28	25–28	
Register-Word					34–37	34–37	
Memory-Byte					31–34	32–34	
Memory-Word					40–43	40–43*	
IMUL = Integer Immediate multiply (signed)	011010s1	mod reg r/m	data	data if s=0	22–25/ 29–32	22–25/ 29–32	
DIV = Divide (unsigned):	1111011w	mod 110 r/m					
Register-Byte					29	29	
Register-Word					38	38	
Memory-Byte					35	35	
Memory-Word					44	44*	
IDIV = Integer divide (signed):	1111011w	mod 111 r/m					
Register-Byte					44–52	44–52	
Register-Word					53–61	53–61	
Memory-Byte					50–58	50–58	
Memory-Word					59–67	59–67*	
AAM = ASCII adjust for multiply	11010100	00001010			19	19	
AAD = ASCII adjust for divide	11010101	00001010			15	15	
CBW = Convert byte to word	10011000				2	2	
CWD = Convert word to double word	10011001				4	4	
LOGIC							
Shift/Rotate Instructions:							
Register/Memory by 1	1101000w	mod TTT r/m			2/15	2/15	
Register/Memory by CL	1101001w	mod TTT r/m			5+n/17+n	5+n/17+n	
Register/Memory by Count	1100000w	mod TTT r/m	count		5+n/17+n	5+n/17+n	
	TTT Instruction						
	000 ROL						
	001 ROR						
	010 RCL						
	011 RCR						
	100 SHL/SAL						
	101 SHR						
	111 SAR						
AND = And:							
Reg/memory and register to either	001000dw	mod reg r/m			3/10	3/10*	
Immediate to register/memory	1000000w	mod 100 r/m	data	data if w=1	4/16	4/16*	
Immediate to accumulator	0010010w	data	data if w=1		3/4	3/4*	8/16-bit
TEST = And function to flags, no result:							
Register/memory and register	1000010w	mod reg r/m			3/10	3/10*	
Immediate data and register/memory	1111011w	mod 000 r/m	data	data if w=1	4/10	4/10*	
Immediate data and accumulator	1010100w	data	data if w=1		3/4	3/4	8/16-bit
OR = Or:							
Reg/memory and register to either	000010dw	mod reg r/m			3/10	3/10*	
Immediate to register/memory	1000000w	mod 001 r/m	data	data if w=1	4/16	4/16*	
Immediate to accumulator	0000110w	data	data if w=1		3/4	3/4*	8/16-bit

Shaded areas indicate instructions not available in 8086/8088 microsystems.

NOTE:
*Clock cycles shown for byte transfers. For word operations, add 4 clock cycles for all memory transfers.

2

INSTRUCTION SET SUMMARY (Continued)

Function	Format	80C186XL Clock Cycles	80C188XL Clock Cycles	Comments
LOGIC (Continued)				
XOR = Exclusive or:				
Reg/memory and register to either	0 0 1 1 0 0 d w | mod reg r/m	3/10	3/10*	
Immediate to register/memory	1 0 0 0 0 0 0 w | mod 1 1 0 r/m | data | data if w=1	4/16	4/16*	
Immediate to accumulator	0 0 1 1 0 1 0 w | data | data if w=1	3/4	3/4	8/16-bit
NOT = Invert register/memory	1 1 1 1 0 1 1 w | mod 0 1 0 r/m	3/10	3/10*	
STRING MANIPULATION				
MOVS = Move byte/word	1 0 1 0 0 1 0 w	14	14*	
CMPS = Compare byte/word	1 0 1 0 0 1 1 w	22	22*	
SCAS = Scan byte/word	1 0 1 0 1 1 1 w	15	15*	
LODS = Load byte/wd to AL/AX	1 0 1 0 1 1 0 w	12	12*	
STOS = Store byte/wd from AL/AX	1 0 1 0 1 0 1 w	10	10*	
INS = Input byte/wd from DX port	0 1 1 0 1 1 0 w	14	14	
OUTS = Output byte/wd to DX port	0 1 1 0 1 1 1 w	14	14	
Repeated by count in CX (REP/REPE/REPZ/REPNE/REPNZ)				
MOVS = Move string	1 1 1 1 0 0 1 0 | 1 0 1 0 0 1 0 w	8+8n	8+8n*	
CMPS = Compare string	1 1 1 1 0 0 1 z | 1 0 1 0 0 1 1 w	5+22n	5+22n*	
SCAS = Scan string	1 1 1 1 0 0 1 z | 1 0 1 0 1 1 1 w	5+15n	5+15n*	
LODS = Load string	1 1 1 1 0 0 1 0 | 1 0 1 0 1 1 0 w	6+11n	6+11n*	
STOS = Store string	1 1 1 1 0 0 1 0 | 1 0 1 0 1 0 1 w	6+9n	6+9n*	
INS = Input string	1 1 1 1 0 0 1 0 | 0 1 1 0 1 1 0 w	8+8n	8+8n*	
OUTS = Output string	1 1 1 1 0 0 1 0 | 0 1 1 0 1 1 1 w	8+8n	8+8n*	
CONTROL TRANSFER				
CALL = Call:				
Direct within segment	1 1 1 0 1 0 0 0 | disp-low | disp-high	15	19	
Register/memory indirect within segment	1 1 1 1 1 1 1 1 | mod 0 1 0 r/m	13/19	17/27	
Direct intersegment	1 0 0 1 1 0 1 0 | segment offset | segment selector	23	31	
Indirect intersegment	1 1 1 1 1 1 1 1 | mod 0 1 1 r/m (mod ≠ 11)	38	54	
JMP = Unconditional jump:				
Short/long	1 1 1 0 1 0 1 1 | disp-low	14	14	
Direct within segment	1 1 1 0 1 0 0 1 | disp-low | disp-high	14	14	
Register/memory indirect within segment	1 1 1 1 1 1 1 1 | mod 1 0 0 r/m	11/17	11/21	
Direct intersegment	1 1 1 0 1 0 1 0 | segment offset | segment selector	14	14	
Indirect intersegment	1 1 1 1 1 1 1 1 | mod 1 0 1 r/m (mod ≠ 11)	26	34	

Shaded areas indicate instructions not available in 8086/8088 microsystems.

NOTE:
*Clock cycles shown for byte transfers. For word operations, add 4 clock cycles for all memory transfers.

INSTRUCTION SET SUMMARY (Continued)

Function	Format				80C186XL Clock Cycles	80C188XL Clock Cycles	Comments
CONTROL TRANSFER (Continued)							
RET = Return from CALL:							
Within segment	11000011				16	20	
Within seg adding immed to SP	11000010	data-low	data-high		18	22	
Intersegment	11001011				22	30	
Intersegment adding immediate to SP	11001010	data-low	data-high		25	33	
JE/JZ = Jump on equal/zero	01110100	disp			4/13	4/13	JMP not taken/JMP taken
JL/JNGE = Jump on less/not greater or equal	01111100	disp			4/13	4/13	
JLE/JNG = Jump on less or equal/not greater	01111110	disp			4/13	4/13	
JB/JNAE = Jump on below/not above or equal	01110010	disp			4/13	4/13	
JBE/JNA = Jump on below or equal/not above	01110110	disp			4/13	4/13	
JP/JPE = Jump on parity/parity even	01111010	disp			4/13	4/13	
JO = Jump on overflow	01110000	disp			4/13	4/13	
JS = Jump on sign	01111000	disp			4/13	4/13	
JNE/JNZ = Jump on not equal/not zero	01110101	disp			4/13	4/13	
JNL/JGE = Jump on not less/greater or equal	01111101	disp			4/13	4/13	
JNLE/JG = Jump on not less or equal/greater	01111111	disp			4/13	4/13	
JNB/JAE = Jump on not below/above or equal	01110011	disp			4/13	4/13	
JNBE/JA = Jump on not below or equal/above	01110111	disp			4/13	4/13	
JNP/JPO = Jump on not par/par odd	01111011	disp			4/13	4/13	
JNO = Jump on not overflow	01110001	disp			4/13	4/13	
JNS = Jump on not sign	01111001	disp			4/13	4/13	
JCXZ = Jump on CX zero	11100011	disp			5/15	5/15	
LOOP = Loop CX times	11100010	disp			6/16	6/16	LOOP not taken/LOOP taken
LOOPZ/LOOPE = Loop while zero/equal	11100001	disp			6/16	6/16	
LOOPNZ/LOOPNE = Loop while not zero/equal	11100000	disp			6/16	6/16	
ENTER = Enter Procedure	11001000	data-low	data-high	L			
L = 0					15	19	
L = 1					25	29	
L > 1					22+16(n−1)	26+20(n−1)	
LEAVE = Leave Procedure	11001001				8	8	
INT = **Interrupt:**							
Type specified	11001101	type			47	47	
Type 3	11001100				45	45	if INT. taken/ if INT. not taken
INTO = Interrupt on overflow	11001110				48/4	48/4	
IRET = Interrupt return	11001111				28	28	
BOUND = Detect value out of range	01100010	mod reg r/m			33–35	33–35	

Shaded areas indicate instructions not available in 8086/8088 microsystems.

NOTE:
*Clock cycles shown for byte transfers. For word operations, add 4 clock cycles for all memory transfers.

INSTRUCTION SET SUMMARY (Continued)

Function	Format	80C186XL Clock Cycles	80C188XL Clock Cycles	Comments
PROCESSOR CONTROL				
CLC = Clear carry	11111000	2	2	
CMC = Complement carry	11110101	2	2	
STC = Set carry	11111001	2	2	
CLD = Clear direction	11111100	2	2	
STD = Set direction	11111101	2	2	
CLI = Clear interrupt	11111010	2	2	
STI = Set interrupt	11111011	2	2	
HLT = Halt	11110100	2	2	
WAIT = Wait	10011011	6	6	if $\overline{TEST}$ = 0
LOCK = Bus lock prefix	11110000	2	2	
NOP = No Operation	10010000	3	3	
	(TTT LLL are opcode to processor extension)			

Shaded areas indicate instructions not available in 8086/8088 microsystems.

NOTE:
*Clock cycles shown for byte transfers. For word operations, add 4 clock cycles for all memory transfers.

The Effective Address (EA) of the memory operand is computed according to the mod and r/m fields:

if mod = 11 then r/m is treated as a REG field
if mod = 00 then DISP = 0*, disp-low and disp-high are absent
if mod = 01 then DISP = disp-low sign-extended to 16-bits, disp-high is absent
if mod = 10 then DISP = disp-high: disp-low
if r/m = 000 then EA = (BX) + (SI) + DISP
if r/m = 001 then EA = (BX) + (DI) + DISP
if r/m = 010 then EA = (BP) + (SI) + DISP
if r/m = 011 then EA = (BP) + (DI) + DISP
if r/m = 100 then EA = (SI) + DISP
if r/m = 101 then EA = (DI) + DISP
if r/m = 110 then EA = (BP) + DISP*
if r/m = 111 then EA = (BX) + DISP

DISP follows 2nd byte of instruction (before data if required)

*except if mod = 00 and r/m = 110 then EA = disp-high: disp-low.

EA calculation time is 4 clock cycles for all modes, and is included in the execution times given whenever appropriate.

Segment Override Prefix

0	0	1	reg	1	1	0

reg is assigned according to the following:

reg	Segment Register
00	ES
01	CS
10	SS
11	DS

REG is assigned according to the following table:

16-Bit (w = 1)	8-Bit (w = 0)
000 AX	000 AL
001 CX	001 CL
010 DX	010 DL
011 BX	011 BL
100 SP	100 AH
101 BP	101 CH
110 SI	110 DH
111 DI	111 BH

The physical addresses of all operands addressed by the BP register are computed using the SS segment register. The physical addresses of the destination operands of the string primitive operations (those addressed by the DI register) are computed using the ES segment, which may not be overridden.

REVISION HISTORY

This data sheet replaces the following data sheets:

- 272031-002 80C186XL
- 270975-002 80C188XL
- 272309-001 SB80C186XL
- 272310-001 SB80C188XL

ERRATA

An A or B step 80C186XL/80C188XL has the following errata. The A or B step 80C186XL/80C188XL can be identified by the presence of an "A" or "B" alpha character, respectively, next to the FPO number. The FPO number location is shown in Figure 4.

1. An internal condition with the interrupt controller can cause no acknowledge cycle on the INTA1 line in response to INT1. This errata only occurs when Interrupt 1 is configured in cascade mode and a higher priority interrupt exists. This errata will not occur consistently, it is dependent on interrupt timing.

The C step 80C186XL/80C188XL has no known errata. The C step can be identified by the presence of a "C" alpha character next to the FPO number. The FPO number location is shown in Figure 4.

PRODUCT IDENTIFICATION

Intel 80C186XL devices are marked with a 9-character alphanumeric Intel FPO number underneath the product number. This data sheet (272431-001) is valid for devices with an "A", "B" or "C" as the ninth character in the FPO number, as illustrated in Figure 4.

PRELIMINARY

80C186EA/80C188EA AND 80L186EA/80L188EA 16-BIT HIGH-INTEGRATION EMBEDDED PROCESSORS

- **80C186 Upgrade for Power Critical Applications**
- **Fully Static Operation**
- **True CMOS Inputs and Outputs**

- **Integrated Feature Set**
  - Static 186 CPU Core
  - Power Save, Idle and Powerdown Modes
  - Clock Generator
  - 2 Independent DMA Channels
  - 3 Programmable 16-Bit Timers
  - Dynamic RAM Refresh Control Unit
  - Programmable Memory and Peripheral Chip Select Logic
  - Programmable Wait State Generator
  - Local Bus Controller
  - System-Level Testing Support (High Impedance Test Mode)
- **Speed Versions Available (5V):**
  - 20 MHz (80C186EA20/80C188EA20)
  - 12 MHz (80C186EA13/80C188EA13)
- **Speed Versions Available (3V):**
  - 13 MHz (80L186EA13/80L188EA13)
  - 8 MHz (80L186EA8/80L188EA8)
- **Direct Addressing Capability to 1 Mbyte Memory and 64 Kbyte I/O**
- **Complete System Development Support**
  - ASM86 Assembler, iC-86, PL/M-86 and System Utilities
  - In-Circuit-Emulator
- **Supports 80C187 Numeric Coprocessor Interface (80C186EA only)**
- **Available in the Following Packages:**
  - 68-Pin Plastic Leaded Chip Carrier (PLCC)
  - 80-Pin EIAJ Quad Flat Pack (QFP)
  - 80-Pin Shrink Quad Flat Pack (SQFP)
- **Available in Extended Temperature Range (−40°C to +85°C)**

The 80C186EA is a CHMOS high integration embedded microprocessor. The 80C186EA includes all of the features of an "Enhanced Mode" 80C186 while adding the additional capabilities of Idle and Powerdown Modes. In Numerics Mode, the 80C186EA interfaces directly with an 80C187 Numerics Coprocessor.

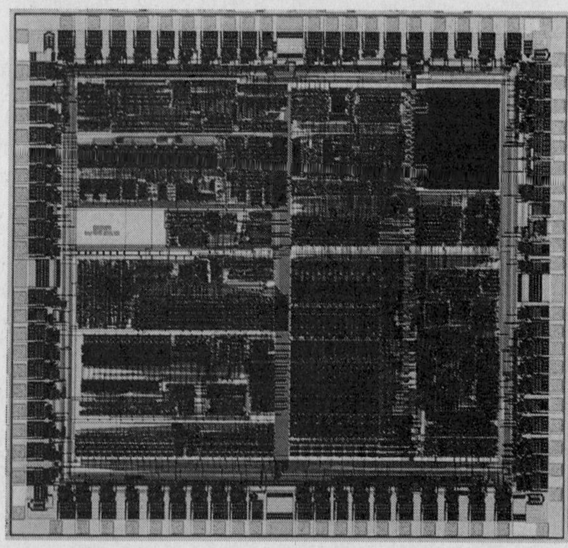

272432–1

November 1993
Order Number: 272432-001

80C186EA/80C188EA AND 80L186EA/80L188EA 16-Bit High Integration Embedded Processor

CONTENTS

CONTENTS	PAGE
INTRODUCTION	2-85
80C186EA CORE ARCHITECTURE	2-85
Bus Interface Unit	2-85
Clock Generator	2-85
80C186EA PERIPHERAL ARCHITECTURE	2-86
Interrupt Control Unit	2-86
Timer/Counter Unit	2-86
DMA Control Unit	2-88
Chip-Select Unit	2-88
Refresh Control Unit	2-88
Power Management	2-88
80C187 Interface (80C186EA Only)	2-89
ONCE Test Mode	2-89
DIFFERENCES BETWEEN THE 80C186XL AND THE 80C186EA	2-89
Pinout Compatibility	2-89
Operating Modes	2-89
TTL vs CMOS Inputs	2-89
Timing Specifications	2-89
PACKAGE INFORMATION	2-90
Prefix Identification	2-90
Pin Descriptions	2-90
80C186EA Pinout	2-96
PACKAGE THERMAL SPECIFICATIONS	2-101
ELECTRICAL SPECIFICATIONS	2-102
Absolute Maximum Ratings	2-102
Recommended Connections	2-102
DC SPECIFICATIONS	2-103
I_{CC} versus Frequency and Voltage	2-105
PDTMR Pin Delay Calculation	2-105
AC SPECIFICATIONS	2-106
AC Characteristics—80C186EA20/13	2-106
AC Characteristics—80L186EA13/8	2-108
Relative Timings	2-110
AC TEST CONDITIONS	2-111
AC TIMING WAVEFORMS	2-111
DERATING CURVES	2-114
RESET	2-114
BUS CYCLE WAVEFORMS	2-117
EXECUTION TIMINGS	2-124
INSTRUCTION SET SUMMARY	2-125
REVISION HISTORY	2-131
ERRATA	2-131

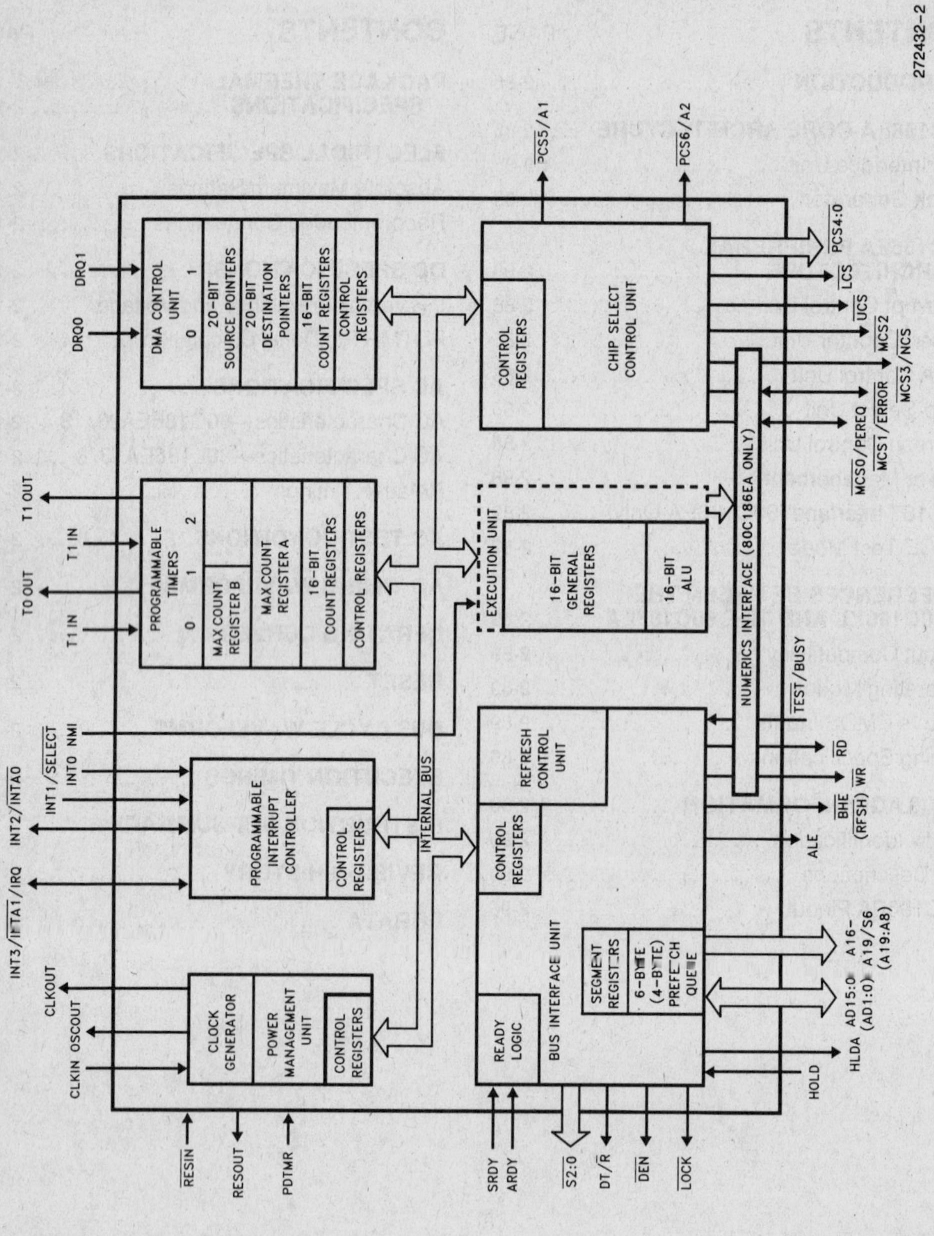

272432-2

NOTE:
Pin names in parentheses apply to the 80C186EA/80L188EA

Figure 1. 80C186EA/80C188EA Block Diagram

INTRODUCTION

Unless specifically noted, all references to the 80C186EA apply to the 80C188EA, 80L186EA, and 80L188EA. References to pins that differ between the 80C186EA/80L186EA and the 80C188EA/80L188EA are given in parentheses. The "L" in the part number denotes low voltage operation. Physically and functionally, the "C" and "L" devices are identical.

The 80C186EA is the second product in a new generation of low-power, high-integration microprocessors. It enhances the existing 80C186XL family by offering new features and operating modes. The 80C186EA is object code compatible with the 80C186XL embedded processor.

The 80L186EA is the 3V version of the 80C186EA. The 80L186EA is functionally identical to the 80C186EA embedded processor. Current 80C186EA customers can easily upgrade their designs to use the 80L186EA and benefit from the reduced power consumption inherent in 3V operation.

The feature set of the 80C186EA/80L186EA meets the needs of low-power, space-critical applications. Low-power applications benefit from the static design of the CPU core and the integrated peripherals as well as low voltage operation. Minimum current consumption is achieved by providing a Powerdown Mode that halts operation of the device, and freezes the clock circuits. Peripheral design enhancements ensure that non-initialized peripherals consume little current.

Space-critical applications benefit from the integration of commonly used system peripherals. Two flexible DMA channels perform CPU-independent data transfers. A flexible chip select unit simplifies memory and peripheral interfacing. The interrupt unit provides sources for up to 128 external interrupts and will prioritize these interrupts with those generated from the on-chip peripherals. Three general purpose timer/counters round out the feature set of the 80C186EA.

Figure 1 shows a block diagram of the 80C186EA/80C188EA. The Execution Unit (EU) is an enhanced 8086 CPU core that includes: dedicated hardware to speed up effective address calculations, enhance execution speed for multiple-bit shift and rotate instructions and for multiply and divide instructions, string move instructions that operate at full bus bandwidth, ten new instructions, and static operation. The Bus Interface Unit (BIU) is the same as that found on the original 80C186 family products. An independent internal bus is used to allow communication between the BIU and internal peripherals.

80C186EA CORE ARCHITECTURE

Bus Interface Unit

The 80C186EA core incorporates a bus controller that generates local bus control signals. In addition, it employs a HOLD/HLDA protocol to share the local bus with other bus masters.

The bus controller is responsible for generating 20 bits of address, read and write strobes, bus cycle status information and data (for write operations) information. It is also responsible for reading data off the local bus during a read operation. SRDY and ARDY input pins are provided to extend a bus cycle beyond the minimum four states (clocks).

The local bus controller also generates two control signals ($\overline{DEN}$ and DT/$\overline{R}$) when interfacing to external transceiver chips. This capability allows the addition of transceivers for simple buffering of the mulitplexed address/data bus.

Clock Generator

The processor provides an on-chip clock generator for both internal and external clock generation. The clock generator features a crystal oscillator, a divide-by-two counter, and two low-power operating modes.

The oscillator circuit is designed to be used with either a **parallel resonant** fundamental or third-overtone mode crystal network. Alternatively, the oscillator circuit may be driven from an external clock source. Figure 2 shows the various operating modes of the oscillator circuit.

The crystal or clock frequency chosen must be twice the required processor operating frequency due to the internal divide-by-two counter. This counter is used to drive all internal phase clocks and the external CLKOUT signal. CLKOUT is a 50% duty cycle processor clock and can be used to drive other system components. All AC timings are referenced to CLKOUT.

The following parameters are recommended when choosing a crystal:

Temperature Range:	Application Specific
ESR (Equivalent Series Resistance):	60Ω max
C0 (Shunt Capacitance of Crystal):	7.0 pF max
C_L (Load Capacitance):	20 pF ± 2 pF
Drive Level:	2 mW max

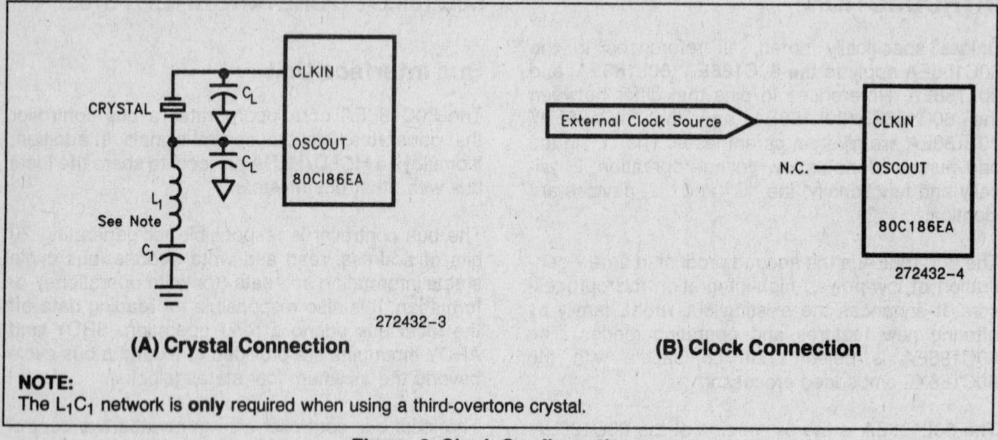

Figure 2. Clock Configurations

80C186EA PERIPHERAL ARCHITECTURE

The 80C186EA has integrated several common system peripherals with a CPU core to create a compact, yet powerful system. The integrated peripherals are designed to be flexible and provide logical interconnections between supporting units (e.g., the interrupt control unit supports interrupt requests from the timer/counters or DMA channels).

The list of integrated peripherals include:

- 4-Input Interrupt Control Unit
- 3-Channel Timer/Counter Unit
- 2-Channel DMA Unit
- 13-Output Chip-Select Unit
- Refresh Control Unit
- Power Management logic

The registers associated with each integrated periheral are contained within a 128 x 16 register file called the Peripheral Control Block (PCB). The PCB can be located in either memory or I/O space on any 256 byte address boundary.

Figure 3 provides a list of the registers associated with the PCB when the processor's Interrupt Control Unit is in Master Mode. In Slave Mode, the definitions of some registers change. Figure 4 provides register definitions specific to Slave Mode.

Interrupt Control Unit

The 80C186EA can receive interrupts from a number of sources, both internal and external. The Interrupt Control Unit (ICU) serves to merge these requests on a priority basis, for individual service by the CPU. Each interrupt source can be independently masked by the Interrupt Control Unit or all interrupts can be globally masked by the CPU.

Internal interrupt sources include the Timers and DMA channels. External interrupt sources come from the four input pins INT3:0. The NMI interrupt pin is not controlled by the ICU and is passed directly to the CPU. Although the timers only have one request input to the ICU, separate vector types are generated to service individual interrupts within the Timer Unit.

Timer/Counter Unit

The 80C186EA Timer/Counter Unit (TCU) provides three 16-bit programmable timers. Two of these are highly flexible and are connected to external pins for control or clocking. A third timer is not connected to any external pins and can only be clocked internally. However, it can be used to clock the other two timer channels. The TCU can be used to count external events, time external events, generate non-repetitive waveforms, generate timed interrupts, etc.

PCB Offset	Function	PCB Offset	Function	PCB Offset	Function	PCB Offset	Function
00H	Reserved	40H	Reserved	80H	Reserved	C0H	DMA0 Src. Lo
02H	Reserved	42H	Reserved	82H	Reserved	C2H	DMA0 Src. Hi
04H	Reserved	44H	Reserved	84H	Reserved	C4H	DMA0 Dest. Lo
06H	Reserved	46H	Reserved	86H	Reserved	C6H	DMA0 Dest. Hi
08H	Reserved	48H	Reserved	88H	Reserved	C8H	DMA0 Count
0AH	Reserved	4AH	Reserved	8AH	Reserved	CAH	DMA0 Control
0CH	Reserved	4CH	Reserved	8CH	Reserved	CCH	Reserved
0EH	Reserved	4EH	Reserved	8EH	Reserved	CEH	Reserved
10H	Reserved	50H	Timer 0 Count	90H	Reserved	D0H	DMA1 Src. Lo
12H	Reserved	52H	Timer 0 Compare A	92H	Reserved	D2H	DMA1 Src. Hi
14H	Reserved	54H	Timer 0 Compare B	94H	Reserved	D4H	DMA1 Dest. Lo
16H	Reserved	56H	Timer 0 Control	96H	Reserved	D6H	DMA1 Dest. Hi
18H	Reserved	58H	Timer 1 Count	98H	Reserved	D8H	DMA1 Count
1AH	Reserved	5AH	Timer 1 Compare A	9AH	Reserved	DAH	DMA1 Control
1CH	Reserved	5CH	Timer 1 Compare B	9CH	Reserved	DCH	Reserved
1EH	Reserved	5EH	Timer 1 Control	9EH	Reserved	DEH	Reserved
20H	Reserved	60H	Timer 2 Count	A0H	UMCS	E0H	Refresh Base
22H	End of Interrupt	62H	Timer 2 Compare	A2H	LMCS	E2H	Refresh Time
24H	Poll	64H	Reserved	A4H	PACS	E4H	Refresh Control
26H	Poll Status	66H	Timer 2 Control	A6H	MMCS	E6H	Reserved
28H	Interrupt Mask	68H	Reserved	A8H	MPCS	E8H	Reserved
2AH	Priority Mask	6AH	Reserved	AAH	Reserved	EAH	Reserved
2CH	In-Service	6CH	Reserved	ACH	Reserved	ECH	Reserved
2EH	Interrupt Request	6EH	Reserved	AEH	Reserved	EEH	Reserved
30H	Interrupt Status	70H	Reserved	B0H	Reserved	F0H	Power-Save
32H	Timer Control	72H	Reserved	B2H	Reserved	F2H	Power Control
34H	DMA0 Int. Control	74H	Reserved	B4H	Reserved	F4H	Reserved
36H	DMA1 Int. Control	76H	Reserved	B6H	Reserved	F6H	Step ID
38H	INT0 Control	78H	Reserved	B8H	Reserved	F8H	Reserved
3AH	INT1 Control	7AH	Reserved	BAH	Reserved	FAH	Reserved
3CH	INT2 Control	7CH	Reserved	BCH	Reserved	FCH	Reserved
3EH	INT3 Control	7EH	Reserved	BEH	Reserved	FEH	Relocation

Figure 3. Peripheral Control Block Registers

PCB Offset	Function
20H	Interrupt Vector
22H	Specific EOI
24H	Reserved
26H	Reserved
28H	Interrupt Mask
2AH	Priority Mask
2C	In-Service
2E	Interrupt Request
30	Interrupt Status
32	TMR0 Interrupt Control
34	DMA0 Interrupt Control
36	DMA1 Interrupt Control
38	TMR1 Interrupt Control
3A	TMR2 Interrupt Control
3C	Reserved
3E	Reserved

Figure 4. 80C186EA Slave Mode Peripheral Control Block Registers

DMA Control Unit

The 80C186EA DMA Contol Unit provides two independent high-speed DMA channels. Data transfers can occur between memory and I/O space in any combination: memory to memory, memory to I/O, I/O to I/O or I/O to memory. Data can be transferred either in bytes or words. Transfers may proceed to or from either even or odd addresses, but even-aligned word transfers proceed at a faster rate. Each data transfer consumes two bus cycles (a minimum of eight clocks), one cycle to fetch data and the other to store data. The chip-select/ready logic may be programmed to point to the memory or I/O space subject to DMA transfers in order to provide hardware chip select lines. DMA cycles run at higher priority than general processor execution cycles.

Chip-Select Unit

The 80C186EA Chip-Select Unit integrates logic which provides up to 13 programmable chip-selects to access both memories and peripherals. In addition, each chip-select can be programmed to automatically terminate a bus cycle independent of the condition of the SRDY and ARDY input pins. The chip-select lines are available for all memory and I/O bus cycles, whether they are generated by the CPU, the DMA unit, or the Refresh Control Unit.

Refresh Control Unit

The Refresh Control Unit (RCU) automatically generates a periodic memory read bus cycle to keep dynamic or pseudo-static memory refreshed. A 9-bit counter controls the number of clocks between refresh requests.

A 9-bit address generator is maintained by the RCU with the address presented on the A9:1 address lines during the refresh bus cycle. Address bits A19:13 are programmable to allow the refresh address block to be located on any 8 Kbyte boundary.

Power Management

The 80C186EA has three operational modes to control the power consumption of the device. They are Power Save Mode, Idle Mode, and Powerdown Mode.

Power Save Mode divides the processor clock by a programmable value to take advantage of the fact that current is linearly proportional to frequency. An unmasked interrupt, NMI, or reset will cause the 80C186EA to exit Power Save Mode.

Idle Mode freezes the clocks of the Execution Unit and the Bus Interface Unit at a logic zero state while all peripherals operate normally.

Powerdown Mode freezes all internal clocks at a logic zero level and disables the crystal oscillator. All internal registers hold their values provided V_{CC} is maintained. Current consumption is reduced to transistor leakage only.

80C187 Interface (80C186EA Only)

The 80C187 Numerics Coprocessor may be used to extend the 80C186EA instruction set to include floating point and advanced integer instructions. Connecting the 80C186EA RESOUT and $\overline{\text{TEST}}$/BUSY pins to the 80C187 enables Numerics Mode operation. In Numerics Mode, three of the four Mid-Range Chip Select ($\overline{\text{MCS}}$) pins become handshaking pins for the interface. The exchange of data and control information proceeds through four dedicated I/O ports.

If an 80C187 is not present, the 80C186EA configures itself for regular operation at reset.

NOTE:
The 80C187 is not specified for 3V operation and therefore does not interface directly to the 80L186EA.

ONCE Test Mode

To facilitate testing and inspection of devices when fixed into a target system, the 80C186EA has a test mode available which forces all output and input/output pins to be placed in the high-impedance state. ONCE stands for "ON Circuit Emulation". The ONCE mode is selected by forcing the $\overline{\text{UCS}}$ and $\overline{\text{LCS}}$ pins LOW (0) during a processor reset (these pins are weakly held to a HIGH (1) level) while $\overline{\text{RESIN}}$ is active.

DIFFERENCES BETWEEN THE 80C186XL AND THE 80C186EA

The 80C186EA is intended as a direct functional upgrade for 80C186XL designs. In many cases, it will be possible to replace an existing 80C186XL with little or no hardware redesign. The following sections describe differences in pinout, operating modes, and AC and DC specifications to keep in mind.

Pinout Compatibility

The 80C186EA requires a PDTMR pin to time the processor's exit from Powerdown Mode. The original pin arrangement for the 80C186XL in the PLCC package did not have any spare leads to use for PDTMR, so the DT/$\overline{\text{R}}$ pin was sacrificed. The arrangement of all the other leads in the 68-lead PLCC is identical between the 80C186XL and the 80C186EA. DT/$\overline{\text{R}}$ may be synthesized by latching the $\overline{\text{S1}}$ status output. Therefore, upgrading a PLCC 80C186XL to PLCC 80C186EA is straightforward.

The 80-lead QFP (EIAJ) pinouts are different between the 80C186XL and the 80C186EA. In addition to the PDTMR pin, the 80C186EA has more power and ground pins and the overall arrangement of pins was shifted. A new circuit board layout for the 80C186EA is required.

Operating Modes

The 80C186XL has two operating modes, Compatible and Enhanced. Compatible Mode is a pin-to-pin replacement for the NMOS 80186, except for numerics coprocessing. In Enhanced Mode, the processor has a Refresh Control Unit, the Power-Save feature and an interface to the 80C187 Numerics Coprocessor. The $\overline{\text{MCS0}}$, $\overline{\text{MCS1}}$, and $\overline{\text{MCS3}}$ pins change their functions to constitute handshaking pins for the 80C187.

The 80C186EA allows all non-80C187 users to use all the $\overline{\text{MCS}}$ pins for chip-selects. In regular operation, all 80C186EA features (including those of the Enhanced Mode 80C186) are present except for the interface to the 80C187. Numerics Mode disables the three chip-select pins and reconfigures them for connection to the 80C187.

TTL vs CMOS Inputs

The inputs of the 80C186EA are rated for CMOS switching levels for improved noise immunity, but the 80C186XL inputs are rated for TTL switching levels. In particular, the 80C186EA requires a minimum V_{IH} of 3.5V to recognize a logic one while the 80C186XL requires a minimum V_{IH} of only 1.9V (assuming 5.0V operation). The solution is to drive the 80C186EA with true CMOS devices, such as those from the HC and AC logic families, or to use pullup resistors where the added current draw is not a problem.

Timing Specifications

80C186EA timing relationships are expressed in a simplified format over the 80C186XL. The AC performance of an 80C186EA at a specified frequency will be very close to that of an 80C186XL at the same frequency. Check the timings applicable to your design prior to replacing the 80C186XL.

PACKAGE INFORMATION

This section describes the pins, pinouts, and thermal characteristics for the 80C186EA in the Plastic Leaded Chip Carrier (PLCC) package, Shrink Quad Flat Pack (SQFP), and Quad Flat Pack (QFP) package. For complete package specifications and information, see the Intel Packaging Outlines and Dimensions Guide (Order Number: 231369).

With the extended temperature range operational characteristics are guaranteed over a temperature range corresponding to −40°C to +85°C ambient. Package types are identified by a two-letter prefix to the part number. The prefixes are listed in Table 1.

Table 1. Prefix Identification

Prefix	Package Type	Temperature Range
TN	PLCC	Extended
TS	QFP (EIAJ)	Extended
SB	SQFP	Extended

Pin Descriptions

Each pin or logical set of pins is described in Table 3. There are three columns for each entry in the Pin Description Table.

The **Pin Name** column contains a mnemonic that describes the pin function. Negation of the signal name (for example, $\overline{\text{RESIN}}$) denotes a signal that is active low.

The **Pin Type** column contains two kinds of information. The first symbol indicates whether a pin is power (P), ground (G), input only (I), output only (O) or input/output (I/O). Some pins have multiplexed functions (for example, A19/S6). Additional symbols indicate additional characteristics for each pin. Table 3 lists all the possible symbols for this column.

The **Input Type** column indicates the type of input (asynchronous or synchronous).

Asynchronous pins require that setup and hold times be met only in order to guarantee *recognition* at a particular clock edge. Synchronous pins require that setup and hold times be met to guarantee proper *operation.* For example, missing the setup or hold time for the SRDY pin (a synchronous input) will result in a system failure or lockup. Input pins may also be edge- or level-sensitive. The possible characteristics for input pins are S(E), S(L), A(E) and A(L).

The **Output States** column indicates the output state as a function of the device operating mode. Output states are dependent upon the current activity of the processor. There are four operational states that are different from regular operation: bus hold, reset, Idle Mode and Powerdown Mode. Appropriate characteristics for these states are also indicated in this column, with the legend for all possible characteristics in Table 2.

The **Pin Description** column contains a text description of each pin.

As an example, consider AD15:0. I/O signifies the pins are bidirectional. S(L) signifies that the input function is synchronous and level-sensitive. H(Z) signifies that, as outputs, the pins are high-impedance upon acknowledgement of bus hold. R(Z) signifies that the pins float during reset. P(X) signifies that the pins retain their states during Powerdown Mode.

Table 2. Pin Description Nomenclature

Symbol	Description
P G I O I/O	Power Pin (Apply $+V_{CC}$ Voltage) Ground (Connect to V_{SS}) Input Only Pin Output Only Pin Input/Output Pin
S(E) S(L) A(E) A(L)	Synchronous, Edge Sensitive Synchronous, Level Sensitive Asynchronous, Edge Sensitive Asynchronous, Level Sensitive
H(1) H(0) H(Z) H(Q) H(X)	Output Driven to V_{CC} during Bus Hold Output Driven to V_{SS} during Bus Hold Output Floats during Bus Hold Output Remains Active during Bus Hold Output Retains Current State during Bus Hold
R(WH) R(1) R(0) R(Z) R(Q) R(X)	Output Weakly Held at V_{CC} during Reset Output Driven to V_{CC} during Reset Output Driven to V_{SS} during Reset Output Floats during Reset Output Remains Active during Reset Output Retains Current State during Reset
I(1) I(0) I(Z) I(Q) I(X)	Output Driven to V_{CC} during Idle Mode Output Driven to V_{SS} during Idle Mode Output Floats during Idle Mode Output Remains Active during Idle Mode Output Retains Current State during Idle Mode
P(1) P(0) P(Z) P(Q) P(X)	Output Driven to V_{CC} during Powerdown Mode Output Driven to V_{SS} during Powerdown Mode Output Floats during Powerdown Mode Output Remains Active during Powerdown Mode Output Retains Current State during Powerdown Mode

2

Table 3. Pin Descriptions

Pin Name	Pin Type	Input Type	Output States	Description
V_{CC}	P			**POWER** connections consist of six pins which must be shorted externally to a V_{CC} board plane.
V_{SS}	G			**GROUND** connections consist of five pins which must be shorted externally to a V_{SS} board plane.
CLKIN	I	A(E)		**CLocK INput** is an input for an external clock. An external oscillator operating at two times the required processor operating frequency can be connected to CLKIN. For crystal operation, CLKIN (along with OSCOUT) are the crystal connections to an internal Pierce oscillator.
OSCOUT	O		H(Q) R(Q) P(Q)	**OSCillator OUTput** is only used when using a crystal to generate the external clock. OSCOUT (along with CLKIN) are the crystal connections to an internal Pierce oscillator. This pin is not to be used as 2X clock output for non-crystal applications (i.e., this pin is N.C. for non-crystal applications). OSCOUT does not float in ONCE mode.
CLKOUT	O		H(Q) R(Q) P(Q)	**CLocK OUTput** provides a timing reference for inputs and outputs of the processor, and is one-half the input clock (CLKIN) frequency. CLKOUT has a 50% duty cycle and transistions every falling edge of CLKIN.
$\overline{\text{RESIN}}$	I	A(L)		**RESet IN** causes the processor to immediately terminate any bus cycle in progress and assume an initialized state. All pins will be driven to a known state, and RESOUT will also be driven active. The rising edge (low-to-high) transition synchronizes CLKOUT with CLKIN before the processor begins fetching opcodes at memory location 0FFFF0H.
RESOUT	O		H(0) R(1) P(0)	**RESet OUTput** that indicates the processor is currently in the reset state. RESOUT will remain active as long as $\overline{\text{RESIN}}$ remains active. When tied to the $\overline{\text{TEST}}$/BUSY pin, RESOUT forces the 80C186EA into Numerics Mode.
PDTMR	I/O	A(L)	H(WH) R(Z) P(1)	**Power-Down TiMeR** pin (normally connected to an external capacitor) that determines the amount of time the processor waits after an exit from power down before resuming normal operation. The duration of time required will depend on the startup characteristics of the crystal oscillator.
NMI	I	A(E)		**Non-Maskable Interrupt** input causes a Type 2 interrupt to be serviced by the CPU. NMI is latched internally.
$\overline{\text{TEST}}$/BUSY ($\overline{\text{TEST}}$)	I	A(E)		**$\overline{\text{TEST}}$/BUSY** is sampled upon reset to determine whether the 80C186EA is to enter Numerics Mode. In regular operation, the pin is **$\overline{\text{TEST}}$.** $\overline{\text{TEST}}$ is used during the execution of the WAIT instruction to suspend CPU operation until the pin is sampled active (low). In Numerics Mode, the pin is **BUSY**. BUSY notifies the 80C186EA of 80C187 Numerics Coprocessor activity.
AD15:0 (AD7:0)	I/O	S(L)	H(Z) R(Z) P(X)	These pins provide a multiplexed **Address** and **Data** bus. During the address phase of the bus cycle, address bits 0 through 15 (0 through 7 on the 8-bit bus versions) are presented on the bus and can be latched using ALE. 8- or 16-bit data information is transferred during the data phase of the bus cycle.

NOTE:
Pin names in parentheses apply to the 80C188EA and 80L188EA.

Table 3. Pin Descriptions (Continued)

<table>
<tr><th>Pin Name</th><th>Pin Type</th><th>Input Type</th><th>Output States</th><th>Description</th></tr>
<tr><td>A18:16
A19/S6–A16
(A19–A8)</td><td>O</td><td></td><td>H(Z)
R(Z)
P(X)</td><td>These pins provide multiplexed Address during the address phase of the bus cycle. Address bits 16 through 19 are presented on these pins and can be latched using ALE. A18:16 are driven to a logic 0 during the data phase of the bus cycle. On the 8-bit bus versions, A15–A8 provide valid address information for the entire bus cycle. Also during the data phase, S6 is driven to a logic 0 to indicate a CPU-initiated bus cycle or logic 1 to indicate a DMA-initiated bus cycle or a refresh cycle.</td></tr>
<tr><td>$\overline{S2:0}$</td><td>O</td><td></td><td>H(Z)
R(Z)
P(1)</td><td>Bus cycle Status are encoded on these pins to provide bus transaction information. $\overline{S2:0}$ are encoded as follows:
<table>
<tr><th>$\overline{S2}$</th><th>$\overline{S1}$</th><th>$\overline{S0}$</th><th>Bus Cycle Initiated</th></tr>
<tr><td>0</td><td>0</td><td>0</td><td>Interrupt Acknowledge</td></tr>
<tr><td>0</td><td>0</td><td>1</td><td>Read I/O</td></tr>
<tr><td>0</td><td>1</td><td>0</td><td>Write I/O</td></tr>
<tr><td>0</td><td>1</td><td>1</td><td>Processor HALT</td></tr>
<tr><td>1</td><td>0</td><td>0</td><td>Queue Instruction Fetch</td></tr>
<tr><td>1</td><td>0</td><td>1</td><td>Read Memory</td></tr>
<tr><td>1</td><td>1</td><td>0</td><td>Write Memory</td></tr>
<tr><td>1</td><td>1</td><td>1</td><td>Passive (no bus activity)</td></tr>
</table></td></tr>
<tr><td>ALE/QS0</td><td>O</td><td></td><td>H(0)
R(0)
P(0)</td><td>Address Latch Enable output is used to strobe address information into a transparent type latch during the address phase of the bus cycle. In Queue Status Mode, QS0 provides queue status information along with QS1.</td></tr>
<tr><td>$\overline{BHE}$
($\overline{RFSH}$)</td><td>O</td><td></td><td>H(Z)
R(Z)
P(X)</td><td>Byte High Enable output to indicate that the bus cycle in progress is transferring data over the upper half of the data bus. $\overline{BHE}$ and A0 have the following logical encoding:
<table>
<tr><th>A0</th><th>$\overline{BHE}$</th><th>Encoding (For 80C186EA/80L186EA Only)</th></tr>
<tr><td>0</td><td>0</td><td>Word Transfer</td></tr>
<tr><td>0</td><td>1</td><td>Even Byte Transfer</td></tr>
<tr><td>1</td><td>0</td><td>Odd Byte Transfer</td></tr>
<tr><td>1</td><td>1</td><td>Refresh Operation</td></tr>
</table>
On the 80C188EA/80L188EA, $\overline{RFSH}$ is asserted low to indicate a Refresh bus cycle.</td></tr>
<tr><td>$\overline{RD}/\overline{QSMD}$</td><td>O</td><td></td><td>H(Z)
R(WH)
P(1)</td><td>ReaD output signals that the accessed memory or I/O device must drive data information onto the data bus. Upon reset, this pin has an alternate function. As $\overline{QSMD}$, it enables Queue Status Mode when grounded. In Queue Status Mode, the ALE/QS0 and $\overline{WR}$/QS1 pins provide the following information about processor/instruction queue interaction:
<table>
<tr><th>QS1</th><th>QS0</th><th>Queue Operation</th></tr>
<tr><td>0</td><td>0</td><td>No Queue Operation</td></tr>
<tr><td>0</td><td>1</td><td>First Opcode Byte Fetched from the Queue</td></tr>
<tr><td>1</td><td>1</td><td>Subsequent Byte Fetched from the Queue</td></tr>
<tr><td>1</td><td>0</td><td>Empty the Queue</td></tr>
</table></td></tr>
</table>

NOTE:
Pin names in parentheses apply to the 80C188EA and 80L188EA.

Table 3. Pin Descriptions (Continued)

Pin Name	Pin Type	Input Type	Output States	Description
$\overline{WR}$/QS1	O		H(Z) R(Z) P(1)	**WRite** output signals that data available on the data bus are to be written into the accessed memory or I/O device. In Queue Status Mode, QS1 provides queue status information along with QS0.
ARDY	I	A(L) S(L)		**Asychronous ReaDY** is an input to signal for the end of a bus cycle. ARDY is asynchronous on rising CLKOUT and synchronous on falling CLKOUT. ARDY or SRDY must be active to terminate any processor bus cycle, unless they are ignored due to correct programming of the Chip Select Unit.
SRDY	I	S(L)		**Synchronous ReaDY** is an input to signal for the end of a bus cycle. ARDY or SRDY must be active to terminate any processor bus cycle, unless they are ignored due to correct programming of the Chip Select Unit.
$\overline{DEN}$	O	H(Z) R(Z) P(1)		**Data ENable** output to control the enable of bidirectional transceivers when buffering a system. $\overline{DEN}$ is active only when data is to be transferred on the bus.
DT/$\overline{R}$	O		H(Z) R(Z) P(X)	**Data Transmit/Receive** output controls the direction of a bi-directional buffer in a buffered system. DT/$\overline{R}$ is only available on the QFP (EIAJ) package and the SQFP package.
$\overline{LOCK}$	O		H(Z) R(WH) P(1)	**LOCK** output indicates that the bus cycle in progress is not to be interrupted. The processor will not service other bus requests (such as HOLD) while $\overline{LOCK}$ is active. This pin is configured as a weakly held high input while $\overline{RESIN}$ is active and must not be driven low.
HOLD	I	A(L)		**HOLD** request input to signal that an external bus master wishes to gain control of the local bus. The processor will relinquish control of the local bus between instruction boundaries not conditioned by a LOCK prefix.
HLDA	O		H(1) R(0) P(0)	**HoLD Acknowledge** output to indicate that the processor has relinquished control of the local bus. When HLDA is asserted, the processor will (or has) floated its data bus and control signals allowing another bus master to drive the signals directly.
$\overline{UCS}$	O		H(1) R(1) P(1)	**Upper Chip Select** will go active whenever the address of a memory or I/O bus cycle is within the address limitations programmed by the user. After reset, $\overline{UCS}$ is configured to be active for memory accesses between 0FFC00H and 0FFFFFH. During a processor reset, $\overline{UCS}$ and $\overline{LCS}$ are used to enable ONCE Mode.
$\overline{LCS}$	O		H(1) R(1) P(1)	**Lower Chip Select** will go active whenever the address of a memory bus cycle is within the address limitations programmed by the user. $\overline{LCS}$ is inactive after a reset. During a processor reset, $\overline{UCS}$ and $\overline{LCS}$ are used to enable ONCE Mode.

NOTE:
Pin names in parentheses apply to the 80C188EA and 80L188EA.

Table 3. Pin Descriptions (Continued)

Pin Name	Pin Type	Input Type	Output States	Description
$\overline{MCS0}$/PEREQ $\overline{MCS1}$/$\overline{ERROR}$ $\overline{MCS2}$ $\overline{MCS3}$/$\overline{NCS}$	I/O	A(L)	H(1) R(1) P(1)	These pins provide a multiplexed function. If enablod, these pins normally comprise a block of **Mid-Range Chip Select** outputs which will go active whenever the address of a memory bus cycle is within the address limitations programmed by the user. In Numerics Mode (80C186EA only), three of the pins become handshaking pins for the 80C187. The **CoProcessor REQuest** input signals that a data transfer is pending. **$\overline{ERROR}$** is an input which indicates that the previous numerics coprocessor operation resulted in an exception condition. An interrupt Type 16 is generated when $\overline{ERROR}$ is sampled active at the beginning of a numerics operation. **Numerics Coprocessor Select** is an output signal generated when the processor accesses the 80C187.
$\overline{PCS4:0}$	O		H(1) R(1) P(1)	**Peripheral Chip Selects** go active whenever the address of a memory or I/O bus cycle is within the address limitations programmed by the user.
$\overline{PCS5}$/A1 $\overline{PCS6}$/A2	O		H(1)/H(X) R(1) P(1)	These pins provide a multiplexed function. As additional **Peripheral Chip Selects,** they go active whenever the address of a memory or I/O bus cycle is within the address limitations by the user. They may also be programmed to provide latched **Address** A2:1 signals.
T0OUT T1OUT	O		H(Q) R(1) P(Q)	**Timer OUTput** pins can be programmed to provide a single clock or continuous waveform generation, depending on the timer mode selected.
T0IN T1IN	I	A(L) A(E)		**Timer INput** is used either as clock or control signals, depending on the timer mode selected.
DRQ0 DRQ1	I	A(L)		**DMA ReQuest** is asserted by an external request when it is prepared for a DMA transfer.
INT0 INT1/$\overline{SELECT}$	I	A(E,L)		Maskable **INTerrupt** input will cause a vector to a specific Type interrupt routine. To allow interrupt expansion, INT0 and/or INT1 can be used with $\overline{INTA0}$ and $\overline{INTA1}$ to interface with an external slave controller. INT1 becomes $\overline{SELECT}$ when the ICU is configured for Slave Mode.
INT2/$\overline{INTA0}$ INT3/$\overline{INTA1}$/IRQ	I/O	A(E,L)	H(1) R(Z) P(1)	These pins provide multiplexed functions. As inputs, they provide a maskable **INTerrupt** that will cause the CPU to vector to a specific Type interrupt routine. As outputs, each is programmatically controlled to provide an **INTerrupt Acknowledge** handshake signal to allow interrupt expansion. INT3/$\overline{INTA1}$ becomes **IRQ** when the ICU is configured for Slave Mode.
N.C.				**No Connect.** For compatibility with future products, do not connect to these pins.

NOTE:
Pin names in parentheses apply to the 80C188EA and 80L188EA.

2

80C186EA PINOUT

Tables 4 and 5 list the 80C186EA pin names with package location for the 68-pin Plastic Leaded Chip Carrier (PLCC) component. Figure 9 depicts the complete 80C186EA/80L186EA pinout (PLCC package) as viewed from the top side of the component (i.e., contacts facing down).

Tables 6 and 7 list the 80C186EA pin names with package location for the 80-pin Quad Flat Pack (EIAJ) component. Figure 6 depicts the complete 80C186EA/80C188EA (EIAJ QFP package) as viewed from the top side of the component (i.e., contacts facing down).

Tables 8 and 9 list the 80C186EA/80C188EA pin names with package location for the 80-pin Shrink Quad Flat Pack (SQFP) component. Figure 7 depicts the complete 80C186EA/80C188EA (SQFP) as viewed from the top side of the component (i.e., contacts facing down).

Table 4. PLCC Pin Names with Package Location

Address/Data Bus	
Name	**Location**
AD0	17
AD1	15
AD2	13
AD3	11
AD4	8
AD5	6
AD6	4
AD7	2
AD8 (A8)	16
AD9 (A9)	14
AD10 (A10)	12
AD11 (A11)	10
AD12 (A12)	7
AD13 (A13)	5
AD14 (A14)	3
AD15 (A15)	1
A16	68
A17	67
A18	66
A19/S6	65

Bus Control	
Name	**Location**
ALE/QS0	61
$\overline{\text{BHE}}$ ($\overline{\text{RFSH}}$)	64
$\overline{\text{S0}}$	52
$\overline{\text{S1}}$	53
$\overline{\text{S2}}$	54
$\overline{\text{RD}}$/QSMD	62
$\overline{\text{WR}}$/QS1	63
ARDY	55
SRDY	49
$\overline{\text{DEN}}$	39
$\overline{\text{LOCK}}$	48
HOLD	50
HLDA	51

Power	
Name	**Location**
V_{SS}	26, 60
V_{CC}	9, 43

Processor Control	
Name	**Location**
$\overline{\text{RESIN}}$	24
RESOUT	57
CLKIN	59
OSCOUT	58
CLKOUT	56
$\overline{\text{TEST}}$/BUSY	47
PDTMR	40
NMI	46
INT0	45
INT1/SELECT	44
INT2/$\overline{\text{INTA0}}$	42
INT3/$\overline{\text{INTA1}}$/IRQ	41

I/O	
Name	**Location**
$\overline{\text{UCS}}$	34
$\overline{\text{LCS}}$	33
$\overline{\text{MCS0}}$/PEREQ	38
$\overline{\text{MCS1}}$/$\overline{\text{ERROR}}$	37
$\overline{\text{MCS2}}$	36
$\overline{\text{MCS3}}$/$\overline{\text{NCS}}$	35
$\overline{\text{PCS0}}$	25
$\overline{\text{PCS1}}$	27
$\overline{\text{PCS2}}$	28
$\overline{\text{PCS3}}$	29
$\overline{\text{PCS4}}$	30
$\overline{\text{PCS5}}$/A1	31
$\overline{\text{PCS6}}$/A2	32
T0OUT	22
T0IN	20
T1OUT	23
T1IN	21
DRQ0	18
DRQ1	19

NOTE:
Pin names in parentheses apply to the 80C188EA/80L188EA.

Table 5. PLCC Package Location with Pin Names

Location	Name	Location	Name	Location	Name	Location	Name
1	AD15 (A15)	18	DRQ0	35	$\overline{MCS3}$/NCS	52	$\overline{S0}$
2	AD7	19	DRQ1	36	$\overline{MCS2}$	53	$\overline{S1}$
3	AD14 (A14)	20	T0IN	37	$\overline{MCS1}$/$\overline{ERROR}$	54	$\overline{S2}$
4	AD6	21	T1IN	38	$\overline{MCS0}$/PEREQ	55	ARDY
5	AD13 (A13)	22	T0OUT	39	$\overline{DEN}$	56	CLKOUT
6	AD5	23	T1OUT	40	PDTMR	57	RESOUT
7	AD12 (A12)	24	$\overline{RESIN}$	41	INT3/$\overline{INTA1}$/IRQ	58	OSCOUT
8	AD4	25	$\overline{PCS0}$	42	INT2/$\overline{INTA0}$	59	CLKIN
9	V_{CC}	26	V_{SS}	43	V_{CC}	60	V_{SS}
10	AD11 (A11)	27	$\overline{PCS1}$	44	INT1/SELECT	61	ALE/QS0
11	AD3	28	$\overline{PCS2}$	45	INT0	62	$\overline{RD}$/$\overline{QSMD}$
12	AD10 (A10)	29	$\overline{PCS3}$	46	NMI	63	$\overline{WR}$/QS1
13	AD2	30	$\overline{PCS4}$	47	$\overline{TEST}$/BUSY	64	$\overline{BHE}$ ($\overline{RFSH}$)
14	AD9 (A9)	31	$\overline{PCS5}$/A1	48	LOCK	65	A19/S6
15	AD1	32	$\overline{PCS6}$/A2	49	SRDY	66	A18
16	AD8 (A8)	33	$\overline{LCS}$	50	HOLD	67	A17
17	AD0	34	$\overline{UCS}$	51	HLDA	68	A16

NOTE:
Pin names in parentheses apply to the 80C186EA/80L188EA.

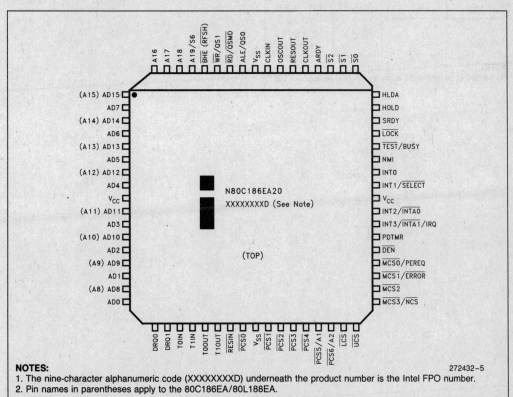

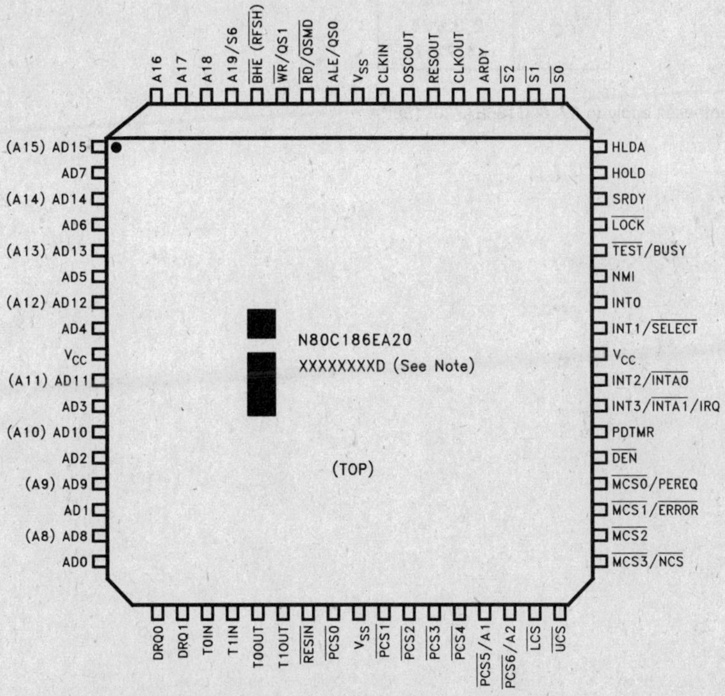

A16 A17 A18 A19/S6 $\overline{BHE}$ ($\overline{RFSH}$) $\overline{WR}$/QS1 $\overline{RD}$/$\overline{QSMD}$ ALE/QS0 V_{SS} CLKIN OSCOUT RESOUT CLKOUT ARDY $\overline{S2}$ $\overline{S1}$ $\overline{S0}$

(A15) AD15, AD7, (A14) AD14, AD6, (A13) AD13, AD5, (A12) AD12, AD4, V_{CC}, (A11) AD11, AD3, (A10) AD10, AD2, (A9) AD9, AD1, (A8) AD8, AD0

HLDA, HOLD, SRDY, $\overline{LOCK}$, $\overline{TEST}$/BUSY, NMI, INT0, INT1/$\overline{SELECT}$, V_{CC}, INT2/$\overline{INTA0}$, INT3/$\overline{INTA1}$/IRQ, PDTMR, $\overline{DEN}$, $\overline{MCS0}$/PEREQ, $\overline{MCS1}$/$\overline{ERROR}$, $\overline{MCS2}$, $\overline{MCS3}$/NCS

N80C186EA20
XXXXXXXXD (See Note)

(TOP)

DRQ0 DRQ1 T0IN T1IN T0OUT T1OUT $\overline{RESIN}$ $\overline{PCS0}$ V_{SS} $\overline{PCS1}$ $\overline{PCS2}$ $\overline{PCS3}$ $\overline{PCS4}$ $\overline{PCS5}$/A1 $\overline{PCS6}$/A2 $\overline{LCS}$ $\overline{UCS}$

272432-5

NOTES:
1. The nine-character alphanumeric code (XXXXXXXXD) underneath the product number is the Intel FPO number.
2. Pin names in parentheses apply to the 80C186EA/80L188EA.

Figure 5. 68-Lead PLCC Pinout Diagram

2

Table 6. QFP (EIAJ) Pin Names with Package Location

Address/Data Bus

Name	Location
AD0	64
AD1	66
AD2	68
AD3	70
AD4	74
AD5	76
AD6	78
AD7	80
AD8 (A8)	65
AD9 (A9)	67
AD10 (A10)	69
AD11 (A11)	71
AD12 (A12)	75
AD13 (A13)	77
AD14 (A14)	79
AD15 (A15)	1
A16	3
A17	4
A18	5
A19/S6	6

Bus Control

Name	Location
ALE/QS0	10
$\overline{\text{BHE}}$ ($\overline{\text{RFSH}}$)	7
$\overline{\text{S0}}$	23
$\overline{\text{S1}}$	22
$\overline{\text{S2}}$	21
$\overline{\text{RD}}$/$\overline{\text{QSMD}}$	9
$\overline{\text{WR}}$/QS1	8
ARDY	20
SRDY	27
DT/$\overline{\text{R}}$	37
$\overline{\text{DEN}}$	39
$\overline{\text{LOCK}}$	28
HOLD	26
HLDA	25

Power

Name	Location
V_{SS}	12, 13, 24, 53, 62
V_{CC}	2, 33, 34, 44, 72, 73

Processor Control

Name	Location
$\overline{\text{RESIN}}$	55
RESOUT	18
CLKIN	16
OSCOUT	17
CLKOUT	19
$\overline{\text{TEST}}$/BUSY	29
PDTMR	38
NMI	30
INT0	31
INT1/$\overline{\text{SELECT}}$	32
INT2/$\overline{\text{INTA0}}$	35
INT3/$\overline{\text{INTA1}}$/IRQ	36
N.C.	11, 14, 15, 63

I/O

Name	Location
$\overline{\text{UCS}}$	45
$\overline{\text{LCS}}$	46
$\overline{\text{MCS0}}$/PEREQ	40
$\overline{\text{MCS1}}$/$\overline{\text{ERROR}}$	41
$\overline{\text{MCS2}}$	42
$\overline{\text{MCS3}}$/$\overline{\text{NCS}}$	43
$\overline{\text{PCS0}}$	54
$\overline{\text{PCS1}}$	52
$\overline{\text{PCS2}}$	51
$\overline{\text{PCS3}}$	50
$\overline{\text{PCS4}}$	49
$\overline{\text{PCS5}}$/A1	48
$\overline{\text{PCS6}}$/A2	47
T0OUT	57
T0IN	59
T1OUT	56
T1IN	58
DRQ0	61
DRQ1	60

NOTE:
Pin names in parentheses apply to the 80C186EA/80L188EA.

Table 7. QFP (EIAJ) Package Location with Pin Names

Location	Name	Location	Name	Location	Name	Location	Name
1	AD15 (A15)	21	$\overline{S2}$	41	$\overline{MCS1}/\overline{ERROR}$	61	DRQ0
2	V_{CC}	22	$\overline{S1}$	42	$\overline{MCS2}$	62	V_{SS}
3	A16	23	$\overline{S0}$	43	$\overline{MCS3}/\overline{NCS}$	63	N.C.
4	A17	24	V_{SS}	44	V_{CC}	64	AD0
5	A18	25	HLDA	45	$\overline{UCS}$	65	AD8 (A8)
6	A19/S6	26	HOLD	46	$\overline{LCS}$	66	AD1
7	$\overline{BHE}$ ($\overline{RFSH}$)	27	SRDY	47	$\overline{PCS6}$/A2	67	AD9 (A9)
8	$\overline{WR}$/QS1	28	$\overline{LOCK}$	48	$\overline{PCS5}$/A1	68	AD2
9	$\overline{RD}/\overline{QSMD}$	29	$\overline{TEST}$/BUSY	49	$\overline{PCS4}$	69	AD10 (A10)
10	ALE/QS0	30	NMI	50	$\overline{PCS3}$	70	AD3
11	N.C.	31	INT0	51	$\overline{PCS2}$	71	AD11 (A11)
12	V_{SS}	32	INT1/$\overline{SELECT}$	52	$\overline{PCS1}$	72	V_{CC}
13	V_{SS}	33	V_{CC}	53	V_{SS}	73	V_{CC}
14	N.C.	34	V_{CC}	54	$\overline{PCS0}$	74	AD4
15	N.C.	35	INT2/$\overline{INTA0}$	55	$\overline{RESIN}$	75	AD12 (A12)
16	CLKIN	36	INT3/$\overline{INTA1}$/ IRQ	56	T1OUT	76	AD5
17	OSCOUT	37	DT/$\overline{R}$	57	T0OUT	77	AD13 (A13)
18	RESOUT	38	PDTMR	58	T1IN	78	AD6
19	CLKOUT	39	$\overline{DEN}$	59	T0IN	79	AD14 (A14)
20	ARDY	40	$\overline{MCS0}$/PEREQ	60	DRQ1	80	AD7

NOTE:
Pin names in parentheses apply to the 80C186EA/80L188EA.

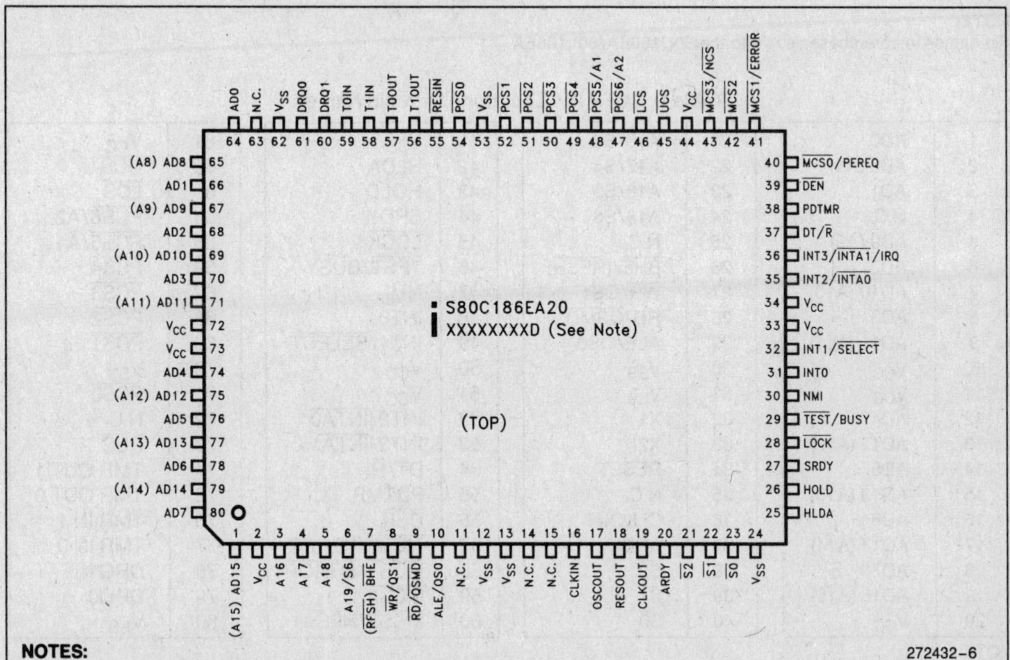

NOTES:
1. The nine-character alphanumeric code (XXXXXXXXD) underneath the product number is the Intel FPO number.
2. Pin names in parentheses apply to the 80C186EA/80L188EA.

Figure 6. Quad Flat Pack (EIAJ) Pinout Diagram

Table 8. SQFP Pin Functions with Package Location

AD Bus	
AD0	1
AD1	3
AD2	6
AD3	8
AD4	12
AD5	14
AD6	16
AD7	18
AD8 (A8)	2
AD9 (A9)	5
AD10 (A10)	7
AD11 (A11)	9
AD12 (A12)	13
AD13 (A13)	15
AD14 (A14)	17
AD15 (A15)	19
A16/S3	21
A17/S4	22
A18/S5	23
A19/S6	24

Bus Control	
ALE/QS0	29
$\overline{\text{BHE}}$/($\overline{\text{RFSH}}$)	26
$\overline{\text{S0}}$	40
$\overline{\text{S1}}$	39
$\overline{\text{S2}}$	38
$\overline{\text{RD}}$/$\overline{\text{QSMD}}$	28
$\overline{\text{WR}}$/QS1	27
ARDY	37
SRDY	44
$\overline{\text{DEN}}$	56
DT/$\overline{\text{R}}$	54
$\overline{\text{LOCK}}$	45
HOLD	43
HLDA	42

No Connection	
N.C.	4
N.C.	25
N.C.	35
N.C.	72

Processor Control	
$\overline{\text{RESIN}}$	73
RESOUT	34
CLKIN	32
OSCOUT	33
CLKOUT	36
$\overline{\text{TEST}}$/BUSY	46
NMI	47
INT0	48
INT1/$\overline{\text{SELECT}}$	49
INT2/$\overline{\text{INTA0}}$	52
INT3/$\overline{\text{INTA1}}$	53
PDTMR	55

Power and Ground	
V_{CC}	10
V_{CC}	11
V_{CC}	20
V_{CC}	50
V_{CC}	51
V_{CC}	61
V_{SS}	30
V_{SS}	31
V_{SS}	41
V_{SS}	70
V_{SS}	80

I/O	
$\overline{\text{UCS}}$	62
$\overline{\text{LCS}}$	63
$\overline{\text{MCS0}}$/PEREQ	57
$\overline{\text{MCS1}}$/$\overline{\text{ERROR}}$	58
$\overline{\text{MCS2}}$	59
$\overline{\text{MCS3}}$/$\overline{\text{NPS}}$	60
$\overline{\text{PCS0}}$	71
$\overline{\text{PCS1}}$	69
$\overline{\text{PCS2}}$	68
$\overline{\text{PCS3}}$	67
$\overline{\text{PCS4}}$	66
$\overline{\text{PCS5}}$/A1	65
$\overline{\text{PCS6}}$/A2	64
TMR IN 0	77
TMR IN 1	76
TMR OUT 0	75
TMR OUT 1	74
DRQ0	79
DRQ1	78

NOTE:
Pin names in parentheses apply to the 80C186EA/80L188EA.

Table 9. SQFP Pin Locations with Pin Names

1	AD0	21	A16/S3	41	V_{SS}	61	V_{CC}
2	AD8 (A8)	22	A17/S4	42	HLDA	62	$\overline{\text{UCS}}$
3	AD1	23	A18/S5	43	HOLD	63	$\overline{\text{LCS}}$
4	N.C.	24	A19/S6	44	SRDY	64	$\overline{\text{PCS6}}$/A2
5	AD9 (A9)	25	N.C.	45	$\overline{\text{LOCK}}$	65	$\overline{\text{PCS5}}$/A1
6	AD2	26	$\overline{\text{BHE}}$/($\overline{\text{RFSH}}$)	46	$\overline{\text{TEST}}$/BUSY	66	$\overline{\text{PCS4}}$
7	AD10 (A10)	27	$\overline{\text{WR}}$/QS1	47	NMI	67	$\overline{\text{PCS3}}$
8	AD3	28	$\overline{\text{RD}}$/$\overline{\text{QSMD}}$	48	INT0	68	$\overline{\text{PCS2}}$
9	AD11 (A11)	29	ALE/QS0	49	INT1/$\overline{\text{SELECT}}$	69	$\overline{\text{PCS1}}$
10	V_{CC}	30	V_{SS}	50	V_{CC}	70	V_{SS}
11	V_{CC}	31	V_{SS}	51	V_{CC}	71	$\overline{\text{PCS0}}$
12	AD4	32	X1	52	INT2/$\overline{\text{INTA0}}$	72	N.C.
13	AD12 (A12)	33	X2	53	INT3/$\overline{\text{INTA1}}$	73	$\overline{\text{RES}}$
14	AD5	34	RESET	54	DT/$\overline{\text{R}}$	74	TMR OUT 1
15	AD13 (A13)	35	N.C.	55	PDTMR	75	TMR OUT 0
16	AD6	36	CLKOUT	56	$\overline{\text{DEN}}$	76	TMR IN 1
17	AD14 (A14)	37	ARDY	57	$\overline{\text{MCS0}}$/PEREQ	77	TMR IN 0
18	AD7	38	$\overline{\text{S2}}$	58	$\overline{\text{MCS1}}$/$\overline{\text{ERROR}}$	78	DRQ1
19	AD15 (A15)	39	$\overline{\text{S1}}$	59	$\overline{\text{MCS2}}$	79	DRQ0
20	V_{CC}	40	$\overline{\text{S0}}$	60	$\overline{\text{MCS3}}$/$\overline{\text{NPS}}$	80	V_{SS}

NOTE:
Pin names in parentheses apply to the 80C186EA/80L188EA.

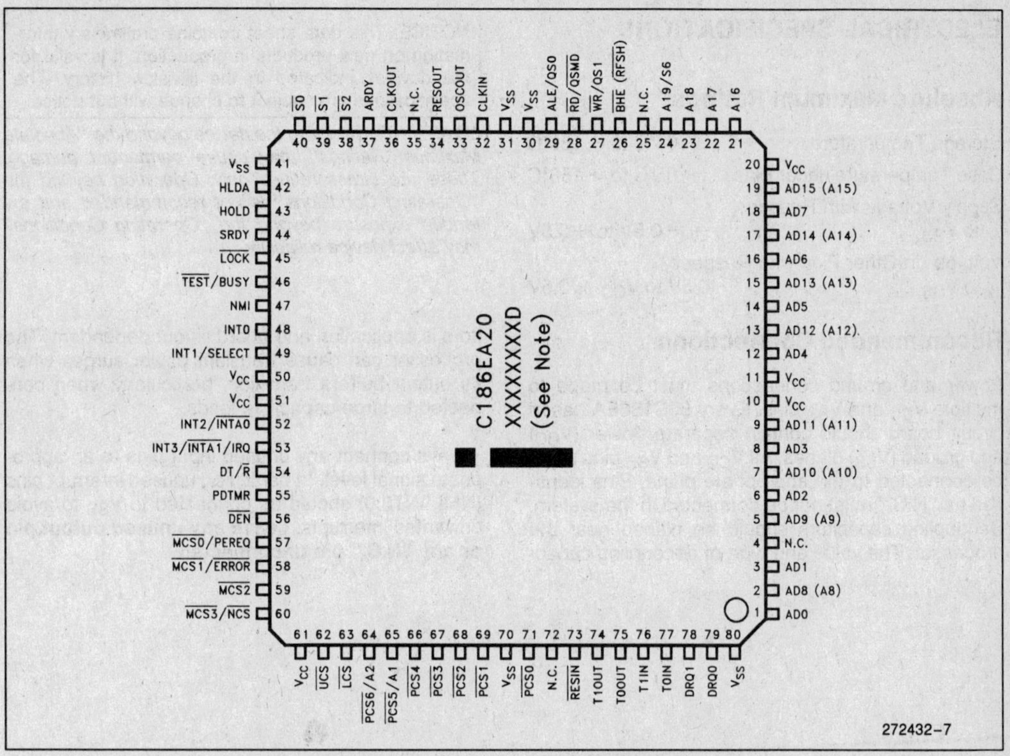

40 $\overline{S0}$, 39 $\overline{S1}$, 38 $\overline{S2}$, 37 ARDY, 36 CLKOUT, 35 N.C., 34 RESOUT, 33 OSCOUT, 32 CLKIN, 31 V_{SS}, 30 V_{SS}, 29 ALE/QS0, 28 $\overline{RD}$/$\overline{QSMD}$, 27 $\overline{WR}$/QS1, 26 $\overline{BHE}$ ($\overline{RFSH}$), 25 N.C., 24 A19/S6, 23 A18, 22 A17, 21 A16

41 V_{SS}, 42 HLDA, 43 HOLD, 44 SRDY, 45 $\overline{LOCK}$, 46 $\overline{TEST}$/BUSY, 47 NMI, 48 INT0, 49 INT1/SELECT, 50 V_{CC}, 51 V_{CC}, 52 INT2/$\overline{INTA0}$, 53 INT3/$\overline{INTA1}$/IRQ, 54 DT/$\overline{R}$, 55 PDTMR, 56 $\overline{DEN}$, 57 $\overline{MCS0}$/PEREQ, 58 $\overline{MCS1}$/$\overline{ERROR}$, 59 $\overline{MCS2}$, 60 $\overline{MCS3}$/$\overline{NCS}$

20 V_{CC}, 19 AD15 (A15), 18 AD7, 17 AD14 (A14), 16 AD6, 15 AD13 (A13), 14 AD5, 13 AD12 (A12), 12 AD4, 11 V_{CC}, 10 V_{CC}, 9 AD11 (A11), 8 AD3, 7 AD10 (A10), 6 AD2, 5 AD9 (A9), 4 N.C., 3 AD1, 2 AD8 (A8), 1 AD0

61 V_{CC}, 62 $\overline{UCS}$, 63 $\overline{LCS}$, 64 $\overline{PCS6}$/A2, 65 $\overline{PCS5}$/A1, 66 $\overline{PCS4}$, 67 $\overline{PCS3}$, 68 $\overline{PCS2}$, 69 $\overline{PCS1}$, 70 V_{SS}, 71 $\overline{PCS0}$, 72 N.C., 73 $\overline{RESIN}$, 74 T1OUT, 75 T0OUT, 76 T1IN, 77 T0IN, 78 DRQ1, 79 DRQ0, 80 V_{SS}

C186EA20
XXXXXXXXD
(See Note)

272432–7

Figure 7. Shrink Quad Flat Pack (SQFP) Pinout Diagram

NOTES:
1. XXXXXXXXD indicates the Intel FPO number.
2. Pin names in parentheses apply to the 80C188EA.

PACKAGE THERMAL SPECIFICATIONS

The 80C186EA/80L186EA is specified for operation when T_C (the case temperature) is within the range of 0°C to 85°C (PLCC package) or 0°C to 106°C (QFP-EIAJ) package. T_C may be measured in any environment to determine whether the processor is within the specified operating range. The case temperature must be measured at the center of the top surface.

T_A (the ambient temperature) can be calculated from θ_{CA} (thermal resistance from the case to ambient) with the following equation:

$$T_A = T_C - P \times \theta_{CA}$$

Typical values for θ_{CA} at various airflows are given in Table 10.

P (the maximum power consumption, specified in watts) is calculated by using the maximum ICC as tabulated in the DC specifications and V_{CC} of 5.5V.

Table 10. Thermal Resistance (θ_{CA}) at Various Airflows (in °C/Watt)

	Airflow Linear ft/min (m/sec)					
	0 (0)	200 (1.01)	400 (2.03)	600 (3.04)	800 (4.06)	1000 (5.07)
θ_{CA} (PLCC)	29	25	21	19	17	16.5
θ_{CA} (QFP)	66	63	60.5	59	58	57
θ_{CA} (SQFP)	70					

ELECTRICAL SPECIFICATIONS

Absolute Maximum Ratings*

Storage Temperature .... −65°C to +150°C

Case Temperature under Bias ... −65°C to +150°C

Supply Voltage with Respect to V_{SS} .... −0.5V to +6.5V

Voltage on Other Pins with Respect to V_{SS} .... −0.5V to V_{CC} + 0.5V

NOTICE: This data sheet contains preliminary information on new products in production. It is valid for the devices indicated in the revision history. The specifications are subject to change without notice.

******WARNING: Stressing the device beyond the "Absolute Maximum Ratings" may cause permanent damage. These are stress ratings only. Operation beyond the "Operating Conditions" is not recommended and extended exposure beyond the "Operating Conditions" may affect device reliability.*

Recommended Connections

Power and ground connections must be made to multiple V_{CC} and V_{SS} pins. Every 80C186EA based circuit board should contain separate power (V_{CC}) and ground (V_{SS}) planes. All V_{CC} and V_{SS} pins **must** be connected to the appropriate plane. Pins identified as "N.C." must not be connected in the system. Decoupling capacitors should be placed near the processor. The value and type of decoupling capacitors is application and board layout dependent. The processor can cause transient power surges when its output buffers transition, particularly when connected to large capacitive loads.

Always connect any unused input pins to an appropriate signal level. In particular, unused interrupt pins (NMI, INT3:0) should be connected to V_{SS} to avoid unwanted interrupts. **Leave any unused output pin or any "N.C." pin unconnected.**

DC SPECIFICATIONS (80C186EA/80C188EA)

Symbol	Parameter	Min	Max	Units	Conditions
V_{CC}	Supply Voltage	4.5	5.5	V	
V_{IL}	Input Low Voltage for All Pins	−0.5	0.3 V_{CC}	V	
V_{IH}	Input High Voltage for All Pins	0.7 V_{CC}	V_{CC} + 0.5	V	
V_{OL}	Output Low Voltage		0.45	V	I_{OL} = 3 mA (min)
V_{OH}	Output High Voltage	V_{CC} − 0.5		V	I_{OH} = −2 mA (min)
V_{HYR}	Input Hysterisis on $\overline{RESIN}$	0.30		V	
I_{IL1}	Input Leakage Current (except $\overline{RD}$/$\overline{QSMD}$, $\overline{UCS}$, $\overline{LCS}$, $\overline{MCS0}$/PEREQ, $\overline{MCS1}$/$\overline{ERROR}$, $\overline{LOCK}$ and $\overline{TEST}$/BUSY)		±10	μA	0V ≤ V_{IN} ≤ V_{CC}
I_{IL2}	Input Leakage Current ($\overline{RD}$/$\overline{QSMD}$, $\overline{UCS}$, $\overline{LCS}$, $\overline{MCS0}$/PEREQ, $\overline{MCS1}$, $\overline{ERROR}$, $\overline{LOCK}$ and $\overline{TEST}$/BUSY	−275		μA	V_{IN} = 0.7 V_{CC} (Note 1)
I_{OL}	Output Leakage Current		±10	μA	0.45 ≤ V_{OUT} ≤ V_{CC} (Note 2)
I_{CC}	Supply Current Cold (RESET) 80C186EA20/80C188EA20 80C186EA13/80C188EA13		 100 65	 mA mA	 (Note 3)
I_{ID}	Supply Current In Idle Mode 80C186EA20/80C188EA20 80C186EA13/80C188EA13		 70 46	 mA mA	
I_{PD}	Supply Current In Powerdown Mode 80C186EA20/80C188EA20 80C186EA13/80C188EA13		 100 100	 μA μA	
C_{OUT}	Output Pin Capacitance	0	15	pF	T_F = 1 MHz (Note 4)
C_{IN}	Input Pin Capacitance	0	15	pF	T_F = 1 MHz

NOTES:
1. $\overline{RD}$/$\overline{QSMD}$, $\overline{UCS}$, $\overline{LCS}$, $\overline{MCS0}$/PEREQ, $\overline{MCS1}$/$\overline{ERROR}$, $\overline{LOCK}$ and $\overline{TEST}$/BUSY have internal pullups that are only activated during RESET. Loading these pins above I_{OL} = −275 μA will cause the processor to enter alternate modes of operation.
2. Output pins are floated using HOLD or ONCE Mode.
3. Measured at worst case temperature and V_{CC} with all outputs loaded as specified in the AC Test Conditions, and with the device in RESET ($\overline{RESIN}$ held low). RESET is worst case for I_{CC}.
4. Output capacitance is the capacitive load of a floating output pin.

2

DC SPECIFICATIONS (80L186EA/80L188EA)

Symbol	Parameter	Min	Max	Units	Conditions
V_{CC}	Supply Voltage	2.7	5.5	V	
V_{IL}	Input Low Voltage for All Pins	−0.5	0.3 V_{CC}	V	
V_{IH}	Input High Voltage for All Pins	0.7 V_{CC}	V_{CC} + 0.5	V	
V_{OL}	Output Low Voltage		0.45	V	I_{OL} = 1.6 mA (min)
V_{OH}	Output High Voltage	V_{CC} − 0.5		V	I_{OH} = −1 mA (min)
V_{HYR}	Input Hysterisis on $\overline{RESIN}$	0.30		V	
I_{IL1}	Input Leakage Current (except $\overline{RD}/\overline{QSMD}$, $\overline{UCS}$, $\overline{LCS}$, $\overline{MCS0}$/PEREQ, $\overline{MCS1}$, $\overline{LOCK}$ and $\overline{TEST}$)		±10	μA	0V ≤ V_{IN} ≤ V_{CC}
I_{IL2}	Input Leakage Current ($\overline{RD}/\overline{QSMD}$, $\overline{UCS}$, $\overline{LCS}$, $\overline{MCS0}$, $\overline{MCS1}$, $\overline{LOCK}$ and $\overline{TEST}$)	−275		μA	V_{IN} = 0.7 V_{CC} (Note 1)
I_{OL}	Output Leakage Current		±10	μA	0.45 ≤ V_{OUT} ≤ V_{CC} (Note 2)
I_{CC5}	Supply Current (RESET, 5.5V) 80L186EA-13 80L186EA-8		 65 40	 mA mA	 (Note 3) (Note 3)
I_{CC3}	Supply Current (RESET, 2.7V) 80L186EA-13 80L186EA-8		 34 20	 mA mA	 (Note 3) (Note 3)
I_{ID5}	Supply Current Idle (5.5V) 80L186EA-13 80L186EA-8		 46 28	 mA mA	
I_{ID5}	Supply Current Idle (2.7V) 80L186EA-13 80L186EA-8		 24 14	 mA mA	
I_{PD5}	Supply Current Powerdown (5.5V) 80L186EA-13 80L186EA-8		 100 100	 μA μA	
I_{PD3}	Supply Current Powerdown (2.7V) 80L186EA-13 80L186EA-8		 50 50	 μA μA	
C_{OUT}	Output Pin Capacitance	0	15	pF	T_F = 1 MHz (Note 4)
C_{IN}	Input Pin Capacitance	0	15	pF	T_F = 1 MHz

NOTES:

1. $\overline{RD}/\overline{QSMD}$, $\overline{UCS}$, $\overline{LCS}$, $\overline{MCS0}$, $\overline{MCS1}$, $\overline{LOCK}$ and $\overline{TEST}$ have internal pullups that are only activated during RESET. Loading these pins above I_{OL} = −275 μA will cause the processor to enter alternate modes of operation.
2. Output pins are floated using HOLD or ONCE Mode.
3. Measured at worst case temperature and V_{CC} with all outputs loaded as specified in the AC Test Conditions, and with the device in RESET ($\overline{RESIN}$ held low).
4. Output capacitance is the capacitive load of a floating output pin.

I_{CC} VERSUS FREQUENCY AND VOLTAGE

The current (I_{CC}) consumption of the processor is essentially composed of two components; I_{PD} and I_{CCS}.

I_{PD} is the **quiescent** current that represents internal device leakage, and is measured with all inputs or floating outputs at GND or V_{CC} (no clock applied to the device). I_{PD} is equal to the Powerdown current and is typically less than 50 μA.

I_{CCS} is the **switching** current used to charge and discharge parasitic device capacitance when changing logic levels. Since I_{CCS} is typically much greater than I_{PD}, I_{PD} can often be ignored when calculating I_{CC}.

I_{CCS} is related to the voltage and frequency at which the device is operating. It is given by the formula:

$$Power = V \times I = V^2 \times C_{DEV} \times f$$

$$\therefore I = I_{CC} = I_{CCS} = V \times C_{DEV} \times f$$

Where: V = Device operating voltage (V_{CC})

C_{DEV} = Device capacitance

f = Device operating frequency

I_{CCS} = I_{CC} = Device current

Measuring C_{DEV} on a device like the 80C186EA would be difficult. Instead, C_{DEV} is calculated using the above formula by measuring I_{CC} at a known V_{CC} and frequency (see Table 11). Using this C_{DEV} value, I_{CC} can be calculated at any voltage and frequency within the specified operating range.

EXAMPLE: Calculate the typical I_{CC} when operating at 20 MHz, 4.8V.

$$I_{CC} = I_{CCS} = 4.8 \times 0.515 \times 20 \approx 49 \text{ mA}$$

PDTMR PIN DELAY CALCULATION

The PDTMR pin provides a delay between the assertion of NMI and the enabling of the internal clocks when exiting Powerdown. A delay is required only when using the on-chip oscillator to allow the crystal or resonator circuit time to stabilize.

NOTE:

The PDTMR pin function does not apply when $\overline{RESIN}$ is asserted (i.e., a device reset during Powerdown is similar to a cold reset and $\overline{RESIN}$ must remain active until after the oscillator has stabilized).

To calculate the value of capacitor required to provide a desired delay, use the equation:

$$440 \times t = C_{PD} \quad (5V, 25°C)$$

Where: t = desired delay in **seconds**

C_{PD} = capacitive load on PDTMR in **microfarads**

EXAMPLE: To get a delay of 300 μs, a capacitor value of $C_{PD} = 440 \times (300 \times 10^{-6}) = 0.132$ μF is required. Round up to standard (available) capacitive values.

NOTE:

The above equation applies to delay times greater than 10 μs and will compute the **TYPICAL** capacitance needed to achieve the desired delay. A delay variance of +50% or −25% can occur due to temperature, voltage, and device process extremes. In general, higher V_{CC} and/or lower temperature will decrease delay time, while lower V_{CC} and/or higher temperature will increase delay time.

2

Table 11. C_{DEV} Values

Parameter	Typ	Max	Units	Notes
C_{DEV} (Device in Reset)	0.515	0.905	mA/V*MHz	1, 2
C_{DEV} (Device in Idle)	0.391	0.635	mA/V*MHz	1, 2

1. Max C_{DEV} is calculated at −40°C, all floating outputs driven to V_{CC} or GND, and all outputs loaded to 50 pF (including CLKOUT and OSCOUT).
2. Typical C_{DEV} is calculated at 25°C with all outputs loaded to 50 pF except CLKOUT and OSCOUT, which are not loaded.

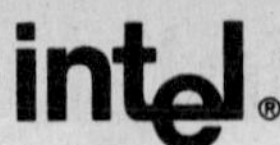

AC SPECIFICATIONS

AC Characteristics—80C186EA20/80C186EA13

Symbol	Parameter	Min	Max	Min	Max	Units	Notes
INPUT CLOCK		20 MHz		13 MHz			
T_F	CLKIN Frequency	0	40	0	26	MHz	1
T_C	CLKIN Period	25	∞	38.5	∞	ns	1
T_{CH}	CLKIN High Time	10	∞	12	∞	ns	1, 2
T_{CL}	CLKIN Low Time	10	∞	12	∞	ns	1, 2
T_{CR}	CLKIN Rise Time	1	8	1	8	ns	1, 3
T_{CF}	CLKIN Fall Time	1	8	1	8	ns	1, 3
OUTPUT CLOCK							
T_{CD}	CLKIN to CLKOUT Delay	0	17	0	23	ns	1, 4
T	CLKOUT Period		2*T_C		2*T_C	ns	1
T_{PH}	CLKOUT High Time	(T/2) − 5		(T/2) − 5		ns	1
T_{PL}	CLKOUT Low Time	(T/2) − 5		(T/2) − 5		ns	1
T_{PR}	CLKOUT Rise Time	1	6	1	6	ns	1, 5
T_{PF}	CLKOUT Fall Time	1	6	1	6	ns	1, 5
OUTPUT DELAYS							
T_{CHOV1}	ALE, $\overline{S2:0}$, $\overline{DEN}$, DT/$\overline{R}$, $\overline{BHE}$, ($\overline{RFSH}$), $\overline{LOCK}$, A19:16	3	22	3	25	ns	1, 4, 6, 7
T_{CHOV2}	$\overline{MCS3:0}$, $\overline{LCS}$, $\overline{UCS}$, $\overline{PCS6:0}$, $\overline{NCS}$, $\overline{RD}$, $\overline{WR}$	3	27	3	30	ns	1, 4, 6, 8
T_{CLOV1}	$\overline{BHE}$ ($\overline{RFSH}$), $\overline{DEN}$, $\overline{LOCK}$, RESOUT, HLDA, T0OUT, T1OUT, A19:16	3	22	3	25	ns	1, 4, 6
T_{CLOV2}	$\overline{RD}$, $\overline{WR}$, $\overline{MCS3:0}$, $\overline{LCS}$, $\overline{UCS}$, $\overline{PCS6:0}$, AD15:0 (A15:8, AD7:0), $\overline{NCS}$, $\overline{INTA1:0}$, $\overline{S2:0}$	3	27	3	30	ns	1, 4, 6
T_{CHOF}	$\overline{RD}$, $\overline{WR}$, $\overline{BHE}$ ($\overline{RFSH}$), DT/$\overline{R}$, $\overline{LOCK}$, $\overline{S2:0}$, A19:16	0	25	0	25	ns	1
T_{CLOF}	$\overline{DEN}$, AD15:0 (A15:8, AD7:0)	0	20	0	25	ns	1

AC SPECIFICATIONS (Continued)

AC Characteristics—80C186EA20/80C186EA13

Symbol	Parameter	Min	Max	Min	Max	Units	Notes
SYNCHRONOUS INPUTS		20 MHz		13 MHz			
T_{CHIS}	$\overline{TEST}$, NMI, INT3:0, T1:0IN, ARDY	10		10		ns	1, 9
T_{CHIH}	$\overline{TEST}$, NMI, INT3:0, T1:0IN, ARDY	3		3		ns	1, 9
T_{CLIS}	AD15:0 (AD7:0), ARDY, SRDY, DRQ1:0	10		10		ns	1, 10
T_{CLIH}	AD15:0 (AD7:0), ARDY, SRDY, DRQ1:0	3		3		ns	1, 10
T_{CLIS}	HOLD, PEREQ, $\overline{ERROR}$ (80C186EA Only)	10		10		ns	1, 9
T_{CLIH}	HOLD, PEREQ, $\overline{ERROR}$ (80C186EA Only)	3		3		ns	1, 9
T_{CLIS}	$\overline{RESIN}$ (to CLKIN)	10		10		ns	1, 9
T_{CLIH}	$\overline{RESIN}$ (from CLKIN)	3		3		ns	1, 9

NOTES:
1. See **AC Timing Waveforms**, for waveforms and definition.
2. Measured at V_{IH} for high time, V_{IL} for low time.
3. Only required to guarantee I_{CC}. Maximum limits are bounded by T_C, T_{CH} and T_{CL}.
4. Specified for a 50 pF load, see Figure 13 for capacitive derating information.
5. Specified for a 50 pF load, see Figure 14 for rise and fall times outside 50 pF.
6. See Figure 14 for rise and fall times.
7. T_{CHOV1} applies to $\overline{BHE}$ ($\overline{RFSH}$), $\overline{LOCK}$ and A19:16 only after a HOLD release.
8. T_{CHOV2} applies to $\overline{RD}$ and $\overline{WR}$ only after a HOLD release.
9. Setup and Hold are required to guarantee recognition.
10. Setup and Hold are required for proper operation.
11. T_{CHOVS} applies to $\overline{BHE}$ ($\overline{RFSH}$) and A19:16 only after a HOLD release.

Pin names in parentheses apply to the 80C188EA/80L188EA.

2

AC SPECIFICATIONS

AC Characteristics—80L186EA13/80L186EA8

Symbol	Parameter	Min	Max	Min	Max	Units	Notes
INPUT CLOCK		**13 MHz**		**8 MHz**			
T_F	CLKIN Frequency	0	26	0	16	MHz	1
T_C	CLKIN Period	38.5	∞	62.5	∞	ns	1
T_{CH}	CLKIN High Time	12	∞	12	∞	ns	1, 2
T_{CL}	CLKIN Low Time	12	∞	12	∞	ns	1, 2
T_{CR}	CLKIN Rise Time	1	8	1	8	ns	1, 3
T_{CF}	CLKIN Fall Time	1	8	1	8	ns	1, 3
OUTPUT CLOCK							
T_{CD}	CLKIN to CLKOUT Delay	0	45	0	95	ns	1, 4
T	CLKOUT Period		$2{*}T_C$		$2{*}T_C$	ns	1
T_{PH}	CLKOUT High Time	(T/2) − 5		(T/2) − 5		ns	1
T_{PL}	CLKOUT Low Time	(T/2) − 5		(T/2) − 5		ns	1
T_{PR}	CLKOUT Rise Time	1	12	1	12	ns	1, 5
T_{PF}	CLKOUT Fall Time	1	12	1	12	ns	1, 5
OUTPUT DELAYS							
T_{CHOV1}	ALE, $\overline{LOCK}$	3	27	3	27	ns	1, 4, 6, 7
T_{CHOV2}	$\overline{MCS3:0}$, $\overline{LCS}$, $\overline{UCS}$, $\overline{PCS6:0}$, $\overline{RD}$, $\overline{WR}$	3	32	3	32	ns	1, 4, 6, 8
T_{CHOV3}	$\overline{S2:0}$ ($\overline{DEN}$), DT/$\overline{R}$, $\overline{BHE}$ ($\overline{RFSH}$), A19:16	3	30	3	30	ns	1
T_{CLOV1}	$\overline{LOCK}$, RESOUT, HLDA, T0OUT, T1OUT	3	27	3	27	ns	1, 4, 6
T_{CLOV2}	$\overline{RD}$, $\overline{WR}$, $\overline{MCS3:0}$, $\overline{LCS}$, $\overline{UCS}$, $\overline{PCS6:0}$, $\overline{INTA1:0}$	3	32	3	35	ns	1, 4, 6
T_{CLOV3}	$\overline{BHE}$ ($\overline{RFSH}$), $\overline{DEN}$, A19:16	3	30	3	30	ns	1, 4, 6
T_{CLOV4}	AD15:0 (A15:8, AD7:0)	3	34	3	35	ns	1, 4, 6
T_{CLOV5}	$\overline{S2:0}$	3	38	3	40	ns	1, 4, 6
T_{CHOF}	$\overline{RD}$, $\overline{WR}$, $\overline{BHE}$ ($\overline{RFSH}$), DT/$\overline{R}$, $\overline{LOCK}$, $\overline{S2:0}$, A19:16	0	27	0	27	ns	1
T_{CLOF}	$\overline{DEN}$, AD15:0 (A15:8, AD7:0)	0	27	0	27	ns	1

NOTES:
1. See **AC Timing Waveforms**, for waveforms and definition.
2. Measured at V_{IH} for high time, V_{IL} for low time.
3. Only required to guarantee I_{CC}. Maximum limits are bounded by T_C, T_{CH} and T_{CL}.
4. Specified for a 50 pF load, see Figure 13 for capacitive derating information.
5. Specified for a 50 pF load, see Figure 14 for rise and fall times outside 50 pF.
6. See Figure 14 for rise and fall times.
7. T_{CHOV1} applies to $\overline{BHE}$ ($\overline{RFSH}$), $\overline{LOCK}$ and A19:16 only after a HOLD release.
8. T_{CHOV2} applies to $\overline{RD}$ and $\overline{WR}$ only after a HOLD release.
9. Setup and Hold are required to guarantee recognition.
10. Setup and Hold are required for proper operation.
11. T_{CHOVS} applies to $\overline{BHE}$ ($\overline{RFSH}$) and A19:16 only after a HOLD release.
12. Pin names in parentheses apply to the 80C188EA/80L188EA.

AC SPECIFICATIONS

AC Characteristics—80L186EA13/80L186EA8

Symbol	Parameter	Min	Max	Min	Max	Units	Notes
SYNCHRONOUS INPUTS		13 MHz		8 MHz			
T_{CHIS}	$\overline{TEST}$, NMI, INT3:0, T1:0IN, ARDY	22		22		ns	1, 9
T_{CHIH}	$\overline{TEST}$, NMI, INT3:0, T1:0IN, ARDY	3		3		ns	1, 9
T_{CLIS}	AD15:0 (AD7:0), ARDY, SRDY, DRQ1:0	22		22		ns	1, 10
T_{CLIH}	AD15:0 (AD7:0), ARDY, SRDY, DRQ1:0	3		3		ns	1, 10
T_{CLIS}	HOLD	22		22		ns	1, 9
T_{CLIH}	HOLD	3		3		ns	1, 9
T_{CLIS}	$\overline{RESIN}$ (to CLKIN)	22		22		ns	1, 9
T_{CLIH}	$\overline{RESIN}$ (from CLKIN)	3		3		ns	1, 9

NOTES:
1. See **AC Timing Waveforms**, for waveforms and definition.
2. Measured at V_{IH} for high time, V_{IL} for low time.
3. Only required to guarantee I_{CC}. Maximum limits are bounded by T_C, T_{CH} and T_{CL}.
4. Specified for a 50 pF load, see Figure 13 for capacitive derating information.
5. Specified for a 50 pF load, see Figure 14 for rise and fall times outside 50 pF.
6. See Figure 14 for rise and fall times.
7. T_{CHOV1} applies to $\overline{BHE}$ ($\overline{RFSH}$), $\overline{LOCK}$ and A19:16 only after a HOLD release.
8. T_{CHOV2} applies to $\overline{RD}$ and $\overline{WR}$ only after a HOLD release.
9. Setup and Hold are required to guarantee recognition.
10. Setup and Hold are required for proper operation.
11. T_{CHOVS} applies to $\overline{BHE}$ ($\overline{RFSH}$) and A19:16 only after a HOLD release.
12. Pin names in parentheses apply to the 80C188EA/80L188EA.

AC SPECIFICATIONS (Continued)

Relative Timings (80C186EA20/13, 80L186EA13/8)

Symbol	Parameter	Min	Max	Unit	Notes
RELATIVE TIMINGS					
T_{LHLL}	ALE Rising to ALE Falling	T − 15		ns	
T_{AVLL}	Address Valid to ALE Falling	½T − 10		ns	
T_{PLLL}	Chip Selects Valid to ALE Falling	½T − 10		ns	1
T_{LLAX}	Address Hold from ALE Falling	½T − 10		ns	
T_{LLWL}	ALE Falling to $\overline{WR}$ Falling	½T − 15		ns	1
T_{LLRL}	ALE Falling to $\overline{RD}$ Falling	½T − 15		ns	1
T_{RHLH}	$\overline{RD}$ Rising to ALE Rising	½T − 10		ns	1
T_{WHLH}	$\overline{WR}$ Rising to ALE Rising	½T − 10		ns	1
T_{AFRL}	Address Float to $\overline{RD}$ Falling	0		ns	
T_{RLRH}	$\overline{RD}$ Falling to $\overline{RD}$ Rising	(2*T) − 5		ns	2
T_{WLWH}	$\overline{WR}$ Falling to $\overline{WR}$ Rising	(2*T) − 5		ns	2
T_{RHAV}	$\overline{RD}$ Rising to Address Active	T − 15		ns	
T_{WHDX}	Output Data Hold after $\overline{WR}$ Rising	T − 15		ns	
T_{WHDEX}	$\overline{WR}$ Rising to $\overline{DEN}$ Rising	½T − 10		ns	1
T_{WHPH}	$\overline{WR}$ Rising to Chip Select Rising	½T − 10		ns	1, 4
T_{RHPH}	$\overline{RD}$ Rising to Chip Select Rising	½T − 10		ns	1, 4
T_{PHPL}	$\overline{CS}$ Inactive to $\overline{CS}$ Active	½T − 10		ns	1
T_{DXDL}	$\overline{DEN}$ Inactive to DT/$\overline{R}$ Low	0		ns	5
T_{OVRH}	ONCE ($\overline{UCS}$, $\overline{LCS}$) Active to $\overline{RESIN}$ Rising	T		ns	3
T_{RHOX}	ONCE ($\overline{UCS}$, $\overline{LCS}$) to $\overline{RESIN}$ Rising	T		ns	3

NOTES:
1. Assumes equal loading on both pins.
2. Can be extended using wait states.
3. Not tested.
4. Not applicable to latched A2:1. These signals change only on falling T_1.
5. For write cycle followed by read cycle.

AC TEST CONDITIONS

The AC specifications are tested with the 50 pF load shown in Figure 8. See the Derating Curves section to see how timings vary with load capacitance.

Specifications are measured at the $V_{CC}/2$ crossing point, unless otherwise specified. See AC Timing Waveforms, for AC specification definitions, test pins, and illustrations.

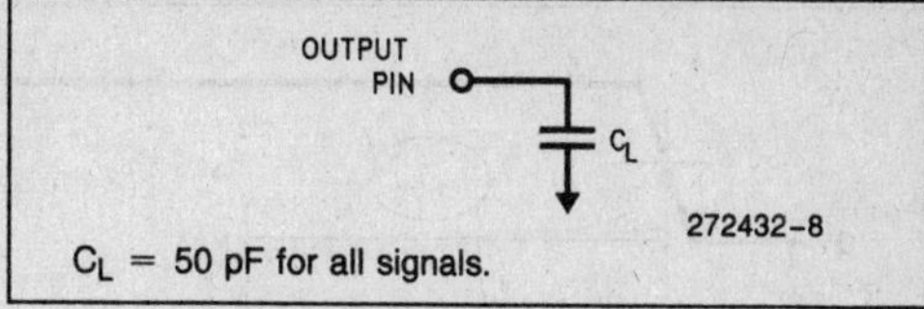

Figure 8. AC Test Load

AC TIMING WAVEFORMS

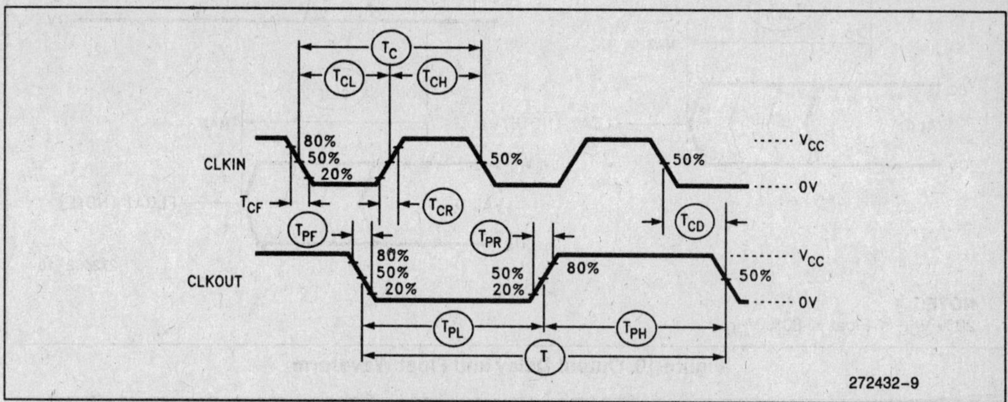

Figure 9. Input and Output Clock Waveform

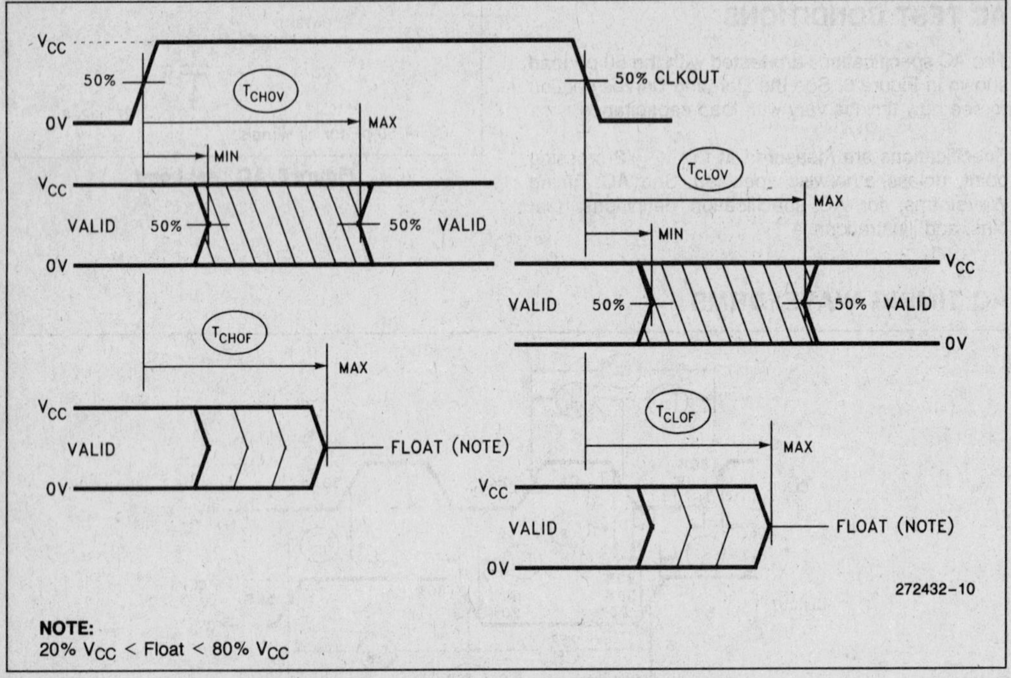

NOTE:
20% V_{CC} < Float < 80% V_{CC}

Figure 10. Output Delay and Float Waveform

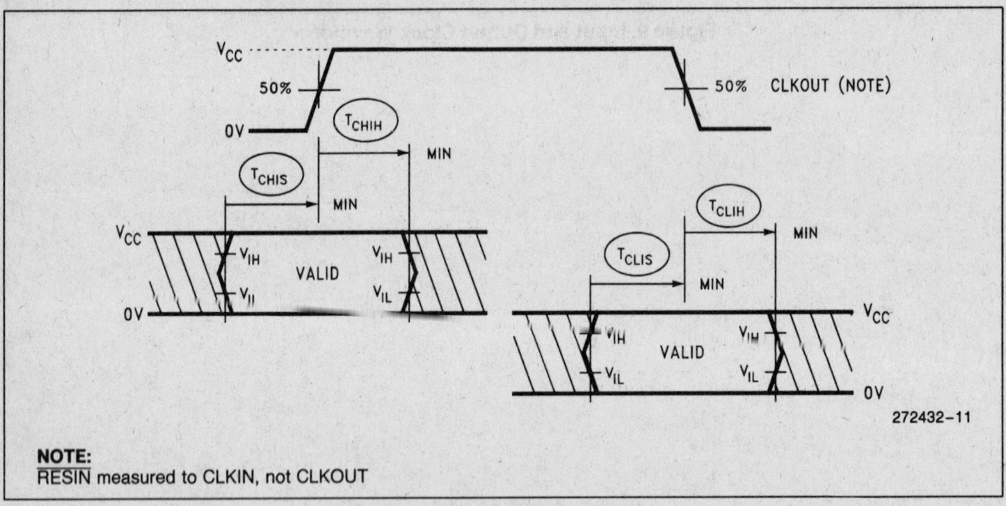

NOTE:
$\overline{\text{RESIN}}$ measured to CLKIN, not CLKOUT

Figure 11. Input Setup and Hold

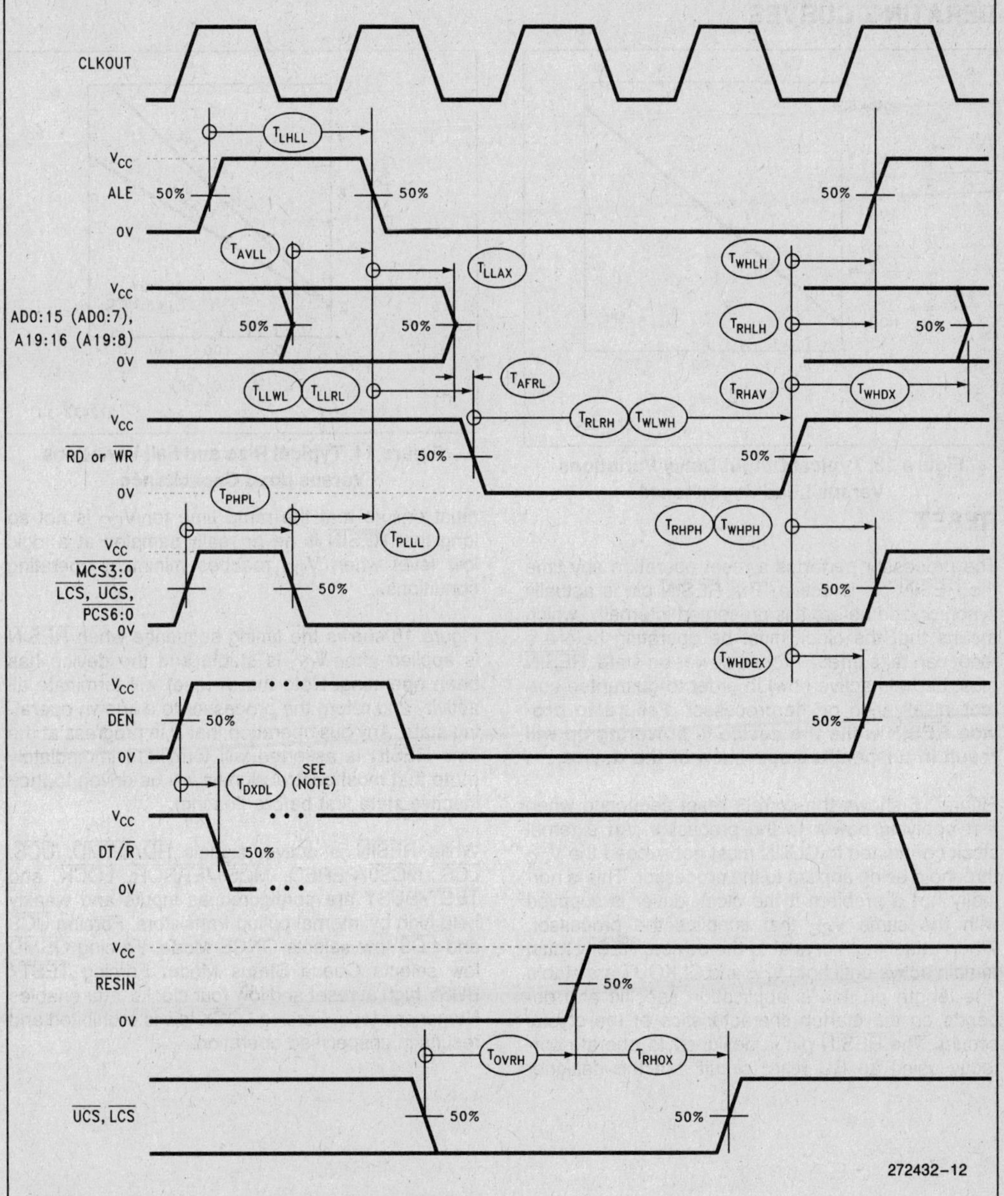

NOTES:

1. T_{DXDL} for write cycle followed by read cycle.
2. Pin names in parentheses apply to tthe 80C188EA.

Figure 12. Relative Signal Waveform

DERATING CURVES

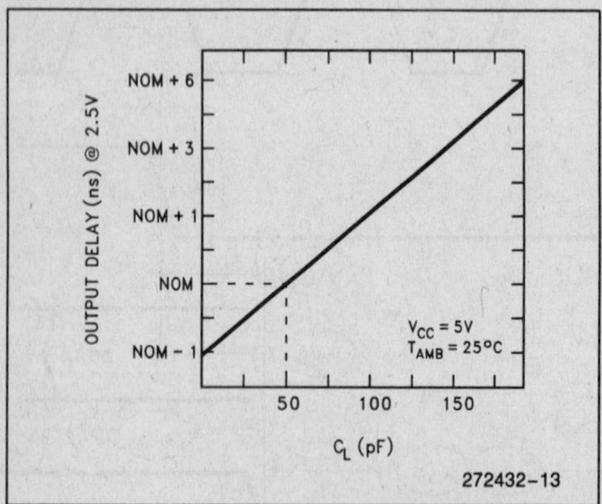

Figure 13. Typical Output Delay Variations Versus Load Capacitance

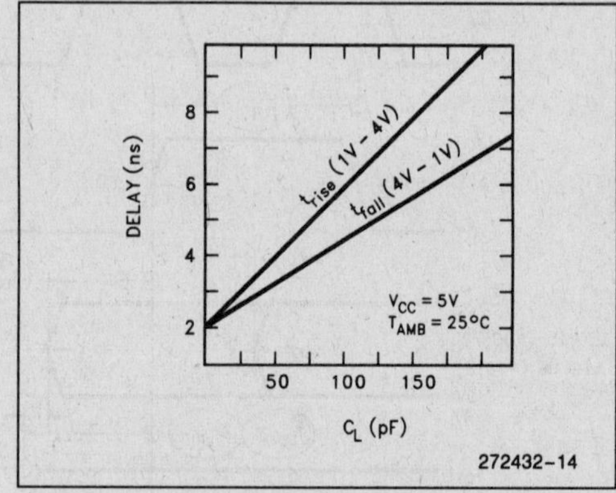

Figure 14. Typical Rise and Fall Variations Versus Load Capacitance

RESET

The processor performs a reset operation any time the $\overline{\text{RESIN}}$ pin is active. The $\overline{\text{RESIN}}$ pin is actually synchronized before it is presented internally, which means that the clock must be operating before a reset can take effect. From a power-on state, $\overline{\text{RESIN}}$ must be held active (low) in order to guarantee correct initialization of the processor. **Failure to provide $\overline{\text{RESIN}}$ while the device is powering up will result in unspecified operation of the device.**

Figure 15 shows the correct reset sequence when first applying power to the processor. An external clock connected to CLKIN must not exceed the V_{CC} threshold being applied to the processor. This is normally not a problem if the clock driver is supplied with the same V_{CC} that supplies the processor. When attaching a crystal to the device, $\overline{\text{RESIN}}$ must remain active until both V_{CC} and CLKOUT are stable (the length of time is application specific and depends on the startup characteristics of the crystal circuit). The $\overline{\text{RESIN}}$ pin is designed to operate correctly using an RC reset circuit, but the designer must ensure that the ramp time for V_{CC} is not so long that $\overline{\text{RESIN}}$ is never really sampled at a logic low level when V_{CC} reaches minimum operating conditions.

Figure 16 shows the timing sequence when $\overline{\text{RESIN}}$ is applied after V_{CC} is stable and the device has been operating. Note that a reset will terminate all activity and return the processor to a known operating state. Any bus operation that is in progress at the time $\overline{\text{RESIN}}$ is asserted will terminate immediately (note that most control signals will be driven to their inactive state first before floating).

While $\overline{\text{RESIN}}$ is active, signals $\overline{\text{RD}}/\overline{\text{QSMD}}$, $\overline{\text{UCS}}$, $\overline{\text{LCS}}$, $\overline{\text{MCS0}}$/PEREQ, $\overline{\text{MCS1}}/\overline{\text{ERROR}}$, $\overline{\text{LOCK}}$, and $\overline{\text{TEST}}$/BUSY are configured as inputs and weakly held high by internal pullup transistors. Forcing $\overline{\text{UCS}}$ and $\overline{\text{LCS}}$ low selects ONCE Mode. Forcing $\overline{\text{QSMD}}$ low selects Queue Status Mode. Forcing $\overline{\text{TEST}}$/BUSY high at reset and low four clocks later enables Numerics Mode. Forcing $\overline{\text{LOCK}}$ low is prohibited and results in unspecified operation.

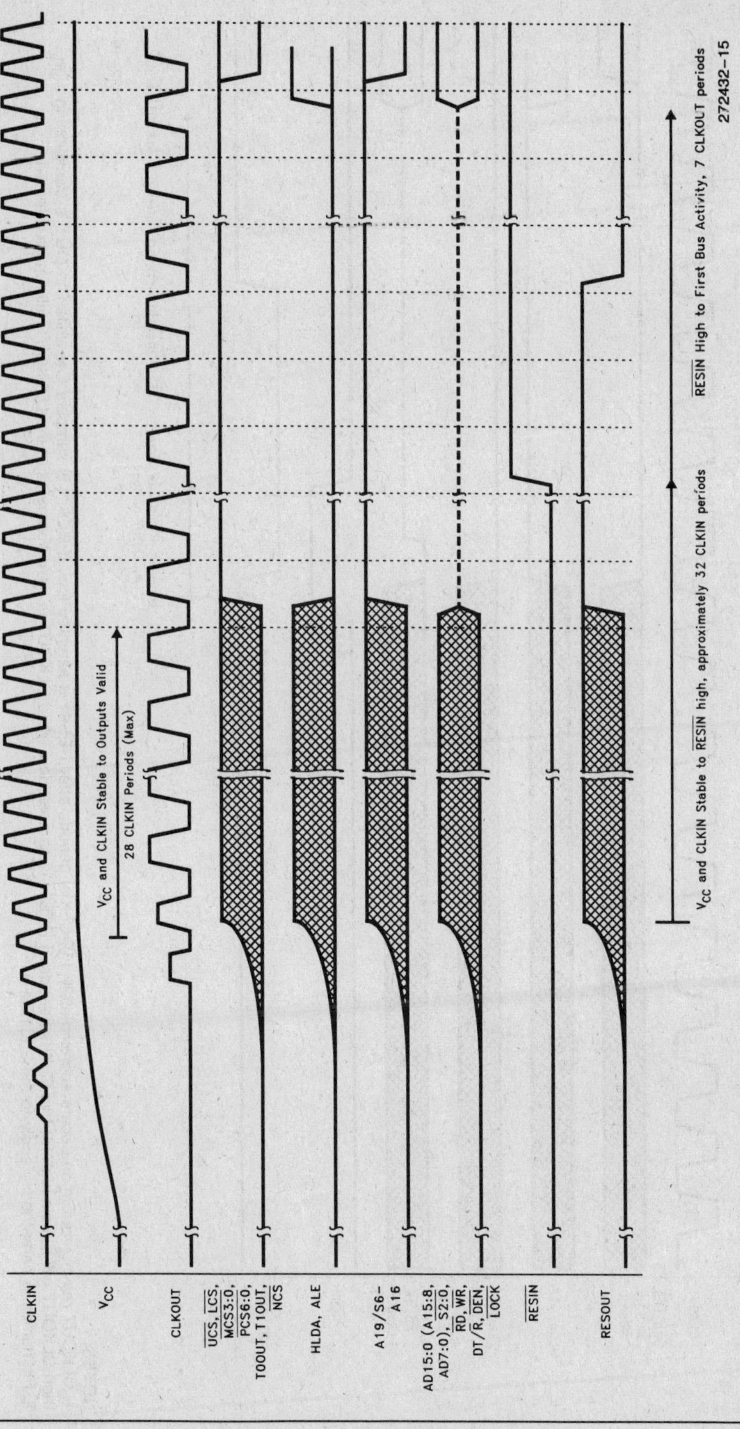

NOTES:
1. CLKOUT synchronization occurs approximately 1½ CLKIN periods after $\overline{\text{RESIN}}$ is sampled low.
2. Pin names in parentheses apply to the 80C188EA.

272432–15

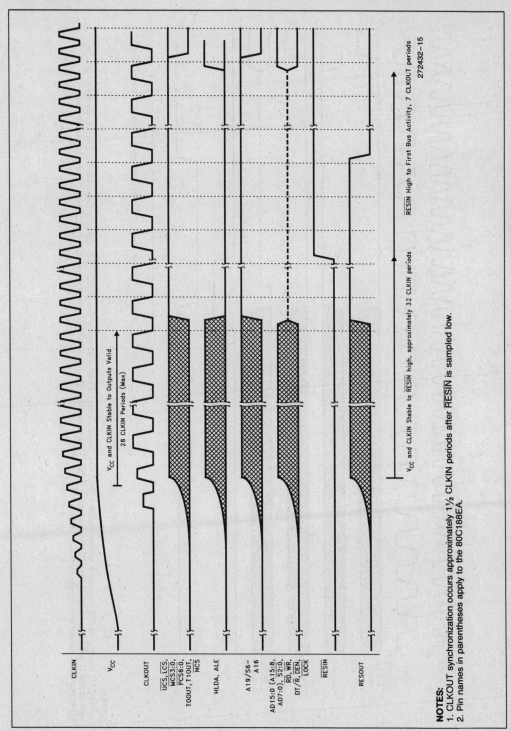

Figure 15. Powerup Reset Waveforms

272432–16

NOTES:
1. CLKOUT resynchronization occurs approximately 1½ CLKIN periods after $\overline{\text{RESIN}}$ is sampled low. If $\overline{\text{RESIN}}$ is sampled low while CLKOUT is transitioning high, then CLKOUT will remain high for two CLKIN periods. If $\overline{\text{RESIN}}$ is sampled low while CLKOUT is transitioning high, then CLKOUT will not be affected.
2. Pin names in parentheses apply to the 80C188EA.

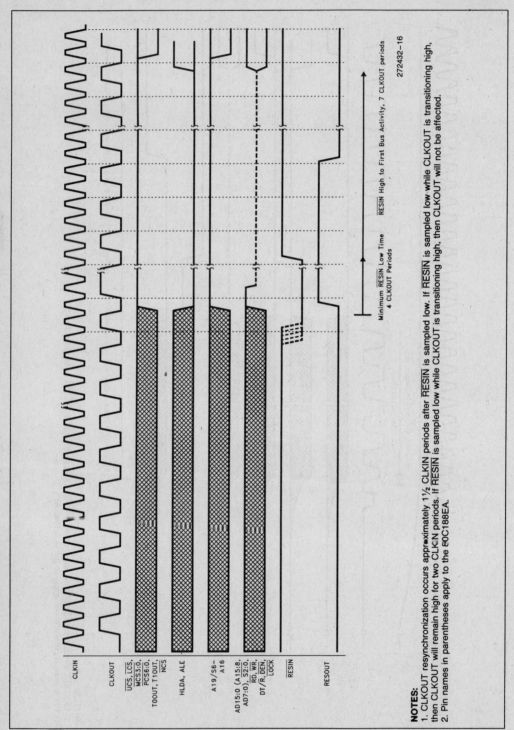

Figure 16. Warm Reset Waveforms

BUS CYCLE WAVEFORMS

Figures 17 through 23 present the various bus cycles that are generated by the processor. What is shown in the figure is the relationship of the various bus signals to CLKOUT. These figures along with the information present in **AC Specifications** allow the user to determine all the critical timing analysis needed for a given application.

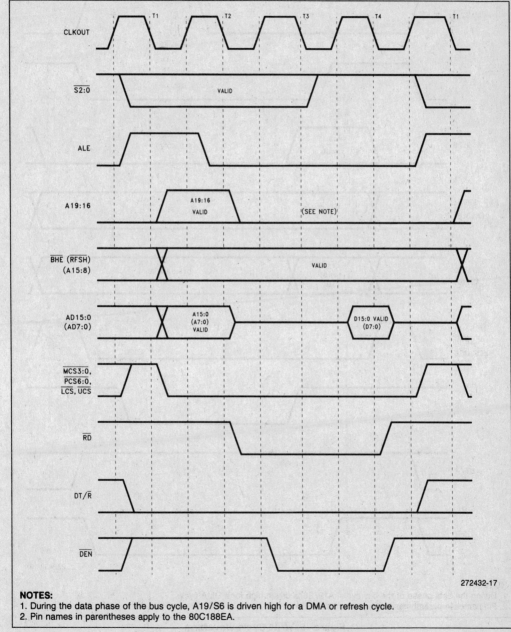

NOTES:
1. During the data phase of the bus cycle, A19/S6 is driven high for a DMA or refresh cycle.
2. Pin names in parentheses apply to the 80C188EA.

Figure 17. Read, Fetch and Refresh Cycle Waveform

2

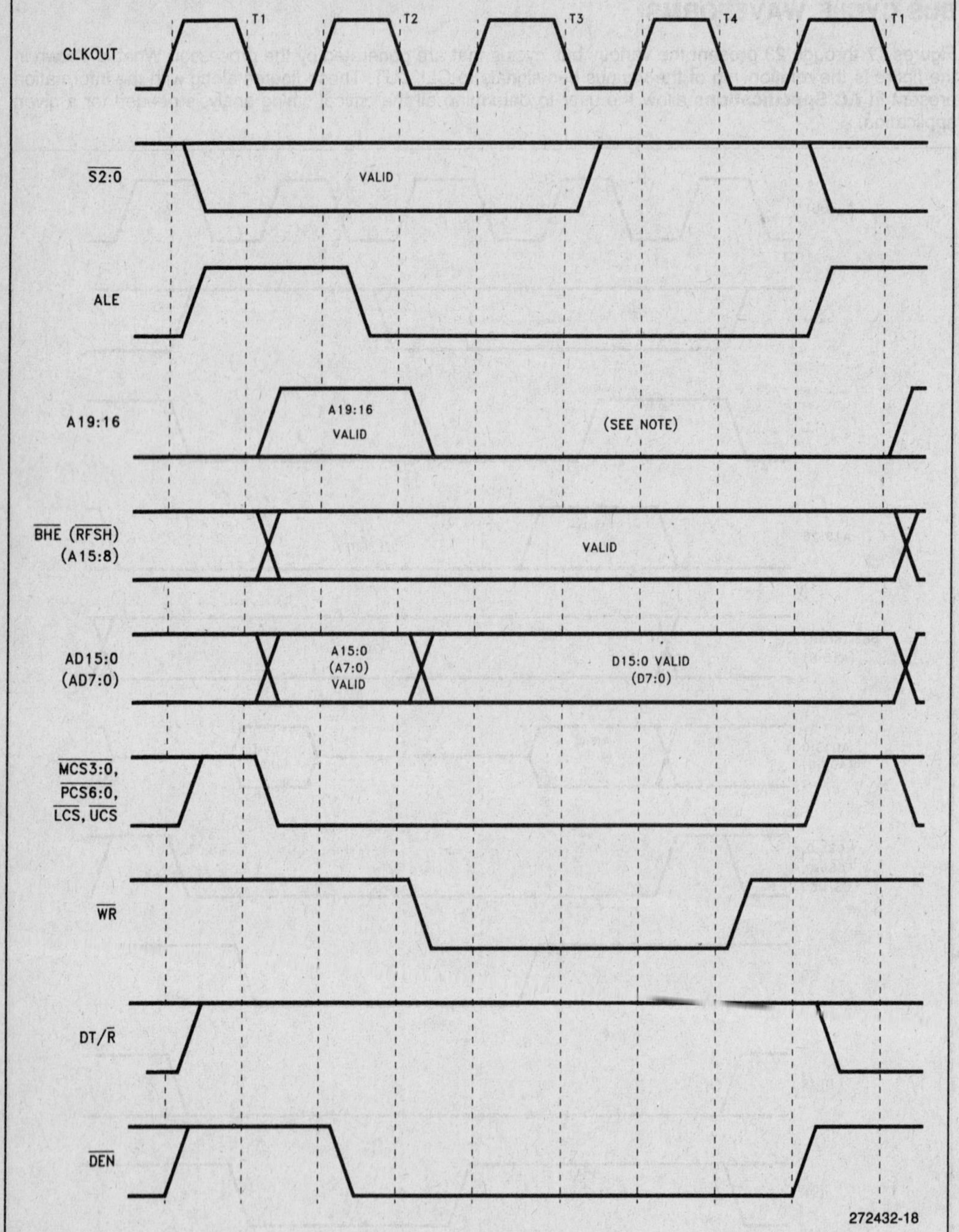

NOTES:

1. During the data phase of the bus cycle, A19/S6 is driven high for a DMA cycle.
2. Pin names in parentheses apply to the 80C188EA.

Figure 18. Write Cycle Waveform

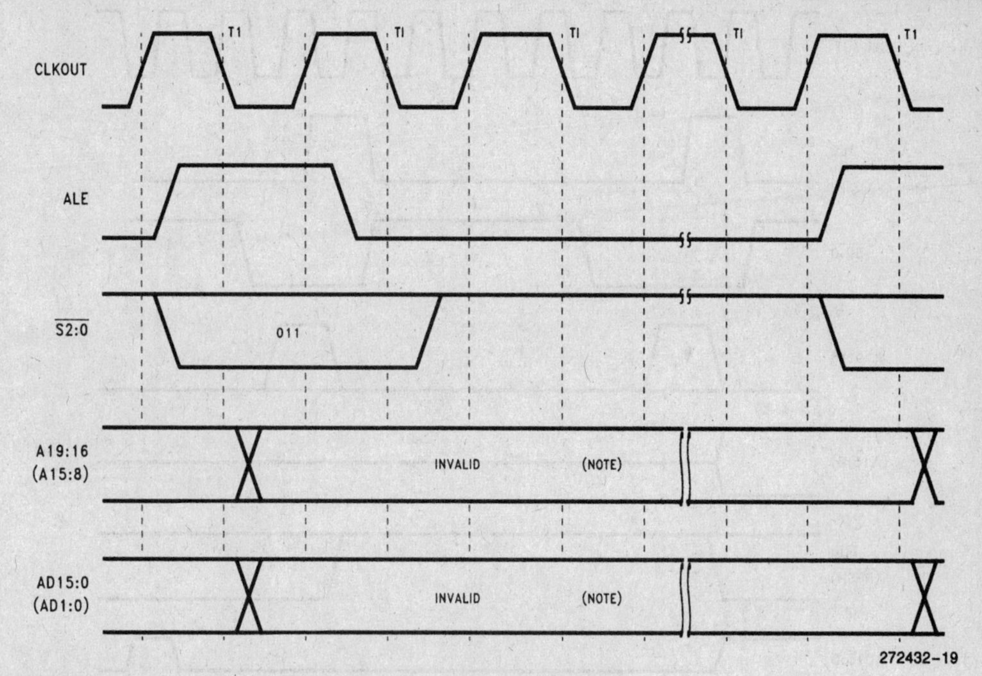

NOTES:
1. The processor drives these pins to 0 during Idle and Powerdown Modes.
2. Pin names in parentheses apply to the 80C188EA.

Figure 19. Halt Cycle Waveform

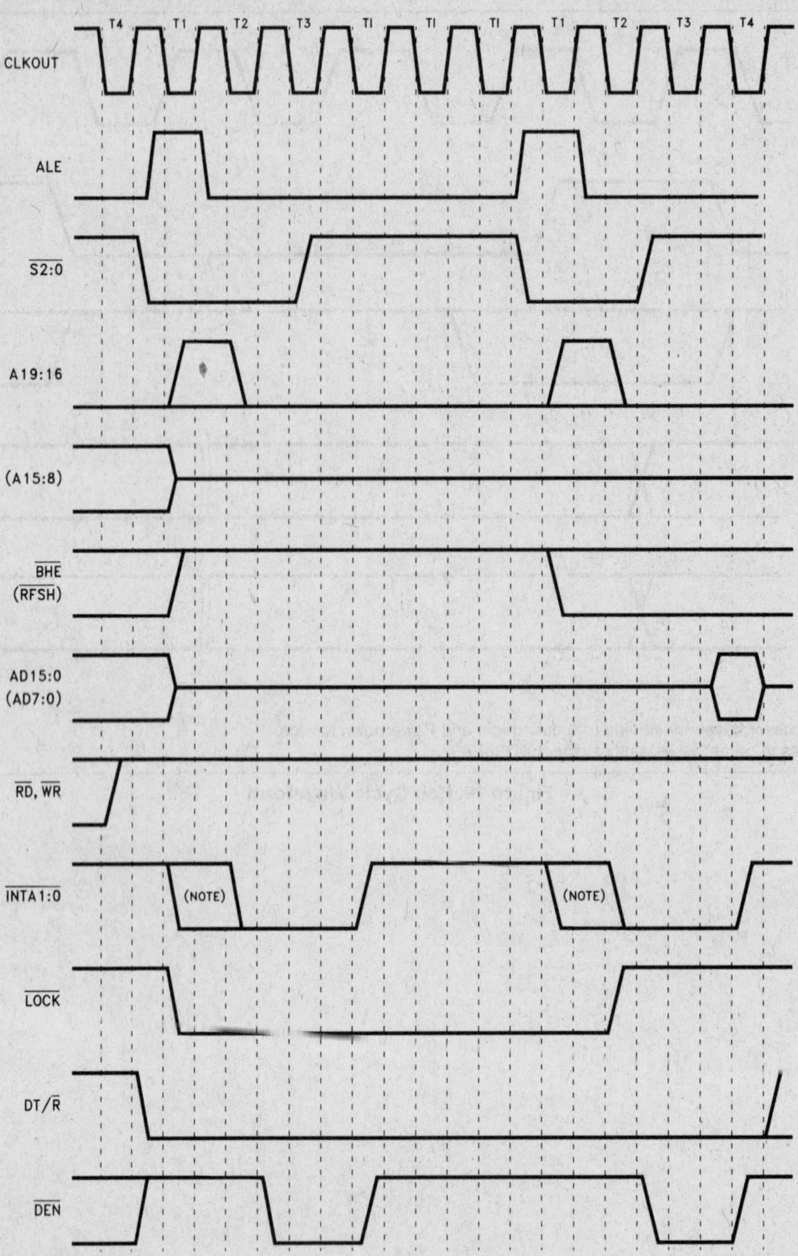

NOTES:
1. INTA occurs one clock later in Slave Mode.
2. Pin names in parentheses apply to the 80C188EA.

Figure 20. INTA Cycle Waveform

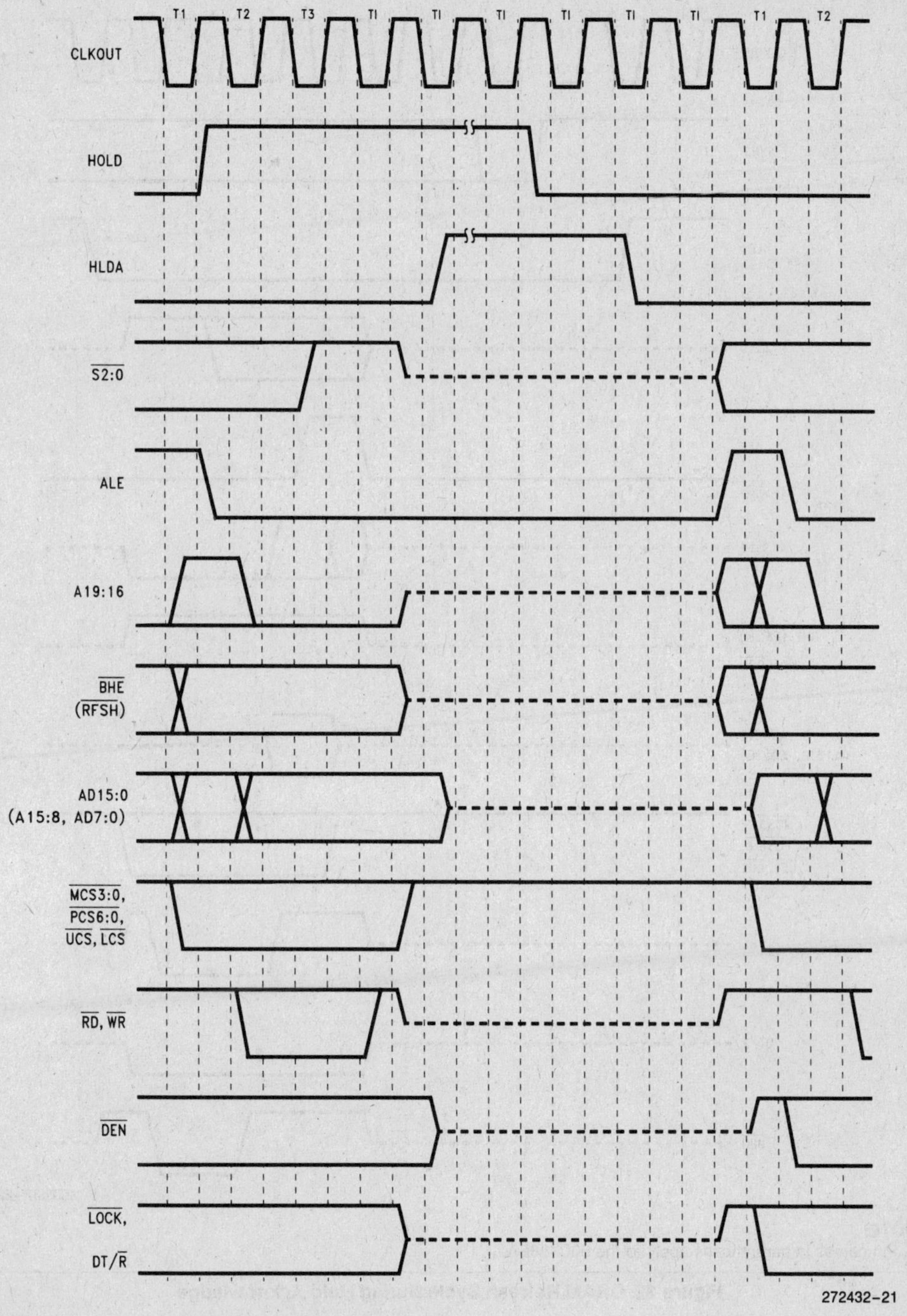

T1 T2 T3 TI TI TI TI TI TI T1 T2

CLKOUT

HOLD

HLDA

$\overline{\text{S2:0}}$

ALE

A19:16

$\overline{\text{BHE}}$
($\overline{\text{RFSH}}$)

AD15:0
(A15:8, AD7:0)

$\overline{\text{MCS3:0}}$,
$\overline{\text{PCS6:0}}$,
$\overline{\text{UCS}}$, $\overline{\text{LCS}}$

$\overline{\text{RD}}$, $\overline{\text{WR}}$

$\overline{\text{DEN}}$

$\overline{\text{LOCK}}$,
DT/$\overline{\text{R}}$

272432–21

NOTE:
1. Pin names in parentheses apply to the 80C188EA.

Figure 21. HOLD/HLDA Waveform

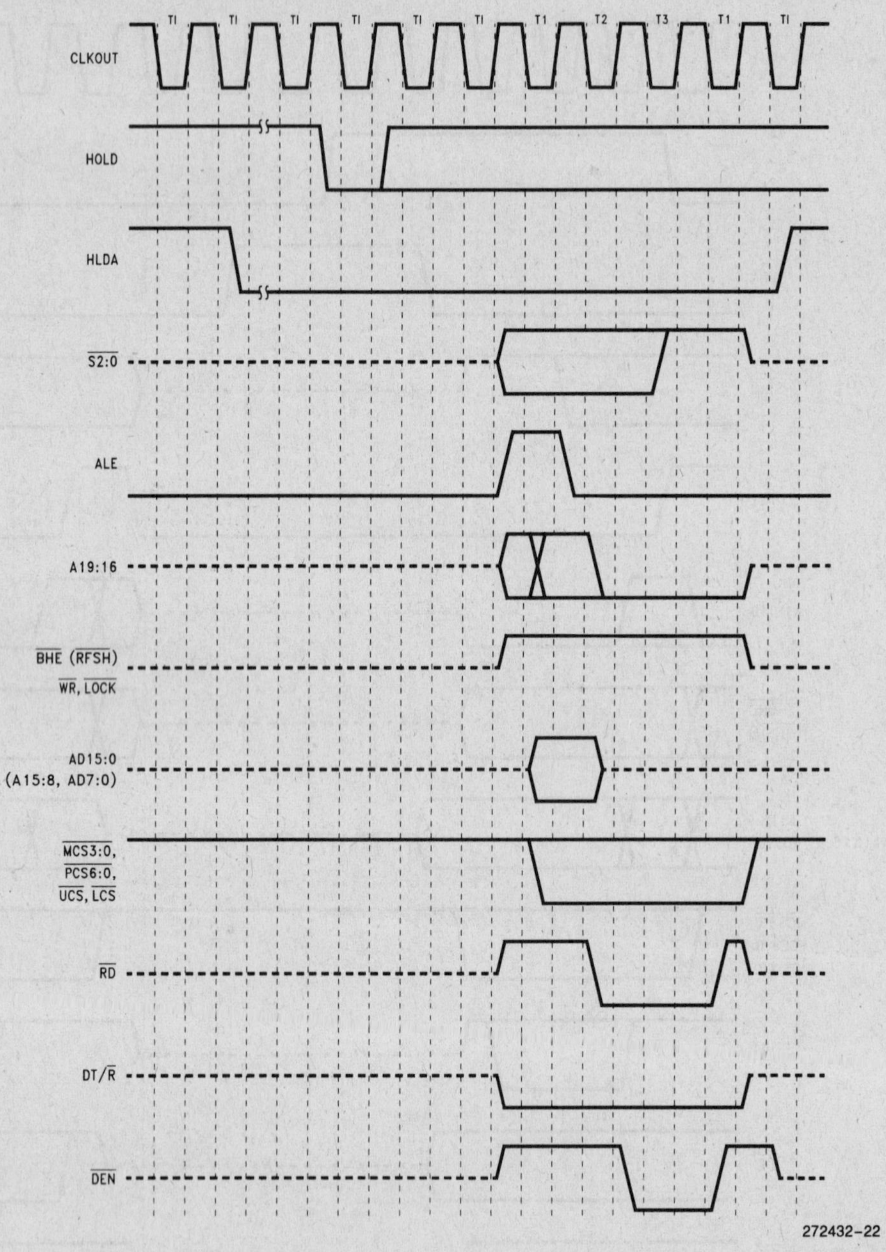

TI TI TI TI TI TI T1 T2 T3 T1 TI

CLKOUT

HOLD

HLDA

$\overline{S2:0}$

ALE

A19:16

$\overline{BHE}$ ($\overline{RFSH}$)

$\overline{WR}$, $\overline{LOCK}$

AD15:0

(A15:8, AD7:0)

$\overline{MCS3:0}$,

$\overline{PCS6:0}$,

$\overline{UCS}$, $\overline{LCS}$

$\overline{RD}$

DT/$\overline{R}$

$\overline{DEN}$

272432–22

NOTE:

1. Pin names in parentheses apply to the 80C188EA.

Figure 22. DRAM Refresh Cycle During Hold Acknowledge

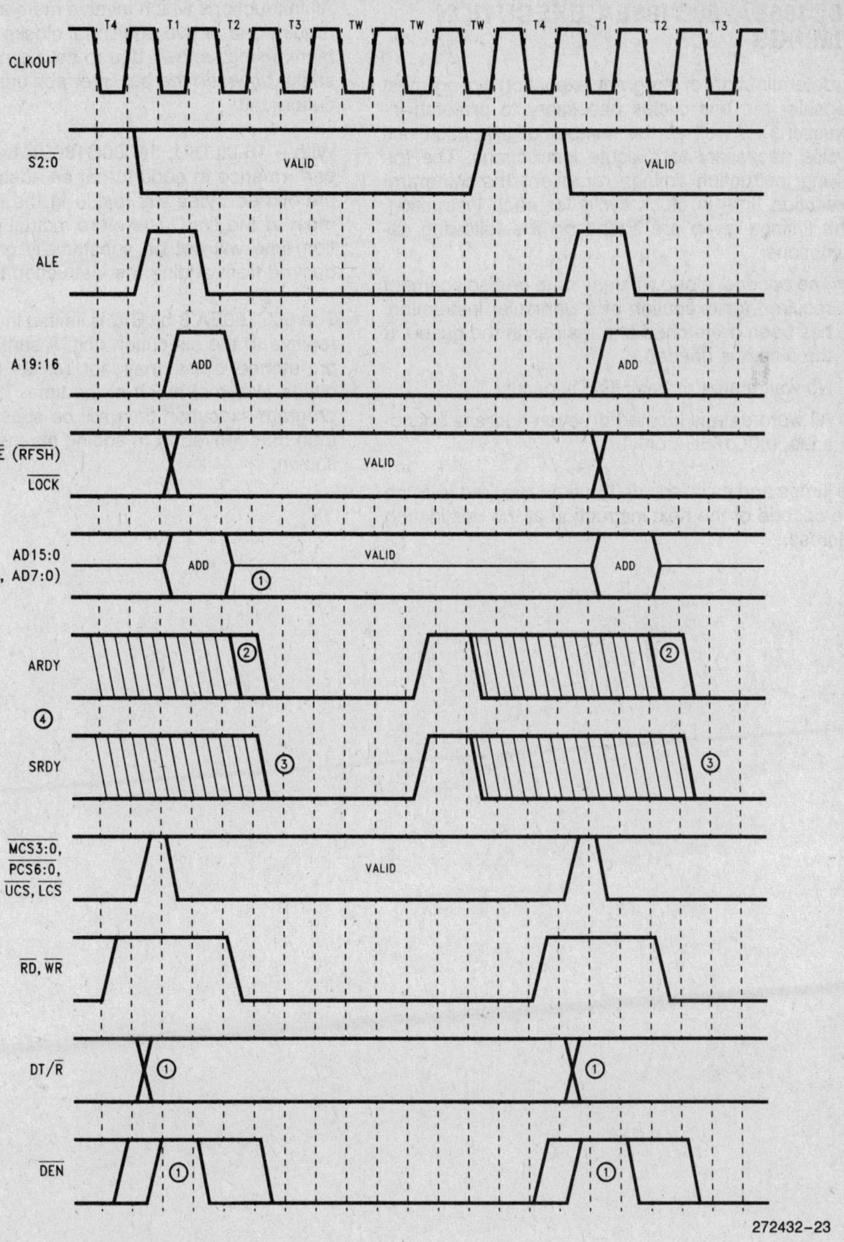

NOTES:
1. Generalized diagram for READ or WRITE.
2. ARDY low by either edge causes a wait state. Only rising ARDY is fully synchronized.
3. SRDY low causes a wait state. SRDY must meet setup and hold times to ensure correct device operation.
4. Either ARDY or SRDY active high will terminate a bus cycle.
5. Pin names in parentheses apply to the 80C188EA.

Figure 23. Ready Waveform

2

80C186EA/80C188EA EXECUTION TIMINGS

A determination of program exeution timing must consider the bus cycles necessary to prefetch instructions as well as the number of execution unit cycles necessary to execute instructions. The following instruction timings represent the **minimum** execution time in clock cycle for each instruction. The timings given are based on the following assumptions:

- The opcode, along with any data or displacement required for execution of a particular instruction, has been prefetched and resides in the queue at the time it is needed.
- No wait states or bus HOLDs occur.
- All word-data is located on even-address boundaries. (80C186EA only)

All jumps and calls include the time required to fetch the opcode of the next instruction at the destination address.

All instructions which involve memory accesses can require one or two additional clocks above the minimum timings shown due to the asynchronous handshake between the bus interface unit (BIU) and execution unit.

With a 16-bit BIU, the 80C186EA has sufficient bus performance to endure that an adequate number of prefetched bytes will reside in the queue (6 bytes) most of the time. Therefore, actual program exeuction time will not be substanially greater than that derived from adding the instruction timings shown.

The 80C188EA 8-bit BIU is limited in its performance relative to the execution unit. A sufficient number of prefetched bytes may not reside in the prefetch queue (4 bytes) much of the time. Therefore, actual program execution time will be substantially greater than that derived from adding the instruction timings shown.

INSTRUCTION SET SUMMARY

Function	Format				80C186EA Clock Cycles	80C188EA Clock Cycles	Comments
DATA TRANSFER							
MOV = Move:							
Register to Register/Memory	1000100w	mod reg r/m			2/12	2/12*	
Register/memory to register	1000101w	mod reg r/m			2/9	2/9	
Immediate to register/memory	1100011w	mod 000 r/m	data	data if w=1	12–13	12–13	8/16-bit
Immediate to register	1011w reg	data	data if w=1		3–4	3–4	8/16-bit
Memory to accumulator	1010000w	addr-low	addr-high		8	8*	
Accumulator to memory	1010001w	addr-low	addr-high		9	9*	
Register/memory to segment register	10001110	mod 0 reg r/m			2/9	2/13	
Segment register to register/memory	10001100	mod 0 reg r/m			2/11	2/15	
PUSH = Push:							
Memory	11111111	mod 110 r/m			16	20	
Register	01010 reg				10	14	
Segment register	000reg110				9	13	
Immediate	011010s0	data	data if s=0		10	14	
PUSHA = Push All	01100000				36	68	
POP = Pop:							
Memory	10001111	mod 000 r/m			20	24	
Register	01011 reg				10	14	
Segment register	000reg111	(reg≠01)			8	12	
POPA = Pop All	01100001				51	83	
XCHG = Exchange:							
Register/memory with register	1000011w	mod reg r/m			4/17	4/17*	
Register with accumulator	10010 reg				3	3	
IN = Input from:							
Fixed port	1110010w	port			10	10*	
Variable port	1110110w				8	7*	
OUT = Output to:							
Fixed port	1110011w	port			9	9*	
Variable port	1110111w				7	7*	
XLAT = Translate byte to AL	11010111				11	15	
LEA = Load EA to register	10001101	mod reg r/m			6	6	
LDS = Load pointer to DS	11000101	mod reg r/m	(mod≠11)		18	26	
LES = Load pointer to ES	11000100	mod reg r/m	(mod≠11)		18	26	
LAHF = Load AH with flags	10011111				2	2	
SAHF = Store AH into flags	10011110				3	3	
PUSHF = Push flags	10011100				9	13	
POPF = Pop flags	10011101				8	12	

Shaded areas indicate instructions not available in 8086/8088 microsystems.

NOTE:
*Clock cycles shown for byte transfers. For word operations, add 4 clock cycles for all memory transfers.

INSTRUCTION SET SUMMARY (Continued)

Function	Format	80C186EA Clock Cycles	80C188EA Clock Cycles	Comments
DATA TRANSFER (Continued)				
SEGMENT = Segment Override:				
CS	00101110	2	2	
SS	00110110	2	2	
DS	00111110	2	2	
ES	00100110	2	2	
ARITHMETIC				
ADD = Add:				
Reg/memory with register to either	000000dw | mod reg r/m	3/10	3/10*	
Immediate to register/memory	100000sw | mod 0 0 0 r/m | data | data if s w=01	4/16	4/16*	
Immediate to accumulator	0000010w | data | data if w=1	3/4	3/4	8/16-bit
ADC = Add with carry:				
Reg/memory with register to either	000100dw | mod reg r/m	3/10	3/10*	
Immediate to register/memory	100000sw | mod 0 1 0 r/m | data | data if s w=01	4/16	4/16*	
Immediate to accumulator	0001010w | data | data if w=1	3/4	3/4	8/16-bit
INC = Increment:				
Register/memory	1111111w | mod 0 0 0 r/m	3/15	3/15*	
Register	01000 reg	3	3	
SUB = Subtract:				
Reg/memory and register to either	001010dw | mod reg r/m	3/10	3/10*	
Immediate from register/memory	100000sw | mod 1 0 1 r/m | data | data if s w=01	4/16	4/16*	
Immediate from accumulator	0010110w | data | data if w=1	3/4	3/4	8/16-bit
SBB = Subtract with borrow:				
Reg/memory and register to either	000110dw | mod reg r/m	3/10	3/10*	
Immediate from register/memory	100000sw | mod 0 1 1 r/m | data | data if s w=01	4/16	4/16*	
Immediate from accumulator	0001110w | data | data if w=1	3/4	3/4*	8/16-bit
DEC = Decrement				
Register/memory	1111111w | mod 0 0 1 r/m	3/15	3/15*	
Register	01001 reg	3	3	
CMP = Compare:				
Register/memory with register	0011101w | mod reg r/m	3/10	3/10*	
Register with register/memory	0011100w | mod reg r/m	3/10	3/10*	
Immediate with register/memory	100000sw | mod 1 1 1 r/m | data | data if s w=01	3/10	3/10*	
Immediate with accumulator	0011110w | data | data if w=1	3/4	3/4	8/16-bit
NEG = Change sign register/memory	1111011w | mod 0 1 1 r/m	3/10*	3/10*	
AAA = ASCII adjust for add	00110111	8	8	
DAA = Decimal adjust for add	00100111	4	4	
AAS = ASCII adjust for subtract	00111111	7	7	
DAS = Decimal adjust for subtract	00101111	4	4	
MUL = Multiply (unsigned):	1111011w | mod 100 r/m			
Register-Byte		26–28	26–28	
Register-Word		35–37	35–37	
Memory-Byte		32–34	32–34	
Memory-Word		41–43	41–48*	

Shaded areas indicate instructions not available in 8086/8088 microsystems.

NOTE:
*Clock cycles shown for byte transfers. For word operations, add 4 clock cycles for all memory transfers.

INSTRUCTION SET SUMMARY (Continued)

Function	Format				80C186EA Clock Cycles	80C188EA Clock Cycles	Comments
ARITHMETIC (Continued)							
IMUL = Integer multiply (signed):	1111011w	mod 101 r/m					
Register-Byte					25–28	25–28	
Register-Word					34–37	34–37	
Memory-Byte					31–34	32–34	
Memory-Word					40–43	40–43*	
IMUL = Integer Immediate multiply (signed)	011010s1	mod reg r/m	data	data if s=0	22–25 29–32	22–25 29–32	
DIV = Divide (unsigned):	1111011w	mod 110 r/m					
Register-Byte					29	29	
Register-Word					38	38	
Memory-Byte					35	35	
Memory-Word					44	44*	
IDIV = Integer divide (signed):	1111011w	mod 111 r/m					
Register-Byte					44–52	44–52	
Register-Word					53–61	53–61	
Memory-Byte					50–58	50–58	
Memory-Word					59–67	59–67*	
AAM = ASCII adjust for multiply	11010100	00001010			19	19	
AAD = ASCII adjust for divide	11010101	00001010			15	15	
CBW = Convert byte to word	10011000				2	2	
CWD = Convert word to double word	10011001				4	4	
LOGIC **Shift/Rotate Instructions:**							
Register/Memory by 1	1101000w	mod TTT r/m			2/15	2/15	
Register/Memory by CL	1101001w	mod TTT r/m			5+n/17+n	5+n/17+n	
Register/Memory by Count	1100000w	mod TTT r/m	count		5+n/17+n	5+n/17+n	
	TTT Instruction 000 ROL 001 ROR 010 RCL 011 RCR 100 SHL/SAL 101 SHR 111 SAR						
AND = And:							
Reg/memory and register to either	001000dw	mod reg r/m			3/10	3/10*	
Immediate to register/memory	1000000w	mod 100 r/m	data	data if w=1	4/16	4/16*	
Immediate to accumulator	0010010w	data	data if w=1		3/4	3/4*	8/16-bit
TEST = And function to flags, no result:							
Register/memory and register	1000010w	mod reg r/m			3/10	3/10*	
Immediate data and register/memory	1111011w	mod 000 r/m	data	data if w=1	4/10	4/10*	
Immediate data and accumulator	1010100w	data	data if w=1		3/4	3/4	8/16-bit
OR = Or:							
Reg/memory and register to either	000010dw	mod reg r/m			3/10	3/10*	
Immediate to register/memory	1000000w	mod 001 r/m	data	data if w=1	4/16	4/16*	
Immediate to accumulator	0000110w	data	data if w=1		3/4	3/4*	8/16-bit

Shaded areas indicate instructions not available in 8086/8088 microsystems.

NOTE:
*Clock cycles shown for byte transfers. For word operations, add 4 clock cycles for all memory transfers.

INSTRUCTION SET SUMMARY (Continued)

Function	Format				80C186EA Clock Cycles	80C188EA Clock Cycles	Comments
LOGIC (Continued)							
XOR = Exclusive or:							
Reg/memory and register to either	0 0 1 1 0 0 d w	mod reg r/m			3/10	3/10*	
Immediate to register/memory	1 0 0 0 0 0 0 w	mod 1 1 0 r/m	data	data if w=1	4/16	4/16*	
Immediate to accumulator	0 0 1 1 0 1 0 w	data	data if w=1		3/4	3/4	8/16-bit
NOT = Invert register/memory	1 1 1 1 0 1 1 w	mod 0 1 0 r/m			3/10	3/10*	
STRING MANIPULATION							
MOVS = Move byte/word	1 0 1 0 0 1 0 w				14	14*	
CMPS = Compare byte/word	1 0 1 0 0 1 1 w				22	22*	
SCAS = Scan byte/word	1 0 1 0 1 1 1 w				15	15*	
LODS = Load byte/wd to AL/AX	1 0 1 0 1 1 0 w				12	12*	
STOS = Store byte/wd from AL/AX	1 0 1 0 1 0 1 w				10	10*	
INS = Input byte/wd from DX port	0 1 1 0 1 1 0 w				14	14	
OUTS = Output byte/wd to DX port	0 1 1 0 1 1 1 w				14	14	
Repeated by count in CX (REP/REPE/REPZ/REPNE/REPNZ)							
MOVS = Move string	1 1 1 1 0 0 1 0	1 0 1 0 0 1 0 w			8+8n	8+8n*	
CMPS = Compare string	1 1 1 1 0 0 1 z	1 0 1 0 0 1 1 w			5+22n	5+22n	
SCAS = Scan string	1 1 1 1 0 0 1 z	1 0 1 0 1 1 1 w			5+15n	5+15n*	
LODS = Load string	1 1 1 1 0 0 1 0	1 0 1 0 1 1 0 w			6+11n	6+11n*	
STOS = Store string	1 1 1 1 0 0 1 0	1 0 1 0 1 0 1 w			6+9n	6+9n*	
INS = Input string	1 1 1 1 0 0 1 0	0 1 1 0 1 1 0 w			8+8n	8+8n*	
OUTS = Output string	1 1 1 1 0 0 1 0	0 1 1 0 1 1 1 w			8+8n	8+8n*	
CONTROL TRANSFER							
CALL = Call:							
Direct within segment	1 1 1 0 1 0 0 0	disp-low	disp-high		15	19	
Register/memory indirect within segment	1 1 1 1 1 1 1 1	mod 0 1 0 r/m			13/19	17/27	
Direct intersegment	1 0 0 1 1 0 1 0	segment offset			23	31	
		segment selector					
Indirect intersegment	1 1 1 1 1 1 1 1	mod 0 1 1 r/m	(mod ≠ 11)		38	51	
JMP = Unconditional jump:							
Short/long	1 1 1 0 1 0 1 1	disp-low			14	14	
Direct within segment	1 1 1 0 1 0 0 1	disp-low	disp-high		14	14	
Register/memory indirect within segment	1 1 1 1 1 1 1 1	mod 1 0 0 r/m			11/17	11/21	
Direct intersegment	1 1 1 0 1 0 1 0	segment offset			14	14	
		segment selector					
Indirect intersegment	1 1 1 1 1 1 1 1	mod 1 0 1 r/m	(mod ≠ 11)		26	34	

Shaded areas indicate instructions not available in 8086/8088 microsystems.

NOTE:
*Clock cycles shown for byte transfers. For word operations, add 4 clock cycles for all memory transfers.

INSTRUCTION SET SUMMARY (Continued)

Function	Format				80C186EA Clock Cycles	80C188EA Clock Cycles	Comments
CONTROL TRANSFER (Continued)							
RET = Return from CALL:							
Within segment	11000011				16	20	
Within seg adding immed to SP	11000010	data-low	data-high		18	22	
Intersegment	11001011				22	30	
Intersegment adding immediate to SP	11001010	data-low	data-high		25	33	
JE/JZ = Jump on equal/zero	01110100	disp			4/13	4/13	JMP not taken/JMP taken
JL/JNGE = Jump on less/not greater or equal	01111100	disp			4/13	4/13	
JLE/JNG = Jump on less or equal/not greater	01111110	disp			4/13	4/13	
JB/JNAE = Jump on below/not above or equal	01110010	disp			4/13	4/13	
JBE/JNA = Jump on below or equal/not above	01110110	disp			4/13	4/13	
JP/JPE = Jump on parity/parity even	01111010	disp			4/13	4/13	
JO = Jump on overflow	01110000	disp			4/13	4/13	
JS = Jump on sign	01111000	disp			4/13	4/13	
JNE/JNZ = Jump on not equal/not zero	01110101	disp			4/13	4/13	
JNL/JGE = Jump on not less/greater or equal	01111101	disp			4/13	4/13	
JNLE/JG = Jump on not less or equal/greater	01111111	disp			4/13	4/13	
JNB/JAE = Jump on not below/above or equal	01110011	disp			4/13	4/13	
JNBE/JA = Jump on not below or equal/above	01110111	disp			4/13	4/13	
JNP/JPO = Jump on not par/par odd	01111011	disp			4/13	4/13	
JNO = Jump on not overflow	01110001	disp			4/13	4/13	
JNS = Jump on not sign	01111001	disp			4/13	4/13	
JCXZ = Jump on CX zero	11100011	disp			5/15	5/15	
LOOP = Loop CX times	11100010	disp			6/16	6/16	LOOP not taken/LOOP taken
LOOPZ/LOOPE = Loop while zero/equal	11100001	disp			6/16	6/16	
LOOPNZ/LOOPNE = Loop while not zero/equal	11100000	disp			6/16	6/16	
ENTER = Enter Procedure	11001000	data-low	data-high	L			
L = 0					15	19	
L = 1					25	29	
L > 1					22 + 16(n − 1)	26 + 20(n − 1)	
LEAVE = Leave Procedure	11001001				8	8	
INT = Interrupt:							
Type specified	11001101	type			47	47	
Type 3	11001100			45	45	45	if INT. taken/ if INT. not taken
INTO = Interrupt on overflow	11001110				48/4	48/4	
IRET = Interrupt return	11001111				28	28	
BOUND = Detect value out of range	01100010	mod reg r/m			33–35	33–35	

Shaded areas indicate instructions not available in 8086/8088 microsystems.

NOTE:
*Clock cycles shown for byte transfers. For word operations, add 4 clock cycles for all memory transfers.

INSTRUCTION SET SUMMARY (Continued)

Function	Format	80C186EA Clock Cycles	80C188EA Clock Cycles	Comments
PROCESSOR CONTROL				
CLC = Clear carry	11111000	2	2	
CMC = Complement carry	11110101	2	2	
STC = Set carry	11111001	2	2	
CLD = Clear direction	11111100	2	2	
STD = Set direction	11111101	2	2	
CLI = Clear interrupt	11111010	2	2	
STI = Set interrupt	11111011	2	2	
HLT = Halt	11110100	2	2	
WAIT = Wait	10011011	6	6	if $\overline{TEST}$ = 0
LOCK = Bus lock prefix	11110000	2	2	
NOP = No Operation	10010000	3	3	
	(TTT LLL are opcode to processor extension)			

Shaded areas indicate instructions not available in 8086/8088 microsystems.

NOTE:
*Clock cycles shown for byte transfers. For word operations, add 4 clock cycles for all memory transfers.

The Effective Address (EA) of the memory operand is computed according to the mod and r/m fields:

if mod = 11 then r/m is treated as a REG field
if mod = 00 then DISP = 0*, disp-low and disp-high are absent
if mod = 01 then DISP = disp-low sign-extended to 16-bits, disp-high is absent
if mod = 10 then DISP = disp-high: disp-low
if r/m = 000 then EA = (BX) + (SI) + DISP
if r/m = 001 then EA = (BX) + (DI) + DISP
if r/m = 010 then EA = (BP) + (SI) + DISP
if r/m = 011 then EA = (BP) + (DI) + DISP
if r/m = 100 then EA = (SI) + DISP
if r/m = 101 then EA = (DI) + DISP
if r/m = 110 then EA = (BP) + DISP*
if r/m = 111 then EA = (BX) + DISP

DISP follows 2nd byte of instruction (before data if required)

*except if mod = 00 and r/m = 110 then EA = disp-high: disp-low.

EA calculation time is 4 clock cycles for all modes, and is included in the execution times given whenever appropriate.

Segment Override Prefix

0	0	1	reg	1	1	0

reg is assigned according to the following:

reg	Segment Register
00	ES
01	CS
10	SS
11	DS

REG is assigned according to the following table:

16-Bit (w = 1)	8-Bit (w = 0)
000 AX	000 AL
001 CX	001 CL
010 DX	010 DL
011 BX	011 BL
100 SP	100 AH
101 BP	101 CH
110 SI	110 DH
111 DI	111 BH

The physical addresses of all operands addressed by the BP register are computed using the SS segment register. The physical addresses of the destination operands of the string primitive operations (those addressed by the DI register) are computed using the ES segment, which may not be overridden.

REVISION HISTORY

Intel 80C186EA/80L186EA devices are marked with a 9-character alphanumeric Intel FPO number underneath the product number. This data sheet update is valid for devices with an "A", "B", "C", or "D" as the ninth character in the FPO number, as illustrated in Figure 5 for the 68-lead PLCC package, Figure 6 for the 84-lead QFP (EIAJ) package, and Figure 7 for the 80-lead SQFP device. Such devices may also be identified by reading a value of 01H, 02H, 03H from the STEPID register.

This data sheet replaces the following data sheets:

272019-002—80C186EA
272020-002—80C188EA
272021-002—80L186EA
272022-002—80L188EA
272307-001—SB80C186EA/SB80L186EA
272308-001—SB80C188EA/SB80L188EA

ERRATA

An 80C186EA/80L186EA with a STEPID value of 01H or 02H has the following known errata. A device with a STEPID of 01H or 02H can be visually identified by noting the presence of an "A", "B", or "C" alpha character, next to the FPO number. The FPO number location is shown in Figures 5, 6, and 7.

1. An internal condition with the interrupt controller can cause no acknowledge cycle on the INTA1 line in response to INT1. This errata only occurs when Interrupt 1 is configured in cascade mode and a higher priority interrupt exists. This errata will not occur consistantly, it is dependent on interrupt timing.

An 80C186EA/80L186EA with a STEPID value of 03H has no known errata. A device with a STEPID of 03H can be visually identified by noting the presence of a "D" alpha character next to the FPO number. The FPO number location is shown in Figures 5, 6, and 7.

PRELIMINARY

80C186EB/80C188EB AND 80L186EB/80L188EB 16-BIT HIGH-INTEGRATION EMBEDDED PROCESSORS

- **Full Static Operation**
- **True CMOS Inputs and Outputs**
- **−40°C to +85°C Operating Temperature Range**

- **Integrated Feature Set**
  - Low-Power Static CPU Core
  - Two Independent UARTs each with an Integral Baud Rate Generator
  - Two 8-Bit Multiplexed I/O Ports
  - Programmable Interrupt Controller
  - Three Programmable 16-Bit Timer/Counters
  - Clock Generator
  - Ten Programmable Chip Selects with Integral Wait-State Generator
  - Memory Refresh Control Unit
  - System Level Testing Support (ONCE Mode)
- **Direct Addressing Capability to 1 Mbyte Memory and 64 Kbyte I/O**
- **Speed Versions Available (5V):**
  - 20 MHz (80C186EB20/80C188EB20)
  - 13 MHz (80C186EB13/80C188EB13)
- **Speed Versions Available (3V):**
  - 13 MHz (80L186EB13/80L188EB13)
  - 8 MHz (80L186EB8/80L188EB8)
- **Low-Power Operating Modes:**
  - Idle Mode Freezes CPU Clocks but keeps Peripherals Active
  - Powerdown Mode Freezes All Internal Clocks
- **Complete System Development Support**
  - ASM86 Assembler, PL/M 86, C-86, and System Utilities
  - In-Circuit Emulator
- **Supports 80C187 Numeric Coprocessor Interface (80C186EB PLCC Only)**
- **Available In:**
  - 80-Pin Quad Flat Pack (QFP)
  - 84-Pin Plastic Leaded Chip Carrier (PLCC)
  - 80-Pin Shrink Quad Flat Pack (SQFP)

The 80C186EB is a second generation CHMOS High-Integration microprocessor. It has features that are new to the 80C186 family and include a STATIC CPU core, an enhanced Chip Select decode unit, two independent Serial Channels, I/O ports, and the capability of Idle or Powerdown low power modes.

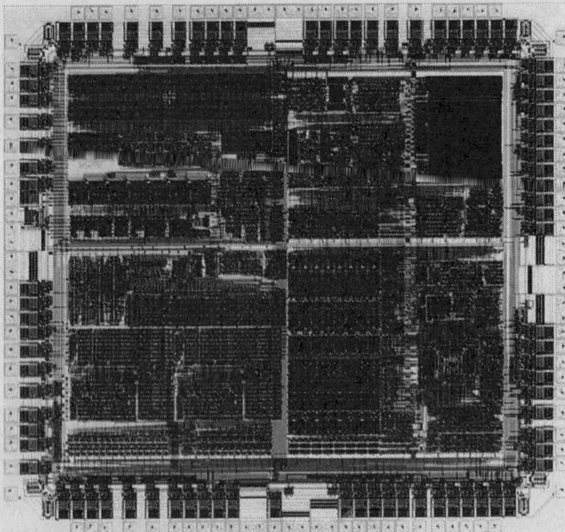

272433–1

November 1993
Order Number: 272433-001

80C186EB/80C188EB and 80L186EB/80L188EB
16-Bit High-Integration Embedded Processors

CONTENTS PAGE

INTRODUCTION 2-135

CORE ARCHITECTURE 2-135

Bus Interface Unit 2-135

Clock Generator 2-135

80C186EC PERIPHERAL ARCHITECTURE 2-136

Interrupt Control Unit 2-136

Timer/Counter Unit 2-136

Serial Communications Unit 2-138

Chip-Select Unit 2-138

I/O Port Unit 2-138

Refresh Control Unit 2-138

Power Management Unit 2-138

80C187 Interface (80C186EB Only) 2-138

ONCE Test Mode 2-138

PACKAGE INFORMATION 2-139

Prefix Identification 2-139

Pin Descriptions 2-139

80C186EB PINOUT 2-145

PACKAGE THERMAL SPECIFICATIONS 2-153

ELECTRICAL SPECIFICATIONS 2-154

Absolute Maximum Ratings 2-154

CONTENTS PAGE

Recommended Connections 2-154

DC SPECIFICATIONS 2-155

I_{CC} versus Frequency and Voltage 2-157

PDTMR Pin Delay Calculation 2-157

AC SPECIFICATIONS 2-158

AC Characteristics—80C186EB20/13 2-158

AC Characteristics—80L186EB13/8 2-160

Relative Timings 2-162

Serial Port Mode 0 Timings 2-163

AC TEST CONDITIONS 2-164

AC TIMING WAVEFORMS 2-164

DERATING CURVES 2-167

RESET 2-168

BUS CYCLE WAVEFORMS 2-171

EXECUTION TIMINGS 2-178

INSTRUCTION SET SUMMARY 2-179

ERRATA 2-185

REVISION HISTORY 2-185

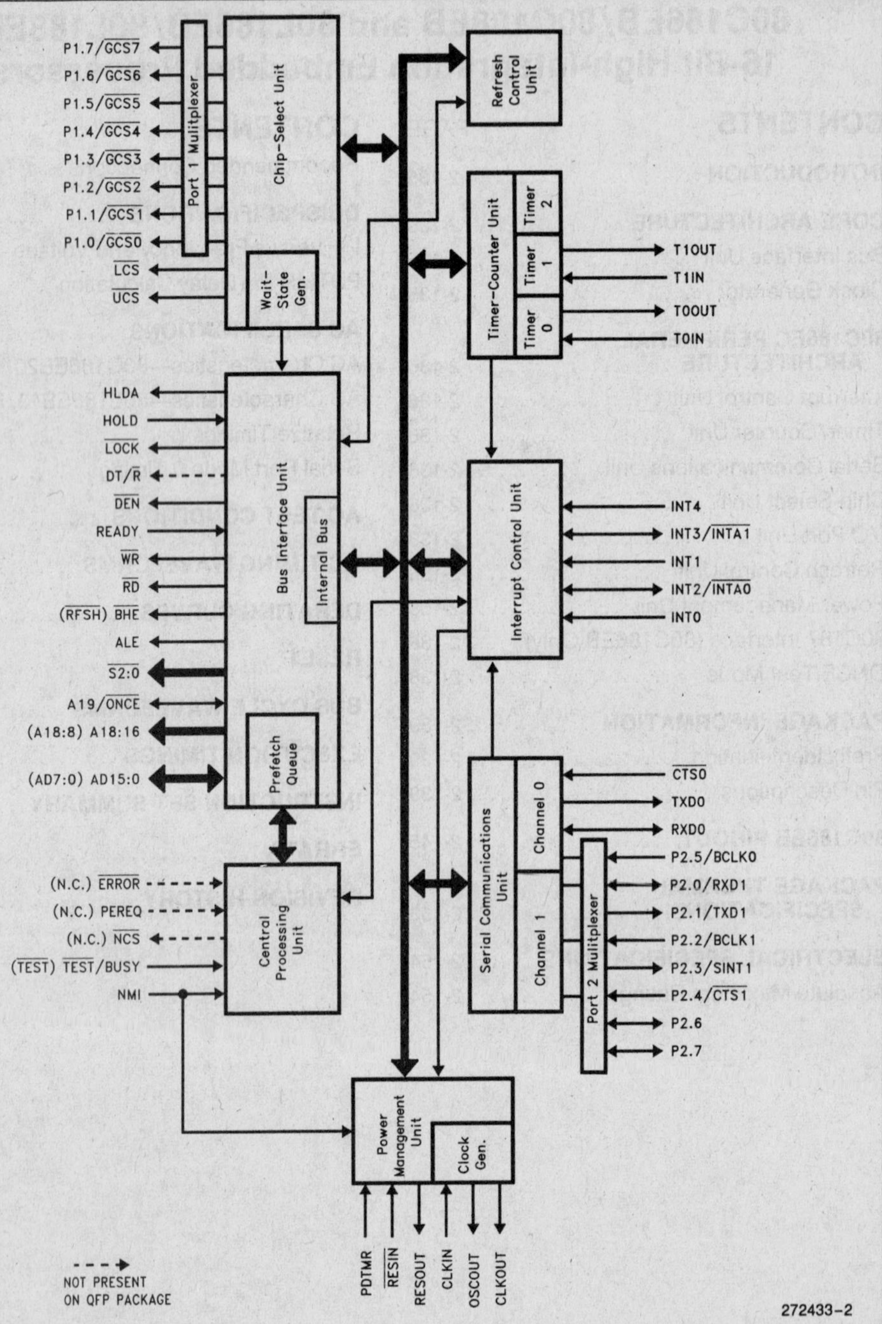

Chip-Select Unit
Port 1 Mulitplexer
P1.7/$\overline{GCS7}$
P1.6/$\overline{GCS6}$
P1.5/$\overline{GCS5}$
P1.4/$\overline{GCS4}$
P1.3/$\overline{GCS3}$
P1.2/$\overline{GCS2}$
P1.1/$\overline{GCS1}$
P1.0/$\overline{GCS0}$
$\overline{LCS}$
$\overline{UCS}$
Wait-State Gen.
Refresh Control Unit
Timer-Counter Unit
Timer 2
Timer 1
Timer 0
T1OUT
T1IN
T0OUT
T0IN
Bus Interface Unit
Internal Bus
HLDA
HOLD
$\overline{LOCK}$
DT/$\overline{R}$
$\overline{DEN}$
READY
$\overline{WR}$
$\overline{RD}$
($\overline{RFSH}$) $\overline{BHE}$
ALE
$\overline{S2:0}$
A19/$\overline{ONCE}$
(A18:8) A18:16
(AD7:0) AD15:0
Prefetch Queue
Interrupt Control Unit
INT4
INT3/$\overline{INTA1}$
INT1
INT2/$\overline{INTA0}$
INT0
Serial Communications Unit
Channel 0
Channel 1
Port 2 Mulitplexer
$\overline{CTS0}$
TXD0
RXD0
P2.5/BCLK0
P2.0/RXD1
P2.1/TXD1
P2.2/BCLK1
P2.3/SINT1
P2.4/$\overline{CTS1}$
P2.6
P2.7
Central Processing Unit
(N.C.) $\overline{ERROR}$
(N.C.) PEREQ
(N.C.) $\overline{NCS}$
($\overline{TEST}$) $\overline{TEST}$/BUSY
NMI
Power Management Unit
Clock Gen.
PDTMR
$\overline{RESIN}$
RESOUT
CLKIN
OSCOUT
CLKOUT
NOT PRESENT ON QFP PACKAGE
272433-2

NOTE:
Pin names in parentheses apply to the 80C188EB/80L188EB

Figure 1. 80C186EB/80C188EB Block Diagram

INTRODUCTION

Unless specifically noted, all references to the 80C186EB apply to the 80C188EB, 80L186EB, and 80L188EB. References to pins that differ between the 80C186EB/80L186EB and the 80C188EB/80L188EB are given in parentheses. The "L" in the part number denotes low voltage operation. Physically and functionally, the "C" and "L" devices are identical.

The 80C186EB is the first product in a new generation of low-power, high-integration microprocessors. It enhances the existing 186 family by offering new features and new operating modes. The 80C186EB is object code compatible with the 80C186XL/80C188XL microprocessors.

The 80L186EB is the 3V version of the 80C186EB. The 80L186EB is functionally identical to the 80C186EB embedded processor. Current 80C186EB users can easily upgrade their designs to use the 80L186EB and benefit from the reduced power consumption inherent in 3V operation.

The feature set of the 80C186EB meets the needs of low power, space critical applications. Low-Power applications benefit from the static design of the CPU core and the integrated peripherals as well as low voltage operation. Minimum current consumption is achieved by providing a Powerdown mode that halts operation of the device, and freezes the clock circuits. Peripheral design enhancements ensure that non-initialized peripherals consume little current.

Space critical applications benefit from the integration of commonly used system peripherals. Two serial channels are provided for services such as diagnostics, inter-processor communication, modem interface, terminal display interface, and many others. A flexible chip select unit simplifies memory and peripheral interfacing. The interrupt unit provides sources for up to 129 external interrupts and will prioritize these interrupts with those generated from the on-chip peripherals. Three general purpose timer/counters and sixteen multiplexed I/O port pins round out the feature set of the 80C186EB.

Figure 1 shows a block diagram of the 80C186EB/80C188EB. The Execution Unit (EU) is an enhanced 8086 CPU core that includes: dedicated hardware to speed up effective address calculations, enhance execution speed for multiple-bit shift and rotate instructions and for multiply and divide instructions, string move instructions that operate at full bus bandwidth, ten new instruction, and fully static operation. The Bus Interface Unit (BIU) is the same as that found on the original 186 family products, except the queue status mode has been deleted and buffer interface control has been changed to ease system design timings. An independent internal bus is used to allow communication between the BIU and internal peripherals.

CORE ARCHITECTURE

Bus Interface Unit

The 80C186EB core incorporates a bus controller that generates local bus control signals. In addition, it employs a HOLD/HLDA protocol to share the local bus with other bus masters.

The bus controller is responsible for generating 20 bits of address, read and write strobes, bus cycle status information, and data (for write operations) information. It is also responsible for reading data off the local bus during a read operation. A READY input pin is provided to extend a bus cycle beyond the minimum four states (clocks).

The local bus controller also generates two control signals ($\overline{\text{DEN}}$ and DT/$\overline{\text{R}}$) when interfacing to external transceiver chips. (Both $\overline{\text{DEN}}$ and DT/$\overline{\text{R}}$ are available on the PLCC devices, only $\overline{\text{DEN}}$ is available on the QFP and SQFP devices.) This capability allows the addition of transceivers for simple buffering of the multiplexed address/data bus.

Clock Generator

The processor provides an on-chip clock generator for both internal and external clock generation. The clock generator features a crystal oscillator, a divide-by-two counter, and two low-power operating modes.

The oscillator circuit is designed to be used with either a **parallel resonant** fundamental or third-overtone mode crystal network. Alternatively, the oscillator circuit may be driven from an external clock source. Figure 2 shows the various operating modes of the oscillator circuit.

The crystal or clock frequency chosen must be twice the required processor operating frequency due to the internal divide-by-two counter. This counter is used to drive all internal phase clocks and the external CLKOUT signal. CLKOUT is a 50% duty cycle processor clock and can be used to drive other system components. All AC timings are referenced to CLKOUT.

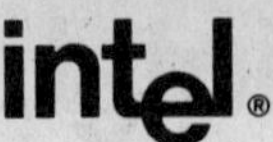

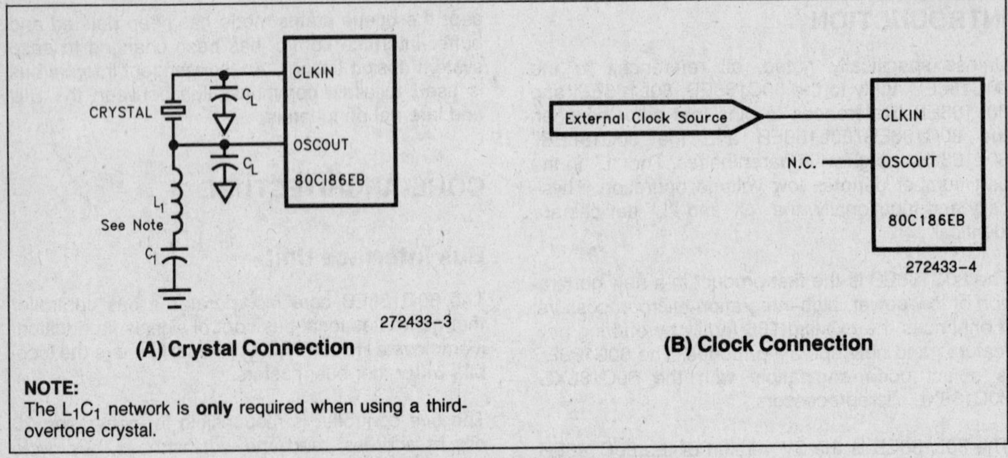

(A) Crystal Connection

(B) Clock Connection

NOTE:
The L_1C_1 network is **only** required when using a third-overtone crystal.

Figure 2. Clock Configurations

The following parameters are recommended when choosing a crystal:

Temperature Range:	Application Specific
ESR (Equivalent Series Resistance):	40Ω max
C0 (Shunt Capacitance of Crystal):	7.0 pF max
C_L (Load Capacitance):	20 pF ± 2 pF
Drive Level:	1 mW max

80C186EB PERIPHERAL ARCHITECTURE

The 80C186EB has integrated several common system peripherals with a CPU core to create a compact, yet powerful system. The integrated peripherals are designed to be flexible and provide logical interconnections between supporting units (e.g., the interrupt control unit supports interrupt requests from the timer/counters or serial channels).

The list of integrated peripherals includes:

- 7-Input Interrupt Control Unit
- 3-Channel Timer/Counter Unit
- 2-Channel Serial Communications Unit
- 10-Output Chip-Select Unit
- I/O Port Unit
- Refresh Control Unit
- Power Management Unit

The registers associated with each integrated peripheral are contained within a 128 x 16 register file called the Peripheral Control Block (PCB). The PCB can be located in either memory or I/O space on any 256 Byte address boundary.

Figure 3 provides a list of the registers associated with the PCB. The Register Bit Summary at the end of this specification individually lists all of the registers and identifies each of their programming attributes.

Interrupt Control Unit

The 80C186EB can receive interrupts from a number of sources, both internal and external. The interrupt control unit serves to merge these requests on a priority basis, for individual service by the CPU. Each interrupt source can be independently masked by the Interrupt Control Unit (ICU) or all interrupts can be globally masked by the CPU.

Internal interrupt sources include the Timers and Serial channel 0. External interrupt sources come from the five input pins INT4:0. The NMI interrupt pin is not controlled by the ICU and is passed directly to the CPU. Although the Timer and Serial channel each have only one request input to the ICU, separate vector types are generated to service individual interrupts within the Timer and Serial channel units.

Timer/Counter Unit

The 80C186EB Timer/Counter Unit (TCU) provides three 16-bit programmable timers. Two of these are highly flexible and are connected to external pins for control or clocking. A third timer is not connected to any external pins and can only be clocked internally. However, it can be used to clock the other two timer channels. The TCU can be used to count external events, time external events, generate non-repetitive waveforms, generate timed interrupts. etc.

PCB Offset	Function	PCB Offset	Function	PCB Offset	Function	PCB Offset	Function
00H	Reserved	40H	Timer2 Count	80H	GCS0 Start	C0H	Reserved
02H	End Of Interrupt	42H	Timer2 Compare	82H	GCS0 Stop	C2H	Reserved
04H	Poll	44H	Reserved	84H	GCS1 Start	C4H	Reserved
06H	Poll Status	46H	Timer2 Control	86H	GCS1 Stop	C6H	Reserved
08H	Interrupt Mask	48H	Reserved	88H	GCS2 Start	C8H	Reserved
0AH	Priority Mask	4AH	Reserved	8AH	GCS2 Stop	CAH	Reserved
0CH	In-Service	4CH	Reserved	8CH	GCS3 Start	CCH	Reserved
0EH	Interrupt Request	4EH	Reserved	8EH	GCS3 Stop	CEH	Reserved
10H	Interrupt Status	50H	Reserved	90H	GCS4 Start	D0H	Reserved
12H	Timer Control	52H	Port0 Pin	92H	GCS4 Stop	D2H	Reserved
14H	Serial Control	54H	Port0 Control	94H	GCS5 Start	D4H	Reserved
16H	INT4 Control	56H	Port0 Latch	96H	GCS5 Stop	D6H	Reserved
18H	INT0 Control	58H	Port1 Direction	98H	GCS6 Start	D8H	Reserved
1AH	INT1 Control	5AH	Port1 Pin	9AH	GCS6 Stop	DAH	Reserved
1CH	INT2 Control	5CH	Port1 Control	9CH	GCS7 Start	DCH	Reserved
1EH	INT3 Control	5EH	Port1 Latch	9EH	GCS7 Stop	DEH	Reserved
20H	Reserved	60H	Serial0 Baud	A0H	LCS Start	E0H	Reserved
22H	Reserved	62H	Serial0 Count	A2H	LCS Stop	E2H	Reserved
24H	Reserved	64H	Serial0 Control	A4H	UCS Start	E4H	Reserved
26H	Reserved	66H	Serial0 Status	A6H	UCS Stop	E6H	Reserved
28H	Reserved	68H	Serial0 RBUF	A8H	Relocation	E8H	Reserved
2AH	Reserved	6AH	Serial0 TBUF	AAH	Reserved	EAH	Reserved
2CH	Reserved	6CH	Reserved	ACH	Reserved	ECH	Reserved
2EH	Reserved	6EH	Reserved	AEH	Reserved	EEH	Reserved
30H	Timer0 Count	70H	Serial1 Baud	B0H	Refresh Base	F0H	Reserved
32H	Timer0 Compare A	72H	Serial1 Count	B2H	Refresh Time	F2H	Reserved
34H	Timer0 Compare B	74H	Serial1 Control	B4H	Refresh Control	F4H	Reserved
36H	Timer0 Control	76H	Serial1 Status	B6H	Refresh Address	F6H	Reserved
38H	Timer1 Count	78H	Serial1 RBUF	B8H	Power Control	F8H	Reserved
3AH	Timer1 Compare A	7AH	Serial1 TBUF	BAH	Reserved	FAH	Reserved
3CH	Timer1 Compare B	7CH	Reserved	BCH	Step ID	FCH	Reserved
3EH	Timer1 Control	7EH	Reserved	BEH	Reserved	FEH	Reserved

Figure 3. Peripheral Control Block Registers

2

Serial Communications Unit

The Serial Control Unit (SCU) of the 80C186EB contains two independent channels. Each channel is identical in operation except that only channel 0 is supported by the integrated interrupt controller (channel 1 has an external interrupt pin). Each channel has its own baud rate generator that is independent of the Timer/Counter Unit, and can be internally or externally clocked at up to one half the 80C186EB operating frequency.

Independent baud rate generators are provided for each of the serial channels. For the asynchronous modes, the generator supplies an 8x baud clock to both the receive and transmit register logic. A 1x baud clock is provided in the synchronous mode.

Chip-Select Unit

The 80C186EB Chip-Select Unit (CSU) integrates logic which provides up to ten programmable chip-selects to access both memories and peripherals. In addition, each chip-select can be programmed to automatically insert additional clocks (wait-states) into the current bus cycle and automatically terminate a bus cycle independent of the condition of the READY input pin.

I/O Port Unit

The I/O Port Unit (IPU) on the 80C186EB supports two 8-bit channels of input, output, or input/output operation. Port 1 is multiplexed with the chip select pins and is output only. Most of Port 2 is multiplexed with the serial channel pins. Port 2 pins are limited to either an output or input function depending on the operation of the serial pin it is multiplexed with.

Refresh Control Unit

The Refresh Control Unit (RCU) automatically generates a periodic memory read bus cycle to keep dynamic or pseudo-static memory refreshed. A 9-bit counter controls the number of clocks between refresh requests.

A 12-bit address generator is maintained by the RCU and is presented on the A12:1 address lines during the refresh bus cycle. Address bits A19:13 are programmable to allow the refresh address block to be located on any 8 Kbyte boundary.

Power Management Unit

The 80C186EB Power Management Unit (PMU) is provided to control the power consumption of the device. The PMU provides three power modes: Active, Idle, and Powerdown.

Active Mode indicates that all units on the 80C186EB are functional and the device consumes maximum power (depending on the level of peripheral operation). Idle Mode freezes the clocks of the Execution and Bus units at a logic zero state (all peripherals continue to operate normally).

The Powerdown mode freezes all internal clocks at a logic zero level and disables the crystal oscillator. All internal registers hold their values provided V_{CC} is maintained. Current consumption is reduced to just transistor junction leakage.

80C187 Interface (80C186EB Only)

The 80C186EB (PLCC package only) supports the direct connection of the 80C187 Numerics Coprocessor.

ONCE Test Mode

To facilitate testing and inspection of devices when fixed into a target system, the 80C186EB has a test mode available which forces all output and input/output pins to be placed in the high-impedance state. ONCE stands for "ON Circuit Emulation". The ONCE mode is selected by forcing the A19/$\overline{ONCE}$ pin LOW (0) during a processor reset (this pin is weakly held to a HIGH (1) level) while $\overline{RESIN}$ is active.

PACKAGE INFORMATION

This section describes the pins, pinouts, and thermal characteristics for the 80C186EB in the Plastic Leaded Chip Carrier (PLCC) package, Shrink Quad Flat Pack (SQFP), and Quad Flat Pack (QFP) package. For complete package specifications and information, see the Intel Packaging Outlines and Dimensions Guide (Order Number: 231369).

Prefix Identification

With the extended temperature range, operational characteristics are guaranteed over the temperature range corresponding to −40°C to +85°C ambient. Package types are identified by a two-letter prefix to the part number. The prefixes are listed in Table 1.

Table 1. Prefix Identification

Prefix	Package Type	Temperature Type
TN	PLCC	Extended
TS	QFP	Extended
SB	SQFP	Extended

Pin Descriptions

Each pin or logical set of pins is described in Table 3. There are three columns for each entry in the Pin Description Table.

The **Pin Name** column contains a mnemonic that describes the pin function. Negation of the signal name (for example, $\overline{\text{RESIN}}$) denotes a signal that is active low.

The **Pin Type** column contains two kinds of information. The first symbol indicates whether a pin is power (P), ground (G), input only (I), output only (O) or input/output (I/O). Some pins have multiplexed functions (for example, A19/S6). Additional symbols indicate additional characteristics for each pin. Table 2 lists all the possible symbols for this column.

The **Input Type** column indicates the type of input (Asynchronous or Synchronous).

Asynchronous pins require that setup and hold times be met only in order to guarantee *recognition* at a particular clock edge. Synchronous pins require that setup and hold times be met to guarantee proper *operation*. For example, missing the setup or hold time for the SRDY pin (a synchronous input) will result in a system failure or lockup. Input pins may also be edge- or level-sensitive. The possible characteristics for input pins are S(E), S(L), A(E) and A(L).

The **Output States** column indicates the output state as a function of the device operating mode. Output states are dependent upon the current activity of the processor. There are four operational states that are different from regular operation: bus hold, reset, Idle Mode and Powerdown Mode. Appropriate characteristics for these states are also indicated in this column, with the legend for all possible characteristics in Table 2.

The **Pin Description** column contains a text description of each pin.

As an example, consider AD15:0. I/O signifies the pins are bidirectional. S(L) signifies that the input function is synchronous and level-sensitive. H(Z) signifies that, as outputs, the pins are high-impedance upon acknowledgement of bus hold. R(Z) signifies that the pins float during reset. P(X) signifies that the pins retain their states during Powerdown Mode.

Table 2. Pin Description Nomenclature

Symbol	Description
P G I O I/O	Power Pin (Apply $+V_{CC}$ Voltage) Ground (Connect to V_{SS}) Input Only Pin Output Only Pin Input/Output Pin
S(E) S(L) A(E) A(L)	Synchronous, Edge Sensitive Synchronous, Level Sensitive Asynchronous, Edge Sensitive Asynchronous, Level Sensitive
H(1) H(0) H(Z) H(Q) H(X)	Output Driven to V_{CC} during Bus Hold Output Driven to V_{SS} during Bus Hold Output Floats during Bus Hold Output Remains Active during Bus Hold Output Retains Current State during Bus Hold
R(WH) R(1) R(0) R(Z) R(Q) R(X)	Output Weakly Held at V_{CC} during Reset Output Driven to V_{CC} during Reset Output Driven to V_{SS} during Reset Output Floats during Reset Output Remains Active during Reset Output Retains Current State during Reset
I(1) I(0) I(Z) I(Q) I(X)	Output Driven to V_{CC} during Idle Mode Output Driven to V_{SS} during Idle Mode Output Floats during Idle Mode Output Remains Active during Idle Mode Output Retains Current State during Idle Mode
P(1) P(0) P(Z) P(Q) P(X)	Output Driven to V_{CC} during Powerdown Mode Output Driven to V_{SS} during Powerdown Mode Output Floats during Powerdown Mode Output Remains Active during Powerdown Mode Output Retains Current State during Powerdown Mode

Table 3. Pin Descriptions

Pin Name	Pin Type	Input Type	Output States	Description
V_{CC}	P	—	—	**POWER** connections consist of four pins which must be shorted externally to a V_{CC} board plane.
V_{SS}	G	—	—	**GROUND** connections consist of six pins which must be shorted externally to a V_{SS} board plane.
CLKIN	I	A(E)	—	**CLocK INput** is an input for an external clock. An external oscillator operating at two times the required processor operating frequency can be connected to CLKIN. For crystal operation, CLKIN (along with OSCOUT) are the crystal connections to an internal Pierce oscillator.
OSCOUT	O	—	H(Q) R(Q) P(Q)	**OSCillator OUTput** is only used when using a crystal to generate the external clock. OSCOUT (along with CLKIN) are the crystal connections to an internal Pierce oscillator. This pin is not to be used as 2X clock output for non-crystal applications (i.e., this pin is N.C. for non-crystal applications). OSCOUT does not float in ONCE mode.
CLKOUT	O	—	H(Q) R(Q) P(Q)	**CLocK OUTput** provides a timing reference for inputs and outputs of the processor, and is one-half the input clock (CLKIN) frequency. CLKOUT has a 50% duty cycle and transistions every falling edge of CLKIN.
$\overline{\text{RESIN}}$	I	A(L)	—	**RESet IN** causes the processor to immediately terminate any bus cycle in progress and assume an initialized state. All pins will be driven to a known state, and RESOUT will also be driven active. The rising edge (low-to-high) transition synchronizes CLKOUT with CLKIN before the processor begins fetching opcodes at memory location 0FFFF0H.
RESOUT	O	—	H(0) R(1) P(0)	**RESet OUTput** that indicates the processor is currently in the reset state. RESOUT will remain active as long as $\overline{\text{RESIN}}$ remains active.
PDTMR	I/O	A(L)	H(WH) R(Z) P(1)	**Power-Down TiMeR** pin (normally connected to an external capacitor) that determines the amount of time the processor waits after an exit from power down before resuming normal operation. The duration of time required will depend on the startup characteristics of the crystal oscillator.
NMI	I	A(E)	—	**Non-Maskable Interrupt** input causes a TYPE-2 interrupt to be serviced by the CPU. NMI is latched internally.
$\overline{\text{TEST}}$/BUSY ($\overline{\text{TEST}}$)	I	A(E)	—	**TEST** is used during the execution of the WAIT instruction to suspend CPU operation until the pin is sampled active (LOW). $\overline{\text{TEST}}$ is alternately known as BUSY when interfacing with an 80C187 numerics coprocessor (80C186EB only).
AD15:0 (AD7:0)	I/O	S(L)	H(Z) R(Z) P(X)	These pins provide a multiplexed **Address** and **Data** bus. During the address phase of the bus cycle, address bits 0 through 15 (0 through 7 on the 80C188EB) are presented on the bus and can be latched using ALE. 8- or 16-bit data information is transferred during the data phase of the bus cycle.

NOTE:
Pin names in parentheses apply to the 80C188EB/80L188EB.

Table 3. Pin Descriptions (Continued)

Pin Name	Pin Type	Input Type	Output States	Description
A18:16 A19/$\overline{ONCE}$ (A15:A8) (A18:16) (A19/ONCE)	I/O	A(L)	H(Z) R(WH) P(X)	These pins provide multiplexed **Address** during the address phase of the bus cycle. Address bits 16 through 19 are presented on these pins and can be latched using ALE. These pins are driven to a logic 0 during the data phase of the bus cycle. On the 80C188EB, A15–A8 provide valid address information for the entire bus cycle. During a processor reset ($\overline{RESIN}$ active), A19/$\overline{ONCE}$ is used to enable ONCE mode. A18:16 must not be driven low during reset or improper operation may result.
$\overline{S2:0}$	O	—	H(Z) R(Z) P(1)	Bus cycle **Status** are encoded on these pins to provide bus transaction information. $\overline{S2:0}$ are encoded as follows: **$\overline{S2}$ $\overline{S1}$ $\overline{S0}$ Bus Cycle Initiated** 0 0 0 Interrupt Acknowledge 0 0 1 Read I/O 0 1 0 Write I/O 0 1 1 Processor HALT 1 0 0 Queue Instruction Fetch 1 0 1 Read Memory 1 1 0 Write Memory 1 1 1 Passive (no bus activity)
ALE	O	—	H(0) R(0) P(0)	**Address Latch Enable** output is used to strobe address information into a transparent type latch during the address phase of the bus cycle.
$\overline{BHE}$ ($\overline{RFSH}$)	O	—	H(Z) R(Z) P(X)	**Byte High Enable** output to indicate that the bus cycle in progress is transferring data over the upper half of the data bus. $\overline{BHE}$ and A0 have the following logical encoding **A0 $\overline{BHE}$ Encoding** (for the 80C186EB/80L186EB only) 0 0 Word Transfer 0 1 Even Byte Transfer 1 0 Odd Byte Transfer 1 1 Refresh Operation On the 80C188EB/80L188EB, $\overline{RFSH}$ is asserted low to indicate a refresh bus cycle.
$\overline{RD}$	O	—	H(Z) R(Z) P(1)	**ReaD** output signals that the accessed memory or I/O device must drive data information onto the data bus.
$\overline{WR}$	O	—	H(Z) R(Z) P(1)	**WRite** output signals that data available on the data bus are to be written into the accessed memory or I/O device.
READY	I	A(L) S(L)	—	**READY** input to signal the completion of a bus cycle. READY must be active to terminate any bus cycle, unless it is ignored by correctly programming the Chip-Select Unit.
$\overline{DEN}$	O	—	H(Z) R(Z) P(1)	**Data ENable** output to control the enable of bi-directional transceivers in a buffered system. $\overline{DEN}$ is active only when data is to be transferred on the bus.

NOTE:
Pin names in parentheses apply to the 80C188EB/80L188EB.

Table 3. Pin Descriptions (Continued)

Pin Name	Pin Type	Input Type	Output States	Description
DT/$\overline{R}$	O	—	H(Z) R(Z) P(X)	**Data Transmit/Receive** output controls the direction of a bi-directional buffer in a buffered system. DT/$\overline{R}$ is only available for the PLCC package.
$\overline{LOCK}$	O	—	H(Z) R(WH) P(1)	**LOCK** output indicates that the bus cycle in progress is not to be interrupted. The processor will not service other bus requests (such as HOLD) while $\overline{LOCK}$ is active. This pin is configured as a weakly held high input while $\overline{RESIN}$ is active and must not be driven low.
HOLD	I	A(L)	—	**HOLD** request input to signal that an external bus master wishes to gain control of the local bus. The processor will relinquish control of the local bus between instruction boundaries not conditioned by a LOCK prefix.
HLDA	O	—	H(1) R(0) P(0)	**HoLD Acknowledge** output to indicate that the processor has relinquished control of the local bus. When HLDA is asserted, the processor will (or has) floated its data bus and control signals allowing another bus master to drive the signals directly.
$\overline{NCS}$ (N.C.)	O	—	H(1) R(1) P(1)	**Numerics Coprocessor Select** output is generated when accessing a numerics coprocessor. $\overline{NCS}$ is not provided on the QFP or SQFP packages. This signal does not exist on the 80C188EB/80L188EB.
$\overline{ERROR}$ (N.C.)	I	A(L)	—	**ERROR** input that indicates the last numerics coprocessor operation resulted in an exception condition. An interrupt TYPE 16 is generated if $\overline{ERROR}$ is sampled active at the beginning of a numerics operation. $\overline{ERROR}$ is not provided on the QFP or SQFP packages. This signal does not exist on the 80C188EB/80L188EB.
PEREQ (N.C.)	I	A(L)	—	**CoProcessor REQuest** signals that a data transfer between an External Numerics Coprocessor and Memory is pending. PEREQ is not provided on the QFP or SQFP packages. This signal does not exist on the 80C188EB/80L188EB.
$\overline{UCS}$	O	—	H(1) R(1) P(1)	**Upper Chip Select** will go active whenever the address of a memory or I/O bus cycle is within the address limitations programmed by the user. After reset, $\overline{UCS}$ is configured to be active for memory accesses between 0FFC00H and 0FFFFFH.
$\overline{LCS}$	O	—	H(1) R(1) P(1)	**Lower Chip Select** will go active whenever the address of a memory bus cycle is within the address limitations programmed by the user. $\overline{LCS}$ is inactive after a reset.
P1.0/$\overline{GCS0}$ P1.1/$\overline{GCS1}$ P1.2/$\overline{GCS2}$ P1.3/$\overline{GCS3}$ P1.4/$\overline{GCS4}$ P1.5/$\overline{GCS5}$ P1.6/$\overline{GCS6}$ P1.7/$\overline{GCS7}$	O	—	H(X)/H(1) R(1) P(X)/P(1)	These pins provide a multiplexed function. If enabled, each pin can provide a **Generic Chip Select** output which will go active whenever the address of a memory or I/O bus cycle is within the address limitations programmed by the user. When not programmed as a Chip-Select, each pin may be used as a general purpose output **Port.** As an output port pin, the value of the pin can be read internally.

NOTE:
Pin names in parentheses apply to the 80C188EB/80L188EB.

Table 3. Pin Descriptions (Continued)

Pin Name	Pin Type	Input Type	Output States	Description
T0OUT T1OUT	O	—	H(Q) R(1) P(Q)	**Timer OUTput** pins can be programmed to provide a single clock or continuous waveform generation, depending on the timer mode selected.
T0IN T1IN	I	A(L) A(E)	—	**Timer INput** is used either as clock or control signals, depending on the timer mode selected.
INT0 INT1 INT4	I	A(E,L)	—	Maskable **INTerrupt** input will cause a vector to a specific Type interrupt routine. To allow interrupt expansion, INT0 and/or INT1 can be used with $\overline{\text{INTA0}}$ and $\overline{\text{INTA1}}$ to interface with an external slave controller.
INT2/$\overline{\text{INTA0}}$ INT3/$\overline{\text{INTA1}}$	I/O	A(E,L)	H(1) R(Z) P(1)	These pins provide a multiplexed function. As inputs, they provide a maskable **INTerrupt** that will cause the CPU to vector to a specific Type interrupt routine. As outputs, each is programmatically controlled to provide an INTERRUPT ACKNOWLEDGE handshake signal to allow interrupt expansion.
P2.7 P2.6	I/O	A(L)	H(X) R(Z) P(X)	BI-DIRECTIONAL, open-drain **Port** pins.
$\overline{\text{CTS0}}$ P2.4/$\overline{\text{CTS1}}$	I	A(L)	—	**Clear-To-Send** input is used to prevent the transmission of serial data on their respective TXD signal pin. $\overline{\text{CTS1}}$ is multiplexed with an input only port function.
TXD0 P2.1/TXD1	O	—	H(X)/H(Q) R(1) P(X)/P(Q)	**Transmit Data** output provides serial data information. TXD1 is multiplexed with an output only **Port** function. During synchronous serial communications, TXD will function as a clock output.
RXD0 P2.0/RXD1	I/O	A(L)	R(Z) H(Q) P(X)	**Receive Data** input accepts serial data information. RXD1 is multiplexed with an input only **Port** function. During synchronous serial communications, RXD is bi-directional and will become an output for transmission or data (TXD becomes the clock).
P2.5/BCLK0 P2.2/BCLK1	I	A(L)/A(E)	—	**Baud CLocK** input can be used as an alternate clock source for each of the integrated serial channels. BCLKx is multiplexed with an input only **Port** function, and cannot exceed a clock rate greater than one-half the operating frequency of the processor.
P2.3/SINT1	O	—	H(X)/H(Q) R(0) P(X)/P(Q)	**Serial INTerrupt** output will go active to indicate serial channel 1 requires service. SINT1 is multiplexed with an output only **Port** function.

NOTE:
Pin names in parentheses apply to the 80C188EB/80L188EB.

80C186EB PINOUT

Tables 4 and 5 list the 80C186EB/80C188EB pin names with package location for the 84-pin Plastic Leaded Chip Carrier (PLCC) component. Figure 5 depicts the complete 80C186EB/80C188EB pinout (PLCC package) as viewed from the top side of the component (i.e., contacts facing down).

Tables 6 and 7 list the 80C186EB/80C188EB pin names with package location for the 80-pin Quad Flat Pack (QFP) component. Figure 6 depicts the complete 80C186EB/80C188EB (QFP package) as viewed from the top side of the component (i.e., contacts facing down).

Tables 8 and 9 list the 80186EB/80188EB pin names with package location for the 80-pin Shrink Quad Flat Pack (SQFP) component. Figure 7 depicts the complete 80C186EB/80C188EB (SQFP package) as viewed from the top side of the component (i.e., contacts facing down).

Table 4. PLCC Pin Names with Package Location

Address/Data Bus	
Name	**Location**
AD0	61
AD1	66
AD2	68
AD3	70
AD4	72
AD5	74
AD6	76
AD7	78
AD8 (A8)	62
AD9 (A9)	67
AD10 (A10)	69
AD11 (A11)	71
AD12 (A12)	73
AD13 (A13)	75
AD14 (A14)	77
AD15 (A15)	79
A16	80
A17	81
A18	82
A19/$\overline{\text{ONCE}}$	83

Bus Control	
Name	**Location**
ALE	6
$\overline{\text{BHE}}$ ($\overline{\text{RFSH}}$)	7
$\overline{\text{S0}}$	10
$\overline{\text{S1}}$	9
$\overline{\text{S2}}$	8
$\overline{\text{RD}}$	4
$\overline{\text{WR}}$	5
READY	18
$\overline{\text{DEN}}$	11
DT/$\overline{\text{R}}$	16
$\overline{\text{LOCK}}$	15
HOLD	13
HLDA	12

Power	
Name	**Location**
V_{SS}	2, 22, 43 63, 65, 84
V_{CC}	1, 23 42, 64

Processor Control	
Name	**Location**
$\overline{\text{RESIN}}$	37
RESOUT	38
CLKIN	41
OSCOUT	40
CLKOUT	44
$\overline{\text{TEST}}$/BUSY	14
$\overline{\text{NCS}}$ (N.C.)	60
PEREQ (N.C.)	39
$\overline{\text{ERROR}}$ (N.C.)	3
PDTMR	36
NMI	17
INT0	31
INT1	32
INT2/$\overline{\text{INTA0}}$	33
INT3/$\overline{\text{INTA1}}$	34
INT4	35

I/O	
Name	**Location**
$\overline{\text{UCS}}$	30
$\overline{\text{LCS}}$	29
P1.0/$\overline{\text{GCS0}}$	28
P1.1/$\overline{\text{GCS1}}$	27
P1.2/$\overline{\text{GCS2}}$	26
P1.3/$\overline{\text{GCS3}}$	25
P1.4/$\overline{\text{GCS4}}$	24
P1.5/$\overline{\text{GCS5}}$	21
P1.6/$\overline{\text{GCS6}}$	20
P1.7/$\overline{\text{GCS7}}$	19
T0OUT	45
T0IN	46
T1OUT	47
T1IN	48
RXD0	53
TXD0	52
P2.5/BCLK0	54
$\overline{\text{CTS0}}$	51
P2.0/RXD1	57
P2.1/TXD1	58
P2.2/BCLK1	59
P2.3/SINT1	55
P2.4/$\overline{\text{CTS1}}$	56
P2.6	50
P2.7	49

NOTE:
Pin names in parentheses apply to the 80C188EB/80L188EB.

Table 5. PLCC Package Locations with Pin Name

Location	Name	Location	Name	Location	Name	Location	Name
1	V_{CC}	22	V_{SS}	43	V_{SS}	64	V_{CC}
2	V_{SS}	23	V_{CC}	44	CLKOUT	65	V_{SS}
3	$\overline{\text{ERROR}}$ (N.C.)	24	P1.4/$\overline{\text{GCS4}}$	45	T0OUT	66	AD1
4	$\overline{\text{RD}}$	25	P1.3/$\overline{\text{GCS3}}$	46	T0IN	67	AD9 (A9)
5	$\overline{\text{WR}}$	26	P1.2/$\overline{\text{GCS2}}$	47	T1OUT	68	AD2
6	ALE	27	P1.1/$\overline{\text{GCS1}}$	48	T1IN	69	AD10 (A10)
7	$\overline{\text{BHE}}$ ($\overline{\text{RFSH}}$)	28	P1.0/$\overline{\text{GCS0}}$	49	P2.7	70	AD3
8	$\overline{\text{S2}}$	29	$\overline{\text{LCS}}$	50	P2.6	71	AD11 (A11)
9	$\overline{\text{S1}}$	30	$\overline{\text{UCS}}$	51	$\overline{\text{CTS0}}$	72	AD4
10	$\overline{\text{S0}}$	31	INT0	52	TXD0	73	AD12 (A12)
11	$\overline{\text{DEN}}$	32	INT1	53	RXD0	74	AD5
12	HLDA	33	INT2/$\overline{\text{INTA0}}$	54	P2.5/BCLK0	75	AD13 (A13)
13	HOLD	34	INT3/$\overline{\text{INTA1}}$	55	P2.3/SINT1	76	AD6
14	$\overline{\text{TEST}}$/BUSY	35	INT4	56	P2.4/$\overline{\text{CTS1}}$	77	AD14 (A14)
15	$\overline{\text{LOCK}}$	36	PDTMR	57	P2.0/RXD1	78	AD7
16	DT/$\overline{\text{R}}$	37	$\overline{\text{RESIN}}$	58	P2.1/TXD1	79	AD15 (A15)
17	NMI	38	RESOUT	59	P2.2/BCLK1	80	A16
18	READY	39	PEREQ (N.C.)	60	$\overline{\text{NCS}}$ (N.C.)	81	A17
19	P1.7/$\overline{\text{GCS7}}$	40	OSCOUT	61	AD0	82	A18
20	P1.6/$\overline{\text{GCS6}}$	41	CLKIN	62	AD8 (A8)	83	A19/$\overline{\text{ONCE}}$
21	P1.5/$\overline{\text{GCS5}}$	42	V_{CC}	63	V_{SS}	84	V_{SS}

NOTE:
Pin names in parentheses apply to the 80C188EB/80L188EB.

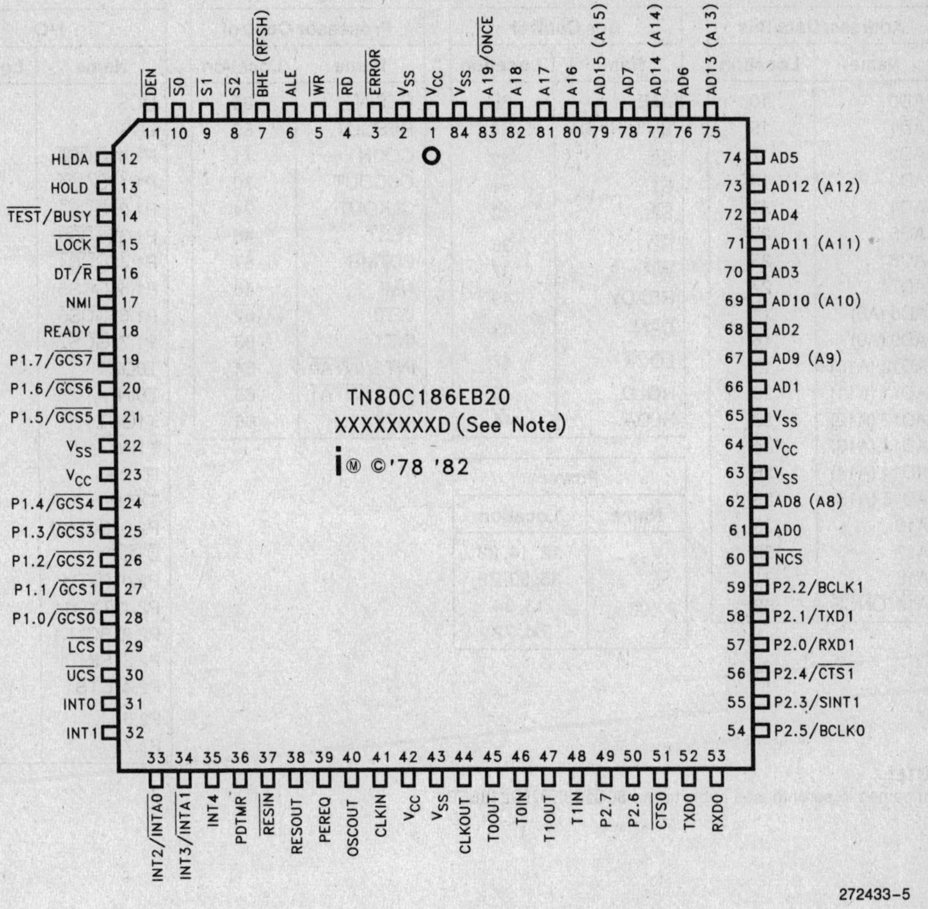

NOTE:
This is the FPO number location (indicated by X's).
Pin names in parentheses apply to the 80C188EB/80L188EB.

Figure 4. 84-Pin Plastic Leaded Chip Carrier Pinout Diagram

Table 6. QFP Pin Name with Package Location

Address/Data Bus

Name	Location
AD0	10
AD1	15
AD2	17
AD3	19
AD4	21
AD5	23
AD6	25
AD7	27
AD8 (A8)	11
AD9 (A9)	16
AD10 (A10)	18
AD11 (A11)	20
AD12 (A12)	22
AD13 (A13)	24
AD14 (A14)	26
AD15 (A15)	28
A16	29
A17	30
A18	31
A19/$\overline{\text{ONCE}}$	32

Bus Control

Name	Location
ALE	38
$\overline{\text{BHE}}$ (RFSH)	39
$\overline{\text{S0}}$	42
$\overline{\text{S1}}$	41
$\overline{\text{S2}}$	40
$\overline{\text{RD}}$	36
$\overline{\text{WR}}$	37
READY	49
$\overline{\text{DEN}}$	43
$\overline{\text{LOCK}}$	47
HOLD	45
HLDA	44

Power

Name	Location
V_{SS}	12, 14, 33 35, 53, 73
V_{CC}	13, 34 54, 72

Processor Control

Name	Location
$\overline{\text{RESIN}}$	68
RESOUT	69
CLKIN	71
OSCOUT	70
CLKOUT	74
$\overline{\text{TEST}}$	46
PDTMR	67
NMI	48
INT0	62
INT1	63
INT2/$\overline{\text{INTA0}}$	64
INT3/$\overline{\text{INTA1}}$	65
INT4	66

I/O

Name	Location
$\overline{\text{UCS}}$	61
$\overline{\text{LCS}}$	60
P1.0/$\overline{\text{GCS0}}$	59
P1.1/$\overline{\text{GCS1}}$	58
P1.2/$\overline{\text{GCS2}}$	57
P1.3/$\overline{\text{GCS3}}$	56
P1.4/$\overline{\text{GCS4}}$	55
P1.5/$\overline{\text{GCS5}}$	52
P1.6/$\overline{\text{GCS6}}$	51
P1.7/$\overline{\text{GCS7}}$	50
T0OUT	75
T0IN	76
T1OUT	77
T1IN	78
RXD0	3
TXD0	2
P2.5/BCLK0	4
$\overline{\text{CTS0}}$	1
P2.0/RXD1	7
P2.1/TXD1	8
P2.2/BCLK1	9
P2.3/SINT1	5
P2.4/$\overline{\text{CTS1}}$	6
P2.6	80
P2.7	79

NOTE:
Pin names in parentheses apply to the 80C188EB/80L188EB.

Table 7. QFP Package Location with Pin Names

Location	Name	Location	Name	Location	Name	Location	Name
1	$\overline{\text{CTS0}}$	21	AD4	41	$\overline{\text{S1}}$	61	$\overline{\text{UCS}}$
2	TXD0	22	AD12 (A12)	42	$\overline{\text{S0}}$	62	INT0
3	RXD0	23	AD5	43	$\overline{\text{DEN}}$	63	INT1
4	P2.5/BCLK0	24	AD13 (A13)	44	HLDA	64	INT2/$\overline{\text{INTA0}}$
5	P2.3/SINT1	25	AD6	45	HOLD	65	INT3/$\overline{\text{INTA1}}$
6	P2.4/$\overline{\text{CTS1}}$	26	AD14 (A14)	46	$\overline{\text{TEST}}$	66	INT4
7	P2.0/RXD1	27	AD7	47	$\overline{\text{LOCK}}$	67	PDTMR
8	P2.1/TXD1	28	AD15 (A15)	48	NMI	68	$\overline{\text{RESIN}}$
9	P2.2/BCLK1	29	A16	49	READY	69	RESOUT
10	AD0	30	A17	50	P1.7/$\overline{\text{GCS7}}$	70	OSCOUT
11	AD8 (A8)	31	A18	51	P1.6/$\overline{\text{GCS6}}$	71	CLKIN
12	V_{SS}	32	A19/$\overline{\text{ONCE}}$	52	P1.5/$\overline{\text{GCS5}}$	72	V_{CC}
13	V_{CC}	33	V_{SS}	53	V_{SS}	73	V_{SS}
14	V_{SS}	34	V_{CC}	54	V_{CC}	74	CLKOUT
15	AD1	35	V_{SS}	55	P1.4/$\overline{\text{GCS4}}$	75	T0OUT
16	AD9 (A9)	36	$\overline{\text{RD}}$	56	P1.3/$\overline{\text{GCS3}}$	76	T0IN
17	AD2	37	$\overline{\text{WR}}$	57	P1.2/$\overline{\text{GCS2}}$	77	T1OUT
18	AD10 (A10)	38	ALE	58	P1.1/$\overline{\text{GCS1}}$	78	T1IN
19	AD3	39	$\overline{\text{BHE}}$ ($\overline{\text{RFSH}}$)	59	P1.0/$\overline{\text{GCS0}}$	79	P2.7
20	AD11 (A11)	40	$\overline{\text{S2}}$	60	$\overline{\text{LCS}}$	80	P2.6

NOTE:
Pin names in parentheses apply to the 80C188EB/80L188EB.

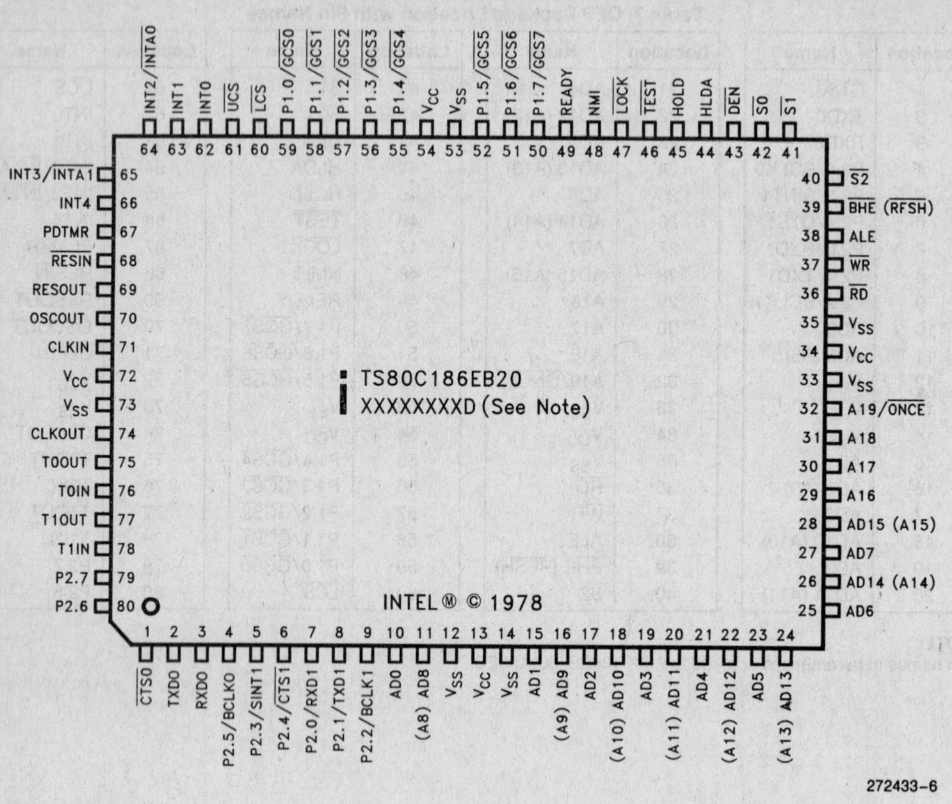

NOTE:
This is the FPO number location (indicated by X's).
Pin names in parentheses apply to the 80C188EB/80L188EB.

Figure 5. Quad Flat Pack Pinout Diagram

Table 8. SQFP Pin Functions with Location

AD Bus	
AD0	47
AD1	52
AD2	54
AD3	56
AD4	58
AD5	60
AD6	62
AD7	64
AD8 (A8)	48
AD9 (A9)	53
AD10 (A10)	55
AD11 (A11)	57
AD12 (A12)	59
AD13 (A13)	61
AD14 (A14)	63
AD15 (A15)	65
A16	66
A17	67
A18	68
A19/ONCE	69

Bus Control	
ALE	75
BHE# (RFSH#)	76
S0#	79
S1#	78
S2#	77
RD#	73
WR#	74
READY	6
DEN#	80
LOCK#	4
HOLD	2
HLDA	1

Processor Control	
RESIN#	25
RESOUT	26
CLKIN	28
OSCOUT	27
CLKOUT	31
TEST#/BUSY	3
NMI	5
INT0	19
INT1	20
INT2/INTA0#	21
INT3/INTA1#	22
INT4	23
PDTMR	24

Power and Ground	
V_{CC}	11
V_{CC}	29
V_{CC}	50
V_{CC}	71
V_{SS}	10
V_{SS}	30
V_{SS}	49
V_{SS}	51
V_{SS}	70
V_{SS}	72

I/O	
UCS#	18
LCS#	17
P1.0/GCS0#	16
P1.1/GCS1#	15
P1.2/GCS2#	14
P1.3/GCS3#	13
P1.4/GCS4#	12
P1.5/GCS5#	9
P1.6/GCS6#	8
P1.7/GCS7#	7
P2.0/RXD1	44
P2.1/TXD1	45
P2.2/BCLK1	46
P2.3/SINT1	42
P2.4/CTS1#	43
P2.5/BCLK0	41
P2.6	37
P2.7	36
CTS0#	38
TXD0	39
RXD0	40
T0IN	33
T1IN	35
T0OUT	32
T1OUT	34

Table 9. SQFP Pin Locations with Pin Names

1	HLDA	21	INT1/INTA0#	41	P2.5/BCLK0	61	AD13 (A13)
2	HOLD	22	INT3/INTA1#	42	P2.3/SINT1	62	AD6
3	TEST#	23	INT4	43	P2.4/CTS1#	63	AD14 (A14)
4	LOCK#	24	PDTMR	44	P2.0/RXD1	64	AD7
5	NMI	25	RESIN#	45	P2.1/TXD1	65	AD15 (A15)
6	READY	26	RESOUT	46	P2.2/BCLK1	66	A16
7	P1.7/GCS7#	27	OSCOUT	47	AD0	67	A17
8	P1.6/GCS6#	28	CLKIN	48	AD8 (A8)	68	A18
9	P1.5/GCS5#	29	V_{CC}	49	V_{SS}	69	A19/ONCE
10	V_{SS}	30	V_{SS}	50	V_{CC}	70	V_{SS}
11	V_{CC}	31	CLKOUT	51	V_{SS}	71	V_{CC}
12	P1.4/GCS4#	32	T0OUT	52	AD1	72	V_{SS}
13	P1.3/GCS3#	33	T0IN	53	AD9 (A9)	73	RD#
14	P1.2/GCS2#	34	T1OUT	54	AD2	74	WR#
15	P1.1/GCS1#	35	T1IN	55	AD10 (A10)	75	ALE
16	P1.0/GCS0#	36	P2.7	56	AD3	76	BHE# (RFSH#)
17	LCS#	37	P2.6	57	AD11 (A11)	77	S2#
18	UCS#	38	CTS0#	58	AD4	78	S1#
19	INT0	39	TXD0	59	AD12 (A12)	79	S0#
20	INT1	40	RXD0	60	AD5	80	DEN#

NOTE:
Pin names in parentheses apply to the 80C188EB/80L188EB.

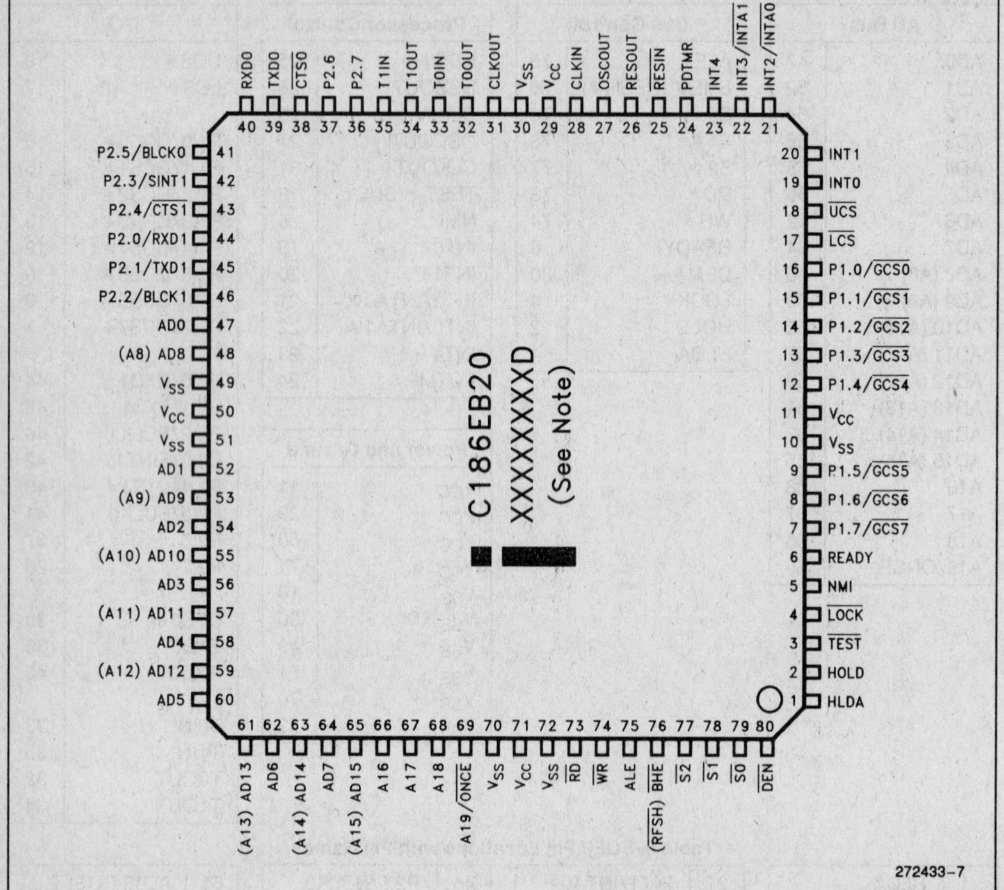

NOTE:
XXXXXXXXC indicates Intel FPO number.
Pin names in parentheses apply to the 80C188EB/80L188EB.

Figure 6. CQFP Package

PACKAGE THERMAL SPECIFICATIONS

The 80C186EB/80L186EB is specified for operation when T_C (the case temperature) is within the range of −40°C to +100°C (PLCC package) or −40°C to +114°C (QFP package). T_C may be measured in any environment to determine whether the processor is within the specified operating range. The case temperature must be measured at the center of the top surface.

T_A (the ambient temperature) can be calculated from θ_{CA} (thermal resistance from the case to ambient) with the following equation:

$$T_A = T_C - P^* \theta_{CA}$$

Typical values for θ_{CA} at various airflows are given in Table 10. P (the maximum power consumption, specified in watts) is calculated by using the maximum ICC as tabulated in the DC specifications and V_{CC} of 5.5V.

Table 10. Thermal Resistance (θ_{CA}) at Various Airflows (in °C/Watt)

	Airflow Linear ft/min (m/sec)					
	0 (0)	**200 (1.01)**	**400 (2.03)**	**600 (3.04)**	**800 (4.06)**	**1000 (5.07)**
θ_{CA} (PLCC)	30	24	21	19	17	16.5
θ_{CA} (QFP)	58	47	43	40	38	36
θ_{CA} (SQFP)	70	TBD	TBD	TBD	TBD	TBD

2

ELECTRICAL SPECIFICATIONS

Absolute Maximum Ratings

Storage Temperature .... −65°C to +150°C
Case Temp under Bias .... −65°C to +120°C
Supply Voltage
with Respect to V_{SS}........... −0.5V to + 6.5V
Voltage on other Pins
with Respect to V_{SS} ...... −0.5V to V_{CC} + 0.5V

NOTICE: This data sheet contains preliminary information on new products in production. It is valid for the devices indicated in the revision history. The specifications are subject to change without notice.

**WARNING: Stressing the device beyond the "Absolute Maximum Ratings" may cause permanent damage. These are stress ratings only. Operation beyond the "Operating Conditions" is not recommended and extended exposure beyond the "Operating Conditions" may affect device reliability.*

Recommended Connections

Power and ground connections must be made to multiple V_{CC} and V_{SS} pins. Every 80C186EB-based circuit board should include separate power (V_{CC}) and ground (V_{SS}) planes. Every V_{CC} pin must be connected to the power plane, and every V_{SS} pin must be connected to the ground plane. Pins identified as "NC" must not be connected in the system. Liberal decoupling capacitance should be placed near the processor. The processor can cause transient power surges when its output buffers transition, particularly when connected to large capacitive loads.

Low inductance capacitors and interconnects are recommended for best high frequency electrical performance. Inductance is reduced by placing the decoupling capacitors as close as possible to the processor V_{CC} and V_{SS} package pins.

Always connect any unused input to an appropriate signal level. In particular, unused interrupt inputs (INT0:4) should be connected to V_{CC} through a pull-up resistor (in the range of 50 KΩ). **Leave any unused output pin or any NC pin unconnected.**

DC SPECIFICATIONS (80C186EB/80C188EB)

Symbol	Parameter	Min	Max	Units	Notes
V_{CC}	Supply Voltage	4.5	5.5	V	
V_{IL}	Input Low Voltage	−0.5	0.3 V_{CC}	V	
V_{IH}	Input High Voltage	0.7 V_{CC}	V_{CC} + 0.5	V	
V_{OL}	Output Low Voltage		0.45	V	I_{OL} = 3 mA (Min)
V_{OH}	Output High Voltage	V_{CC} − 0.5		V	I_{OH} = −2 mA (Min)
V_{HYR}	Input Hysterisis on $\overline{RESIN}$	0.50		V	
I_{LI1}	Input Leakage Current for Pins: AD15:0 (AD7:0), READY, HOLD, $\overline{RESIN}$, CLKIN, $\overline{TEST}$, NMI, INT4:0, T0IN, T1IN, RXD0, $\overline{BCLK0}$, $\overline{CTS0}$, RXD1, $\overline{BCLK1}$, $\overline{CTS1}$, P2.6, P2.7		±15	μA	0V ≤ V_{IN} ≤ V_{CC}
I_{LI2}	Input Leakage Current for Pins: $\overline{ERROR}$, PEREQ	±0.275	±7	mA	0V ≤ V_{IN} < V_{CC}
I_{LI3}	Input Leakage Current for Pins: A19/$\overline{ONCE}$, A18:16, $\overline{LOCK}$	−0.275	−5.0	mA	V_{IN} = 0.7 V_{CC} (Note 1)
I_{LO}	Output Leakage Current		±15	μA	0.45 ≤ V_{OUT} ≤ V_{CC} (Note 2)
I_{CC}	Supply Current Cold (RESET) 80C186EB20		108	mA	(Note 3)
	80C186EB13		73	mA	(Note 3)
I_{ID}	Supply Current Idle 80C186EB20		76	mA	(Note 4)
	80C186EB13		48	mA	(Note 4)
I_{PD}	Supply Current Powerdown 80C186EB20		100	μA	(Note 5)
	80C186EB13		100	μA	(Note 5)
C_{IN}	Input Pin Capacitance	0	15	pF	T_F = 1 MHz
C_{OUT}	Output Pin Capacitance	0	15	pF	T_F = 1 MHz (Note 6)

NOTES:
1. These pins have an internal pull-up device that is active while $\overline{RESIN}$ is low and ONCE Mode is not active. Sourcing more current than specified (on any of these pins) may invoke a factory test mode.
2. Tested by outputs being floated by invoking ONCE Mode or by asserting HOLD.
3. Measured with the device in RESET and at worst case frequency, V_{CC}, and temperature with **ALL** outputs loaded as specified in AC Test Conditions, and all floating outputs driven to V_{CC} or GND.
4. Measured with the device in HALT (IDLE Mode active) and at worst case frequency, V_{CC}, and temperature with **ALL** outputs loaded as specified in AC Test Conditions, and all floating outputs driven to V_{CC} or GND.
5. Measured with the device in HALT (Powerdown Mode active) and at worst case frequency, V_{CC}, and temperature with **ALL** outputs loaded as specified in AC Test Conditions, and all floating outputs driven to V_{CC} or GND.
6. Output Capacitance is the capacitive load of a floating output pin.

DC SPECIFICATIONS (80L186EB/80L188EB)

Symbol	Parameter	Min	Max	Units	Notes
V_{CC}	Supply Voltage	2.7	5.5	V	
V_{IL}	Input Low Voltage	−0.5	0.3 V_{CC}	V	
V_{IH}	Input High Voltage	0.7 V_{CC}	V_{CC} + 0.5	V	
V_{OL}	Output Low Voltage		0.45	V	I_{OL} = 1.6 mA (Min) (Note 1)
V_{OH}	Output High Voltage	V_{CC} − 0.5		V	I_{OH} = −1 mA (Min) (Note 1)
V_{HYR}	Input Hysterisis on $\overline{RESIN}$	0.50		V	
I_{LI1}	Input Leakage Current for pins: AD15:0 (AD7:0), READY, HOLD, $\overline{RESIN}$, CLKIN, $\overline{TEST}$, NMI, INT4:0, T0IN, T1IN, RXD0, $\overline{BCLK0}$, $\overline{CTS0}$, RXD1, $\overline{BCLK1}$, $\overline{CTS1}$, SINT1, P2.6, P2.7		±15	μA	0V ≤ V_{IN} ≤ V_{CC}
I_{LI2}	Input Leakage Current for Pins: A19/$\overline{ONCE}$, A18:16, $\overline{LOCK}$	−0.275	−2	mA	V_{IN} = 0.7 V_{CC} (Note 2)
I_{LO}	Output Leakage Current		±15	μA	0.45 ≤ V_{OUT} ≤ V_{CC} (Note 3)
I_{CC5}	Supply Current (RESET, 5.5V) 80L186EB13 80L186EB8		 73 45	 mA mA	 (Note 4) (Note 4)
I_{CC3}	Supply Current (RESET, 2.7V) 80L186EB13 80L186EB8		 36 22	 mA mA	 (Note 4) (Note 4)
I_{ID5}	Supply Current Idle (5.5V) 80L186EB13 80L186EB8		 48 31	 mA mA	 (Note 5) (Note 5)
I_{ID3}	Supply Current Idle (2.7V) 80L186EB13 80L186EB8		 24 15	 mA mA	 (Note 5) (Note 5)
I_{PD5}	Supply Current Powerdown (5.5V) 80L186EB13 80L186EB8		 100 100	 μA μA	 (Note 6) (Note 6)
I_{PD3}	Supply Current Powerdown (2.7V) 80L186EB13 80L186EB8		 30 30	 μA μA	 (Note 6) (Note 6)
C_{IN}	Input Pin Capacitance	0	15	pF	T_F = 1 MHz
C_{OUT}	Output Pin Capacitance	0	15	pF	T_F = 1 MHz (Note 7)

NOTES:
1. I_{OL} and I_{OH} measured at V_{CC} = 2.7V.
2. These pins have an internal pull-up device that is active while $\overline{RESIN}$ is low and ONCE Mode is not active. Sourcing more current than specified (on any of these pins) may invoke a factory test mode.
3. Tested by outputs being floated by invoking ONCE Mode or by asserting HOLD.
4. Measured with the device in RESET and at worst case frequency, V_{CC}, and temperature with **ALL** outputs loaded as specified in AC Test Conditions, and all floating outputs driven to V_{CC} or GND.
5. Measured with the device in HALT (IDLE Mode active) and at worst case frequency, V_{CC}, and temperature with **ALL** outputs loaded as specified in AC Test Conditions, and all floating outputs driven to V_{CC} or GND.
6. Measured with the device in HALT (Powerdown Mode active) and at worst case frequency, V_{CC}, and temperature with **ALL** outputs loaded as specified in AC Test Conditions, and all floating outputs driven to V_{CC} or GND.
7. Output Capacitance is the capacitive load of a floating output pin.

I_{CC} VERSUS FREQUENCY AND VOLTAGE

The current (I_{CC}) consumption of the processor is essentially composed of two components; I_{PD} and I_{CCS}.

I_{PD} is the **quiescent** current that represents internal device leakage, and is measured with all inputs or floating outputs at GND or V_{CC} (no clock applied to the device). I_{PD} is equal to the Powerdown current and is typically less than 50 μA.

I_{CCS} is the **switching** current used to charge and discharge parasitic device capacitance when changing logic levels. Since I_{CCS} is typically much greater than I_{PD}, I_{PD} can often be ignored when calculating I_{CC}.

I_{CCS} is related to the voltage and frequency at which the device is operating. It is given by the formula:

$$\text{Power} = V \times I = V^2 \times C_{DEV} \times f$$

$$\therefore I = I_{CC} = I_{CCS} = V \times C_{DEV} \times f$$

Where: V = Device operating voltage (V_{CC})

C_{DEV} = Device capacitance

f = Device operating frequency

$I_{CCS} = I_{CC}$ = Device current

Measuring C_{DEV} on a device like the 80C186EB would be difficult. Instead, C_{DEV} is calculated using the above formula by measuring I_{CC} at a known V_{CC} and frequency (see Table 11). Using this C_{DEV} value, I_{CC} can be calculated at any voltage and frequency within the specified operating range.

EXAMPLE: Calculate the typical I_{CC} when operating at 10 MHz, 4.8V.

$$I_{CC} = I_{CCS} = 4.8 \times 0.583 \times 10 \approx 28 \text{ mA}$$

PDTMR PIN DELAY CALCULATION

The PDTMR pin provides a delay between the assertion of NMI and the enabling of the internal clocks when exiting Powerdown. A delay is required only when using the on-chip oscillator to allow the crystal or resonator circuit time to stabilize.

NOTE:
The PDTMR pin function does not apply when $\overline{\text{RESIN}}$ is asserted (i.e., a device reset during Powerdown is similar to a cold reset and $\overline{\text{RESIN}}$ must remain active until after the oscillator has stabilized).

To calculate the value of capacitor required to provide a desired delay, use the equation:

$$440 \times t = C_{PD} \quad (5V, 25°C)$$

Where: t = desired delay in **seconds**

C_{PD} = capacitive load on PDTMR in **microfarads**

EXAMPLE: To get a delay of 300 μs, a capacitor value of $C_{PD} = 440 \times (300 \times 10^{-6}) = 0.132$ μF is required. Round up to standard (available) capacitive values.

NOTE:
The above equation applies to delay times greater than 10 μs and will compute the **TYPICAL** capacitance needed to achieve the desired delay. A delay variance of +50% or −25% can occur due to temperature, voltage, and device process extremes. In general, higher V_{CC} and/or lower temperature will decrease delay time, while lower V_{CC} and/or higher temperature will increase delay time.

Table 11. Device Capacitance (C_{DEV}) Values

Parameter	Typ	Max	Units	Notes
C_{DEV} (Device in Reset)	0.583	1.02	mA/V*MHz	1, 2
C_{DEV} (Device in Idle)	0.408	0.682	mA/V*MHz	1, 2

1. Max C_{DEV} is calculated at −40°C, all floating outputs driven to V_{CC} or GND, and all outputs loaded to 50 pF (including CLKOUT and OSCOUT).
2. Typical C_{DEV} is calculated at 25°C with all outputs loaded to 50 pF except CLKOUT and OSCOUT, which are not loaded.

AC SPECIFICATIONS

AC Characteristics—80C186EB20/80C186EB13

Symbol	Parameter	20 MHz		13 MHz		Units	Notes
		Min	Max	Min	Max		
INPUT CLOCK							
T_F	CLKIN Frequency	0	40	0	26	MHz	1
T_C	CLKIN Period	25	∞	38.5	∞	ns	1
T_{CH}	CLKIN High Time	10	∞	12	∞	ns	1, 2
T_{CL}	CLKIN Low Time	10	∞	12	∞	ns	1, 2
T_{CR}	CLKIN Rise Time	1	8	1	8	ns	1, 3
T_{CF}	CLKIN Fall Time	1	8	1	8	ns	1, 3
OUTPUT CLOCK							
T_{CD}	CLKIN to CLKOUT Delay	0	17	0	23	ns	1, 4
T	CLKOUT Period		$2{*}T_C$		$2{*}T_C$	ns	1
T_{PH}	CLKOUT High Time	(T/2) − 5	(T/2) + 5	(T/2) − 5	(T/2) + 5	ns	1
T_{PL}	CLKOUT Low Time	(T/2) − 5	(T/2) + 5	(T/2) − 5	(T/2) + 5	ns	1
T_{PR}	CLKOUT Rise Time	1	6	1	6	ns	1, 5
T_{PF}	CLKOUT Fall Time	1	6	1	6	ns	1, 5
OUTPUT DELAYS							
T_{CHOV1}	ALE, S2:0, DEN, DT/R, BHE (RFSH), LOCK, A19:16	3	22	3	25	ns	1, 4, 6, 7
T_{CHOV2}	GCS0:7, LCS, UCS, NCS, RD, WR	3	27	3	30	ns	1, 4, 6, 8
T_{CLOV1}	BHE (RFSH), DEN, LOCK, RESOUT, HLDA, T0OUT, T1OUT, A19:16	3	22	3	25	ns	1, 4, 6
T_{CLOV2}	RD, WR, GCS7:0, LCS, UCS, AD15:0 (AD7:0, A15:8), NCS, INTA1:0, S2:0	3	27	3	30	ns	1, 4, 6
T_{CHOF}	RD, WR, BHE (RFSH), DT/R, LOCK, S2:0, A19:16	0	25	0	25	ns	1
T_{CLOF}	DEN, AD15:0 (AD7:0, A15:8)	0	25	0	25	ns	1

AC SPECIFICATIONS

AC Characteristics—80C186EB20/80C186EB13 (Continued)

Symbol	Parameter	20 MHz		13 MHz		Units	Notes
		Min	Max	Min	Max		
SYNCHRONOUS INPUTS							
T_{CHIS}	$\overline{TEST}$, NMI, INT4:0, BCLK1:0, T1:0IN, READY, $\overline{CTS1:0}$, P2.6, P2.7	10		10		ns	1, 9
T_{CHIH}	$\overline{TEST}$, NMI, INT4:0, BCLK1:0, T1:0IN, READY, $\overline{CTS1:0}$	3		3		ns	1, 9
T_{CLIS}	AD15:0 (AD7:0), READY	10		10		ns	1, 10
T_{CLIH}	READY, AD15:0 (AD7:0)	3		3		ns	1, 10
T_{CLIS}	HOLD, PEREQ, $\overline{ERROR}$	10		10		ns	1, 9
T_{CLIH}	HOLD, PEREQ, $\overline{ERROR}$	3		3		ns	1, 9

NOTES:
1. See **AC Timing Waveforms**, for waveforms and definition.
2. Measure at V_{IH} for high time, V_{IL} for low time.
3. Only required to guarantee I_{CC}. Maximum limits are bounded by T_C, T_{CH} and T_{CL}.
4. Specified for a 50 pF load, see Figure 13 for capacitive derating information.
5. Specified for a 50 pF load, see Figure 14 for rise and fall times outside 50 pF.
6. See Figure 14 for rise and fall times.
7. T_{CHOV1} applies to $\overline{BHE}$ ($\overline{RFSH}$), $\overline{LOCK}$ and A19:16 only after a HOLD release.
8. T_{CHOV2} applies to $\overline{RD}$ and $\overline{WR}$ only after a HOLD release.
9. Setup and Hold are required to guarantee recognition.
10. Setup and Hold are required for proper operation.

AC SPECIFICATIONS

AC Characteristics—80L186EB13/80L186EB8

Symbol	Parameter	13 MHz		8 MHz		Units	Notes
		Min	Max	Min	Max		
INPUT CLOCK							
T_F	CLKIN Frequency	0	26	0	16	MHz	1
T_C	CLKIN Period	38.5	∞	62.5	∞	ns	1
T_{CH}	CLKIN High Time	15	∞	15	∞	ns	1, 2
T_{CL}	CLKIN Low Time	15	∞	15	∞	ns	1, 2
T_{CR}	CLKIN Rise Time	1	8	1	8	ns	1, 3
T_{CF}	CLKIN Fall Time	1	8	1	8	ns	1, 3
OUTPUT CLOCK							
T_{CD}	CLKIN to CLKOUT Delay	0	40	0	50	ns	1, 4
T	CLKOUT Period		2^*T_C		2^*T_C	ns	1
T_{PH}	CLKOUT High Time	(T/2) − 5	(T/2) + 5	(T/2) − 5	(T/2) + 5	ns	1
T_{PL}	CLKOUT Low Time	(T/2) − 5	(T/2) + 5	(T/2) − 5	(T/2) + 5	ns	1
T_{PR}	CLKOUT Rise Time	1	10	1	15	ns	1, 5
T_{PF}	CLKOUT Fall Time	1	10	1	15	ns	1, 5
OUTPUT DELAYS							
T_{CHOV1}	ALE, $\overline{S2:0}$, $\overline{DEN}$, DT/$\overline{R}$, $\overline{BHE}$ ($\overline{RFSH}$), $\overline{LOCK}$, A19:16	3	25	3	30	ns	1, 4, 6, 7
T_{CHOV2}	$\overline{GCS0:7}$, $\overline{LCS}$, $\overline{UCS}$, $\overline{NCS}$, $\overline{RD}$, $\overline{WR}$	3	30	3	35	ns	1, 4, 6, 8
T_{CLOV1}	$\overline{BHE}$ ($\overline{RFSH}$), $\overline{DEN}$, $\overline{LOCK}$, RESOUT, HLDA, T0OUT, T1OUT, A19:16	3	25	3	30	ns	1, 4, 6
T_{CLOV2}	$\overline{S2:0}$, $\overline{RD}$, $\overline{WR}$, $\overline{GCS7:0}$, $\overline{LCS}$, $\overline{UCS}$, $\overline{NCS}$, $\overline{INTA1:0}$, AD15:0 (AD7:0, A15:8)	3	30	3	35	ns	1, 4, 6
T_{CHOF}	$\overline{RD}$, $\overline{WR}$, $\overline{BHE}$ ($\overline{RFSH}$), DT/$\overline{R}$, $\overline{LOCK}$, $\overline{S2:0}$, A19:16	0	30	0	30	ns	1
T_{CLOF}	$\overline{DEN}$, AD15:0 (AD7:0, A15:8)	0	30	0	35	ns	1

AC SPECIFICATIONS

AC Characteristics—80L186EB13/80L186EB8 (Continued)

Symbol	Parameter	13 MHz		8 MHz		Units	Notes
		Min	Max	Min	Max		
SYNCHRONOUS INPUTS							
T_{CHIS}	$\overline{TEST}$, NMI, INT4:0, BCLK1:0, T1:0IN, READY, $\overline{CTS1:0}$, P2.6, P2.7	20		25		ns	1, 9
T_{CHIH}	$\overline{TEST}$, NMI, INT4:0, T1:0IN, BCLK1:0, READY, $\overline{CTS1:0}$	3		3		ns	1, 9
T_{CLIS}	AD15:0 (AD7:0), READY	20		25		ns	1, 10
T_{CLIH}	READY, AD15:0 (AD7:0)	3		3		ns	1, 10
T_{CLIS}	HOLD	20		25		ns	1, 9
T_{CLIH}	HOLD	3		3		ns	1, 9

NOTES:
1. See **AC Timing Waveforms**, for waveforms and definition.
2. Measure at V_{IH} for high time, V_{IL} for low time.
3. Only required to guarantee I_{CC}. Maximum limits are bounded by T_C, T_{CH} and T_{CL}.
4. Specified for a 50 pF load, see Figure 13 for capacitive derating information.
5. Specified for a 50 pF load, see Figure 14 for rise and fall times outside 50 pF.
6. See Figure 14 for rise and fall times.
7. T_{CHOV1} applies to $\overline{BHE}$ ($\overline{RFSH}$), $\overline{LOCK}$ and A19:16 only after a HOLD release.
8. T_{CHOV2} applies to $\overline{RD}$ and $\overline{WR}$ only after a HOLD release.
9. Setup and Hold are required to guarantee recognition.
10. Setup and Hold are required for proper operation.

2

AC SPECIFICATIONS (Continued)

Relative Timings (80C186EB20, 13/80L186EB13, 8)

Symbol	Parameter	Min	Max	Units	Notes
RELATIVE TIMINGS					
T_{LHLL}	ALE Rising to ALE Falling	T − 15		ns	
T_{AVLL}	Address Valid to ALE Falling	½T − 10		ns	
T_{PLLL}	Chip Selects Valid to ALE Falling	½T − 10		ns	1
T_{LLAX}	Address Hold from ALE Falling	½T − 10		ns	
T_{LLWL}	ALE Falling to $\overline{WR}$ Falling	½T − 15		ns	1
T_{LLRL}	ALE Falling to $\overline{RD}$ Falling	½T − 15		ns	1
T_{WHLH}	$\overline{WR}$ Rising to ALE Rising	½T − 10		ns	1
T_{AFRL}	Address Float to $\overline{RD}$ Falling	0		ns	
T_{RLRH}	$\overline{RD}$ Falling to $\overline{RD}$ Rising	(2*T) − 5		ns	2
T_{WLWH}	$\overline{WR}$ Falling to $\overline{WR}$ Rising	(2*T) − 5		ns	2
T_{RHAV}	$\overline{RD}$ Rising to Address Active	T − 15		ns	
T_{WHDX}	Output Data Hold after $\overline{WR}$ Rising	T − 15		ns	
T_{WHPH}	$\overline{WR}$ Rising to Chip Select Rising	½T − 10		ns	1
T_{RHPH}	$\overline{RD}$ Rising to Chip Select Rising	½T − 10		ns	1
T_{PHPL}	$\overline{CS}$ Inactive to $\overline{CS}$ Active	½T − 10		ns	1
T_{OVRH}	$\overline{ONCE}$ Active to $\overline{RESIN}$ Rising	T		ns	3
T_{RHOX}	$\overline{ONCE}$ Hold from $\overline{RESIN}$ Rising	T		ns	3

NOTES:
1. Assumes equal loading on both pins.
2. Can be extended using wait states.
3. Not tested

AC SPECIFICATIONS (Continued)

Serial Port Mode 0 Timings (80C186EB20, 13/80L186EB13, 8)

Symbol	Parameter	Min	Max	Unit	Notes
T_{XLXL}	TXD Clock Period	T (n + 1)		ns	1, 2
T_{XLXH}	TXD Clock Low to Clock High (n > 1)	2T − 35	2T + 35	ns	1
T_{XLXH}	TXD Clock Low to Clock High (n = 1)	T − 35	T + 35	ns	1
T_{XHXL}	TXD Clock High to Clock Low (n > 1)	(n − 1) T − 35	(n − 1) T + 35	ns	1, 2
T_{XHXL}	TXD Clock High to Clock Low (n = 1)	T − 35	T + 35	ns	1
T_{QVXH}	RXD Output Data Setup to TXD Clock High (n > 1)	(n − 1) T − 35		ns	1, 2
T_{QVXH}	RXD Output Data Setup to TXD Clock High (n = 1)	T − 35		ns	1
T_{XHQX}	RXD Output Data Hold after TXD Clock High (n > 1)	2T − 35		ns	1
T_{XHQX}	RXD Output Data Hold after TXD Clock High (n = 1)	T − 35		ns	1
T_{XHQZ}	RXD Output Data Float after Last TXD Clock High		T + 20	ns	1
T_{DVXH}	RXD Input Data Setup to TXD Clock High	T + 20		ns	1
T_{XHDX}	RXD Input Data Hold after TXD Clock High	0		ns	1

NOTES:
1. See Figure 12 for waveforms.
2. n is the value of the BxCMP register ignoring the ICLK Bit (i.e., ICLK = 0).

2

AC TEST CONDITIONS

The AC specifications are tested with the 50 pF load shown in Figure 7. See the Derating Curves section to see how timings vary with load capacitance.

Specifications are measured at the $V_{CC}/2$ crossing point, unless otherwise specified. See AC Timing Waveforms, for AC specification definitions, test pins, and illustrations.

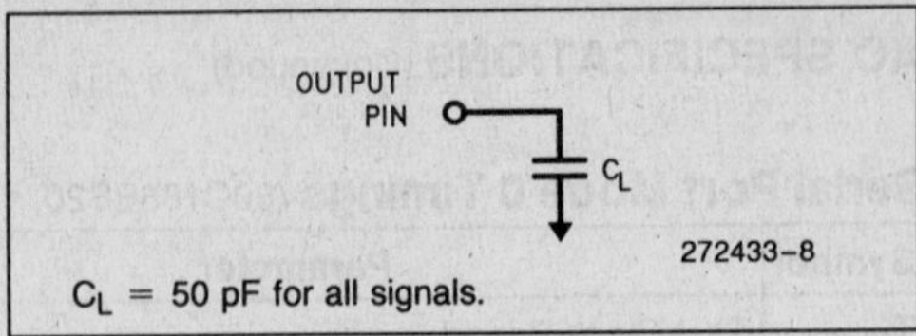

Figure 7. AC Test Load

AC TIMING WAVEFORMS

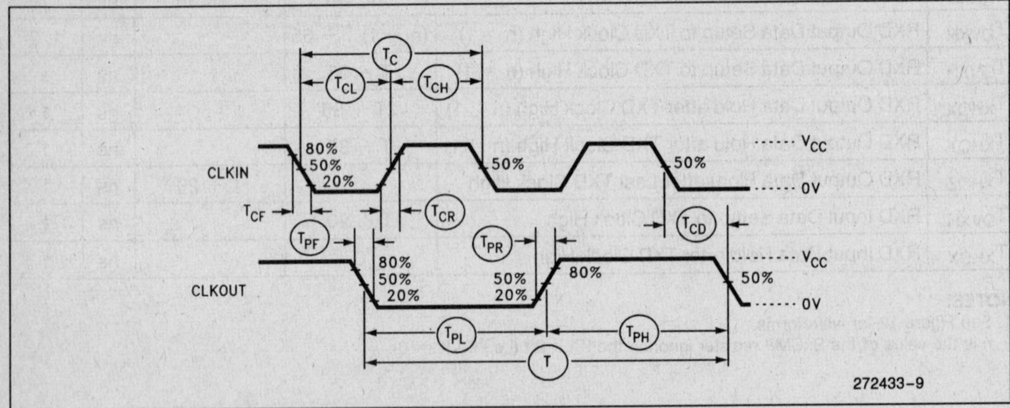

Figure 8. Input and Output Clock Waveform

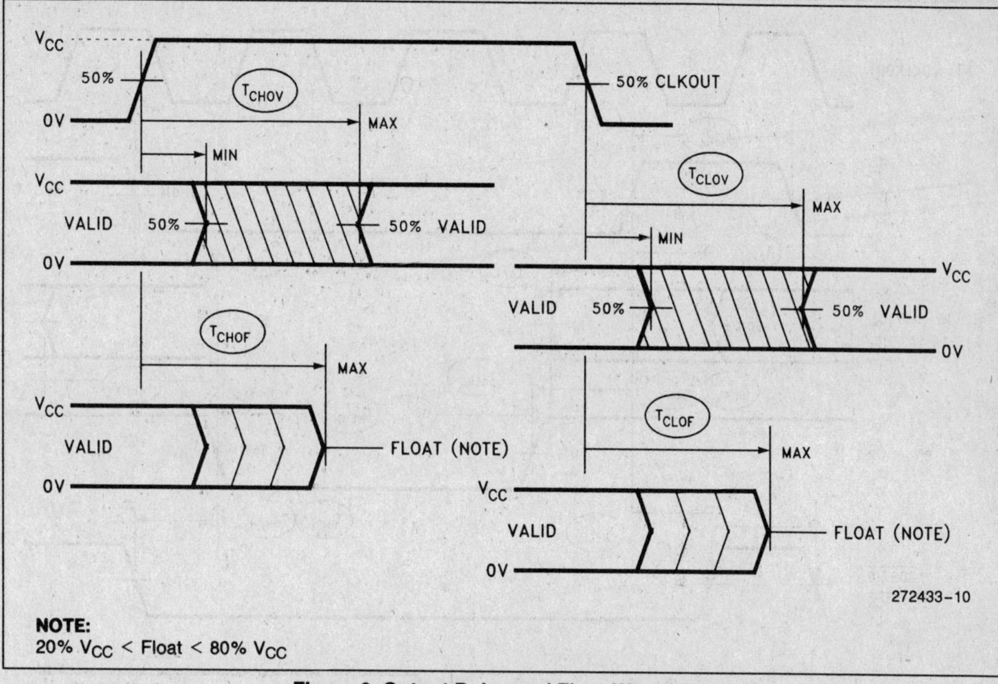

NOTE:
20% V_{CC} < Float < 80% V_{CC}

Figure 9. Output Delay and Float Waveform

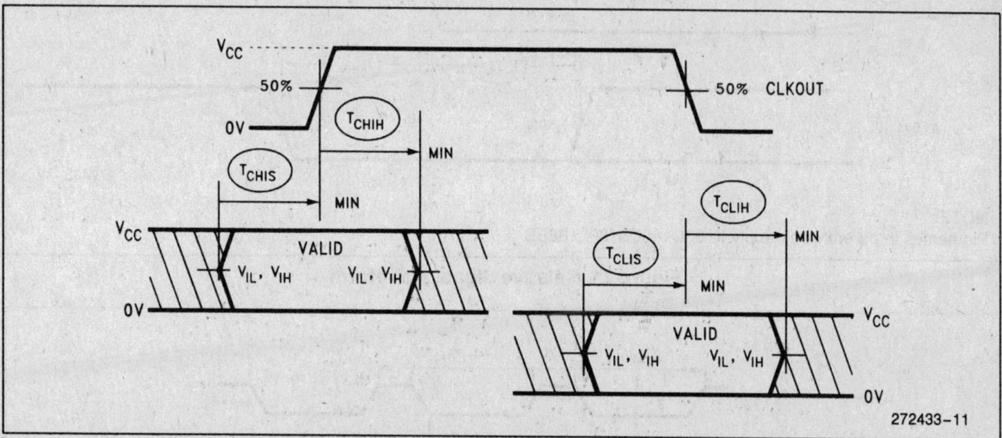

Figure 10. Input Setup and Hold

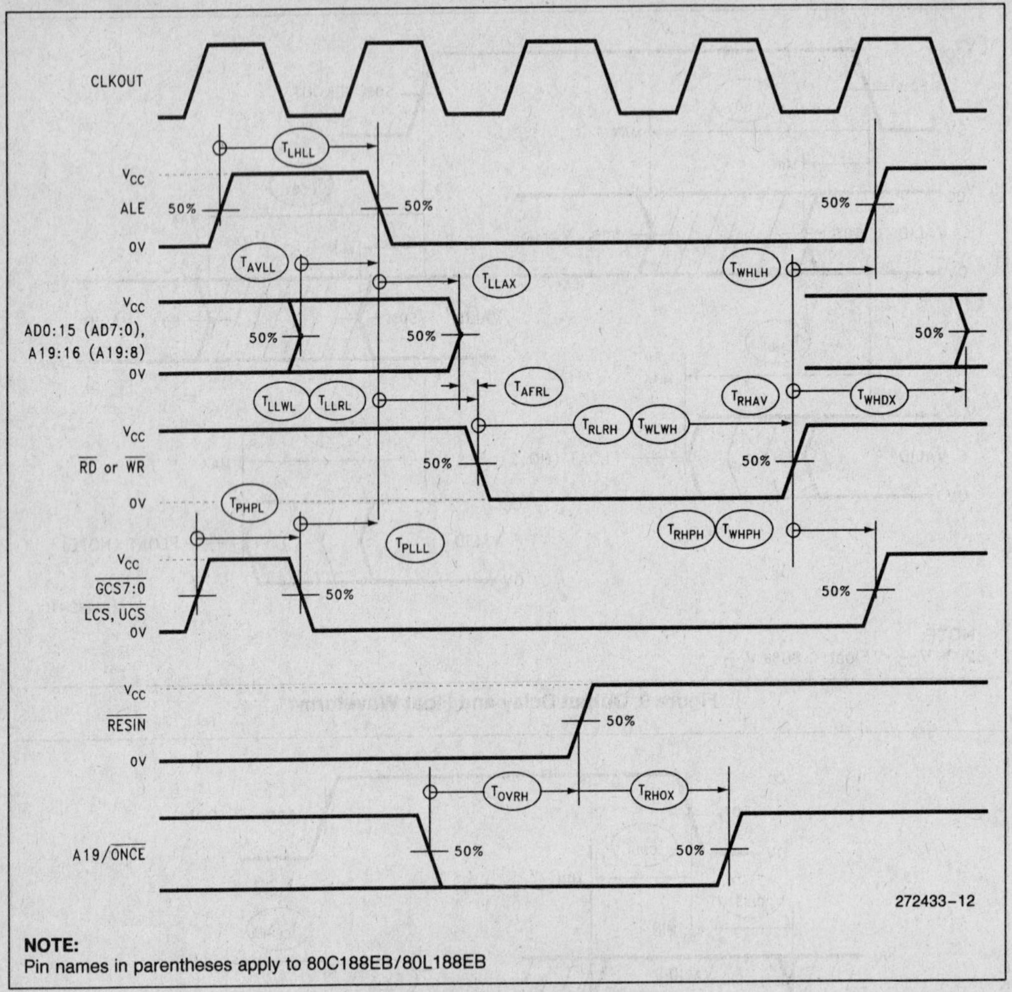

CLKOUT
T_{LHLL}
V_{CC}
ALE 50% 50% 50%
0V
T_{AVLL} T_{LLAX} T_{WHLH}
V_{CC}
AD0:15 (AD7:0), A19:16 (A19:8) 50% 50% 50%
0V
T_{LLWL} T_{LLRL} T_{AFRL} T_{RHAV} T_{WHDX}
V_{CC}
$\overline{RD}$ or $\overline{WR}$ T_{RLRH} T_{WLWH} 50% 50%
0V
T_{PHPL} T_{PLLL} T_{RHPH} T_{WHPH}
V_{CC}
$\overline{GCS7:0}$
$\overline{LCS}$, $\overline{UCS}$ 50% 50%
0V
V_{CC}
$\overline{RESIN}$ 50%
0V
T_{OVRH} T_{RHOX}
A19/$\overline{ONCE}$ 50% 50%

272433-12

NOTE:
Pin names in parentheses apply to 80C188EB/80L188EB

Figure 11. Relative Signal Waveform

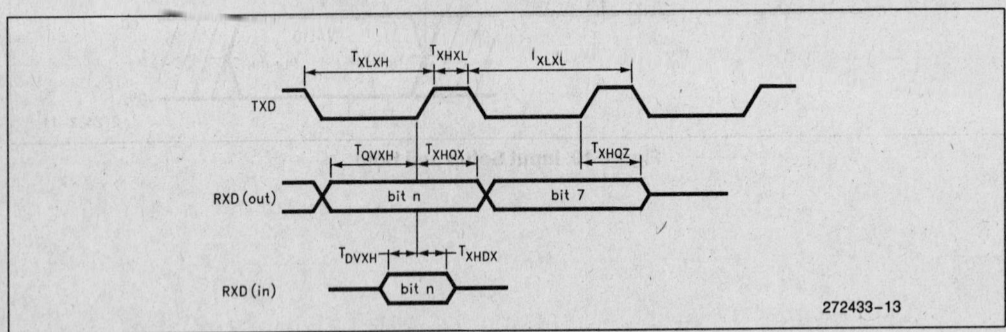

Figure 12. Serial Port Mode 0 Waveform

DERATING CURVES

TYPICAL OUTPUT DELAY VARIATIONS VERSUS LOAD CAPACITANCE

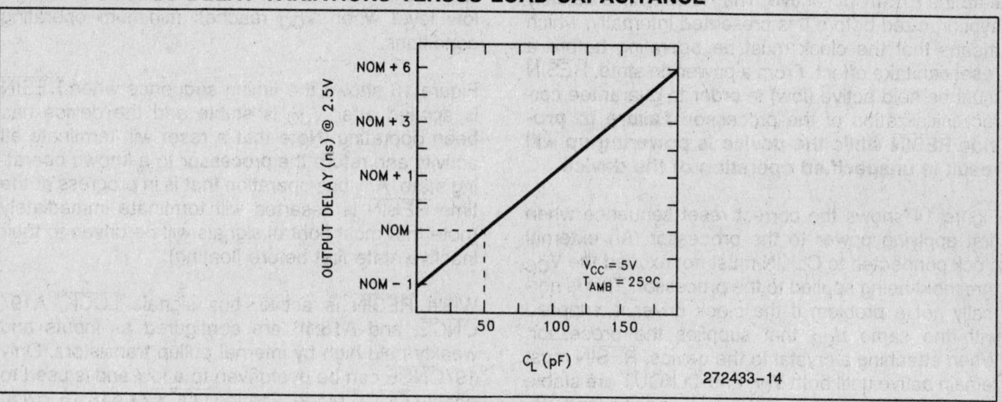

Figure 13

TYPICAL RISE AND FALL VARIATIONS VERSUS LOAD CAPACITANCE

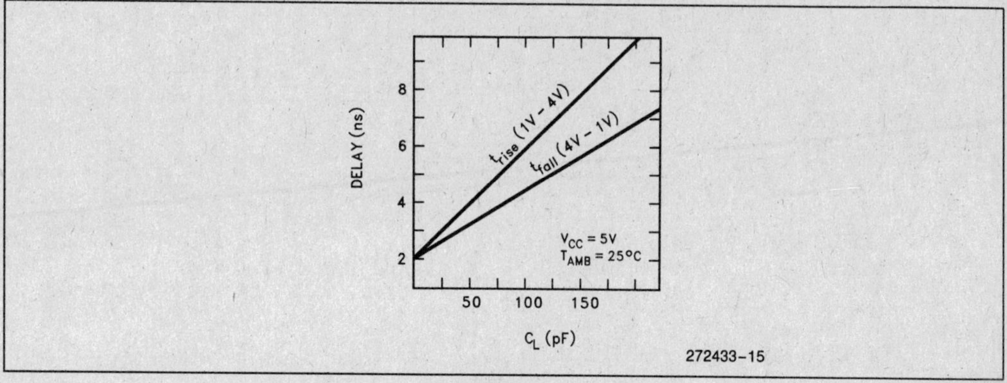

Figure 14

RESET

The processor will perform a reset operation any time the $\overline{RESIN}$ pin active. The $\overline{RESIN}$ pin is actually synchronized before it is presented internally, which means that the clock must be operating before a reset can take effect. From a power-on state, $\overline{RESIN}$ must be held active (low) in order to guarantee correct initialization of the processor. **Failure to provide $\overline{RESIN}$ while the device is powering up will result in unspecified operation of the device.**

Figure 14 shows the correct reset sequence when first applying power to the processor. An external clock connected to CLKIN must not exceed the V_{CC} threshold being applied to the processor. This is normally not a problem if the clock driver is supplied with the same V_{CC} that supplies the processor. When attaching a crystal to the device, $\overline{RESIN}$ must remain active until both V_{CC} and CLKOUT are stable (the length of time is application specific and depends on the startup characteristics of the crystal circuit). The $\overline{RESIN}$ pin is designed to operate correctly using an RC reset circuit, but the designer must ensure that the ramp time for V_{CC} is not so long that $\overline{RESIN}$ is never really sampled at a logic low level when V_{CC} reaches minimum operating conditions.

Figure 16 shows the timing sequence when $\overline{RESIN}$ is applied after V_{CC} is stable and the device has been operating. Note that a reset will terminate all activity and return the processor to a known operating state. Any bus operation that is in progress at the time $\overline{RESIN}$ is asserted will terminate immediately (note that most control signals will be driven to their inactive state first before floating).

While $\overline{RESIN}$ is active, bus signals $\overline{LOCK}$, A19/$\overline{ONCE}$, and A18:16 are configured as inputs and weakly held high by internal pullup transistors. Only 19/$\overline{ONCE}$ can be overdriven to a low and is used to enable $\overline{ONCE}$ Mode. Forcing $\overline{LOCK}$ or A18:16 low at any time while $\overline{RESIN}$ is low is prohibited and will cause unspecified device operation.

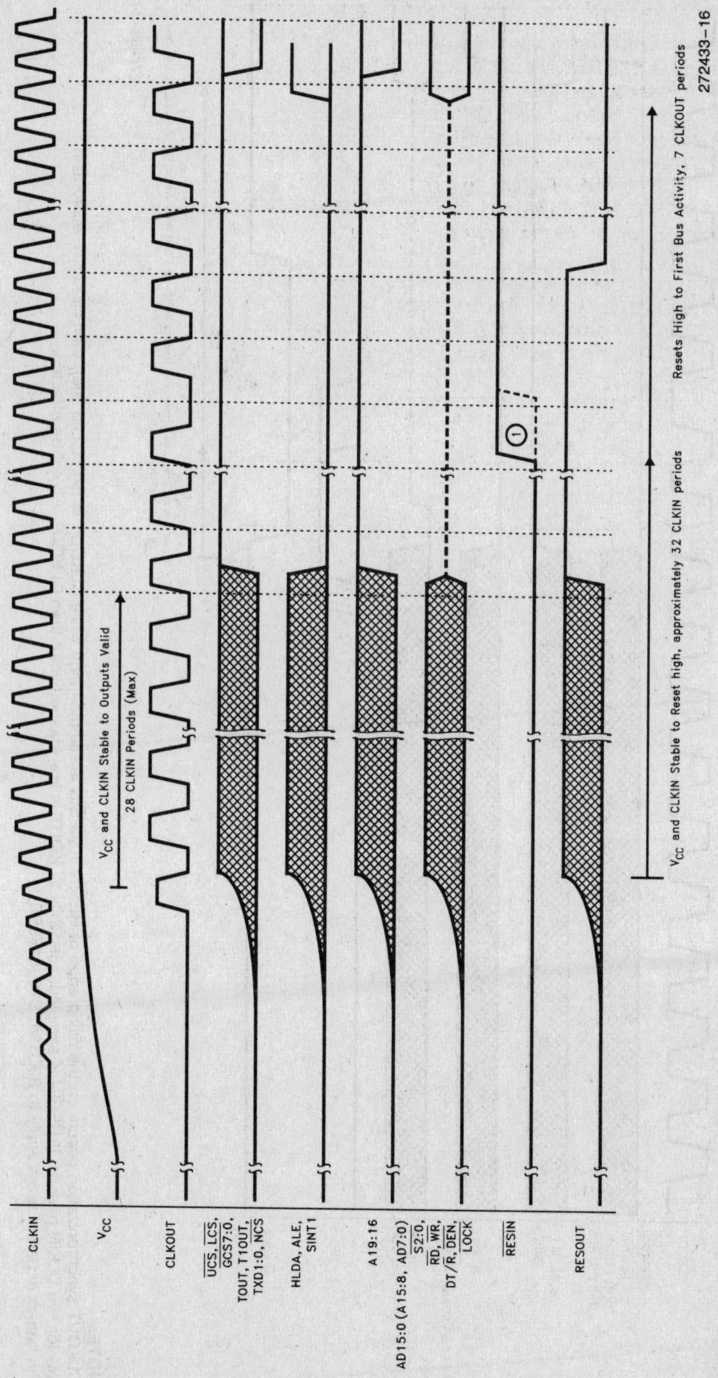

CLKIN

V_{CC}

CLKOUT

$\overline{UCS}$, $\overline{LCS}$, $\overline{GCS7:0}$, TOUT, T1OUT, TXD1:0, $\overline{NCS}$

HLDA, ALE, SINT1

A19:16

AD15:0 (A15:8, AD7:0) $\overline{S2:0}$, $\overline{RD}$, $\overline{WR}$, DT/$\overline{R}$, $\overline{DEN}$, $\overline{LOCK}$

$\overline{RESIN}$

RESOUT

V_{CC} and CLKIN Stable to Outputs Valid
28 CLKIN Periods (Max)

V_{CC} and CLKIN Stable to Reset high, approximately 32 CLKIN periods

Resets High to First Bus Activity, 7 CLKOUT periods

272433–16

NOTE:
CLKOUT synchronization occurs on the rising edge of $\overline{RESIN}$. If $\overline{RESIN}$ is sampled high while CLKOUT is high (solid line), then CLKOUT will remain low for two CLKIN periods. If $\overline{RESIN}$ is sampled high while CLKOUT is low (dashed line), then CLKOUT will not be affected.
Pin names in parentheses apply to 80C188EB/80L188EB

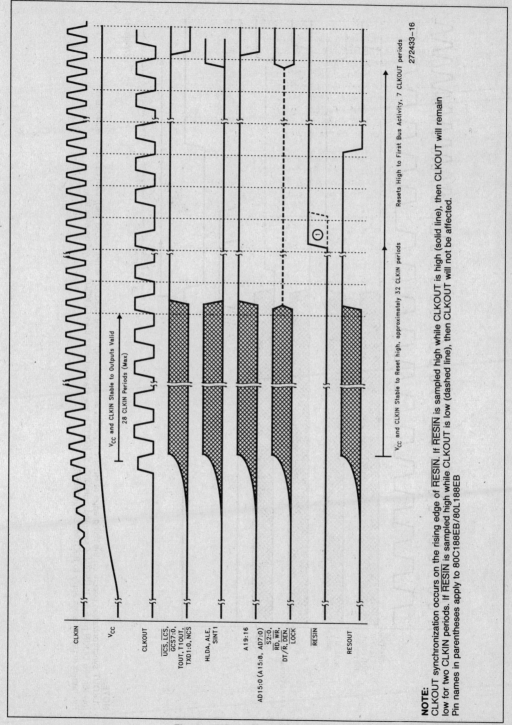

Figure 15. Cold Reset Waveforms

CLKIN

CLKOUT

UCS, LCS, GCS7:0, T0OUT, T1OUT, TXD1:0, NCS

HLDA, ALE, SINT1

A19:16

AD15:0 (AD7:0, A15:8) S2:0, RD, WR, DT/R, DEN, LOCK

RESIN

RESOUT

Minimum RESIN Low Time 4 CLKOUT Periods

Resets High to First Bus Activity, 7 CLKOUT periods

272433–17

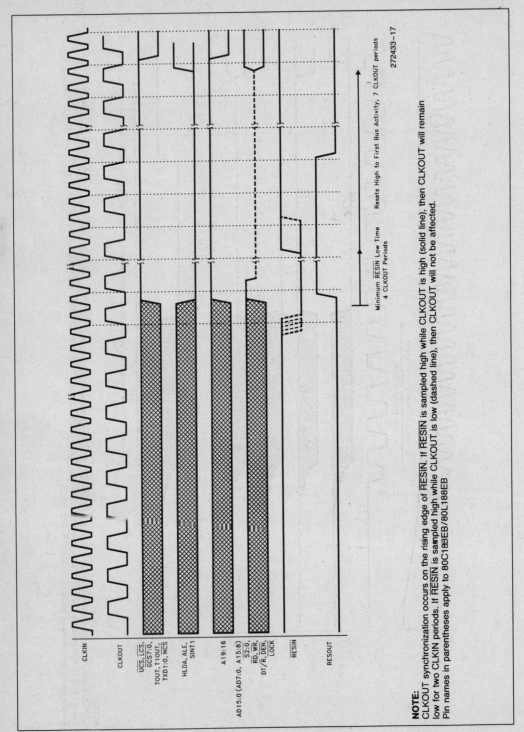

NOTE:
CLKOUT synchronization occurs on the rising edge of RESIN. If RESIN is sampled high while CLKOUT is high (solid line), then CLKOUT will remain low for two CLKIN periods. If RESIN is sampled high while CLKOUT is low (dashed line), then CLKOUT will not be affected.
Pin names in parentheses apply to 80C188EB/80L188EB

Figure 16. Warm Reset Waveforms

BUS CYCLE WAVEFORMS

Figures 17 through 23 present the various bus cycles that are generated by the processor. What is shown in the figure is the relationship of the various bus signals to CLKOUT. These figures along with the information present in **AC Specifications** allow the user to determine all the critical timing analysis needed for a given application.

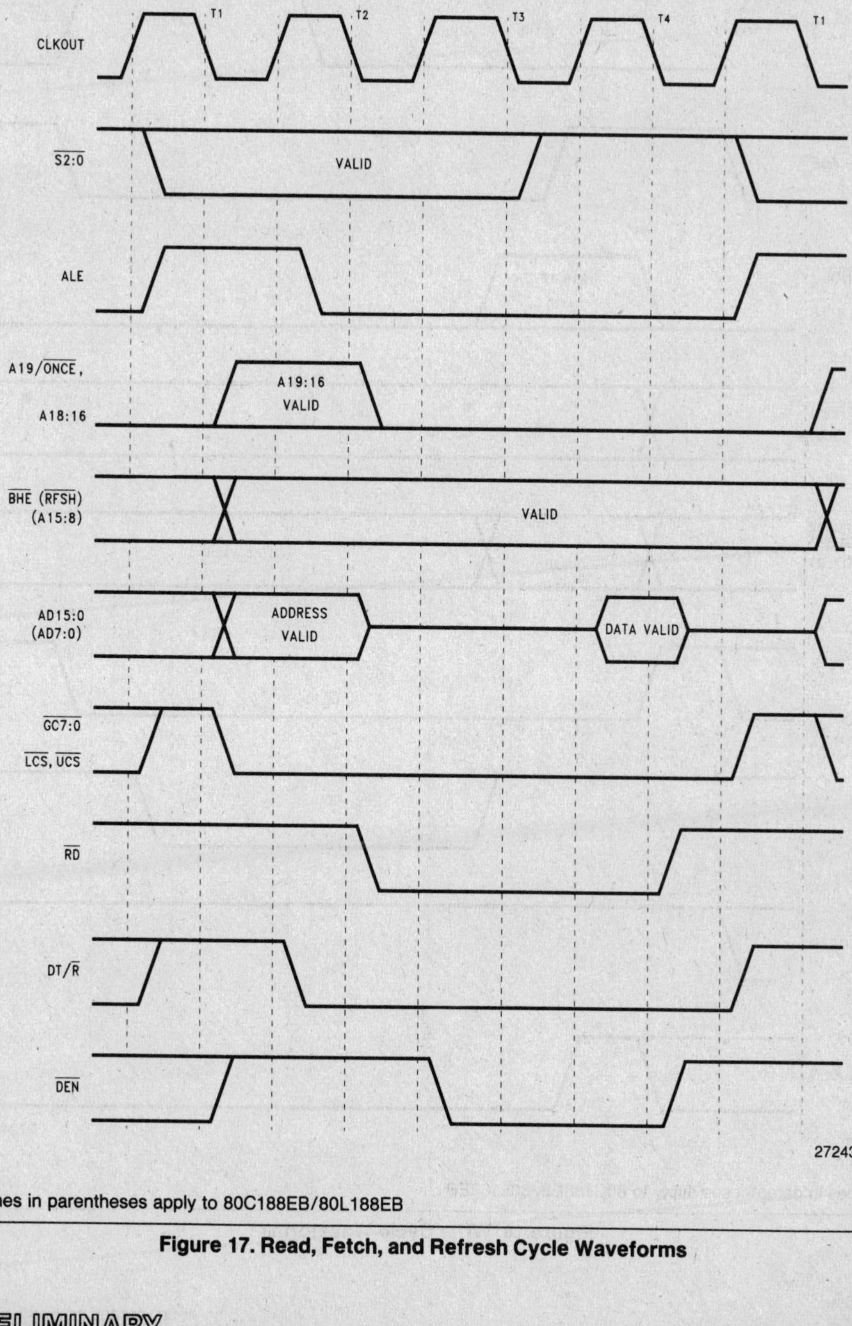

272433-18

NOTE:
Pin names in parentheses apply to 80C188EB/80L188EB

Figure 17. Read, Fetch, and Refresh Cycle Waveforms

T1 T2 T3 T4 T1

CLKOUT

$\overline{S2:0}$ VALID

ALE

A19/$\overline{ONCE}$, A18:16 — A19:16 VALID

BHE ($\overline{RFSH}$) (A15:8) — VALID

AD15:0 (AD7:0) — A15:0 VALID — D15:0 VALID

$\overline{GC7:0}$ $\overline{LCS}$, $\overline{UCS}$

$\overline{WR}$

DT/$\overline{R}$

$\overline{DEN}$

272433–19

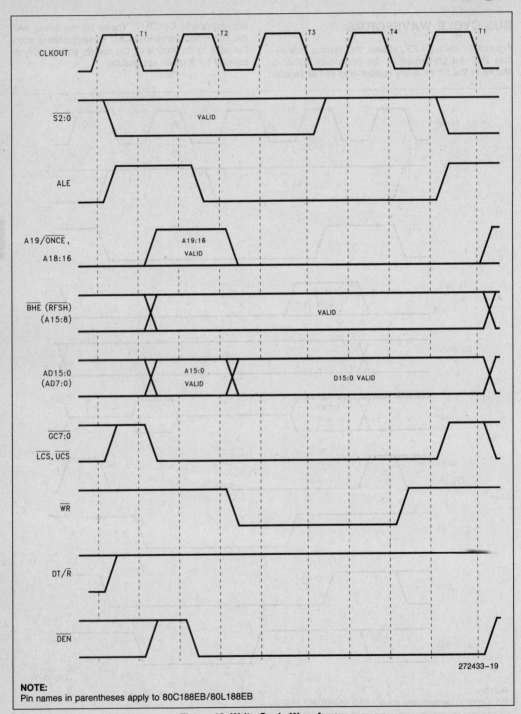

NOTE:
Pin names in parentheses apply to 80C188EB/80L188EB

Figure 18. Write Cycle Waveforms

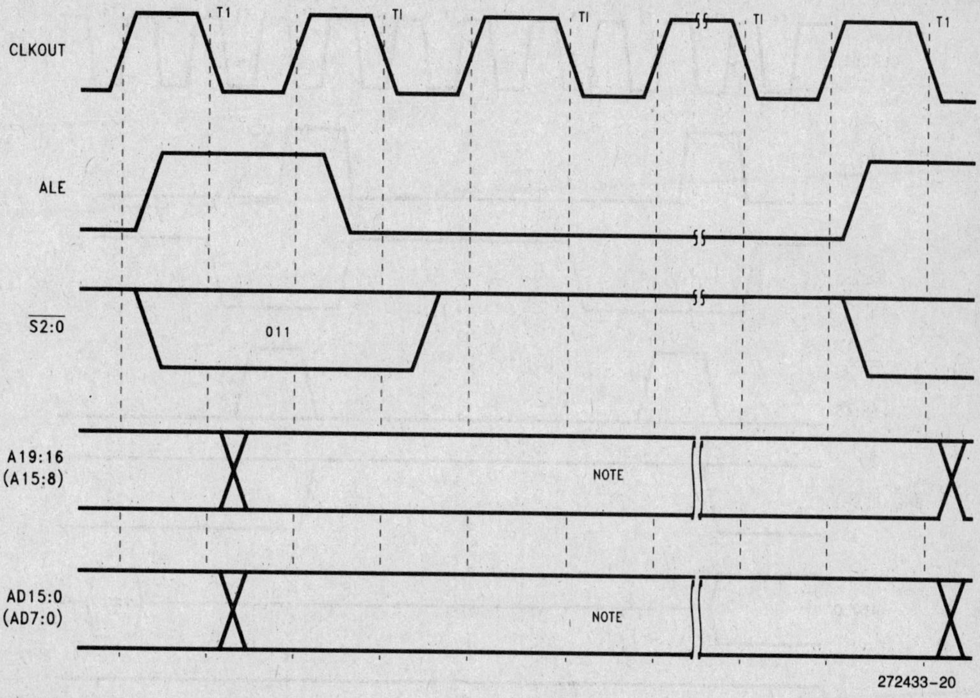

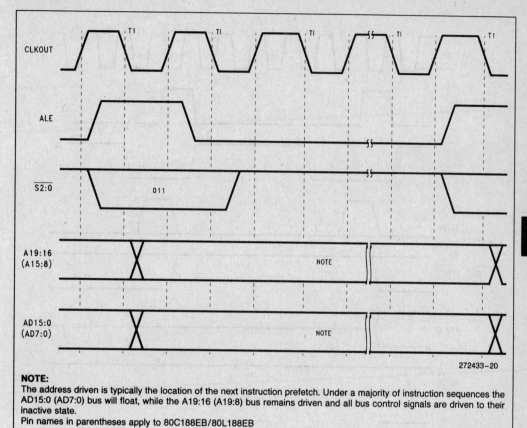

NOTE:
The address driven is typically the location of the next instruction prefetch. Under a majority of instruction sequences the AD15:0 (AD7:0) bus will float, while the A19:16 (A19:8) bus remains driven and all bus control signals are driven to their inactive state.
Pin names in parentheses apply to 80C188EB/80L188EB

Figure 19. Halt Cycle Waveforms

2

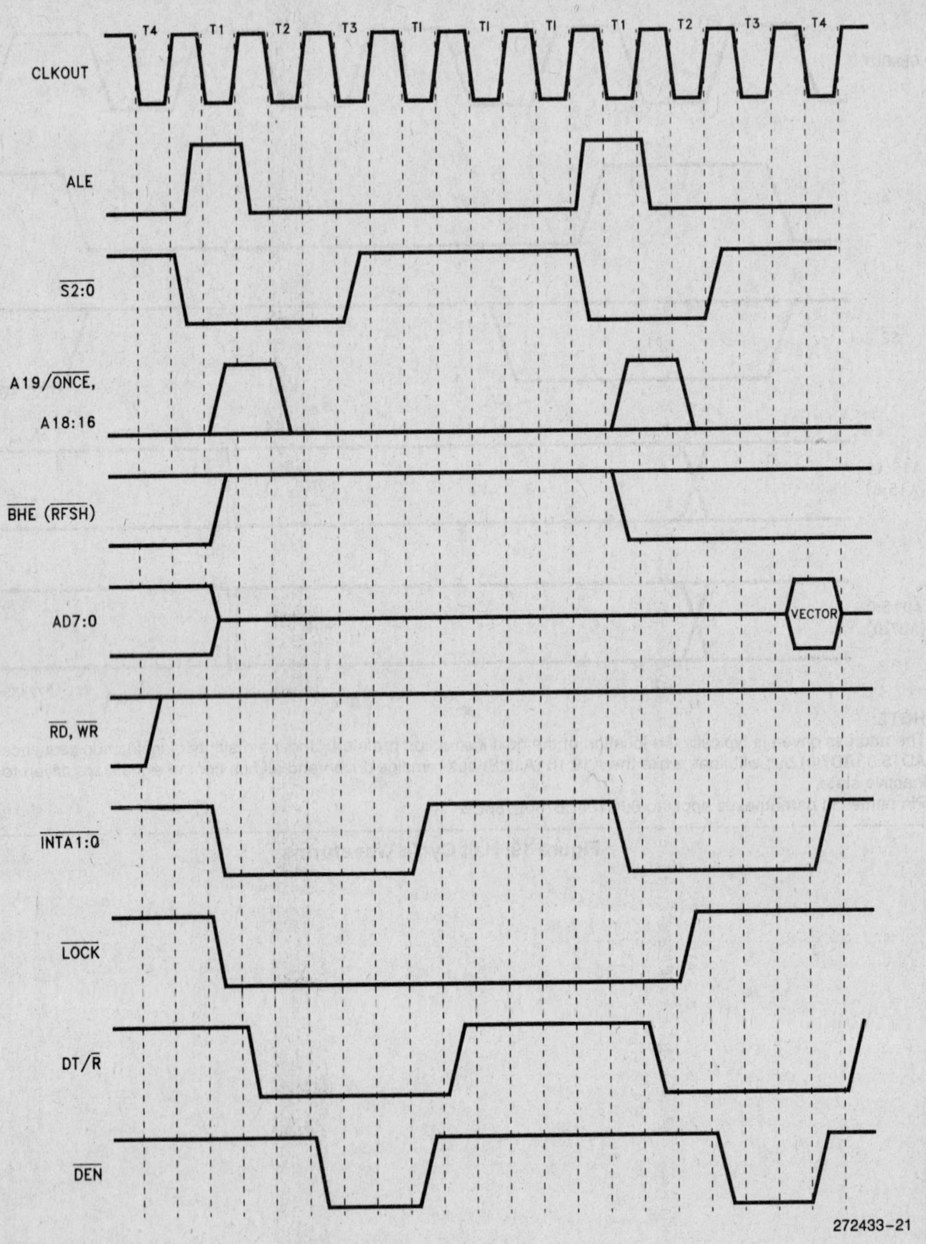

T4 T1 T2 T3 TI TI TI T1 T2 T3 T4

CLKOUT

ALE

S2:0

A19/ONCE,
A18:16

BHE (RFSH)

AD7:0

VECTOR

RD, WR

INTA1:0

LOCK

DT/R

DEN

272433-21

NOTE:
Pin names in parentheses apply to 80C188EB/80L188EB

Figure 20. Interrupt Acknowledge Cycle Waveform

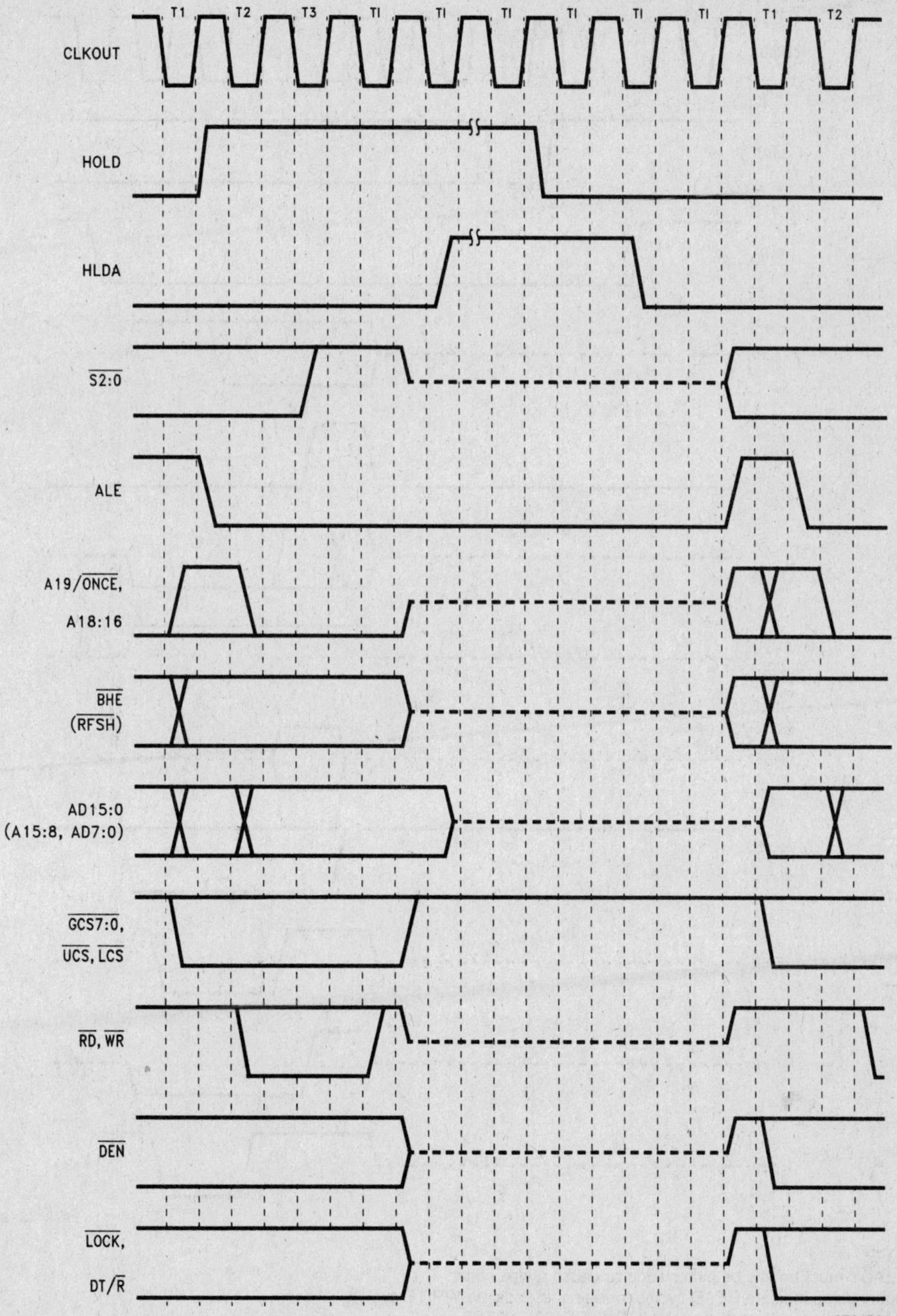

T1 T2 T3 TI TI TI TI TI TI T1 T2

CLKOUT

HOLD

HLDA

$\overline{S2:0}$

ALE

A19/$\overline{ONCE}$,
A18:16

$\overline{BHE}$
($\overline{RFSH}$)

AD15:0
(A15:8, AD7:0)

$\overline{GCS7:0}$,
$\overline{UCS}$, $\overline{LCS}$

$\overline{RD}$, $\overline{WR}$

$\overline{DEN}$

$\overline{LOCK}$,
DT/$\overline{R}$

272433–22

NOTE:
Pin names in parentheses apply to 80C188EB/80L188EB

Figure 21. HOLD/HLDA Waveforms

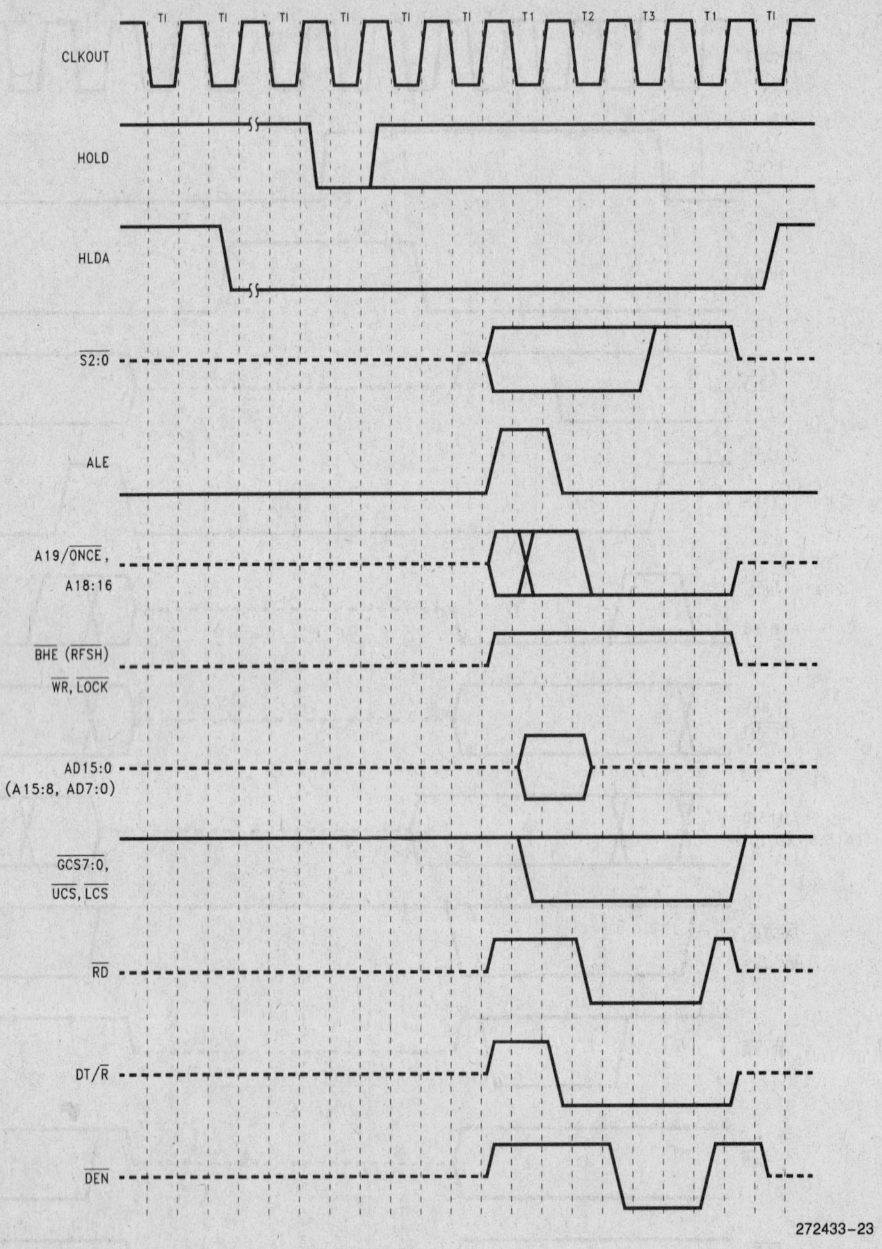

TI TI TI TI TI TI T1 T2 T3 T1 TI

CLKOUT

HOLD

HLDA

$\overline{\text{S2:0}}$

ALE

A19/$\overline{\text{ONCE}}$,
A18:16

$\overline{\text{BHE}}$ ($\overline{\text{RFSH}}$)
$\overline{\text{WR}}$, $\overline{\text{LOCK}}$

AD15:0
(A15:8, AD7:0)

$\overline{\text{GCS7:0}}$,
$\overline{\text{UCS}}$, $\overline{\text{LCS}}$

$\overline{\text{RD}}$

DT/$\overline{\text{R}}$

$\overline{\text{DEN}}$

272433–23

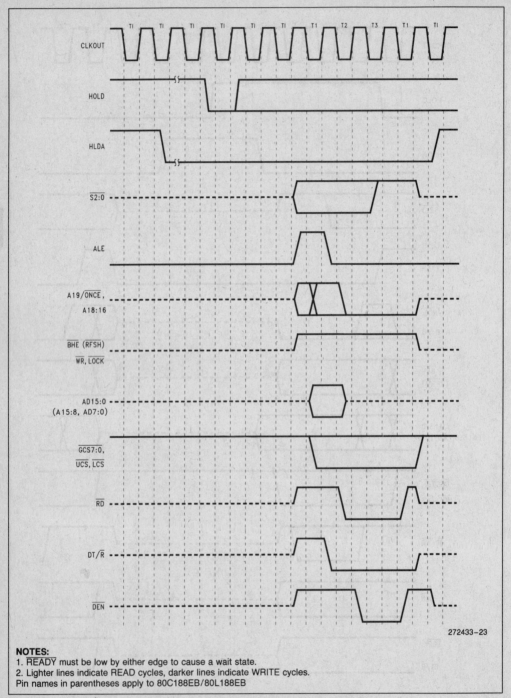

NOTES:
1. $\overline{\text{READY}}$ must be low by either edge to cause a wait state.
2. Lighter lines indicate READ cycles, darker lines indicate WRITE cycles.
Pin names in parentheses apply to 80C188EB/80L188EB

Figure 22. Refresh during Hold Acknowledge

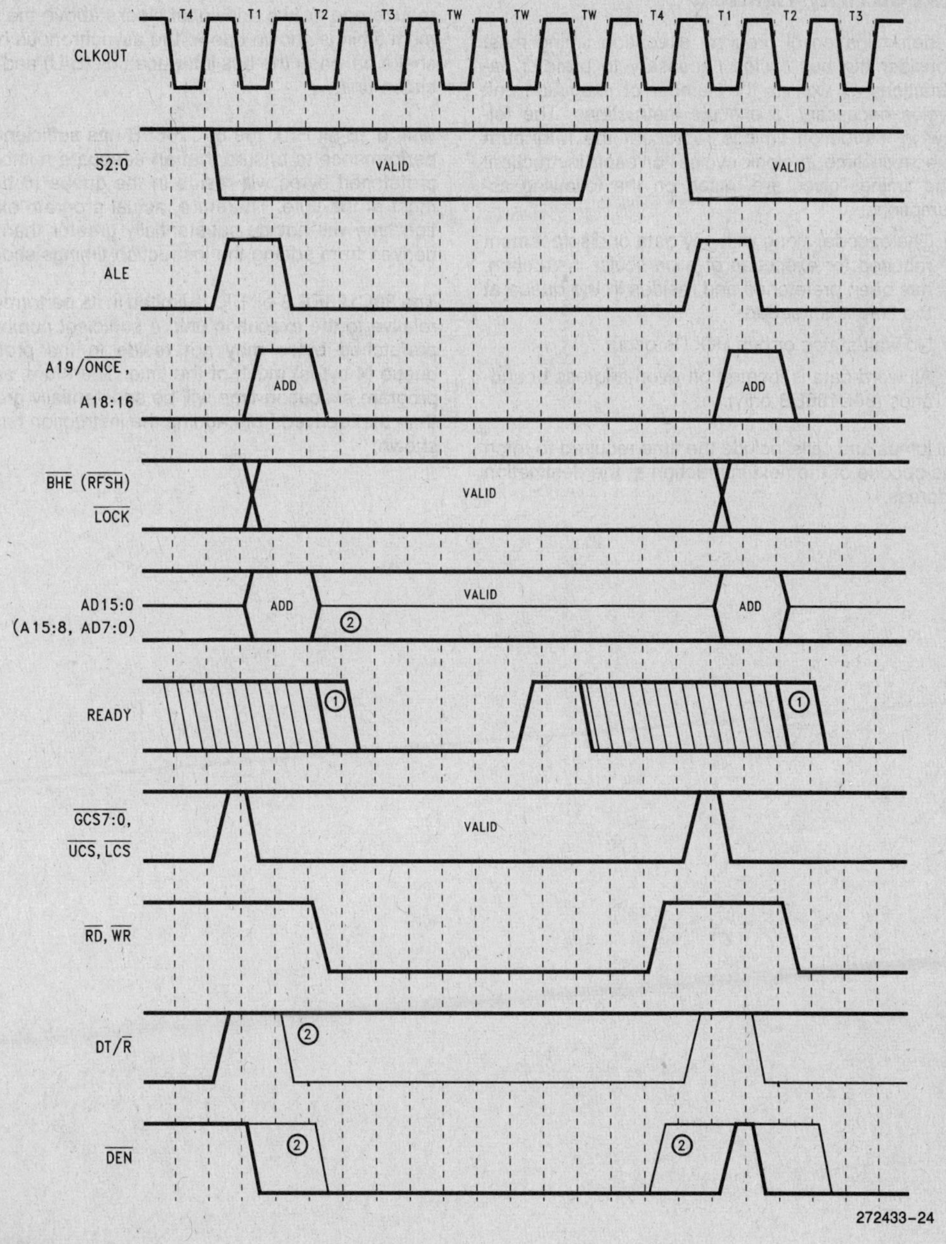

NOTES:
1. READY must be low by either edge to cause a wait state.
2. Lighter lines indicate READ cycles, darker lines indicate WRITE cycles.
Pin names in parentheses apply to 80C188EB/80L188EB

Figure 23. Ready Waveforms

2

EXECUTION TIMINGS

A determination of program execution timing must consider the bus cycles necessary to prefetch instructions as well as the number of execution unit cycles necessary to execute instructions. The following instruction timings represent the **minimum** execution time in clock cycles for each instruction. The timings given are based on the following assumptions:

- The opcode, along with any data or displacement required for execution of a particular instruction, has been prefetched and resides in the queue at the time it is needed.
- No wait states or bus HOLDs occur.
- All word-data is located on even-address boundaries (80C186EB only).

All jumps and calls include the time required to fetch the opcode of the next instruction at the destination address.

All instructions which involve memory accesses can require one or two additional clocks above the minimum timings shown due to the asynchronous handshake between the bus interface unit (BIU) and execution unit.

With a 16-bit BIU, the 80C186EB has sufficient bus performance to ensure that an adequate number of prefetched bytes will reside in the queue (6 bytes) most of the time. Therefore, actual program execution time will not be substantially greater than that derived from adding the instruction timings shown.

The 80C188EB 8-bit BIU is limited in its performance relative to the execution unit. A sufficient number of prefetched bytes may not reside in the prefetch queue (4 bytes) much of the time. Therefore, actual program execution time will be substantially greater than that derived from adding the instruction timings shown.

INSTRUCTION SET SUMMARY

Function	Format				80C186EB Clock Cycles	80C188EB Clock Cycles	Comments
DATA TRANSFER							
MOV = Move:							
Register to Register/Memory	1000100w	mod reg r/m			2/12	2/12*	
Register/memory to register	1000101w	mod reg r/m			2/9	2/9*	
Immediate to register/memory	1100011w	mod 000 r/m	data	data if w=1	12/13	12/13	8/16-bit
Immediate to register	1011w reg	data	data if w=1		3/4	3/4	8/16-bit
Memory to accumulator	1010000w	addr-low	addr-high		8	8*	
Accumulator to memory	1010001w	addr-low	addr-high		9	9*	
Register/memory to segment register	10001110	mod 0 reg r/m			2/9	2/13	
Segment register to register/memory	10001100	mod 0 reg r/m			2/11	2/15	
PUSH = Push:							
Memory	11111111	mod 110 r/m			16	20	
Register	01010 reg				10	14	
Segment register	000reg110				9	13	
Immediate	011010s0	data	data if s=0		10	14	
PUSHA = Push All	01100000				36	68	
POP = Pop:							
Memory	10001111	mod 000 r/m			20	24	
Register	01011 reg				10	14	
Segment register	000reg111	(reg≠01)			8	12	
POPA = Pop All	01100001				51	83	
XCHG = Exchange:							
Register/memory with register	1000011w	mod reg r/m			4/17	4/17*	
Register with accumulator	10010 reg				3	3	
IN = Input from:							
Fixed port	1110010w	port			10	10*	
Variable port	1110110w				8	8*	
OUT = Output to:							
Fixed port	1110011w	port			9	9*	
Variable port	1110111w				7	7*	
XLAT = Translate byte to AL	11010111				11	15	
LEA = Load EA to register	10001101	mod reg r/m			6	6	
LDS = Load pointer to DS	11000101	mod reg r/m	(mod≠11)		18	26	
LES = Load pointer to ES	11000100	mod reg r/m	(mod≠11)		18	26	
LAHF = Load AH with flags	10011111				2	2	
SAHF = Store AH into flags	10011110				3	3	
PUSHF = Push flags	10011100				9	13	
POPF = Pop flags	10011101				8	12	

Shaded areas indicate instructions not available in 8086/8088 microsystems.

NOTE:
*Clock cycles shown for byte transfers. For word operations, add 4 clock cycles for all memory transfers.

INSTRUCTION SET SUMMARY (Continued)

Function	Format				80C186EB Clock Cycles	80C188EB Clock Cycles	Comments
DATA TRANSFER (Continued)							
SEGMENT = Segment Override:							
CS	00101110				2	2	
SS	00110110				2	2	
DS	00111110				2	2	
ES	00100110				2	2	
ARITHMETIC							
ADD = Add:							
Reg/memory with register to either	000000dw	mod reg r/m			3/10	3/10*	
Immediate to register/memory	100000sw	mod 0 0 0 r/m	data	data if s w=01	4/16	4/16*	
Immediate to accumulator	0000010w	data	data if w=1		3/4	3/4	8/16-bit
ADC = Add with carry:							
Reg/memory with register to either	000100dw	mod reg r/m			3/10	3/10*	
Immediate to register/memory	100000sw	mod 0 1 0 r/m	data	data if s w=01	4/16	4/16*	
Immediate to accumulator	0001010w	data	data if w=1		3/4	3/4	8/16-bit
INC = Increment:							
Register/memory	1111111w	mod 0 0 0 r/m			3/15	3/15*	
Register	01000 reg				3	3	
SUB = Subtract:							
Reg/memory and register to either	001010dw	mod reg r/m			3/10	3/10*	
Immediate from register/memory	100000sw	mod 1 0 1 r/m	data	data if s w=01	4/16	4/16*	
Immediate from accumulator	0010110w	data	data if w=1		3/4	3/4	8/16-bit
SBB = Subtract with borrow:							
Reg/memory and register to either	000110dw	mod reg r/m			3/10	3/10*	
Immediate from register/memory	100000sw	mod 0 1 1 r/m	data	data if s w=01	4/16	4/16*	
Immediate from accumulator	0001110w	data	data if w=1		3/4	3/4*	8/16-bit
DEC = Decrement							
Register/memory	1111111w	mod 0 0 1 r/m			3/15	3/15*	
Register	01001 reg				3	3	
CMP = Compare:							
Register/memory with register	0011101w	mod reg r/m			3/10	3/10*	
Register with register/memory	0011100w	mod reg r/m			3/10	3/10*	
Immediate with register/memory	100000sw	mod 1 1 1 r/m	data	data if s w=01	3/10	3/10*	
Immediate with accumulator	0011110w	data	data if w=1		3/4	3/4	8/16-bit
NEG = Change sign register/memory	1111011w	mod 0 1 1 r/m			3/10	3/10*	
AAA = ASCII adjust for add	00110111				8	8	
DAA = Decimal adjust for add	00100111				4	4	
AAS = ASCII adjust for subtract	00111111				7	7	
DAS = Decimal adjust for subtract	00101111				4	4	
MUL = Multiply (unsigned):	1111011w	mod 100 r/m					
Register-Byte					26–28	26–28	
Register-Word					35–37	35–37	
Memory-Byte					32–34	32–34	
Memory-Word					41–43	41–43*	

Shaded areas indicate instructions not available in 8086/8088 microsystems.

NOTE:
*Clock cycles shown for byte transfers. For word operations, add 4 clock cycles for all memory transfers.

INSTRUCTION SET SUMMARY (Continued)

Function	Format				80C186EB Clock Cycles	80C188EB Clock Cycles	Comments
ARITHMETIC (Continued)							
IMUL = Integer multiply (signed):	1 1 1 1 0 1 1 w	mod 1 0 1 r/m					
Register-Byte					25–28	25–28	
Register-Word					34–37	34–37	
Memory-Byte					31–34	31–34	
Memory-Word					40–43	40–43*	
IMUL = Integer Immediate multiply (signed)	0 1 1 0 1 0 s 1	mod reg r/m	data	data if s=0	22–25/ 29–32	22–25/ 29–32	
DIV = Divide (unsigned):	1 1 1 1 0 1 1 w	mod 1 1 0 r/m					
Register-Byte					29	29	
Register-Word					38	38	
Memory-Byte					35	35	
Memory-Word					44	44*	
IDIV = Integer divide (signed):	1 1 1 1 0 1 1 w	mod 1 1 1 r/m					
Register-Byte					44–52	44–52	
Register-Word					53–61	53–61	
Memory-Byte					50–58	50–58	
Memory-Word					59–67	59–67*	
AAM = ASCII adjust for multiply	1 1 0 1 0 1 0 0	0 0 0 0 1 0 1 0			19	19	
AAD = ASCII adjust for divide	1 1 0 1 0 1 0 1	0 0 0 0 1 0 1 0			15	15	
CBW = Convert byte to word	1 0 0 1 1 0 0 0				2	2	
CWD = Convert word to double word	1 0 0 1 1 0 0 1				4	4	
LOGIC							
Shift/Rotate Instructions:							
Register/Memory by 1	1 1 0 1 0 0 0 w	mod TTT r/m			2/15	2/15	
Register/Memory by CL	1 1 0 1 0 0 1 w	mod TTT r/m			5+n/17+n	5+n/17+n	
Register/Memory by Count	1 1 0 0 0 0 0 w	mod TTT r/m	count		5+n/17+n	5+n/17+n	
		TTT Instruction					
		0 0 0 ROL					
		0 0 1 ROR					
		0 1 0 RCL					
		0 1 1 RCR					
		1 0 0 SHL/SAL					
		1 0 1 SHR					
		1 1 1 SAR					
AND = And:							
Reg/memory and register to either	0 0 1 0 0 0 d w	mod reg r/m			3/10	3/10*	
Immediate to register/memory	1 0 0 0 0 0 0 w	mod 1 0 0 r/m	data	data if w=1	4/16	4/16*	
Immediate to accumulator	0 0 1 0 0 1 0 w	data	data if w=1		3/4	3/4*	8/16-bit
TEST = And function to flags, no result:							
Register/memory and register	1 0 0 0 0 1 0 w	mod reg r/m			3/10	3/10*	
Immediate data and register/memory	1 1 1 1 0 1 1 w	mod 0 0 0 r/m	data	data if w=1	4/10	4/10*	
Immediate data and accumulator	1 0 1 0 1 0 0 w	data	data if w=1		3/4	3/4	8/16-bit
OR = Or:							
Reg/memory and register to either	0 0 0 0 1 0 d w	mod reg r/m			3/10	3/10*	
Immediate to register/memory	1 0 0 0 0 0 0 w	mod 0 0 1 r/m	data	data if w=1	4/16	4/16*	
Immediate to accumulator	0 0 0 0 1 1 0 w	data	data if w=1		3/4	3/4*	8/16-bit

Shaded areas indicate instructions not available in 8086/8088 microsystems.

NOTE:
*Clock cycles shown for byte transfers. For word operations, add 4 clock cycles for all memory transfers.

2

INSTRUCTION SET SUMMARY (Continued)

Function	Format				80C186EB Clock Cycles	80C188EB Clock Cycles	Comments
LOGIC (Continued)							
XOR = Exclusive or:							
Reg/memory and register to either	0 0 1 1 0 0 d w	mod reg r/m			3/10	3/10*	
Immediate to register/memory	1 0 0 0 0 0 0 w	mod 1 1 0 r/m	data	data if w = 1	4/16	4/16*	
Immediate to accumulator	0 0 1 1 0 1 0 w	data	data if w = 1		3/4	3/4	8/16-bit
NOT = Invert register/memory	1 1 1 1 0 1 1 w	mod 0 1 0 r/m			3/10	3/10*	
STRING MANIPULATION							
MOVS = Move byte/word	1 0 1 0 0 1 0 w				14	14*	
CMPS = Compare byte/word	1 0 1 0 0 1 1 w				22	22*	
SCAS = Scan byte/word	1 0 1 0 1 1 1 w				15	15*	
LODS = Load byte/wd to AL/AX	1 0 1 0 1 1 0 w				12	12*	
STOS = Store byte/wd from AL/AX	1 0 1 0 1 0 1 w				10	10*	
INS = Input byte/wd from DX port	0 1 1 0 1 1 0 w				14	14	
OUTS = Output byte/wd to DX port	0 1 1 0 1 1 1 w				14	14	
Repeated by count in CX (REP/REPE/REPZ/REPNE/REPNZ)							
MOVS = Move string	1 1 1 1 0 0 1 0	1 0 1 0 0 1 0 w			8+8n	8+8n*	
CMPS = Compare string	1 1 1 1 0 0 1 z	1 0 1 0 0 1 1 w			5+22n	5+22n*	
SCAS = Scan string	1 1 1 1 0 0 1 z	1 0 1 0 1 1 1 w			5+15n	5+15n*	
LODS = Load string	1 1 1 1 0 0 1 0	1 0 1 0 1 1 0 w			6+11n	6+11n*	
STOS = Store string	1 1 1 1 0 0 1 0	1 0 1 0 1 0 1 w			6+9n	6+9n*	
INS = Input string	1 1 1 1 0 0 1 0	0 1 1 0 1 1 0 w			8+8n	8+8n*	
OUTS = Output string	1 1 1 1 0 0 1 0	0 1 1 0 1 1 1 w			8+8n	8+8n*	
CONTROL TRANSFER							
CALL = Call:							
Direct within segment	1 1 1 0 1 0 0 0	disp-low	disp-high		15	19	
Register/memory indirect within segment	1 1 1 1 1 1 1 1	mod 0 1 0 r/m			13/19	17/27	
Direct intersegment	1 0 0 1 1 0 1 0	segment offset			23	31	
		segment selector					
Indirect intersegment	1 1 1 1 1 1 1 1	mod 0 1 1 r/m	(mod ≠ 11)		38	34	
JMP = Unconditional jump:							
Short/long	1 1 1 0 1 0 1 1	disp-low			14	14	
Direct within segment	1 1 1 0 1 0 0 1	disp-low	disp-high		14	14	
Register/memory indirect within segment	1 1 1 1 1 1 1 1	mod 1 0 0 r/m			11/17	11/21	
Direct intersegment	1 1 1 0 1 0 1 0	segment offset			14	14	
		segment selector					
Indirect intersegment	1 1 1 1 1 1 1 1	mod 1 0 1 r/m	(mod ≠ 11)		26	34	

Shaded areas indicate instructions not available in 8086/8088 microsystems.

NOTE:
*Clock cycles shown for byte transfers. For word operations, add 4 clock cycles for all memory transfers.

INSTRUCTION SET SUMMARY (Continued)

Function	Format				80C186EB Clock Cycles	80C188EB Clock Cycles	Comments
CONTROL TRANSFER (Continued)							
RET = Return from CALL:							
Within segment	11000011				16	20	
Within seg adding immed to SP	11000010	data-low	data-high		18	22	
Intersegment	11001011				22	30	
Intersegment adding immediate to SP	11001010	data-low	data-high		25	33	
JE/JZ = Jump on equal/zero	01110100	disp			4/13	4/13	JMP not taken/JMP taken
JL/JNGE = Jump on less/not greater or equal	01111100	disp			4/13	4/13	
JLE/JNG = Jump on less or equal/not greater	01111110	disp			4/13	4/13	
JB/JNAE = Jump on below/not above or equal	01110010	disp			4/13	4/13	
JBE/JNA = Jump on below or equal/not above	01110110	disp			4/13	4/13	
JP/JPE = Jump on parity/parity even	01111010	disp			4/13	4/13	
JO = Jump on overflow	01110000	disp			4/13	4/13	
JS = Jump on sign	01111000	disp			4/13	4/13	
JNE/JNZ = Jump on not equal/not zero	01110101	disp			4/13	4/13	
JNL/JGE = Jump on not less/greater or equal	01111101	disp			4/13	4/13	
JNLE/JG = Jump on not less or equal/greater	01111111	disp			4/13	4/13	
JNB/JAE = Jump on not below/above or equal	01110011	disp			4/13	4/13	
JNBE/JA = Jump on not below or equal/above	01110111	disp			4/13	4/13	
JNP/JPO = Jump on not par/par odd	01111011	disp			4/13	4/13	
JNO = Jump on not overflow	01110001	disp			4/13	4/13	
JNS = Jump on not sign	01111001	disp			4/13	4/13	
JCXZ = Jump on CX zero	11100011	disp			5/15	5/15	
LOOP = Loop CX times	11100010	disp			6/16	6/16	LOOP not taken/LOOP taken
LOOPZ/LOOPE = Loop while zero/equal	11100001	disp			6/16	6/16	
LOOPNZ/LOOPNE = Loop while not zero/equal	11100000	disp			6/16	6/16	
ENTER = Enter Procedure	11001000	data-low	data-high	L			
L = 0					15	19	
L = 1					25	29	
L > 1					22 + 16(n − 1)	26 + 20(n − 1)	
LEAVE = Leave Procedure	11001001				8	8	
INT = Interrupt:							
Type specified	11001101	type			47	47	
Type 3	11001100				45	45	if INT. taken/ if INT. not taken
INTO = Interrupt on overflow	11001110				48/4	48/4	
IRET = Interrupt return	11001111				28	28	
BOUND = Detect value out of range	01100010	mod reg r/m			33–35	33–35	

Shaded areas indicate instructions not available in 8086/8088 microsystems.

NOTE:
*Clock cycles shown for byte transfers. For word operations, add 4 clock cycles for all memory transfers.

INSTRUCTION SET SUMMARY (Continued)

Function	Format	80C186EB Clock Cycles	80C188EB Clock Cycles	Comments
PROCESSOR CONTROL				
CLC = Clear carry	11111000	2	2	
CMC = Complement carry	11110101	2	2	
STC = Set carry	11111001	2	2	
CLD = Clear direction	11111100	2	2	
STD = Set direction	11111101	2	2	
CLI = Clear interrupt	11111010	2	2	
STI = Set interrupt	11111011	2	2	
HLT = Halt	11110100	2	2	
WAIT = Wait	10011011	6	6	if $\overline{TEST}$ = 0
LOCK = Bus lock prefix	11110000	2	2	
NOP = No Operation	10010000	3	3	
	(TTT LLL are opcode to processor extension)			

Shaded areas indicate instructions not available in 8086/8088 microsystems.

NOTE:
*Clock cycles shown for byte transfers. For word operations, add 4 clock cycles for all memory transfers.

FOOTNOTES

The Effective Address (EA) of the memory operand is computed according to the mod and r/m fields:

if mod = 11 then r/m is treated as a REG field
if mod = 00 then DISP = 0*, disp-low and disp-high are absent
if mod = 01 then DISP = disp-low sign-extended to 16-bits, disp-high is absent
if mod = 10 then DISP = disp-high: disp-low
if r/m = 000 then EA = (BX) + (SI) + DISP
if r/m = 001 then EA = (BX) + (DI) + DISP
if r/m = 010 then EA = (BP) + (SI) + DISP
if r/m = 011 then EA = (BP) + (DI) + DISP
if r/m = 100 then EA = (SI) + DISP
if r/m = 101 then EA = (DI) + DISP
if r/m = 110 then EA = (BP) + DISP*
if r/m = 111 then EA = (BX) + DISP

DISP follows 2nd byte of instruction (before data if required)

*except if mod = 00 and r/m = 110 then EA = disp-high: disp-low.

EA calculation time is 4 clock cycles for all modes, and is included in the execution times given whenever appropriate.

Segment Override Prefix

0	0	1	reg	1	1	0

reg is assigned according to the following:

reg	Segment Register
00	ES
01	CS
10	SS
11	DS

REG is assigned according to the following table:

16-Bit (w = 1)	8-Bit (w = 0)
000 AX	000 AL
001 CX	001 CL
010 DX	010 DL
011 BX	011 BL
100 SP	100 AH
101 BP	101 CH
110 SI	110 DH
111 DI	111 BH

The physical addresses of all operands addressed by the BP register are computed using the SS segment register. The physical addresses of the destination operands of the string primitive operations (those addressed by the DI register) are computed using the ES segment, which may not be overridden.

ERRATA

An 80C186EB/80L186EB with a STEPID value of 0001H has the following known errata. A device with a STEPID of 0001H can be visually identified by the **presence** of an **"A"** alpha character next to the FPO number. The FPO number location is shown in Figures 4, 5 and 6.

1. A19/$\overline{\text{ONCE}}$ is not latched by the rising edge of $\overline{\text{RESIN}}$. A19/$\overline{\text{ONCE}}$ must remain active (LOW) at all times to remain in the ONCE Mode. Removing A19/$\overline{\text{ONCE}}$ after $\overline{\text{RESIN}}$ is high will return all output pins to a driving state, however, the 80C186EB will remain in a reset state.
2. During interrupt acknowledge (INTA) bus cycles, the bus controller will ignore the state of the READY pin if the previous bus cycle ignored the state of the READY pin. This errata can only occur if the Chip-Select Unit is being used. All active chip-selects must be programmed to use READY (RDY bit must be programmed to a 1) if wait-states are required for INTA bus cycles.
3. CLKOUT will transition off the **rising** edge of CLKIN rather than the falling edge of CLKIN. This does not affect any bus timings other than T_{CD}.
4. $\overline{\text{RESIN}}$ has a hysterisis of only 130 mV. It is recommended that $\overline{\text{RESIN}}$ be driven by a Schmitt triggered device to avoid processor lockup during reset using an RC circuit.
5. SINT1 will only go active for one clock period when a receive or transmit interrupt is pending (i.e., it does not remain active until the S1STS register is read). If SINT1 is to be connected to any of the processor interrupt lines (INT0–INT4), then it must be latched by user logic.

An 80C186EB/80L186EB with a STEPID value of 0001H or 0002H has the following known errata. A device with a STEPID of 0002H can be visually identified by noting the presence of a "B", "C" or "D" alpha character next to the FPO number. The FPO number location is shown in Figures 4, 5 and 6.

1. An internal condition with the interrupt controller can cause no acknowledge cycle on the $\overline{\text{INTA1}}$ line in response to INT1. This errata only occurs when Interrupt 1 is configured in cascade mode and a higher priority interrupt exists. This errata will not occur consistantly, it is dependent on interrupt timing.

REVISION HISTORY

This data sheet replaces the following data sheets:

270803-004 80C186EB
270885-003 80C188EB
270921-003 80L186EB
270920-003 80L188EB
272311-001 SB80C188EB/SB80L188EB
272312-001 SB80C186EB/SB80L186EB

PRELIMINARY

80C186EC/80C188EC AND 80L186EC/80L188EC 16-BIT HIGH-INTEGRATION EMBEDDED PROCESSORS

- **Fully Static Operation**
- **True CMOS Inputs and Outputs**
- **−40°C to +85°C Operating Temperature Range**

- **Integrated Feature Set:**
  - — Low-Power, Static, Enhanced 8086 CPU Core
  - — Two Independent DMA Supported UARTs, each with an Integral Baud Rate Generator
  - — Four Independent DMA Channels
  - — 22 Multiplexed I/O Port Pins
  - — Two 8259A Compatible Programmable Interrupt Controllers
  - — Three Programmable 16-Bit Timer/Counters
  - — 32-Bit Watchdog Timer
  - — Ten Programmable Chip Selects with Integral Wait-State Generator
  - — Memory Refresh Control Unit
  - — Power Management Unit
  - — On-Chip Oscillator
  - — System Level Testing Support (ONCE Mode)
- **Direct Addressing Capability to 1 Mbyte Memory and 64 Kbyte I/O**
- **Low-Power Operating Modes:**
  - — Idle Mode Freezes CPU Clocks but Keeps Peripherals Active
  - — Powerdown Mode Freezes All Internal Clocks
  - — Powersave Mode Divides All Clocks by Programmable Prescalar
- **Complete System Development Support**
  - — ASM86 Assembler, iC-86 and System Utilities
  - — In-Circuit Emulator
- **Supports 80C187 Numerics Processor Extension (80C186EC only)**
- **Package Types:**
  - — 100-Pin EIAJ Quad Flat Pack (QFP)
  - — 100-Pin Plastic Quad Flat Pack (PQFP)
  - — 100-Pin Shrink Quad Flat Pack (SQFP)
- **Speed Versions Available (5V):**
  - — 20 MHz (80C186EC20/80C188EC20)
  - — 13 MHz (80C186EC13/80C188EC13)
- **Speed Version Available (3V):**
  - — 13 MHz (80L186EC13/80L188EC13)
  - — 8 MHz (80L186EC8/80L188EC8)

The 80C186EC is a member of the 186 Integrated Processor Family. The 186 Integrated Processor Family incorporates several different VLSI devices all of which share a common CPU architecture: the 8086/8088. The 80C186EC uses the latest high density CHMOS technology to integrate several of the most common system peripherals with an enhanced 8086 CPU core to create a powerful system on a single monolithic silicon die.

November 1993
Order Number: 272434-001

80C186EC/80C188EC and 80L186EC/80L188EC 16-Bit High-Integration Embedded Processor

CONTENTS PAGE

INTRODUCTION 2-189

80C186EC CORE ARCHITECTURE 2-189

Bus Interface Unit 2-189

Clock Generator 2-189

80C186EC PERIPHERAL ARCHITECTURE 2-190

Programmable Interrupt Controllers 2-192

Timer/Counter Unit 2-192

Serial Communications Unit 2-192

DMA Unit 2-192

Chip-Select Unit 2-192

I/O Port Unit 2-192

Refresh Control Unit 2-192

Watchdog Timer Unit 2-192

Power Management Unit 2-193

80C187 Interface (80C186EC only) 2-193

ONCE Test Mode 2-193

PACKAGE INFORMATION 2-193

Prefix Identification 2-193

Pin Descriptions 2-193

Pinout 2-200

Package Thermal Specifications 2-209

ELECTRICAL SPECIFICATIONS 2-210

Absolute Maximum Ratings 2-210

CONTENTS PAGE

Recommended Connections 2-210

DC SPECIFICATIONS 2-211

I_{CC} versus Frequency and Voltage 2-213

PDTMR Pin Delay Calculation 2-213

AC SPECIFICATIONS 2-214

AC Characteristics—80C186EC20/13 2-214

AC Characteristics—80L186EC13 2-215

Relative Timings 2-216

Serial Port Mode 0 Timings 2-217

AC TEST CONDITIONS 2-218

AC TIMING WAVEFORMS 2-218

DERATING CURVES 2-221

RESET 2-221

BUS CYCLE WAVEFORMS 2-224

EXECUTION TIMINGS 2-231

INSTRUCTION SET SUMMARY 2-232

ERRATA 2-238

REVISION HISTORY 2-238

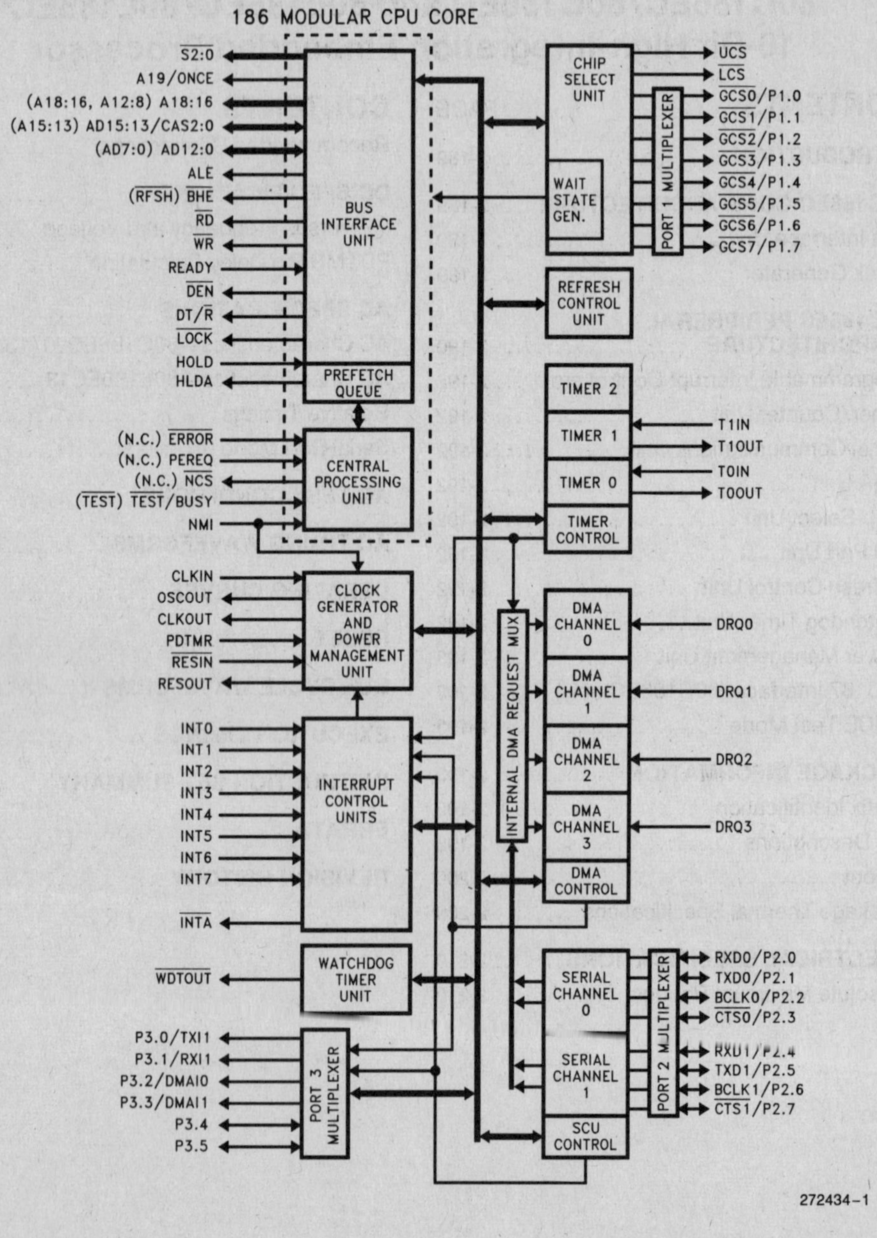

186 MODULAR CPU CORE

S2:0
A19/ONCE
(A18:16, A12:8) A18:16
(A15:13) AD15:13/CAS2:0
(AD7:0) AD12:0
ALE
(RFSH) BHE
RD
WR
READY
DEN
DT/R
LOCK
HOLD
HLDA

BUS INTERFACE UNIT
PREFETCH QUEUE

(N.C.) ERROR
(N.C.) PEREQ
(N.C.) NCS
(TEST) TEST/BUSY
NMI

CENTRAL PROCESSING UNIT

CLKIN
OSCOUT
CLKOUT
PDTMR
RESIN
RESOUT

CLOCK GENERATOR AND POWER MANAGEMENT UNIT

INT0
INT1
INT2
INT3
INT4
INT5
INT6
INT7
INTA

INTERRUPT CONTROL UNITS

WDTOUT

WATCHDOG TIMER UNIT

P3.0/TXI1
P3.1/RXI1
P3.2/DMAI0
P3.3/DMAI1
P3.4
P3.5

PORT 3 MULTIPLEXER

CHIP SELECT UNIT
WAIT STATE GEN.
PORT 1 MULTIPLEXER

UCS
LCS
GCS0/P1.0
GCS1/P1.1
GCS2/P1.2
GCS3/P1.3
GCS4/P1.4
GCS5/P1.5
GCS6/P1.6
GCS7/P1.7

REFRESH CONTROL UNIT

TIMER 2
TIMER 1
TIMER 0
TIMER CONTROL

T1IN
T1OUT
T0IN
T0OUT

INTERNAL DMA REQUEST MUX

DMA CHANNEL 0
DMA CHANNEL 1
DMA CHANNEL 2
DMA CHANNEL 3
DMA CONTROL

DRQ0
DRQ1
DRQ2
DRQ3

SERIAL CHANNEL 0
SERIAL CHANNEL 1
SCU CONTROL
PORT 2 MULTIPLEXER

RXD0/P2.0
TXD0/P2.1
BCLK0/P2.2
CTS0/P2.3
RXD1/P2.4
TXD1/P2.5
BCLK1/P2.6
CTS1/P2.7

272434–1

NOTE:
Pin names in parentheses apply to the 80C188EC/80L188EC

Figure 1. 80C186EC/80L186EC Block Diagram

INTRODUCTION

Unless specifically noted, all references to the 80C186EC apply to the 80C188EC, 80L186EC, and 80L188EC. References to pins that differ between the 80C186EC/80L186EC and the 80C188EC/80L188EC are given in parentheses. The "L" in the part number denotes low voltage operation. Physically and functionally, the "C" and "L" devices are identical.

The 80C186EC is one of the highest integration members of the 186 Integrated Processor Family. Two serial ports are provided for services such as interprocessor communication, diagnostics and modem interfacing. Four DMA channels allow for high speed data movement as well as support of the onboard serial ports. A flexible chip select unit simplifies memory and peripheral interfacing. The three general purpose timer/counters can be used for a variety of time measurement and waveform generation tasks. A watchdog timer is provided to insure system integrity even in the most hostile of environments. Two 8259A compatible interrupt controllers handle internal interrupts, and, up to 57 external interrupt requests. A DRAM refresh unit and 24 multiplexed I/O ports round out the feature set of the 80C186EC.

The future set of the 80C186EC meets the needs of low-power, space-critical applications. Low-power applications benefit from the static design of the CPU and the integrated peripherals as well as low voltage operation. Minimum current consumption is achieved by providing a powerdown mode that halts operaton of the device and freezes the clock circuits. Peripheral design enhancements ensure that non-initialized peripherals consume little current.

The 80L186EC is the 3V version of the 80C186EC. The 80L186EC is functionally identical to the 80C186EC embedded processor. Current 80C186EC users can easily upgrade their designs to use the 80L186EC and benefit from the reduced power consumption inherent in 3V operation.

Figure 1 shows a block diagram of the 80C186EC/80C188EC. The execution unit (EU) is an enhanced 8086 CPU core that includes: dedicated hardware to speed up effective address calculations, enhanced execution speed for multiple-bit shift and rotate instructions and for multiply and divide instructions, string move instructions that operate at full bus bandwidth, ten new instructions and fully static operation. The bus interface unit (BIU) is the same as that found on the original 186 family products, except the queue-status mode has been deleted and buffer interface control has been changed to ease system design timings. An independent internal bus is used for communication between the BIU and onchip peripherals.

80C186EC CORE ARCHITECTURE

Bus Interface Unit

The 80C186EC core incorporates a bus controller that generates local bus control signals. In addition, it employs a HOLD/HLDA protocol to share the local bus with other bus masters.

The bus controller is responsible for generating 20 bits of address, read and write strobes, bus cycle status information and data (for write operations) information. It is also responsible for reading data from the local bus during a read operation. A ready input pin is provided to extend a bus cycle beyond the minimum four states (clocks).

The bus controller also generates two control signals ($\overline{\text{DEN}}$ and DT/$\overline{\text{R}}$) when interfacing to external transceiver chips. This capability allows the addition of transceivers for simple buffering of the multiplexed address/data bus.

Clock Generator

The 80C186EC provides an on-chip clock generator for both internal and external clock generation. The clock generator features a crystal oscillator, a divide-by-two counter and three low-power operating modes.

The oscillator circuit is designed to be used with either a parallel resonant fundamental or third-overtone mode crystal network. Alternatively, the oscillator circuit may be driven from an external clock source. Figure 2 shows the various operating modes of the oscillator circuit.

The crystal or clock frequency chosen must be twice the required processor operating frequency due to the internal divide-by-two counter. This counter is used to drive all internal phase clocks and the external CLKOUT signal. CLKOUT is a 50% duty cycle processor clock and can be used to drive other system components. All AC timings are referenced to CLKOUT.

The following parameters are recommended when choosing a crystal:

Temperature Range:	Application Specific
ESR (Equivalent Series Res.):	40Ω max
C0 (Shunt Capacitance of Crystal):	7.0 pF max
C_L (Load Capacitance):	20 pF ±2 pF
Drive Level:	1 mW (max)

2

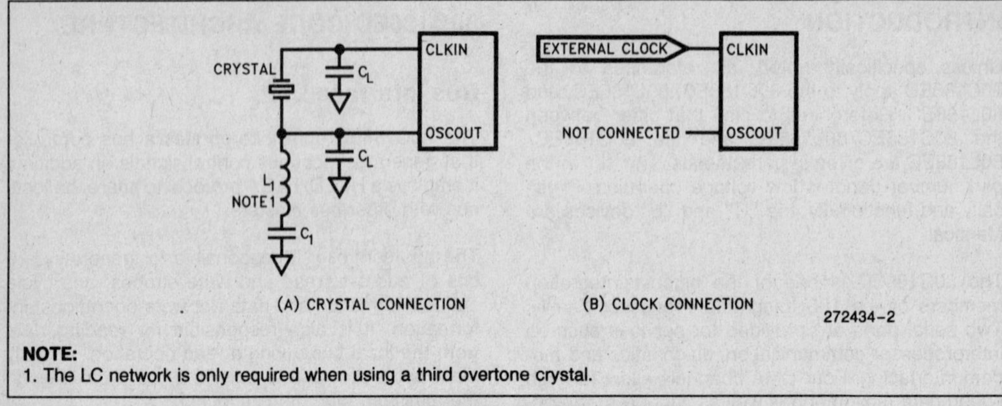

NOTE:
1. The LC network is only required when using a third overtone crystal.

Figure 2. 80C186EC Clock Connections

80C186EC PERIPHERAL ARCHITECTURE

The 80C186EC integrates several common system peripherals with a CPU core to create a compact, yet powerful system. The integrated peripherals are designed to be flexbile and provide logical interconnections between supporting units (e.g., the DMA unit can accept requests from the Serial Communications Unit).

The list of integrated peripherals includes:

- Two cascaded, 8259A compatible, Programmable Interrupt Controllers
- 3-Channel Timer/Counter Unit
- 2-Channel Serial Communications Unit
- 4-Channel DMA Unit
- 10-Output Chip-Select Unit
- 32-bit Watchdog Timer Unit
- I/O Port Unit
- Refresh Control Unit
- Power Management Unit

The registers associated with each integrated peripheral are contained within a 128 x 16-bit register file called the Peripheral Control Block (PCB). The base address of the PCB is programmable and can be located on any 256 byte address boundary in either memory or I/O space.

Figure 3 provides a list of the registers associated with the PCB. The Register Bit Summary individually lists all of the registers and identifies each of their programming attributes.

PCB Offset	Function	PCB Offset	Function	PCB Offset	Function	PCB Offset	Function
00H	Master PIC Port 0	40H	T2 Count	80H	GCS0 Start	C0H	DMA 0 Source Low
02H	Master PIC Port 1	42H	T2 Compare	82H	GCS0 Stop	C2H	DMA 0 Source High
04H	Slave PIC Port 0	44H	Reserved	84H	GCS1 Start	C4H	DMA 0 Dest. Low
06H	Slave PIC Port 1	46H	T2 Control	86H	GCS1 Stop	C6H	DMA 0 Dest. High
08H	Reserved	48H	Port 3 Direction	88H	GCS2 Start	C8H	DMA 0 Count
0AH	SCU Int. Req. Ltch.	4AH	Port 3 Pin State	8AH	GCS2 Stop	CAH	DMA 0 Control
0CH	DMA Int. Req. Ltch.	4CH	Port 3 Mux Control	8CH	GCS3 Start	CCH	DMA Module Pri.
0EH	TCU Int. Req. Ltch.	4EH	Port 3 Data Latch	8EH	GCS3 Stop	CEH	DMA Halt
10H	Reserved	50H	Port 1 Direction	90H	GCS4 Start	D0H	DMA 1 Source Low
12H	Reserved	52H	Port 1 Pin State	92H	GCS4 Stop	D2H	DMA 1 Source High
14H	Reserved	54H	Port 1 Mux Control	94H	GCS5 Start	D4H	DMA 1 Dest. Low
16H	Reserved	56H	Port 1 Data Latch	96H	GCS5 Stop	D6H	DMA 1 Dest. High
18H	Reserved	58H	Port 2 Direction	98H	GCS6 Start	D8H	DMA 1 Count
1AH	Reserved	5AH	Port 2 Pin State	9AH	GCS6 Stop	DAH	DMA 1 Control
1CH	Reserved	5CH	Port 2 Mux Control	9CH	GCS7 Start	DCH	Reserved
1EH	Reserved	5EH	Port 2 Data Latch	9EH	GCS7 Stop	DEH	Reserved
20H	WDT Reload High	60H	SCU 0 Baud	A0H	LCS Start	E0H	DMA 2 Source Low
22H	WDT Reload Low	62H	SCU 0 Count	A2H	LCS Stop	E2H	DMA 2 Source High
24H	WDT Count High	64H	SCU 0 Control	A4H	UCS Start	E4H	DMA 2 Dest. Low
26H	WDT Count Low	66H	SCU 0 Status	A6H	UCS Stop	E6H	DMA 2 Dest. High
28H	WDT Clear	68H	SCU 0 RBUF	A8H	Relocation Register	E8H	DMA 2 Count
2AH	WDT Disable	6AH	SCU 0 TBUF	AAH	Reserved	EAH	DMA 2 Control
2CH	Reserved	6CH	Reserved	ACH	Reserved	ECH	Reserved
2EH	Reserved	6EH	Reserved	AEH	Reserved	EEH	Reserved
30H	T0 Count	70H	SCU 1 Baud	B0H	Refresh Base Addr.	F0H	DMA 3 Source Low
32H	T0 Compare A	72H	SCU 1 Count	B2H	Refresh Time	F2H	DMA 3 Source High
34H	T0 Compare B	74H	SCU 1 Control	B4H	Refresh Control	F4H	DMA 3 Dest. Low
46H	T0 Control	76H	SCU 1 Status	B6H	Refresh Address	F6H	DMA 3 Dest. High
38H	T1 Count	78H	SCU 1 RBUF	B8H	Power Control	F8H	DMA 3 Count
3AH	T1 Compare A	7AH	SCU 1 TBUF	BAH	Reserved	FAH	DMA 3 Control
3CH	T1 Compare B	7CH	Reserved	BCH	Step ID	FCH	Reserved
3EH	T1 Control	7EH	Reserved	BEH	Powersave	FEH	Reserved

Figure 3. Peripheral Control Block Registers

Programmable Interrupt Controllers

The 80C186EC utilizes two 8259A compatible Programmable Interrupt Controllers (PIC) to manage both internal and external interrupts. The 8259A modules are configured in a master/slave arrangement.

Seven of the external interrupt pins, INT0 through INT6, are connected to the master 8259A module. The eighth external interrupt pin, INT7, is connected to the slave 8259A module.

There are a total of 11 internal interrupt sources from the integrated peripherals: 4 Serial, 4 DMA and 3 Timer/Counter.

Timer/Counter Unit

The 80C186EC Timer/Counter Unit (TCU) provides three 16-bit programmable timers. Two of these are highly flexible and are connected to external pins for external control or clocking. The third timer is not connected to any external pins and can only be clocked internally. However, it can be used to clock the other two timer channels. The TCU can be used to count external events, time external events, generate non-repetitive waveforms or generate timed interrupts.

Serial Communications Unit

The 80C186EC Serial Communications Unit (SCU) contains two independent channels. Each channel is identical in operation except that only channel 0 is directly supported by the integrated interrupt controller (the channel 1 interrupts are routed to external interrupt pins). Each channel has its own baud rate generator and can be internally or externally clocked up to one half the processor operating frequency. Both serial channels can request service from the DMA unit thus providing block reception and transmission without CPU intervention.

Independent baud rate generators are provided for each of the serial channels. For the asynchronous modes, the generator supplies an 8x baud clock to both the receive and transmit shifting register logic. A 1x baud clock is provided in the synchronous mode.

DMA Unit

The four channel Direct Memory Access (DMA) Unit is comprised of two modules with two channels each. All four channels are identical in operation. DMA transfers can take place from memory to memory, I/O to memory, memory to I/O or I/O to I/O. DMA requests can be external (on the DRQ pins), internal (from Timer 2 or a serial channel) or software initiated.

The DMA Unit transfers data as bytes only. Each data transfer requires at least two bus cycles, one to fetch data and one to deposit. The minimum clock count for each transfer is 8, but this will vary depending on synchronization and wait states.

Chip-Select Unit

The 80C186EC Chip-Select Unit (CSU) integrates logic which provides up to ten programmable chip-selects to access both memories and peripherals. In addition, each chip-select can be programmed to automatically insert additional clocks (wait states) into the current bus cycle, and/or automatically terminate a bus cycle independent of the condition of the READY input pin.

I/O Port Unit

The I/O Port Unit on the 80C186EC supports two 8-bit channels and one 6-bit channel of input, output or input/output operation. Port 1 is multiplexed with the chip select pins and is output only. Port 2 is multiplexed with the pins for serial channels 1 and 2. All Port 2 pins are input/output. Port 3 has a total of 6 pins: four that are multiplexed with DMA and serial port interrupts and two that are non-multiplexed, open drain I/O.

Refresh Control Unit

The Refresh Control Unit (RCU) automatically generates a periodic memory read bus cycle to keep dynamic or pseudo-static memory refreshed. A 9-bit counter controls the number of clocks between refresh requests.

A 12-bit address generator is maintained by the RCU and is presented on the A12:1 address lines during the refresh bus cycle. Address bits A19:13 are programmable to allow the refresh address block to be located on any 8 Kbyte boundary.

Watchdog Timer Unit

The Watchdog Timer Unit (WDT) allows for graceful recovery from unexpected hardware and software upsets. The WDT consists of a 32-bit counter that decrements every clock cycle. If the counter reaches zero before being reset, the $\overline{\text{WDTOUT}}$ pin is pulled low for four clock cycles. Logically ANDing the $\overline{WDTOUT}$ pin with the power-on reset signal allows the WDT to reset the device in the event of a WDT timeout. If a less drastic method of recovery is desired, $\overline{WDTOUT}$ can be connected directly to NMI or one of the INT input pins. The WDT may also be used as a general purpose timer.

Power Management Unit

The 80C186EC Power Management Unit (PMU) is provided to control the power consumption of the device. The PMU provides four power management modes: Active, Powersave, Idle and Powerdown.

Active Mode indicates that all units on the 80C186EC are operating at ½ the CLKIN frequency.

Idle Mode freezes the clocks of the Execution and Bus units at a logic zero state (all peripherals continue to operate normally).

The Powerdown Mode freezes all internal clocks at a logic zero level and disables the crystal oscillator.

In Powersave Mode, all internal clock signals are divided by a programmable prescalar (up to 1⁄64 the normal frequency). Powersave Mode can be used with Idle Mode as well as during normal (Active Mode) operation.

80C187 Interface (80C186EC only)

The 80C186EC supports the direct connection of the 80C187 Numerics Processor Extension. The 80C187 can dramatically improve the performance of calculation intensive applications.

ONCE Test Mode

To facilitate testing and inspection of devices when fixed into a target system, the 80C186EC has a test mode available which forces all output and input/output pins to be placed in the high-impedance state. ONCE stands for "ON Circuit Emulation". The ONCE mode is selected by forcing the A19/S6/$\overline{ONCE}$ pin low during a processor reset (this pin is weakly held high during reset to prevent inadvertant entrance into ONCE Mode).

PACKAGE INFORMATION

This section describes the pin functions, pinout and thermal characteristics for the 80C186EC in the Plastic Quad Flat Pack (JEDEC PQFP), the EIAJ Quad Flat Pack (QFP) and the Shrink Quad Flat Pack (SQFP). For complete package specifications and information, see the Intel Packaging Outlines and Dimensions Guide (Order Number: 231369).

Prefix Identification

Table 1 lists the prefix identifications.

Table 1. Prefix Identification

Prefix	Package Type	Temperature Range
S	QFP (EIAJ)	Extended
KU	PQFP	Extended
JB	SQFP	Extended

Pin Descriptions

Each pin or logical set of pins is described in Table 2. There are four columns for each entry in the Pin Description Table. The following sections describe each column.

Column 1: Pin Name

In this column is a mnemonic that describes the pin function. Negation of the signal name (i.e. $\overline{RESIN}$) implies that the signal is active low.

Column 2: Pin Type

A pin may be either power (P), ground (G), input only (I), output only (O) or input/output (I/O). Please note that some pins have more than 1 function. A19/S6/$\overline{ONCE}$, for example, is normally an output but functions as an input during reset. For this reason A19/S6/$\overline{ONCE}$ is classified as an input/output pin.

Column 3: Input Type (for I and I/O types only)

There are two different types of input pins on the 80C186EC: asynchronous and synchronous. **Asynchronous** pins require that setup and hold times be met only to *guarantee recognition*. **Synchronous** input pins require that the setup and hold times be met to *guarantee proper operation*. Stated simply, missing a setup or hold on an asynchronous pin will result in something minor (i.e. a timer count will be missed) whereas missing a setup or hold on a synchronous pin will result in system failure (the system will "lock up").

An input pin may also be edge or level sensitive.

2

Column 4: Output States (for O and I/O types only)

The state of an output or I/O pin is dependent on the operating mode of the device. There are four modes of operation that are different from normal active mode: Bus Hold, Reset, Idle Mode, Powerdown Mode. This column describes the output pin state in each of these modes.

The legend for interpreting the information in the Pin Descriptions is shown in Table 1.

As an example, please refer to the table entry for AD12:0. The "I/O" signifies that the pins are bidirectional (i.e. have both an input and output function). The "S" indicates that, as an input the signal must be synchronized to CLKOUT for proper operation. The "H(Z)" indicates that these pins will float while the processor is in the Hold Acknowledge state. R(Z) indicates that these pins will float while $\overline{RESIN}$ is low. P(0) and I(0) indicate that these pins will drive 0 when the device is in either Powerdown or Idle Mode.

Some pins, the I/O Ports for example, can be programmed to perform more than one function. Multi-function pins have a "/" in their signal name between the different functions (i.e. P3.0/RXI1). If the input pin type or output pin state differ between functions, then that will be indicated by separating the state (or type) with a "/" (i.e. H(X)/H(Q)). In this example when the pin is configured as P3.0 then its hold output state is H(X); when configured as RXI1 its output state is H(Q).

All pins float while the processor is in the ONCE Mode (with the exception of OSCOUT).

Table 1. Pin Description Nomenclature

Symbol	Description
P	Power Pin (apply + V_{CC} voltage)
G	Ground (connect to V_{SS})
I	Input only pin
O	Output only pin
I/O	Input/Output pin
S(E)	Synchronous, edge sensitive
S(L)	Synchronous, level sensitive
A(E)	Asynchronous, edge sensitive
A(L)	Asynchronous, level sensitive
H(1)	Output driven to V_{CC} during bus hold
H(0)	Output driven to V_{SS} during bus hold
H(Z)	Output floats during bus hold
H(Q)	Output remains active during bus hold
H(X)	Output retains current state during bus hold
R(WH)	Output weakly held at V_{CC} during reset
R(1)	Output driven to V_{CC} during reset
R(0)	Output driven to V_{SS} during reset
R(Z)	Output floats during reset
R(Q)	Output remains active during reset
R(X)	Output retains current state during reset
I(1)	Output driven to V_{CC} during Idle Mode
I(0)	Output driven to V_{SS} during Idle Mode
I(Z)	Output floats during Idle Mode
I(Q)	Output remains active during Idle Mode
I(X)	Output retains current state during Idle Mode
P(1)	Output driven to V_{CC} during Powerdown Mode
P(0)	Output driven to V_{SS} during Powerdown Mode
P(Z)	Output floats during Powerdown Mode
P(Q)	Output remains active during Powerdown Mode
P(X)	Output retains current state during Powerdown Mode

Table 2. Pin Descriptions

Pin Name	Pin Type	Input Type	Output States	Pin Description
V_{CC}	P	—	—	**POWER** +5V ±10% power supply connection
V_{SS}	G	—	—	**GROUND**
CLKIN	I	A(E)	—	**CLocK INput** is the external clock input. An external oscillator operating at two times the required processor operating frequency can be connected to CLKIN. For crystal operation, CLKIN (along with OSCOUT) are the crystal connections to an internal Pierce oscillator.
OSCOUT	O	—	H(Q) R(Q) I(Q) P(X)	**OSCillator OUTput** is only used when using a crystal to generate the internal clock. OSCOUT (along with CLKIN) are the crystal connections to an internal Pierce oscillator. This pin can not be used as 2X clock output for non-crystal applications (i.e. this pin is not connected for non-crystal applications).
CLKOUT	O	—	H(Q) R(Q) I(Q) P(X)	**CLocK OUTput** provides a timing reference for inputs and outputs of the processor, and is one-half the input clock (CLKIN) frequency. CLKOUT has a 50% duty cycle and transitions every falling edge of CLKIN.
$\overline{\text{RESIN}}$	I	A(L)	—	**RESet IN** causes the processor to immediately terminate any bus cycle in progress and assume an initialized state. All pins will be driven to a known state, and RESOUT will also be driven active. The rising edge (low-to-high) transition synchronizes CLKOUT with CLKIN before the processor begins fetching opcodes at memory location 0FFFF0H.
RESOUT	O	—	H(0) R(1) I(0) P(0)	**RESet OUTput** that indicates the processor is currently in the reset state. RESOUT will remain active as long as $\overline{\text{RESIN}}$ remains active.
PDTMR	I/O	A(L)	H(WH) R(Z) P(WH) I(WH)	**Power-Down TiMeR** pin (normally connected to an external capacitor) that determines the amount of time the processors waits after an exit from Powerdown before resuming normal operation. The duration of time required will depend on the startup characteristics of the crystal oscillator.
NMI	I	A(E)	—	**Non-Maskable Interrupt** input causes a TYPE-2 interrupt to be serviced by the CPU. NMI is latched internally.
$\overline{\text{TEST}}$/BUSY ($\overline{\text{TEST}}$)	I	A(E)	—	**TEST** is used during the execution of the WAIT instruction to suspend CPU operation until the pin is sampled active (LOW). $\overline{\text{TEST}}$ is alternately known as **BUSY** when interfacing with an 80C187 numerics coprocessor (80C186EC only).
A19/S6/$\overline{\text{ONCE}}$	I/O	A(L)	H(Z) R(WH) I(0) P(0)	This pin drives address bit 19 during the address phase of the bus cycle. During T2 and T3 this pin functions as status bit 6. S6 is low to indicate CPU bus cycles and high to indicate DMA or refresh bus cycles. During a processor reset ($\overline{\text{RESIN}}$ active) this pin becomes the ONCE input pin. Holding this pin low during reset will force the part into ONCE Mode.

NOTE:
Pin names in parentheses apply to the 80C188EC/80L188EC.

Table 2. Pin Descriptions (Continued)

Pin Name	Pin Type	Input Type	Output States	Pin Description
A18/S5 A17/S4 A16/S3 (A15:8)	I/O	A(L)	H(Z) R(WH) I(0) P(0)	These pins drive address information during the address phase of the bus cycle. During T2 and T3 these pins drive status information (which is always 0 on the 80C186EC). These pins are used as inputs during factory test; driving these pins low during reset will cause unspecified operation. On the 80C188EC, A15:8 provide valid address information for the entire bus cycle.
AD15/CAS2 AD14/CAS1 AD13/CAS0	I/O	S(L)	H(Z) R(Z) I(0) P(0)	These pins are part of the multiplexed ADDRESS and DATA bus. During the address phase of the bus cycle, address bits 15 through 13 are presented on these pins and can be latched using ALE. Data information is transferred during the data phase of the bus cycle. Pins AD15:13/CAS2:0 drive the 82C59 slave address information during interrupt acknowledge cycles.
AD12:0 (AD7:0)	I/O	S(L)	H(Z) R(Z) I(0) P(0)	These pins provide a multiplexed ADDRESS and DATA bus. During the address phase of the bus cycle, address bits 0 through 12 (0 through 7 on the 80C188EC) are presented on the bus and can be latched using ALE. Data information is transferred during the data phase of the bus cycle.
$\overline{S2:0}$	O	—	H(Z) R(1) I(1) P(1)	Bus cycle Status are encoded on these pins to provide bus transaction information. $\overline{S2:0}$ are encoded as follows:

$\overline{S2}$	$\overline{S1}$	$\overline{S0}$	Bus Cycle Initiated
0	0	0	Interrupt Acknowledge
0	0	1	Read I/O
0	1	0	Write I/O
0	1	1	Processor HALT
1	0	0	Instruction Queue Fetch
1	0	1	Read Memory
1	1	0	Write Memory
1	1	1	Passive (No bus activity)

Pin Name	Pin Type	Input Type	Output States	Pin Description
ALE	O	—	H(0) R(0) I(0) P(0)	**Address Latch Enable** output is used to strobe address information into a transparent type latch during the address phase of the bus cycle.
$\overline{BHE}$ ($\overline{RFSH}$)	O	—	H(Z) R(Z) I(1) P(1)	**Byte High Enable** output to indicate that the bus cycle in progress is transferring data over the upper half of the data bus. $\overline{BHE}$ and A0 have the following logical encoding:

A0	$\overline{BHE}$	Encoding (for 80C186EC/ 80L186EC only)
0	0	Word transfer
0	1	Even Byte transfer
1	0	Odd Byte transfer
1	1	Refresh operation

On the 80C188EC/80L188EC, $\overline{RFSH}$ is asserted low to indicate a refresh bus cycle.

NOTE:
Pin names in parentheses apply to the 80C188EC/80L188EC.

Table 2. Pin Descriptions (Continued)

Pin Name	Pin Type	Input Type	Output States	Pin Description
$\overline{\text{RD}}$	O	—	H(Z) R(Z) I(1) P(1)	**ReaD** output signals that the accessed memory or I/O device should drive data information onto the data bus.
$\overline{\text{WR}}$	O	—	H(Z) R(Z) I(1) P(1)	**WRite** output signals that data available on the data bus are to be written into the accessed memory or I/O device.
READY	I	A(L) S(L) (Note 1)	—	**READY** input to signal the completion of a bus cycle. READY must be active to terminate any 80C186EC bus cycle, unless it is ignored by correctly programming the Chip-Select unit.
$\overline{\text{DEN}}$	O	—	H(Z) R(Z) I(1) P(1)	**Data ENable** output to control the enable of bi-directional transceivers in a buffered system. $\overline{\text{DEN}}$ is active only when data is to be transferred on the bus.
DT/$\overline{\text{R}}$	O	—	H(Z) R(Z) I(X) P(X)	**Data Transmit/Receive** output controls the direction of a bi-directional buffer in a buffered system.
$\overline{\text{LOCK}}$	I/O	A(L)	H(Z) R(Z) I(X) P(X)	**LOCK** output indicates that the bus cycle in progress is not interruptable. The processor will not service other bus requests (such as HOLD) while $\overline{\text{LOCK}}$ is active. This pin is configured as a weakly held high input while $\overline{\text{RESIN}}$ is active and must not be driven low.
HOLD	I	A(L)	—	**HOLD** request input to signal that an external bus master wishes to gain control of the local bus. The processor will relinquish control of the local bus between instruction boundaries that are not LOCKed.
HLDA	O	—	H(1) R(0) I(0) P(0)	**HoLD Acknowledge** output to indicate that the processor has relinquished control of the local bus. When HLDA is asserted, the processor will (or has) floated its data bus and control signals allowing another bus master to drive the signals directly.
$\overline{\text{NCS}}$	O	—	H(1) R(1) I(1) P(1)	**Numerics Coprocessor Select** output is generated when acessing a numerics coprocessor. This signal does not exist on the 80C188EC/80L188EC.
$\overline{\text{ERROR}}$	I	A(L)	—	**ERROR** input that indicates the last numerics processor extension operation resulted in an exception condition. An interrupt TYPE 16 is generated if $\overline{\text{ERROR}}$ is sampled active at the beginning of a numerics operation. Systems not using an 80C187 must tie $\overline{\text{ERROR}}$ to V_{CC}. This signal does not exist on the 80C188EC/80L188EC.

NOTE:
Pin names in parentheses apply to the 80C188EC/80L188EC.

Table 2. Pin Descriptions (Continued)

Pin Name	Pin Type	Input Type	Output States	Pin Description
PEREQ	I	A(L)	—	**Processor Extension REQuest** signals that a data transfer between an 80C187 Numerics Processor Extension and Memory is pending. Systems not using an 80C187 must tie this pin to V_{SS}. This signal does not exist on the 80C188EC/80L188EC.
$\overline{UCS}$	O	—	H(1) R(1) I(1) P(1)	**Upper Chip Select** will go active whenever the address of a memory or I/O bus cycle is within the address range programmed by the user. After reset, $\overline{UCS}$ is configured to be active for memory accesses between 0FFC00H and 0FFFFFH.
$\overline{LCS}$	O	—	H(1) R(1) I(1) P(1)	**Lower Chip Select** will go active whenever the address of a memory or I/O bus cycle is within the address range programmed by the user. $\overline{LCS}$ is inactive after a reset.
P1.0/$\overline{GCS0}$ P1.1/$\overline{GCS1}$ P1.2/$\overline{GCS2}$ P1.3/$\overline{GCS3}$ P1.4/$\overline{GCS4}$ P1.5/$\overline{GCS5}$ P1.6/$\overline{GCS6}$ P1.7/$\overline{GCS7}$	O	—	H(X)/H(1) R(1) I(X)/I(1) P(X)/P(1)	These pins provide a multiplexed function. If enabled, each pin can provide a **General purpose Chip Select** output which will go active whenever the address of a memory or I/O bus cycle is within the address limitations programmed by the user. When not programmed as a Chip-Select, each pin may be used as a general purpose output port.
T0OUT T1OUT	O	—	H(Q) R(1) I(Q) P(X)	**Timer OUTput** pins can be programmed to provide single clock or continuous waveform generation, depending on the timer mode selected.
T0IN T1IN	I	A(L) A(E)	—	**Timer INput** is used either as clock or control signals, depending on the timer mode selected. This pin may be either level or edge sensitive depending on the programming mode.
INT7:0	I	A(L) A(E)	—	**Maskable INTerrupt** input will cause a vector to a specific Type interrupt routine. The INT6:0 pins can be used as cascade inputs from slave 8259A devices. The INT pins can be configured as level or edge sensitive.
$\overline{INTA}$	O	—	H(1) R(1) I(1) P(1)	**INTerrupt Acknowledge** output is a handshaking signal used by external 82C59A Programmable Interrupt Controllers.
P3.5 P3.4	I/O	A(L)	H(X) R(Z) I(X) H(X)	Bidirectional, open-drain port pins.
P3.3/DMAI1 P3.2/DMAI0	O	—	H(X) R(0) I(Q) P(X)	**DMA Interrupt** output goes active to indicate that the channel has completed a transfer. DMAI1 and DMAI0 are multiplexed with output only port functions.

NOTE:
Pin names in parentheses apply to the 80C188EC/80L188EC.

Table 2. Pin Descriptions (Continued)

Pin Name	Pin Type	Input Type	Output States	Pin Description
P3.1/TXI1	O	—	H(X)/H(Q) R(0) I(Q) P(X)	**Transmit Interrupt** output goes active to indicate that serial channel 1 has completed a transfer. TXI1 is multiplexed with an output only Port function.
P3.0/RXI1	O	—	H(X)/H(Q) R(0) I(Q) P(X)	**Receive Interrupt** output goes active to indicate that serial channel 1 has completed a reception. RXI1 is multiplexed with an output only port function.
$\overline{\text{WDTOUT}}$	O	—	H(Q) R(1) I(Q) P(X)	**WatchDog Timer OUTput** is driven low for four clock cycles when the watchdog timer reaches zero. $\overline{\text{WDTOUT}}$ may be ANDed with the power-on reset signal to reset the processor when the watchdog timer is not properly reset.
P2.7/$\overline{\text{CTS1}}$ P2.3/$\overline{\text{CTS0}}$	I/O	A(L)	H(X) R(Z) I(X) P(X)	**Clear-To-Send** input is used to prevent the transmission of serial data on the TXD signal pin. $\overline{\text{CTS1}}$ and $\overline{\text{CTS0}}$ are multiplexed with an I/O Port function.
P2.6/BCLK1 P2.2/BCLK0	I/O	A(L)/ A(E)	H(X) R(Z) I(X) P(X)	**Baud CLocK** input can be used as an alternate clock source for each of the integrated serial channels. The BCLK inputs are multiplexed with I/O Port functions. The BCLK input frequency cannot exceed ½ the operating frequency of the processor .
P2.5/TXD1 P2.1/TXD0	I/O	A(L)	H(Q) R(Z) I(X)/I(Q) P(X)	**Transmit Data** output provides serial data information. The TXD outputs are multiplexed with I/O Port functions. During synchronous serial communications, TXD will function as a clock output.
P2.4/RXD1 P2.0/RXD0	I/O	A(L)	H(X)/H(Q) R(Z) I(X)/I(Q) P(X)	**Receive Data** input accepts serial data information. The RXD pins are multiplexed with I/O Port functions. During synchronous serial communications, RXD is bi-directional and will become an output for transmission of data (TXD becomes the clock).
DRQ3:0	I	A(L)	—	**DMA ReQuest** input pins are used to request a DMA transfer. The timing of the request is dependent on the programmed synchronization mode.

NOTES:
1. READY is A(E) for the rising edge of CLKOUT, S(E) for the falling edge of CLKOUT.
2. Pin names in parentheses apply to the 80C188EC/80L188EC.

2

Pinout

Tables 3 and 4 list the pin names with package location for the 100-pin Plastic Quad Flat Pack (PQFP) component. Figure 4 depicts the PQFP package as viewed from the top side of the component (i.e. contacts facing down).

Tables 5 and 6 list the pin names with package location for the 100-pin EIAJ Quad Flat Pack (QFP) component. Figure 5 depicts the QFP package as viewed from the top side of the component (i.e. contacts facing down).

Tables 7 and 8 list the pin names with package location for the 100-pin Shrink Quad Flat Pack (SQFP) component. Figure 6 depicts the SQFP package as viewed from the top side of the component (i.e., contacts facing down).

Table 3. PQFP Pin Functions with Location

AD Bus	
Name	**Pin**
AD0	73
AD1	72
AD2	71
AD3	70
AD4	66
AD5	65
AD6	64
AD7	63
AD8 (A8)	60
AD9 (A9)	59
AD10 (A10)	58
AD11 (A11)	57
AD12 (A12)	56
AD13/CAS0 (A13/CAS0)	55
AD14/CAS1 (A14/CAS1)	54
AD15/CAS2 (A15/CAS2)	53
A16/S3	77
A17/S4	76
A18/S5	75
A19/S6/$\overline{\text{ONCE}}$	74

Bus Control	
Name	**Pin**
ALE	52
$\overline{\text{BHE}}$ ($\overline{\text{RFSH}}$)	51
$\overline{\text{S0}}$	78
$\overline{\text{S1}}$	79
$\overline{\text{S2}}$	80
$\overline{\text{RD}}$	50
$\overline{\text{WR}}$	49
READY	85
$\overline{\text{DEN}}$	47
DT/$\overline{\text{R}}$	46
$\overline{\text{LOCK}}$	48
HOLD	44
HLDA	45
$\overline{\text{INTA}}$	34

Power and Ground	
Name	**Pin**
V_{CC}	13
V_{CC}	14
V_{CC}	38
V_{CC}	62
V_{CC}	67
V_{CC}	69
V_{CC}	86
V_{SS}	12
V_{SS}	15
V_{SS}	37
V_{SS}	39
V_{SS}	61
V_{SS}	68
V_{SS}	87

Processor Control	
Name	**Pin**
$\overline{\text{RESIN}}$	8
RESOUT	7
CLKIN	10
OSCOUT	11
CLKOUT	6
$\overline{\text{TEST}}$/BUSY ($\overline{\text{TEST}}$)	83
PEREQ (V_{SS})	81
$\overline{\text{NCS}}$ (N.C.)	35
$\overline{\text{ERROR}}$ (V_{CC})	84
PDTMR	9
NMI	82
INT0	30
INT1	31
INT2	32
INT3	33
INT4	40
INT5	41
INT6	42
INT7	43

I/O	
Name	**Pin**
$\overline{\text{UCS}}$	88
$\overline{\text{LCS}}$	89
P1.7/$\overline{\text{GCS7}}$	90
P1.6/$\overline{\text{GCS6}}$	91
P1.5/$\overline{\text{GCS5}}$	92
P1.4/$\overline{\text{GCS4}}$	93
P1.3/$\overline{\text{GCS3}}$	94
P1.2/$\overline{\text{GCS2}}$	95
P1.1/$\overline{\text{GCS1}}$	96
P1.0/$\overline{\text{GCS0}}$	97
P2.7/$\overline{\text{CTS1}}$	23
P2.6/BCLK1	22
P2.5/TXD1	21
P2.4/RXD1	20
P2.3/$\overline{\text{CTS0}}$	19
P2.2/BCLK0	18
P2.1/TXD0	17
P2.0/RXD0	16
P3.5	29
P3.4	28
P3.3/DMAI1	27
P3.2/DMAI0	26
P3.1/TXI1	25
P3.0/RXI1	24
T0IN	3
T0OUT	2
T1IN	5
T1OUT	4
DRQ0	98
DRQ1	99
DRQ2	100
DRQ3	1
$\overline{\text{WDTOUT}}$	36

Table 4. PQFP Pin Locations with Pin Name

Pin	Name	Pin	Name	Pin	Name	Pin	Name
1	DRQ3	26	DMAI0/P3.2	51	$\overline{BHE}$ ($\overline{RFSH}$)	76	A17/S4
2	T0OUT	27	DMAI1/P3.3	52	ALE	77	A16/S3
3	T0IN	28	P3.4	53	AD15 (A15)	78	$\overline{S0}$
4	T1OUT	29	P3.5	54	AD14 (A14)	79	$\overline{S1}$
5	T1IN	30	INT0	55	AD13 (A13)	80	$\overline{S2}$
6	CLKOUT	31	INT1	56	AD12 (A12)	81	PEREQ (V_{SS})
7	RESOUT	32	INT2	57	AD11 (A11)	82	NMI
8	$\overline{RESIN}$	33	INT3	58	AD10 (A10)	83	$\overline{TEST}$
9	PDTMR	34	$\overline{INTA}$	59	AD9 (A9)	84	$\overline{ERROR}$ (V_{CC})
10	CLKIN	35	$\overline{NCS}$ (N.C.)	60	AD8 (A8)	85	READY
11	OSCOUT	36	$\overline{WDTOUT}$	61	V_{SS}	86	V_{CC}
12	V_{SS}	37	V_{SS}	62	V_{CC}	87	V_{SS}
13	V_{CC}	38	V_{CC}	63	AD7	88	$\overline{UCS}$
14	V_{CC}	39	V_{SS}	64	AD6	89	$\overline{LCS}$
15	V_{SS}	40	INT4	65	AD5	90	P1.7/$\overline{GCS7}$
16	P2.0/RXD0	41	INT5	66	AD4	91	P1.6/$\overline{GCS6}$
17	P2.1/TXD0	42	INT6	67	V_{CC}	92	P1.5/$\overline{GCS5}$
18	P2.2/BCLK0	43	INT7	68	V_{SS}	93	P1.4/$\overline{GCS4}$
19	P2.3/$\overline{CTS0}$	44	HOLD	69	V_{CC}	94	P1.3/$\overline{GCS3}$
20	P2.4/RXD1	45	HLDA	70	AD3	95	P1.2/$\overline{GCS2}$
21	P2.5/TXD1	46	DT/$\overline{R}$	71	AD2	96	P1.1/$\overline{GCS1}$
22	P2.6/BCLK1	47	$\overline{DEN}$	72	AD1	97	P1.0/$\overline{GCS0}$
23	P2.7/$\overline{CTS1}$	48	$\overline{LOCK}$	73	AD0	98	DRQ0
24	P3.0/RXI1	49	$\overline{WR}$	74	A19/S6/$\overline{ONCE}$	99	DRQ1
25	P3.1/TXI1	50	$\overline{RD}$	75	A18/S5	100	DRQ2

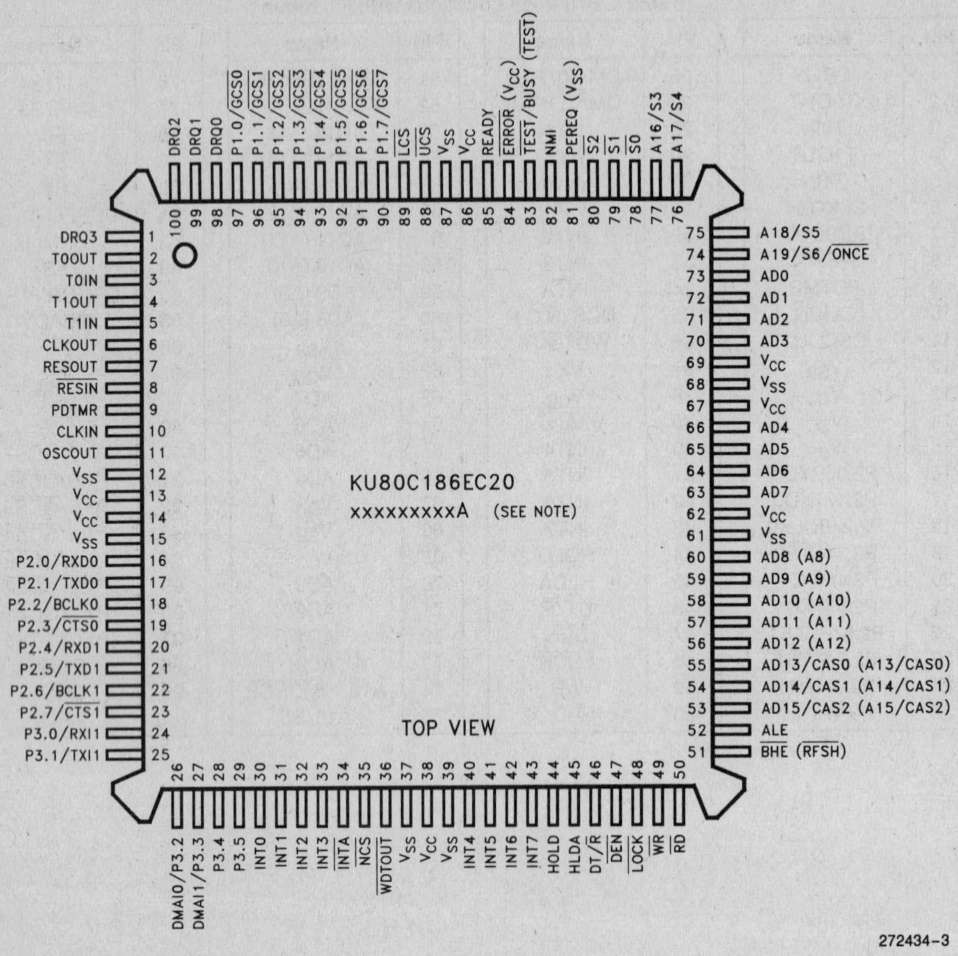

Pin	Name
1	DRQ3
2	T0OUT
3	T0IN
4	T1OUT
5	T1IN
6	CLKOUT
7	RESOUT
8	$\overline{\text{RESIN}}$
9	PDTMR
10	CLKIN
11	OSCOUT
12	V_{SS}
13	V_{CC}
14	V_{CC}
15	V_{SS}
16	P2.0/RXD0
17	P2.1/TXD0
18	P2.2/BCLK0
19	P2.3/$\overline{\text{CTS0}}$
20	P2.4/RXD1
21	P2.5/TXD1
22	P2.6/BCLK1
23	P2.7/$\overline{\text{CTS1}}$
24	P3.0/RXI1
25	P3.1/TXI1
26	DMAI0/P3.2
27	DMAI1/P3.3
28	P3.4
29	P3.5
30	INT0
31	INT1
32	INT2
33	INT3
34	$\overline{\text{INTA}}$
35	$\overline{\text{NCS}}$
36	$\overline{\text{WDTOUT}}$
37	V_{SS}
38	V_{CC}
39	V_{SS}
40	INT4
41	INT5
42	INT6
43	INT7
44	HOLD
45	HLDA
46	DT/$\overline{\text{R}}$
47	$\overline{\text{DEN}}$
48	$\overline{\text{LOCK}}$
49	$\overline{\text{WR}}$
50	$\overline{\text{RD}}$
51	$\overline{\text{BHE}}$ (RFSH)
52	ALE
53	AD15/CAS2 (A15/CAS2)
54	AD14/CAS1 (A14/CAS1)
55	AD13/CAS0 (A13/CAS0)
56	AD12 (A12)
57	AD11 (A11)
58	AD10 (A10)
59	AD9 (A9)
60	AD8 (A8)
61	V_{SS}
62	V_{CC}
63	AD7
64	AD6
65	AD5
66	AD4
67	V_{CC}
68	V_{SS}
69	V_{CC}
70	AD3
71	AD2
72	AD1
73	AD0
74	A19/S6/$\overline{\text{ONCE}}$
75	A18/S5
76	A17/S4
77	A16/S3
78	$\overline{\text{S0}}$
79	$\overline{\text{S1}}$
80	$\overline{\text{S2}}$
81	PEREQ (V_{SS})
82	NMI
83	$\overline{\text{TEST}}$/BUSY ($\overline{\text{TEST}}$)
84	$\overline{\text{ERROR}}$ (V_{CC})
85	READY
86	V_{CC}
87	V_{SS}
88	$\overline{\text{UCS}}$
89	$\overline{\text{LCS}}$
90	P1.7/$\overline{\text{GCS7}}$
91	P1.6/$\overline{\text{GCS6}}$
92	P1.5/$\overline{\text{GCS5}}$
93	P1.4/$\overline{\text{GCS4}}$
94	P1.3/$\overline{\text{GCS3}}$
95	P1.2/$\overline{\text{GCS2}}$
96	P1.1/$\overline{\text{GCS1}}$
97	P1.0/$\overline{\text{GCS0}}$
98	DRQ0
99	DRQ1
100	DRQ2

KU80C186EC20
xxxxxxxxxA (SEE NOTE)

TOP VIEW

272434-3

NOTE:
This is the FPO number location (indicated by X's).

Figure 4. 100-Pin Plastic Quad Flat Pack Package (PQFP)

Table 5. QFP Pin Names with Package Location

AD Bus	
Name	**Pin**
AD0	76
AD1	75
AD2	74
AD3	73
AD4	69
AD5	68
AD6	67
AD7	66
AD8 (A8)	63
AD9 (A9)	62
AD10 (A10)	61
AD11 (A11)	60
AD12 (A12)	59
AD13/CAS0 (A13/CAS0)	58
AD14/CAS1 (A14/CAS1)	57
AD15/CAS2 (A15/CAS2)	56
A16/S3	80
A17/S4	79
A18/S5	78
A19/S6/$\overline{ONCE}$	77

Bus Control	
Name	**Pin**
ALE	55
$\overline{BHE}$ ($\overline{RFSH}$)	54
$\overline{S0}$	81
$\overline{S1}$	82
$\overline{S2}$	83
$\overline{RD}$	53
$\overline{WR}$	52
READY	88
$\overline{DEN}$	50
DT/$\overline{R}$	49
$\overline{LOCK}$	51
HOLD	47
HLDA	48
$\overline{INTA}$	37

Power and Ground	
Name	**Pin**
V_{CC}	16
V_{CC}	17
V_{CC}	41
V_{CC}	65
V_{CC}	70
V_{CC}	72
V_{CC}	89
V_{SS}	15
V_{SS}	18
V_{SS}	40
V_{SS}	42
V_{SS}	64
V_{SS}	71
V_{SS}	90

Processor Control	
Name	**Pin**
$\overline{RESIN}$	11
RESOUT	10
CLKIN	13
OSCOUT	14
CLKOUT	9
$\overline{TEST}$/BUSY ($\overline{TEST}$)	86
PEREQ (V_{SS})	84
$\overline{NCS}$ (N.C.)	38
$\overline{ERROR}$ (V_{CC})	87
PDTMR	12
NMI	85
INT0	33
INT1	34
INT2	35
INT3	36
INT4	43
INT5	44
INT6	45
INT7	46

I/O	
Name	**Pin**
$\overline{UCS}$	91
$\overline{LCS}$	92
P1.7/$\overline{GCS7}$	93
P1.6/$\overline{GCS6}$	94
P1.5/$\overline{GCS5}$	95
P1.4/$\overline{GCS4}$	96
P1.3/$\overline{GCS3}$	97
P1.2/$\overline{GCS2}$	98
P1.1/$\overline{GCS1}$	99
P1.0/$\overline{GCS0}$	100
P2.7/$\overline{CTS1}$	26
P2.6/BCLK1	25
P2.5/TXD1	24
P2.4/RXD1	23
P2.3/$\overline{CTS0}$	22
P2.2/BCLK0	21
P2.1/TXD0	20
P2.0/RXD0	19
P3.5	32
P3.4	31
P3.3/DMAI1	30
P3.2/DMAI0	29
P3.1/TXI1	28
P3.0/RXI1	27
T0IN	6
T0OUT	5
T1IN	8
T1OUT	7
DRQ0	1
DRQ1	2
DRQ2	[illegible]
DRQ3	4
$\overline{WDTOUT}$	39

Table 6. QFP Package Location with Pin Names

Pin	Name	Pin	Name	Pin	Name	Pin	Name
1	DRQ0	26	P2.7/$\overline{\text{CTS1}}$	51	$\overline{\text{LOCK}}$	76	AD0
2	DRQ1	27	P3.0/RXI1	52	$\overline{\text{WR}}$	77	A19/S6/$\overline{\text{ONCE}}$
3	DRQ2	28	P3.1/TXI1	53	$\overline{\text{RD}}$	78	A18/S5
4	DRQ3	29	DMAI0/P3.2	54	$\overline{\text{BHE}}$ ($\overline{\text{RFSH}}$)	79	A17/S4
5	T0OUT	30	DMAI1/P3.3	55	ALE	80	A16/S3
6	T0IN	31	P3.4	56	AD15 (A15)	81	$\overline{\text{S0}}$
7	T1OUT	32	P3.5	57	AD14 (A14)	82	$\overline{\text{S1}}$
8	T1IN	33	INT0	58	AD13 (A13)	83	$\overline{\text{S2}}$
9	CLKOUT	34	INT1	59	AD12 (A12)	84	PEREQ (V_{SS})
10	RESOUT	35	INT2	60	AD11 (A11)	85	NMI
11	$\overline{\text{RESIN}}$	36	INT3	61	AD10 (A10)	86	$\overline{\text{TEST}}$
12	PDTMR	37	$\overline{\text{INTA}}$	62	AD9 (A9)	87	$\overline{\text{ERROR}}$ (V_{CC})
13	CLKIN	38	$\overline{\text{NCS}}$ (N.C.)	63	AD8 (A8)	88	READY
14	OSCOUT	39	$\overline{\text{WDTOUT}}$	64	V_{SS}	89	V_{CC}
15	V_{SS}	40	V_{SS}	65	V_{CC}	90	V_{SS}
16	V_{CC}	41	V_{CC}	66	AD7	91	$\overline{\text{UCS}}$
17	V_{CC}	42	V_{SS}	67	AD6	92	$\overline{\text{LCS}}$
18	V_{SS}	43	INT4	68	AD5	93	P1.7/$\overline{\text{GCS7}}$
19	P2.0/RXD0	44	INT5	69	AD4	94	P1.6/$\overline{\text{GCS6}}$
20	P2.1/TXD0	45	INT6	70	V_{CC}	95	P1.5/$\overline{\text{GCS5}}$
21	P2.2/BCLK0	46	INT7	71	V_{SS}	96	P1.4/$\overline{\text{GCS4}}$
22	P2.3/$\overline{\text{CTS0}}$	47	HOLD	72	V_{CC}	97	P1.3/$\overline{\text{GCS3}}$
23	P2.4/RXD1	48	HLDA	73	AD3	98	P1.2/$\overline{\text{GCS2}}$
24	P2.5/TXD1	49	DT/$\overline{\text{R}}$	74	AD2	99	P1.1/$\overline{\text{GCS1}}$
25	P2.6/BCLK1	50	$\overline{\text{DEN}}$	75	AD1	100	P1.0/$\overline{\text{GCS0}}$

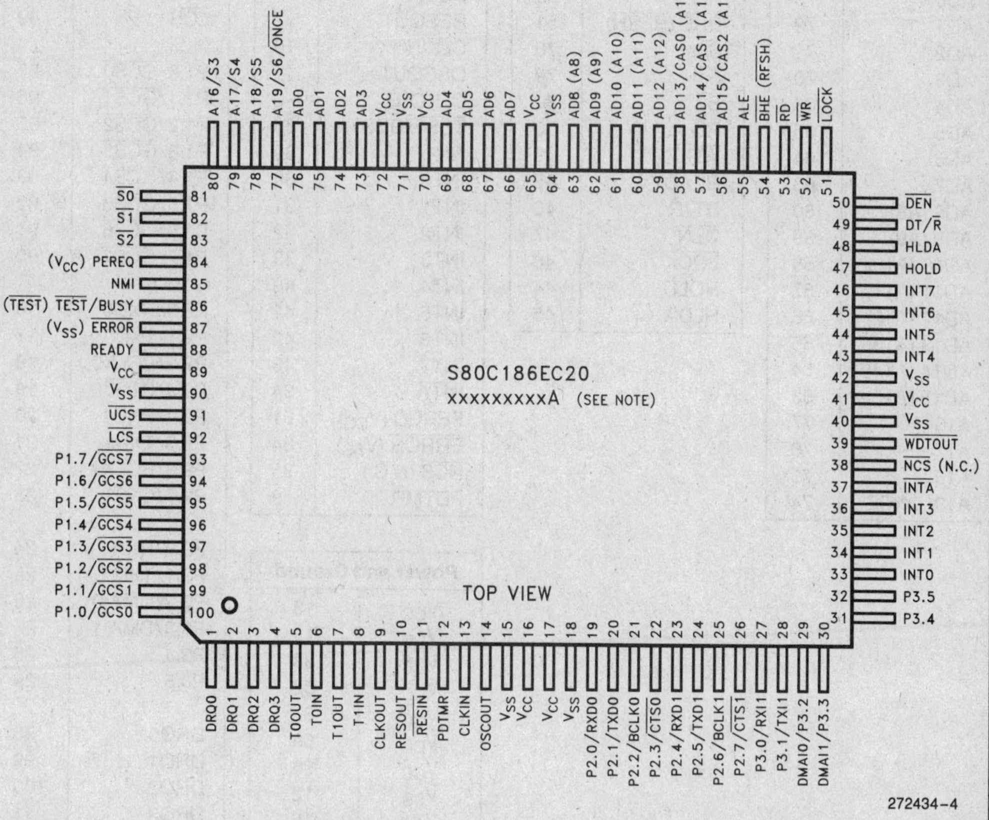

NOTE:
This is the FPO number location (indicated by X's).

Figure 5. Quad Flat Pack (EIAJ) Pinout Diagram

Table 7. SQFP Pin Functions with Location

AD Bus	
AD0	73
AD1	72
AD2	71
AD3	70
AD4	66
AD5	65
AD6	64
AD7	63
AD8 (A8)	60
AD9 (A9)	59
AD10 (A10)	58
AD11 (A11)	57
AD12 (A12)	56
AD13 (A13)	55
AD14 (A14)	54
AD15 (A15)	53
A16	77
A17	76
A18	75
A19/ONCE	74

Bus Control	
ALE	52
$\overline{\text{BHE}}$ ($\overline{\text{RFSH}}$)	51
$\overline{\text{S0}}$	78
$\overline{\text{S1}}$	79
$\overline{\text{S2}}$	80
$\overline{\text{RD}}$	50
$\overline{\text{WR}}$	49
READY	85
DT/$\overline{\text{R}}$	46
$\overline{\text{DEN}}$	47
$\overline{\text{LOCK}}$	48
HOLD	44
HLDA	45

Processor Control	
$\overline{\text{RESIN}}$	8
RESOUT	7
CLKIN	10
OSCOUT	11
CLKOUT	6
$\overline{\text{TEST}}$/BUSY	83
NMI	82
INT0	30
INT1	31
INT2	32
INT3	33
INT4	40
INT5	41
INT6	42
INT7	43
$\overline{\text{INTA}}$	34
PEREQ (V_{CC})	81
$\overline{\text{ERROR}}$ (V_{SS})	84
$\overline{\text{NCS}}$ (N.C.)	35
PDTMR	9

Power and Ground	
V_{CC}	13
V_{CC}	14
V_{CC}	38
V_{CC}	62
V_{CC}	67
V_{CC}	69
V_{CC}	86
V_{SS}	12
V_{SS}	15
V_{SS}	37
V_{SS}	39
V_{SS}	61
V_{SS}	68
V_{SS}	87

I/O	
$\overline{\text{UCS}}$	81
$\overline{\text{LCS}}$	89
P1.0/$\overline{\text{GCS0}}$	97
P1.1/$\overline{\text{GCS1}}$	96
P1.2/$\overline{\text{GCS2}}$	95
P1.3/$\overline{\text{GCS3}}$	94
P1.4/$\overline{\text{GCS4}}$	93
P1.5/$\overline{\text{GCS5}}$	92
P1.6/$\overline{\text{GCS6}}$	91
P1.7/$\overline{\text{GCS7}}$	90
P2.0/RXD0	16
P2.1/TXD0	17
P2.2/BCLK0	18
P2.3/$\overline{\text{CTS0}}$	19
P2.4/RXD1	20
P2.5/TXD1	21
P2.6/BCLK1	22
P2.7/$\overline{\text{CTS1}}$	23
P3.0/RXI1	24
P3.1/TXI1	25
P3.2/DMAI0	26
P3.3/DMAI1	27
P3.4	28
P3.5	29
DRQ0	98
DRQ1	99
DRQ2	100
DRQ3	1
T0IN	3
T0OUT	5
T1IN	2
T1OUT	4
WDTOUT	36

Table 8. SQFP Pin Locations with Pin Names

Pin	Name	Pin	Name	Pin	Name	Pin	Name
1	DRQ3	26	P3.2/DMAI0	51	$\overline{\text{BHE}}$ ($\overline{\text{RFSH}}$)	76	A17
2	T0OUT	27	P3.3/DMAI1	52	ALE	77	A16
3	T0IN	28	P3.4	53	AD15 (A15)	78	$\overline{\text{S0}}$
4	T1OUT	29	P3.5	54	AD14 (A14)	79	$\overline{\text{S1}}$
5	T1IN	30	INT0	55	AD13 (A13)	80	$\overline{\text{S2}}$
6	CLKOUT	31	INT1	56	AD12 (A12)	81	PEREQ (V_{CC})
7	RESOUT	32	INT2	57	AD11 (A11)	82	MNI
8	$\overline{\text{RESIN}}$	33	INT3	58	AD10 (A10)	83	$\overline{\text{TEST}}$/BUSY ($\overline{\text{TEST}}$)
9	PDTMR	34	$\overline{\text{INTA}}$	59	AD9 (A9)	84	$\overline{\text{ERROR}}$ (V_{SS})
10	CLKIN	35	$\overline{\text{NSC}}$ (N.C.)	60	AD8 (A8)	85	READY
11	OSCOUT	36	$\overline{\text{WDTOUT}}$	61	V_{SS}	86	V_{CC}
12	V_{SS}	37	V_{SS}	62	V_{CC}	87	V_{SS}
13	V_{CC}	38	V_{CC}	63	AD7 (A7)	88	$\overline{\text{UCS}}$
14	V_{CC}	39	V_{SS}	64	AD6 (A6)	89	$\overline{\text{LCS}}$
15	V_{SS}	40	INT4	65	AD5	90	P1.7/$\overline{\text{GCS7}}$
16	P2.0/RXD0	41	INT5	66	AD4	91	P1.6/$\overline{\text{GS6}}$
17	P2.1/TXD0	42	INT6	67	V_{CC}	92	P1.5/$\overline{\text{GCS5}}$
18	P2.2/BCLK0	43	INT7	68	V_{SS}	93	P1.4/$\overline{\text{GCS4}}$
19	P2.3/$\overline{\text{CTS0}}$	44	HOLD	69	V_{CC}	94	P1.3/$\overline{\text{GCS3}}$
20	P2.4/RXD1	45	HLDA	70	AD3	95	P1.2/$\overline{\text{GCS2}}$
21	P2.5/TXD1	46	DT/$\overline{\text{R}}$	71	AD2	96	P1.1/$\overline{\text{GCS1}}$
22	P2.6/BCLK1	47	$\overline{\text{DEN}}$	72	AD1	97	P1.0/$\overline{\text{GCS0}}$
23	P2.7/$\overline{\text{CTS1}}$	48	$\overline{\text{LOCK}}$	73	AD0	98	DRQ0
24	P3.0/RXI1	49	$\overline{\text{WR}}$	74	A19/ONCE	99	DRQ1
25	P3.1/TXI1	50	$\overline{\text{RD}}$	75	AD18	100	DRQ2

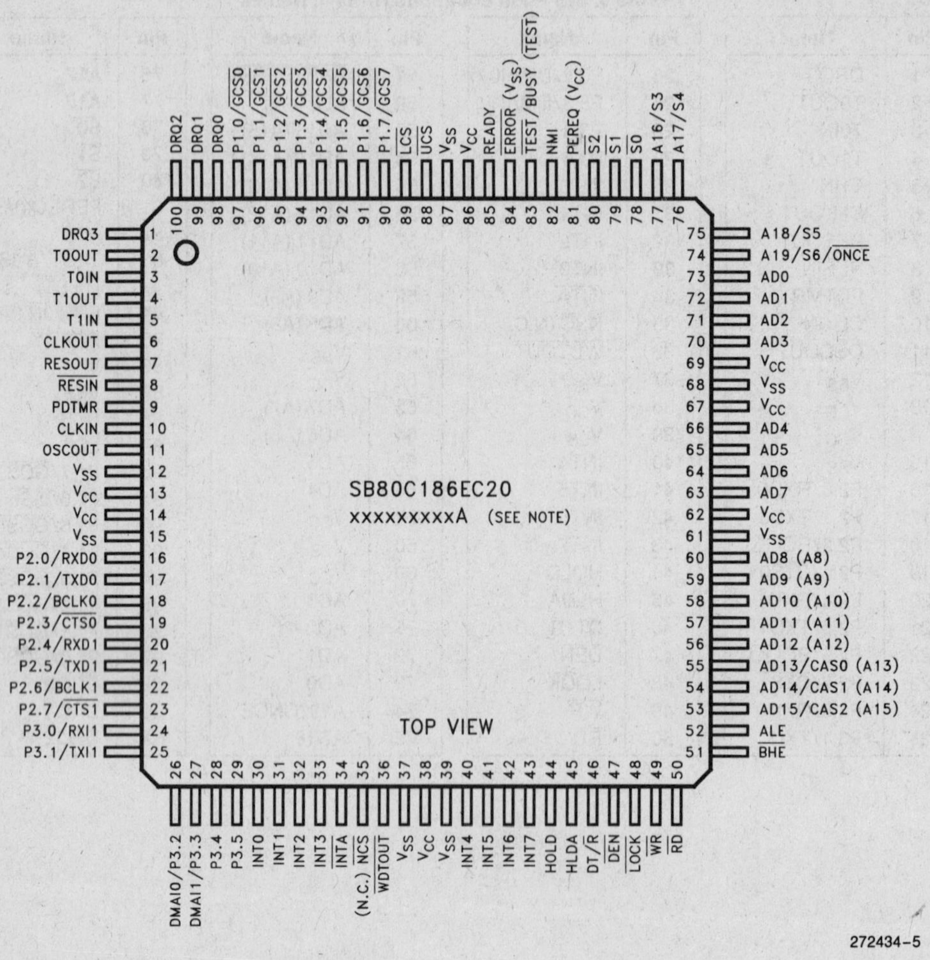

SB80C186EC20

xxxxxxxxxA (SEE NOTE)

TOP VIEW

Pin	Name	Pin	Name	Pin	Name	Pin	Name
1	DRQ3	26	DMAI0/P3.2	51	$\overline{\text{BHE}}$	76	A17/S4
2	T0OUT	27	DMAI1/P3.3	52	ALE	77	A16/S3
3	T0IN	28	P3.4	53	AD15/CAS2 (A15)	78	$\overline{\text{S0}}$
4	T1OUT	29	P3.5	54	AD14/CAS1 (A14)	79	$\overline{\text{S1}}$
5	T1IN	30	INT0	55	AD13/CAS0 (A13)	80	$\overline{\text{S2}}$
6	CLKOUT	31	INT1	56	AD12 (A12)	81	PEREQ (V_{CC})
7	RESOUT	32	INT2	57	AD11 (A11)	82	NMI
8	$\overline{\text{RESIN}}$	33	INT3	58	AD10 (A10)	83	$\overline{\text{TEST}}$/BUSY ($\overline{\text{TEST}}$)
9	PDTMR	34	$\overline{\text{INTA}}$	59	AD9 (A9)	84	$\overline{\text{ERROR}}$ (V_{SS})
10	CLKIN	35	(N.C.) $\overline{\text{NCS}}$	60	AD8 (A8)	85	READY
11	OSCOUT	36	$\overline{\text{WDTOUT}}$	61	V_{SS}	86	V_{CC}
12	V_{SS}	37	V_{SS}	62	V_{CC}	87	V_{SS}
13	V_{CC}	38	V_{CC}	63	AD7	88	$\overline{\text{UCS}}$
14	V_{CC}	39	V_{SS}	64	AD6	89	$\overline{\text{LCS}}$
15	V_{SS}	40	INT4	65	AD5	90	P1.7/$\overline{\text{GCS7}}$
16	P2.0/RXD0	41	INT5	66	AD4	91	P1.6/$\overline{\text{GCS6}}$
17	P2.1/TXD0	42	INT6	67	V_{CC}	92	P1.5/$\overline{\text{GCS5}}$
18	P2.2/BCLK0	43	INT7	68	V_{SS}	93	P1.4/$\overline{\text{GCS4}}$
19	P2.3/$\overline{\text{CTS0}}$	44	HOLD	69	V_{CC}	94	P1.3/$\overline{\text{GCS3}}$
20	P2.4/RXD1	45	HLDA	70	AD3	95	P1.2/$\overline{\text{GCS2}}$
21	P2.5/TXD1	46	DT/$\overline{\text{R}}$	71	AD2	96	P1.1/$\overline{\text{GCS1}}$
22	P2.6/BCLK1	47	$\overline{\text{DEN}}$	72	AD1	97	P1.0/$\overline{\text{GCS0}}$
23	P2.7/$\overline{\text{CTS1}}$	48	$\overline{\text{LOCK}}$	73	AD0	98	DRQ0
24	P3.0/RXI1	49	$\overline{\text{WR}}$	74	A19/S6/$\overline{\text{ONCE}}$	99	DRQ1
25	P3.1/TXI1	50	$\overline{\text{RD}}$	75	A18/S5	100	DRQ2

272434–5

NOTE:
This is the FPO number location (indicated by X's)

Figure 6. 100-Pin Shrink Quad Flat Pack Package (SQFP)

Package Thermal Specifications

The 80C186EC/80L186EC is specified for operation when T_C (the case temperature) is within the range of −40°C to +100°C. T_C may be measured in any environment to determine whether the processor is within the specified operating range. The case temperature must be measured at the center of the top surface.

T_A (the ambient temperature) can be calculated from θ_{CA} (thermal resistance from the case to ambient) with the following equation:

$$T_A = T_C - P * \theta_{CA}$$

Typical values for θ_{CA} at various airflows are given in Table 9. P (the maximum power consumption—specified in Watts) is calculated by using the maximum I_{CC} and V_{CC} of 5.5V.

Table 9. Thermal Resistance (θ_{CA}) at Various Airflows (in °C/Watt)

	Airflow in ft/min (m/sec)					
	0 (0)	**200 (1.01)**	**400 (2.03)**	**600 (3.04)**	**800 (4.06)**	**1000 (5.07)**
θ_{CA} (PQFP)	27.0	22.0	18.0	15.0	14.0	13.5
θ_{CA} (QFP)	64.5	55.5	51.0	TBD	TBD	TBD
θ_{CA} (SQFP)	62.0	TBD	TBD	TBD	TBD	TBD

2

ELECTRICAL SPECIFICATIONS

Absolute Maximum Ratings

Storage Temperature .... −65°C to +150°C

Case Temperature Under Bias... −65°C to +100°C

Supply Voltage
with Respect to V_{SS} .... −0.5V to +6.5V

Voltage on Other Pins
with Respect to V_{SS} ...... −0.5V to V_{CC} + 0.5V

NOTICE: This data sheet contains preliminary information on new products in production. The specifications are subject to change without notice. Verify with your local Intel Sales office that you have the latest data sheet before finalizing a design.

**WARNING: Stressing the device beyond the "Absolute Maximum Ratings" may cause permanent damage. These are stress ratings only. Operation beyond the "Operating Conditions" is not recommended and extended exposure beyond the "Operating Conditions" may affect device reliability.*

Recommended Connections

Power and ground connections must be made to multiple V_{CC} and V_{SS} pins. Every 80C186EC-based circuit board should include separate power (V_{CC}) and ground (V_{SS}) planes. Every V_{CC} pin must be connected to the power plane, and every V_{SS} pin must be connected to the ground plane. Liberal decoupling capacitance should be placed near the processor. The processor can cause transient power surges when its output buffers transition, particularly when connected to large capacitive loads.

Low inductance capacitors and interconnects are recommended for best high frequency electrical performance. Inductance is reduced by placing the decoupling capacitors as close as possible to the processor V_{CC} and V_{SS} package pins.

Always connect any unused input to an appropriate signal level. In particular, unused interrupt inputs (NMI, INT0:7) should be connected to V_{SS} through a pull-down resistor. Leave any unused output pin unconnected.

DC SPECIFICATIONS (80C186EC/80C188EC)

Symbol	Parameter	Min	Max	Units	Notes
V_{CC}	Supply Voltage	4.5	5.5	V	
V_{IL}	Input Low Voltage	−0.5	0.3 V_{CC}	V	
V_{IH}	Input High Voltage	0.7 V_{CC}	V_{CC} + 0.5	V	
V_{OL}	Output Low Voltage		0.45	V	I_{OL} = 3 mA (Min)
V_{OH}	Output High Voltage	V_{CC} − 0.5		V	I_{OH} = −2 mA (Min)
V_{HYR}	Input Hysteresis on $\overline{RESIN}$	0.5		V	
I_{LI}	Input Leakage Current for Pins: AD15:0 (AD7:0, A15:8), READY, HOLD, $\overline{RESIN}$, CLKIN, $\overline{TEST}$/BUSY, NMI, INT7:0, T0IN, T1IN, P2.7–P2.0, P3.5–P3.0, DRQ3:0, PEREQ, $\overline{ERROR}$		±15	μA	$0 \leq V_{IN} \leq V_{CC}$
I_{LIU}	Input Leakage for Pins with Pullups Active During Reset: A19:16, $\overline{LOCK}$	−0.275	−5	mA	V_{IN} = 0.7 V_{CC} (Note 1)
I_{LO}	Output Leakage for Floated Output Pins		±15	μA	$0.45 \leq V_{OUT} \leq V_{CC}$ (Note 2)
I_{CC}	Supply Current Cold (in RESET) 80C186EC20 80C186EC13		 100 70	 mA mA	(Note 3)
I_{ID}	Supply Current in Idle Mode 80C186EC20 80C186EC13		 76 50	 mA mA	(Note 4)
I_{PD}	Supply Current in Powerdown Mode 80C186EC20 80C186EC13		 100 100	 μA μA	(Note 5)
C_{IN}	Input Pin Capacitance	0	15	pF	T_F = 1 MHz
C_{OUT}	Output Pin Capacitance	0	15	pF	T_F = 1 MHz (Note 6)

NOTES:
1. These pins have an internal pull-up device that is active while $\overline{RESIN}$ is low and ONCE Mode is not active. Sourcing more current than specified (on any of these pins) may invoke a factory test mode.
2. Tested by outputs being floated by invoking ONCE Mode or by asserting HOLD.
3. Measured with the device in RESET and at worst case frequency, V_{CC}, and temperature with **ALL** outputs loaded as specified in AC Test Conditions, and all floating outputs driven to V_{CC} or GND.
4. Measured with the device in HALT (IDLE Mode active) and at worst case frequency, V_{CC}, and temperature with **ALL** outputs loaded as specified in AC Test Conditions, and all floating outputs driven to V_{CC} or GND.
5. Measured with the device in HALT (Powerdown Mode active) and at worst case frequency, V_{CC}, and temperature with **ALL** outputs loaded as specified in AC Test Conditions, and all floating outputs driven to V_{CC} or GND.
6. Output Capacitance is the capacitive load of a floating output pin.

DC SPECIFICATIONS (80L186EC/80L188EC)

Symbol	Parameter	Min	Max	Units	Notes
V_{CC}	Supply Voltage	2.7	5.5	V	
V_{IL}	Input Low Voltage	−0.5	0.3 V_{CC}	V	
V_{IH}	Input High Voltage	0.7 V_{CC}	V_{CC} + 0.5	V	
V_{OL}	Output Low Voltage		0.45	V	I_{OL} = 3 mA (Min)
V_{OH}	Output High Voltage	V_{CC} − 0.5		V	I_{OH} = −2 mA (Min)
V_{HYR}	Input Hysteresis on $\overline{RESIN}$	0.5		V	
I_{LI}	Input Leakage Current for Pins: AD15:0 (AD7:0, A15:8), READY, HOLD, $\overline{RESIN}$, CLKIN, $\overline{TEST}$/BUSY, NMI, INT7:0, T0IN, T1IN, P2.7–P2.0, P3.5–P3.0, DRQ3:0, PEREQ, $\overline{ERROR}$		±15	μA	$0 \le V_{IN} \le V_{CC}$
I_{LIU}	Input Leakage for Pins with Pullups Active During Reset: A19:16, $\overline{LOCK}$	−0.275	−5	mA	V_{IN} = 0.7 V_{CC} (Note 1)
I_{LO}	Output Leakage for Floated Output Pins		±15	μA	$0.45 \le V_{OUT} \le V_{CC}$ (Note 2)
I_{CC}	Supply Current Cold (in RESET) 80L186EC-13		36	mA	(Note 3)
I_{ID}	Supply Current in Idle Mode 80C186EC-13		24	mA	(Note 4)
I_{PD}	Supply Current in Powerdown Mode 80C186EC-13		30	μA	(Note 5)
C_{IN}	Input Pin Capacitance	0	15	pF	T_F = 1 MHz
C_{OUT}	Output Pin Capacitance	0	15	pF	T_F = 1 MHz (Note 6)

NOTES:
1. These pins have an internal pull-up device that is active while $\overline{RESIN}$ is low and ONCE Mode is not active. Sourcing more current than specified (on any of these pins) may invoke a factory test mode.
2. Tested by outputs being floated by invoking ONCE Mode or by asserting HOLD.
3. Measured with the device in RESET and at worst case frequency, V_{CC}, and temperature with **ALL** outputs loaded as specified in AC Test Conditions, and all floating outputs driven to V_{CC} or GND.
4. Measured with the device in HALT (IDLE Mode active) and at worst case frequency, V_{CC}, and temperature with **ALL** outputs loaded as specified in AC Test Conditions, and all floating outputs driven to V_{CC} or GND.
5. Measured with the device in HALT (Powerdown Mode active) and at worst case frequency, V_{CC}, and temperature with **ALL** outputs loaded as specified in AC Test Conditions, and all floating outputs driven to V_{CC} or GND.
6. Output Capacitance is the capacitive load of a floating output pin.

I_{CC} versus Frequency and Voltage

The I_{CC} consumed by the processor is composed of two components:

1. I_{PD}—The quiescent current that represents internal device leakage. Measured with all inputs at either V_{CC} or ground and no clock applied.
2. I_{CCS}—The switching current used to charge and discharge internal parasitic capacitance when changing logic levels. I_{CCS} is related to both the frequency of operation and the device supply voltage (V_{CC}). I_{CCS} is given by the formula:

$$\text{Power} = V * I = V^2 * C_{DEV} * f$$

$$\therefore I_{CCS} = V * C_{DEV} * f$$

Where:

V = Supply Voltage (V_{CC})

C_{DEV} = Device Capacitance

f = Operating Frequency

Measuring C_{PD} on a device like the 80C186EC would be difficult. Instead, C_{PD} is calculated using the above formula with I_{CC} values measured at known V_{CC} and frequency. Using the C_{PD} value, the user can calculate I_{CC} at any voltage and frequency within the specified operating range.

Example. Calculate typical I_{CC} at 14 MHz, 5.2V V_{CC}.

$$I_{CC} = I_{PD} + I_{CCS}$$
$$= 0.1\text{ mA} + 5.2\text{V} * 0.77 * 14\text{ MHz}$$
$$= 56.2\text{ mA}$$

PDTMR Pin Delay Calculation

The PDTMR pin provides a delay between the assertion of NMI and the enabling of the internal clocks when exiting Powerdown Mode. A delay is required only when using the on chip oscillator to allow the crystal or resonator circuit to stabilize.

NOTE:
The PDTMR pin function does not apply when $\overline{\text{RESIN}}$ is asserted (i.e. a device reset while in Powerdown is similar to a cold reset and $\overline{\text{RESIN}}$ must remain active until after the oscillator has stabilized.

To calculate the value of capacitor to use to provide a desired delay, use the equation:

$$440 \times t = C_{PD}\ (5V, 25°C)$$

Where:

t = desired delay in **seconds**

C_{PD} = capacitive load on PDTMR in **microfarads**

Example. For a delay of 300 μs, a capacitor value of $C_{PD} = 440 \times (300 \times 10^{-6} = 0.132\ \mu$F is required. Round up to a standard (available) capacitor value.

NOTE:
The above equation applies to delay time longer than 10 μs and will compute the **TYPICAL** capacitance needed to achieve the desired delay. A delay variance of +50% to −25% can occur due to temperature, voltage, and device process extremes. In general, higher V_{CC} and/or lower temperatures will decrease delay time, while lower V_{CC} and/or higher temperature will increase delay time.

Parameter	Typical	Max	Units	Notes
CPD	0.77	1.37	mA/V*MHz	1, 2
CPD (Idle Mode)	0.55	0.96	mA/V*MHz	1, 2

NOTES:
1. Maximum C_{PD} is measured at −40°C with all outputs loaded as specified in the AC test conditions and the device in reset (or Idle Mode). Due to tester limitations, CLKOUT and OSCOUT also have 50 pF loads that increase I_{CC} by V*C*F.
2. Typical C_{PD} is calculated at 25°C assuming no loads on CLKOUT or OSCOUT and the device in reset (or Idle Mode).

AC SPECIFICATIONS

AC Characteristics—80C186EC-20/80C186EC-13

Symbol	Parameter	Min	Max	Min	Max	Unit	Notes
INPUT CLOCK		**20 MHz**		**13 MHz**			
TF	CLKIN Frequency	0	40	0	26	MHz	1
TC	CLKIN Period	25	∞	38.5	∞	ns	1
TCH	CLKIN High Time	10	∞	12	∞	ns	1, 2
TCL	CLKIN Low Time	10	∞	12	∞	ns	1, 2
TCR	CLKIN Rise Time	1	10	1	10	ns	1, 3
TCF	CLKIN Fall Time	1	10	1	10	ns	1, 3
OUTPUT CLOCK							
T_{CD}	CLKIN to CLKOUT Delay	0	17	0	23	ns	1, 4
T	CLKOUT Period		2 * TC		2 * TC	ns	1
T_{PH}	CLKOUT High Time	(T/2) − 5	(T/2) + 5	(T/2) − 5	(T/2) + 5	ns	1
T_{PL}	CLKOUT Low Time	(T/2) − 5	(T/2) + 5	(T/2) − 5	(T/2) + 5	ns	1
T_{PR}	CLKOUT Rise Time	1	6	1	6	ns	1, 5
T_{PF}	CLKOUT Fall Time	1	6	1	6	ns	1, 5
OUTPUT DELAYS							
T_{CHOV1}	ALE, $\overline{S2:0}$, $\overline{DEN}$, DT/$\overline{R}$, $\overline{BHE}$ ($\overline{RFSH}$), $\overline{LOCK}$, A19:16	3	20	3	25	ns	1, 4, 6, 7
T_{CHOV2}	$\overline{GCS7:0}$, $\overline{LCS}$, $\overline{UCS}$, $\overline{RD}$, $\overline{WR}$, $\overline{NCS}$, $\overline{WDTOUT}$	3	23	3	30	ns	1, 4, 6, 8
T_{CLOV1}	$\overline{BHE}$ ($\overline{RFSH}$), $\overline{DEN}$, $\overline{LOCK}$, RESOUT, HLDA, T0OUT, T1OUT	3	20	3	25	ns	1, 4, 6
T_{CLOV2}	$\overline{RD}$, $\overline{WR}$, $\overline{GSC7:0}$, $\overline{LCS}$, $\overline{UCS}$, AD15:0 (AD7:0, A15:8), $\overline{NCS}$, $\overline{INTA}$, $\overline{S2:0}$, A19:16	3	23	3	30	ns	1, 4, 6
T_{CHOF}	$\overline{RD}$, $\overline{WR}$, $\overline{BHE}$ ($\overline{RFSH}$), DT/$\overline{R}$, $\overline{LOCK}$, $\overline{S2:0}$, A19:16	0	25	0	30	ns	1
T_{CLOF}	$\overline{DEN}$, AD15:0 (AD7:0, A15:8)	0	25	0	30	ns	1
INPUT REQUIREMENTS							
T_{CHIS}	$\overline{TEST}$, NMI, T1IN, T0IN, READY, $\overline{CTS1:0}$, BCLK1:0, P3.4, P3.5	10		10		ns	1, 9
T_{CHIH}	$\overline{TEST}$, NMI, T1IN, T0IN, READY, $\overline{CTS1:0}$, BCLK1:0, P3.4, P3.5	3		3		ns	1, 9
T_{CLIS}	AD15:0 (AD7:0), READY	10		10		ns	1, 10
T_{CLIH}	AD15:0 (AD7:0), READY	3		3		ns	1, 10
T_{CLIS}	HOLD, $\overline{RESIN}$, PEREQ, $\overline{ERROR}$, DRQ3:0	10		10		ns	1, 9
T_{CLIH}	HOLD, $\overline{RESIN}$, REREQ, $\overline{ERROR}$, DRQ3:0	3		3		ns	1, 9

NOTES:
1. See **AC Timing Waveforms**, for waveforms and definition.
2. Measure at V_{IH} for high time, V_{IL} for low time.
3. Only required to guarantee I_{CC}. Maximum limits are bounded by T_C, T_{CH} and T_{CL}.
4. Specified for a 50 pF load, see Figure 14 for capacitive derating information.
5. Specified for a 50 pF load, see Figure 15 for rise and fall times outside 50 pF.
6. See Figure 15 for rise and fall times.
7. T_{CHOV1} applies to $\overline{BHE}$ ($\overline{RFSH}$), $\overline{LOCK}$ and A19:16 only after a HOLD release.
8. T_{CHOV2} applies to $\overline{RD}$ and $\overline{WR}$ only after a HOLD release.
9. Setup and Hold are required to guarantee recognition.
10. Setup and Hold are required for proper operation.

AC Characteristics—80L186EC

Symbol	Parameter	Min	Max	Unit	Notes
INPUT CLOCK		**13 MHz**			
TF	CLKIN Frequency	0	26	MHz	1
TC	CLKIN Period	38.5	∞	ns	1
TCH	CLKIN High Time	15	∞	ns	1, 2
TCL	CLKIN Low Time	15	∞	ns	1, 2
TCR	CLKIN Rise Time	1	10	ns	1, 3
TCF	CLKIN Fall Time	1	10	ns	1, 3
OUTPUT CLOCK					
T_{CD}	CLKIN to CLKOUT Delay	0	20	ns	1, 4
T	CLKOUT Period		2 * TC	ns	1
T_{PH}	CLKOUT High Time	(T/2) − 5	(T/2) + 5	ns	1
T_{PL}	CLKOUT Low Time	(T/2) − 5	(T/2) + 5	ns	1
T_{PR}	CLKOUT Rise Time	1	10	ns	1, 5
T_{PF}	CLKOUT Fall Time	1	10	ns	1, 5
OUTPUT DELAYS					
T_{CHOV1}	$\overline{\text{S2:0}}$, DT/$\overline{\text{R}}$, $\overline{\text{BHE}}$, $\overline{\text{LOCK}}$	3	28	ns	1, 4, 6, 7
T_{CHOV2}	$\overline{\text{LCS}}$, $\overline{\text{UCS}}$, $\overline{\text{DEN}}$, A19:16, $\overline{\text{RD}}$, $\overline{\text{WR}}$, $\overline{\text{NCS}}$, $\overline{\text{WDTOUT}}$, ALE	3	32	ns	1, 4, 6, 8
T_{CHOV3}	$\overline{\text{GCS7:0}}$	3	34	ns	1, 4, 6
T_{CLOV1}	$\overline{\text{LOCK}}$, RESOUT, HLDA, T0OUT, T1OUT	3	28	ns	1, 4, 6
T_{CLOV2}	$\overline{\text{RD}}$, $\overline{\text{WR}}$, AD15:0 (AD7:0, A15:8), $\overline{\text{BHE}}$ ($\overline{\text{RFSH}}$), $\overline{\text{NCS}}$, $\overline{\text{INTA}}$, $\overline{\text{DEN}}$	3	32	ns	1, 4, 6
T_{CLOV3}	$\overline{\text{GSC7:0}}$, $\overline{\text{LCS}}$, $\overline{\text{UCS}}$	3	34	ns	1, 4, 6
T_{CLOV4}	$\overline{\text{S2:0}}$, A19:16	3	37	ns	1, 4, 6
T_{CHOF}	$\overline{\text{RD}}$, $\overline{\text{WR}}$, $\overline{\text{BHE}}$ ($\overline{\text{RFSH}}$), DT/$\overline{\text{R}}$, $\overline{\text{LOCK}}$, $\overline{\text{S2:0}}$, A19:16	0	30	ns	1
T_{CLOF}	$\overline{\text{DEN}}$, AD15:0 (AD7:0, A15:8)	0	35	ns	1
INPUT REQUIREMENTS					
T_{CHIS}	$\overline{\text{TEST}}$, NMI, T1IN, T0IN, READY, $\overline{\text{CTS1:0}}$, BCLK1:0, P3.4, P3.5	20		ns	1, 9
T_{CHIH}	$\overline{\text{TEST}}$, NMI, T1IN, T0IN, READY, $\overline{\text{CTS1:0}}$, BCLK1:0, P3.4, P3.5	3		ns	1, 9
T_{CLIS}	AD15:0 (AD7:0), READY	20		ns	1, 10
T_{CLIH}	AD15:0 (AD7:0), READY	3		ns	1, 10
T_{CLIS}	HOLD, $\overline{\text{RESIN}}$, PEREQ, $\overline{\text{ERROR}}$, DRQ3:0	20		ns	1, 9
T_{CLIH}	HOLD, $\overline{\text{RESIN}}$, REREQ, $\overline{\text{ERROR}}$, DRQ3:0	3		ns	1, 9

NOTES:
1. See **AC Timing Waveforms**, for waveforms and definition.
2. Measure at V_{IH} for high time, V_{IL} for low time.
3. Only required to guarantee I_{CC}. Maximum limits are bounded by T_C, T_{CH} and T_{CL}.
4. Specified for a 50 pF load, see Figure 14 for capacitive derating information.
5. Specified for a 50 pF load, see Figure 15 for rise and fall times outside 50 pF.

AC Characteristics—80L186EC (Continued)

NOTES:
6. See Figure 15 for rise and fall times.
7. T_{CHOV1} applies to $\overline{BHE}$ ($\overline{RFSH}$), $\overline{LOCK}$ and A19:16 only after a HOLD release.
8. T_{CHOV2} applies to $\overline{RD}$ and $\overline{WR}$ only after a HOLD release.
9. Setup and Hold are required to guarantee recognition.
10. Setup and Hold are required for proper operation.

Relative Timings (80C186EC-20/13, 80L186EC13)

Symbol	Parameter	Min	Max	Unit	Notes
RELATIVE TIMINGS					
T_{LHLL}	ALE Active Pulse Width	T − 15		ns	
T_{AVLL}	AD Valid Setup before ALE Falls	½T − 10		ns	
T_{PLLL}	Chip Select Valid before ALE Falls	½T − 10		ns	1
T_{LLAX}	AD Hold after ALE Falls	½T − 10		ns	
T_{LLWL}	ALE Falling to $\overline{WR}$ Falling	½T − 15		ns	1
T_{LLRL}	ALE Falling to $\overline{RD}$ Falling	½T − 15		ns	1
T_{WHLH}	$\overline{WR}$ Rising to Next ALE Rising	½T − 10		ns	1
T_{AFRL}	AD Float to $\overline{RD}$ Falling	0		ns	
T_{RLRH}	$\overline{RD}$ Active Pulse Width	2T − 5		ns	2
T_{WLWH}	$\overline{WR}$ Active Pulse Width	2T − 5		ns	2
T_{RHAX}	$\overline{RD}$ Rising to Next Address Active	T − 15		ns	
T_{WHDX}	Output Data Hold after $\overline{WR}$ Rising	T − 15		ns	
T_{WHPH}	$\overline{WR}$ Rise to Chip Select Rise	½T − 10		ns	1
T_{RHPH}	$\overline{RD}$ Rise to Chip Select Rise	½T − 10		ns	1
T_{PHPL}	Chip Select Inactive to Next Chip Select Active	½T − 10		ns	1
T_{OVRH}	$\overline{ONCE}$ Active Setup to $\overline{RESIN}$ Rising	T		ns	
T_{RHOX}	$\overline{ONCE}$ Hold after $\overline{RESIN}$ Rise	T		ns	
T_{IIIL}	$\overline{INTA}$ High to Next $\overline{INTA}$ Low during INTA Cycle	4T − 5		ns	4
T_{ILIH}	$\overline{INTA}$ Active Pulse Width	2T − 5		ns	2, 4
T_{CVIL}	CAS2:0 Setup before 2nd $\overline{INTA}$ Pulse Low	8T		ns	2, 4

Relative Timings (80C186EC-20/13, 80L186EC13) (Continued)

Symbol	Parameter	Min	Max	Unit	Notes
RELATIVE TIMINGS					
T_{ILCX}	CAS2:0 Hold after 2nd $\overline{INTA}$ Pulse Low	4T		ns	2, 4
T_{IRES}	Interrupt Resolution Time		150	ns	3
T_{IRLH}	IR Low Time to Reset Edge Detector	50		ns	
T_{IRHIF}	IR Hold Time after 1st $\overline{INTA}$ Falling	25		ns	4, 5

NOTES:
1. Assumes equal loading on both pins.
2. Can be extended using wait states.
3. Interrupt resolution time is the delay between an unmasked interrupt request going active and the interrupt output of the 8259A module going active. This is not directly measureable by the user. For interrupt pin INT7 the delay from an active signal to an active input to the CPU would actually be twice the T_{IRES} value since the signal must pass through two 8259A modules.
4. See INTA Cycle Waveforms for definition.
5. To guarantee interrupt is not spurious.

2

Serial Port Mode 0 Timings (80C186EC-20/13, 80L186EC13)

Symbol	Parameter	Min	Max	Unit	Notes
RELATIVE TIMINGS					
T_{XLXL}	TXD Clock Period	T (n + 1)		ns	1, 2
T_{XLXH}	TXD Clock Low to Clock High (N > 1)	2T − 35	2T + 35	ns	1
T_{XLXH}	TXD Clock Low to Clock High (N = 1)	T − 35	T + 35	ns	1
T_{XHXL}	TXD Clock High to Clock Low (N > 1)	(n − 1) T − 35	(n − 1) T + 35	ns	1, 2
T_{XHXL}	TXD Clock High to Clock Low (N = 1)	T − 35	T + 35	ns	1
T_{QVXH}	RXD Output Data Setup to TXD Clock High (N > 1)	(n − 1)T − 35		ns	1, 2
T_{QVXH}	RXD Output Data Setup to TXD Clock High (N = 1)	T − 35		ns	1
T_{XHQX}	RXD Output Data Hold after TXD Clock High (N > 1)	2T − 35		ns	1
T_{XHQX}	RXD Output Data Hold after TXD Clock High (N = 1)	T − 35		ns	1
T_{XHQZ}	RXD Output Data Float after Last TXD Clock High		T + 20	ns	1
T_{DVXH}	RXD Input Data Setup to TXD Clock High	T + 20		ns	1
T_{XHDX}	RXD Input Data Setup after TXD Clock High	0		ns	1

NOTES:
1. See Figure 13 for Waveforms.
2. n is the value in the BxCMP register ignoring the ICLK bit.

AC TEST CONDITIONS

The AC specifications are tested with the 50 pF load shown in Figure 7. See the Derating Curves section to see how timings vary with load capacitance.

Specifications are measured at the $V_{CC}/2$ crossing point, unless otherwise specified. See AC Timing Waveforms for AC specification definitions, test pins and illustrations.

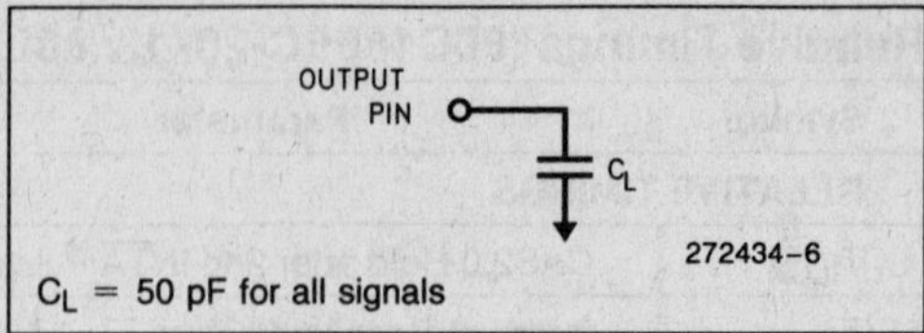

Figure 7. AC Test Load

AC TIMING WAVEFORMS

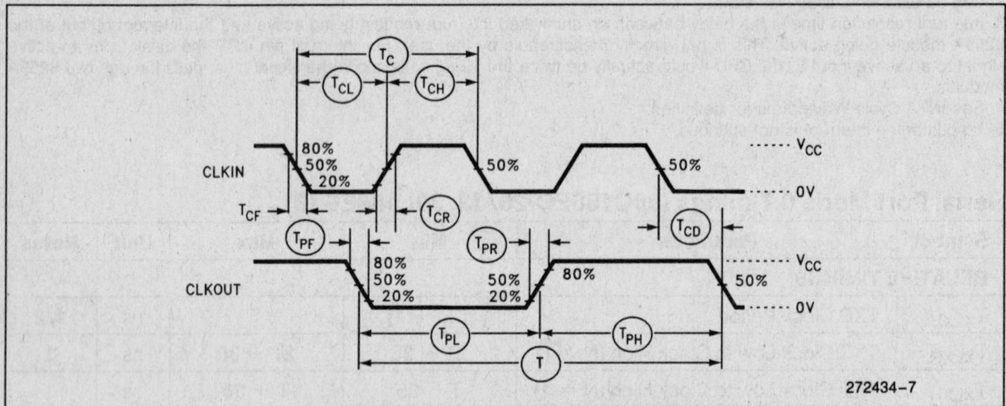

Figure 8. Input and Output Clock Waveforms

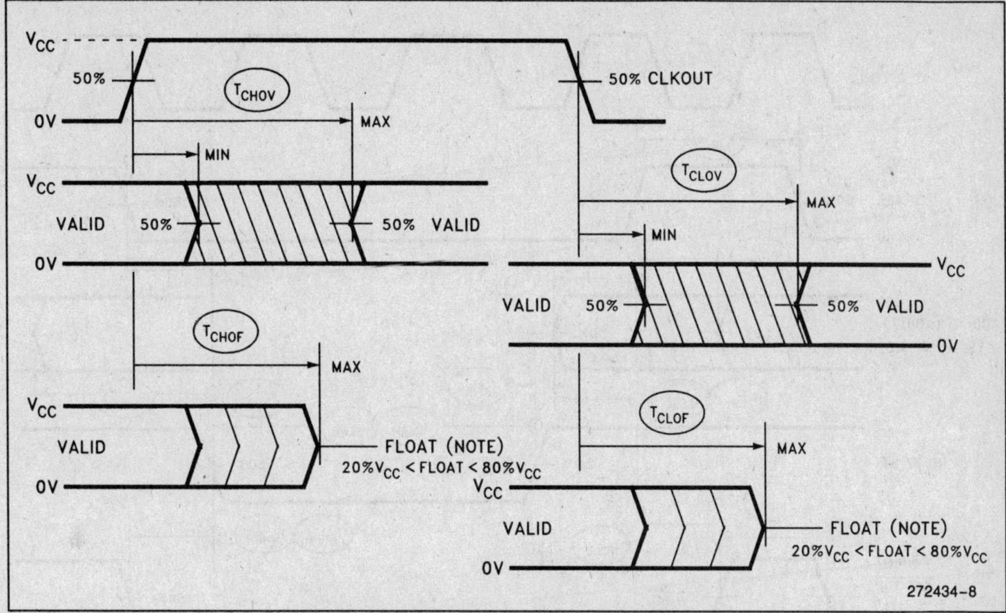

Figure 9. Output Delay and Float Waveforms

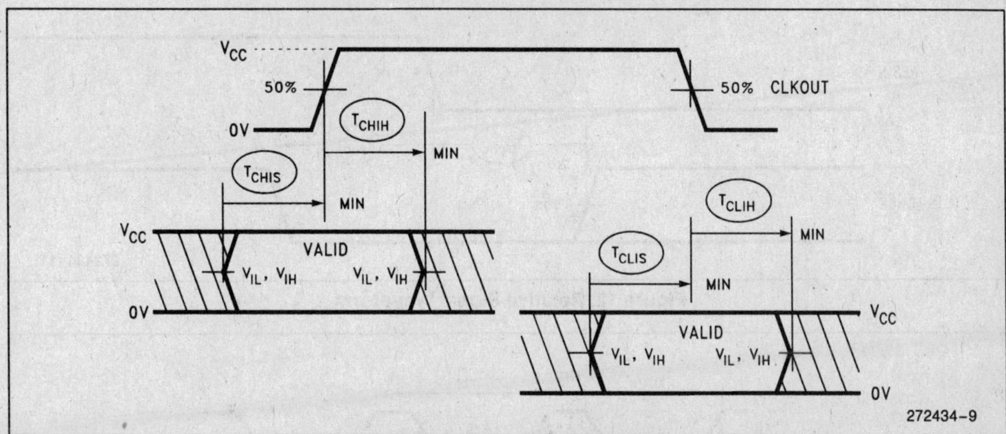

Figure 10. Input Setup and Hold

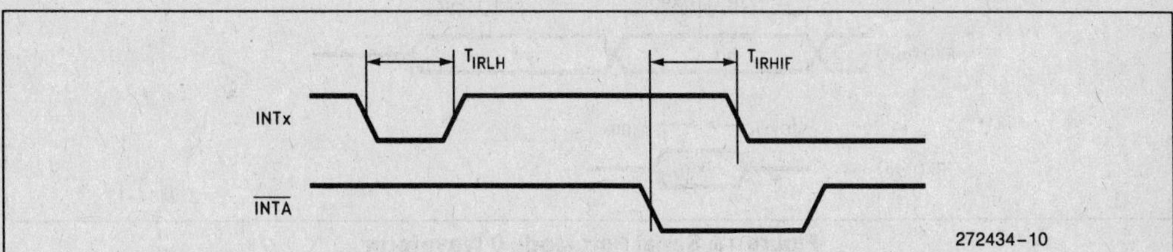

Figure 11. Relative Interrupt Signal Timings

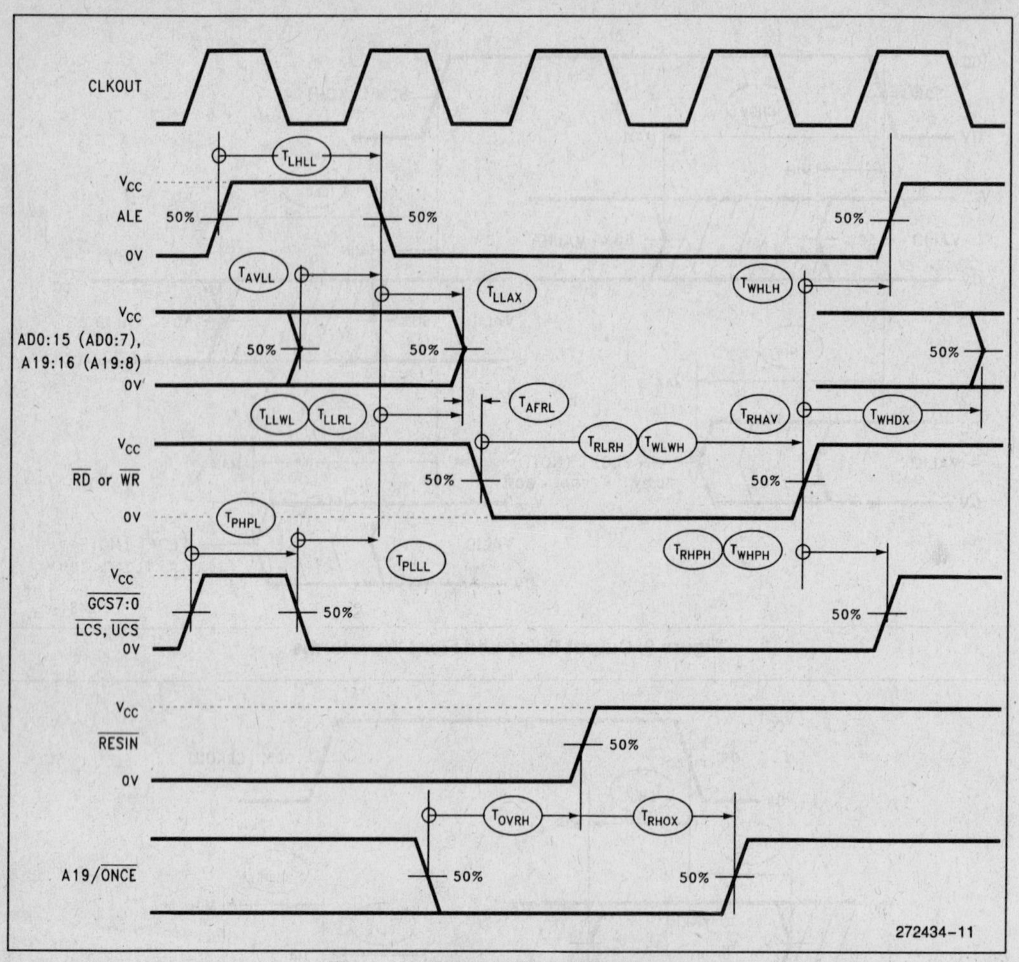

CLKOUT
T_{LHLL}
V_{CC}
ALE 50% 50% 50%
0V
T_{AVLL} T_{LLAX} T_{WHLH}
V_{CC}
AD0:15 (AD0:7), A19:16 (A19:8) 50% 50% 50%
0V
T_{LLWL} T_{LLRL} T_{AFRL} T_{RHAV} T_{WHDX}
V_{CC}
T_{RLRH} T_{WLWH}
$\overline{RD}$ or $\overline{WR}$ 50% 50%
0V
T_{PHPL} T_{PLLL} T_{RHPH} T_{WHPH}
V_{CC}
$\overline{GCS7:0}$
$\overline{LCS}$, $\overline{UCS}$ 50% 50%
0V
V_{CC}
$\overline{RESIN}$ 50%
0V
T_{OVRH} T_{RHOX}
A19/$\overline{ONCE}$ 50% 50%
272434-11

Figure 12. Relative Signal Waveform

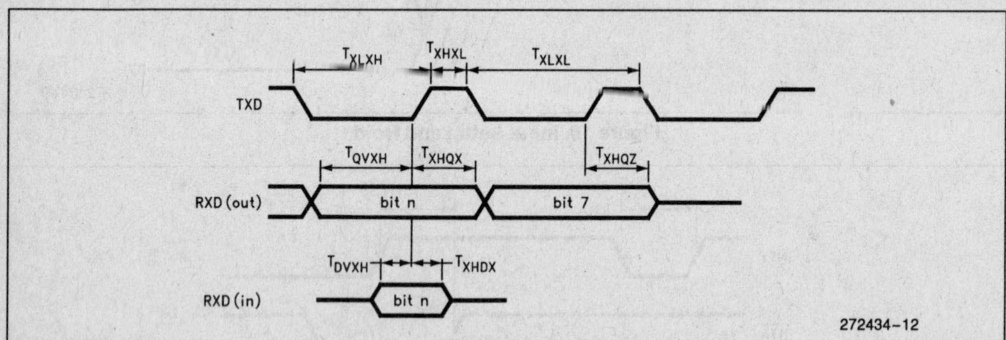

Figure 13. Serial Port Mode 0 Waveform

DERATING CURVES

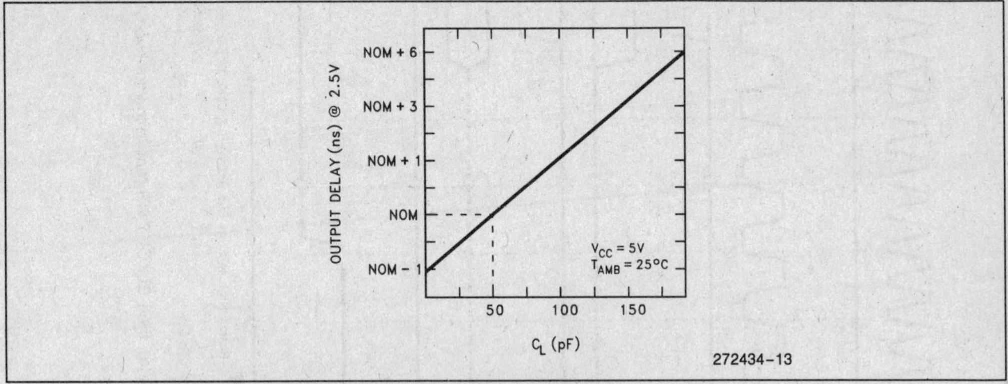

Figure 14. Typical Output Delay Variations versus Load Capacitance

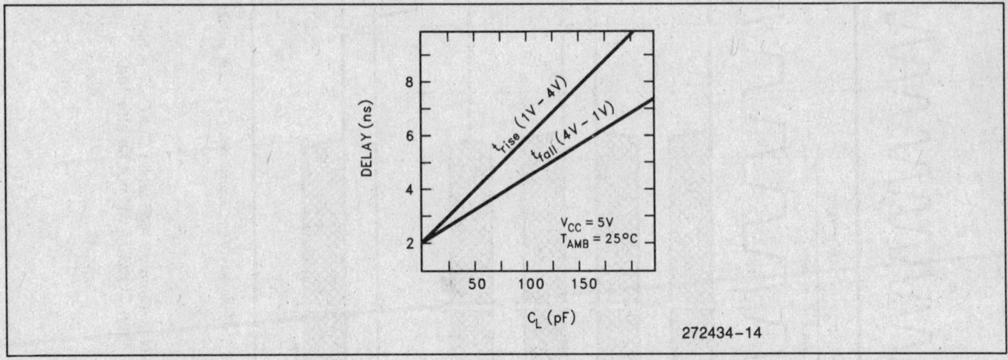

Figure 15. Typical Rise and Fall Variations versus Load Capacitance

RESET

The processor will perform a reset operation any time the $\overline{RESIN}$ pin is active. The $\overline{RESIN}$ pin is synchronized before it is presented internally, which means that the clock must be operating before a reset can take effect. From a power-on state, $\overline{RESIN}$ must be held active (low) in order to guarantee correct initialization of the processor. **Failure to provide $\overline{RESIN}$ while the device is powering up will result in unspecified operation of the device.**

Figure 16 shows the correct reset sequence when first applying power to the processor. An external clock connected to CLKIN must not exceed the V_{CC} threshold being applied to the processor. This is normally not a problem if the clock driver is supplied with the same V_{CC} that supplies the processor. When attaching a crystal to the device, $\overline{RESIN}$ must remain active until both V_{CC} and CLKOUT are stable (the length of time is application specific and depends on the startup characteristics of the crystal circuit). The $\overline{RESIN}$ pin is designed to operate correctly using a RC reset circuit, but the designer must ensure that the ramp time for V_{CC} is not so long that $\overline{RESIN}$ is never sampled at a logic low level when V_{CC} reaches minimum operating conditions.

Figure 17 shows the timing sequence when $\overline{RESIN}$ is applied after V_{CC} is stable and the device has been operating. Note that a reset will terminate all activity and return the processor to a known operating state. Any bus operation that is in progress at the time $\overline{RESIN}$ is asserted will terminate immediately (note that most control signals will be driven to their inactive state first before floating).

While $\overline{RESIN}$ is active, bus signals $\overline{LOCK}$, A19/S16/$\overline{ONCE}$ and A18:16 are configured as inputs and weakly held high by internal pullup transistors. Only A19/$\overline{ONCE}$ can be overdriven to a low and is used to enable the ONCE Mode. Forcing $\overline{LOCK}$ or A18:16 low at any time while $\overline{RESIN}$ is low is prohibited and will cause unspecified device operation.

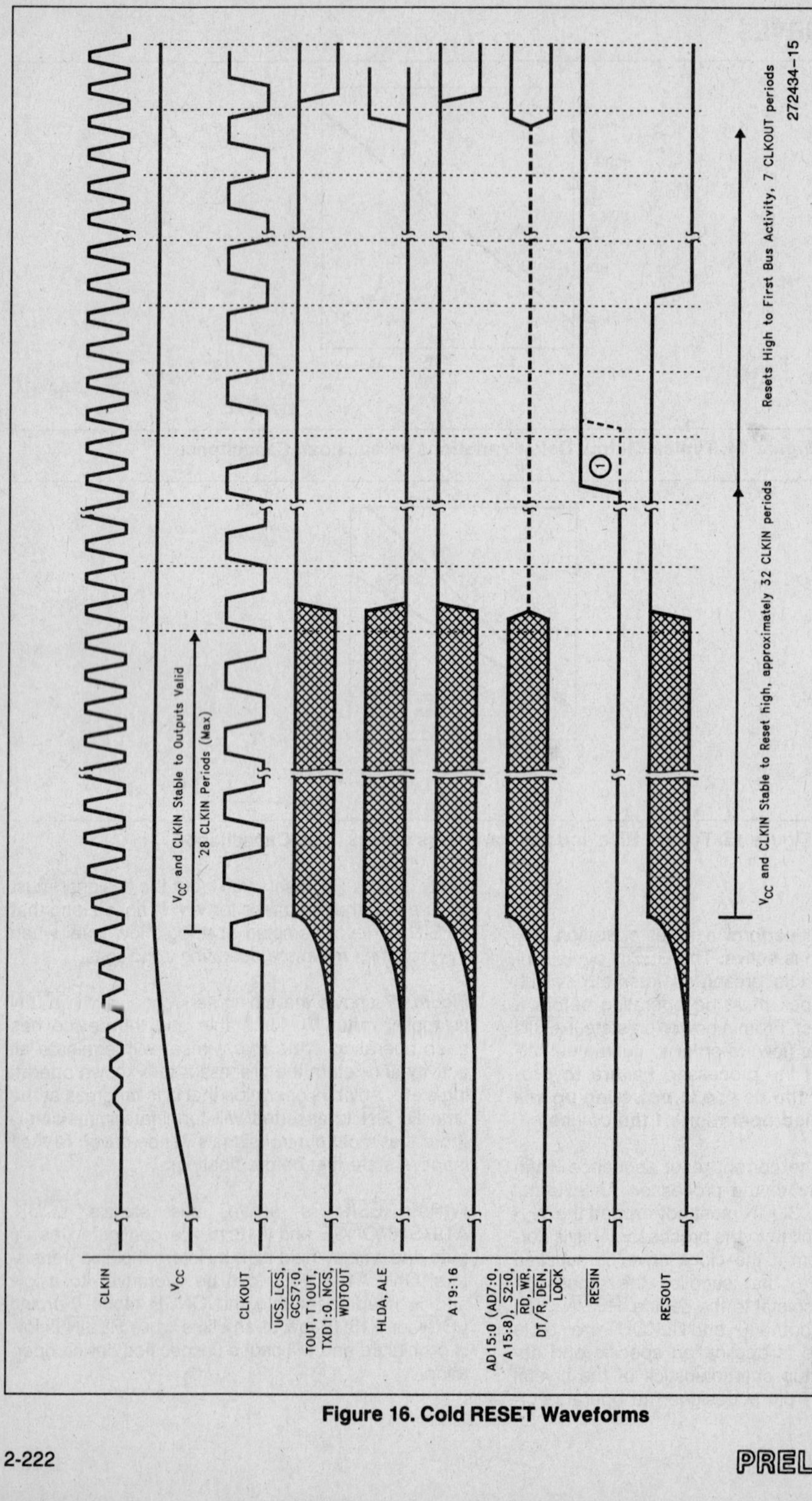

CLKIN

V_{CC}

CLKOUT

$\overline{UCS}$, $\overline{LCS}$, $\overline{GCS7:0}$, TOUT, T1OUT, TXD1:0, $\overline{NCS}$, $\overline{WDTOUT}$

HLDA, ALE

A19:16

AD15:0 (AD7:0, A15:8), $\overline{S2:0}$, $\overline{RD}$, $\overline{WR}$, DT/$\overline{R}$, $\overline{DEN}$, $\overline{LOCK}$

$\overline{RESIN}$

RESOUT

V_{CC} and CLKIN Stable to Outputs Valid 28 CLKIN Periods (Max)

V_{CC} and CLKIN Stable to Reset high, approximately 32 CLKIN periods

Resets High to First Bus Activity, 7 CLKOUT periods

272434–15

NOTE:
CLKOUT synchronization occurs on the rising edge of $\overline{RESIN}$. If $\overline{RESIN}$ is sampled high while CLKOUT is high (solid line), then CLKOUT will remain low for two CLKIN periods. If $\overline{RESIN}$ is sampled high while CLKOUT is low (dashed line), then CLKOUT will not be affected.
Pin names in parentheses apply to 80C188EC/80L188EC.

Figure 16. Cold RESET Waveforms

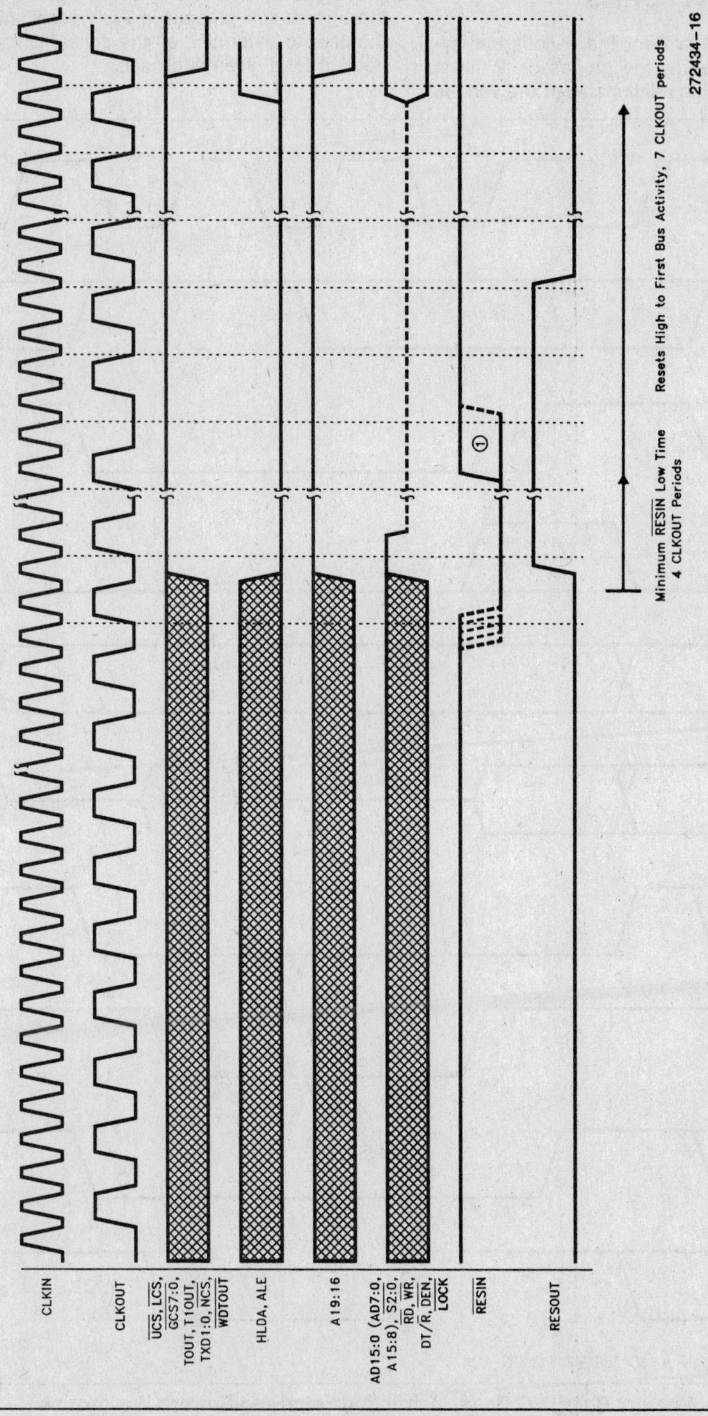

CLKIN

CLKOUT

UCS, LCS, GCS7:0, TOUT, T1OUT, TXD1:0, NCS, WDTOUT

HLDA, ALE

A19:16

AD15:0 (AD7:0, A15:8), S2:0, RD, WR, DT/R, DEN, LOCK

RESIN

RESOUT

①

Minimum RESIN Low Time 4 CLKOUT Periods

Resets High to First Bus Activity, 7 CLKOUT periods

272434–16

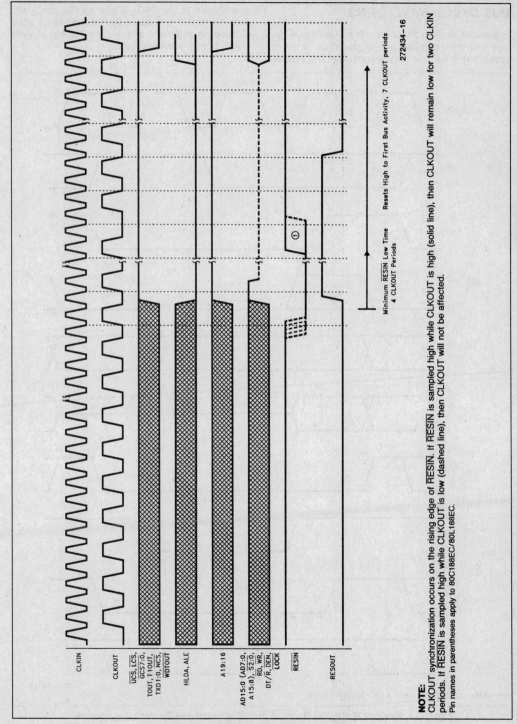

NOTE:
CLKOUT synchronization occurs on the rising edge of RESIN. If RESIN is sampled high while CLKOUT is high (solid line), then CLKOUT will remain low for two CLKIN periods. If RESIN is sampled high while CLKOUT is low (dashed line), then CLKOUT will not be affected.
Pin names in parentheses apply to 80C188EC/80L188EC.

Figure 17. Warm RESET Waveforms

BUS CYCLE WAVEFORMS

Figures 18 through 24 present the various bus cycles that are generated by the processor. What is shown in the figure is the relationship of the various bus signals to CLKOUT. These figures along with the information present in AC Specifications allow the user to determine all the critical timing analysis needed for a given application.

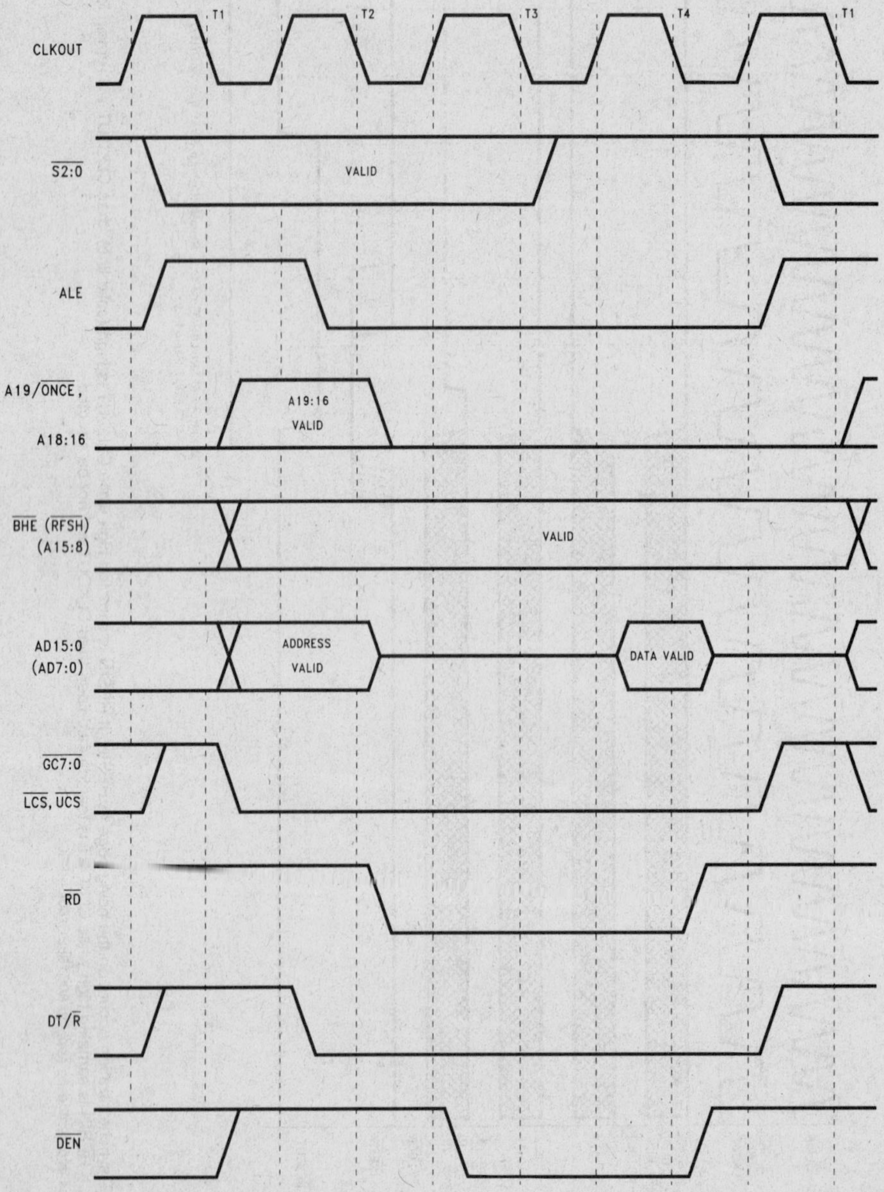

Pin names in parentheses apply to 80C188EC/80L188EC.

272434–17

Figure 18. Memory Read, I/O Read, Instruction Fetch and Refresh Waveforms

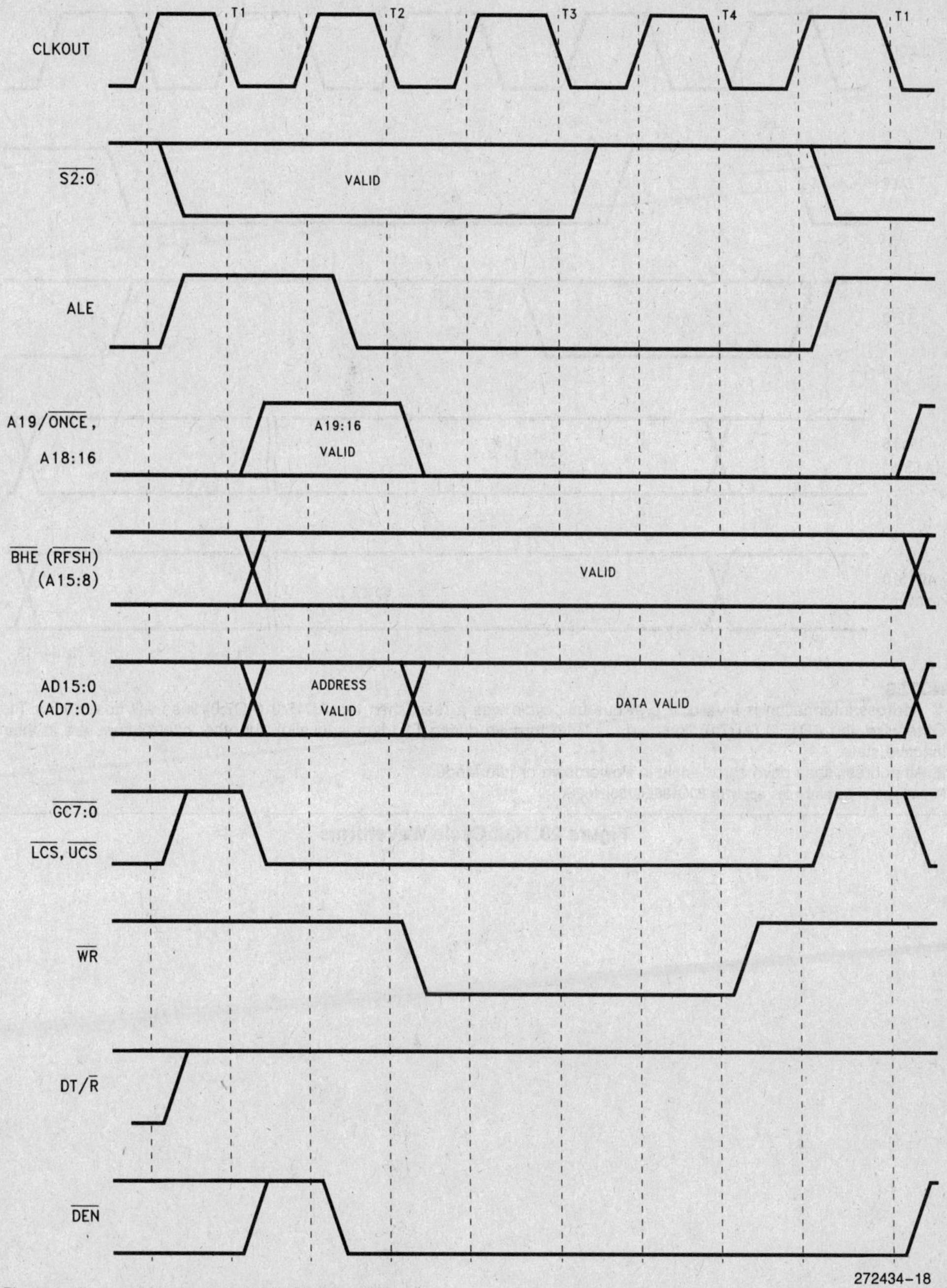

Pin names in parentheses apply to 80C188EC/80L188EC.

Figure 19. Memory Write and I/O Write Cycle Waveforms

2

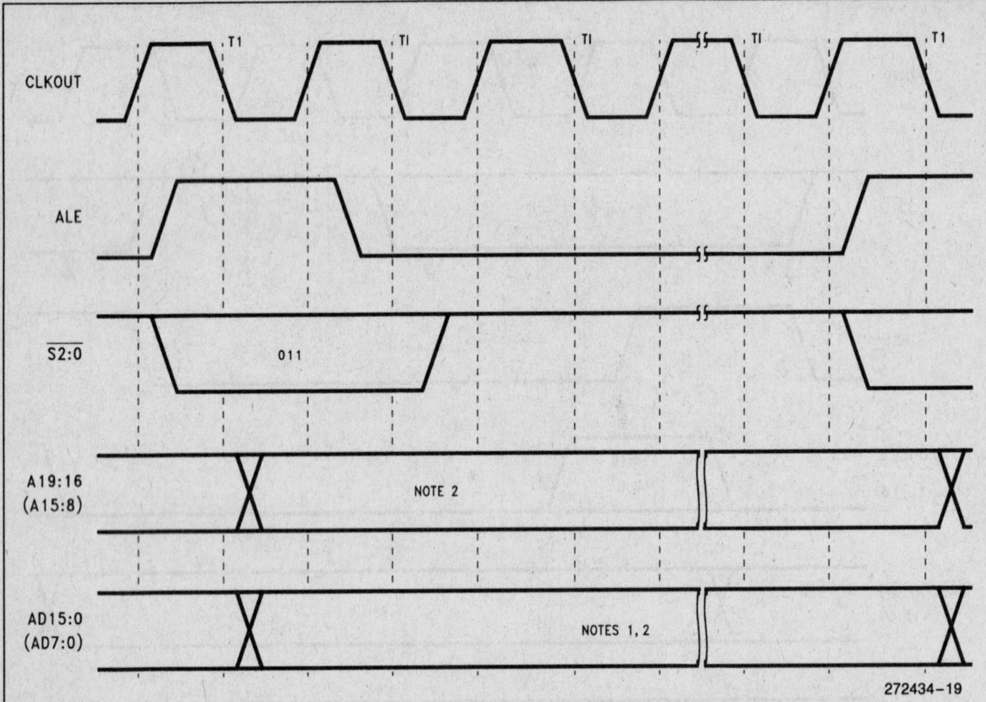

NOTES:

1. Address information is invalid. If previous bus cycle was a read, then the AD15:0 (AD7:0) lines will float during T1. Otherwise, the AD15:0 (AD7:0) lines will continue to drive during T1 (data is invalid). All other control lines are in their inactive state.
2. All address lines drive zeros while in Powerdown or Idle Mode.

Pin names in parentheses apply to 80C188EC/80L188EC.

Figure 20. Halt Cycle Waveforms

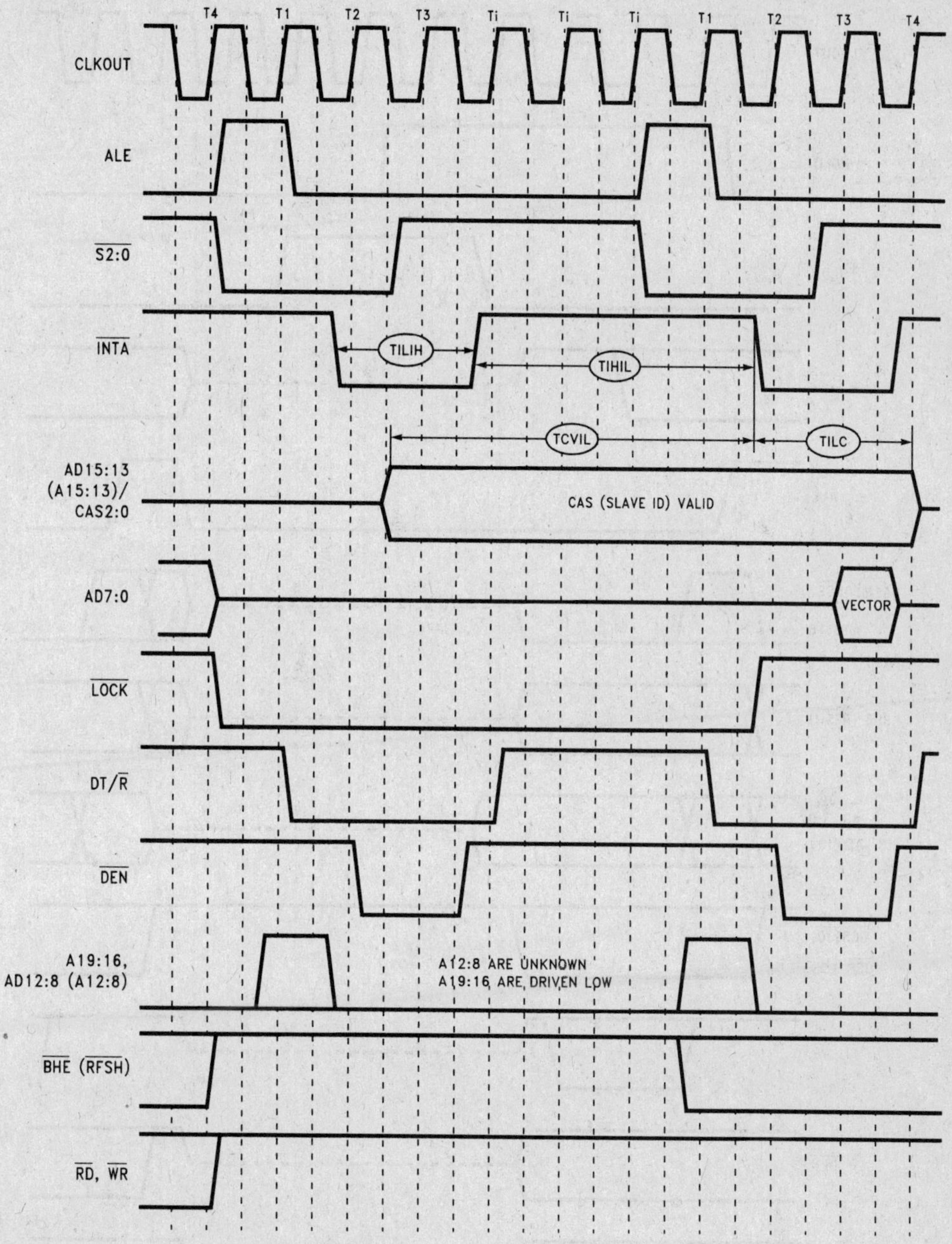

Pin names in parentheses apply to 80C188EC/80L188EC.

Figure 21. Interrupt Acknowledge Cycle Waveforms

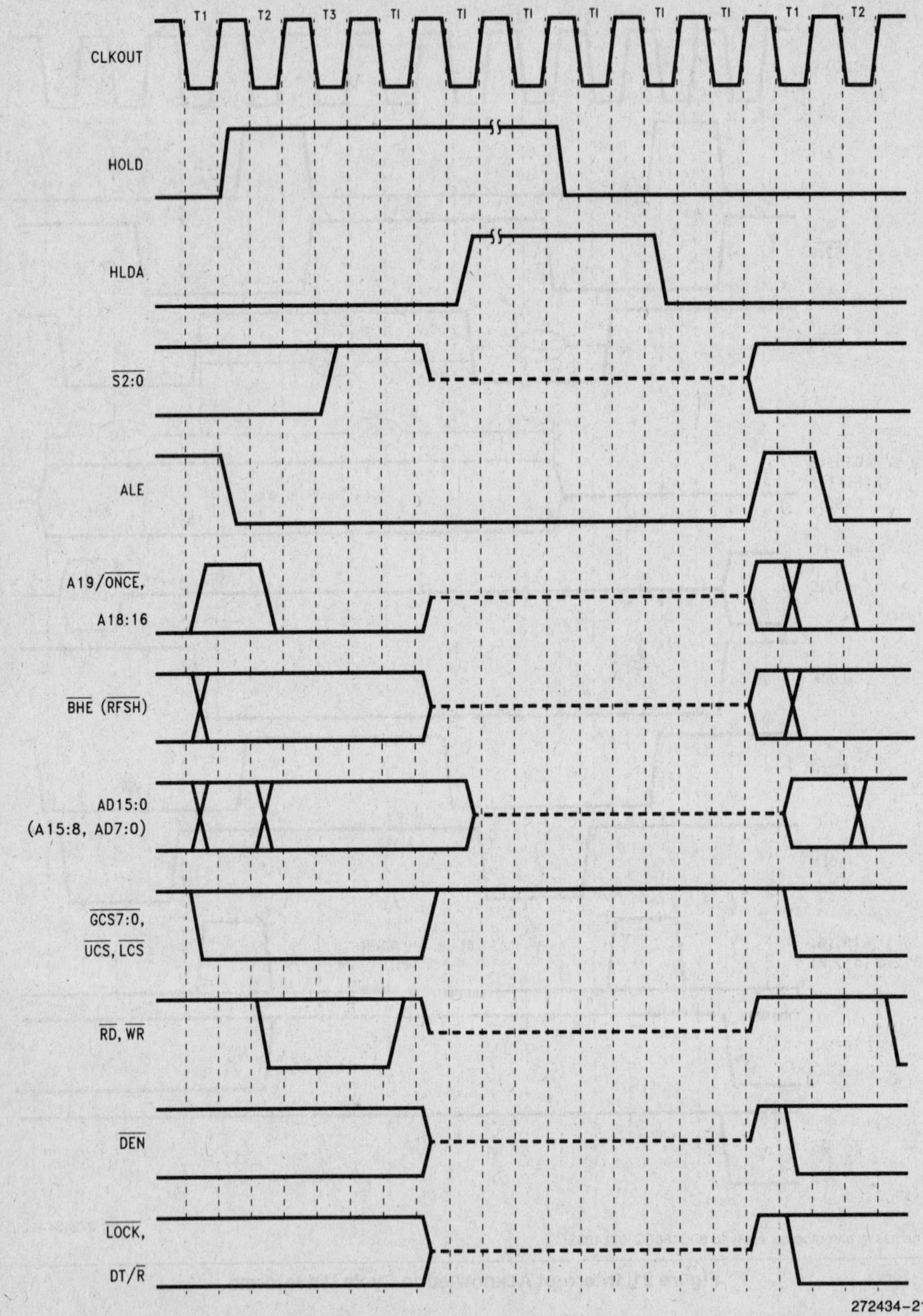

Pin names in parentheses apply to 80C188EC/80L188EC.

272434-21

Figure 22. HOLD/HLDA Cycle Waveforms

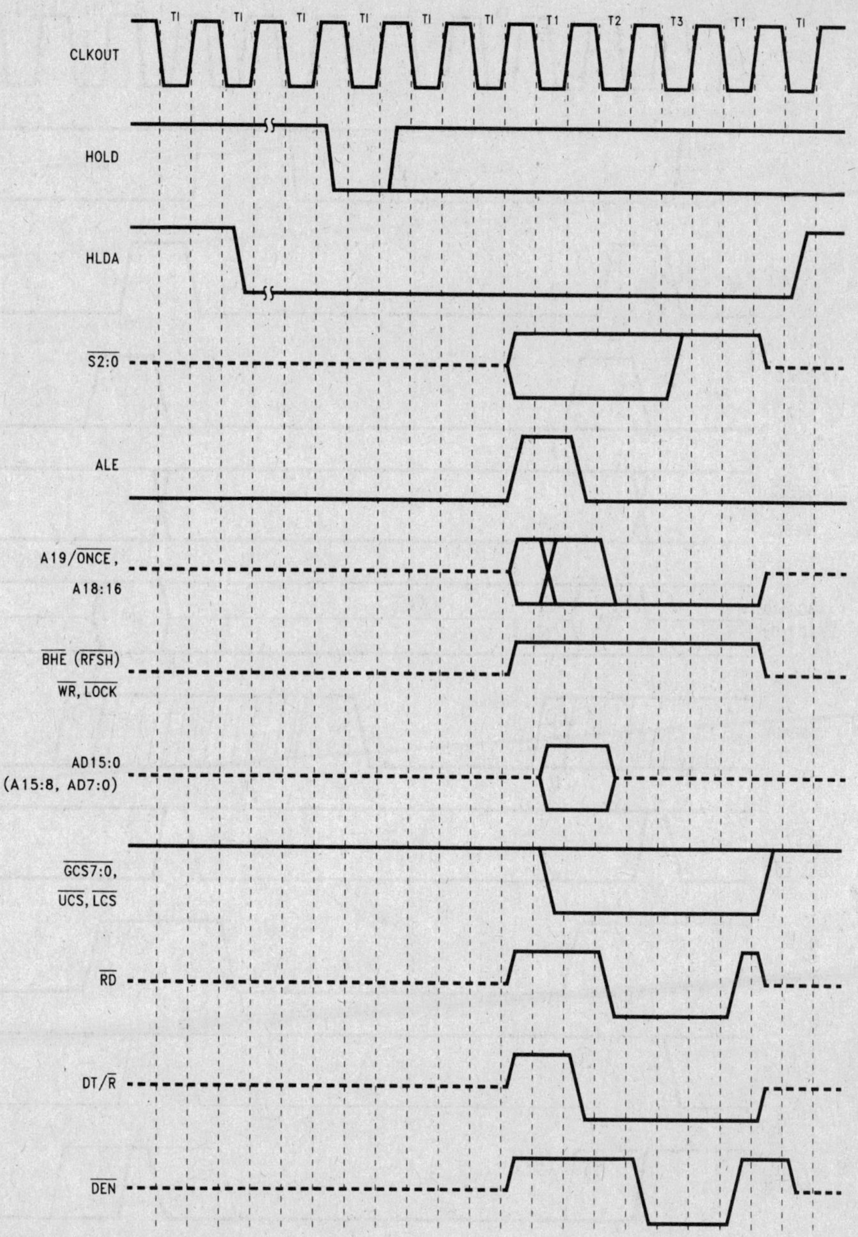

Pin names in parentheses apply to 80C188EC/80L188EC.

Figure 23. Refresh during HLDA Waveforms

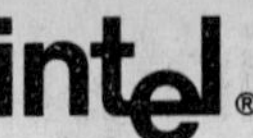

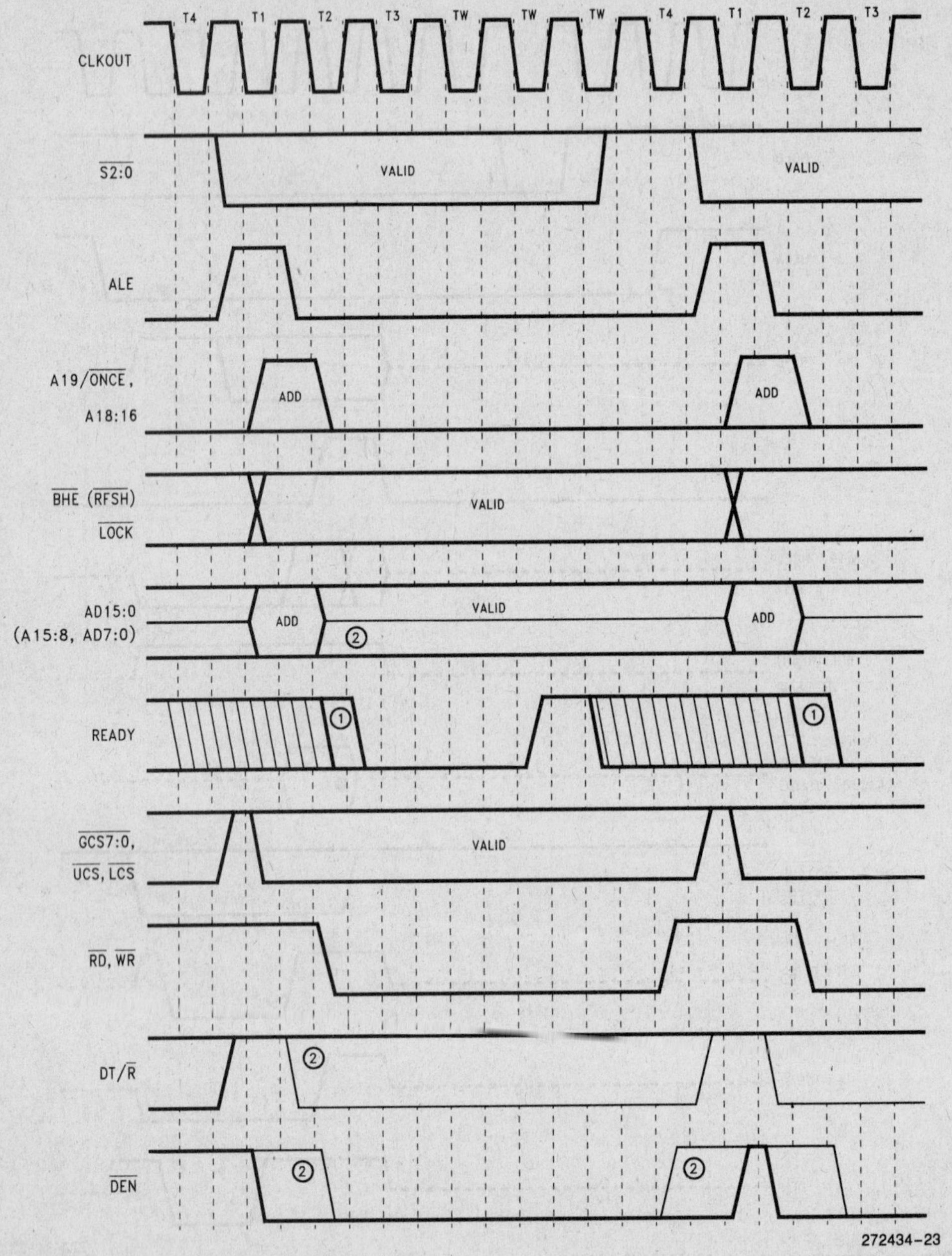

NOTES:
1. $\overline{READY}$ must be low by either edge to cause a wait state.
2. Lighter lines indicate READ cycles, darker lines indicate WRITE cycles.

Pin names in parentheses apply to 80C188EC/80L188EC.

Figure 24. READY Cycle Waveforms

80C186EC/80C188EC EXECUTION TIMINGS

A determination of program execution timing must consider the bus cycles necessary to prefetch instructions as well as the number of execution unit cycles necessary to execute instructions. The following instruction timings represent the **minimum** execution time in clock cycles for each instruction. The timings given are based on the following assumptions:

- The opcode, along with any data or displacement required for execution of a particular instruction, has been prefetched and resides in the queue at the time it is needed.
- No wait states or bus HOLDs occur.
- All word-data is located on even-address boundaries (80C186EC only).

All jumps and calls include the time required to fetch the opcode of the next instruction at the destination address.

All instructions which involve memory accesses can require one or two additional clocks above the minimum timings shown due to the asynchronous handshake between the bus interface unit (BIU) and execution unit.

With a 16-bit BIU, the 80C186EC has sufficient bus performance to ensure that an adequate number of prefetched bytes will reside in the queue (6 bytes) most of the time. Therefore, actual program execution time will not be substantially greater than that derived from adding the instruction timings shown.

The 80C188EC 8-bit BIU is limited in its performance relative to the execution unit. A sufficient number of prefetched bytes may not reside in the prefetch queue (4 bytes) much of the time. Therefore, actual program execution time will be substantially greater than that derived from adding the instruction timings shown.

INSTRUCTION SET SUMMARY

Function	Format				80C186EC Clock Cycles	80C188EC Clock Cycles	Comments
DATA TRANSFER							
MOV = **Move:**							
Register to Register/Memory	1000100w	mod reg r/m			2/12	2/12*	
Register/memory to register	1000101w	mod reg r/m			2/9	2/9*	
Immediate to register/memory	1100011w	mod 000 r/m	data	data if w=1	12/13	12/13	8/16-bit
Immediate to register	1011w reg	data	data if w=1		3/4	3/4	8/16-bit
Memory to accumulator	1010000w	addr-low	addr-high		8	8*	
Accumulator to memory	1010001w	addr-low	addr-high		9	9*	
Register/memory to segment register	10001110	mod 0 reg r/m			2/9	2/13	
Segment register to register/memory	10001100	mod 0 reg r/m			2/11	2/15	
PUSH = **Push:**							
Memory	11111111	mod 110 r/m			16	20	
Register	01010 reg				10	14	
Segment register	000reg110				9	13	
Immediate	011010s0	data	data if s=0		10	14	
PUSHA = **Push All**	01100000				36	68	
POP = **Pop:**							
Memory	10001111	mod 000 r/m			20	24	
Register	01011 reg				10	14	
Segment register	000reg111	(reg≠01)			8	12	
POPA = Pop All	01100001				51	83	
XCHG = **Exchange:**							
Register/memory with register	1000011w	mod reg r/m			4/17	4/17*	
Register with accumulator	10010 reg				3	3	
IN = **Input from:**							
Fixed port	1110010w	port			10	10*	
Variable port	1110110w				8	8*	
OUT = **Output to:**							
Fixed port	1110011w	port			9	9*	
Variable port	1110111w				7	7*	
XLAT = Translate byte to AL	11010111				11	15	
LEA = Load EA to register	10001101	mod reg r/m			6	6	
LDS = Load pointer to DS	11000101	mod reg r/m	(mod≠11)		18	26	
LES = Load pointer to ES	11000100	mod reg r/m	(mod≠11)		18	26	
LAHF = Load AH with flags	10011111				2	2	
SAHF = Store AH into flags	10011110				3	3	
PUSHF = Push flags	10011100				9	13	
POPF = Pop flags	10011101				8	12	

Shaded areas indicate instructions not available in 8086/8088 microsystems.

NOTE:
*Clock cycles shown for byte transfers, for word operations, add 4 clock cycles for all memory transfers.

INSTRUCTION SET SUMMARY (Continued)

Function	Format				80C186EC Clock Cycles	80C188EC Clock Cycles	Comments
DATA TRANSFER (Continued)							
SEGMENT = Segment Override:							
CS	00101110				2	2	
SS	00110110				2	2	
DS	00111110				2	2	
ES	00100110				2	2	
ARITHMETIC							
ADD = Add:							
Reg/memory with register to either	000000dw	mod reg r/m			3/10	3/10*	
Immediate to register/memory	100000sw	mod 000 r/m	data	data if s w=01	4/16	4/16*	
Immediate to accumulator	0000010w	data	data if w=1		3/4	3/4	8/16-bit
ADC = Add with carry:							
Reg/memory with register to either	000100dw	mod reg r/m			3/10	3/10*	
Immediate to register/memory	100000sw	mod 010 r/m	data	data if s w=01	4/16	4/16*	
Immediate to accumulator	0001010w	data	data if w=1		3/4	3/4	8/16-bit
INC = Increment:							
Register/memory	1111111w	mod 000 r/m			3/15	3/15*	
Register	01000 reg				3	3	
SUB = Subtract:							
Reg/memory and register to either	001010dw	mod reg r/m			3/10	3/10*	
Immediate from register/memory	100000sw	mod 101 r/m	data	data if s w=01	4/16	4/16*	
Immediate from accumulator	0010110w	data	data if w=1		3/4	3/4*	8/16-bit
SBB = Subtract with borrow:							
Reg/memory and register to either	000110dw	mod reg r/m			3/10	3/10*	
Immediate from register/memory	100000sw	mod 011 r/m	data	data if s w=01	4/16	4/16*	
Immediate from accumulator	0001110w	data	data if w=1		3/4	3/4*	8/16-bit
DEC = Decrement							
Register/memory	1111111w	mod 001 r/m			3/15	3/15*	
Register	01001 reg				3	3	
CMP = Compare:							
Register/memory with register	0011101w	mod reg r/m			3/10	3/10*	
Register with register/memory	0011100w	mod reg r/m			3/10	3/10*	
Immediate with register/memory	100000sw	mod 111 r/m	data	data if s w=01	3/10	3/10*	
Immediate with accumulator	0011110w	data	data if w=1		3/4	3/4	8/16-bit
NEG = Change sign register/memory	1111011w	mod 011 r/m			3/10	3/10*	
AAA = ASCII adjust for add	00110111				8	8	
DAA = Decimal adjust for add	00100111				4	4	
AAS = ASCII adjust for subtract	00111111				7	7	
DAS = Decimal adjust for subtract	00101111				4	4	
MUL = Multiply (unsigned):	1111011w	mod 100 r/m					
Register-Byte					26–28	26–28	
Register-Word					35–37	35–37	
Memory-Byte					32–34	32–34	
Memory-Word					41–43	41–43*	

Shaded areas indicate instructions not available in 8086/8088 microsystems.

NOTE:
*Clock cycles shown for byte transfers, for word operations, add 4 clock cycles for all memory transfers.

INSTRUCTION SET SUMMARY (Continued)

Function	Format				80C186EC Clock Cycles	80C188EC Clock Cycles	Comments
ARITHMETIC (Continued)							
IMUL = Integer multiply (signed):	1111011w	mod 101 r/m					
Register-Byte					25–28	25–28	
Register-Word					34–37	34–37	
Memory-Byte					31–34	32–34	
Memory-Word					40–43	40–43*	
IMUL = Integer Immediate multiply (signed)	011010s1	mod reg r/m	data	data if s=0	22–25/ 29–32	22–25/ 29–32	
DIV = Divide (unsigned):	1111011w	mod 110 r/m					
Register-Byte					29	29	
Register-Word					38	38	
Memory-Byte					35	35	
Memory-Word					44	44*	
IDIV = Integer divide (signed):	1111011w	mod 111 r/m					
Register-Byte					44–52	44–52	
Register-Word					53–61	53–61	
Memory-Byte					50–58	50–58	
Memory-Word					59–67	59–67*	
AAM = ASCII adjust for multiply	11010100	00001010			19	19	
AAD = ASCII adjust for divide	11010101	00001010			15	15	
CBW = Convert byte to word	10011000				2	2	
CWD = Convert word to double word	10011001				4	4	
LOGIC							
Shift/Rotate Instructions:							
Register/Memory by 1	1101000w	mod TTT r/m			2/15	2/15	
Register/Memory by CL	1101001w	mod TTT r/m			5+n/17+n	5+n/17+n	
Register/Memory by Count	1100000w	mod TTT r/m	count		5+n/17+n	5+n/17+n	
	TTT Instruction						
	000 ROL						
	001 ROR						
	010 RCL						
	011 RCR						
	100 SHL/SAL						
	101 SHR						
	111 SAR						
AND = And:							
Reg/memory and register to either	001000dw	mod reg r/m			3/10	3/10*	
Immediate to register/memory	1000000w	mod 100 r/m	data	data if w=1	4/16	4/16*	
Immediate to accumulator	0010010w	data	data if w=1		3/4	3/4*	8/16-bit
TEST = And function to flags, no result:							
Register/memory and register	1000010w	mod reg r/m			3/10	3/10	
Immediate data and register/memory	1111011w	mod 000 r/m	data	data if w=1	4/10	4/10*	
Immediate data and accumulator	1010100w	data	data if w=1		3/4	3/4	8/16-bit
OR = Or:							
Reg/memory and register to either	000010dw	mod reg r/m			3/10	3/10*	
Immediate to register/memory	1000000w	mod 001 r/m	data	data if w=1	4/16	4/16*	
Immediate to accumulator	0000110w	data	data if w=1		3/4	3/4*	8/16-bit

Shaded areas indicate instructions not available in 8086/8088 microsystems.

NOTE:
*Clock cycles shown for byte transfers, for word operations, add 4 clock cycles for all memory transfers.

INSTRUCTION SET SUMMARY (Continued)

Function	Format				80C186EC Clock Cycles	80C188EC Clock Cycles	Comments
LOGIC (Continued)							
XOR = Exclusive or:							
Reg/memory and register to either	001100dw	mod reg r/m			3/10	3/10*	
Immediate to register/memory	1000000w	mod 1 1 0 r/m	data	data if w=1	4/16	4/16*	
Immediate to accumulator	0011010w	data	data if w=1		3/4	3/4	8/16-bit
NOT = Invert register/memory	1111011w	mod 0 1 0 r/m			3/10	3/10*	
STRING MANIPULATION							
MOVS = Move byte/word	1010010w				14	14*	
CMPS = Compare byte/word	1010011w				22	22*	
SCAS = Scan byte/word	1010111w				15	15*	
LODS = Load byte/wd to AL/AX	1010110w				12	12*	
STOS = Store byte/wd from AL/AX	1010101w				10	10*	
INS = Input byte/wd from DX port	0110110w				14	14	
OUTS = Output byte/wd to DX port	0110111w				14	14	
Repeated by count in CX (REP/REPE/REPZ/REPNE/REPNZ)							
MOVS = Move string	11110010	1010010w			8+8n	8+8n*	
CMPS = Compare string	1111001z	1010011w			5+22n	5+22n*	
SCAS = Scan string	1111001z	1010111w			5+15n	5+15n*	
LODS = Load string	11110010	1010110w			6+11n	6+11n*	
STOS = Store string	11110010	1010101w			6+9n	6+9n*	
INS = Input string	11110010	0110110w			8+8n	8+8n*	
OUTS = Output string	11110010	0110111w			8+8n	8+8n*	
CONTROL TRANSFER							
CALL = Call:							
Direct within segment	11101000	disp-low	disp-high		15	19	
Register/memory indirect within segment	11111111	mod 0 1 0 r/m			13/19	17/27	
Direct intersegment	10011010	segment offset			23	31	
		segment selector					
Indirect intersegment	11111111	mod 0 1 1 r/m	(mod ≠ 11)		38	54	
JMP = Unconditional jump:							
Short/long	11101011	disp-low			14	14	
Direct within segment	11101001	disp-low	disp-high		14	14	
Register/memory indirect within segment	11111111	mod 1 0 0 r/m			11/17	11/21	
Direct intersegment	11101010	segment offset			14	14	
		segment selector					
Indirect intersegment	11111111	mod 1 0 1 r/m	(mod ≠ 11)		26	34	

Shaded areas indicate instructions not available in 8086/8088 microsystems.

NOTE:
*Clock cycles shown for byte transfers, for word operations, add 4 clock cycles for all memory transfers.

2

INSTRUCTION SET SUMMARY (Continued)

Function	Format	80C186EC Clock Cycles	80C188EC Clock Cycles	Comments
CONTROL TRANSFER (Continued)				
RET = Return from CALL:				
Within segment	11000011	16	20	
Within seg adding immed to SP	11000010 | data-low | data-high	18	22	
Intersegment	11001011	22	30	
Intersegment adding immediate to SP	11001010 | data-low | data-high	25	33	
JE/JZ = Jump on equal/zero	01110100 | disp	4/13	4/13	JMP not taken/JMP taken
JL/JNGE = Jump on less/not greater or equal	01111100 | disp	4/13	4/13	
JLE/JNG = Jump on less or equal/not greater	01111110 | disp	4/13	4/13	
JB/JNAE = Jump on below/not above or equal	01110010 | disp	4/13	4/13	
JBE/JNA = Jump on below or equal/not above	01110110 | disp	4/13	4/13	
JP/JPE = Jump on parity/parity even	01111010 | disp	4/13	4/13	
JO = Jump on overflow	01110000 | disp	4/13	4/13	
JS = Jump on sign	01111000 | disp	4/13	4/13	
JNE/JNZ = Jump on not equal/not zero	01110101 | disp	4/13	4/13	
JNL/JGE = Jump on not less/greater or equal	01111101 | disp	4/13	4/13	
JNLE/JG = Jump on not less or equal/greater	01111111 | disp	4/13	4/13	
JNB/JAE = Jump on not below/above or equal	01110011 | disp	4/13	4/13	
JNBE/JA = Jump on not below or equal/above	01110111 | disp	4/13	4/13	
JNP/JPO = Jump on not par/par odd	01111011 | disp	4/13	4/13	
JNO = Jump on not overflow	01110001 | disp	4/13	4/13	
JNS = Jump on not sign	01111001 | disp	4/13	4/13	
JCXZ = Jump on CX zero	11100011 | disp	5/15	5/15	
LOOP = Loop CX times	11100010 | disp	6/16	6/16	LOOP not taken/LOOP taken
LOOPZ/LOOPE = Loop while zero/equal	11100001 | disp	6/16	6/16	
LOOPNZ/LOOPNE = Loop while not zero/equal	11100000 | disp	6/16	6/16	
ENTER = Enter Procedure	11001000 | data-low | data-high | L			
L = 0		15	19	
L = 1		25	29	
L > 1		22 + 16(n − 1)	26 + 20(n − 1)	
LEAVE = Leave Procedure	11001001	8	8	
INT = Interrupt:				
Type specified	11001101 | type	47	47	
Type 3	11001100	45	45	if INT. taken/ if INT. not taken
INTO = Interrupt on overflow	11001110	48/4	48/4	
IRET = Interrupt return	11001111	28	28	
BOUND = Detect value out of range	01100010 | mod reg r/m	33–35	33–35	

Shaded areas indicate instructions not available in 8086/8088 microsystems.

NOTE:
*Clock cycles shown for byte transfers, for word operations, add 4 clock cycles for all memory transfers.

INSTRUCTION SET SUMMARY (Continued)

Function	Format	80C186EC Clock Cycles	80C188EC Clock Cycles	Comments
PROCESSOR CONTROL				
CLC = Clear carry	11111000	2	2	
CMC = Complement carry	11110101	2	2	
STC = Set carry	11111001	2	2	
CLD = Clear direction	11111100	2	2	
STD = Set direction	11111101	2	2	
CLI = Clear interrupt	11111010	2	2	
STI = Set interrupt	11111011	2	2	
HLT = Halt	11110100	2	2	
WAIT = Wait	10011011	6	6	if $\overline{TEST}$ = 0
LOCK = Bus lock prefix	11110000	2	2	
NOP = No Operation	10010000	3	3	
	(TTT LLL are opcode to processor extension)			

Shaded areas indicate instructions not available in 8086/8088 microsystems.

NOTE:
*Clock cycles shown for byte transfers, for word operations, add 4 clock cycles for all memory transfers.

The Effective Address (EA) of the memory operand is computed according to the mod and r/m fields:

if mod = 11 then r/m is treated as a REG field
if mod = 00 then DISP = 0*, disp-low and disp-high are absent
if mod = 01 then DISP = disp-low sign-extended to 16-bits, disp-high is absent
if mod = 10 then DISP = disp-high: disp-low
if r/m = 000 then EA = (BX) + (SI) + DISP
if r/m = 001 then EA = (BX) + (DI) + DISP
if r/m = 010 then EA = (BP) + (SI) + DISP
if r/m = 011 then EA = (BP) + (DI) + DISP
if r/m = 100 then EA = (SI) + DISP
if r/m = 101 then EA = (DI) + DISP
if r/m = 110 then EA = (BP) + DISP*
if r/m = 111 then EA = (BX) + DISP

DISP follows 2nd byte of instruction (before data if required)

*except if mod = 00 and r/m = 110 then EA = disp-high: disp-low.

EA calculation time is 4 clock cycles for all modes, and is included in the execution times given whenever appropriate.

Segment Override Prefix

0	0	1	reg	1	1	0

reg is assigned according to the following:

reg	Segment Register
00	ES
01	CS
10	SS
11	DS

REG is assigned according to the following table:

16-Bit (w = 1)	8-Bit (w = 0)
000 AX	000 AL
001 CX	001 CL
010 DX	010 DL
011 BX	011 BL
100 SP	100 AH
101 BP	101 CH
110 SI	110 DH
111 DI	111 BH

The physical addresses of all operands addressed by the BP register are computed using the SS segment register. The physical addresses of the destination operands of the string primitive operations (those addressed by the DI register) are computed using the ES segment, which may not be overridden.

ERRATA

An 80C186EC/80L186EC with a STEPID value of 0002H has no known errata. A device with a STEPID of 0002H can be visually identified by noting the **presence** of an "A" alpha character next to the FPO number or the absence of any alpha character. The FPO number location is shown in Figures 4, 5 and 6.

REVISION HISTORY

This data sheet replaces the following data sheets:

272072-003	80C186EC
272076-003	80C188EC
272332-001	80L186EC
272333-001	80L188EC
272373-001	SB80C188EC/SB80L188EC
272372-001	SB80C186EC/SB80L186EC

80C187
80-BIT MATH COPROCESSOR

- High Performance 80-Bit Internal Architecture
- Implements ANSI/IEEE Standard 754-1985 for Binary Floating-Point Arithmetic
- Upward Object-Code Compatible from 8087
- Fully Compatible with 387DX and 387SX Math Coprocessors. Implements all 387 Architectural Enhancements over 8087
- Directly Interfaces with 80C186 CPU
- 80C186/80C187 Provide a Software/Binary Compatible Upgrade from 80186/82188/8087 Systems
- Expands 80C186's Data Types to Include 32-, 64-, 80-Bit Floating-Point, 32-, 64-Bit Integers and 18-Digit BCD Operands
- Directly Extends 80C186's Instruction Set to Trigonometric, Logarithmic, Exponential, and Arithmetic Instructions for All Data Types
- Full-Range Transcendental Operations for SINE, COSINE, TANGENT, ARCTANGENT, and LOGARITHM
- Built-In Exception Handling
- Eight 80-Bit Numeric Registers, Usable as Individually Addressable General Registers or as a Register Stack
- Available in 40-Pin CERDIP and 44-Pin PLCC Package
  (See Packaging Outlines and Dimensions, Order #231369)

2

The Intel 80C187 is a high-performance math coprocessor that extends the architecture of the 80C186 with floating-point, extended integer, and BCD data types. A computing system that includes the 80C187 fully conforms to the IEEE Floating-Point Standard. The 80C187 adds over seventy mnemonics to the instruction set of the 80C186, including support for arithmetic, logarithmic, exponential, and trigonometric mathematical operations. The 80C187 is implemented with 1.5 micron, high-speed CHMOS III technology and packaged in both a 40-pin CERDIP and a 44-pin PLCC package. The 80C187 is upward object-code compatible from the 8087 math coprocessor and will execute code written for the 80387DX and 80387SX math coprocessors.

November 1992
Order Number: 270640-004

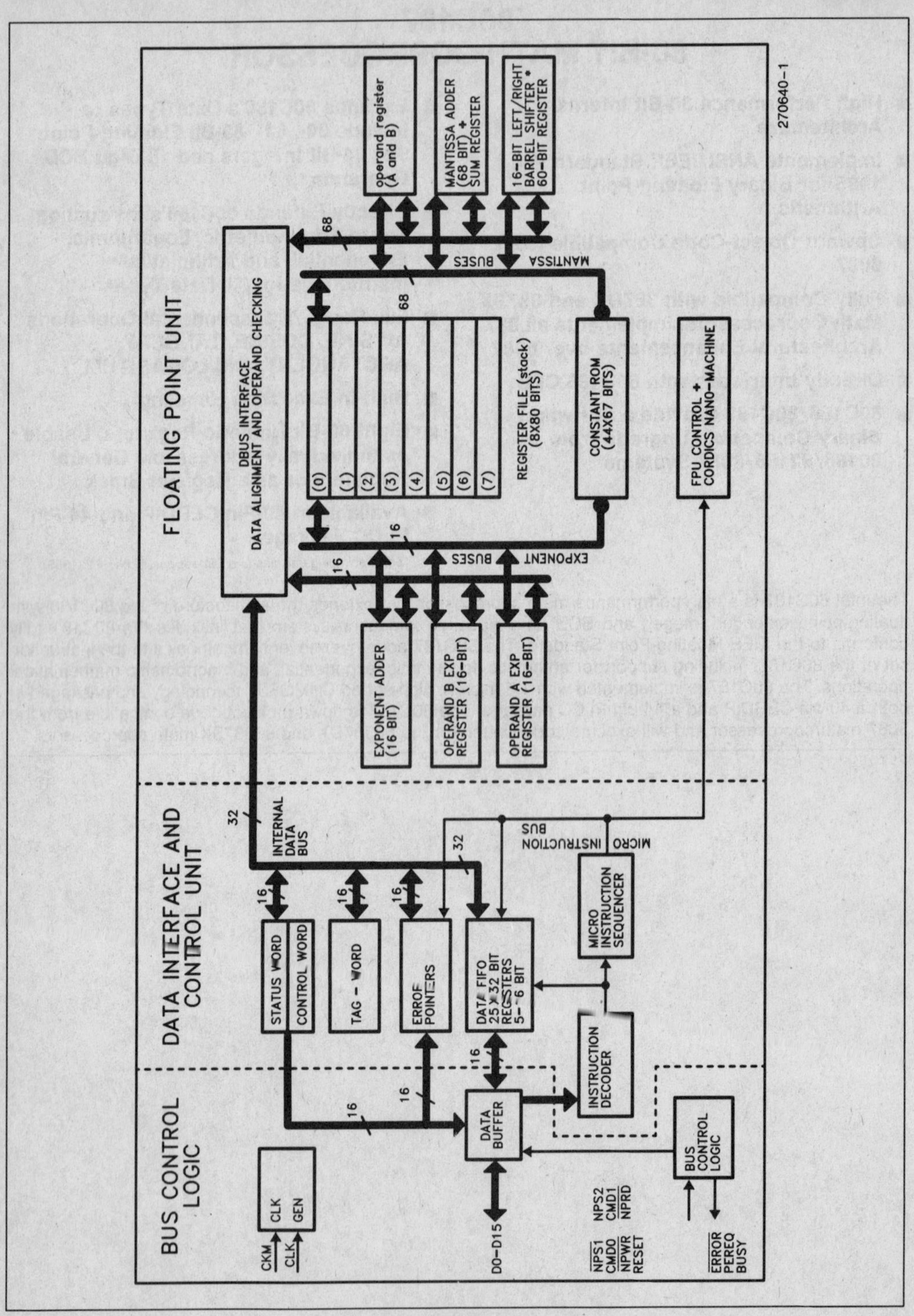

Figure 1. 80C187 Block Diagram

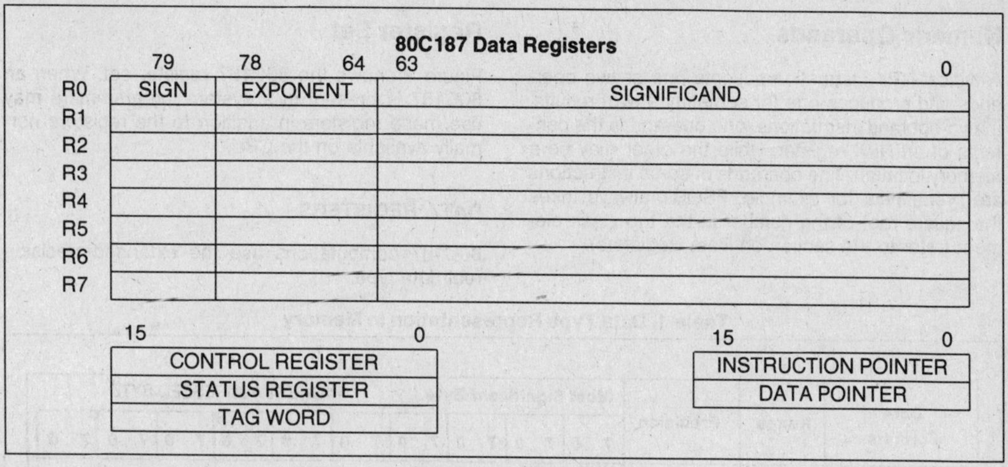

80C187 Data Registers

	79 SIGN	78 EXPONENT 64	63 SIGNIFICAND 0
R0			
R1			
R2			
R3			
R4			
R5			
R6			
R7			

15 0
CONTROL REGISTER
STATUS REGISTER
TAG WORD

15 0
INSTRUCTION POINTER
DATA POINTER

Figure 2. Register Set

FUNCTIONAL DESCRIPTION

The 80C187 Math Coprocessor provides arithmetic instructions for a variety of numeric data types. It also executes numerous built-in transcendental functions (e.g. tangent, sine, cosine, and log functions). The 80C187 effectively extends the register and instruction set of the 80C186 CPU for existing data types and adds several new data types as well. Figure 2 shows the additional registers visible to programs in a system that includes the 80C187. Essentially, the 80C187 can be treated as an additional resource or an extension to the CPU. The 80C186 CPU together with an 80C187 can be used as a single unified system.

A 80C186 system that includes the 80C187 is completely upward compatible with software for the 8086/8087.

The 80C187 interfaces only with the 80C186 CPU. The interface hardware for the 80C187 is not implemented on the 80C188.

PROGRAMMING INTERFACE

The 80C187 adds to the CPU additional data types, registers, instructions, and interrupts specifically designed to facilitate high-speed numerics processing. All new instructions and data types are directly supported by the assembler and compilers for high-level languages. The 80C187 also supports the full 80387DX instruction set.

All communication between the CPU and the 80C187 is transparent to applications software. The CPU automatically controls the 80C187 whenever a numerics instruction is executed. All physical memory and virtual memory of the CPU are available for storage of the instructions and operands of programs that use the 80C187. All memory addressing modes are available for addressing numerics operands.

The end of this data sheet lists by class the instructions that the 80C187 adds to the instruction set.

NOTE:
The 80C187 Math Coprocessor is also referred to as a Numeric Processor Extension (NPX) in this document.

Data Types

Table 1 lists the seven data types that the 80C187 supports and presents the format for each type. Operands are stored in memory with the least significant digit at the lowest memory address. Programs retrieve these values by generating the lowest address. For maximum system performance, all operands should start at even physical-memory addresses; operands may begin at odd addresses, but will require extra memory cycles to access the entire operand.

Internally, the 80C187 holds all numbers in the extended-precision real format. Instructions that load operands from memory automatically convert operands represented in memory as 16-, 32-, or 64-bit integers, 32- or 64-bit floating-point numbers, or 18-digit packed BCD numbers into extended-precision real format. Instructions that store operands in memory perform the inverse type conversion.

Numeric Operands

A typical NPX instruction accepts one or two operands and produces one (or sometimes two) results. In two-operand instructions, one operand is the contents of an NPX register, while the other may be a memory location. The operands of some instructions are predefined; for example, FSQRT always takes the square root of the number in the top stack element (refer to the section on Data Registers).

Register Set

Figure 2 shows the 80C187 register set. When an 80C187 is present in a system, programmers may use these registers in addition to the registers normally available on the CPU.

DATA REGISTERS

80C187 computations use the extended-precision real data type.

Table 1. Data Type Representation in Memory

Data Formats	Range	Precision	Most Significant Byte — HIGHEST ADDRESSED BYTE (7 0 | 7 0 | 7 0 | 7 0 | 7 0 | 7 0 | 7 0 | 7 0 | 7 0 | 7 0)
Word Integer	$\pm 10^4$	16 Bits	(TWO S COMPLEMENT) bits 15 … 0
Short Integer	$\pm 10^9$	32 Bits	(TWO S COMPLEMENT) bits 31 … 0
Long Integer	$\pm 10^{18}$	64 Bits	(TWO S COMPLEMENT) bits 63 … 0
Packed BCD	$\pm 10^{18}$	18 Digits	S (bit 79), X (bits 78–72), MAGNITUDE: d_{17} d_{16} d_{15} d_{14} d_{13} d_{12} d_{11} d_{10} d_9 d_8 d_7 d_6 d_5 d_4 d_3 d_2 d_1 d_0 (… bit 0)
Single Precision	$\pm 10^{\pm 38}$	24 Bits	S (bit 31), BIASED EXPONENT, SIGNIFICAND (bit 23 … 0); I ▲ at 23
Double Precision	$\pm 10^{\pm 308}$	53 Bits	S (bit 63), BIASED EXPONENT, SIGNIFICAND (bit 52 … 0); I ▲ at 52
Extended Precision	$\pm 10^{\pm 4932}$	64 Bits	S (bit 79), BIASED EXPONENT (… 64), I (bit 63), SIGNIFICAND (… 0)

070640-2

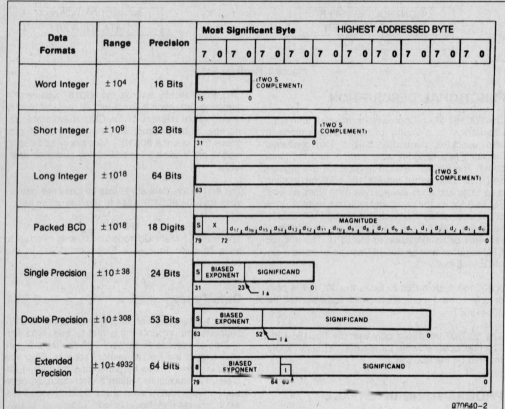

NOTES:
1. S = Sign bit (0 = Positive, 1 = Negative)
2. d_n = Decimal digit (two per byte)
3. X = Bits have no significance; 80C187 ignores when loading, zeros when storing
4. ▲ = Position of implicit binary point
5. I = Integer bit of significand; stored in temporary real, implicit in single and double precision
6. Exponent Bias (normalized values):
   Single: 127 (7FH)
   Double: 1023 (3FFH)
   Extended Real: 16383 (3FFFH)
7. Packed BCD: $(-1)^S (D_{17} \ldots D_0)$
8. Real: $(-1)^S (2^{E-BIAS}) (F_0, F_1 \ldots)$

The 80C187 register set can be accessed either as a stack, with instructions operating on the top one or two stack elements, or as individually addressable registers. The TOP field in the status word identifies the current top-of-stack register. A "push" operation decrements TOP by one and loads a value into the new top register. A "pop" operation stores the value from the current top register and then increments TOP by one. The 80C187 register stack grows "down" toward lower-addressed registers.

Instructions may address the data registers either implicitly or explicitly. Many instructions operate on the register at the TOP of the stack. These instructions implicitly address the register at which TOP points. Other instructions allow the programmer to explicitly specify which register to use. This explicit addressing is also relative to TOP.

TAG WORD

The tag word marks the content of each numeric data register, as Figure 3 shows. Each two-bit tag represents one of the eight data registers. The principal function of the tag word is to optimize the NPX's performance and stack handling by making it possible to distinguish between empty and nonempty register locations. It also enables exception handlers to identify special values (e.g. NaNs or denormals) in the contents of a stack location without the need to perform complex decoding of the actual data.

STATUS WORD

The 16-bit status word (in the status register) shown in Figure 4 reflects the overall state of the 80C187. It may be read and inspected by programs.

Bit 15, the B-bit (busy bit) is included for 8087 compatibility only. It always has the same value as the ES bit (bit 7 of the status word); it does **not** indicate the status of the BUSY output of 80C187.

Bits 13–11 (TOP) point to the 80C187 register that is the current top-of-stack.

The four numeric condition code bits (C_3–C_0) are similar to the flags in a CPU; instructions that perform arithmetic operations update these bits to reflect the outcome. The effects of these instructions on the condition code are summarized in Tables 2 through 5.

Bit 7 is the error summary (ES) status bit. This bit is set if any unmasked exception bit is set; it is clear otherwise. If this bit is set, the $\overline{\text{ERROR}}$ signal is asserted.

Bit 6 is the stack flag (SF). This bit is used to distinguish invalid operations due to stack overflow or underflow from other kinds of invalid operations. When SF is set, bit 9 (C_1) distinguishes between stack overflow ($C_1 = 1$) and underflow ($C_1 = 0$).

Figure 4 shows the six exception flags in bits 5–0 of the status word. Bits 5–0 are set to indicate that the 80C187 has detected an exception while executing an instruction. A later section entitled "Exception Handling" explains how they are set and used.

Note that when a new value is loaded into the status word by the FLDENV or FRSTOR instruction, the value of ES (bit 7) and its reflection in the B-bit (bit 15) are not derived from the values loaded from memory but rather are dependent upon the values of the exception flags (bits 5–0) in the status word and their corresponding masks in the control word. If ES is set in such a case, the $\overline{\text{ERROR}}$ output of the 80C187 is activated immediately.

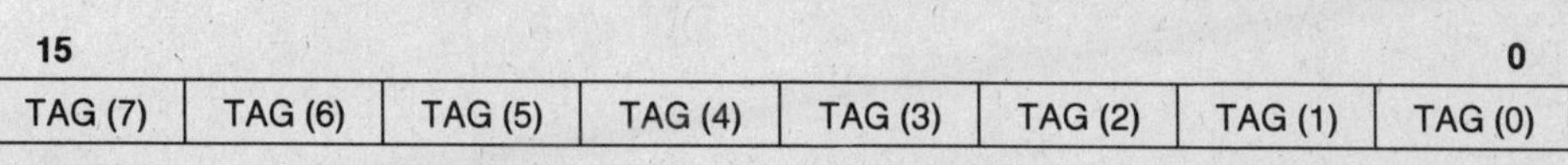

NOTE:
The index i of tag(i) is **not** top-relative. A program typically uses the "top" field of Status Word to determine which tag(i) field refers to logical top of stack.
TAG VALUES:
00 = Valid
01 = Zero
10 = QNaN, SNaN, Infinity, Denormal and Unsupported Formats
11 = Empty

Figure 3. Tag Word

BUSY
TOP OF STACK POINTER
CONDITION CODE
15
7
0
B
C3
TOP
C2
C1
C0
ES
SF
PE
UE
OE
ZE
DE
IE
ERROR SUMMARY STATUS
STACK FLAG
EXCEPTION FLAGS:
PRECISION
UNDERFLOW
OVERFLOW
ZERO DIVIDE
DENORMALIZED OPERAND
INVALID OPERATION
270640-3
ES is set if any unmasked exception bit is set; cleared otherwise.
See Table 2 for interpretation of condition code.
TOP values:
000 = Register 0 is Top of Stack
001 = Register 1 is Top of Stack
•
•
•
111 = Register 7 is Top of Stack
For definitions of exceptions, refer to the section entitled, "Exception Handling"

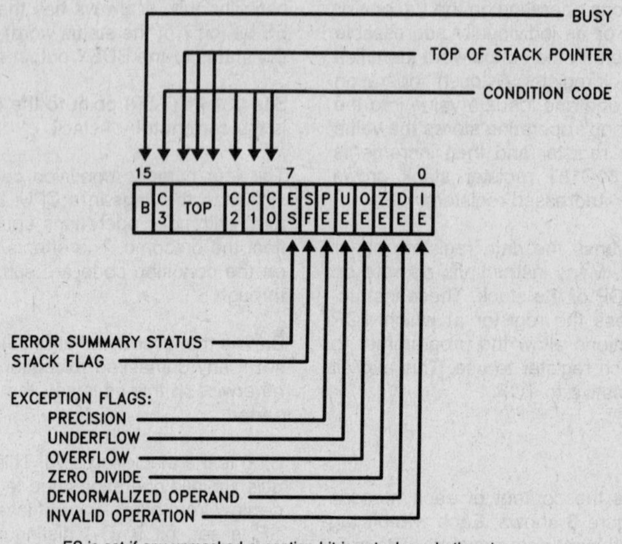

Figure 4. Status Word

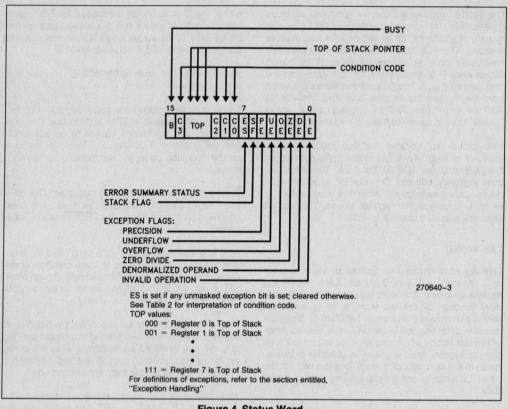

CONTROL WORD

The NPX provides several processing options that are selected by loading a control word from memory into the control register. Figure 5 shows the format and encoding of fields in the control word.

Table 2. Condition Code Interpretation

Instruction	C0(S)	C3(Z)	C1(A)	C2(C)
FPREM, FPREM1 (See Table 3)	Three Least Significant Bits of Quotient Q2	Q0	Q1 or O/Ū	Reduction 0 = Complete 1 = Incomplete
FCOM, FCOMP, FCOMPP, FTST FUCOM, FUCOMP, FUCOMPP, FICOM, FICOMP	Result of Comparison (See Table 4)		Zero or O/Ū	Operand is not Comparable (Table 4)
FXAM	Operand Class (See Table 5)		Sign or O/Ū	Operand Class (Table 5)
FCHS, FABS, FXCH, FINCSTP, FDECSTP, Constant Loads, FXTRACT, FLD, FILD, FBLD, FSTP (Ext Real)	UNDEFINED		Zero or O/Ū	UNDEFINED
FIST, FBSTP, FRNDINT, FST, FSTP, FADD, FMUL, FDIV, FDIVR, FSUB, FSUBR, FSCALE, FSQRT, FPATAN, F2XM1, FYL2X, FYL2XP1	UNDEFINED		Roundup or O/Ū	UNDEFINED
FPTAN, FSIN, FCOS, FSINCOS	UNDEFINED		Roundup or O/Ū, Undefined if C2 = 1	Reduction 0 = Complete 1 = Incomplete
FLDENV, FRSTOR	Each Bit Loaded from Memory			
FLDCW, FSTENV, FSTCW, FSTSW, FCLEX, FINIT, FSAVE	UNDEFINED			

O/Ū — When both IE and SF bits of status word are set, indicating a stack exception, this bit distinguishes between stack overflow (C1 = 1) and underflow (C1 = 0).

Reduction — If FPREM or FPREM1 produces a remainder that is less than the modulus, reduction is complete. When reduction is incomplete the value at the top of the stack is a partial remainder, which can be used as input to further reduction. For FPTAN, FSIN, FCOS, and FSINCOS, the reduction bit is set if the operand at the top of the stack is too large. In this case the original operand remains at the top of the stack.

Roundup — When the PE bit of the status word is set, this bit indicates whether one was added to the least significant bit of the result during the last rounding.

UNDEFINED — Do not rely on finding any specific value in these bits.

The low-order byte of this control word configures exception masking. Bits 5–0 of the control word contain individual masks for each of the six exceptions that the 80C187 recognizes.

The high-order byte of the control word configures the 80C187 operating mode, including precision, rounding, and infinity control.

- The "infinity control bit" (bit 12) is not meaningful to the 80C187, and programs must ignore its value. To maintain compatibility with the 8087, this bit can be programmed; however, regardless of its value, the 80C187 always treats infinity in the affine sense ($-\infty < +\infty$). This bit is initialized to zero both after a hardware reset and after the FINIT instruction.
- The rounding control (RC) bits (bits 11–10) provide for directed rounding and true chop, as well as the unbiased round to nearest even mode specified in the IEEE standard. Rounding control affects only those instructions that perform rounding at the end of the operation (and thus can generate a precision exception); namely, FST, FSTP, FIST, all arithmetic instructions (except FPREM, FPREM1, FXTRACT, FABS, and FCHS), and all transcendental instructions.
- The precision control (PC) bits (bits 9–8) can be used to set the 80C187 internal operating precision of the significand at less than the default of 64 bits (extended precision). This can be useful in providing compatibility with early generation arithmetic processors of smaller precision. PC affects only the instructions ADD, SUB, DIV, MUL, and SQRT. For all other instructions, either the precision is determined by the opcode or extended precision is used.

Table 3. Condition Code Interpretation after FPREM and FPREM1 Instructions

Condition Code					Interpretation after FPREM and FPREM1
C2	C3	C1	C0		
1	X	X	X		Incomplete Reduction: Further Iteration Required for Complete Reduction
0	Q1	Q0	Q2	Q MOD 8	Complete Reduction: C0, C3, C1 Contain Three Least Significant Bits of Quotient
	0	0	0	0	
	0	1	0	1	
	1	0	0	2	
	1	1	0	3	
	0	0	1	4	
	0	1	1	5	
	1	0	1	6	
	1	1	1	7	

Table 4. Condition Code Resulting from Comparison

Order	C3	C2	C0
TOP > Operand	0	0	0
TOP < Operand	0	0	1
TOP = Operand	1	0	0
Unordered	1	1	1

Table 5. Condition Code Defining Operand Class

C3	C2	C1	C0	Value at TOP
0	0	0	0	+ Unsupported
0	0	0	1	+ NaN
0	0	1	0	− Unsupported
0	0	1	1	− NaN
0	1	0	0	+ Normal
0	1	0	1	+ Infinity
0	1	1	0	− Normal
0	1	1	1	− Infinity
1	0	0	0	+ 0
1	0	0	1	+ Empty
1	0	1	0	− 0
1	0	1	1	− Empty
1	1	0	0	+ Denormal
1	1	1	1	− Denormal

2

INSTRUCTION AND DATA POINTERS

Because the NPX operates in parallel with the CPU, any exceptions detected by the NPX may be reported after the CPU has executed the ESC instruction which caused it. To allow identification of the failing numerics instruction, the 80C187 contains registers that aid in diagnosis. These registers supply the opcode of the failing numerics instruction, the address of the instruction, and the address of its numerics memory operand (if appropriate).

The instruction and data pointers are provided for user-written exception handlers. Whenever the 80C187 executes a new ESC instruction, it saves the address of the instruction (including any prefixes that may be present), the address of the operand (if present), and the opcode.

The instruction and data pointers appear in the format shown by Figure 6. The ESC instruction FLDENV, FSTENV, FSAVE and FRSTOR are used to transfer these values between the registers and memory. Note that the value of the data pointer is *undefined* if the prior ESC instruction did not have a memory operand.

Interrupt Description

CPU interrupt 16 is used to report exceptional conditions while executing numeric programs. Interrupt 16 indicates that the previous numerics instruction caused an unmasked exception. The address of the faulty instruction and the address of its operand are stored in the instruction pointer and data pointer registers. Only ESC instructions can cause this interrupt. The CPU return address pushed onto the stack of the exception handler points to an ESC instruction (including prefixes). This instruction can be restarted after clearing the exception condition in the NPX. FNINIT, FNCLEX, FNSTSW, FNSTENV, and FNSAVE cannot cause this interrupt.

Exception Handling

The 80C187 detects six different exception conditions that can occur during instruction execution. Table 6 lists the exception conditions in order of precedence, showing for each the cause and the default action taken by the 80C187 if the exception is masked by its corresponding mask bit in the control word.

Any exception that is not masked by the control word sets the corresponding exception flag of the status word, sets the ES bit of the status word, and asserts the $\overline{\text{ERROR}}$ signal. When the CPU attempts to execute another ESC instruction, interrupt 16 occurs. The exception condition must be resolved via an interrupt service routine. The return address pushed onto the CPU stack upon entry to the service routine does not necessarily point to the failing instruction nor to the following instruction. The 80C187 saves the address of the floating-point instruction that caused the exception and the address of any memory operand required by that instruction.

If error trapping is required at the end of a series of numerics instructions (specifically, when the last ESC instruction modifies memory data and that data is used in subsequent nonnumerics instructions), it is necessary to insert the FNOP instruction to force the 80C187 to check its $\overline{\text{ERROR}}$ input.

RESERVED
(INFINITY CONTROL) *
ROUNDING CONTROL
PRECISION CONTROL

15 7 0

X X X X RC PC X X PM UM OM ZM DM IM

RESERVED

EXCEPTION MARKS:
PRECISION
UNDERFLOW
OVERFLOW
ZERO DIVIDE
DENORMALIZED OPERAND
INVALID OPERATION

270640–4

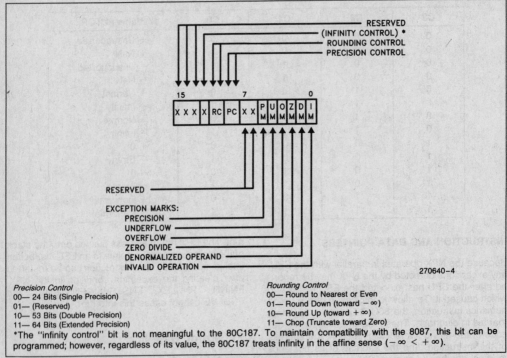

Precision Control
00— 24 Bits (Single Precision)
01— (Reserved)
10— 53 Bits (Double Precision)
11— 64 Bits (Extended Precision)

Rounding Control
00— Round to Nearest or Even
01— Round Down (toward $-\infty$)
10— Round Up (toward $+\infty$)
11— Chop (Truncate toward Zero)

*The "infinity control" bit is not meaningful to the 80C187. To maintain compatibility with the 8087, this bit can be programmed; however, regardless of its value, the 80C187 treats infinity in the affine sense ($-\infty < +\infty$).

Figure 5. Control Word

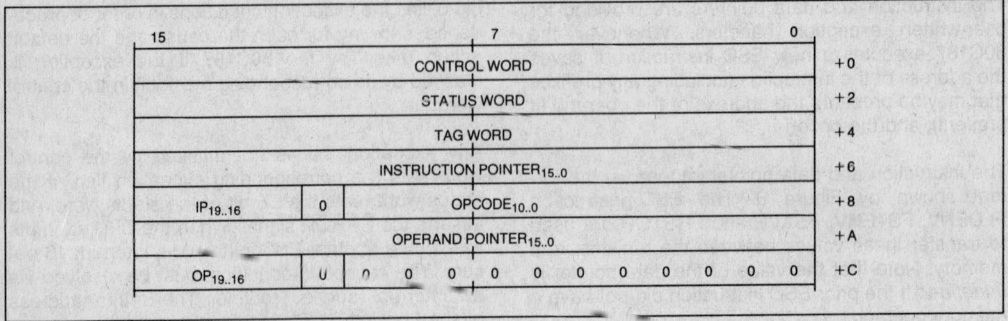

Figure 6. Instruction and Data Pointer Image in Memory

Table 6. Exceptions

Exception	Cause	Default Action (If Exception is Masked)
Invalid Operation	Operation on a signalling NaN, unsupported format, indeterminate form ($0*\infty$, 0/0), $(+\infty) + (-\infty)$, etc.), or stack overflow/underflow (SF is also set)	Result is a quiet NaN, integer indefinite, or BCD indefinite
Denormalized Operand	At least one of the operands is denormalized, i.e. it has the smallest exponent but a nonzero significand	The operand is normalized, and normal processing continues
Zero Divisor	The divisor is zero while the dividend is a noninfinite, nonzero number	Result is ∞
Overflow	The result is too large in magnitude to fit in the specified format	Result is largest finite value or ∞
Underflow	The true result is nonzero but too small to be represented in the specified format, and, if underflow exception is masked, denormalization causes loss of accuracy	Result is denormalized or zero
Inexact Result (Precision)	The true result is not exactly representable in the specified format (e.g. 1/3); the result is rounded according to the rounding mode	Normal processing continues

Initialization

After FNINIT or RESET, the control word contains the value 037FH (all exceptions masked, precision control 64 bits, rounding to nearest) the same values as in an 8087 after RESET. For compatibility with the 8087, the bit that used to indicate infinity control (bit 12) is set to zero; however, regardless of its setting, infinity is treated in the affine sense. After FNINIT or RESET, the status word is initialized as follows:

- All exceptions are set to zero.
- Stack TOP is zero, so that after the first push the stack top will be register seven (111B).
- The condition code C_3–C_0 is **undefined**.
- The B-bit is zero.

The tag word contains FFFFH (all stack locations are empty).

80C186/80C187 initialization software should execute an FNINIT instruction (i.e. an FINIT without a preceding WAIT) after RESET. The FNINIT is not strictly required for 80C187 software, but Intel recommends its use to help ensure upward compatibility with other processors.

8087 Compatibility

This section summarizes the differences between the 80C187 and the 8087. Many changes have been designed into the 80C187 to directly support the IEEE standard in hardware. These changes result in increased performance by elminating the need for software that supports the standard.

GENERAL DIFFERENCES

The 8087 instructions FENI/FNENI and FDISI/FNDISI perform no useful function in the 80C187 Numeric Processor Extension. They do not alter the state of the 80C187 Numeric Processor Extension. (They are treated similarly to FNOP, except that $\overline{\text{ERROR}}$ is not checked.) While 8086/8087 code containing these instructions can be executed on the 80C186/80C187, it is unlikely that the exception-handling routines containing these instructions will be completely portable to the 80C187 Numeric Processor Extension.

The 80C187 differs from the 8087 with respect to instruction, data, and exception synchronization. Except for the processor control instructions, all of the 80C187 numeric instructions are automatically synchronized by the 80C186 CPU. When necessary, the

2

80C186 automatically tests the BUSY line from the 80C187 Numeric Processor Extension to ensure that the 80C187 Numeric Processor Extension has completed its previous instruction before executing the next ESC instruction. No explicit WAIT instructions are required to assure this synchronization. For the 8087 used with 8086 and 8088 CPUs, explicit WAITs are required before each numeric instruction to ensure synchronization. Although 8086/8087 programs having explicit WAIT instructions will execute on the 80C186/80C187, these WAIT instructions are unnecessary.

The 80C187 supports only affine closure for infinity arithmetic, not projective closure.

Operands for FSCALE and FPATAN are no longer restricted in range (except for $\pm\infty$); F2XM1 and FPTAN accept a wider range of operands.

Rounding control is in effect for FLD *constant*.

Software cannot change entries of the tag word to values (other than empty) that differ from actual register contents.

After reset, FINIT, and incomplete FPREM, the 80C187 resets to zero the condition code bits C_3–C_0 of the status word.

In conformance with the IEEE standard, the 80C187 does not support the special data formats pseudozero, pseudo-NaN, pseudoinfinity, and unnormal.

The denormal exception has a different purpose on the 80C187. A system that uses the denormal-exception handler solely to normalize the denormal operands, would better mask the denormal exception on the 80C187. The 80C187 automatically normalizes denormal operands when the denormal exception is masked.

EXCEPTIONS

A number of differences exist due to changes in the IEEE standard and to functional improvements to the architecture of the 80C186/80C187:

1. The 80C186/80C187 traps exceptions only on the next ESC instruction; i.e. the 80C186 does not notice unmasked 80C187 exceptions on the 80C186 $\overline{\text{ERROR}}$ input line until a later numerics instruction is executed. Because the 80C186 does not sample $\overline{\text{ERROR}}$ on WAIT and FWAIT instructions, programmers should place an FNOP instruction at the end of a sequence of numerics instructions to force the 80C186 to sample its $\overline{\text{ERROR}}$ input.
2. The 80C187 Numeric Processor Extension signals exceptions through a dedicated $\overline{\text{ERROR}}$ line to the CPU. The 80C187 error signal does not pass through an interrupt controller (the 8087 INT signal does). Therefore, any interrupt-controller-oriented instructions in numerics exception handlers for the 8086/8087 should be deleted.
3. Interrupt vector 16 must point to the numerics exception handling routine.
4. The ESC instruction address saved in the 80C187 Numeric Processor Extension includes any leading prefixes before the ESC opcode. The corresponding address saved in the 8087 does not include leading prefixes.
5. When the overflow or underflow exception is masked, the 80C187 differs from the 8087 in rounding when overflow or underflow occurs. The 80C187 produces results that are consistent with the rounding mode.
6. When the underflow exception is masked, the 80C187 sets its underflow flag only if there is also a loss of accuracy during denormalization.
7. Fewer invalid-operation exceptions due to denormal operands, because the instructions FSQRT, FDIV, FPREM, and conversions to BCD or to integer normalize denormal operands before proceeding.
8. The FSQRT, FBSTP, and FPREM instructions may cause underflow, because they support denormal operands.
9. The denormal exception can occur during the transcendental instructions and the FXTRACT instruction.
10. The denormal exception no longer takes precedence over all other exceptions.
11. When the denormal exception is masked, the 80C187 automatically normalizes denormal operands. The 8087 performs unnormal arithmetic, which might produce an unnormal result.
12. When the operand is zero, the FXTRACT instruction reports a zero-divide exception and leaves $-\infty$ in ST(1).
13. The status word has a new bit (SF) that signals when invalid-operation exceptions are due to stack underflow or overflow.
14. FLD *extended precision* no longer reports denormal exceptions, because the instruction is not numeric.
15. FLD *single/double precision* when the operand is denormal converts the number to extended precision and signals the denormalized oper-

and exception. When loading a signalling NaN, FLD *single/double precision* signals an invalid-operand exception.

16. The 80C187 only generates quiet NaNs (as on the 8087); however, the 80C187 distinguishes between quiet NaNs and signalling NaNs. Signalling NaNs trigger exceptions when they are used as operands; quiet NaNs do not (except for FCOM, FIST, and FBSTP which also raise IE for quiet NaNs).

17. When stack overflow occurs during FPTAN and overflow is masked, both ST(0) and ST(1) contain quiet NaNs. The 8087 leaves the original operand in ST(1) intact.

18. When the scaling factor is ±∞, the FSCALE (ST(0), ST(1) instruction behaves as follows (ST(0) and ST(1) contain the scaled and scaling operands respectively):
    - FSCALE (0, ∞) generates the invalid operation exception.
    - FSCALE (finite, −∞) generates zero with the same sign as the scaled operand.
    - FSCALE (finite, +∞) generates ∞ with the same sign as the scaled operand.

    The 8087 returns zero in the first case and raises the invalid-operation exception in the other cases.

19. The 80C187 returns signed infinity/zero as the unmasked response to massive overflow/underflow. The 8087 supports a limited range for the scaling factor; within this range either massive overflow/underflow do not occur or undefined results are produced.

2

Table 7. Pin Summary

Pin Name	Function	Active State	Input/ Output
CLK	CLocK		I
CKM	ClocKing Mode		I
RESET	System reset	High	I
PEREQ	Processor Extension REQuest	High	O
BUSY	Busy status	High	O
$\overline{\text{ERROR}}$	Error status	Low	O
$D_{15}-D_0$	Data pins	High	I/O
$\overline{\text{NPRD}}$	Numeric Processor ReaD	Low	I
$\overline{\text{NPWR}}$	Numeric Processor WRite	Low	I
$\overline{\text{NPS1}}$	NPX select #1	Low	I
NPS2	NPX select #2	High	I
CMD0	CoMmanD 0	High	I
CMD1	CoMmanD 1	High	I
V_{CC}	System power		I
V_{SS}	System ground		I

HARDWARE INTERFACE

In the following description of hardware interface, an overbar above a signal name indicates that the active or asserted state occurs when the signal is at a low voltage. When no overbar is present above the signal name, the signal is asserted when at the high voltage level.

Signal Description

In the following signal descriptions, the 80C187 pins are grouped by function as follows:

1. Execution Control— CLK, CKM, RESET
2. NPX Handshake— PEREQ, BUSY, $\overline{ERROR}$
3. Bus Interface Pins— D_{15}–D_0, $\overline{NPWR}$, $\overline{NPRD}$
4. Chip/Port Select— $\overline{NPS1}$, NPS2, CMD0, CMD1
5. Power Supplies— V_{CC}, V_{SS}

Table 7 lists every pin by its identifier, gives a brief description of its function, and lists some of its characteristics. Figure 7 shows the locations of pins on the CERDIP package, while Figure 8 shows the locations of pins on the PLCC package. Table 8 helps to locate pin identifiers in Figures 7 and 8.

Clock (CLK)

This input provides the basic timing for internal operation. This pin does not require MOS-level input; it will operate at either TTL or MOS levels up to the maximum allowed frequency. A minimum frequency must be provided to keep the internal logic properly functioning. Depending on the signal on CKM, the signal on CLK can be divided by two to produce the internal clock signal (in which case CLK may be up to 32 MHz in frequency), or can be used directly (in which case CLK may be up to 12.5 MHz).

Clocking Mode (CKM)

This pin is a strapping option. When it is strapped to V_{CC} (HIGH), the CLK input is used directly; when strapped to V_{SS} (LOW), the CLK input is divided by two to produce the internal clock signal. During the RESET sequence, this input must be stable at least four internal clock cycles (i.e. CLK clocks when CKM is HIGH; 2 × CLK clocks when CKM is LOW) before RESET goes LOW.

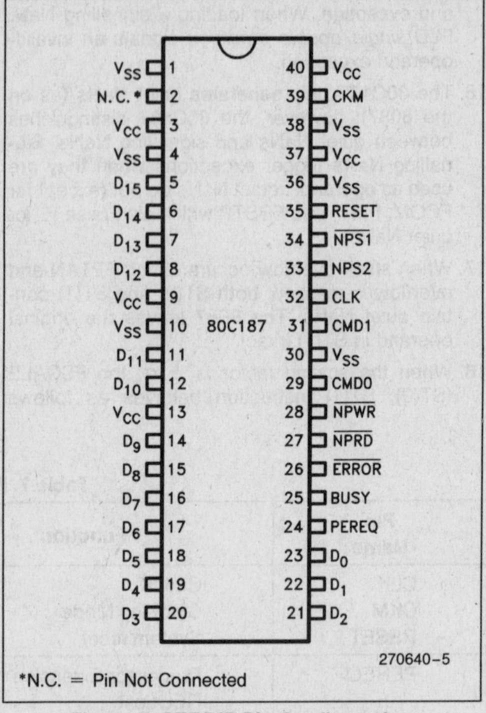

*N.C. = Pin Not Connected

Figure 7. CERDIP Pin Configuration

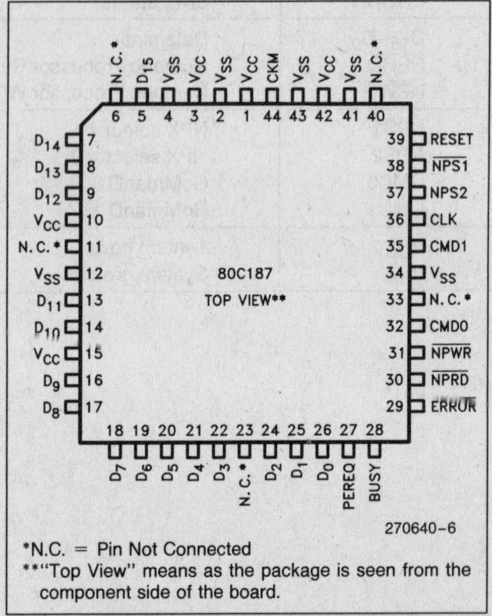

*N.C. = Pin Not Connected
**"Top View" means as the package is seen from the component side of the board.

Figure 8. PLCC Pin Configuration

Table 8. PLCC Pin Cross-Reference

Pin Name	CERDIP Package	PLCC Package
BUSY	25	28
CKM	39	44
CLK	32	36
CMD0	29	32
CMD1	31	35
D_0	23	26
D_1	22	25
D_2	21	24
D_3	20	22
D_4	19	21
D_5	18	20
D_6	17	19
D_7	16	18
D_8	15	17
D_9	14	16
D_{10}	12	14
D_{11}	11	13
D_{12}	8	9
D_{13}	7	8
D_{14}	6	7
D_{15}	5	5
$\overline{ERROR}$	26	29
No Connect	2	6, 11, 23, 33, 40
$\overline{NPRD}$	27	30
$\overline{NPS1}$	34	38
NPS2	33	37
$\overline{NPWR}$	28	31
PEREQ	24	27
RESET	35	39
V_{CC}	3, 9, 13, 37, 40	1, 3, 10, 15, 42
V_{SS}	1, 4, 10, 30, 36, 38	2, 4, 12, 34, 41, 43

System Reset (RESET)

A LOW to HIGH transition on this pin causes the 80C187 to terminate its present activity and to enter a dormant state. RESET must remain active (HIGH) for at least four internal clock periods. (The relation of the internal clock period to CLK depends on CLKM; the internal clock may be different from that of the CPU.) Note that the 80C187 is active internally for 25 clock periods after the termination of the RESET signal (the HIGH to LOW transition of RESET); therefore, the first instruction should not be written to the 80C187 until 25 internal clocks after the falling edge of RESET. Table 9 shows the status of the output pins during the reset sequence. After a reset, all output pins return to their inactive states.

Table 9. Output Pin Status during Reset

Output Pin Name	Value during Reset
BUSY	HIGH
$\overline{ERROR}$	HIGH
PEREQ	LOW
D_{15}–D_0	TRI-STATE OFF

Processor Extension Request (PEREQ)

When active, this pin signals to the CPU that the 80C187 is ready for data transfer to/from its data FIFO. When there are more than five data transfers,

PEREQ is deactivated after the first three transfers and subsequently after every four transfers. This signal always goes inactive before BUSY goes inactive.

Busy Status (BUSY)

When active, this pin signals to the CPU that the 80C187 is currently executing an instruction. This pin is active HIGH. It should be connected to the 80C186's $\overline{\text{TEST}}$/BUSY pin. During the RESET sequence this pin is HIGH. The 80C186 uses this HIGH state to detect the presence of an 80C187.

Error Status ($\overline{\text{ERROR}}$)

This pin reflects the ES bit of the status register. When active, it indicates that an unmasked exception has occurred. This signal can be changed to inactive state only by the following instructions (without a preceding WAIT): FNINIT, FNCLEX, FNSTENV, FNSAVE, FLDCW, FLDENV, and FRSTOR. This pin should be connected to the $\overline{\text{ERROR}}$ pin of the CPU. $\overline{\text{ERROR}}$ can change state only when BUSY is active.

Data Pins (D_{15}–D_0)

These bidirectional pins are used to transfer data and opcodes between the CPU and 80C187. They are normally connected directly to the corresponding CPU data pins. Other buffers/drivers driving the local data bus must be disabled when the CPU reads from the NPX. High state indicates a value of one. D_0 is the least significant data bit.

Numeric Processor Write ($\overline{\text{NPWR}}$)

A signal on this pin enables transfers of data from the CPU to the NPX. This input is valid only when $\overline{\text{NPS1}}$ and NPS2 are both active.

Numeric Processor Read ($\overline{\text{NPRD}}$)

A signal on this pin enables transfers of data from the NPX to the CPU. This input is valid only when $\overline{\text{NPS1}}$ and NPS2 are both active.

Numeric Processor Selects ($\overline{\text{NPS1}}$ and NPS2)

Concurrent assertion of these signals indicates that the CPU is performing an escape instruction and enables the 80C187 to execute that instruction. No data transfer involving the 80C187 occurs unless the device is selected by these lines.

Command Selects (CMD0 and CMD1)

These pins along with the select pins allow the CPU to direct the operation of the 80C187.

System Power (V_{CC})

System power provides the +5V ±10% DC supply input. All V_{CC} pins should be tied together on the circuit board and local decoupling capacitors should be used between V_{CC} and V_{SS}.

System Ground (V_{SS})

All V_{SS} pins should be tied together on the circuit board and local decoupling capacitors should be used between V_{CC} and V_{SS}.

Processor Architecture

As shown by the block diagram (Figure 1), the 80C187 NPX is internally divided into three sections: the bus control logic (BCL), the data interface and control unit, and the floating-point unit (FPU). The FPU (with the support of the control unit which contains the sequencer and other support units) executes all numerics instructions. The data interface and control unit is responsible for the data flow to and from the FPU and the control registers, for receiving the instructions, decoding them, and sequencing the microinstructions, and for handling some of the administrative instructions. The BCL is responsible for CPU bus tracking and interface.

BUS CONTROL LOGIC

The BCL communicates solely with the CPU using I/O bus cycles. The BCL appears to the CPU as a special peripheral device. It is special in two respects: the CPU initiates I/O automatically when it encounters ESC instructions, and the CPU uses reserved I/O addresses to communicate with the BCL. The BCL does not communicate directly with memory. The CPU performs all memory access, transferring input operands from memory to the 80C187 and transferring outputs from the 80C187 to memory. A dedicated communication protocol makes possible high-speed transfer of opcodes and operands between the CPU and 80C187.

Table 10. Bus Cycles Definition

$\overline{NPS1}$	NPS2	CMD0	CMD1	$\overline{NPRD}$	$\overline{NPWR}$	Bus Cycle Type
x	0	x	x	x	x	80C187 Not Selected
1	x	x	x	x	x	80C187 Not Selected
0	1	0	0	1	0	Opcode Write to 80C187
0	1	0	0	0	1	CW or SW Read from 80C187
0	1	1	0	0	1	Read Data from 80C187
0	1	1	0	1	0	Write Data to 80C187
0	1	0	1	1	0	Write Exception Pointers
0	1	0	1	0	1	Reserved
0	1	1	1	0	1	Read Opcode Status
0	1	1	1	1	0	Reserved

DATA INTERFACE AND CONTROL UNIT

The data interface and control unit latches the data and, subject to BCL control, directs the data to the FIFO or the instruction decoder. The instruction decoder decodes the ESC instructions sent to it by the CPU and generates controls that direct the data flow in the FIFO. It also triggers the microinstruction sequencer that controls execution of each instruction. If the ESC instruction is FINIT, FCLEX, FSTSW, FSTSW AX, FSTCW, FSETPM, or FRSTPM, the control executes it independently of the FPU and the sequencer. The data interface and control unit is the one that generates the BUSY, PEREQ, and $\overline{ERROR}$ signals that synchronize 80C187 activities with the CPU.

FLOATING-POINT UNIT

The FPU executes all instructions that involve the register stack, including arithmetic, logical, transcendental, constant, and data transfer instructions. The data path in the FPU is 84 bits wide (68 significant bits, 15 exponent bits, and a sign bit) which allows internal operand transfers to be performed at very high speeds.

Bus Cycles

The pins $\overline{NPS1}$, NPS2, CMD0, CMD1, $\overline{NPRD}$ and $\overline{NPWR}$ identify bus cycles for the NPX. Table 10 defines the types of 80C187 bus cycles.

80C187 ADDRESSING

The $\overline{NPS1}$, NPS2, CMD0, and CMD1 signals allow the NPX to identify which bus cycles are intended for the NPX. The NPX responds to I/O cycles when the I/O address is 00F8H, 00FAH, 00FCH, or 00FEH. The correspondence betwen I/O addresses and control signals is defined by Table 11. To guarantee correct operation of the NPX, programs must not perform any I/O operations to these reserved port addresses.

Table 11. I/O Address Decoding

I/O Address (Hexadecimal)	80C187 Select and Command Inputs			
	NPS2	$\overline{NPS1}$	CMD1	CMD0
00F8	1	0	0	0
00FA	1	0	0	1
00FC	1	0	1	0
00FE	1	0	1	1

CPU/NPX SYNCHRONIZATION

The pins BUSY, PEREQ, and $\overline{\text{ERROR}}$ are used for various aspects of synchronization between the CPU and the NPX.

BUSY is used to synchronize instruction transfer from the CPU to the 80C187. When the 80C187 recognizes an ESC instruction, it asserts BUSY. For most ESC instructions, the CPU waits for the 80C187 to deassert BUSY before sending the new opcode.

The NPX uses the PEREQ pin of the CPU to signal that the NPX is ready for data transfer to or from its data FIFO. The NPX does not directly access memory; rather, the CPU provides memory access services for the NPX.

Once the CPU initiates an 80C187 instruction that has operands, the CPU waits for PEREQ signals that indicate when the 80C187 is ready for operand transfer. Once all operands have been transferred (or if the instruction has no operands) the CPU continues program execution while the 80C187 executes the ESC instruction.

In 8086/8087 systems, WAIT instructions are required to achieve synchronization of both commands and operands. The 80C187, however, does not require WAIT instructions. The WAIT or FWAIT instruction commonly inserted by high-level compilers and assembly-language programmers for exception synchronization is not treated as an instruction by the 80C186 and does not provide exception trapping. (Refer to the section "System Configuration for 8087-Compatible Exception Trapping".)

Once it has started to execute a numerics instruction and has transferred the operands from the CPU, the 80C187 can process the instruction in parallel with and independent of the host CPU. When the NPX detects an exception, it asserts the $\overline{\text{ERROR}}$ signal, which causes a CPU interrupt.

OPCODE INTERPRETATION

The CPU and the NPX use a bus protocol that adapts to the numerics opcode being executed. Only the NPX directly interprets the opcode. Some of the results of this interpretation are relevant to the CPU. The NPX records these results (opcode status information) in an internal 16-bit register. The 80C186 accesses this register only via reads from NPX port 00FEH. Tables 10 and 11 define the signal combinations that correspond to each of the following steps.

1. The CPU writes the opcode to NPX port 00F8H. This write can occur even when the NPX is busy or is signalling an exception. The NPX does not necessarily begin executing the opcode immediately.
2. The CPU reads the opcode status information from NPX port 00FEH.
3. The CPU initiates subsequent bus cycles according to the opcode status information. The opcode status information specifies whether to wait until the NPX is not busy, when to transfer exception pointers to port 00FCH, when to read or write operands and results at port 00FAH, etc.

For most instructions, the NPX does not start executing the previously transferred opcode until the CPU (guided by the opcode status information) first writes exception pointer information to port 00FCH of the NPX. This protocol is completely transparent to programmers.

Bus Operation

With respect to bus interface, the 80C187 is fully asynchronous with the CPU, even when it operates from the same clock source as the CPU. The CPU initiates a bus cycle for the NPX by activating both $\overline{\text{NPS1}}$ and NPS2, the NPX select signals. During the CLK period in which $\overline{\text{NPS1}}$ and NPS2 are activated, the 80C187 also examines the $\overline{\text{NPRD}}$ and $\overline{\text{NPRW}}$

input signals to determine whether the cycle is a read or a write cycle and examines the CMD0 and CMD1 inputs to determine whether an opcode, operand, or control/status register transfer is to occur. The 80C187 activates its BUSY output some time after the leading edge of the $\overline{NPRD}$ or $\overline{NPRW}$ signal. Input and ouput data are referenced to the trailing edges of the $\overline{NPRD}$ and $\overline{NPRW}$ signals.

The 80C187 activates the PEREQ signal when it is ready for data transfer. The 80C187 deactivates PEREQ automatically.

System Configuration

The 80C187 can be connected to the 80C186 CPU as shown by Figure 9. (Refer to the 80C186 Data Sheet for an explanation of the 80C186's signals.) This interface has the following characteristics:

- The 80C187's $\overline{NPS1}$, $\overline{ERROR}$, PEREQ, and BUSY pins are connected directly to the corresponding pins of the 80C186.
- The 80C186 pin $\overline{MCS3}/\overline{NPS}$ is connected to $\overline{NPS1}$; NPS2 is connected to V_{CC}. Note that if the 80C186 CPU's $\overline{DEN}$ signal is used to gate external data buffers, it must be combined with the $\overline{NPS}$ signal to insure numeric accesses will not activate these buffers.
- The $\overline{NPRD}$ and $\overline{NPRW}$ pins are connected to the $\overline{RD}$ and $\overline{WR}$ pins of the 80C186.
- CMD1 and CMD0 come from the latched A_2 and A_1 of the 80C186, respectively.
- The 80C187 BUSY output connects to the 80C186 $\overline{TEST}$/BUSY input. During RESET, the signal at the 80C187 BUSY output automatically programs the 80C186 to use the 80C187.
- The 80C187 can use the CLKOUT signal of the 80C186 to conserve board space when operating at 12.5 MHz or less. In this case, the 80C187 CKM input must be pulled HIGH. For operation in excess of 12.5 MHz, a double-frequency external oscillator for CLK input is needed. In this case, CKM must be pulled LOW.

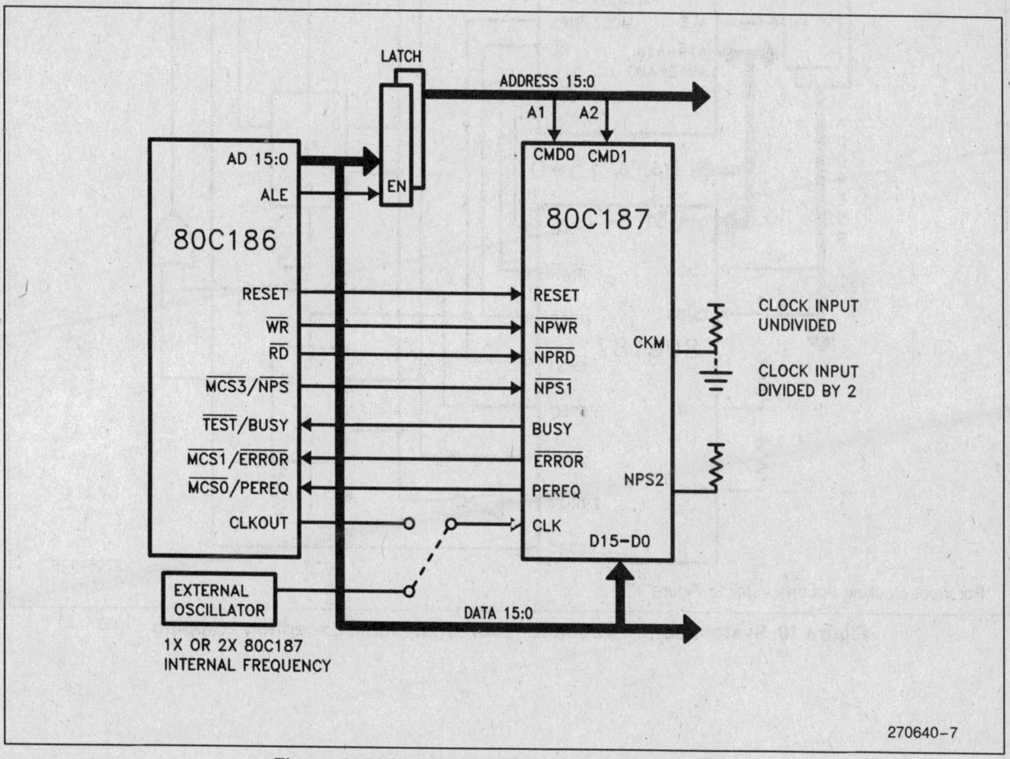

2

LATCH
ADDRESS 15:0
A1 A2
AD 15:0
ALE
EN
CMD0 CMD1
80C186
80C187
RESET
$\overline{WR}$
$\overline{RD}$
$\overline{MCS3}/\overline{NPS}$
$\overline{TEST}$/BUSY
$\overline{MCS1}/\overline{ERROR}$
$\overline{MCS0}$/PEREQ
CLKOUT
RESET
$\overline{NPWR}$
$\overline{NPRD}$
$\overline{NPS1}$
BUSY
$\overline{ERROR}$
PEREQ
CLK
CKM
NPS2
D15–D0
CLOCK INPUT UNDIVIDED
CLOCK INPUT DIVIDED BY 2
EXTERNAL OSCILLATOR
1X OR 2X 80C187 INTERNAL FREQUENCY
DATA 15:0
270640–7

Figure 9. 80C186/80C187 System Configuration

System Configuration for 80186/80187-Compatible Exception Trapping

When the 80C187 ERROR output signal is connected directly to the 80C186 ERROR input, floating-point exceptions cause interrupt #16. However, existing software may be programmed to expect floating-point exceptions to be signalled over an external interrupt pin via an interrupt controller.

For exception handling compatible with the 80186/82188/8087, the 80C186 can be wired to recognize exceptions through an external interrupt pin, as Figure 10 shows. (Refer to the 80C186 Data Sheet for an explanation of the 80C186's signals.) With this arrangement, a flip-flop is needed to latch BUSY upon assertion of ERROR. The latch can then be cleared during the exception-handler routine by forcing a PCS pin active. The latch must also be cleared at RESET in order for the 80C186 to work with the 80C187.

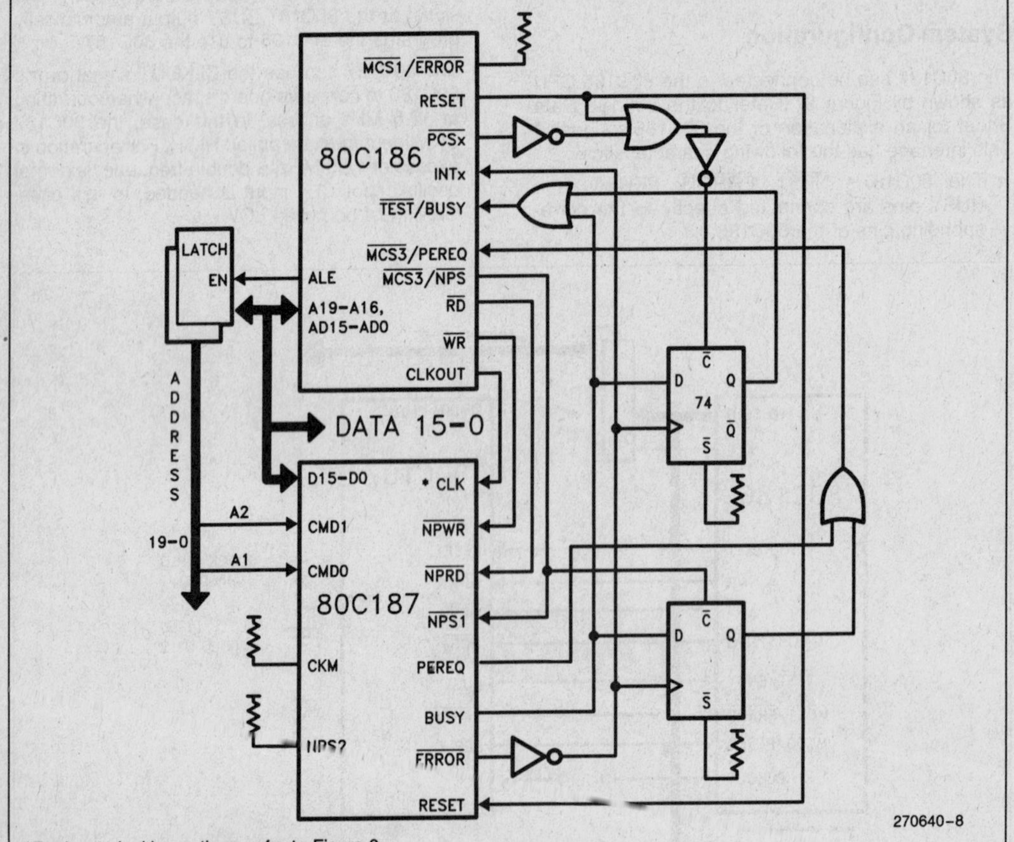

*For input clocking options, refer to Figure 9.

270640–8

Figure 10. System Configuration for 8087-Compatible Exception Trapping

ELECTRICAL DATA

Absolute Maximum Ratings*

Case Temperature Under Bias (T_C) . . . 0°C to +85°C

Storage Temperature . . . . −65°C to +150°C

Voltage on Any Pin
with Respect to Ground . . . . −0.5V to V_{CC} +0.5V

Power Dissipation 1.5W

NOTICE: This is a production data sheet. The specifications are subject to change without notice.

**WARNING: Stressing the device beyond the "Absolute Maximum Ratings" may cause permanent damage. These are stress ratings only. Operation beyond the "Operating Conditions" is not recommended and extended exposure beyond the "Operating Conditions" may affect device reliability.*

Power and Frequency Requirements

The typical relationship between I_{CC} and the frequency of operation F is as follows:

$I_{CC_{typ}} = 55 + 5 \cdot F$ mA where F is in MHz.

When the frequency is reduced below the minimum operating frequency specified in the AC Characteristics table, the internal states of the 80C187 may become indeterminate. The 80C187 clock cannot be stopped; otherwise, I_{CC} would increase significantly beyond what the equation above indicates.

DC Characteristics T_C = 0°C to +85°C, V_{CC} = +5V ±10%

Symbol	Parameter	Min	Max	Units	Test Conditions
V_{IL}	Input LOW Voltage	−0.5	+0.8	V	
V_{IH}	Input HIGH Voltage	2.0	V_{CC} +0.5	V	
V_{ICL}	Clock Input LOW Voltage	−0.5	+0.8	V	
V_{ICH}	Clock Input HIGH Voltage	2.0	V_{CC} +0.5	V	
V_{OL}	Output LOW Voltage		0.45	V	I_{OL} = 3.0 mA
V_{OH}	Output HIGH Voltage	2.4		V	I_{OH} = −0.4 mA
I_{CC}	Power Supply Current		156 135	mA mA	16 MHz 12.5 MHz
I_{LI}	Input Leakage Current		±10	μA	0V ≤ V_{IN} ≤ V_{CC}
I_{LO}	I/O Leakage Current		±10	μA	0.45V ≤ V_{OUT} ≤ V_{CC} − 0.45V
C_{IN}	Input Capacitance		10	pF	F_C = 1 MHz
C_O	I/O or Output Capacitance		12	pF	F_C = 1 MHz
C_{CLK}	Clock Capacitance		20	pF	F_C = 1 MHz

AC Characteristics

T_C = 0°C to +85°C, V_{CC} = 5V ±10%
All timings are measured at 1.5V unless otherwise specified

Symbol	Parameter	12.5 MHz		16 MHz		Test Conditions
		Min (ns)	Max (ns)	Min (ns)	Max (ns)	
T_{dvwh} (t6) T_{whdx} (t7)	Data Setup to $\overline{\text{NPWR}}$ Data Hold from $\overline{\text{NPWR}}$	43 14		33 14		
T_{rlrh} (t8) T_{wlwh} (t9)	$\overline{\text{NPRD}}$ Active Time $\overline{\text{NPWR}}$ Active Time	59 59		54 54		
T_{avwl} (t10) T_{avrl} (t11)	Command Valid to $\overline{\text{NPWR}}$ Command Valid to $\overline{\text{NPRD}}$	0 0		0 0		
T_{mhrl} (t12)	Min Delay from PEREQ Active to $\overline{\text{NPRD}}$ Active	40		30		
T_{whax} (t18) T_{rhax} (t19)	Command Hold from $\overline{\text{NPWR}}$ Command Hold from $\overline{\text{NPRD}}$	12 12		8 8		
T_{ivcl} (t20)	$\overline{\text{NPRD}}$, $\overline{\text{NPWR}}$, RESET to CLK Setup Time	46		38		Note 1
T_{clih} (t21)	$\overline{\text{NPRD}}$, $\overline{\text{NPWR}}$, RESET from CLK Hold Time	26		18		Note 1
T_{rscl} (t24)	RESET to CLK Setup	21		19		Note 1
T_{clrs} (t25)	RESET from CLK Hold	14		9		Note 1
T_{cmdi} (t26)	Command Inactive Time Write to Write Read to Read Read to Write Write to Read	 69 69 69 69		 59 59 59 59		

NOTE:
1. This is an asynchronous input. This specification is given for testing purposes only, to assure recognition at a specific CLK edge.

Timing Responses

All timings are measured at 1.5V unless otherwise specified

Symbol	Parameter	12.5 MHz		16 MHz		Test Conditions
		Min (ns)	Max (ns)	Min (ns)	Max (ns)	
T_{rhqz} (t27) T_{rlqv} (t28)	$\overline{NPRD}$ Inactive to Data Float* $\overline{NPRD}$ Active to Data Valid		18 50		18 45	Note 2 Note 3
T_{ilbh} (t29)	$\overline{ERROR}$ Active to Busy Inactive	104		104		Note 4
T_{wlbv} (t30)	$\overline{NPWR}$ Active to Busy Active		80		60	Note 4
T_{klml} (t31)	$\overline{NPRD}$ or $\overline{NPWR}$ Active to PEREQ Inactive		80		60	Note 5
T_{rhqh} (t32)	Data Hold from $\overline{NPRD}$ Inactive	2		2		Note 3
T_{rlbh} (t33)	RESET Inactive to BUSY Inactive		80		60	

NOTES:
*The data float delay is not tested.
2. The float condition occurs when the measured output current is less than I_{OL} on $D_{15}-D_0$.
3. $D_{15}-D_0$ loading: $C_L = 100$ pF.
4. BUSY loading: $C_L = 100$ pF.
5. On last data transfer of numeric instruction.

2

Clock Timings

Symbol	Parameter		12.5 MHz		16 MHz*		Test Conditions
			Min (ns)	Max (ns)	Min (ns)	Max (ns)	
T_{clcl} (t1a) (t1B)	CLK Period	CKM = 1 CKM = 0	80 40	250 125	N/A 31.25	N/A 125	Note 6 Note 6
T_{clch} (t2a) (t2b)	CLK Low Time	CKM = 1 CKM = 0	35 9		N/A 7		Note 6 Note 7
T_{chcl} (t3a) (t3b)	CLK High Time	CKM = 1 CKM = 0	35 13		N/A 9		Note 6 Note 8
T_{ch2ch1}(t4)				10		8	Note 9
T_{ch1ch2}(t5)				10		8	Note 10

NOTES:
*16 MHz operation is available only in divide-by-2 mode (CKM strapped LOW).
6. At 1.5V
7. At 0.8V
8. At 2.0V
9. CKM = 1: 3.7V to 0.8V at 16 MHz, 3.5V to 1.0V at 12.5 MHz
10. CKM = 1: 0.8V to 3.7V at 16 MHz, 1.0V to 3.5V at 12.5 MHz

AC DRIVE AND MEASUREMENT POINTS—CLK INPUT

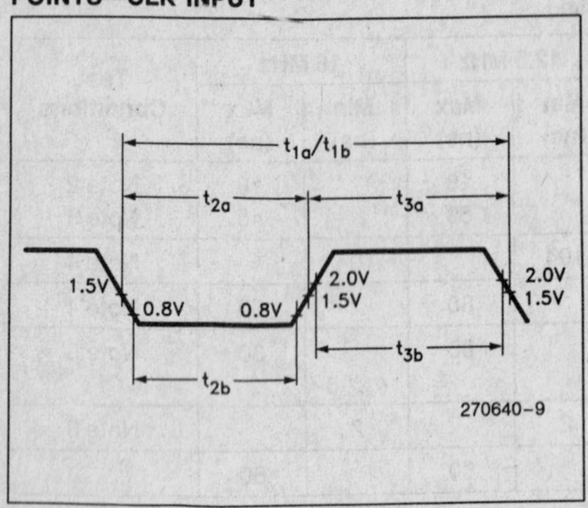

270640-9

AC SETUP, HOLD, AND DELAY TIME MEASUREMENTS—GENERAL

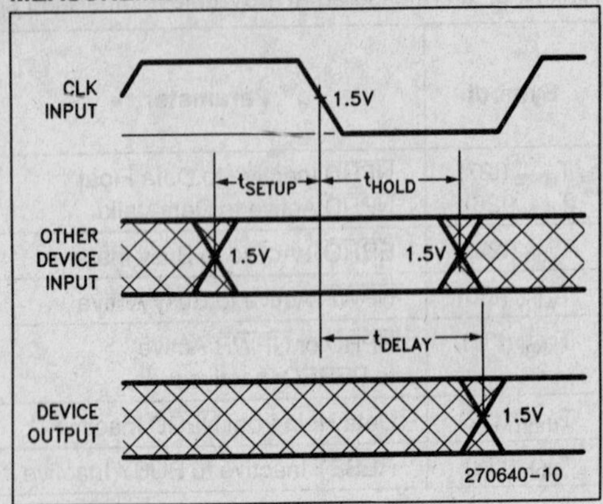

270640-10

AC TEST LOADING ON OUTPUTS

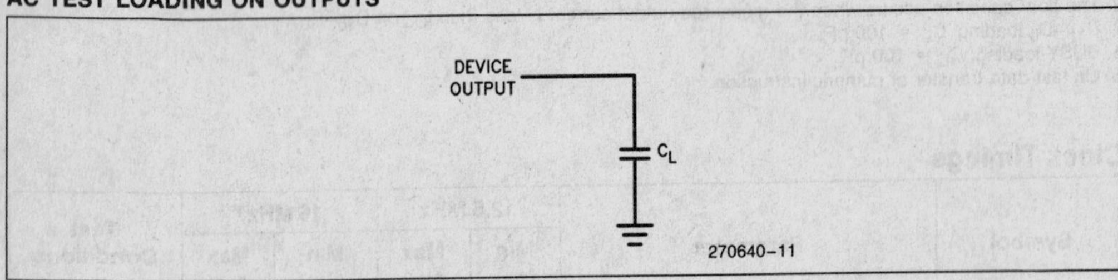

270640-11

DATA TRANSFER TIMING (INITIATED BY CPU)

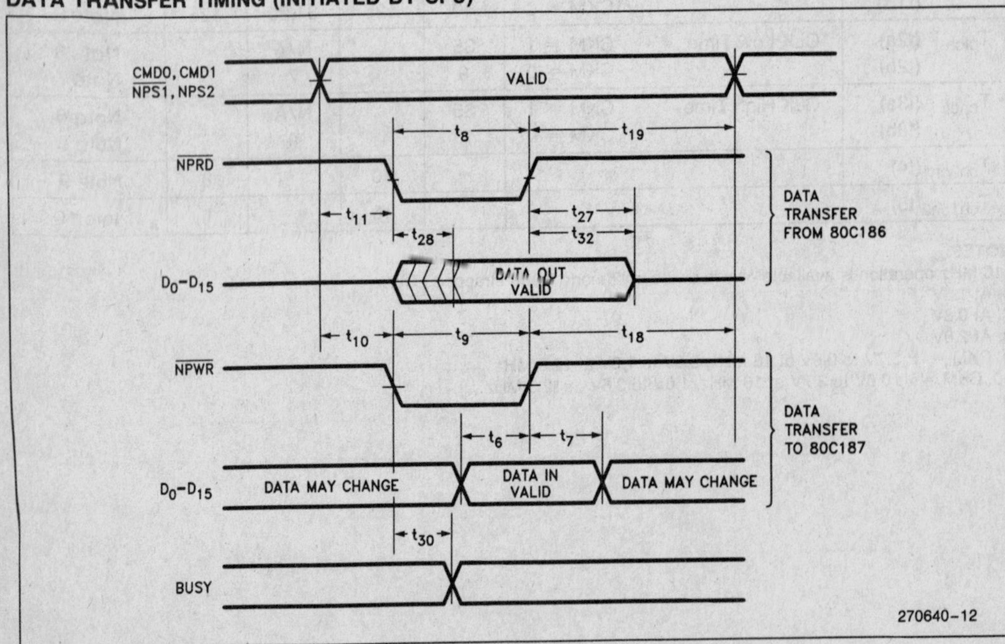

270640-12

DATA CHANNEL TIMING (INITIATED BY 80C187)

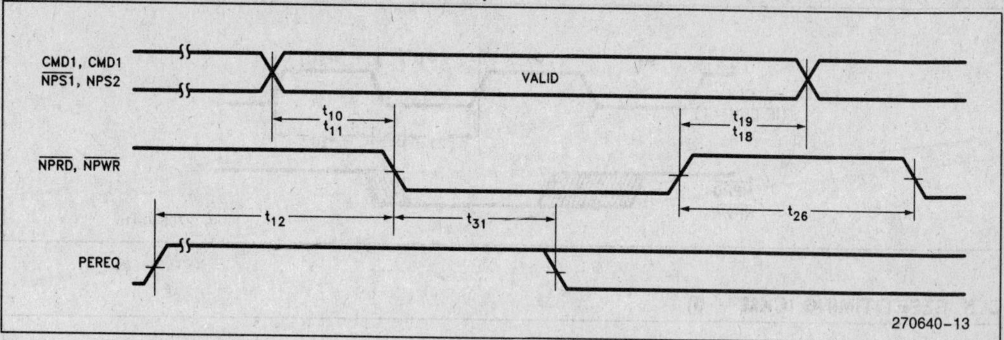

270640-13

ERROR OUTPUT TIMING

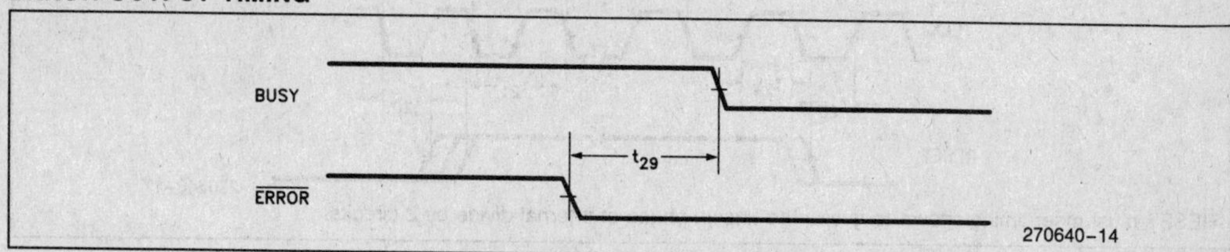

270640-14

CLK, RESET TIMING (CKM = 1)

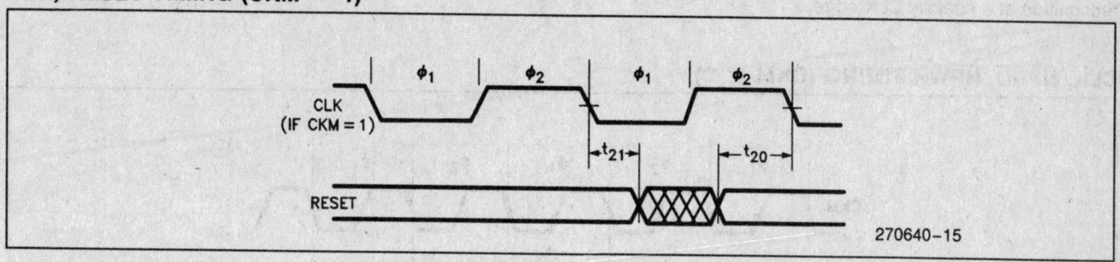

270640-15

2

CLK, $\overline{NPRD}$, $\overline{NPWR}$ TIMING (CKM = 1)

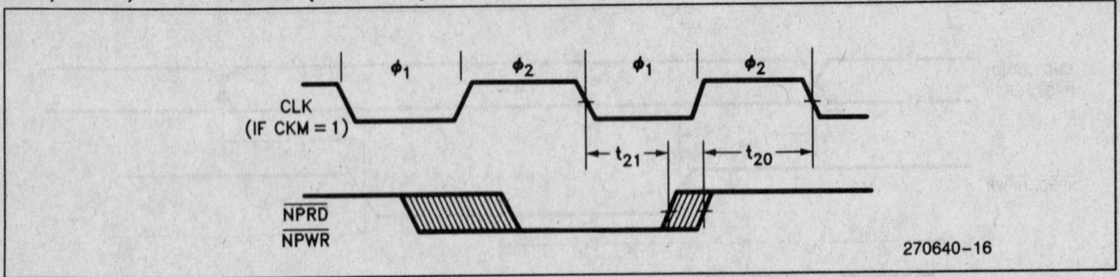

270640-16

CLK, RESET TIMING (CKM = 0)

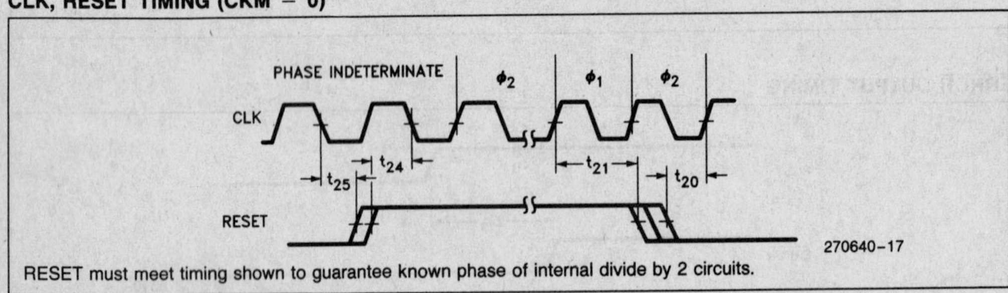

270640-17

RESET must meet timing shown to guarantee known phase of internal divide by 2 circuits.

NOTE:
RESET, $\overline{NPWR}$, $\overline{NPRD}$ inputs are asynchronous to CLK. Timing requirements are given for testing purposes only, to assure recognition at a specific CLK edge.

CLK, $\overline{NPRD}$, $\overline{NPWR}$ TIMING (CKM = 0)

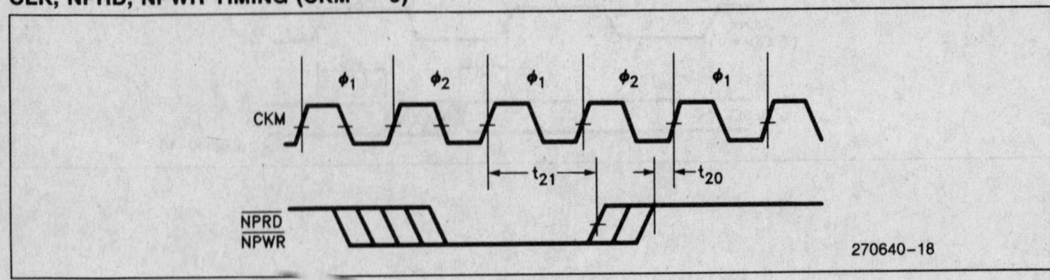

270640-18

RESET, BUSY TIMING

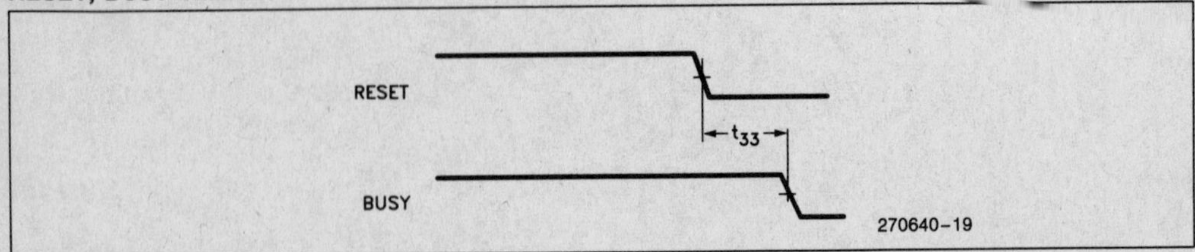

270640-19

80C187 EXTENSIONS TO THE CPU's INSTRUCTION SET

Instructions for the 80C187 assume one of the five forms shown in Table 12. In all cases, instructions are at least two bytes long and begin with the bit pattern 11011B, which identifies the ESCAPE class of instruction. Instructions that refer to memory operands specify addresses using the CPU's addressing modes.

MOD (Mode field) and R/M (Register/Memory specifier) have the same interpretation as the corresponding fields of CPU instructions (refer to Programmer's Reference Manual for the CPU). The DISP (displacement) is optionally present in instructions that have MOD and R/M fields. Its presence depends on the values of MOD and R/M, as for instructions of the CPU.

The instruction summaries that follow assume that the instruction has been prefetched, decoded, and is ready for execution; that bus cycles do not require wait states; that there are no local bus HOLD requests delaying processor access to the bus; and that no exceptions are detected during instruction execution. Timings are given in internal 80C187 clocks and include the time for opcode and data transfer between the CPU and the NPX. If the instruction has MOD and R/M fields that call for both base and index registers, add one clock.

2

Table 12. Instruction Formats

<table>
<tr><th rowspan="2"></th><th colspan="9">Instruction</th><th rowspan="2">Optional Field</th></tr>
<tr><th colspan="4">First Byte</th><th colspan="5">Second Byte</th></tr>
<tr><td>1</td><td>11011</td><td colspan="2">OPA</td><td>1</td><td colspan="2">MOD</td><td>1</td><td>OPB</td><td>R/M</td><td>DISP</td></tr>
<tr><td>2</td><td>11011</td><td colspan="2">MF</td><td>OPA</td><td colspan="2">MOD</td><td colspan="2">OPB *</td><td>R/M</td><td>DISP</td></tr>
<tr><td>3</td><td>11011</td><td>d</td><td>P</td><td>OPA</td><td>1</td><td>1</td><td colspan="2">OPB *</td><td>ST (i)</td><td></td></tr>
<tr><td>4</td><td>11011</td><td>0</td><td>0</td><td>1</td><td>1</td><td>1</td><td>1</td><td colspan="2">OP</td><td></td></tr>
<tr><td>5</td><td>11011</td><td>0</td><td>1</td><td>1</td><td>1</td><td>1</td><td>1</td><td colspan="2">OP</td><td></td></tr>
<tr><td></td><td>15–11</td><td>10</td><td>9</td><td>8</td><td>7</td><td>6</td><td>5</td><td>4 3</td><td>2 1 0</td><td></td></tr>
</table>

NOTES:

OP = Instruction opcode, possibly split into two fields OPA and OPB

MF = Memory Format
- 00— 32-Bit Real
- 01— 32-Bit Integer
- 10— 64-Bit Real
- 11— 16-Bit Integer

d = Destination
- 0— Destination is ST(0)
- 0— Destination is ST(i)

R XOR d = 0— Destination (op) Source
R XOR d = 1— Source (op) Destination

*In FSUB and FDIV, the low-order bit of OPB is the R (reversed) bit

P = Pop
- 0— Do not pop stack
- 1— Pop stack after operation

ST(i) = Register Stack Element *i*
- 000 = Stack Top
- 001 = Second Stack Element
- •
- •
- •
- 111 = Eighth Stack Element

ESC = 11011

80C187 Extensions to the 80C186 Instruction Set

Instruction	Encoding			Clock Count Range			
	Byte 0	Byte 1	Optional Bytes 2–3	32-Bit Real	32-Bit Integer	64-Bit Real	16-Bit Integer
DATA TRANSFER							
FLD = Load[a]							
Integer/real memory to ST(0)	ESC MF 1	MOD 000 R/M	DISP	40	65–72	59	67–71
Long integer memory to ST(0)	ESC 111	MOD 101 R/M	DISP		90–101		
Extended real memory to ST(0)	ESC 011	MOD 101 R/M	DISP		74		
BCD memory to ST(0)	ESC 111	MOD 100 R/M	DISP		296–305		
ST(i) to ST(0)	ESC 001	11000 ST(i)			16		
FST = Store							
ST(0) to integer/real memory	ESC MF 1	MOD 010 R/M	DISP	58	93–107	73	80–93
ST(0) to ST(i)	ESC 101	11010 ST(i)			13		
FSTP = Store and Pop							
ST(0) to integer/real memory	ESC MF 1	MOD 011 R/M	DISP	58	93–107	73	80–93
ST(0) to long integer memory	ESC 111	MOD 111 R/M	DISP		116–133		
ST(0) to extended real	ESC 011	MOD 111 R/M	DISP		83		
ST(0) to BCD memory	ESC 111	MOD 110 R/M	DISP		542–564		
ST(0) to ST(i)	ESC 101	11001 ST (i)			14		
FXCH = Exchange							
ST(i) and ST(0)	ESC 001	11001 ST(i)			20		
COMPARISON							
FCOM = Compare							
Integer/real memory to ST(0)	ESC MF 0	MOD 010 R/M	DISP	48	78–85	67	77–81
ST(i) to ST(0)	ESC 000	11010 ST(i)			26		
FCOMP = Compare and pop							
Integer/real memory to ST	ESC MF 0	MOD 011 R/M	DISP	48	78–85	67	77–81
ST(i) to ST(0)	ESC 000	11011 ST(i)			28		
FCOMPP = Compare and pop twice							
ST(1) to ST(0)	ESC 110	1101 1001			28		
FTST = Test ST(0)	ESC 001	1110 0100			30		
FUCOM = Unordered compare	ESC 101	11100 ST(i)			26		
FUCOMP = Unordered compare and pop	ESC 101	11101 ST(i)			28		
FUCOMPP = Unordered compare and pop twice	ESC 010	1110 1001			28		
FXAM = Examine ST(0)	ESC 001	11100101			32-40		
CONSTANTS							
FLDZ = Load +0.0 into ST(0)	ESC 001	1110 1110			22		
FLD1 = Load +1.0 into ST(0)	ESC 001	1110 1000			26		
FLDPI = Load pi into ST(0)	ESC 001	1110 1011			42		
FLDL2T = Load $\log_2(10)$ into ST(0)	ESC 001	1110 1001			42		

Shaded areas indicate instructions not available in 8087.

NOTE:
a. When loading single- or double-precision zero from memory, add 5 clocks.

80C187 Extensions to the 80C186 Instruction Set (Continued)

Instruction	Encoding			Clock Count Range			
	Byte 0	Byte 1	Optional Bytes 2–3	32-Bit Real	32-Bit Integer	64-Bit Real	16-Bit Integer
CONSTANTS (Continued)							
FLDL2E = Load $\log_2(e)$ into ST(0)	ESC 001	1110 1010		42			
FLDLG2 = Load $\log_{10}(2)$ into ST(0)	ESC 001	1110 1100		43			
FLDLN2 = Load $\log_e(2)$ into ST(0)	ESC 001	1110 1101		43			
ARITHMETIC							
FADD = Add							
Integer/real memory with ST(0)	ESC MF 0	MOD 000 R/M	DISP	44–52	77–92	65–73	77–91
ST(i) and ST(0)	ESC d P 0	11000 ST(i)		25–33[b]			
FSUB = Subtract							
Integer/real memory with ST(0)	ESC MF 0	MOD 10 R R/M	DISP	44–52	77–92	65–73	77–91[c]
ST(i) and ST(0)	ESC d P 0	1110 R R/M		28–36[d]			
FMUL = Multiply							
Integer/real memory with ST(0)	ESC MF 0	MOD 001 R/M	DISP	47–57	81–102	68–93	82–93
ST(i) and ST(0)	ESC d P 0	1100 1 R/M		31–59[e]			
FDIV = Divide							
Integer/real memory with ST(0)	ESC MF 0	MOD 11 R R/M	DISP	108	140–147[f]	128	142–146[g]
ST(i) and ST(0)	ESC d P 0	1111 R R/M		90[h]			
FSQRT[i] = Square root	ESC 001	1111 1010		124–131			
FSCALE = Scale ST(0) by ST(1)	ESC 001	1111 1101		69–88			
FPREM = Partial remainder of ST(0) ÷ ST(1)	ESC 001	1111 1000		76–157			
FPREM1 = Partial remainder (IEEE)	ESC 001	1111 0101		97–187			
FRNDINT = Round ST(0) to integer	ESC 001	1111 1100		68–82			
FXTRACT = Extract components of ST(0)	ESC 001	1111 0100		72–78			
FABS = Absolute value of ST(0)	ESC 001	1110 0001		24			
FCHS = Change sign of ST(0)	ESC 001	1110 0000		26–27			

Shaded areas indicate instructions not available in 8087.

NOTES:

b. Add 3 clocks to the range when d = 1.
c. Add 1 clock to **each** range when R = 1.
d. Add 3 clocks to the range when d = 0.
e. typical = 54 (When d = 0, 48–56, typical = 51).
f. Add 1 clock to the range when R = 1.
g. 153–159 when R = 1.
h. Add 3 clocks to the range when d = 1.
i. $-0 \leq ST(0) \leq +\infty$.

80C187 Extensions to the 80C186 Instruction Set (Continued)

Instruction	Encoding			Clock Count Range
	Byte 0	Byte 1	Optional Bytes 2–3	
TRANSCENDENTAL				
FCOS = Cosine of ST(0)	ESC 001	1111 1111		125–774[j]
FPTAN[k] = Partial tangent of ST(0)	ESC 001	1111 0010		193–499[j]
FPATAN = Partial arctangent	ESC 001	1111 0011		316–489
FSIN = Sine of ST(0)	ESC 001	1111 1110		124–773[j]
FSINCOS = Sine and cosine of ST(0)	ESC 001	1111 1011		196–811[j]
F2XM1[l] = $2^{ST(0)} - 1$	ESC 001	1111 0000		213–478
FYL2X[m] = $ST(1) * \log_2(ST(0))$	ESC 001	1111 0001		122–540
FYL2XP1[n] = $ST(1) * \log_2(ST(0) + 1.0)$	ESC 001	1111 1001		259–549
PROCESSOR CONTROL				
FINIT = Initialize NPX	ESC 011	1110 0011		35
FSTSW AX = Store status word	ESC 111	1110 0000		17
FLDCW = Load control word	ESC 001	MOD 101 R/M	DISP	23
FSTCW = Store control word	ESC 001	MOD 111 R/M	DISP	21
FSTSW = Store status word	ESC 101	MOD 111 R/M	DISP	21
FCLEX = Clear exceptions	ESC 011	1110 0010		13
FSTENV = Store environment	ESC 001	MOD 110 R/M	DISP	146
FLDENV = Load environment	ESC 001	MOD 100 R/M	DISP	113
FSAVE = Save state	ESC 101	MOD 110 R/M	DISP	550
FRSTOR = Restore state	ESC 101	MOD 100 R/M	DISP	482
FINCSTP = Increment stack pointer	ESC 001	1111 0111		23
FDECSTP = Decrement stack pointer	ESC 001	1111 0110		24
FFREE = Free ST(i)	ESC 101	1100 0 ST(i)		20
FNOP = No operations	ESC 001	1101 0000		14

Shaded areas indicate instructions not available in 8087.

NOTES:
j. These timings hold for operands in the range $|x| < \pi/4$. For operands not in this range, up to 78 clocks may be needed to reduce the operand.
k. $0 \leq |ST(0)| < 2^{63}$.
l. $-1.0 \leq ST(0) \leq 1.0$.
m. $0 \leq ST(0) < \infty, -\infty < ST(1) < +\infty$.
n. $0 \leq |ST(0)| < (2 - \sqrt{2})/2, -\infty < ST(1) < +\infty$.

DATA SHEET REVISION REVIEW

The following list represents the key differences between the -002 and the -001 version of the 80C187 data sheet. Please review this summary carefully.

1. Figure 10, titled "System Configuration for 8087—Compatible Exception Trapping", was replaced with a revised schematic. The previous configuration was faulty. Updated timing diagrams on Data Transfer Timing, Error Output, and RESET/BUSY.

AP-477

APPLICATION NOTE

2

Low Voltage Embedded Design

JOHN WILLIAMS
APPLICATIONS ENGINEER

February 1993

Order Number: 272324-001

Low Voltage Embedded Design

CONTENTS

PAGE

1.0 INTRODUCTION 2-271

1.1 What is 3V? 2-271

2.0 REASONS FOR 3V OPERATION .. 2-271

2.1 Device Geometries 2-271

2.2 System Benefits 2-271

3.0 LOW VOLTAGE SYSTEM DESIGN 2-272

3.1 Power Supply Design 2-272

3.1.1 Batteries 2-272

3.1.2 Voltage Regulation 2-273

3.1.3 Calculating System Power Consumption 2-273

3.1.3.1 Device Current 2-273

3.1.3.2 Discrete Component Current 2-274

3.1.3.3 Leakage Current 2-274

3.1.4 Summary: Calculating Power Consumption 2-275

3.2 Mixed Voltage System Design ... 2-275

3.2.1 Interfacing 3V and 5V Components 2-275

3.2.1.1 3V to 5V Interface 2-275

3.2.1.2 5V to 3V Interface 2-275

3.2.1.3 Voltage Translation with Open Drain Outputs 2-276

3.2.1.4 Bidirectional Translation 2-276

CONTENTS

PAGE

3.2.2 Disadvantages of Mixed Voltage Systems 2-276

3.2.2.1 Multiple Supplies in Mixed Voltage Systems 2-277

3.2.2.2 Additional Current Consumption in Mixed Voltage Systems 2-277

3.2.3 Summary: Mixed Voltage Systems 2-278

3.3 Single Voltage System Design ... 2-278

3.3.1 Devices Designed for Low Voltage Operation 2-278

3.3.2 Devices Derated for Low Voltage Operation 2-278

3.3.3 Noise Generation by Low Voltage Devices 2-279

3.3.4 Noise Margins in Low Voltage Systems 2-279

4.0 SYSTEM POWER MANAGEMENT 2-279

4.1 Device Power Management 2-279

4.2 Software Power Management 2-280

4.2.1 Implementing Delays 2-280

4.2.2 Code Optimization 2-280

1.0 INTRODUCTION

Currently, integrated circuit manufacturers are specifying devices for low voltage operation. Most devices are specified for operation around 3V. This can indicate operation centered around 3.0V, 3.3V or other voltages. Many devices are even specified for operation at 2V and below.

In many embedded designs, the designer wants the lowest system power dissipation possible. Embedded, low voltage designs require maximum battery life which is directly proportional to the current consumption of the system. System current consumption is a linear function of operating voltage.

This application note discusses why low voltage devices and systems are beneficial and how to design low voltage systems. Power supplies, mixed voltage systems, single voltage systems and power management schemes are all discussed. Although 3V systems are specifically discussed, the concepts apply to all low voltage designs.

1.1 What is 3V?

The term "3V" usually refers to 3.3V ±0.3V. This is the JEDEC standard for regulated supplies. The majority of devices are specified for 3.3V operation, the standard being used for portable PC's. JEDEC Standard 8 defines LVCMOS (Low Voltage CMOS) operating voltages and interface levels for low voltages. JEDEC Standard 8.1 defines LVTTL (Low Voltage TTL) compatibility. The LVTTL standard defines specifications for low voltage devices that operate in 5V TTL systems without interface logic.

There is also a standard for unregulated supplies, 2.7V to 3.6V (battery operated systems). Few devices are currently specified for operation in the unregulated region. Many devices used in embedded applications have a wider V_{CC} range and do not conform to this standard. A V_{CC} specification from 2.7V to 5.5V allows operation from an unregulated alkaline battery supply (3 x AA). Older 5V devices derated for 3V operation (specified for 3V operation at a reduced frequency) typically can operate in this region.

2.0 REASONS FOR 3V OPERATION

Components are being specified to operate at 3V for two reasons. First, advanced fabrication technologies incorporating smaller device geometries require lower operating voltages. Second, there are a number of advantages to operating a system at low voltage.

2.1 Device Geometries

One of the driving factors to reduce component operating voltages is technology. As device channel lengths and oxide thicknesses decrease (Figure 2-1), lower operating voltages are required to maintain component reliability. Three main reliability concerns are: oxide breakdown, punch-through, and hot-electron effects.

As feature length and width in a component decrease, depth also decreases. With thinner gate oxides, lower gate voltages are required to avoid dielectric breakdown in the oxide. If oxide breakdown occurs, the gate of the device begins to draw current.

As the channel lengths shorten, lower source and drain voltages are required to keep the depletion regions around the wells from meeting, at this point, the current through the device is no longer controlled by the voltage on the gate.

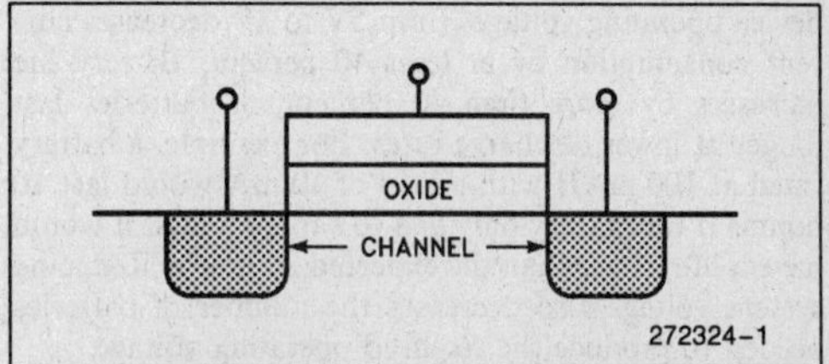

Figure 2-1. Basic Transistor Structure

Finally, lower voltages are required to avoid hot-electron effects. Electrons can lodge in the gate oxide, altering the charge in the oxide. When charge is added to the gate oxide, the turn-on voltage of the device is altered, degrading performance.

2.2 System Benefits

Presently, not all devices are being designed to operate specifically at low voltages. Many devices are 5V designs with their performance derated for low voltage operation. These devices are only rated for low voltage operation because of the benefits it has for system designs. Operating parts at lower voltages has some significant advantages at a system level.

2

Battery powered systems operate significantly longer at 3V. Battery life, rated in Amp-hours, is a function of the current a system draws. The current consumption of a system varies linearly with the operating voltages of the devices. Equation 2.1 expresses this relationship.

Equation 2.1: $I_{CC} = C \int V \bullet dt \cong \Delta V \bullet C \bullet F$

where

I_{CC} = Device current consumption

ΔV = Switching voltage

C = Device capacitance and output capacitive loading

F = Device operating frequency

Determining the current consumption of an entire system is not quite this straightforward, but this topic will be examined in more detail later. The point is, lowering device operating voltages from 5V to 3V decreases current consumption by at least 40 percent. Battery life increases by more than 40 percent, as batteries last longer at lower discharge rates. For example, a battery rated at 100 mAH with a load of 10 mA would last 10 hours. If the battery only had to supply 5 mA, it would have a life longer than the expected 20 hours. Reducing system voltage also decreases the number of batteries needed to produce the required operating voltage.

Heat generated by a device is proportional to the power it consumes. The formula for power consumption of a device is the current (Equation 1) multiplied by the operating voltage (V). Power consumption varies as the square of the operating voltage. Reducing the operating voltage of a device from 5V to 3V decreases power consumption by 64 percent. Heat dissipation is reduced by the same amount. This has a couple of important implications. On a device level, parts that generate less heat do not have as many constraints placed on packaging. Packages with much smaller footprints can be created and plastic packages can be offered for devices previously only offered in ceramic packages. On a system level, if parts produce less heat, they can be placed closer together. These advantages allow reduction of the overall form factor and weight of a system. Additionally, many device failure mechanisms are heat related. Systems producing less heat have higher reliability.

Noise generated by devices is a concern for all system designers. The effects of noise: overshoot, undershoot, ground bounce, etc., are a function of dV/dt. On low voltage devices, dV/dt is lower. This is discussed in more detail in a later section. Decreased noise generation by low voltage systems simplifies design and makes meeting maximum noise limits easier.

The move to lower operating voltages has a number of benefits to the system designer. Smaller, lighter, less noisy systems and longer battery life all contribute to better designs. Low voltage designs also enable older designs to become mobile/portable.

3.0 LOW VOLTAGE SYSTEM DESIGN

Low voltage systems have many aspects in common with standard 5V designs. In addition to the normal design considerations made in any 5V system, low voltage designs have some areas that need specific attention. System power supply, mixed voltage interfaces, and complete low voltage designs all need to be considered.

3.1 Power Supply Design

When designing the power supply for a low voltage system, the characteristics of that system must be taken into account. A supply must exist for each operating voltage on a board. This could mean a number of different voltages for logic, communications, displays, and other functions. For each voltage generated, the designer must determine the worst-case current consumption of the system. Number of supplies and their capacity determine the power supply design.

3.1.1 BATTERIES

A major application of low voltage devices in embedded systems is in portable systems that require battery operation. The type of battery the designer chooses affects the power supply design. Batteries are characterized by two general discharge curves. Alkaline batteries have a constantly decreasing voltage output (Figure 3-1a). NiCad batteries (as well as Nickel-Hydride, Lithium and others) have a relatively constant voltage through the majority of their life (Figure 3-1b). Internal chemical reactions and the number of cells inside each battery determine the output voltage.

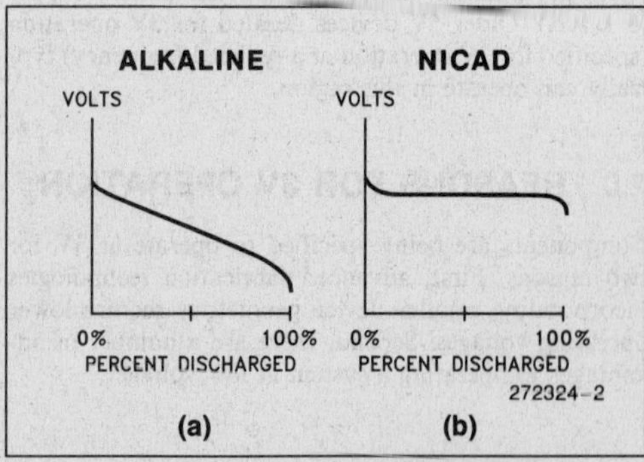

Figure 3-1. Typical Battery Discharge Curves

The battery discharge curve and voltage requirements of the system components determine whether voltage regulation is required. A system utilizing components with narrow voltage specifications (3.3V ±10%, for example) using Alkaline batteries, would require a voltage regulator to translate the battery output voltage to something usable by the system. NiCad batteries, on the other hand, provide a stable enough voltage over their lifetime that the designer could avoid using a regulator.

Although the constant voltage type of batteries may appear to be the most efficient choice, a number of other tradeoffs exist such as overall capacity, rechargeability, temperature sensitivity, safety, volume, weight and cost. When deciding on a battery, these characteristics, or combinations of these characteristics should be considered. For example, an application may require maximum capacity, but minimum weight, so capacity per unit weight may be the most important combination. Also, rechargeability may or may not be important to the design. Secondary batteries, such as NiCad may be recharged, while primary batteries such as alkaline may not.

3.1.2 VOLTAGE REGULATION

Voltage regulators may be required in systems where battery output voltage and system V_{CC} requirements do not match. For example, three Alkaline AA batteries would discharge from about 4.5V to about 2.7V over their lifetime. A device specified for operation from 3V to 3.6V would require this supply to be regulated. Voltage regulated systems have the advantage of having a stable, constant V_{CC} for the life of the batteries. The disadvantages include extra board space needed for the regulator(s) and decreased battery life due to regulator efficiency losses. Most regulator efficiencies run from the mid-80 percent to low-90 percent range.

In low power designs, voltage regulation is usually performed with pulse-skipping regulators, current-mode pulse width modulators (PWM's) or voltage-mode PWM's. Each of these methods has certain advantages and disadvantages. Important regulator characteristics include output ripple amplitude and frequency, efficiency, quiescent current, transient response and physical size requirements. Individual designs will have different requirements, and these issues should be considered when designing the system power supply.

3.1.3 CALCULATING SYSTEM POWER CONSUMPTION

When designing a system power supply, it is important to understand system current requirements. Knowing the worst-case current consumption allows the designer to choose the voltage regulation method, estimate system battery life and determine system packaging requirements (heat dissipation, etc.).

Many factors determine total system current. Device current, discrete component current, and leakage current are all factors. The general formula for current consumption, I is:

Equation 3.1: $I = V \bullet C \bullet f = C \bullet dV/dt$

Where: **V** = voltage, **C** = capacitance, and **f** = frequency. This formula must be used for all components in the system to estimate current consumption. The term "estimate" is used because, until the design is completed, fabricated, and tested, there is no way to know the exact current consumption. Actual current will depend on the way the software controls the hardware in the system, temperature and other factors. To estimate current consumption, some assumptions are required to keep the calculations from becoming too detailed. The various contributors to system current consumption are detailed in the following sections.

3.1.3.1 Device Current

There are two parts to device current consumption: core current and I/O current. Core current is typically a large percentage of the total device current. I/O current is a smaller percentage, but still a major contributor to total system current.

Core current is the current consumed by internal transistors switching and the charging and discharging of internal capacitances. In this situation, V in Equation 3.1 is equal to V_{CC}. All of the internal nodes switch between V_{CC} and ground. The frequency term is the device operating frequency. The Capacitance term, slightly more complicated, is an equivalent capacitance accounting for all internal node and trace capacitances. To determine this value, I_{CC} is measured at a known frequency and voltage with output pins inactive, Equation 3.2 is then solved for the equivalent capacitance (Equation 3.3). This value applies to all operating frequencies.

Equation 3.2: $I_{core} = V_{CC} \bullet C_{eq} \bullet f$

Equation 3.3: $C_{eq} = I_{core}/(V_{CC} \bullet f)$

2

I/O current is the current consumed by outputs switching. To determine I/O current, V in Equation 1 is the voltage swing of the output, V_{CC} in a normal, CMOS system. The capacitance term is the sum of all input capacitances of devices connected to the output plus the capacitance of the PCB trace (approximately 2 pF/in.). The frequency term is the switching frequency of the output, not necessarily the operating frequency of the system. The frequency term can be determined by approximating how often an output switches during a particular time period. The measure of time in an embedded system is typically a processor bus cycle. Using the 80C186 embedded processor as an example, the major contributors to I/O current are the Address/Data bus, RD#, WR# and ALE outputs. Depending on the application, other outputs may switch frequently enough to be included in current calculations. These signals are used as a simple example.

Because of the multiplexed Address/Data bus on the 186 device, data is written and read on the same pins that drive address information. Thus, read and write cycles need to be treated separately. An analysis of bus cycles for a typical application indicates that about 80 percent are read cycles (data reads and instruction fetches) and the remaining 20 percent are write cycles. Equation 3.4 represents the Address/Data bus current for a write cycle.

Equation 3.4: $I_{write} = (V \bullet C \bullet f) \bullet (1/n) \bullet (x + y)$

where:

- V = V_{CC}
- C = Load capacitance per pin
- f = Processor operating frequency
- n = Number of clocks per bus cycle (4 at zero wait states)
- x = Number of pins switching during the address phase
- y = Number of pins switching during the data phase

Because of the random nature of data being read/written, it is a reasonable assumption that approximately half of the Address/Data pins will switch during each phase of the bus cycle (address and data). For a read cycle, the equation will be identical, with y = 0, as shown in Equation 3.5.

Equation 3.5: $I_{read} = (V \bullet C \bullet f) \bullet (1/n) \bullet (x)$

The control signals: RD#, WR# and ALE are driven during each bus cycle. Equation 3.6 shows the current for the combined control signals. Each of these signals switch twice during a bus cycle, once to go active and once to go inactive or vice-versa.

Equation 3.6: $I_{control} = (V \bullet C \bullet f) \bullet (1/n) \bullet (x)$

- V = V_{CC}
- C = Load capacitance on the control signal pin
- f = Processor operating frequency
- n = Number of clocks per bus cycle (4 at zero wait states)
- x = Number of times the control signal switches during a bus cycle
  - ALE: x = 2
  - RD#/WR#: x = 2

Total I/O current, Equation 3.7, is calculated by adding equations 3.4, 3.5 and 3.6.

Equation 3.7: I/O current = $I_{read} \bullet (0.8) + I_{write} \bullet (0.2) + I_{control}$

The 0.8 and 0.2 factors come from the percentage of read and write bus cycles in a typical system. A similar analysis is required for all devices within a system. The system processor will usually be the most difficult. Once this is done, many of the approximations made apply to calculations for the rest of the system.

3.1.3.2 Discrete Component Current

Current consumed by discrete components must also be factored into total system current. Current consumed by pull-up or pull-down resistors, voltage dividers, transistors or other discrete components must be included. These are relatively straightforward calculations, and do not require elaboration.

3.1.3.3 Leakage Current

Leakage currents from devices are typically very small and can usually be ignored when calculating system current consumption. When a CMOS device is in a static condition, all p and n transistors inside the device should have their gates driven to V_{CC} or Ground, turning them on or off. The equivalent resistance of an "off" transistor is approximately 5 MΩ, the equivalent resistance of an "on" transistor is typically less than 100Ω. Some current flows through this resistive path to ground. Typically, this amount will be in the μA range.

Leakage current can become more significant. If a device is running at a given V_{CC}, there may be situations where an input is not driven close to V_{CC}. The p and n transistors of the device input buffers will not be completely turned on or off. This lowers the equivalent resistance through the transistors to ground. On some devices (AC logic, as an example), at $V_{IN} = V_{CC} - 2.1V$, the device may consume as much as 1.5 mA additional current **per input pin**. Typically, this value is from 100 μA to 200 μA per input, but still measurable. This additional current exists unless the input to the device is driven close to V_{CC}. Most logic data sheets list this specification as ΔI_{CC}, given as a maximum current per input pin with the input at $V_{CC} - 2.1V$.

3.1.4 SUMMARY: CALCULATING POWER CONSUMPTION

For a complete system design, total system current consumption must be calculated. This analysis determines power supply design, product packaging and battery life. Although an exact calculation may not be possible (or practical), a worst-case analysis with reasonable approximations allows a reliable system design.

3.2 Mixed Voltage System Design

One of the difficulties in designing a low voltage system is product availability. There are a large number of manufacturers producing low voltage products (3V or lower). Embedded processors, like the Intel 80L186EA, EB and EC have been available at 3V for some time. Memory and logic are also widely available. Some peripheral components are still not available at low voltages. Many of these components require redesign to operate at low voltages. Until these components are replaced with low voltage versions, systems requiring their functionality have to utilize the 5V version. This causes tremendous headaches for system designers. System cost, complexity and power consumption all suffer due to the lack of a complete selection of low voltage devices.

3.2.1 INTERFACING 3V AND 5V COMPONENTS

Somewhere within a mixed voltage design, the designer must interface 3V and 5V devices. This can happen in 3V to 5V translation, 5V to 3V translation, bidirectional translation or 3V and 5V devices residing on the same system bus. As simple as these interfaces may seem, there are still problems to be solved.

3.2.1.1 3V to 5V Interface

One way to translate a 3V output to a 5V CMOS level is with ACT/HCT logic. These parts accept a TTL level input and give a CMOS output. When operating at 5V, these parts see a 3V level input the same as they would see a 5V TTL level input. The output will be a 5V CMOS level. This is a relatively straightforward approach, but it does have the problem of additional current consumption (ΔI_{CC}).

The JEDEC standard for 3.3V outputs is compatible with TTL input requirements. If the 5V device connected to the 3V output already has TTL compatible inputs, no interface logic is required.

3.2.1.2 5V to 3V Interface

Unfortunately, a 5V output cannot be connected directly to a 3V input. Maximum operating conditions for most devices specify the maximum voltage on any input pin. This number is typically $V_{CC} + 0.5V$ (LVTTL and unregulated LVCMOS), and on some 3V devices is $V_{CC} + 1.0V$ (regulated LVCMOS). A 5V CMOS output high typically drives close to V_{CC}. When the maximum input voltage is exceeded, the ESD (Electrostatic Discharge) protection diode on the input of the device forward biases and current flows into the 3V V_{CC} (Figure 3-2). This causes unacceptably high current consumption. Connecting a 5V output to a 3V input leads to reliability problems. Device manufacturers are developing input buffers for low voltage devices that are 5V tolerant, but until these devices are widely available, other solutions are required.

A 5V bipolar TTL device may be connected directly to a 3V input. Some newer 5V CMOS devices have outputs with reduced voltage swings. These devices have 3V compatible outputs and may be connected directly to 3V inputs. The designer must be careful when regulating the 5V and 3V supplies. If the 5V supply goes to 5.5V and the 3.3V supply goes to 3.0V, the 3V input specification could be violated.

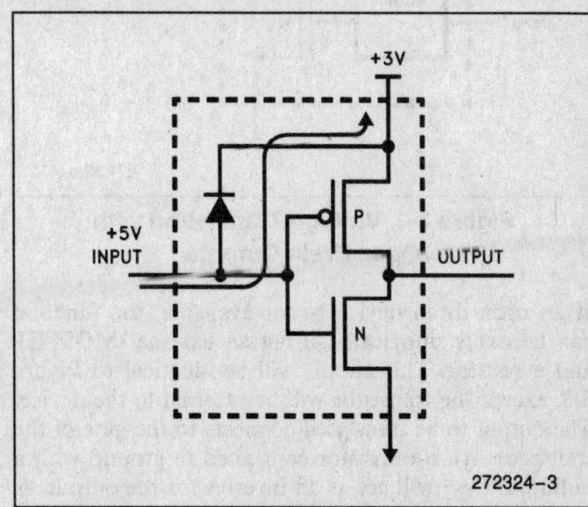

Figure 3-2. 5V Output Driving a 3V Input

There is a way to work around the problem of driving a 3V input with a 5V output. Series resistors can be placed on the outputs of the 5V device. The goal is to drop the voltage to a level acceptable by the 3V device. The value of the resistor must be chosen to limit the

2

current into the 3V device. The major sacrifice in this solution is speed. If the system can handle the speed degradation, then it is a simple, inexpensive way to translate from 5V to 3V. As a final point on this subject, if this solution is implemented, considerations must be made for system power-up. If the 5V supply ramps much faster than the 3V supply, the substrate diode may still be forward biased temporarily, leading to reliability problems. This situation must be taken into account when determining the resistor value. The designer must either assume the worst case where the 5V part V_{CC} = 5.5V and the 3V part has V_{CC} = 0V or the 3V and 5V supplies must be sequenced.

3.2.1.3 Voltage Translation with Open Drain Outputs

Open drain output devices provide a simple way to convert from 3V to 5V and vice-versa (Figure 3-3). All that is required is an external pullup resistor to the desired output voltage. If the open drain device outputs a logic "1", there is virtually no current consumption penalty for the conversion. If the output is a logic "0", there is a current path to ground, but a high resistance pullup will limit the amount of current (at the cost of speed).

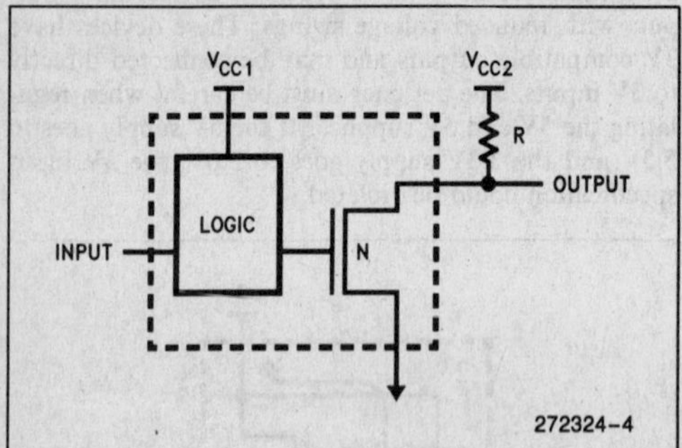

Figure 3-3. Voltage Translation with Open Drain Outputs

If an open drain device is not available, the function can be easily duplicated using an external MOSFET and a resistor. This circuit will be identical to Figure 3-3, except the transistor will be external to the device. The output to be translated connects to the gate of the transistor. An n-transistor connected to ground with a pullup to V_{CC} will act as an inverter for the output. A p-transistor connected to ground with a pullup resistor will not invert the output. The switching time required by the external MOSFET must be considered when determining system timing.

3.2.1.4 Bidirectional Translation

The methods described above all work well for translating unidirectional signals. What happens if a 5V peripheral resides on a 3V bus? Ideally, a designer could place a 5V device and a 3V device on the same system bus. Unfortunately, a floated 3V output will be damaged when a 5V part drives the bus. Depending on the state of the inputs to the 3V device output buffers, it is possible that the p-transistor will turn on (Figure 3-4). If this device turns on, the 5V supply and 3V supply are shorted together. Even if this situation does not occur, the 5V signal still forward biases the ESD protection diodes inside the 3V device, creating a situation similar to a 5V output driving a 3V input. Fortunately, a number of manufacturers are producing buffers with two V_{CC} pins. The devices translate bidirectionally between the two V_{CC} values. These are the most practical solution for bidirectional translation between 3V and 5V. System busses must operate at a single voltage with other voltages buffered.

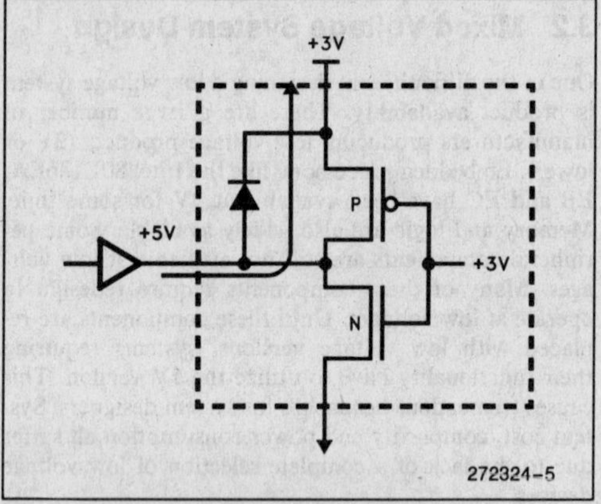

Figure 3-4. 5V Device Driving a Floated 3V Output

3.2.2 DISADVANTAGES OF MIXED VOLTAGE SYSTEMS

It is obvious at this point that there really are no advantages to mixed voltage systems over complete 3V designs. They only exist because of the absence of a complete selection of low voltage devices. During the industry's transition to 3V, the objective of designers is to minimize the disadvantages of mixed voltage systems. Two of the drawbacks of mixed voltage systems are voltage supply requirements and additional current consumption.

3.2.2.1 Multiple Supplies in Mixed Voltage Systems

A major disadvantage of mixed voltage systems is the requirement of multiple voltage supplies. A typical system may require 3V (major components, memory), 5V (older peripherals, small displays), ±12V (RS-232 communications) and even higher voltages (backlit LCD displays, etc.). One goal in designing a mixed voltage system is to minimize the number of required voltages and the number of devices used to create them. To avoid the extra chip-count associated with creating multiple voltages, some manufacturers, offer one-chip solutions to provide multiple voltages from 2 or 3 cells. The designer can also take advantage of parts with internal charge pumps that take 3V or 5V inputs and create the output voltage levels they require. Although multiple voltages can easily be created with a minimal number of chips, the designer still pays the price for having non-3V parts in the system: battery life. As technology moves forward and 3V designs gain momentum, more components will be available at low voltage (3V or less). This eliminates the requirement for multiple system voltages and the added system cost and complexity associated with creating them.

3.2.2.2 Additional Current Consumption in Mixed Voltage Systems

Interfacing 3V and 5V devices in a mixed voltage system is unavoidable. Regardless of how a designer implements these interfaces, they will all have one common characteristic, additional current consumption.

Some devices have an additional specification called ΔI_{CC} (or I_{CCT}). This specification defines the additional current consumed, per input pin, if an input high voltage is at $V_{CC} - 2.1V$. This situation closely resembles using ACT or HCT logic for 3V to 5V translation. This number can be up to 1.5 mA per input pin. Consider a unidirectional, 16-bit bus translated from 3V to 5V using ACT logic. In a worst-case situation, this can be a major source of continuous current consumption. This is a maximum value, typically the extra current amounts to 100 μA to 200 μA per input pin. Additionally, this specification only applies to a logic "1" input, and typically, only a fraction of the 3V inputs are high at any time.

The reason behind the extra current consumption when using ACT/HCT logic for 3V to 5V translation lies in the input buffers (Figure 3-5). If the input of the device is driven all the way to V_{CC}, the p-transistor turns completely off and the n-transistor turns completely on. This can be roughly modeled as 5V connected to ground through a 5 MΩ resistor. As shown by the graph in Figure 3-5, the only current flowing is leakage current, almost nothing.

As the voltage on the input moves farther away from V_{CC}, the input transistors move closer to their saturation region. The resistance path through the transistors to ground decreases from the initial 5 MΩ. This increases the current flow through them. The graph shows this current to be on the order or 150 uA per input with a 3V input (at room temperature).

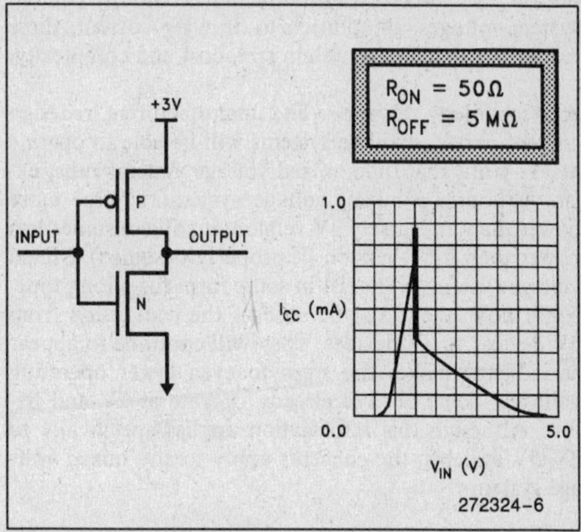

Figure 3-5. Current When Using ACT/HCT Logic for Voltage Conversion

This leads to a valid question. If there is such a penalty for creating mixed voltage systems, is the system better off running at 5V? An analysis of system current consumption must be done for the pure 5V and mixed voltage cases. If only a small part of the system can operate at 3V, the extra power for voltage translation may offset the benefit of using 3V parts. This accents the need to have a complete selection of devices that operate at 3V.

2

3.2.3 SUMMARY: MIXED VOLTAGE SYSTEMS

There are a number of considerations a designer must make when designing a mixed voltage system. Interfacing 3V and 5V logic must be done carefully. There are many solutions to do this, but if done incorrectly, the system eventually fails. Many manufacturers provide simple solutions to do unidirectional and bidirectional transfers. These solutions are probably the easiest to implement and consume a minimal amount of power.

A mixed voltage system, by definition, consumes more current than a pure 3V system. This added current consumption comes from different sources. Any method used to translate from one voltage to another requires additional current. A mixed voltage system also has more devices than a pure 3V system. Extra devices are needed for voltage translation and creating required system voltages. In addition to drawing current, these extra devices increase system size, cost and complexity.

As technology advances and manufacturers redesign current parts, complete systems will be able to operate at 3V. Until that time, mixed voltage systems must exist. Although a mixed voltage system requires more power than an entirely 3V version, it still consumes less power than a 5V version (if properly designed). Mixed voltage systems will exist in some form for a long time. Right now, they exist because of the conversion from 5V devices to 3V devices. They will continue to appear as industry makes the steps to even lower operating voltages. Some devices already operate at 2V and below. Although this information applies specifically to 3V/5V systems, the concepts apply to any mixed voltage system.

3.3 Single Voltage System Design

Complete 3V designs have few disadvantages, the exceptions being operating speed and noise immunity. Advantages include: longer battery life, less heat and lower noise emissions. The advantages of a complete 3V system are significant compared to the minimal design effort required to work around the disadvantages.

3.3.1 DEVICES DESIGNED FOR LOW VOLTAGE OPERATION

Currently, some devices are designed for 3V only operation. Devices optimized for 3V operation are generally specified for operation from 3.0V to 3.6V. These devices exhibit the performance of their 5V counterparts at significantly lower power. The high performance and narrow operating voltages of these parts limits their benefit to embedded, battery operated designs.

If a fabrication process is optimized for 3V operation, gate oxides are thinner. The increased gate capacitance allows a 3V device to function at the same speed as a 5V device produced on a non-3V processes. Oxide breakdown is the major drawback to optimizing a process for 3V. A thinner gate oxide implies a lower oxide breakdown voltage. Devices produced on the optimized process will not be able to operate at 5V without damaging the part.

3.3.2 DEVICES DERATED FOR LOW VOLTAGE OPERATION

Many low voltage products are derated versions of their 5V versions. These devices are specified, typically, for operation from 2.7V to 5.5V. The only sacrifice of running a product designed for 5V at 3V is speed. Device speed is a function of internal switching speeds. Switching speeds are proportional to device current, a function of gate oxide capacitance and gate voltages within a device. A device produced on a process not optimized for 3V will have a thicker gate oxide, decreasing gate capacitance, reducing current The combination of lower gate voltage and capacitance limits operating speeds for derated 5V devices. For many embedded systems, speed is not critical. Using devices that operate from 2.7V to 5.5V allows the designer to use inexpensive alkaline batteries and avoid the added device count and efficiency losses of voltage regulators.

3.3.3 NOISE GENERATION BY LOW VOLTAGE DEVICES

Overshoot, undershoot and ground bounce all relate to dV/dt, dV being the output voltage swing and dt being the output switching time. In low voltage devices, obviously, voltage levels decrease, lowering the dV term. This applies to all low voltage devices. Devices designed specifically for low voltage operation, which have smaller geometries and thinner gate oxides, have switching times comparable to the 5V versions. Therefore, the dt term remains relatively constant. Low voltage devices which are derated versions of 5V parts have slower switching times when operating voltage decreases. The dt term increases for devices derated for low voltage operation. Derated devices generate very little noise.

Regardless of the exact amount of noise a low voltage device generates (derated or not), any low voltage device will produce less noise than its 5V counterpart. dV/dt and practicing good PCB design techniques (multi-layer, bypass capacitors, etc.), should eliminate noise as a problem.

3.3.4 NOISE MARGINS IN LOW VOLTAGE SYSTEMS

In devices with CMOS compatible inputs, input high (V_{IH}) and input low (V_{IL}) voltage specifications are a function of operating voltage. The difference between V_{IH} and V_{IL} defines the noise margin on the input (Equation 3.8).

Equation 3.8: Noise Margin $= V_{IH} - V_{IL}$

Typically, V_{IH} is 0.7^*V_{CC} and V_{IL} is 0.3^*V_{CC} on CMOS compatible inputs. This defines a noise margin of 0.4^*V_{CC}. If operating voltage decreases from 5.0V, noise margins decrease proportionally.

Devices with TTL compatible inputs will not see any change in noise margins when operating at 3V. TTL inputs define V_{IH} as 2.0V and V_{IL} as 0.8V. The standards for input levels on 3.3V devices are defined to be compatible with the TTL standard. This is why a 3.3V output can directly interface with a 5V device with TTL inputs.

Noise susceptibility of low voltage systems is not as significant as it may appear. Low voltage systems generate less noise than 5V systems. If a system generates less noise, decreased noise margins on device inputs become less important. Additionally, good Printed Circuit Board layout techniques should eliminate major noise issues.

4.0 SYSTEM POWER MANAGEMENT

When creating a battery operated system, the designer is concerned with extending battery life as long as possible. Reducing operating voltages is a relatively simple way to achieve a significant reduction in power consumption. Voltage reduction is an excellent start to increasing battery life, but numerous power management techniques exist to provide even lower power consumption.

4.1 Device Power Management

Many Intel embedded processors have modes of operation designed to reduce current consumption. Many static-design embedded processors have Powerdown mode, disabling the clock input to the device. Disabling the clock input eliminates transistor switching within the device, reducing current consumption to leakage current (microamps). Other devices have Idle mode which disables the clock to the CPU, but keeps integrated peripherals active. This decreases current consumption by a smaller amount than Powerdown mode, but is excellent for devices requiring peripherals to remain active at all times. Finally, many embedded processors offer Powersave mode. Powersave mode internally divides the clock input to the device. Because processor current consumption is approximately a linear function of clock frequency, Powersave mode significantly reduces current consumption during execution of noncritical sections of code. Including one or more of these power management functions on silicon reduces board space required to create them separately, if they can be created at all (Idle mode, for example).

Other devices that commonly appear in embedded systems also offer power management features in silicon. Some Intel Flash memory devices offer a powerdown mode, reducing current to leakage levels. Other memories enter a "sleep" mode when not being accessed, reducing current consumption. Even some regulators allow their output to be shut down to decrease current consumption.

Many devices exist offering power management features which enhance low voltage operation. When system designers select components for their systems, parts should be chosen which offer benefits beyond just low voltage operation.

4.2 Software Power Management

Power management schemes need to be implemented in software as well as hardware. Software controls power management modes on Intel embedded processors and can be used to control power management on external devices (using port pins, etc.). Software can also be implemented to reduce switching on address and data busses and processor outputs.

4.2.1 IMPLEMENTING DELAYS

Many applications require time delays. For example, there may be a minimum time required between successive writes to an LCD display or other peripherals. These delays can be implemented either in hardware (controlled by software) or software. When delay loops are implemented in software, every iteration of that loop will execute a given number of bus cycles. Every bus cycle will drive address information onto the bus and all of the relevant control signals that define a bus cycle and turn on the memory device(s) containing program code. With enough iterations of the loop, a large amount of current is consumed. One solution is to divide the processor clock during these delays. Dividing the clock by a factor of x reduces the number of bus cycles required by x, for the same delay.

Implementing a delay with hardware and software is simple. Timers are used to create the delay. A timer can be programmed to cause an interrupt after a set delay. The timer needs to be programmed with the correct count and enabled. If the delay is long enough, it may even make sense to put the processor into a power management mode (such as Idle mode or Powersave mode). This entire process requires a small number of bus cycles. If the overhead associated with interrupt servicing is a limitation, some processors allow the designer to implement delays without interrupts.

The 80C186, for example, has an input called TEST#. The TEST# pin is sampled during the WAIT instruction. The processor stops execution during a WAIT until the TEST# pin is sampled low. If the output of a timer is connected to the TEST# input, the timer times-out and pulls its output low, causing the processor to continue execution. This solution requires only enough bus cycles to program the timer.

4.2.2 CODE OPTIMIZATION

Program code can also be optimized for minimal power consumption. To minimize switching on the address bus, code should be written to reduce the number of jumps that occur. Interrupt driven code is also preferable to code which depends on polling routines. The processor can issue a HLT instruction and wait for an interrupt rather than constantly looping to poll a register bit. The reduction in power consumption by using these methods may be slight but still increases battery life.

Power management is very important to low voltage embedded designs. The effort to add power management is minimal but the benefits are significant. Using hardware and software to minimize power consumption increases battery life with little or no increase in system cost or complexity.

376 Embedded Processors

3

PRELIMINARY

376™ HIGH PERFORMANCE 32-BIT EMBEDDED PROCESSOR

- **Full 32-Bit Internal Architecture**
  - **8-, 16-, 32-Bit Data Types**
  - **8 General Purpose 32-Bit Registers**
  - **Extensive 32-Bit Instruction Set**
- **High Performance 16-Bit Data Bus**
  - **16 or 20 MHz CPU Clock**
  - **Two-Clock Bus Cycles**
  - **16 Mbytes/Sec Bus Bandwidth**
- **16 Mbyte Physical Memory Size**
- **High Speed Numerics Support with the 80387SX**
- **Low System Cost with the 82370 Integrated System Peripheral**
- **On-Chip Debugging Support Including Break Point Registers**
- **Complete Intel Development Support**
  - **C, PL/M, Assembler**
  - **ICE™-376, In-Circuit Emulator**
  - **iRMK Real Time Kernel**
  - **iSDM Debug Monitor**
  - **DOS Based Debug**
- **Extensive Third-Party Support:**
  - **Languages: C, Pascal, FORTRAN, BASIC and ADA***
  - **Hosts: VMS*, UNIX*, MS-DOS*, and Others**
  - **Real-Time Kernels**
- **High Speed CHMOS IV Technology**
- **Available in 100 Pin Plastic Quad Flat-Pack Package and 88-Pin Pin Grid Array**
  (See Packaging Outlines and Dimensions #231369)

3

INTRODUCTION

The 376 32-bit embedded processor is designed for high performance embedded systems. It provides the performance benefits of a highly pipelined 32-bit internal architecture with the low system cost associated with 16-bit hardware systems. The 80376 processor is based on the 80386 and offers a high degree of compatibility with the 80386. All 80386 32-bit programs not dependent on paging can be executed on the 80376 and all 80376 programs can be executed on the 80386. All 32-bit 80386 language translators can be used for software development. With proper support software, any 80386-based computer can be used to develop and test 80376 programs. In addition, any 80386-based PC-AT* compatible computer can be used for hardware prototyping for designs based on the 80376 and its companion product the 82370.

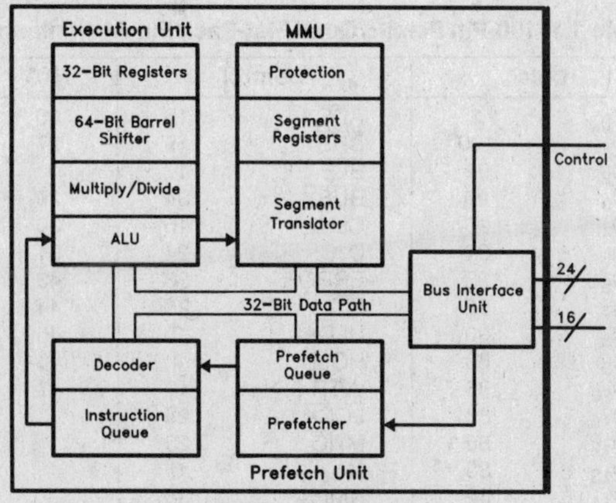

80376 Microarchitecture

Intel, iRMK, ICE, 376, 386, Intel386, iSDM, Intel1376 are trademarks of Intel Corp.
*UNIX is a registered trademark of AT&T.
ADA is a registered trademark of the U.S. Government, Ada Joint Program Office.
PC-AT is a registered trademark of IBM Corporation.
VMS is a trademark of Digital Equipment Corporation.
MS-DOS is a trademark of MicroSoft Corporation.

December 1990
Order Number: 240182-004

1.0 PIN DESCRIPTION

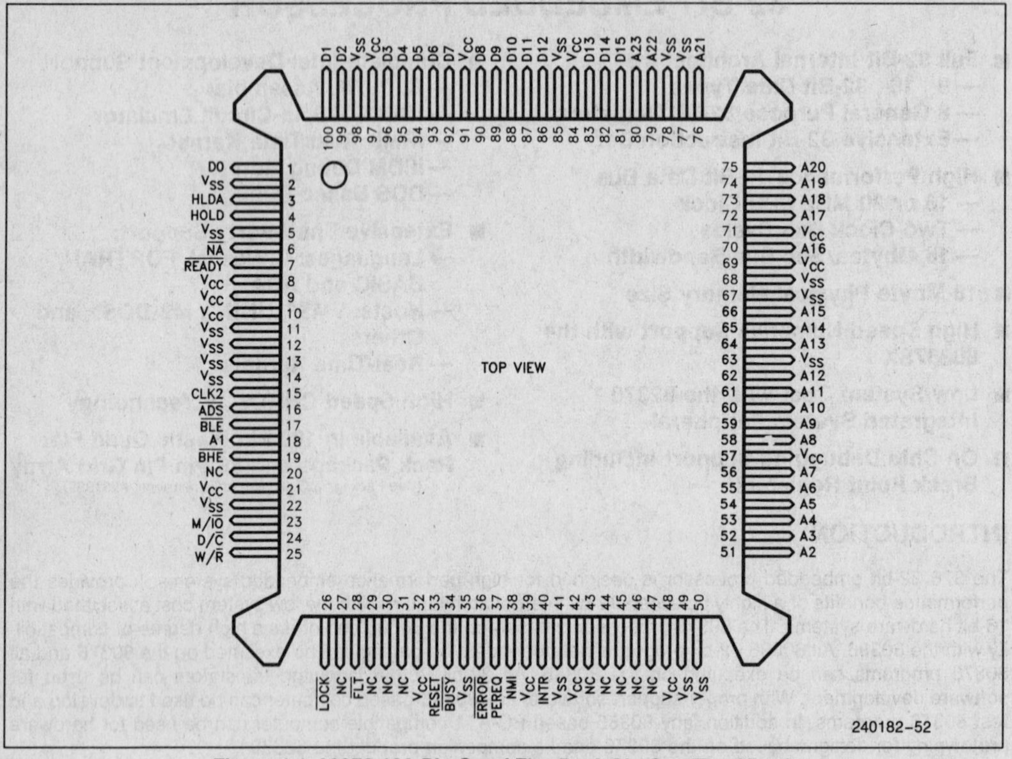

TOP VIEW

Top side (pins 100–76): D1, D2, V_{SS}, V_{CC}, D3, D4, D5, D6, D7, V_{CC}, D8, D9, D10, D11, D12, V_{SS}, V_{CC}, D13, D14, D15, A23, A22, V_{SS}, V_{SS}, A21

Left side (pins 1–25): D0, V_{SS}, HLDA, HOLD, V_{SS}, $\overline{NA}$, $\overline{READY}$, V_{CC}, V_{CC}, V_{CC}, V_{SS}, V_{SS}, V_{SS}, V_{SS}, CLK2, $\overline{ADS}$, $\overline{BLE}$, A1, $\overline{BHE}$, NC, V_{CC}, V_{SS}, M/$\overline{IO}$, D/$\overline{C}$, W/$\overline{R}$

Bottom side (pins 26–50): $\overline{LOCK}$, NC, FLT, NC, NC, NC, NC, V_{CC}, RESET, $\overline{BUSY}$, V_{SS}, $\overline{ERROR}$, PEREQ, NMI, V_{CC}, INTR, V_{SS}, V_{CC}, NC, NC, NC, NC, V_{CC}, V_{SS}, V_{SS}

Right side (pins 75–51): A20, A19, A18, A17, V_{CC}, A16, V_{CC}, V_{SS}, V_{SS}, A15, A14, A13, V_{SS}, A12, A11, A10, A9, A8, V_{CC}, A7, A6, A5, A4, A3, A2

240182–52

Figure 1.1. 80376 100-Pin Quad Flat-Pack Pin Out (Top View)

Table 1.1. 100-Pin Plastic Quad Flat-Pack Pin Assignments

Address		Data		Control		N/C	V_{CC}	V_{SS}
A_1	18	D_0	1	$\overline{ADS}$	16	20	8	2
A_2	51	D_1	100	$\overline{BHE}$	19	27	9	5
A_3	52	D_2	99	$\overline{BLE}$	17		10	11
A_4	53	D_3	96	$\overline{BUSY}$	34	29	21	12
A_5	54	D_4	95	CLK2	15	30	32	13
A_6	55	D_5	94	D/$\overline{C}$	24	31	39	14
A_7	56	D_6	93	$\overline{ERROR}$	36	43	42	22
A_8	58	D_7	92	$\overline{FLT}$	28	44	48	35
A_9	59	D_8	90	HLDA	3	45	57	41
A_{10}	60	D_9	89	HOLD	4	46	69	49
A_{11}	61	D_{10}	88	INTR	40	47	71	50
A_{12}	62	D_{11}	87	$\overline{LOCK}$	26		84	63
A_{13}	64	D_{12}	86	M/$\overline{IO}$	23		91	67
A_{14}	65	D_{13}	83	$\overline{NA}$	6		97	68
A_{15}	66	D_{14}	82	NMI	38			77
A_{16}	70	D_{15}	81	PEREQ	37			78
A_{17}	72			$\overline{READY}$	7			85
A_{18}	73			RESET	33			98
A_{19}	74			W/$\overline{R}$	25			
A_{20}	75							
A_{21}	76							
A_{22}	79							
A_{23}	80							

Top View (Component Side)

	N	M	L	K	J	H	G	F	E	D	C	B	A	
1	V_{CC}	V_{SS}	N/C	A1	$\overline{ADS}$	$\overline{READY}$	HOLD	D0	D2	V_{SS}	V_{CC}	V_{SS}	V_{CC}	1
2	V_{SS}	V_{CC}	M/$\overline{IO}$	$\overline{BHE}$	$\overline{BLE}$	CLK2	$\overline{NA}$	HLDA	D1	D3	V_{SS}	V_{CC}	V_{SS}	2
3	V_{CC}	D/$\overline{C}$										D4	V_{CC}	3
4	V_{SS}	W/$\overline{R}$										D6	D5	4
5	V_{CC}	$\overline{LOCK}$										D7	D8	5
6	V_{SS}	RESET										D9	D10	6
7	PEREQ	$\overline{BUSY}$										D11	D12	7
8	$\overline{ERROR}$	NMI										D13	D14	8
9	V_{SS}	INTR										D15	A23	9
10	V_{CC}	A2										A21	A22	10
11	V_{SS}	A3										V_{SS}	V_{CC}	11
12	V_{SS}	A4	A5	A7	A8	A10	A13	A15	A17	A18	A20	V_{CC}	V_{SS}	12
13	V_{CC}	V_{SS}	V_{CC}	A6	A9	A11	A12	A14	A16	A19	V_{CC}	V_{SS}	V_{CC}	13
	N	M	L	K	J	H	G	F	E	D	C	B	A	

240182–49

Bottom View (Pin Side)

	A	B	C	D	E	F	G	H	J	K	L	M	N	
01	V_{CC}	V_{SS}	V_{CC}	V_{SS}	D_2	D_0	HOLD	$\overline{READY}$	$\overline{ADS}$	A_1	N/C	V_{SS}	V_{CC}	01
02	V_{SS}	V_{CC}	V_{SS}	D_3	D_1	HLDA	$\overline{NA}$	CLK2	$\overline{BLE}$	$\overline{BHE}$	M/$\overline{IO}$	V_{CC}	V_{SS}	02
03	V_{CC}	D_4										D/$\overline{C}$	V_{CC}	03
04	D_5	D_6										W/$\overline{R}$	V_{SS}	04
05	D_8	D_7										$\overline{LOCK}$	V_{CC}	05
06	D_{10}	D_9										RESET	V_{SS}	06
07	D_{12}	D_{11}										$\overline{BUSY}$	PEREQ	07
08	D_{14}	D_{13}										NMI	$\overline{ERROR}$	08
09	A_{23}	D_{15}										INTR	V_{SS}	09
10	A_{22}	A_{21}										A_2	V_{CC}	10
11	V_{CC}	V_{SS}										A_3	V_{SS}	11
12	V_{SS}	V_{CC}	A_{20}	A_{18}	A_{17}	A_{15}	A_{13}	A_{10}	A_8	A_7	A_5	A_4	V_{SS}	12
13	V_{CC}	V_{SS}	V_{CC}	A_{19}	A_{16}	A_{14}	A_{12}	A_{11}	A_9	A_6	V_{CC}	V_{SS}	V_{CC}	13
	A	B	C	D	E	F	G	H	J	K	L	M	N	

240182–2

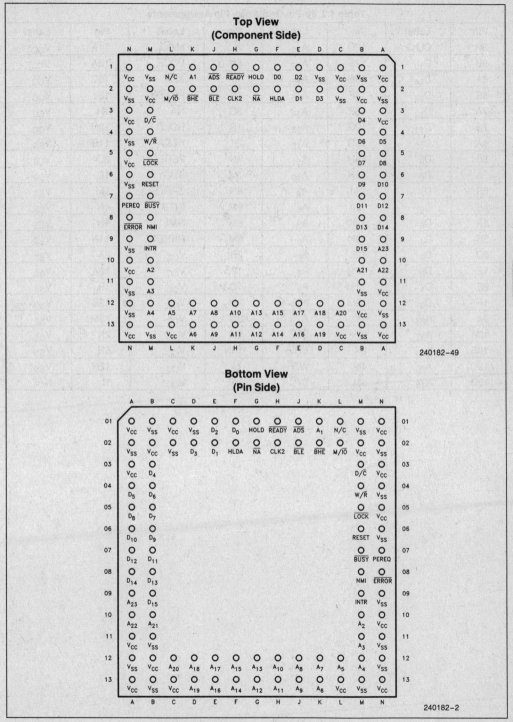

Figure 1.2. 80376 88-Pin Grid Array Pin Out

Table 1.2. 88-Pin Grid Array Pin Assignments

Pin	Label	Pin	Label	Pin	Label	Pin	Label
2H	CLK2	12D	A_{18}	2L	M/$\overline{IO}$	11A	V_{CC}
9B	D_{15}	12E	A_{17}	5M	$\overline{LOCK}$	13A	V_{CC}
8A	D_{14}	13E	A_{16}	1J	$\overline{ADS}$	13C	V_{CC}
8B	D_{13}	12F	A_{15}	1H	$\overline{READY}$	13L	V_{CC}
7A	D_{12}	13F	A_{14}	2G	$\overline{NA}$	1N	V_{CC}
7B	D_{11}	12G	A_{13}	1G	HOLD	13N	V_{CC}
6A	D_{10}	13G	A_{12}	2F	HLDA	11B	V_{SS}
6B	D_9	13H	A_{11}	7N	PEREQ	2C	V_{SS}
5A	D_8	12H	A_{10}	7M	$\overline{BUSY}$	1D	V_{SS}
5B	D_7	13J	A_9	8N	$\overline{ERROR}$	1M	V_{SS}
4B	D_6	12J	A_8	9M	INTR	4N	V_{SS}
4A	D_5	12K	A_7	8M	NMI	9N	V_{SS}
3B	D_4	13K	A_6	6M	RESET	11N	V_{SS}
2D	D_3	12L	A_5	2B	V_{CC}	2A	V_{SS}
1E	D_2	12M	A_4	12B	V_{CC}	12A	V_{SS}
2E	D_1	11M	A_3	1C	V_{CC}	1B	V_{SS}
1F	D_0	10M	A_2	2M	V_{CC}	13B	V_{SS}
9A	A_{23}	1K	A_1	3N	V_{CC}	13M	V_{SS}
10A	A_{22}	2J	$\overline{BLE}$	5N	V_{CC}	2N	V_{SS}
10B	A_{21}	2K	$\overline{BHE}$	10N	V_{CC}	6N	V_{SS}
12C	A_{20}	4M	W/$\overline{R}$	1A	V_{CC}	12N	V_{SS}
13D	A_{19}	3M	D/$\overline{C}$	3A	V_{CC}	1L	N/C

The following table lists a brief description of each pin on the 80376. The following definitions are used in these descriptions:

—	The named signal is active LOW.
I	Input signal.
O	Output signal.
I/O	Input and Output signal.
—	No electrical connection.

Symbol	Type	Name and Function
CLK2	I	**CLK2** provides the fundamental timing for the 80376. For additional information see **Clock** in Section 4.1.
RESET	I	**RESET** suspends any operation in progress and places the 80376 in a known reset state. See **Interrupt Signals** in Section 4.1 for additional information.
$D_{15}-D_0$	I/O	**DATA BUS** inputs data during memory, I/O and interrupt acknowledge read cycles and outputs data during memory and I/O write cycles. See **Data Bus** in Section 4.1 for additional information.
$A_{23}-A_1$	O	**ADDRESS BUS** outputs physical memory or port I/O addresses. See **Address Bus** in Section 4.1 for additional information.
$W/\overline{R}$	O	**WRITE/READ** is a bus cycle definition pin that distinguishes write cycles from read cycles. See **Bus Cycle Definition Signals** in Section 4.1 for additional information.
$D/\overline{C}$	O	**DATA/CONTROL** is a bus cycle definition pin that distinguishes data cycles, either memory or I/O, from control cycles which are: interrupt acknowledge, halt, and instruction fetching. See **Bus Cycle Definition Signals** in Section 4.1 for additional information.
$M/\overline{IO}$	O	**MEMORY I/O** is a bus cycle definition pin that distinguishes memory cycles from input/output cycles. See **Bus Cycle Definition Signals** in Section 4.1 for additional information.
$\overline{LOCK}$	O	**BUS LOCK** is a bus cycle definition pin that indicates that other system bus masters are denied access to the system bus while it is active. See **Bus Cycle Definition Signals** in Section 4.1 for additional information.
$\overline{ADS}$	O	**ADDRESS STATUS** indicates that a valid bus cycle definition and address ($W/\overline{R}$, $D/\overline{C}$, $M/\overline{IO}$, $\overline{BHE}$, $\overline{BLE}$ and $A_{23}-A_1$) are being driven at the 80376 pins. See **Bus Control Signals** in Section 4.1 for additional information.
$\overline{NA}$	I	**NEXT ADDRESS** is used to request address pipelining. See **Bus Control Signals** in Section 4.1 for additional information.
$\overline{READY}$	I	**BUS READY** terminates the bus cycle. See **Bus Control Signals** in Section 4.1 for additional information.
$\overline{BHE}$, $\overline{BLE}$	O	**BYTE ENABLES** indicate which data bytes of the data bus take part in a bus cycle. See **Address Bus** in Section 4.1 for additional information.
HOLD	I	**BUS HOLD REQUEST** input allows another bus master to request control of the local bus. See **Bus Arbitration Signals** in Section 4.1 for additional information.

Symbol	Type	Name and Function
HLDA	O	**BUS HOLD ACKNOWLEDGE** output indicates that the 80376 has surrendered control of its local bus to another bus master. See **Bus Arbitration Signals** in Section 4.1 for additional information.
INTR	I	**INTERRUPT REQUEST** is a maskable input that signals the 80376 to suspend execution of the current program and execute an interrupt acknowledge function. See **Interrupt Signals** in Section 4.1 for additional information.
NMI	I	**NON-MASKABLE INTERRUPT REQUEST** is a non-maskable input that signals the 80376 to suspend execution of the current program and execute an interrupt acknowledge function. See **Interrupt Signals** in Section 4.1 for additional information.
$\overline{BUSY}$	I	**BUSY** signals a busy condition from a processor extension. See **Coprocessor Interface Signals** in Section 4.1 for additional information.
$\overline{ERROR}$	I	**ERROR** signals an error condition from a processor extension. See **Coprocessor Interface Signals** in Section 4.1 for additional information.
PEREQ	I	**PROCESSOR EXTENSION REQUEST** indicates that the processor extension has data to be transferred by the 80376. See **Coprocessor Interface Signals** in Section 4.1 for additional information.
$\overline{FLT}$	I	**FLOAT,** when active, forces all bidirectional and output signals, including HLDA, to the float condition. FLOAT is not available on the PGA package. See **Float** for additional information.
N/C	—	**NO CONNECT** should always remain unconnected. Connection of a N/C pin may cause the processor to malfunction or be incompatible with future steppings of the 80376.
V_{CC}	I	**SYSTEM POWER** provides the +5V nominal D.C. supply input.
V_{SS}	I	**SYSTEM GROUND** provides 0V connection from which all inputs and outputs are measured.

2.0 ARCHITECTURE OVERVIEW

The 80376 supports the protection mechanisms needed by sophisticated multitasking embedded systems and real-time operating systems. The use of these protection mechanisms is completely optional. For embedded applications not needing protection, the 80376 can easily be configured to provide a 16 Mbyte physical address space.

Instruction pipelining, high bus bandwidth, and a very high performance ALU ensure short average instruction execution times and high system throughput. The 80376 is capable of execution at sustained rates of 2.5–3.0 million instructions per second.

The 80376 offers on-chip testability and debugging features. Four break point registers allow conditional or unconditional break point traps on code execution or data accesses for powerful debugging of even ROM based systems. Other testability features include self-test and tri-stating of output buffers during RESET.

The Intel 80376 embedded processor consists of a central processing unit, a memory management unit and a bus interface. The central processing unit consists of the execution unit and instruction unit. The execution unit contains the eight 32-bit general registers which are used for both address calculation and data operations and a 64-bit barrel shifter used to speed shift, rotate, multiply, and divide operations. The instruction unit decodes the instruction opcodes and stores them in the decoded instruction queue for immediate use by the execution unit.

The Memory Management Unit (MMU) consists of a segmentation and protection unit. Segmentation allows the managing of the logical address space by providing an extra addressing component, one that allows easy code and data relocatability, and efficient sharing.

The protection unit provides four levels of protection for isolating and protecting applications and the operating system from each other. The hardware enforced protection allows the design of systems with a high degree of integrity and simplifies debugging.

Finally, to facilitate high performance system hardware designs, the 80376 bus interface offers address pipelining and direct Byte Enable signals for each byte of the data bus.

2.1 Register Set

The 80376 has twenty-nine registers as shown in Figure 2.1. These registers are grouped into the following six categories:

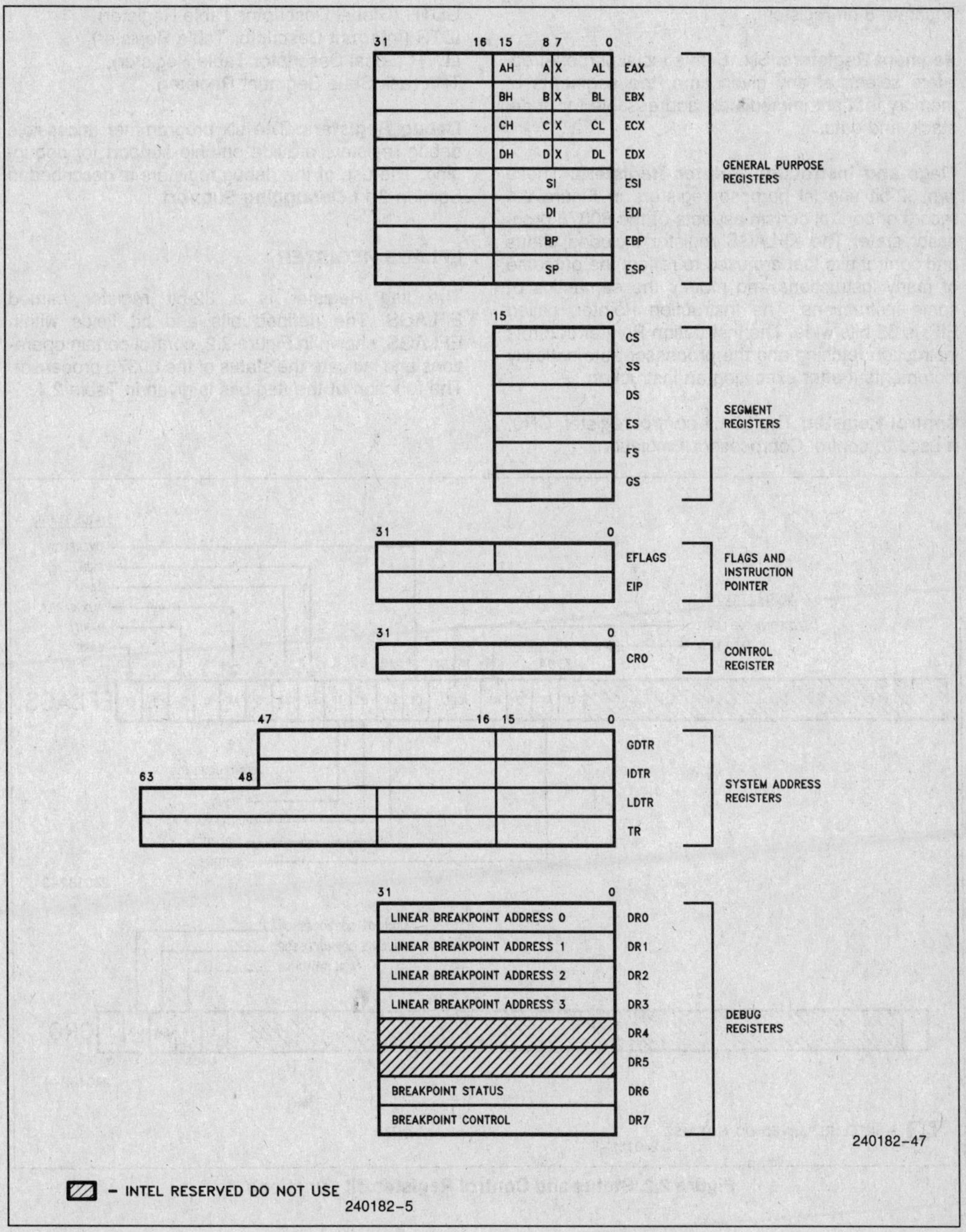

Figure 2.1. 80376 Base Architecture Registers

General Registers: The eight 32-bit general purpose registers are used to contain arithmetic and logical operands. Four of these (EAX, EBX, ECX and EDX) can be used either in their entirety as 32-bit registers, as 16-bit registers, or split into pairs of separate 8-bit registers.

Segment Registers: Six 16-bit special purpose registers select, at any given time, the segments of memory that are immediately addressable for code, stack, and data.

Flags and Instruction Pointer Registers: These two 32-bit special purpose registers in Figure 2.1 record or control certain aspects of the 80376 processor state. The EFLAGS register includes status and control bits that are used to reflect the outcome of many instructions and modify the semantics of some instructions. The Instruction Pointer, called EIP, is 32 bits wide. The Instruction Pointer controls instruction fetching and the processor automatically increments it after executing an instruction.

Control Register: The 32-bit control register, CR0, is used to control Coprocessor Emulation.

System Address Registers: These four special registers reference the tables or segments supported by the 80376/80386 protection model. These tables or segments are:

GDTR (Global Descriptor Table Register),
IDTR (Interrupt Descriptor Table Register),
LDTR (Local Descriptor Table Register),
TR (Task State Segment Register).

Debug Registers: The six programmer accessible debug registers provide on-chip support for debugging. The use of the debug registers is described in Section 2.11 **Debugging Support**.

EFLAGS REGISTER

The flag Register is a 32-bit register named EFLAGS. The defined bits and bit fields within EFLAGS, shown in Figure 2.2, control certain operations and indicate the status of the 80376 processor. The function of the flag bits is given in Table 2.1.

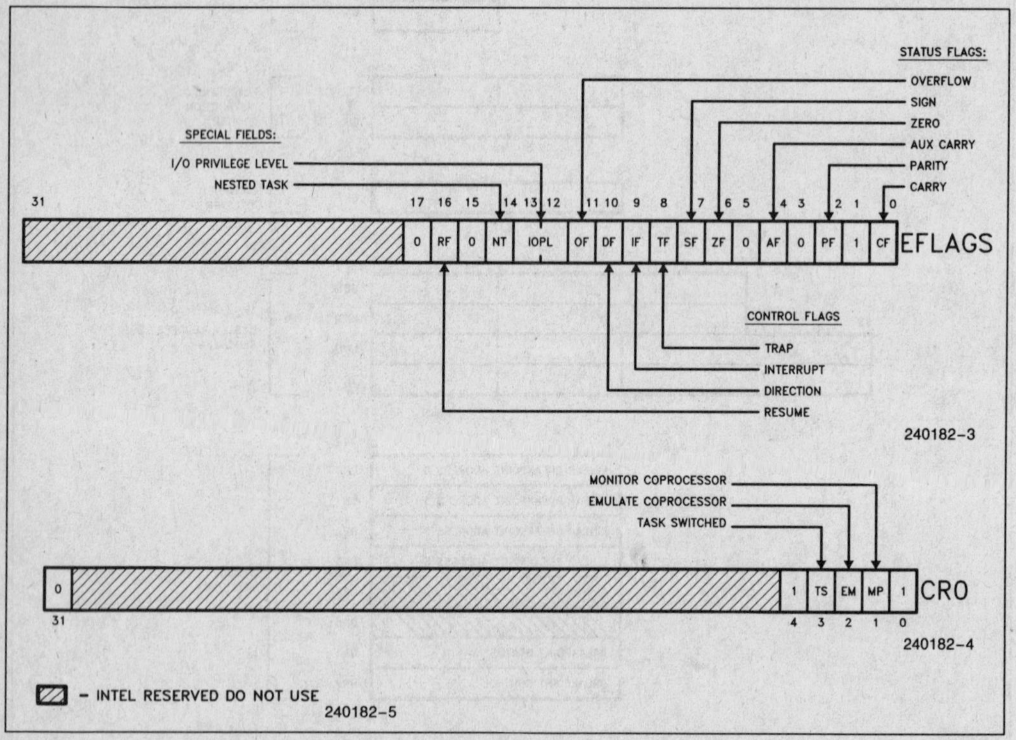

Figure 2.2. Status and Control Register Bit Functions

Table 2.1. Flag Definitions

Bit Position	Name	Function
0	CF	**Carry Flag**—Set on high-order bit carry or borrow; cleared otherwise.
2	PF	**Parity Flag**—Set if low-order 8 bits of result contain an even number of 1-bits; cleared otherwise.
4	AF	**Auxiliary Carry Flag**—Set on carry from or borrow to the low order four bits of AL; cleared otherwise.
6	ZF	**Zero Flag**—Set if result is zero; cleared otherwise.
7	SF	**Sign Flag**—Set equal to high-order bit of result (0 if positive, 1 if negative).
8	TF	**Single Step Flag**—Once set, a single step interrupt occurs after the next instruction executes. TF is cleared by the single step interrupt.
9	IF	**Interrupt-Enable Flag**—When set, external interrupts signaled on the INTR pin will cause the CPU to transfer control to an interrupt vector specified location.
10	DF	**Direction Flag**—Causes string instructions to auto-increment (default) the appropriate index registers when cleared. Setting DF causes auto-decrement.
11	OF	**Overflow Flag**—Set if the operation resulted in a carry/borrow into the sign bit (high-order bit) of the result but did not result in a carry/borrow out of the high-order bit or vice-versa.
12, 13	IOPL	**I/O Privilege Level**—Indicates the maximum CPL permitted to execute I/O instructions without generating an exception 13 fault or consulting the I/O permission bit map. It also indicates the maximum CPL value allowing alteration of the IF bit.
14	NT	**Nested Task**—Indicates that the execution of the current task is nested within another task (see **Task Switching**).
16	RF	**Resume Flag**—Used in conjunction with debug register breakpoints. It is checked at instruction boundaries before breakpoint processing. If set, any debug fault is ignored on the next instruction. It is reset at the successful completion of any instruction except IRET, POPF, and those instructions causing task switches.

CONTROL REGISTER

The 80376 has a 32-bit control register called CR0 that is used to control coprocessor emulation. This register is shown in Figures, 2.1 and 2.2. The defined CR0 bits are described in Table 2.2. Bits 0, 4 and 31 of CR0 have fixed values in the 80376. These values cannot be changed. Programs that load CR0 should always load bits 0, 4 and 31 with values previously there to be compatible with the 80386.

Table 2.2. CR0 Definitions

Bit Position	Name	Function
1	MP	**Monitor Coprocessor Extension**—Allows WAIT instructions to cause a processor extension not present exception (number 7).
2	EM	**Emulate Processor Extension**—When set, this bit causes a processor extension not present exception (number 7) on ESC instructions to allow processor extension emulation.
3	TS	**Task Switched**—When set, this bit indicates the next instruction using a processor extension will cause exception 7, allowing software to test whether the current processor extension context belongs to the current task (see **Task Switching**).

2.2 Instruction Set

The instruction set is divided into nine categories of operations:

Data Transfer
Arithmetic
Shift/Rotate
String Manipulation
Bit Manipulation
Control Transfer
High Level Language Support
Operating System Support
Processor Control

These 80376 processor instructions are listed in Table 8.1 **80376 Instruction Set and Clock Count Summary**.

All 80376 processor instructions operate on either 0, 1, 2 or 3 operands; an operand resides in a register, in the instruction itself, or in memory. Most zero operand instructions (e.g. CLI, STI) take only one byte. One operand instructions generally are two bytes long. The average instruction is 3.2 bytes long. Since the 80376 has a 16-byte prefetch instruction queue an average of 5 instructions can be prefetched. The use of two operands permits the following types of common instructions:

Register to Register
Memory to Register
Immediate to Register
Memory to Memory
Register to Memory
Immediate to Memory

The operands are either 8-, 16- or 32-bit long.

2.3 Memory Organization

Memory on the 80376 is divided into 8-bit quantities (bytes), 16-bit quantities (words), and 32-bit quantities (dwords). Words are stored in two consecutive bytes in memory with the low-order byte at the lowest address. Dwords are stored in four consecutive bytes in memory with the low-order byte at the lowest address. The address of a word or Dword is the byte address of the low-order byte. For maximum performance word and dword values should be at even physical addresses.

In addition to these basic data types the 80376 processor supports segments. Memory can be divided up into one or more variable length segments, which can be shared between programs.

ADDRESS SPACES

The 80376 has three types of address spaces: **logical, linear,** and **physical.** A **logical** address (also known as a **virtual** address) consists of a selector and an offset. A selector is the contents of a segment register. An offset is formed by summing all of the addressing components (BASE, INDEX, and DISPLACEMENT), discussed in Section 2.4 **Addressing Modes,** into an effective address.

Every selector has a **logical base** address associated with it that can be up to 32 bits in length. This 32-bit **logical base** address is added to either a 32-bit offset address or a 16-bit offset address (by using the ***address length prefix***)to form a final 32-bit **linear** address. This final **linear** address is then truncated so that only the lower 24 bits of this address are used to address the 16 Mbytes physical memory address space. The **logical base** address is stored in one of two operating system tables (i.e. the Local Descriptor Table or Global Descriptor Table).

Figure 2.3 shows the relationship between the various address spaces.

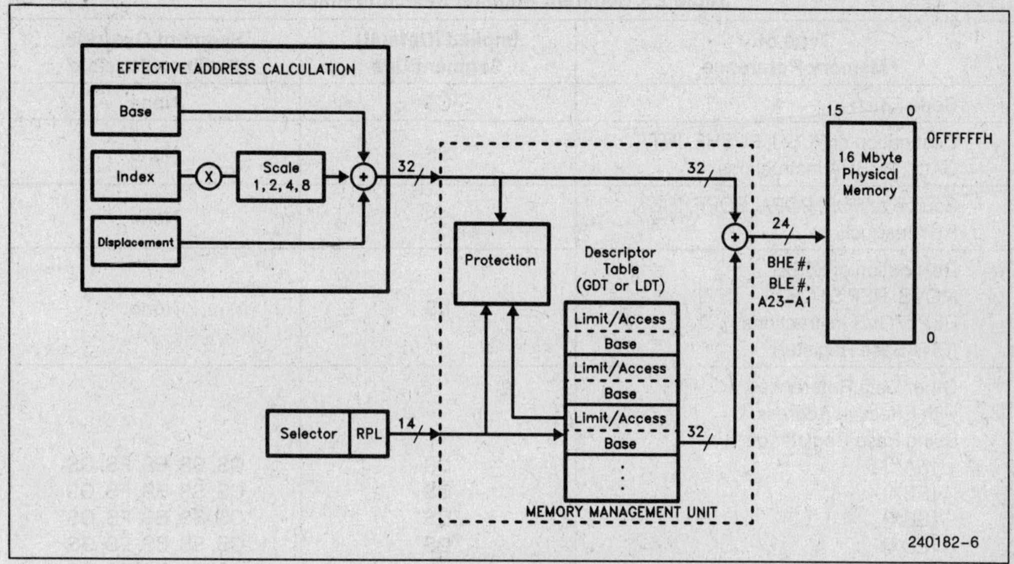

Figure 2.3. Address Translation

SEGMENT REGISTER USAGE

The main data structure used to organize memory is the segment. On the 80376, segments are variable sized blocks of linear addresses which have certain attributes associated with them. There are two main types of segments, code and data. The simplest use of segments is to have one code and data segment. Each segment is 16 Mbytes in size overlapping each other. This allows code and data to be directly addressed by the same offset.

In order to provide compact instruction encoding and increase processor performance, instructions do not need to explicitly specify which segment register is used. The segment register is automatically chosen according to the rules of Table 2.3 (Segment Register Selection Rules). In general, data references use the selector contained in the DS register, stack references use the SS register and instruction fetches use the CS register. The contents of the Instruction Pointer provide the offset. Special segment override prefixes allow the explicit use of a given segment register, and override the implicit rules listed in Table 2.3. The override prefixes also allow the use of the ES, FS and GS segment registers.

There are no restrictions regarding the overlapping of the base addresses of any segments. Thus, all 6 segments could have the base address set to zero. Further details of segmentation are discussed in Section 3.0 Architecture.

Table 2.3. Segment Register Selection Rules

Type of Memory Reference	Implied (Default) Segment Use	Segment Override Prefixes Possible
Code Fetch	CS	None
Destination of PUSH, PUSHF, INT, CALL, PUSHA Instructions	SS	None
Source of POP, POPA, POPF, IRET, RET Instructions	SS	None
Destination of STOS, MOVS, REP STOS, REP MOVS Instructions (DI is Base Register)	ES	None
Other Data References, with Effective Address Using Base Register of:		
[EAX]	DS	CS, SS, ES, FS, GS
[EBX]	DS	CS, SS, ES, FS, GS
[ECX]	DS	CS, SS, ES, FS, GS
[EDX]	DS	CS, SS, ES, FS, GS
[ESI]	DS	CS, SS, ES, FS, GS
[EDI]	DS	CS, SS, ES, FS, GS
[EBP]	SS	CS, SS, ES, FS, GS
[ESP]	SS	CS, SS, ES, FS, GS

2.4 Addressing Modes

The 80376 provides a total of 8 addressing modes for instructions to specify operands. The addressing modes are optimized to allow the efficient execution of high level languages such as C and FORTRAN, and they cover the vast majority of data references needed by high-level languages.

Two of the addressing modes provide for instructions that operate on register or immediate operands:

Register Operand Mode: The operand is located in one of the 8-, 16- or 32-bit general registers.

Immediate Operand Mode: The operand is included in the instruction as part of the opcode.

The remaining 6 modes provide a mechanism for specifying the effective address of an operand. The linear address consists of two components: the segment base address and an effective address. The effective address is calculated by summing any combination of the following three address elements (see Figure 2.3):

DISPLACEMENT: an 8-, 16- or 32-bit immediate value following the instruction.

BASE: The contents of any general purpose register. The base registers are generally used by compilers to point to the start of the local variable area. Note that if the ***Address Length Prefix*** is used, only BX and BP can be used as a BASE register.

INDEX: The contents of any general purpose register except for ESP. The index registers are used to access the elements of an array, or a string of characters. The index register's value can be multiplied by a scale factor, either 1, 2, 4 or 8. The scaled index is especially useful for accessing arrays or structures. Note that if the ***Address Length Prefix*** is used, no Scaling is available and only the registers SI and DI can be used to INDEX.

Combinations of these 3 components make up the 6 additional addressing modes. There is no performance penalty for using any of these addressing combinations, since the effective address calculation is pipelined with the execution of other instructions. The one exception is the simultaneous use of BASE and INDEX components which requires one additional clock.

As shown in Figure 2.4, the effective address (EA) of an operand is calculated according to the following formula:

$$EA = BASE_{Register} + (INDEX_{Register} \times scaling) + DISPLACEMENT$$

1. **Direct Mode:** The operand's offset is contained as part of the instruction as an 8-, 16- or 32-bit DISPLACEMENT.
2. **Register Indirect Mode:** A BASE register contains the address of the operand.
3. **Based Mode:** A BASE register's contents is added to a DISPLACEMENT to form the operand's offset.
4. **Scaled Index Mode:** An INDEX register's contents is multiplied by a SCALING factor which is added to a DISPLACEMENT to form the operand's offset.
5. **Based Scaled Index Mode:** The contents of an INDEX register is multiplied by a SCALING factor and the result is added to the contents of a BASE register to obtain the operand's offset.
6. **Based Scaled Index Mode with Displacement:** The contents of an INDEX register are multiplied by a SCALING factor, and the result is added to the contents of a BASE register and a DISPLACEMENT to form the operand's offset.

240182-7

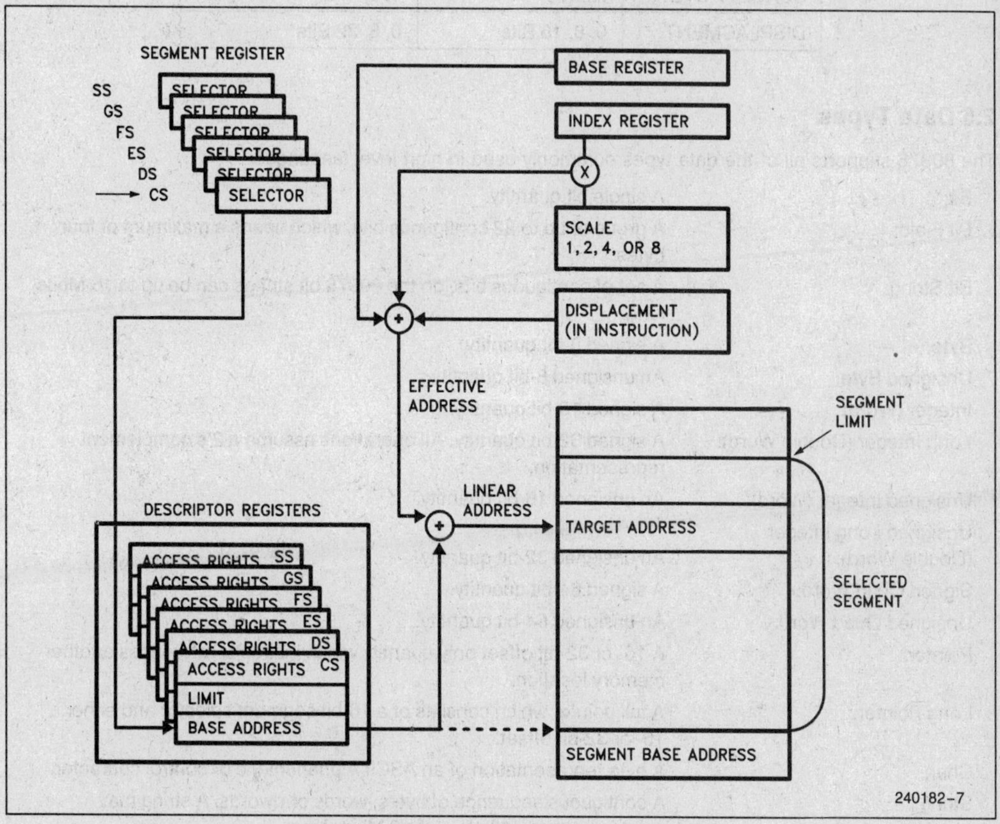

Figure 2.4. Addressing Mode Calculations

GENERATING 16-BIT ADDRESSES

The 80376 executes code with a default length for operands and addresses of 32 bits. The 80376 is also able to execute operands and addresses of 16 bits. This is specified through the use of override prefixes. Two prefixes, the **Operand Length Prefix** and the **Address Length Prefix,** override the default 32-bit length on an individual instruction basis. These prefixes are automatically added by assemblers. The Operand Length and Address Length Prefixes can be applied separately or in combination to any instruction.

The 80376 normally executes 32-bit code and uses either 8- or 32-bit displacements, and any register can be used as based or index registers. When executing 16-bit code (by prefix overrides), the displacements are either 8 or 16 bits, and the base and index register conform to the 16-bit model. Table 2.4 illustrates the differences.

Table 2.4. BASE and INDEX Registers for 16- and 32-Bit Addresses

	16-Bit Addressing	32-Bit Addressing
BASE REGISTER	BX, BP	Any 32-Bit GP Register
INDEX REGISTER	SI, DI	Any 32-Bit GP Register except ESP
SCALE FACTOR	None	1, 2, 4, 8
DISPLACMENT	0, 8, 16 Bits	0, 8, 32 Bits

2.5 Data Types

The 80376 supports all of the data types commonly used in high level languages:

Bit:	A single bit quantity.
Bit Field:	A group of up to 32 contiguous bits, which spans a maximum of four bytes.
Bit String:	A set of contiguous bits, on the 80376 bit strings can be up to 16 Mbits long.
Byte:	A signed 8-bit quantity.
Unsigned Byte:	An unsigned 8-bit quantity.
Integer (Word):	A signed 16-bit quantity.
Long Integer (Double Word):	A signed 32-bit quantity. All operations assume a 2's complement representation.
Unsigned Integer (Word):	An unsigned 16-bit quantity.
Unsigned Long Integer (Double Word):	An unsigned 32-bit quantity
Signed Quad Word:	A signed 64-bit quantity.
Unsigned Quad Word:	An unsigned 64-bit quantity.
Pointer:	A 16- or 32-bit offset only quantity which indirectly references another memory location.
Long Pointer:	A full pointer which consists of a 16-bit segment selector and either a 16- or 32-bit offset.
Char:	A byte representation of an ASCII Alphanumeric or control character.
String:	A contiguous sequence of bytes, words or dwords. A string may contain between 1 byte and 16 Mbytes.
BCD:	A byte (unpacked) representation of decimal digits 0–9.
Packed BCD:	A byte (packed) representation of two decimal digits 0–9 storing one digit in each nibble.

When the 80376 is coupled with a numerics Coprocessor such as the 80387SX then the following common Floating Point types are supported.

Floating Point: A signed 32-, 64- or 80-bit real number representation. Floating point numbers are supported by the 80387SX numerics coprocessor.

Figure 2.5 illustrates the data types supported by the 80376 processor and the 80387SX coprocessor.

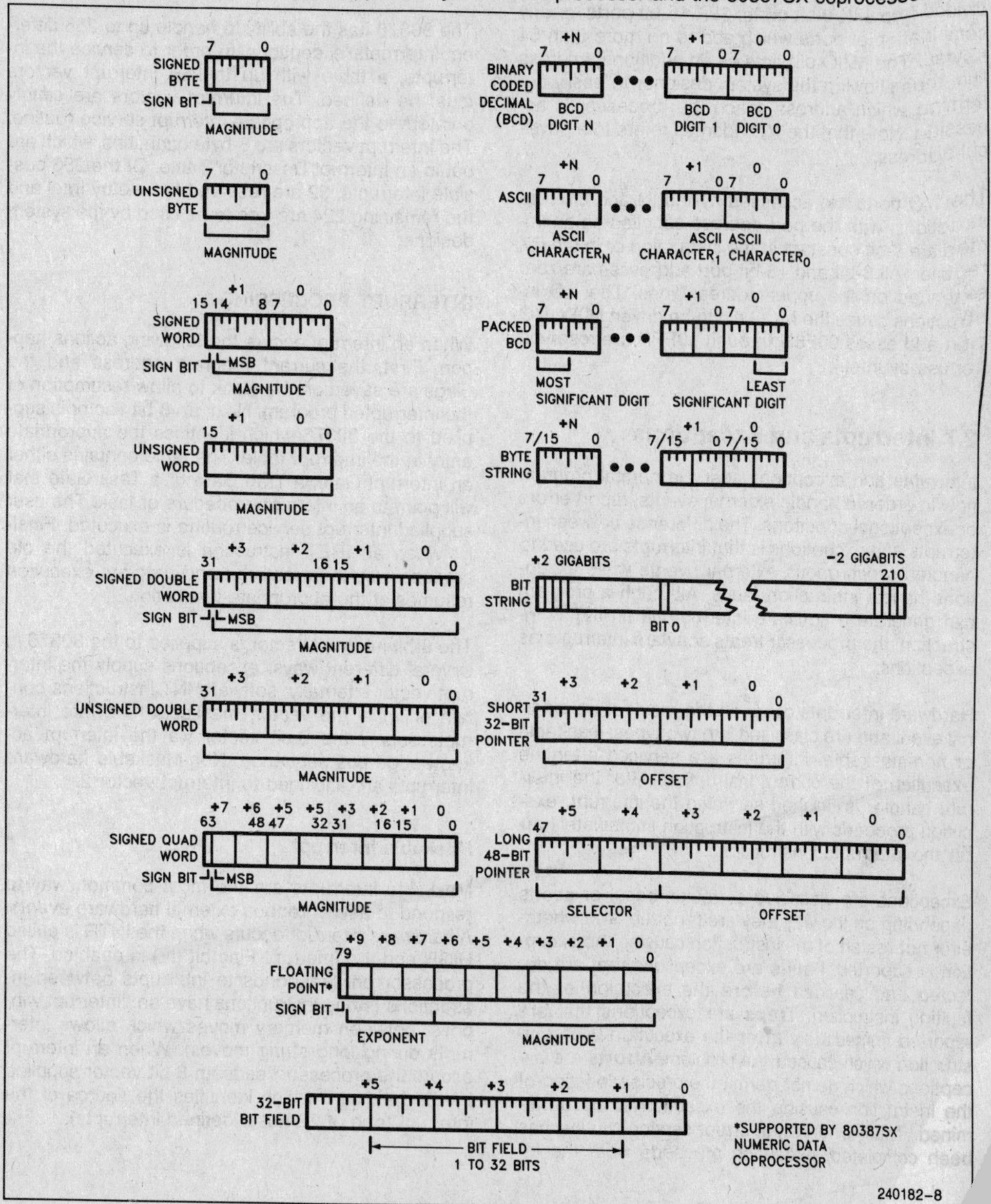

Figure 2.5. 80376 Supported Data Types

3

2.6 I/O Space

The 80376 has two distinct physical address spaces: physical memory and I/O. Generally, peripherals are placed in I/O space although the 80376 also supports memory-mapped peripherals. The I/O space consists of 64 Kbytes which can be divided into 64K 8-bit ports, 32K 16-bit ports, or any combination of ports which add to no more than 64 Kbytes. The M/$\overline{IO}$ pin acts as an additional address line, thus allowing the system designer to easily determine which address space the processor is accessing. Note that the I/O address refers to a physical address.

The I/O ports are accessed by the IN and OUT instructions, with the port address supplied as an immediate 8-bit constant in the instruction or in the DX register. All 8-bit and 16-bit port addresses are zero extended on the upper address lines. The I/O instructions cause the M/$\overline{IO}$ pin to be driven LOW. I/O port addresses 00F8H through 00FFH are reserved for use by Intel.

2.7 Interrupts and Exceptions

Interrupts and exceptions alter the normal program flow in order to handle external events, report errors or exceptional conditons. The difference between interrupts and exceptions is that interrupts are used to handle asynchronous external events while exceptions handle instruction faults. Although a program can generate a software interrupt via an INT N instruction, the processor treats software interrupts as exceptions.

Hardware interrupts occur as the result of an external event and are classified into two types: maskable or non-maskable. Interrupts are serviced after the execution of the current instruction. After the interrupt handler is finished servicing the interrupt, execution proceeds with the instruction immediately **after** the interrupted instruction.

Exceptions are classified as faults, traps, or aborts depending on the way they are reported, and whether or not restart of the instruction causing the exception is suported. **Faults** are exceptions that are detected and serviced **before** the execution of the faulting instruction. **Traps** are exceptions that are reported immediately **after** the execution of the instruction which caused the problem. **Aborts** are exceptions which do not permit the precise location of the instruction causing the exception to be determined. Thus, when an interrupt service routine has completed, execution proceeds from the instruction immediately following the interrupted instruction. On the other hand the return address from an exception/fault routine will always point at the instruction causing the exception and include any leading instruction prefixes. Table 2.5 summarizes the possible interrupts for the 80376 and shows where the return address points to.

The 80376 has the ability to handle up to 256 different interrupts/exceptions. In order to service the interrupts, a table with up to 256 interrupt vectors must be defined. The interrupt vectors are simply pointers to the appropriate interrupt service routine. The interrupt vectors are 8-byte quantities, which are put in an Interrupt Descriptor Table. Of the 256 possible interrupts, 32 are reserved for use by Intel and the remaining 224 are free to be used by the system designer.

INTERRUPT PROCESSING

When an interrupt occurs the following actions happen. First, the current program address and the Flags are saved on the stack to allow resumption of the interrupted program. Next, an 8-bit vector is supplied to the 80376 which identifies the appropriate entry in the interrupt table. The table contains either an Interrupt Gate, a Trap Gate or a Task Gate that will point to an interrupt procedure or task. The user supplied interrupt service routine is executed. Finally, when an IRET instruction is executed the old processor state is restored and program execution resumes at the appropriate instruction.

The 8-bit interrupt vector is supplied to the 80376 in several different ways: exceptions supply the interrupt vector internally; software INT instructions contain or imply the vector; maskable hardware interrupts supply the 8-bit vector via the interrupt acknowledge bus sequence. Non-Maskable hardware interrupts are assigned to interrupt vector 2.

Maskable Interrupt

Maskable interrupts are the most common way to respond to asynchronous external hardware events. A hardware interrupt occurs when the INTR is pulled HIGH and the Interrupt Flag bit (IF) is enabled. The processor only responds to interrupts between instructions (string instructions have an "interrupt window" between memory moves which allows interrupts during long string moves). When an interrupt occurs the processor reads an 8-bit vector supplied by the hardware which identifies the source of the interrupt (one of 224 user defined interrupts).

Table 2.5. Interrupt Vector Assignments

Function	Interrupt Number	Instruction Which Can Cause Exception	Return Address Points to Faulting Instruction	Type
Divide Error	0	DIV, IDIV	Yes	FAULT
Debug Exception	1	Any Instruction	Yes	TRAP*
NMI Interrupt	2	INT 2 or NMI	No	NMI
One-Byte Interrupt	3	INT	No	TRAP
Interrupt on Overflow	4	INTO	No	TRAP
Array Bounds Check	5	BOUND	Yes	FAULT
Invalid OP-Code	6	Any Illegal Instruction	Yes	FAULT
Device Not Available	7	ESC, WAIT	Yes	FAULT
Double Fault	8	Any Instruction That Can Generate an Exception		ABORT
Coprocessor Segment Overrun	9	ESC	No	ABORT
Invalid TSS	10	JMP, CALL, IRET, INT	Yes	FAULT
Segment Not Present	11	Segment Register Instructions	Yes	FAULT
Stack Fault	12	Stack References	Yes	FAULT
General Protection Fault	13	Any Memory Reference	Yes	FAULT
Intel Reserved	14–15	—	—	—
Coprocessor Error	16	ESC, WAIT	Yes	FAULT
Intel Reserved	17–32			
Two-Byte Interrupt	0–255	INT n	No	TRAP

*Some debug exceptions may report both traps on the previous instruction, and faults on the next instruction.

Interrupts through Interrupt Gates automatically reset IF, disabling INTR requests. Interrupts through Trap Gates leave the state of the IF bit unchanged. Interrupts through a Task Gate change the IF bit according to the image of the EFLAGs register in the task's Task State Segment (TSS). When an IRET instruction is executed, the original state of the IF bit is restored.

Non-Maskable Interrupt

Non-maskable interrupts provide a method of servicing very high priority interrupts. When the NMI input is pulled HIGH it causes an interrupt with an internally supplied vector value of 2. Unlike a normal hardware interrupt no interrupt acknowledgement sequence is performed for an NMI.

While executing the NMI servicing procedure, the 80376 will not service any further NMI request, or INT requests, until an interrupt return (IRET) instruction is executed or the processor is reset. If NMI occurs while currently servicing an NMI, its presence will be saved for servicing after executing the first IRET instruction. The disabling of INTR requests depends on the gate in IDT location 2.

Software Interrupts

A third type of interrupt/exception for the 80376 is the software interrupt. An INT n instruction causes the processor to execute the interrupt service routine pointed to by the nth vector in the interrupt table.

A special case of the two byte software interrupt INT n is the one byte INT 3, or breakpoint interrupt. By inserting this one byte instruction in a program, the user can set breakpoints in his program as a debugging tool.

A final type of software interrupt, is the single step interrupt. It is discussed in **Single-Step Trap** (page 22).

INTERRUPT AND EXCEPTION PRIORITIES

Interrupts are externally-generated events. Maskable Interrupts (on the INTR input) and Non-Maskable Interrupts (on the NMI input) are recognized at instruction boundaries. When NMI and maskable INTR are **both** recognized at the **same** instruction boundary, the 80376 invokes the NMI service routine first. If, after the NMI service routine has been invoked, maskable interrupts are still enabled, then the 80376 will invoke the appropriate interrupt service routine.

As the 80376 executes instructions, it follows a consistent cycle in checking for exceptions, as shown in Table 2.6. This cycle is repeated as each instruction is executed, and occurs in parallel with instruction decoding and execution.

INSTRUCTION RESTART

The 80376 fully supports restarting all instructions after faults. If an exception is detected in the instruction to be executed (exception categories 4 through 9 in Table 2.6), the 80376 device invokes the appropriate exception service routine. The 80376 is in a state that permits restart of the instruction.

DOUBLE FAULT

A Double fault (exception 8) results when the processor attempts to invoke an exception service routine for the segment exceptions (10, 11, 12 or 13), but in the process of doing so, detects an exception.

2.8 Reset and Initialization

When the processor is Reset the registers have the values shown in Table 2.7. The 80376 will then start executing instructions near the top of physical memory, at location 0FFFFF0H. A short JMP should be executed within the segment defined for power-up (see Table 2.7). The GDT should then be initialized for a start-up data and code segment followed by a far JMP that will load the segment descriptor cache with the new descriptor values. The IDT table, after reset, is located at physical address 0H, with a limit of 256 entries.

RESET forces the 80376 to terminate all execution and local bus activity. No instruction execution or bus activity will occur as long as Reset is active. Between 350 and 450 CLK2 periods after Reset becomes inactive, the 80376 will start executing instructions at the top of physical memory.

Table 2.6. Sequence of Exception Checking

Consider the case of the 80376 having just completed an instruction. It then performs the following checks before reaching the point where the next instruction is completed:

1. Check for Exception 1 Traps from the instruction just completed (single-step via Trap Flag, or Data Breakpoints set in the Debug Registers).
2. Check for external NMI and INTR.
3. Check for Exception 1 Faults in the next instruction (Instruction Execution Breakpoint set in the Debug Registers for the next instruction).
4. Check for Segmentation Faults that prevented fetching the entire next instruction (exceptions 11 or 13).
5. Check for Faults decoding the next instruction (exception 6 if illegal opcode; or exception 13 if instruction is longer than 15 bytes, or privilege violation (i.e. not at IOPL or at CPL = 0).
6. If WAIT opcode, check if TS = 1 and MP = 1 (exception 7 if both are 1).
7. If ESCape opcode for numeric coprocessor, check if EM = 1 or TS = 1 (exception 7 if either are 1).
8. If WAIT opcode or ESCape opcode for numeric coprocessor, check $\overline{\text{ERROR}}$ input signal (exception 16 if $\overline{\text{ERROR}}$ input is asserted).
9. Check for Segmentation Faults that prevent transferring the entire memory quantity (exceptions 11, 12, 13).

Table 2.7. Register Values after Reset

Flag Word (EFLAGS)	uuuu0002H	(Note 1)
Machine Status Word (CR0)	uuuuuuu1H	(Note 2)
Instruction Pointer (EIP)	0000FFF0H	
Code Segment (CS)	F000H	(Note 3)
Data Segment (DS)	0000H	(Note 4)
Stack Segment (SS)	0000H	
Extra Segment (ES)	0000H	(Note 4)
Extra Segment (FS)	0000H	
Extra Segment (GS)	0000H	
EAX Register	0000H	(Note 5)
EDX Register	Component and Stepping ID	(Note 6)
All Other Registers	Undefined	(Note 7)

NOTES:
1. EFLAG Register. The upper 14 bits of the EFLAGS register are undefined, all defined flag bits are zero.
2. CR0: The defined 4 bits in the CR0 is equal to 1H.
3. The Code Segment Register (CS) will have its Base Address set to 0FFFF0000H and Limit set to 0FFFFH.
4. The Data and Extra Segment Registers (DS and ES) will have their Base Address set to 000000000H and Limit set to 0FFFFH.
5. If self-test is selected, the EAX should contain a 0 value. If a value of 0 is not found the self-test has detected a flaw in the part.
6. EDX register always holds component and stepping identifier.
7. All unidentified bits are Intel Reserved and should not be used.

2.9 Initialization

Because the 80376 processor starts executing in protected mode, certain precautions need be taken during initialization. Before any far jumps can take place the GDT and/or LDT tables need to be setup and their respective registers loaded. Before interrupts can be initialized the IDT table must be setup and the IDTR must be loaded. The example code is shown below:

```
; ********************************************************************
;
; This is an example of startup code to put either an 80376,
; 80386SX or 80386 into flat mode. All of memory is treated as
; simple linear RAM. There are no interrupt routines. The
; Builder creates the GDT-alias and IDT-alias and places them,
; by default, in GDT[1] and GDT[2].  Other entries in the GDT
; are specified in the Build file.  After initialization it jumps
; to a C startup routine. To use this template, change this jmp
; address to that of your code, or make the label of your code
; "c_startup".
;
; This code was assembled and built using version 1.2 of the
; Intel RLL utilities and Intel 386ASM assembler.
;
;             ***    This code was tested    ***
;
; ********************************************************************
```

```
NAME FLAT                ; name of the object module

EXTRN    c_startup:near  ; this is the label jmped to after init

pe_flag          equ 1
data_selc        equ 20h  ; assume code is GDT[3], data GDT[4]

INIT_CODE     SEGMENT ER PUBLIC USE32     ; Segment base at Offffff80h

PUBLIC GDT_DESC

gdt_desc    dq   ?

PUBLIC     START

start:
    cld                          ; clear direction flag
    smsw bx                      ; check for processor (80376) at reset
    test bl,1                    ; use SMSW rather than MOV for speed
    jnz pestart
realstart                        ; is an 80386 and in real mode
    db 66h                       ; force the next operand into 32-bit mode.
    mov eax,offset gdt_desc      ; move address of the GDT descriptor into eax
    xor ebx,ebx                  ; clear ebx
    mov bh,ah                    ; load 8 bits of address into bh
    move bl,al                   ; load 8 bits of address into bl
    db 67h
    db 66h                       ; use the 32-bit form of LGDT to load
    lgdt cs:[ebx]                ; the 32-bits of address into the GDTR
    smsw ax                      ; go into protected mode (set PE bit)
    or al,pe_flag
    lmsw ax
    jmp next                     ; flush prefetch queue
pestart:
    mov ebx,offset gdt_desc
    xor eax,eax
    mov ax,bx                    ; lower portion of address only
    lgdt cs:[eax]
    xor ebx,ebx                  ; initialize data selectors
    mov bl,data_selc             ; GDT[3]
    mov ds,bx
    mov ss,bx
    mov es,bx
    mov fs,bx
    mov gs,bx
    jmp pejump
next:
    xor ebx,ebx                  ; initialize data selectors
    mov bl,data_selc             ; GDT[3]
    mov ds,bx
    mov ss,bx
    mov es,bx
    mov fs,bx
    mov gs,bx
    db 66h                       ; for the 80386, need to make a 32-bit jump
pejump:
    jmp far ptr c_startup        ; but the 80376 is already 32-bit.

    org 70h                      ; only if segment base is at Offffff80h
    jmp short start
INIT_CODE ENDS
END
```

This code should be linked into your application for boot loadable code. The following build file illustrates how this is accomplished.

```
FLAT; -- build program id

SEGMENT
    *segments (dpl=0),              -- Give all user segments a DPL of 0.
    _phantom_code_ (dpl=0),         -- These two segments are created by
    _phantom_data_ (dpl=0),         -- the builder when the FLAT control is used.
    init_code  (base=0ffffff80h); -- Put startup code at the reset vector area.

GATE
    g13 (entry=13, dpl=0, trap),        -- trap gate disables interrupts
    i32 (entry=32, dpl=0, interrupt),  -- interrupt gates doesn't

TABLE
    -- create GDT

    GDT (LOCATION = GDT_DESC,       -- In a buffer starting at GDT_DESC,
                                    -- BLD386 places the GDT base and
                                    -- GDT limit values. Buffer must be
                                    -- 6 bytes long. The base and limit
                                    -- values are places in this buffer
                                    -- as two bytes of limit plus
                                    -- four bytes of base in the format
                                    -- required for use by the LGDT
                                    -- instruction.
        ENTRY = (3:_phantom_code_,      -- Explicitly place segment
                 4:_phantom_data_,      -- entries into the GDT.
                 5:code32,
                 6:data,
                 7:init_code)
        );
TASK
    MAIN_TASK
        (
         DPL  = 0,                  -- Task privilege level is 0.
         DATA = DATA,               -- Points to a segment that
                                    -- indicates initial DS value.
         CODE = main,               -- Entry point is main, which
                                    -- must be a public id.

         STACKS = (DATA),           -- Segment id points to stack
                                    -- segment. Sets the initial SS:ESP.
         NO INTENABLED,             -- Disable interrupts.
         PRESENT                    -- Present bit in TSS set to 1.
        );

    MEMORY
        (RANGE = (EPROM = ROM(0ffff8000h..0ffffffffh),
                  DRAM = RAM(0..0ffffh)),
        ALLOCATE = (EPROM = (MAIN_TASK)));

END

asm386 flatsim.a38 debug
asm386 application.a38 debug
bnd386 application.obj,flatsim.obj nolo debug oj (application.bnd)
bld386 application.bnd bf (flatsim.bld) bl flat
```

Commands to assemble and build a boot-loadable application named "application.a38". The initialization code is called "flatsim.a38", and build file is called "application.bld".

2.10 Self-Test

The 80376 has the capability to perform a self-test. The self-test checks the function of all of the Control ROM and most of the non-random logic of the part. Approximately one-half of the 80376 can be tested during self-test.

Self-Test is initiated on the 80376 when the $\overline{\text{RESET}}$ pin transitions from HIGH to LOW, and the $\overline{\text{BUSY}}$ pin is LOW. The self-test takes about 2^{20} clocks, or approximately 33 ms with a 16 MHz 80376 processor. At the completion of self-test the processor performs reset and begins normal operation. The part has successfully passed self-test if the contents of the EAX register is zero. If the EAX register is not zero then the self-test has detected a flaw in the part. If self-test is not selected after reset, EAX may be non-zero after reset.

2.11 Debugging Support

The 80376 provides several features which simplify the debugging process. The three categories of on-chip debugging aids are:

1. The code execution breakpoint opcode (0CCH).
2. The single-step capability provided by the TF bit in the flag register, and
3. The code and data breakpoint capability provided by the Debug Registers DR0–3, DR6, and DR7.

BREAKPOINT INSTRUCTION

A single-byte software interrupt (Int 3) breakpoint instruction is available for use by software debuggers. The breakpoint opcode is 0CCh, and generates an exception 3 trap when executed.

DEBUG REGISTERS

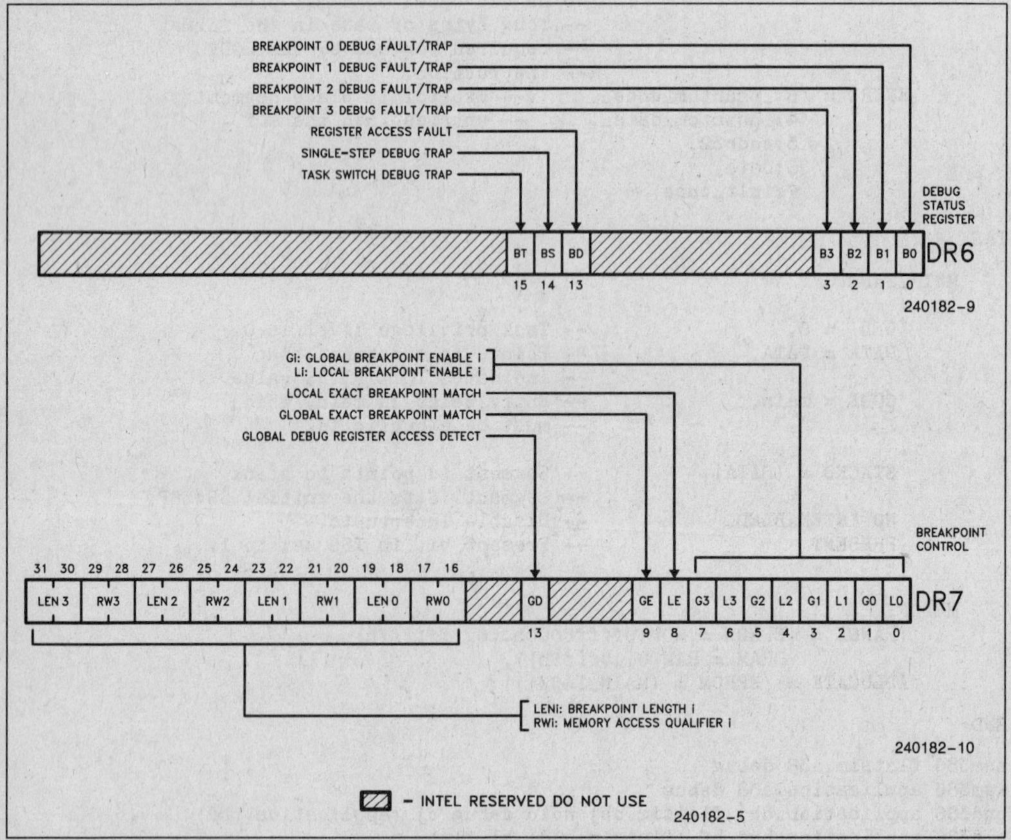

Figure 2.6. Debug Registers

SINGLE-STEP TRAP

If the single-step flag (TF, bit 8) in the EFLAG register is found to be set at the end of an instruction, a single-step exception occurs. The single-step exception is auto vectored to exception number 1.

The Debug Registers are an advanced debugging feature of the 80376. They allow data access breakpoints as well as code execution breakpoints. Since the breakpoints are indicated by on-chip registers, an instruction execution breakpoint can be placed in ROM code or in code shared by several tasks, neither of which can be supported by the INT 3 breakpoint opcode.

The 80376 contains six Debug Registers, consisting of four breakpoint address registers and two breakpoint control registers. Initially after reset, breakpoints are in the disabled state; therefore, no breakpoints will occur unless the debug registers are programmed. Breakpoints set up in the Debug Registers are auto-vectored to exception 1. Figure 2.6 shows the breakpoint status and control registers.

3.0 ARCHITECTURE

The Intel 80376 Embedded Processor has a physical address space of 16 Mbytes (2^{24} bytes) and allows the running of virtual memory programs of almost unlimited size (16 Kbytes × 16 Mbytes or 256 Gbytes (2^{38} bytes)). In addition the 80376 provides a sophisticated memory management and a hardware-assisted protection mechanism.

3.1 Addressing Mechanism

The 80376 uses two components to form the logical address, a 16-bit selector which determines the linear base address of a segment, and a 32-bit effective address. The selector is used to specify an index into an operating system defined table (see Figure 3.1). The table contains the 32-bit base address of a given segment. The linear address is formed by adding the base address obtained from the table to the 32-bit effective address. This value is truncated to 24 bits to form the physical address, which is then placed on the address bus.

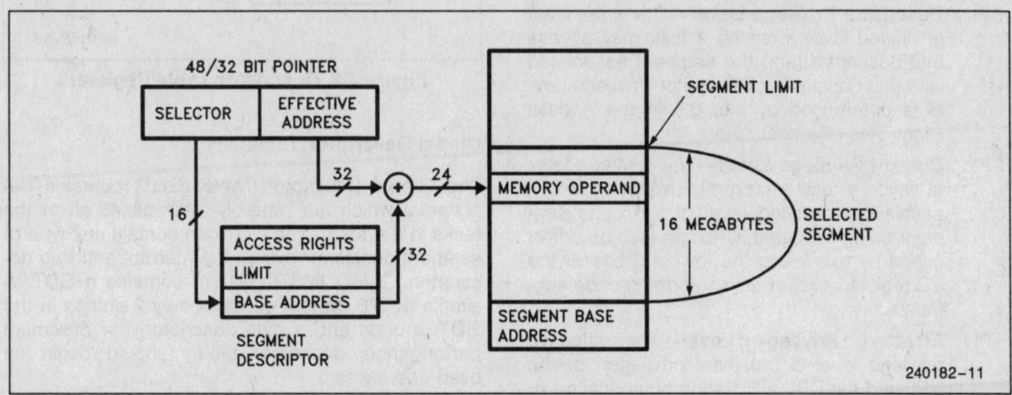

Figure 3.1. Address Calculation

3.2 Segmentation

Segmentation is one method of memory management and provides the basis for protection in the 80376. Segments are used to encapsulate regions of memory which have common attributes. For example, all of the code of a given program could be contained in a segment, or an operating system table may reside in a segment. All information about each segment, is stored in an 8-byte data structure called a descriptor. All of the descriptors in a system are contained in tables recognized by hardware.

TERMINOLOGY

The following terms are used throughout the discussion of descriptors, privilege levels and protection:

PL: **Privilege Level**—One of the four hierarchical privilege levels. Level 0 is the most privileged level and level 3 is the least privileged.

RPL: **Requestor Privilege Level**—The privilege level of the original supplier of the selector. RPL is determined by the least two significant bits of a selector.

DPL: **Descriptor Privilege Level**—This is the least privileged level at which a task may access that descriptor (and the segment associated with that descriptor). Descriptor Privilege Level is determined by bits 6:5 in the Access Right Byte of a descriptor.

CPL: **Current Privilege Level**—The privilege level at which a task is currently executing, which equals the privilege level of the code segment being executed. CPL can also be determined by examining the lowest 2 bits of the CS register, except for conforming code segments.

EPL: **Effective Privilege Level**—The effective privilege level is the least privileged of the RPL and the DPL. EPL is the numerical maximum of RPL and DPL.

Task: One instance of the execution of a program. Tasks are also referred to as processes.

DESCRIPTOR TABLES

The descriptor tables define all of the segments which are used in an 80376 system. There are three types of tables on the 80376 which hold descriptors: the Global Descriptor Table, Local Descriptor Table, and the Interrupt Decriptor Table. All of the tables are variable length memory arrays, they can range in size between 8 bytes and 64 Kbytes. Each table can hold up to 8192 8-byte descriptors. The upper 13 bits of a selector are used as an index into the descriptor table. The tables have registers associated with them which hold the 32-bit linear base address, and the 16-bit limit of each table.

Each of the tables have a register associated with it: GDTR, LDTR and IDTR; see Figure 3.2. The LGDT, LLDT and LIDT instructions load the base and limit of the Global, Local and Interrupt Descriptor Tables into the appropriate register. The SGDT, SLDT and SIDT store these base and limit values. These are privileged instructions.

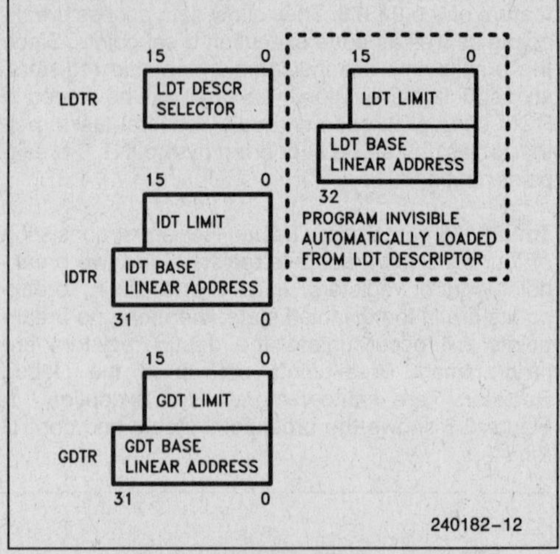

Figure 3.2. Descriptor Table Registers

Global Descriptor Table

The Global Descriptor Table (GDT) contains descriptors which are possibly available to all of the tasks in a system. The GDT can contain any type of segment descriptor except for interrupt and trap descriptors. Every 80376 system contains a GDT. A simple 80376 system contains only 2 entries in the GDT; a code and a data descriptor. For maximum performance, descriptor tables should begin on even addresses.

The first slot of the Global Descriptor Table corresponds to the null selector and is not used. The null selector defines a null pointer value.

Local Descriptor Table

LDTs contain descriptors which are associated with a given task. Generally, operating systems are designed so that each task has a separate LDT. The LDT may contain only code, data, stack, task gate, and call gate descriptors. LDTs provide a mechanism for isolating a given task's code and data segments from the rest of the operating system, while the GDT contains descriptors for segments which are common to all tasks. A segment cannot be accessed by a task if its segment descriptor does not exist in either the current LDT or the GDT. This provides both isolation and protection for a task's segments, while still allowing global data to be shared among tasks.

Unlike the 6-byte GDT or IDT registers which contain a base address and limit, the visible portion of the LDT register contains only a 16-bit selector. This selector refers to a Local Descriptor Table descriptor in the GDT (see Figure 2.1).

INTERRUPT DESCRIPTOR TABLE

The third table needed for 80376 systems is the Interrupt Descriptor Table. The IDT contains the descriptors which point to the location of up to 256 interrupt service routines. The IDT may contain only task gates, interrupt gates and trap gates. The IDT should be at least 256 bytes in size in order to hold the descriptors for the 32 Intel Reserved Interrupts. Every interrupt used by a system must have an entry in the IDT. The IDT entries are referenced by INT instructions, external interrupt vectors, and exceptions.

DESCRIPTORS

The object to which the segment selector points to is called a descriptor. Descriptors are eight-byte quantities which contain attributes about a given region of linear address space. These attributes include the 32-bit logical base address of the segment, the 20-bit length and granularity of the segment, the protection level, read, write or execute privileges, and the type of segment. All of the attribute information about a segment is contained in 12 bits in the segment descriptor. Figure 3.3 shows the general format of a descriptor. All segments on the the 80376 have three attribute fields in common: the Present bit (P), the Descriptor Privilege Level bits (DPL) and the Segment bit (S). P=1 if the segment is loaded in physical memory, if P = 0 then any attempt to access the segment causes a not present exception (exception 11). The DPL is a two-bit field which specifies the protection level, 0–3, associated with a segment.

The 80376 has two main categories of segments: system segments, and non-system segments (for code and data). The segment bit, S, determines if a given segment is a system segment, a code segment or a data segment. If the S bit is 1 then the segment is either a code or data segment, if it is 0 then the segment is a system segment.

Note that although the 80376 is limited to a 16-Mbyte Physical address space (2^{24}), its base address allows a segment to be placed anywhere in a 4-Gbyte linear address space. When writing code for the 80386, users should keep code portability to an 80386 processor (or other processors with a larger physical address space) in mind. A segment base address can be placed anywhere in this 4-Gbyte linear address space, but a physical address will be

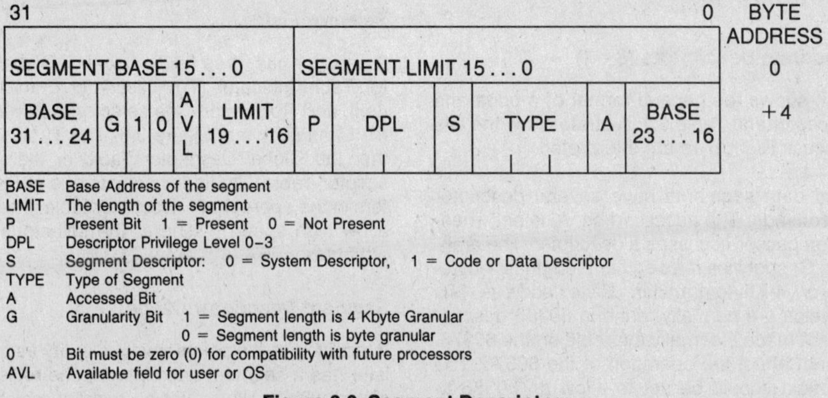

Figure 3.3. Segment Descriptors

31							0	
SEGMENT BASE 15 . . . 0					SEGMENT LIMIT 15 . . . 0			0
BASE 31 . . . 24	G	1	0	AVL	LIMIT 19 . . . 16	ACCESS RIGHTS BYTE	BASE 23 . . . 16	+4

G Granularity Bit 1 = Segment length is 4 Kbyte granular
0 = Segment length is byte granular
0 Bit must be zero (0) for compatibility with future processors
AVL Available field for user or OS

Figure 3.4. Code and Data Descriptors

Table 3.1. Access Rights Byte Definition for Code and Data Descriptors

Bit Position	Name	Function	
7	Present (P)	P = 1 Segment is mapped into physical memory. P = 0 No mapping to physical memory exits	
6–5	Descriptor Privilege Level (DPL)	Segment privilege attribute used in privilege tests.	
4	Segment Descriptor (S)	S = 1 Code or Data (includes stacks) segment descriptor S = 0 System Segment Descriptor or Gate Descriptor	
3	Executable (E)	E = 0 Descriptor type is data segment:	If Data Segment (S = 1, E = 0)
2	Expansion Direction (ED)	ED = 0 Expand up segment, offsets must be ≤ limit. ED = 1 Expand down segment, offsets must be > limit.	
1	Writable (W)	W = 0 Data segment may not be written into. W = 1 Data segment may be written into.	
3	Executable (E)	E = 1 Descriptor type is code segment:	If Code Segment (S = 1, E = 1)
2	Conforming (C)	C = 1 Code segment may only be executed when CPL ≥ DPL and CPL remains unchanged.	
1	Readable (R)	R = 0 Code segment may not be read. R = 1 Code segment may be read.	
0	Accessed (A)	A = 0 Segment has not been accessed. A = 1 Segment selector has been loaded into segment register or used by selector test instructions.	

generated that is a truncated version of this linear address. Truncation will be to the maximum number of address bits. It is recommended to place EPROM at the highest physical address and DRAM at the lowest physical addresses.

Code and Data Descriptors (S = 1)

Figure 3.4 shows the general format of a code and data descriptor and Table 3.1 illustrates how the bits in the Access Right Byte are interpreted.

Code and data segments have several descriptor fields in common. The accessed bit, A, is set whenever the processor accesses a descriptor. The granularity bit, G, specifies if a segment length is 1-byte-granular or 4-Kbyte-granular. Base address bits 31–24, which are normally found in 80386 descriptors, are not made externally available on the 80376. They do not affect the operation of the 80376. The A_{31}–A_{24} field should be set to allow an 80386 to correctly execute with EPROM at the upper 4096 Mbytes of physical memory.

System Descriptor Formats (S = 0)

System segments describe information about operating system tables, tasks, and gates. Figure 3.5 shows the general format of system segment descriptors, and the various types of system segments. 80376 system descriptors (which are the same as 80386 descriptor types 2, 5, 9, B, C, E and F) contain a 32-bit logical base address and a 20-bit segment limit.

Selector Fields

A selector has three fields: Local or Global Descriptor Table Indicator (TI), Descriptor Entry Index (Index), and Requestor (the selector's) Privilege Level (RPL) as shown in Figure 3.6. The TI bit selects either the Global Descriptor Table or the Local Descriptor Table. The Index selects one of 8K descriptors in the appropriate descriptor table. The RPL bits allow high speed testing of the selector's privilege attributes.

Segment Descriptor Cache

In addition to the selector value, every segment register has a segment descriptor cache register associated with it. Whenever a segment register's contents are changed, the 8-byte descriptor associated with that selector is automatically loaded (cached) on the chip. Once loaded, all references to that segment use the cached descriptor information instead of reaccessing the descriptor. The contents of the descriptor cache are not visible to the programmer. Since descriptor caches only change when a segment register is changed, programs which modify the descriptor tables must reload the appropriate segment registers after changing a descriptor's value.

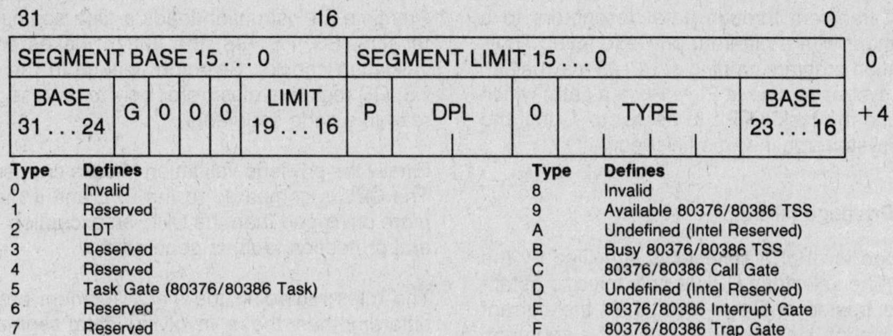

Type	Defines	Type	Defines
0	Invalid	8	Invalid
1	Reserved	9	Available 80376/80386 TSS
2	LDT	A	Undefined (Intel Reserved)
3	Reserved	B	Busy 80376/80386 TSS
4	Reserved	C	80376/80386 Call Gate
5	Task Gate (80376/80386 Task)	D	Undefined (Intel Reserved)
6	Reserved	E	80376/80386 Interrupt Gate
7	Reserved	F	80376/80386 Trap Gate

Figure 3.5. System Descriptors

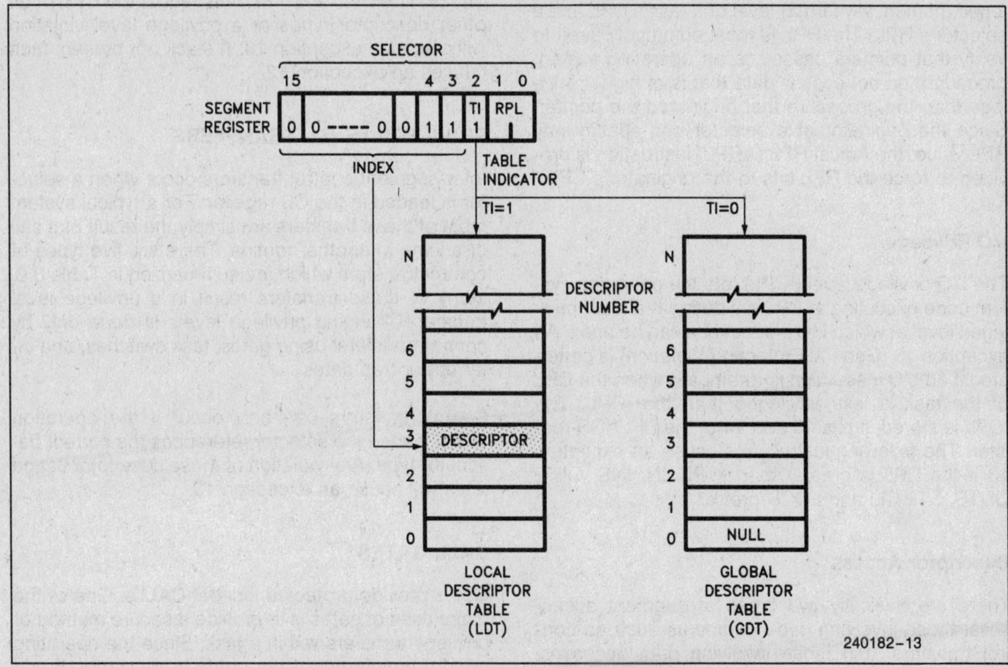

Figure 3.6. Example Descriptor Selection

3.3 Protection

The 80376 offers extensive protection features. These protection features are particularly useful in sophisticated embedded applications which use multitasking real-time operating systems. For simpler embedded applications these protection capabilities can be easily bypassed by making all applications run at privilege level (PL) 0.

RULES OF PRIVILEGE

The 80376 controls access to both data and procedures between levels of a task, according to the following rules.

—Data stored in a segment with privilege level **p** can be accessed only by code executing at a privilege level at least as privileged as **p**.

—A code segment/procedure with privilege level **p** can only be called by a task executing at the same or a lesser privilege level than **p**.

PRIVILEGE LEVELS

At any point in time, a task on the 80376 always executes at one of the four privilege levels. The Current Privilege Level (CPL) specifies what the task's privilege level is. A task's CPL may only be changed

by control transfers through gate descriptors to a code segment with a different privilege level. Thus, an application program running at PL = 3 may call an operating system routine at PL = 1 (via a gate) which would cause the task's CPL to be set to 1 until the operating system routine was finished.

Selector Privilege (RPL)

The privilege level of a selector is specified by the RPL field. The selector's RPL is only used to establish a less trusted privilege level than the current privilege level of the task for the use of a segment. This level is called the task's effective privilege level (EPL). The EPL is defined as being the least privileged (numerically larger) level of a task's CPL and a selector's RPL. The RPL is most commonly used to verify that pointers passed to an operating system procedure do not access data that is of higher privilege than the procedure that originated the pointer. Since the originator of a selector can specify any RPL value, the Adjust RPL (ARPL) instruction is provided to force the RPL bits to the originator's CPL.

I/O Privilege

The I/O privilege level (IOPL) lets the operating system code executing at CPL = 0 define the least privileged level at which I/O instructions can be used. An exception 13 (General Protection Violation) is generated if an I/O instruction is attempted when the CPL of the task is less privileged than the IOPL. The IOPL is stored in bits 13 and 14 of the EFLAGS register. The following instructions cause an exception 13 if the CPL is greater than IOPL: IN, INS, OUT, OUTS, STI, CLI and LOCK prefix.

Descriptor Access

There are basically two types of segment accessess: those involving code segments such as control transfers and those involving data accesses. Determining the ability of a task to access a segment involves the type of segment to be accessed, the instruction used, the type of descriptor used and CPL, RPL, and DPL as described above.

Any time an instruction loads a data segment register (DS, ES, FS, GS) the 80376 makes protection validation checks. Selectors loaded in the DS, ES, FS, GS registers must refer only to data segment or readable code segments.

Finally the privilege validation checks are performed. The CPL is compared to the EPL and if the EPL is more privileged than the CPL, an exception 13 (general protection fault) is generated.

The rules regarding the stack segment are slightly different than those involving data segments. Instructions that load selectors into SS must refer to data segment descriptors for writeable data segments. The DPL and RPL must equal the CPL of all other descriptor types or a privilege level violation will cause an exception 13. A stack not present fault causes an exception 12.

PRIVILEGE LEVEL TRANSFERS

Inter-segment control transfers occur when a selector is loaded in the CS register. For a typical system most of these transfers are simply the result of a call or a jump to another routine. There are five types of control transfers which are summarized in Table 3.2. Many of these transfers result in a privilege level transfer. Changing privilege levels is done only by control transfers, using gates, task switches, and interrupt or trap gates.

Control transfers can only occur if the operation which loaded the selector references the correct descriptor type. Any violation of these descriptor usage rules will cause an exception 13.

CALL GATES

Gates provide protected indirect CALLs. One of the major uses of gates is to provide a secure method of privilege transfers within a task. Since the operating system defines all of the gates in a system, it can ensure that all gates only allow entry into a few trusted procedures.

Table 3.2. Descriptor Types Used for Control Transfer

Control Transfer Types	Operation Types	Descriptor Referenced	Descriptor Table
Intersegment within the same privilege level	JMP, CALL, RET, IRET*	Code Segment	GDT/LDT
Intersegment to the same or higher privilege level Interrupt within task may change CPL	CALL	Call Gate	GDT/LDT
	Interrupt Instruction, Exception, External Interrupt	Trap or Interrupt Gate	IDT
Intersegment to a lower privilege level (changes task CPL)	RET, IRET*	Code Segment	GDT/LDT
	CALL, JMP	Task State Segment	GDT
Task Switch	CALL, JMP	Task Gate	GDT/LDT
	IRET** Interrupt Instruction, Exception, External Interrupt	Task Gate	IDT

*NT (Nested Task bit of flag register) = 0
**NT (Nested Task bit of flag register) = 1

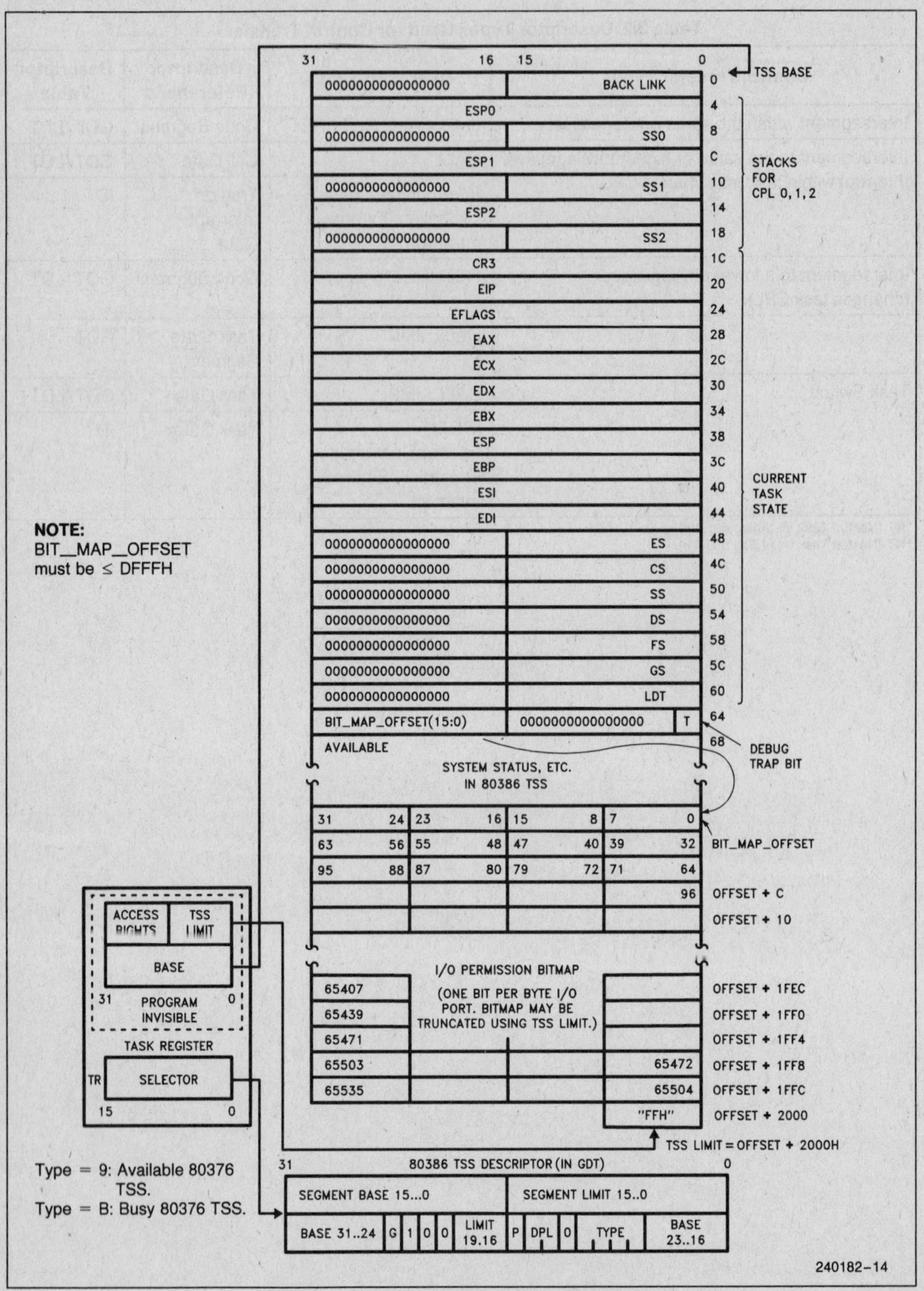

31 … 16	15 … 0	Offset	
0000000000000000	BACK LINK	0	← TSS BASE
ESP0		4	STACKS FOR CPL 0, 1, 2
0000000000000000	SS0	8	
ESP1		C	
0000000000000000	SS1	10	
ESP2		14	
0000000000000000	SS2	18	
CR3		1C	CURRENT TASK STATE
EIP		20	
EFLAGS		24	
EAX		28	
ECX		2C	
EDX		30	
EBX		34	
ESP		38	
EBP		3C	
ESI		40	
EDI		44	
0000000000000000	ES	48	
0000000000000000	CS	4C	
0000000000000000	SS	50	
0000000000000000	DS	54	
0000000000000000	FS	58	
0000000000000000	GS	5C	
0000000000000000	LDT	60	
BIT_MAP_OFFSET(15:0)	000000000000000 T	64	DEBUG TRAP BIT
AVAILABLE		68	

SYSTEM STATUS, ETC. IN 80386 TSS

31 … 24	23 … 16	15 … 8	7 … 0	
31 24	23 16	15 8	7 0	BIT_MAP_OFFSET
63 56	55 48	47 40	39 32	
95 88	87 80	79 72	71 64	
			96	OFFSET + C
				OFFSET + 10

I/O PERMISSION BITMAP (ONE BIT PER BYTE I/O PORT. BITMAP MAY BE TRUNCATED USING TSS LIMIT.)

65407				OFFSET + 1FEC
65439				OFFSET + 1FF0
65471				OFFSET + 1FF4
65503			65472	OFFSET + 1FF8
65535			65504	OFFSET + 1FFC
			"FFH"	OFFSET + 2000

TSS LIMIT = OFFSET + 2000H

NOTE:
BIT__MAP__OFFSET must be ≤ DFFFH

TASK REGISTER: ACCESS RIGHTS | TSS LIMIT | BASE (31 … 0, PROGRAM INVISIBLE); TR SELECTOR (15 … 0)

80386 TSS DESCRIPTOR (IN GDT)

31 … 16									… 0
SEGMENT BASE 15...0					SEGMENT LIMIT 15..0				
BASE 31..24	G	1	0	0	LIMIT 19.16	P	DPL	0	TYPE	BASE 23..16

Type = 9: Available 80376 TSS.
Type = B: Busy 80376 TSS.

240182–14

Figure 3.7. 80376 TSS And TSS Registers

TASK SWITCHING

A very important attribute of any multi-tasking operating system is its ability to rapidly switch between tasks or processes. The 80376 directly supports this operation by providing a task switch instruction in hardware. The 80376 task switch operation saves the entire state of the machine (all of the registers, address space, and a link to the previous task), loads a new execution state, performs protection checks, and commences execution in the new task. Like transfer of control by gates, the task switch operation is invoked by executing an inter-segment JMP or CALL instruction which refers to a Task State Segment (TSS), or a task gate descriptor in the GDT or LDT. An INT n instruction, exception, trap or external interrupt may also invoke the task switch operation if there is a task gate descriptor in the associated IDT descriptor slot. For simple applications, the TSS and task switching may not be used. The TSS or task switch will not be used or occur if no task gates are present in the GDT, LDT or IDT.

The TSS descriptor points to a segment (see Figure 3.7) containing the entire 80376 execution state. A task gate descriptor contains a TSS selector. The limit of an 80376 TSS must be greater than 64H, and can be as large as 16 Mbytes. In the additional TSS space, the operating system is free to store additional information as the reason the task is inactive, the time the task has spent running, and open files belonging to the task. For maximum performance, TSS should start on an even address.

Each Task must have a TSS associated with it. The current TSS is identified by a special register in the 80376 called the Task State Segment Register (TR). This register contains a selector referring to the task state segment descriptor that defines the current TSS. A hidden base and limit register associated with the TSS descriptor is loaded whenever TR is loaded with a new selector. Returning from a task is accomplished by the IRET instruction. When IRET is executed, control is returned to the task which was interrupted. The current executing task's state is saved in the TSS and the old task state is restored from its TSS.

Several bits in the flag register and CR0 register give information about the state of a task which is useful to the operating system. The Nested Task bit, NT, controls the function of the IRET instruction. If NT = 0 the IRET instruction performs the regular return. If NT = 1, IRET performs a task switch operation back to the previous task. The NT bit is set or reset in the following fashion:

> When a CALL or INT instruction initiates a task switch, the new TSS will be marked busy and the back link field of the new TSS set to the old TSS selector. The NT bit of the new task is set by CALL or INT initiated task switches. An interrupt that does not cause a task switch will clear NT (The NT bit will be restored after execution of the interrupt handler). NT may also be set or cleared by POPF or IRET instructions.

The 80376 task state segment is marked busy by changing the descriptor type field from TYPE 9 to TYPE 0BH. Use of a selector that references a busy task state segment causes an exception 13.

The coprocessor's state is not automatically saved when a task switch occurs. The Task Switched Bit, TS, in the CR0 register helps deal with the coprocessor's state in a multi-tasking environment. Whenever the 80376 switches tasks, it sets the TS bit. The 80376 detects the first use of a processor extension instruction after a task switch and causes the processor extension not available exception 7. The exception handler for exception 7 may then decide whether to save the state of the coprocessor.

The T bit in the 80376 TSS indicates that the processor should generate a debug exception when switching to a task. If T = 1 then upon entry to a new task a debug exception 1 will be generated.

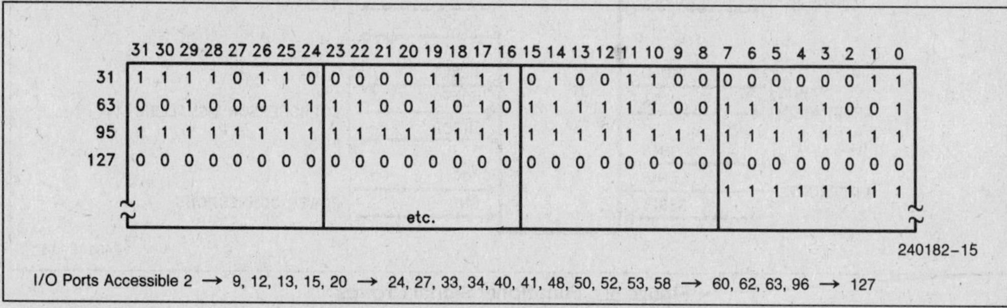

	31	30	29	28	27	26	25	24	23	22	21	20	19	18	17	16	15	14	13	12	11	10	9	8	7	6	5	4	3	2	1	0
31	1	1	1	1	0	1	1	0	0	0	0	0	1	1	1	1	0	1	0	0	1	1	0	0	0	0	0	0	0	0	1	1
63	0	0	1	0	0	0	1	1	1	1	0	0	1	0	1	0	1	1	1	1	1	1	0	0	1	1	1	1	1	0	0	1
95	1	1	1	1	1	1	1	1	1	1	1	1	1	1	1	1	1	1	1	1	1	1	1	1	1	1	1	1	1	1	1	1
127	0	0	0	0	0	0	0	0	0	0	0	0	0	0	0	0	0	0	0	0	0	0	0	0	0	0	0	0	0	0	0	0
																									1	1	1	1	1	1	1	1
										etc.																						

240182–15

I/O Ports Accessible 2 → 9, 12, 13, 15, 20 → 24, 27, 33, 34, 40, 41, 48, 50, 52, 53, 58 → 60, 62, 63, 96 → 127

Figure 3.8. Sample I/O Permission Bit Map

PROTECTION AND I/O PERMISSION BIT MAP

The I/O instructions that directly refer to addresses in the processor's I/O space are IN, INS, OUT and OUTS. The 80376 has the ability to selectively trap references to specific I/O addresses. The structure that enables selective trapping is the ***I/O Permission Bit Map*** in the TSS segment (see Figures 3.7 and 3.8). The I/O permission map is a bit vector. The size of the map and its location in the TSS segment are variable. The processor locates the I/O permission map by means of the **I/O map base** field in the fixed portion of the TSS. The **I/O map base** field is 16 bits wide and contains the offset of the beginning of the I/O permission map.

If an I/O instruction (IN, INS, OUT or OUTS) is encountered, the processor first checks whether CPL $\leq$ IOPL. If this condition is true, the I/O operation may proceed. If not true, the processor checks the I/O permission map.

Each bit in the map corresponds to an I/O port byte address; for example, the bit for port 41 is found at **I/O map base** $+5$ linearly, $(5 \times 8 = 40)$, bit offset 1. The processor tests all the bits that correspond to the I/O addresses spanned by an I/O operation; for example, a double word operation tests four bits corresponding to four adjacent byte addresses. If any tested bit is set, the processor signals a general protection exception. If all the tested bits are zero, the I/O operations may proceed.

It is not necessary for the I/O permission map to represent all the I/O addresses. I/O addresses not spanned by the map are treated as if they had one-bits in the map. The **I/O map base** should be at least one byte less than the TSS limit and the last byte beyond the I/O mapping information must contain all 1's.

Because the I/O permission map is in the TSS segment, different tasks can have different maps. Thus, the operating system can allocate ports to a task by changing the I/O permission map in the task's TSS.

IMPORTANT IMPLEMENTATION NOTE:
Beyond the last byte of I/O mapping information in the I/O permission bit map **must** be a byte containing all 1's. The byte of all 1's must be within the limit of the 80376's TSS segment (see Figure 3.7).

4.0 FUNCTIONAL DATA

The Intel 80376 embedded processor features a straightforward functional interface to the external hardware. The 80376 has separate parallel buses for data and address. The data bus is 16 bits in width, and bidirectional. The address bus outputs 24-bit address values using 23 address lines and two-byte enable signals.

The 80376 has two selectable address bus cycles: pipelined and non-pipelined. The pipelining option allows as much time as possible for data access by

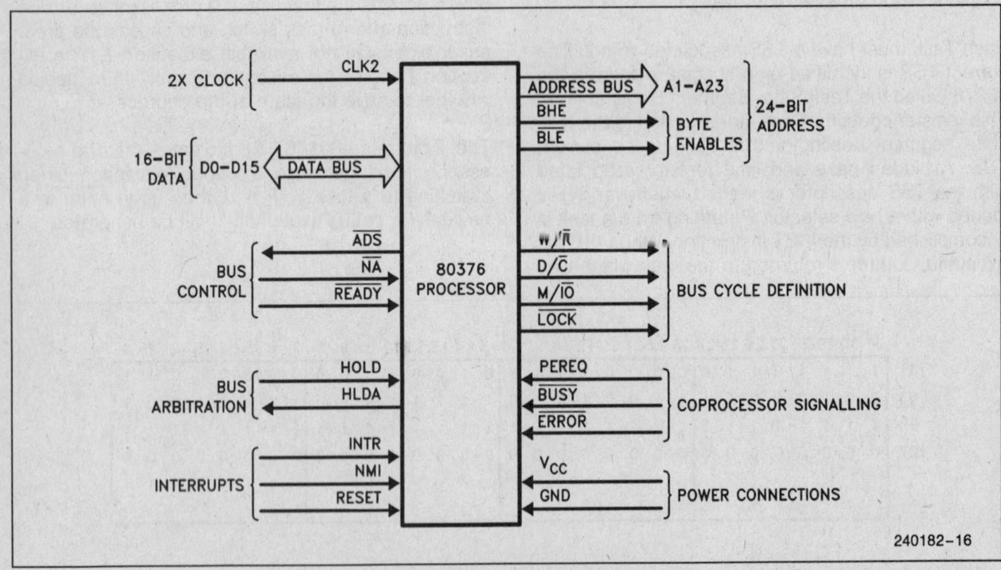

Figure 4.1. Functional Signal Groups

starting the pending bus cycle before the present bus cycle is finished. A non-pipelined bus cycle gives the highest bus performance by executing every bus cycle in two processor clock cycles. For maximum design flexibility, the address pipelining option is selectable on a cycle-by-cycle basis.

The processor's bus cycle is the basic mechanism for information transfer, either from system to processor, or from processor to system. 80376 bus cycles perform data transfer in a minimum of only two clock periods. On a 16-bit data bus, the maximum 80376 transfer bandwidth at 16 MHz is therefore 16 Mbytes/sec. However, any bus cycle will be extended for more than two clock periods if external hardware withholds acknowledgement of the cycle.

The 80376 can relinquish control of its local buses to allow mastership by other devices, such as direct memory access (DMA) channels. When relinquished, HLDA is the only output pin driven by the 80376, providing near-complete isolation of the processor from its system (all other output pins are in a float condition).

4.1 Signal Description Overview

Ahead is a brief description of the 80376 input and output signals arranged by functional groups.

The signal descriptions sometimes refer to A.C. timing parameters, such as "t_{25} Reset Setup Time" and "t_{26} Reset Hold Time." The values of these parameters can be found in Tables 6.4 and 6.5.

CLOCK (CLK2)

CLK2 provides the fundamental timing for the 80376. It is divided by two internally to generate the internal processor clock used for instruction execution. The internal clock is comprised of two

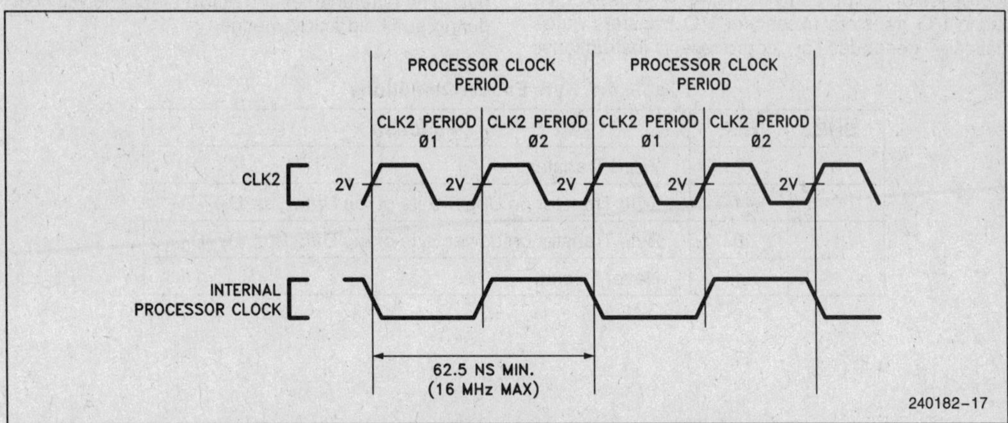

Figure 4.2. CLK2 Signal and Internal Processor Clock

phases, "phase one" and "phase two". Each CLK2 period is a phase of the internal clock. Figure 4.2 illustrates the relationship. If desired, the phase of the internal processor clock can be synchronized to a known phase by ensuring the falling edge of the RESET signal meets the applicable setup and hold times t_{25} and t_{26}.

DATA BUS (D_{15}–D_0)

These three-state bidirectional signals provide the general purpose data path between the 80376 and other devices. The data bus outputs are active HIGH and will float during bus hold acknowledge. Data bus reads require that read-data setup and hold times t_{21} and t_{22} be met relative to CLK2 for correct operation.

ADDRESS BUS ($\overline{BHE}$, $\overline{BLE}$, A_{23}–A_1)

These three-state outputs provide physical memory addresses or I/O port addresses. A_{23}–A_{16} are LOW during I/O transfers except for I/O transfers automatically generated by coprocessor instructions. During coprocessor I/O transfers, A_{22}–A_{16} are driven LOW, and A_{23} is driven HIGH so that this address line can be used by external logic to generate the coprocessor select signal. Thus, the I/O address driven by the 80376 for coprocessor commands is 8000F8H, and the I/O address driven by the 80376 processor for coprocessor data is 8000FCH or 8000FEH.

The address bus is capable of addressing 16 Mbytes of physical memory space (000000H through 0FFFFFFH), and 64 Kbytes of I/O address space (000000H through 00FFFFH) for programmed I/O. The address bus is active HIGH and will float during bus hold acknowledge.

The Byte Enable outputs $\overline{BHE}$ and $\overline{BLE}$ directly indicate which bytes of the 16-bit data bus are involved with the current transfer. $\overline{BHE}$ applies to D_{15}–D_8 and $\overline{BLE}$ applies to D_7–D_0. If both $\overline{BHE}$ and $\overline{BLE}$ are asserted, then 16 bits of data are being transferred. See Table 4.1 for a complete decoding of these signals. The byte enables are active LOW and will float during bus hold acknowledge.

Table 4.1. Byte Enable Definitions

$\overline{BHE}$	$\overline{BLE}$	Function
0	0	Word Transfer
0	1	Byte Transfer on Upper Byte of the Data Bus, D_{15}–D_8
1	0	Byte Transfer on Lower Byte of the Data Bus, D_7–D_0
1	1	Never Occurs

BUS CYCLE DEFINITION SIGNALS (W/$\overline{\text{R}}$, D/$\overline{\text{C}}$, M/$\overline{\text{IO}}$, $\overline{\text{LOCK}}$)

These three-state outputs define the type of bus cycle being performed: W/$\overline{\text{R}}$ distinguishes between write and read cycles, D/$\overline{\text{C}}$ distinguishes between data and control cycles, M/$\overline{\text{IO}}$ distinguishes between memory and I/O cycles, and $\overline{\text{LOCK}}$ distinguishes between locked and unlocked bus cycles. All of these signals are active LOW and will float during bus acknowledge.

The primary bus cycle definition signals are W/$\overline{\text{R}}$, D/$\overline{\text{C}}$ and M/$\overline{\text{IO}}$, since these are the signals driven valid as $\overline{\text{ADS}}$ (Address Status output) becomes active. The $\overline{\text{LOCK}}$ signal is driven valid at the same time the bus cycle begins, which due to address pipelining, could be after $\overline{\text{ADS}}$ becomes active. Exact bus cycle definitions, as a function of W/$\overline{\text{R}}$, D/$\overline{\text{C}}$ and M/$\overline{\text{IO}}$ are given in Table 4.2.

$\overline{\text{LOCK}}$ indicates that other system bus masters are not to gain control of the system bus while it is active. $\overline{\text{LOCK}}$ is activated on the CLK2 edge that begins the first locked bus cycle (i.e., it is not active at the same time as the other bus cycle definition pins) and is deactivated when ready is returned to the end of the last bus cycle which is to be locked. The beginning of a bus cycle is determined when $\overline{\text{READY}}$ is returned in a previous bus cycle and another is pending ($\overline{\text{ADS}}$ is active) or the clock in which $\overline{\text{ADS}}$ is driven active if the bus was idle. This means that it follows more closely with the write data rules when it is valid, but may cause the bus to be locked longer than desired. The $\overline{\text{LOCK}}$ signal may be explicitly activated by the LOCK prefix on certain instructions. $\overline{\text{LOCK}}$ is always asserted when executing the XCHG instruction, during descriptor updates, and during the interrupt acknowledge sequence.

BUS CONTROL SIGNALS ($\overline{\text{ADS}}$, $\overline{\text{READY}}$, $\overline{\text{NA}}$)

The following signals allow the processor to indicate when a bus cycle has begun, and allow other system hardware to control address pipelining and bus cycle termination.

Address Status ($\overline{\text{ADS}}$)

This three-state output indicates that a valid bus cycle definition and address (W/$\overline{\text{R}}$, D/$\overline{\text{C}}$, M/$\overline{\text{IO}}$, $\overline{\text{BHE}}$, $\overline{\text{BLE}}$ and A_{23}–A_1) are being driven at the 80376 pins. $\overline{\text{ADS}}$ is an active LOW output. Once $\overline{\text{ADS}}$ is driven active, valid address, byte enables, and definition signals will not change. In addition, $\overline{\text{ADS}}$ will remain active until its associated bus cycle begins (when $\overline{\text{READY}}$ is returned for the previous bus cycle when running pipelined bus cycles). $\overline{\text{ADS}}$ will float during bus hold acknowledge. See sections **Non-Pipelined Bus Cycles** and **Pipelined Bus Cycles** for additional information on how $\overline{\text{ADS}}$ is asserted for different bus states.

Transfer Acknowledge ($\overline{\text{READY}}$)

This input indicates the current bus cycle is complete, and the active bytes indicated by $\overline{\text{BHE}}$ and $\overline{\text{BLE}}$ are accepted or provided. When $\overline{\text{READY}}$ is sampled active during a read cycle or interrupt acknowledge cycle, the 80376 latches the input data and terminates the cycle. When $\overline{\text{READY}}$ is sampled active during a write cycle, the processor terminates the bus cycle.

Table 4.2. Bus Cycle Definition

M/$\overline{\text{IO}}$	D/$\overline{\text{C}}$	W/$\overline{\text{R}}$	Bus Cycle Type		Locked?
0	0	0	INTERRUPT ACKNOWLEDGE		Yes
0	0	1	Does Not Occur		—
0	1	0	I/O DATA READ		No
0	1	1	I/O DATA WRITE		No
1	0	0	MEMORY CODE READ		No
1	0	1	HALT: Address = 2 $\overline{\text{BHE}}$ = 1 $\overline{\text{BLE}}$ = 0	SHUTDOWN: Address = 0 $\overline{\text{BHE}}$ = 1 $\overline{\text{BLE}}$ = 0	No
1	1	0	MEMORY DATA READ		Some Cycles
1	1	1	MEMORY DATA WRITE		Some Cycles

$\overline{\text{READY}}$ is ignored on the first bus state of all bus cycles, and sampled each bus state thereafter until asserted. $\overline{\text{READY}}$ must eventually be asserted to acknowledge every bus cycle, including Halt Indication and Shutdown Indication bus cycles. When being sampled, $\overline{\text{READY}}$ must always meet setup and hold times t_{19} and t_{20} for correct operation.

Next Address Request ($\overline{\text{NA}}$)

This is used to request pipelining. This input indicates the system is prepared to accept new values of $\overline{\text{BHE}}$, $\overline{\text{BLE}}$, A_{23}–A_1, W/$\overline{\text{R}}$, D/$\overline{\text{C}}$ and M/$\overline{\text{IO}}$ from the 80376 even if the end of the current cycle is not being acknowledged on $\overline{\text{READY}}$. If this input is active when sampled, the next bus cycle's address and status signals are driven onto the bus, provided the next bus request is already pending internally. $\overline{\text{NA}}$ is ignored in clock cycles in which $\overline{\text{ADS}}$ or $\overline{\text{READY}}$ is activated. This signal is active LOW and must satisfy setup and hold times t_{15} and t_{16} for correct operation. See **Pipelined Bus Cycles** and **Read and Write Cycles** for additional information.

BUS ARBITRATION SIGNALS (HOLD, HLDA)

This section describes the mechanism by which the processor relinquishes control of its local buses when requested by another bus master device. See **Entering and Exiting Hold Acknowledge** for additional information.

Bus Hold Request (HOLD)

This input indicates some device other than the 80376 requires bus mastership. When control is granted, the 80376 floats A_{23}–A_1, $\overline{\text{BHE}}$, $\overline{\text{BLE}}$, D_{15}–D_0, $\overline{\text{LOCK}}$, M/$\overline{\text{IO}}$, D/$\overline{\text{C}}$, W/$\overline{\text{R}}$ and $\overline{\text{ADS}}$, and then activates HLDA, thus entering the bus hold acknowledge state. The local bus will remain granted to the requesting master until HOLD becomes inactive. When HOLD becomes inactive, the 80376 will deactivate HLDA and drive the local bus (at the same time), thus terminating the hold acknowledge condition.

HOLD must remain asserted as long as any other device is a local bus master. External pull-up resistors may be required when in the hold acknowledge state since none of the 80376 floated outputs have internal pull-up resistors. See **Resistor Recommendations** for additional information. HOLD is not recognized while RESET is active but is recognized during the time between the high-to-low transistion of RESET and the first instruction fetch. If RESET is asserted while HOLD is asserted, RESET has priority and places the bus into an idle state, rather than the hold acknowledge (high-impedance) state.

HOLD is a level-sensitive, active HIGH, synchronous input. HOLD signals must always meet setup and hold times t_{23} and t_{24} for correct operation.

Bus Hold Acknowledge (HLDA)

When active (HIGH), this output indicates the 80376 has relinquished control of its local bus in response to an asserted HOLD signal, and is in the bus Hold Acknowledge state.

The Bus Hold Acknowledge state offers near-complete signal isolation. In the Hold Acknowledge state, HLDA is the only signal being driven by the 80376. The other output signals or bidirectional signals (D_{15}–D_0, $\overline{\text{BHE}}$, $\overline{\text{BLE}}$, A_{23}–A_1, W/$\overline{\text{R}}$, D/$\overline{\text{C}}$, M/$\overline{\text{IO}}$, $\overline{\text{LOCK}}$ and $\overline{\text{ADS}}$) are in a high-impedance state so the requesting bus master may control them. These pins remain OFF throughout the time that HLDA remains active (see Table 4.3). Pull-up resistors may be desired on several signals to avoid spurious activity when no bus master is driving them. See **Resistor Recommendations** for additional information.

When the HOLD signal is made inactive, the 80376 will deactivate HLDA and drive the bus. One rising edge on the NMI input is remembered for processing after the HOLD input is negated.

Table 4.3. Output Pin State during HOLD

Pin Value	Pin Names
1	HLDA
Float	$\overline{\text{LOCK}}$, M/$\overline{\text{IO}}$, D/$\overline{\text{C}}$, W/$\overline{\text{R}}$, $\overline{\text{ADS}}$, A_{23}–A_1, $\overline{\text{BHE}}$, $\overline{\text{BLE}}$, D_{15}–D_0

Hold Latencies

The maximum possible HOLD latency depends on the software being executed. The actual HOLD latency at any time depends on the current bus activity, the state of the $\overline{\text{LOCK}}$ signal (internal to the CPU) activated by the $\overline{\text{LOCK}}$ prefix, and interrupts. The 80376 will not honor a HOLD request until the current bus operation is complete.

The 80376 breaks 32-bit data or I/O accesses into 2 internally locked 16-bit bus cycles; the $\overline{\text{LOCK}}$ signal is not asserted. The 80376 breaks unaligned 16-bit or 32-bit data or I/O accesses into 2 or 3 internally locked 16-bit bus cycles. Again the $\overline{\text{LOCK}}$ signal is not asserted but a HOLD request will not be recognized until the end of the entire transfer.

Wait states affect HOLD latency. The 80376 will not honor a HOLD request until the end of the current bus operation, no matter how many wait states are required. Systems with DMA where data transfer is critical must insure that $\overline{\text{READY}}$ returns sufficiently soon.

COPROCESSOR INTERFACE SIGNALS (PEREQ, $\overline{\text{BUSY}}$, $\overline{\text{ERROR}}$)

In the following sections are descriptions of signals dedicated to the numeric coprocessor interface. In addition to the data bus, address bus, and bus cycle definition signals, these following signals control communication between the 80376 and the 80387SX processor extension.

Coprocessor Request (PEREQ)

When asserted (HIGH), this input signal indicates a coprocessor request for a data operand to be transferred to/from memory by the 80376. In response, the 80376 transfers information between the coprocessor and memory. Because the 80376 has internally stored the coprocessor opcode being executed, it performs the requested data transfer with the correct direction and memory address.

PEREQ is a level-sensitive active HIGH asynchronous signal. Setup and hold times, t_{29} and t_{30}, relative to the CLK2 signal must be met to guarantee recognition at a particular clock edge. This signal is provided with a weak internal pull-down resistor of around 20 KΩ to ground so that it will not float active when left unconnected.

Coprocessor Busy ($\overline{\text{BUSY}}$)

When asserted (LOW), this input indicates the coprocessor is still executing an instruction, and is not yet able to accept another. When the 80376 encounters any coprocessor instruction which operates on the numerics stack (e.g. load, pop, or arithmetic operation), or the WAIT instruction, this input is first automatically sampled until it is seen to be inactive. This sampling of the $\overline{\text{BUSY}}$ input prevents overrunning the execution of a previous coprocessor instruction.

The F(N)INIT, F(N)CLEX coprocessor instructions are allowed to execute even if $\overline{\text{BUSY}}$ is active, since these instructions are used for coprocessor initialization and exception-clearing.

$\overline{\text{BUSY}}$ is an active LOW, level-sensitive asynchronous signal. Setup and hold times, t_{29} and t_{30}, relative to the CLK2 signal must be met to guarantee recognition at a particular clock edge. This pin is provided with a weak internal pull-up resistor of around 20 KΩ to V_{CC} so that it will not float active when left unconnected.

$\overline{\text{BUSY}}$ serves an additional function. If $\overline{\text{BUSY}}$ is sampled LOW at the falling edge of RESET, the 80376 processor performs an internal self-test (see **Bus Activity During and Following Reset.** If $\overline{\text{BUSY}}$ is sampled HIGH, no self-test is performed.

Coprocessor Error ($\overline{\text{ERROR}}$)

When asserted (LOW), this input signal indicates that the previous coprocessor instruction generated a coprocessor error of a type not masked by the coprocessor's control register. This input is automatically sampled by the 80376 when a coprocessor instruction is encountered, and if active, the 80376 generates exception 16 to access the error-handling software.

Several coprocessor instructions, generally those which clear the numeric error flags in the coprocessor or save coprocessor state, do execute without the 80376 generating exception 16 even if $\overline{\text{ERROR}}$ is active. These instructions are FNINIT, FNCLEX, FNSTSW, FNSTSWAX, FNSTCW, FNSTENV and FNSAVE.

$\overline{\text{ERROR}}$ is an active LOW, level-sensitive asynchronous signal. Setup and hold times t_{29} and t_{30}, relative to the CLK2 signal must be met to guarantee recognition at a particular clock edge. This pin is provided with a weak internal pull-up resistor of around 20 KΩ to V_{CC} so that it will not float active when left unconnected.

3

INTERRUPT SIGNALS (INTR, NMI, RESET)

The following descriptions cover inputs that can interrupt or suspend execution of the processor's current instruction stream.

Maskable Interrupt Request (INTR)

When asserted, this input indicates a request for interrupt service, which can be masked by the 80376 Flag Register IF bit. When the 80376 responds to the INTR input, it performs two interrupt acknowledge bus cycles and, at the end of the second, latches an 8-bit interrupt vector on D_7-D_0 to identify the source of the interrupt.

INTR is an active HIGH, level-sensitive asynchronous signal. Setup and hold times, t_{27} and t_{28}, relative to the CLK2 signal must be met to guarantee recognition at a particular clock edge. To assure recognition of an INTR request, INTR should remain active until the first interrupt acknowledge bus cycle begins. INTR is sampled at the beginning of every instruction. In order to be recognized at a particular instruction boundary, INTR must be active at least eight CLK2 clock periods before the beginning of the execution of the instruction. If recognized, the 80376 will begin execution of the interrupt.

Non-Maskable Interrupt Request (NMI)

This input indicates a request for interrupt service which cannot be masked by software. The non-maskable interrupt request is always processed according to the pointer or gate in slot 2 of the interrupt table. Because of the fixed NMI slot assignment, no interrupt acknowledge cycles are performed when processing NMI.

NMI is an active HIGH, rising edge-sensitive asynchronous signal. Setup and hold times, t_{27} and t_{28}, relative to the CLK2 signal must be met to guarantee recognition at a particular clock edge. To assure recognition of NMI, it must be inactive for at least eight CLK2 periods, and then be active for at least eight CLK2 periods before the beginning of the execution of an instruction.

Once NMI processing has begun, no additional NMI's are processed until after the next IRET instruction, which is typically the end of the NMI service routine. If NMI is re-asserted prior to that time, however, one rising edge on NMI will be remembered for processing after executing the next IRET instruction.

Interrupt Latency

The time that elapses before an interrupt request is serviced (interrupt latency) varies according to several factors. This delay must be taken into account by the interrupt source. Any of the following factors can affect interrupt latency:

1. If interrupts are masked, and INTR request will not be recognized until interrupts are reenabled.
2. If an NMI is currently being serviced, an incoming NMI request will not be recognized until the 80376 encounters the IRET instruction.
3. An interrupt request is recognized only on an instruction boundary of the 80376 ***Execution Unit*** except for the following cases:
   - Repeat string instructions can be interrupted after each iteration.
   - If the instruction loads the Stack Segment register, an interrupt is not processed until after the following instruction, which should be an ESP load. This allows the entire stack pointer to be loaded without interruption.
   - If an instruction sets the interrupt flag (enabling interrupts), an interrupt is not processed until after the next instruction.

   The longest latency occurs when the interrupt request arrives while the 80376 processor is executing a long instruction such as multiplication, division or a task-switch.
4. Saving the Flags register and CS:EIP registers.
5. If interrupt service routine requires a task switch, time must be allowed for the task switch.
6. If the interrupt service routine saves registers that are not automatically saved by the 80376.

RESET

This input signal suspends any operation in progress and places the 80376 in a known reset state. The 80376 is reset by asserting RESET for 15 or more CLK2 periods (80 or more CLK2 periods before requesting self-test). When RESET is active, all other input pins except $\overline{\text{FLT}}$ are ignored, and all other bus pins are driven to an idle bus state as shown in Table 4.4. If RESET and HOLD are both active at a point in time, RESET takes priority even if the 80376 was in a Hold Acknowledge state prior to RESET active.

RESET is an active HIGH, level-sensitive synchronous signal. Setup and hold times, t_{25} and t_{26}, must be met in order to assure proper operation of the 80376.

Table 4.4. Pin State (Bus Idle) during RESET

Pin Name	Signal Level during RESET
$\overline{ADS}$	1
D_{15}–D_0	Float
$\overline{BHE}$, $\overline{BLE}$	0
A_{23}–A_1	1
W/$\overline{R}$	0
D/$\overline{C}$	1
M/$\overline{IO}$	0
$\overline{LOCK}$	1
HLDA	0

4.2 Bus Transfer Mechanism

All data transfers occur as a result of one or more bus cycles. Logical data operands of byte and word lengths may be transferred without restrictions on physical address alignment. Any byte boundary may be used, although two physical bus cycles are performed as required for unaligned operand transfers.

The 80376 processor address signals are designed to simplify external system hardware. $\overline{BHE}$ and $\overline{BLE}$ provide linear selects for the two bytes of the 16-bit data bus.

Byte Enable outputs $\overline{BHE}$ and $\overline{BLE}$ are asserted when their associated data bus bytes are involved with the present bus cycle, as listed in Table 4.5.

Table 4.5. Byte Enables and Associated Data and Operand Bytes

Byte Enable	Associated Data Bus Signals
$\overline{BHE}$	D_{15}–D_8 (Byte 1—Most Significant)
$\overline{BLE}$	D_7–D_0 (Byte 0—Least Significant)

Each bus cycle is composed of at least two bus states. Each bus state requires one processor clock period. Additional bus states added to a single bus cycle are called wait states. See **Bus Functional Description** for additional information.

4.3 Memory and I/O Spaces

Bus cycles may access physical memory space or I/O space. Peripheral devices in the system may either be memory-mapped, or I/O-mapped, or both. As shown in Figure 4.3, physical memory addresses range from 000000H to 0FFFFFFH (16 Mbytes) and I/O addresses from 000000H to 00FFFFH (64 Kbytes). Note the I/O addresses used by the automatic I/O cycles for coprocessor communication are 8000F8H to 8000FFH, beyond the address range of programmed I/O, to allow easy generation of a coprocessor chip select signal using the A_{23} and M/$\overline{IO}$ signals.

OPERAND ALIGNMENT

With the flexibility of memory addressing on the 80376, it is possible to transfer a logical operand that spans more than one physical Dword or word of memory or I/O. Examples are 32-bit Dword or 16-bit word operands beginning at addresses not evenly divisible by 2.

Operand alignment and size dictate when multiple bus cycles are required. Table 4.6 describes the transfer cycles generated for all combinations of logical operand lengths and alignment.

Table 4.6. Transfer Bus Cycles for Bytes, Words and Dwords

	Byte-Length of Logical Operand								
	1	2				4			
Physical Byte Address in Memory (Low-Order Bits)	xx	00	01	10	11	00	01	10	11
Transfer Cycles	b	w	lb, hb	w	hb, l,b	lw, hw	hb, lb, mw	hw, lw	mw, hb, lb

Key: b = byte transfer
w = word transfer
l = low-order portion
m = mid-order portion
x = don't care
h = high-order portion

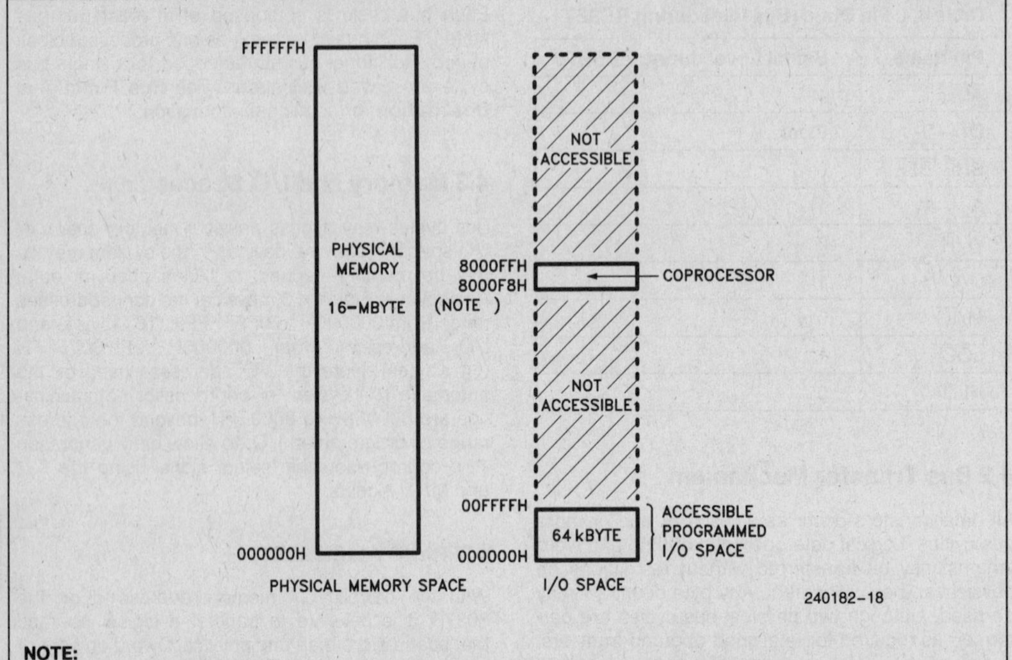

NOTE:
Since A_{23} is HIGH during automatic communication with coprocessor, A_{23} HIGH and M/$\overline{IO}$ LOW can be used to easily generate a coprocessor select signal.

Figure 4.3. Physical Memory and I/O Spaces

4.4 Bus Functional Description

The 80376 has separate, parallel buses for data and address. The data bus is 16 bits in width, and bidirectional. The address bus provides a 24-bit value using 23 signals for the 23 upper-order address bits and 2 Byte Enable signals to directly indicate the active bytes. These buses are interpreted and controlled by several definition signals.

The definition of each bus cycle is given by three signals: M/$\overline{IO}$, W/$\overline{R}$ and D/$\overline{C}$. At the same time, a valid address is present on the byte enable signals, $\overline{BHE}$ and $\overline{BLE}$, and the other address signals A_{23}–A_1. A status signal, $\overline{ADS}$, indicates when the 80376 issues a new bus cycle definition and address.

Collectively, the address bus, data bus and all associated control signals are referred to simply as "the bus". When active, the bus performs one of the bus cycles below:

1. Read from memory space
2. Locked read from memory space
3. Write to memory space
4. Locked write to memory space
5. Read from I/O space (or coprocessor)
6. Write to I/O space (or coprocessor)
7. Interrupt acknowledge (always locked)
8. Indicate halt, or indicate shutdown

Table 4.2 shows the encoding of the bus cycle definition signals for each bus cycle. See **Bus Cycle Definition Signals** for additonal information.

When the 80376 bus is not performing one of the activities listed above, it is either Idle or in the Hold Acknowledge state, which may be detected by external circuitry. The idle state can be identified by the 80376 giving no further assertions on its address strobe output ($\overline{ADS}$) since the beginning of its most recent bus cycle, and the most recent bus cycle having been terminated. The hold acknowledge state is identified by the 80376 asserting its hold acknowledge (HLDA) output.

The shortest time unit of bus activity is a bus state. A bus state is one processor clock period (two CLK2 periods) in duration. A complete data transfer occurs during a bus cycle, composed of two or more bus states.

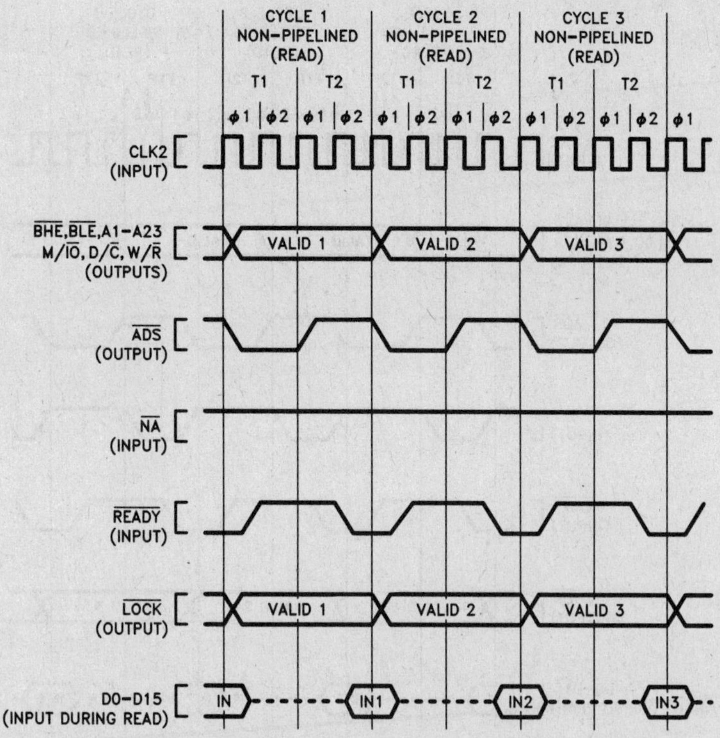

Figure 4.4. Fastest Read Cycles with Non-Pipelined Timing

The fastest 80376 bus cycle requires only two bus states. For example, three consecutive bus read cycles, each consisting of two bus states, are shown by Figure 4.4. The bus states in each cycle are named T1 and T2. Any memory or I/O address may be accessed by such a two-state bus cycle, if the external hardware is fast enough.

Every bus cycle continues until it is acknowledged by the external system hardware, using the 80376 $\overline{\text{READY}}$ input. Acknowledging the bus cycle at the end of the first T2 results in the shortest bus cycle, requiring only T1 and T2. If $\overline{\text{READY}}$ is not immediately asserted however, T2 states are repeated indefinitely until the $\overline{\text{READY}}$ input is sampled active.

The pipelining option provides a choice of bus cycle timings. Pipelined or non-pipelined cycles are selectable on a cycle-by-cycle basis with the Next Address ($\overline{\text{NA}}$) input.

When pipelining is selected the address ($\overline{\text{BHE}}$, $\overline{\text{BLE}}$ and A_{23}–A_1) and definition (W/$\overline{\text{R}}$, D/$\overline{\text{C}}$, M/$\overline{\text{IO}}$ and $\overline{\text{LOCK}}$) of the next cycle are available before the end of the current cycle. To signal their availability, the 80376 address status output ($\overline{\text{ADS}}$) is asserted. Figure 4.5 illustrates the fastest read cycles with pipelined timing.

Note from Figure 4.5 the fastest bus cycles using pipelining require only two bus states, named **T1P** and **T2P**. Therefore pipelined cycles allow the same data bandwidth as non-pipelined cycles, but address-to-data access time is increased by one T-state time compared to that of a non-pipelined cycle.

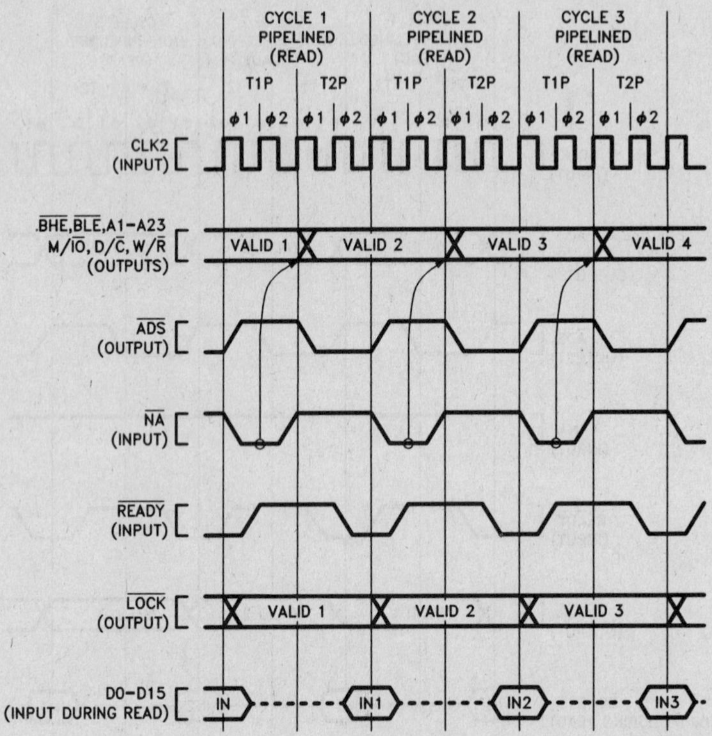

240182–20

Figure 4.5. Fastest Read Cycles with Pipelined Timing

READ AND WRITE CYCLES

Data transfers occur as a result of bus cycles, classified as read or write cycles. During read cycles, data is transferred from an external device to the processor. During write cycles, data is transferred from the processor to an external device.

Two choices of bus cycle timing are dynamically selectable: non-pipelined or pipelined. After an idle bus state, the processor always uses non-pipelined timing. However the $\overline{NA}$ (Next Address) input may be asserted to select pipelined timing for the next bus cycle. When pipelining is selected and the 80376 has a bus request pending internally, the address and definition of the next cycle is made available even before the current bus cycle is acknowledged by $\overline{READY}$.

Terminating a read or write cycle, like any bus cycle, requires acknowledging the cycle by asserting the $\overline{READY}$ input. Until acknowledged, the processor inserts wait states into the bus cycle, to allow adjustment for the speed of any external device. External hardware, which has decoded the address and bus cycle type, asserts the $\overline{READY}$ input at the appropriate time.

At the end of the second bus state within the bus cycle, $\overline{READY}$ is sampled. At that time, if external hardware acknowledges the bus cycle by asserting $\overline{READY}$, the bus cycle terminates as shown in Figure 4.6. If $\overline{READY}$ is negated as in Figure 4.7, the 80376 executes another bus state (a wait state) and $\overline{READY}$ is sampled again at the end of that state. This continues indefinitely until the cycle is acknowledged by $\overline{READY}$ asserted.

When the current cycle is acknowledged, the 80376 terminates it. When a read cycle is acknowledged, the 80376 latches the information present at its data pins. When a write cycle is acknowledged, the write data of the 80376 remains valid throughout phase one of the next bus state, to provide write data hold time.

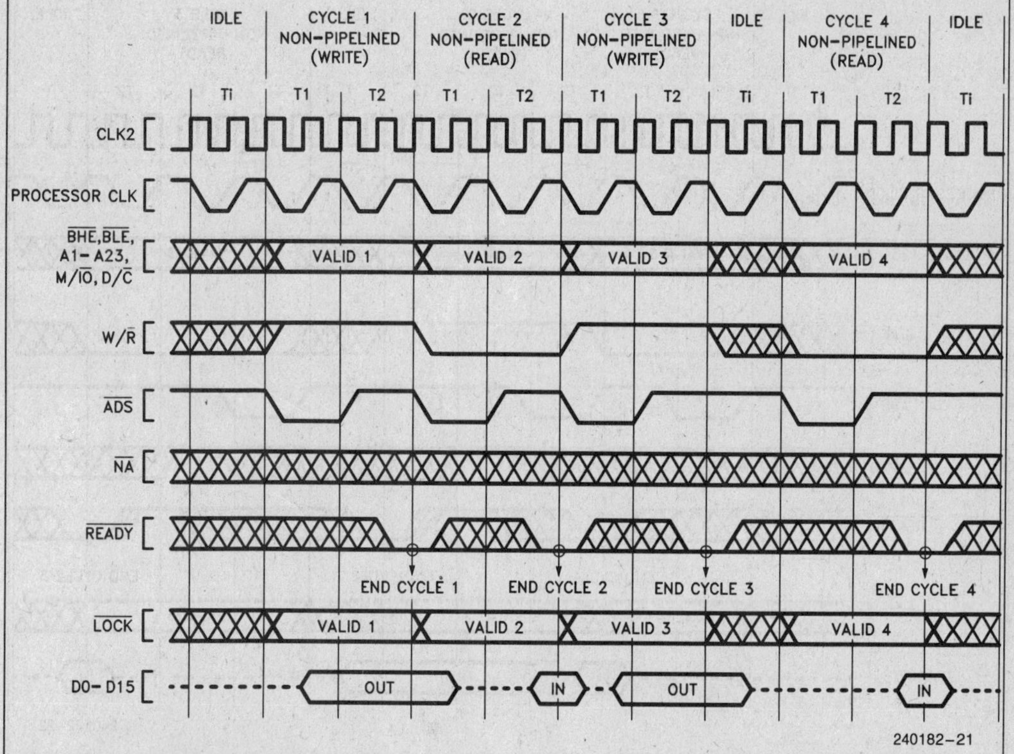

240182-21

Idle states are shown here for diagram variety only. Write cycles are not always followed by an idle state. An active bus cycle can immediately follow the write cycle.

Figure 4.6. Various Non-Pipelined Bus Cycles (Zero Wait States)

Non-Pipelined Bus Cycles

Any bus cycle may be performed with non-pipelined timing. For example, Figure 4.6 shows a mixture of non-pipelined read and write cycles. Figure 4.6 shows that the fastest possible non-pipelined cycles have two bus states per bus cycle. The states are named T1 and T2. In phase one of T1, the address signals and bus cycle definition signals are driven valid and, to signal their availability, address strobe ($\overline{ADS}$) is simultaneously asserted.

During read or write cycles, the data bus behaves as follows. If the cycle is a read, the 80376 floats its data signals to allow driving by the external device being addressed. **The 80376 requires that all data bus pins be at a valid logic state (HIGH or LOW) at the end of each read cycle, when $\overline{READY}$ is asserted. The system MUST be designed to meet this requirement.** If the cycle is a write, data signals are driven by the 80376 beginning in phase two of T1 until phase one of the bus state following cycle acknowledgement.

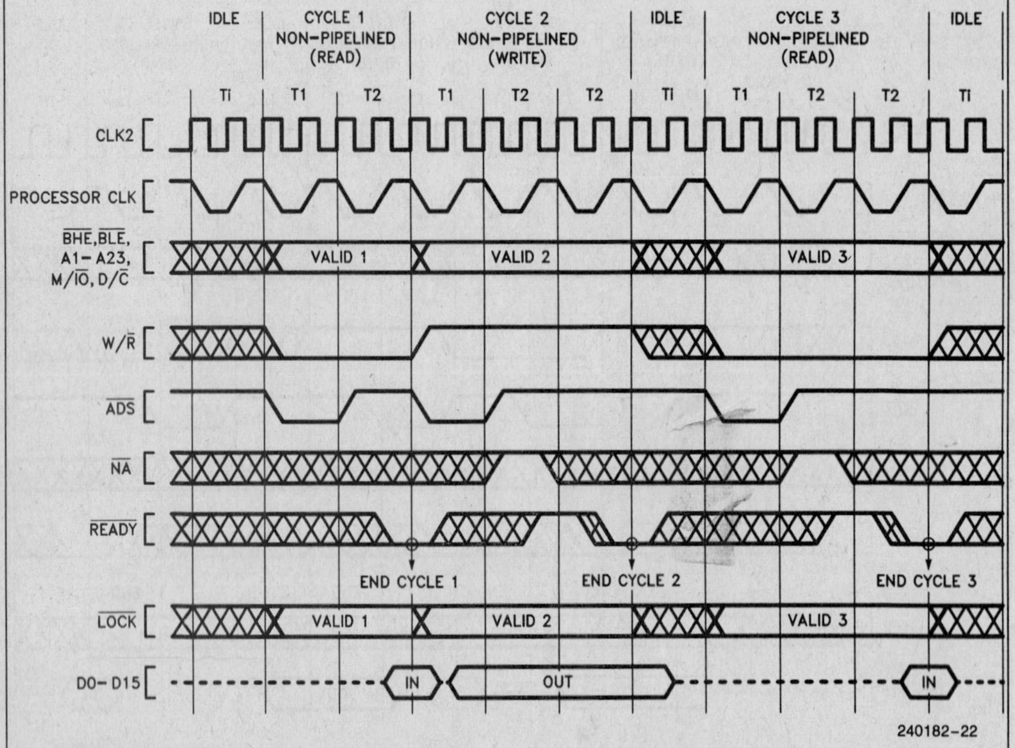

240182-22

Idle states are shown here for diagram variety only. Write cycles are not always followed by an idle state. An active bus cycle can immediately follow the write cycle.

Figure 4.7. Various Non-Pipelined Bus Cycles (Various Number of Wait States)

Figure 4.7 illustrates non-pipelined bus cycles with one wait state added to Cycles 2 and 3. $\overline{READY}$ is sampled inactive at the end of the first T2 in Cycles 2 and 3. Therefore Cycles 2 and 3 have T2 repeated again. At the end of the second T2, $\overline{READY}$ is sampled active.

When address pipelining is not used, the address and bus cycle definition remain valid during all wait states. When wait states are added and it is desirable to maintain non-pipelined timing, it is necessary to negate $\overline{NA}$ during each T2 state except the last one, as shown in Figure 4.7, Cycles 2 and 3. If $\overline{NA}$ is sampled active during a T2 other than the last one, the next state would be T2I or T2P instead of another T2.

When address pipelining is not used, the bus states and transitions are completely illustrated by Figure 4.8. The bus transitions between four possible states, T1, T2, T_i, and T_h. Bus cycles consist of T1 and T2, with T2 being repeated for wait states. Otherwise the bus may be idle, T_i, or in the hold acknowledge state T_h.

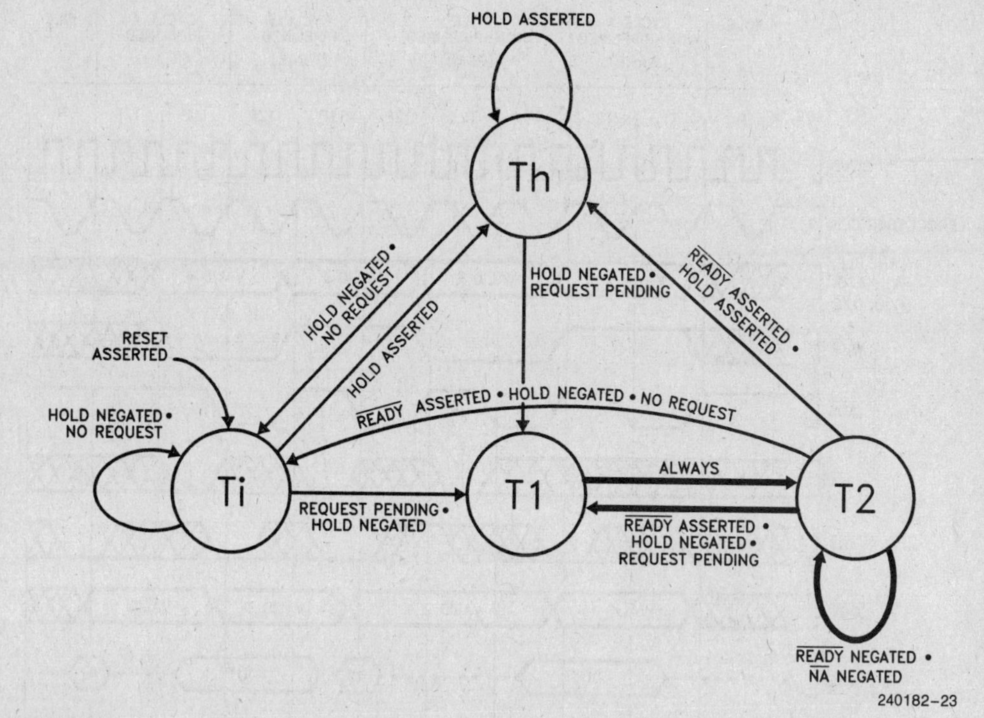

HOLD ASSERTED

Th

HOLD NEGATED • NO REQUEST

HOLD ASSERTED

HOLD NEGATED • REQUEST PENDING

$\overline{\text{READY}}$ ASSERTED • HOLD ASSERTED •

RESET ASSERTED

HOLD NEGATED • NO REQUEST

$\overline{\text{READY}}$ ASSERTED • HOLD NEGATED • NO REQUEST

Ti

T1

T2

REQUEST PENDING • HOLD NEGATED

ALWAYS

$\overline{\text{READY}}$ ASSERTED • HOLD NEGATED • REQUEST PENDING

$\overline{\text{READY}}$ NEGATED • $\overline{\text{NA}}$ NEGATED

240182–23

Bus States:

T1—first clock of a non-pipelined bus cycle (80376 drives new address and asserts $\overline{\text{ADS}}$).
T2—subsequent clocks of a bus cycle when $\overline{\text{NA}}$ has not been sampled asserted in the current bus cycle.
Ti—idle state.
Th—hold acknowledge state (80376 asserts HLDA).

The fastest bus cycle consists of two states: T1 and T2.
Four basic bus states describe bus operation when not using pipelined address.

Figure 4.8. 80376 Bus States (Not Using Pipelined Address)

Bus cycles always begin with T1. T1 always leads to T2. If a bus cycle is not acknowledged during T2 and $\overline{\text{NA}}$ is inactive, T2 is repeated. When a cycle is acknowledged during T2, the following state will be T1 of the next bus cycle if a bus request is pending internally, or T_i if there is no bus request pending, or T_h if the HOLD input is being asserted.

Use of pipelining allows the 80376 to enter three additional bus states not shown in Figure 4.8. Figure 4.12 is the complete bus state diagram, including pipelined cycles.

Pipelined Bus Cycles

Pipelining is the option of requesting the address and the bus cycle definition of the next internally pending bus cycle before the current bus cycle is acknowledged with $\overline{\text{READY}}$ asserted. $\overline{\text{ADS}}$ is asserted by the 80376 when the next address is issued. The pipelining option is controlled on a cycle-by-cycle basis with the $\overline{\text{NA}}$ input signal.

Once a bus cycle is in progress and the current address has been valid for at least one entire bus state, the $\overline{\text{NA}}$ input is sampled at the end of every phase one until the bus cycle is acknowledged. During non-pipelined bus cycles $\overline{\text{NA}}$ is sampled at the end of phase one in every T2. An example is Cycle 2 in Figure 4.9, during which $\overline{\text{NA}}$ is sampled at the end of phase one of every T2 (it was asserted once during the first T2 and has no further effect during that bus cycle).

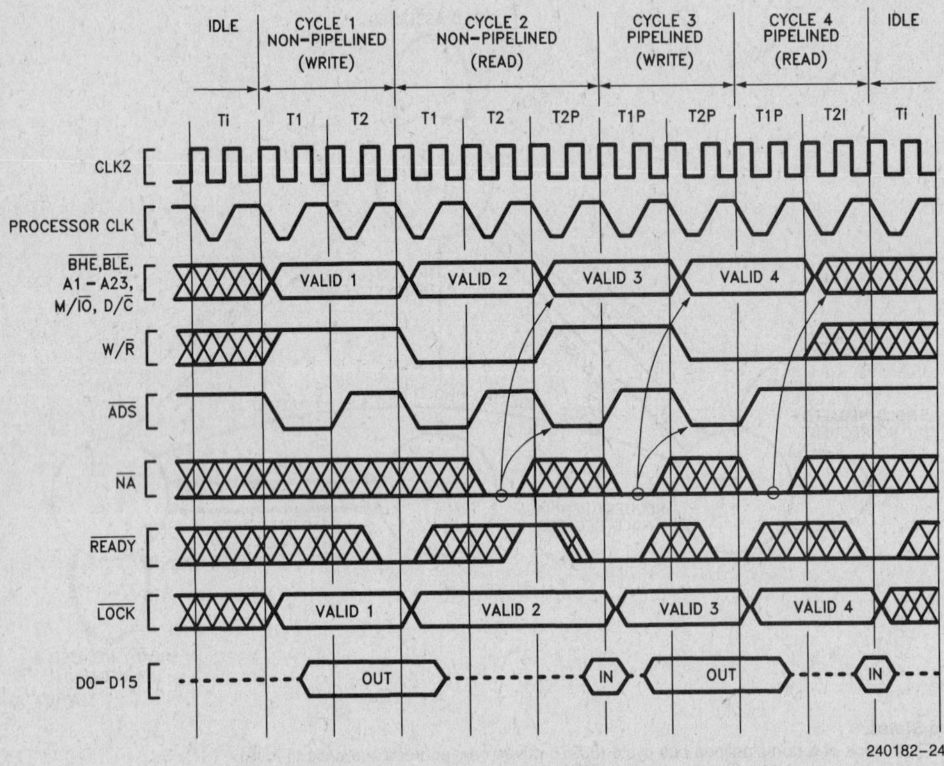

Following any idle bus state (Ti), bus cycles are non-pipelined. Within non-pipelined bus cycles, $\overline{NA}$ is only sampled during wait states. Therefore, to begin pipelining during a group of non-pipelined bus cycles requires a non-pipelined cycle with at least one wait state (Cylcle 2 above).

Figure 4.9. Transitioning to Pipelining during Burst of Bus Cycles

If $\overline{NA}$ is sampled active, the 80376 is free to drive the address and bus cycle definition of the next bus cycle, and assert $\overline{ADS}$, as soon as it has a bus request internally pending. It may drive the next address as early as the next bus state, whether the current bus cycle is acknowledged at that time or not.

Regarding the details of pipelining, the 80376 has the following characteristics:

1. The next address and status may appear as early as the bus state after $\overline{NA}$ was sampled active (see Figures 4.9 or 4.10). In that case, state T2P is entered immediately. However, when there is not an internal bus request already pending, the next address and status will not be available immediately after $\overline{NA}$ is asserted and T2I is entered instead of T2P (see Figure 4.11 Cycle 3). Provided the current bus cycle isn't yet acknowledged by $\overline{READY}$ asserted, T2P will be entered as soon as the 80376 does drive the next address and status. External hardware should therefore observe the $\overline{ADS}$ output as confirmation the next address and status are actually being driven on the bus.
2. Any address and status which are validated by a pulse on the 80376 $\overline{ADS}$ output will remain stable on the address pins for at least two processor clock periods. The 80376 cannot produce a new address and status more frequently than every two processor clock periods (see Figures 4.9, 4.10 and 4.11).
3. Only the address and bus cycle definition of the very next bus cycle is available. The pipelining capability cannot look further than one bus cycle ahead (see Figure 4.11, Cycle 1).

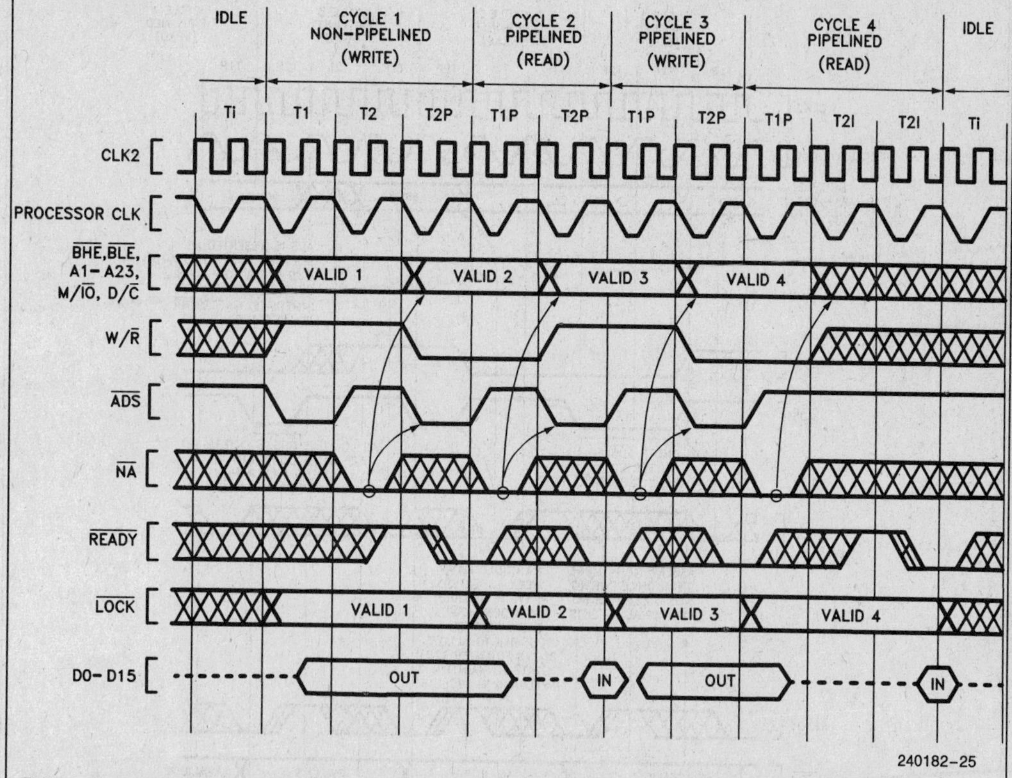

240182-25

Following any idle bus state (Ti) the bus cycle is always non-pipelined and $\overline{\text{NA}}$ is only sampled during wait states. To start, address pipelining after an idle state requires a non-pipelined cycle with at least one wait state (cycle 1 above). The pipelined cycles (2, 3, 4 above) are shown with various numbers of wait states.

Figure 4.10. Fastest Transition to Pipelined Bus Cycle Following Idle Bus State

The complete bus state transition diagram, including pipelining is given by Figure 4.12. Note it is a superset of the diagram for non-pipelined only, and the three additional bus states for pipelining are drawn in bold.

The fastest bus cycle with pipelining consists of just two bus states, T1P and T2P (recall for non-pipelined it is T1 and T2). T1P is the first bus state of a pipelined cycle.

Initiating and Maintaining Pipelined Bus Cycles

Using the state diagram Figure 4.12, observe the transitions from an idle state, T_i, to the beginning of a pipelined bus cycle T1P. From an idle state, T_i, the first bus cycle must begin with T1, and is therefore a non-pipelined bus cycle. The next bus cycle will be pipelined, however, provided $\overline{\text{NA}}$ is asserted and the first bus cycle ends in a T2P state (the address and status for the next bus cycle is driven during T2P). The fastest path from an idle state to a pipelined bus cycle is shown in bold below:

T_i, T_i,	**T1–T2–T2P,**	**T1P–T2P,**
idle states	non-pipelined cycle	pipelined cycle

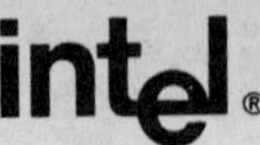

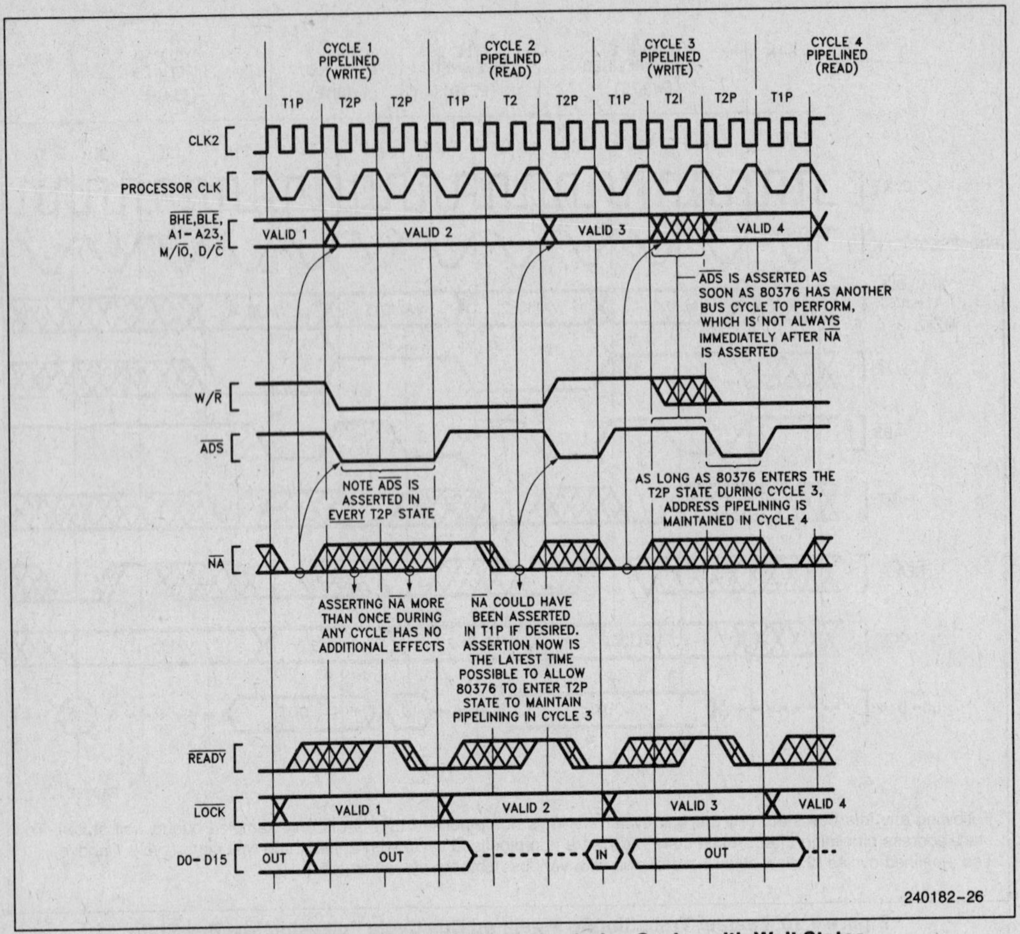

Figure 4.11. Details of Address Pipelining during Cycles with Wait States

T1–T2–T2P are the states of the bus cycle that establishes address pipelining for the next bus cycle, which begins with T1P. The same is true after a bus hold state, shown below:

T_h, T_h, T_h,	T1–T2–T2P,	T1P–T2P,
hold aknowledge states	non-pipelined cycle	pipelined cycle

The transition to pipelined address is shown functionally by Figure 4.10, Cycle 1. Note that Cycle 1 is used to transition into pipelined address timing for the subsequent Cycles 2, 3 and 4, which are pipelined. The $\overline{\text{NA}}$ input is asserted at the appropriate time to select address pipelining for Cycles 2, 3 and 4.

Once a bus cycle is in progress and the current address and status has been valid for one entire bus state, the $\overline{\text{NA}}$ input is sampled at the end of every phase one until the bus cycle is acknowledged.

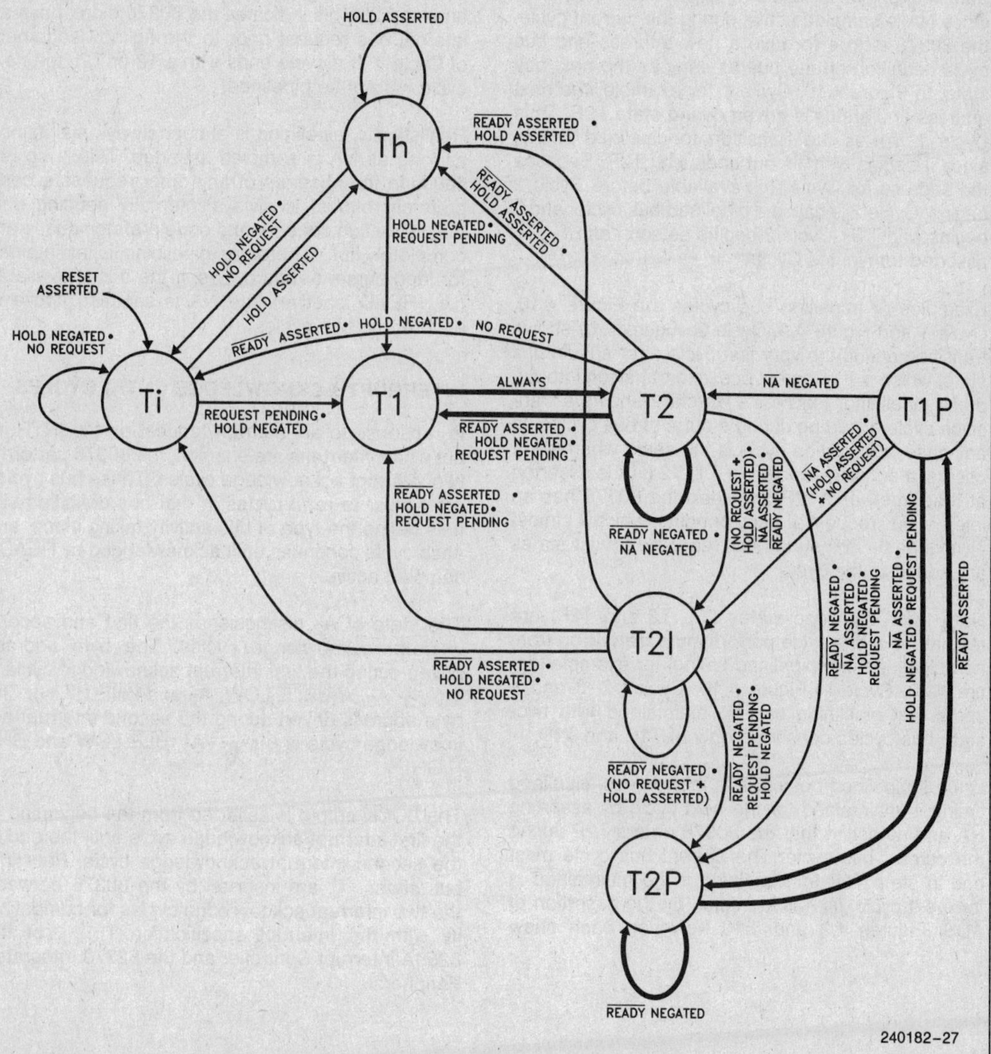

Bus States:

T1—first clock of a non-pipelined bus cycle (80376 drives new address, status and asserts $\overline{\text{ADS}}$).

T2—subsequent clocks of a bus cycle when $\overline{\text{NA}}$ has not been sampled asserted in the current bus cycle.

T2I—subsequent clocks of a bus cycle when $\overline{\text{NA}}$ has been sampled asserted in the current bus cycle but there is not yet an internal bus request pending (80376 will not drive new address, status or assert $\overline{\text{ADS}}$).

T2P—subsequent clocks of a bus cycle when $\overline{\text{NA}}$ has been sampled asserted in the current bus cycle and there is an internal bus request pending (80376 drives new address, status and asserts $\overline{\text{ADS}}$).

T1P—first clock of a pipelined bus cycle.

Ti—idle state.

Th—hold acknowledge state (80376 asserts HLDA).

Asserting $\overline{\text{NA}}$ for pipelined bus cycles gives access to three more bus states: T2I, T2P and T1P.
Using pipelining the fastest bus cycle consists of T1P and T2P.

Figure 4.12. 80376 Processor Complete Bus States (Including Pipelining)

Sampling begins in T2 during Cycle 1 in Figure 4.10. Once $\overline{NA}$ is sampled active during the current cycle, the 80376 is free to drive a new address and bus cycle definition on the bus as early as the next bus state. In Figure 4.10, Cycle 1 for example, the next address and status is driven during state T2P. Thus Cycle 1 makes the transition to pipelined timing, since it begins with T1 but ends with T2P. Because the address for Cycle 2 is available before Cycle 2 begins, Cycle 2 is called a pipelined bus cycle, and it begins with T1P. Cycle 2 begins as soon as $\overline{READY}$ asserted terminates Cycle 1.

Examples of transition bus cycles are Figure 4.10, Cycle 1 and Figure 4.9, Cycle 2. Figure 4.10 shows transition during the very first cycle after an idle bus state, which is the fastest possible transition into address pipelining. Figure 4.9, Cycle 2 shows a transition cycle occurring during a burst of bus cycles. In any case, a transition cycle is the same whenever it occurs: it consists at least of T1, T2 ($\overline{NA}$ is asserted at that time), and T2P (provided the 80376 has an internal bus request already pending, which it almost always has). T2P states are repeated if wait states are added to the cycle.

Note that only three states (T1, T2 and T2P) are required in a bus cycle performing a **transition** from non-pipelined into pipelined timing, for example Figure 4.10, Cycle 1. Figure 4.10, Cycles 2, 3 and 4 show that pipelining can be maintained with two-state bus cycles consisting only of T1P and T2P.

Once a pipelined bus cycle is in progress, pipelined timing is maintained for the next cycle by asserting $\overline{NA}$ and detecting that the 80376 enters T2P during the current bus cycle. The current bus cycle must end in state T2P for pipelining to be maintained in the next cycle. T2P is identified by the assertion of $\overline{ADS}$. Figures 4.9 and 4.10 however, each show pipelining ending after Cycle 4 because Cycle 4 ends in T2I. This indicates the 80376 didn't have an internal bus request prior to the acknowledgement of Cycle 4. If a cycle ends with a T2 or T2I, the next cycle will not be pipelined.

Realistically, pipelining is almost always maintained as long as $\overline{NA}$ is sampled asserted. This is so because in the absence of any other request, a code prefetch request is always internally pending until the instruction decoder and code prefetch queue are completely full. Therefore pipelining is maintained for long bursts of bus cycles, if the bus is available (i.e., HOLD inactive) and $\overline{NA}$ is sampled active in each of the bus cycles.

INTERRUPT ACKNOWLEDGE (INTA) CYCLES

In repsonse to an interrupt request on the INTR input when interrupts are enabled, the 80376 performs two interrupt acknowledge cycles. These bus cycles are similar to read cycles in that bus definition signals define the type of bus activity taking place, and each cycle continues until acknowledged by $\overline{READY}$ sampled active.

The state of A_2 distinguishes the first and second interrupt acknowledge cycles. The byte address driven during the first interrupt acknowledge cycle is 4 (A_{23}–A_3, A_1, $\overline{BLE}$ LOW, A_2 and $\overline{BHE}$ HIGH). The byte address driven during the second interrupt acknowledge cycle is 0 (A_{23}–A_1, $\overline{BLE}$ LOW and $\overline{BHE}$ HIGH).

The $\overline{LOCK}$ output is asserted from the beginning of the first interrupt acknowledge cycle until the end of the second interrupt acknowledge cycle. Four idle bus states, T_i, are inserted by the 80376 between the two interrupt acknowledge cycles for compatibility with the interrupt specification T_{RHRL} of the 8259A Interrupt Controller and the 82370 Integrated Peripheral.

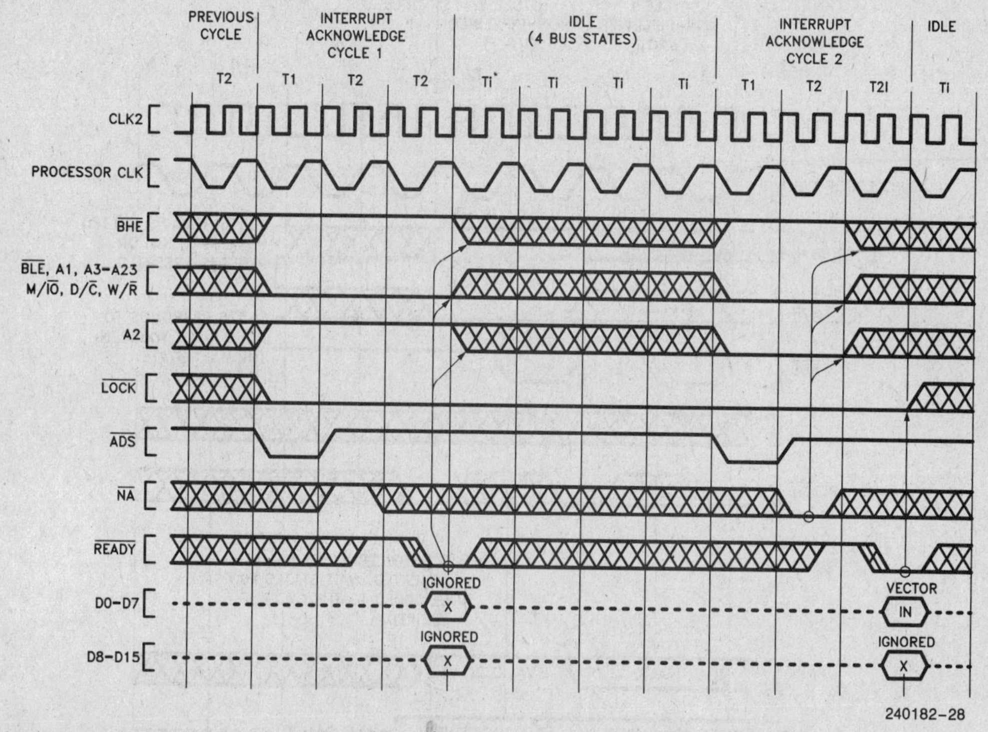

PREVIOUS CYCLE | INTERRUPT ACKNOWLEDGE CYCLE 1 | IDLE (4 BUS STATES) | INTERRUPT ACKNOWLEDGE CYCLE 2 | IDLE

T2 T1 T2 T2 Ti Ti Ti Ti T1 T2 T2I Ti

CLK2

PROCESSOR CLK

$\overline{BHE}$

$\overline{BLE}$, A1, A3–A23
M/$\overline{IO}$, D/$\overline{C}$, W/$\overline{R}$

A2

$\overline{LOCK}$

$\overline{ADS}$

$\overline{NA}$

$\overline{READY}$

D0–D7

D8–D15

IGNORED X

IGNORED X

VECTOR IN

IGNORED X

240182–28

Interrupt Vector (0–255) is read on D0–D7 at end of second Interrupt Acknowledge bus cycle.
Because each Interrupt Acknowledge bus cycle is followed by idle bus states, asserting $\overline{NA}$ has no practical effect.
Choose the approach which is simplest for your system hardware design.

Figure 4.13. Interrupt Acknowledge Cycles

During both interrupt acknowledge cycles, D_{15}–D_0 float. No data is read at the end of the first interrupt acknowledge cycle. At the end of the second interrupt acknowledge cycle, the 80376 will read an external interrupt vector from D_7–D_0 of the data bus. The vector indicates the specific interrupt number (from 0–255) requiring service.

HALT INDICATION CYCLE

The 80376 execution unit halts as a result of executing a HLT instruction. Signaling its entrance into the halt state, a halt indication cycle is performed. The halt indication cycle is identified by the state of the bus definition signals and a byte address of 2. See the **Bus Cycle Definition Signals** section. The halt indication cycle must be acknowledged by $\overline{READY}$ asserted. A halted 80376 resumes execution when INTR (if interrupts are enabled), NMI or RESET is asserted.

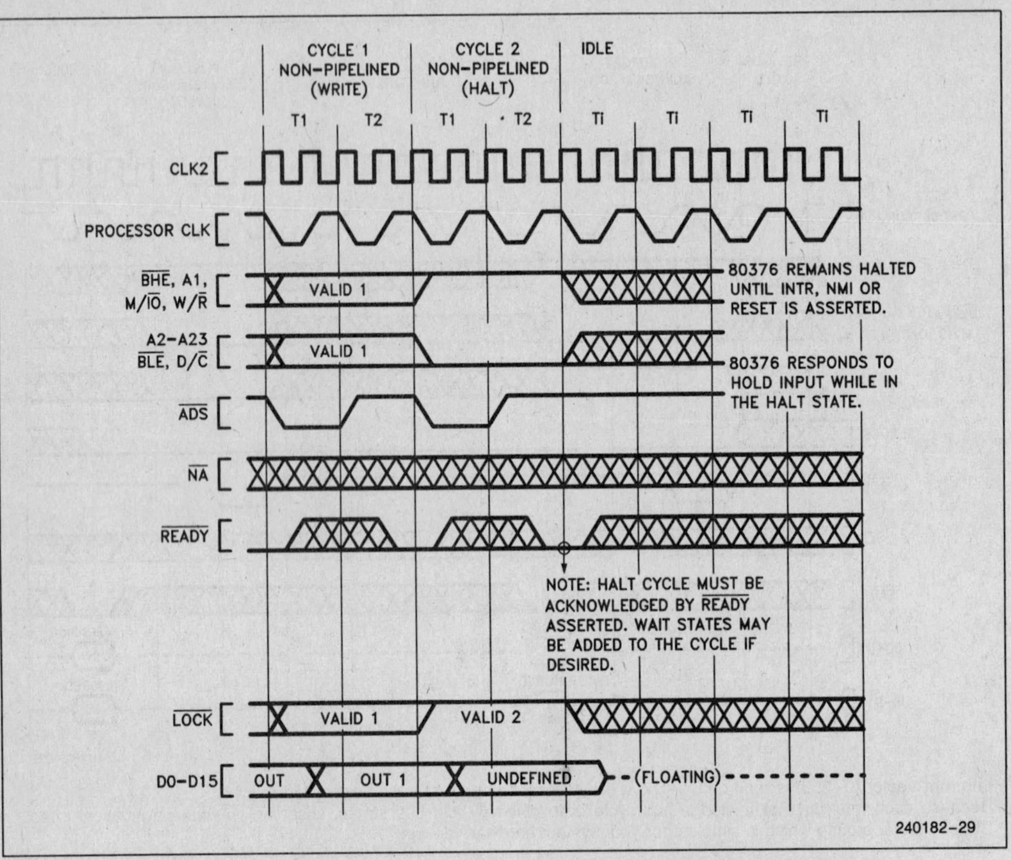

Figure 4.14. Example Halt Indication Cycle from Non-Pipelined Cycle

SHUTDOWN INDICATION CYCLE

The 80376 shuts down as a result of a protection fault while attempting to process a double fault. Signaling its entrance into the shutdown state, a shutdown indication cycle is performed. The shutdown indication cycle is identified by the state of the bus definition signals shown in **Bus Cycle Definition Signals** and a byte address of 0. The shutdown indication cycle must be acknowledged by $\overline{READY}$ asserted. A shutdown 80376 resumes execution when NMI or RESET is asserted.

ENTERING AND EXITING HOLD ACKNOWLEDGE

The bus hold acknowledge state, T_h, is entered in response to the HOLD input being asserted. In the bus hold acknowledge state, the 80376 floats all outputs or bidirectional signals, except for HLDA. HLDA is asserted as long as the 80376 remains in the bus hold acknowledge state. In the bus hold acknowledge state, all inputs except HOLD and RESET are ignored.

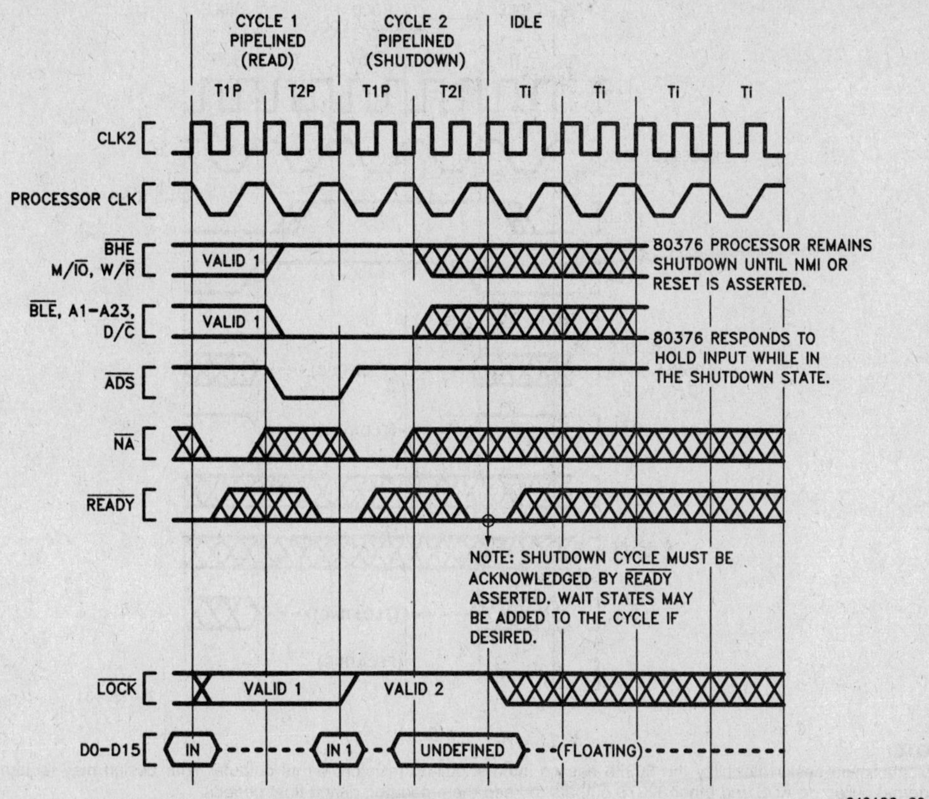

Figure 4.15. Example Shutdown Indication Cycle from Non-Pipelined Cycle

T_h may be entered from a bus idle state as in Figure 4.16 or after the acknowledgement of the current physical bus cycle if the $\overline{\text{LOCK}}$ signal is not asserted, as in Figures 4.17 and 4.18.

T_h is exited in response to the HOLD input being negated. The following state will be T_i as in Figure 4.16 if no bus request is pending. The following bus state will be T1 if a bus request is internally pending, as in Figures 4.17 and 4.18. T_h is exited in response to RESET being asserted.

If a rising edge occurs on the edge-triggered NMI input while in T_h, the event is remembered as a non-maskable interrupt 2 and is serviced when T_h is exited unless the 80376 is reset before T_h is exited.

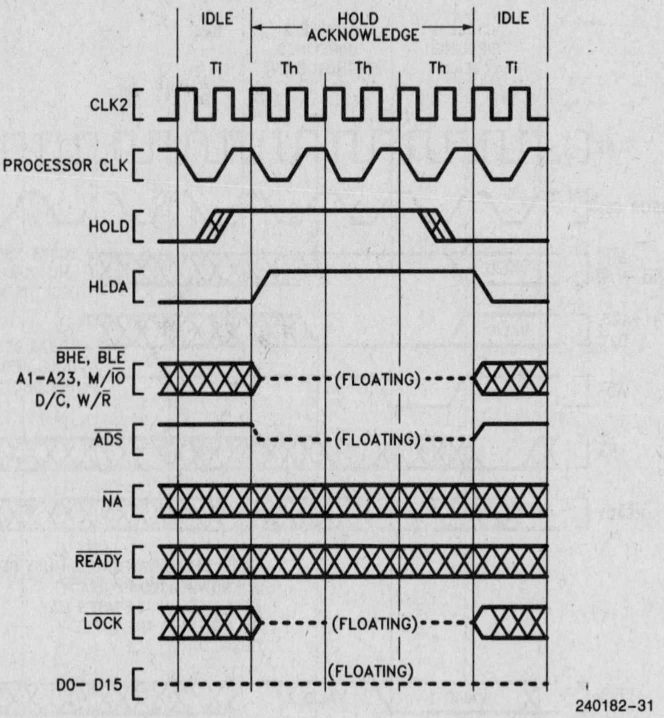

IDLE | HOLD ACKNOWLEDGE | IDLE

Ti Th Th Th Ti

CLK2

PROCESSOR CLK

HOLD

HLDA

$\overline{\text{BHE}}$, $\overline{\text{BLE}}$ A1–A23, M/$\overline{\text{IO}}$ D/$\overline{\text{C}}$, W/$\overline{\text{R}}$ (FLOATING)

$\overline{\text{ADS}}$ (FLOATING)

$\overline{\text{NA}}$

$\overline{\text{READY}}$

$\overline{\text{LOCK}}$ (FLOATING)

D0–D15 (FLOATING)

240182–31

NOTE:
For maximum design flexibility the 80376 has no internal pull-up resistors on its outputs. Your design may require an external pullup on $\overline{\text{ADS}}$ and other 80376 outputs to keep them negated during float periods.

Figure 4.16. Requesting Hold from Idle Bus

RESET DURING HOLD ACKNOWLEDGE

RESET being asserted takes priority over HOLD being asserted. If RESET is asserted while HOLD remains asserted, the 80376 drives its pins to defined states during reset, as in **Table 4.5, Pin State During Reset,** and performs internal reset activity as usual.

If HOLD remains asserted when RESET is inactive, the 80376 enters the hold acknowledge state before performing its first bus cycle, provided HOLD is still asserted when the 80376 processor would otherwise perform its first bus cycle. If HOLD remains asserted when RESET is inactive, the $\overline{\text{BUSY}}$ input is still sampled as usual to determine whether a self test is being requested.

FLOAT

Activating the $\overline{\text{FLT}}$ input floats all 80376 bidirectional and output signals, including HLDA. Asserting $\overline{\text{FLT}}$ isolates the 80376 from the surrounding circuitry.

When an 80376 in a PQFP surface-mount package is used without a socket, it cannot be removed from the printed circuit board. The $\overline{\text{FLT}}$ input allows the 80376 to be electrically isolated to allow testing of external circuitry. This technique is known as ONCE for "ON-Circuit Emulation".

ENTERING AND EXITING FLOAT

$\overline{\text{FLT}}$ is an asynchronous, active-low input. It is recognized on the rising edge of CLK2. When recognized, it aborts the current bus cycle and floats the outputs of the 80376 (Figure 4.20). $\overline{\text{FLT}}$ must be held low for a minimum of 16 CLK2 cycles. Reset should be asserted and held asserted until after $\overline{\text{FLT}}$ is deasserted. This will ensure that the 80376 will exit float in a valid state.

Asserting the $\overline{\text{FLT}}$ input unconditionally aborts the current bus cycle and forces the 80376 into the FLOAT mode. Since activating $\overline{\text{FLT}}$ unconditionally forces the 80376 into FLOAT mode, the 80376 is not

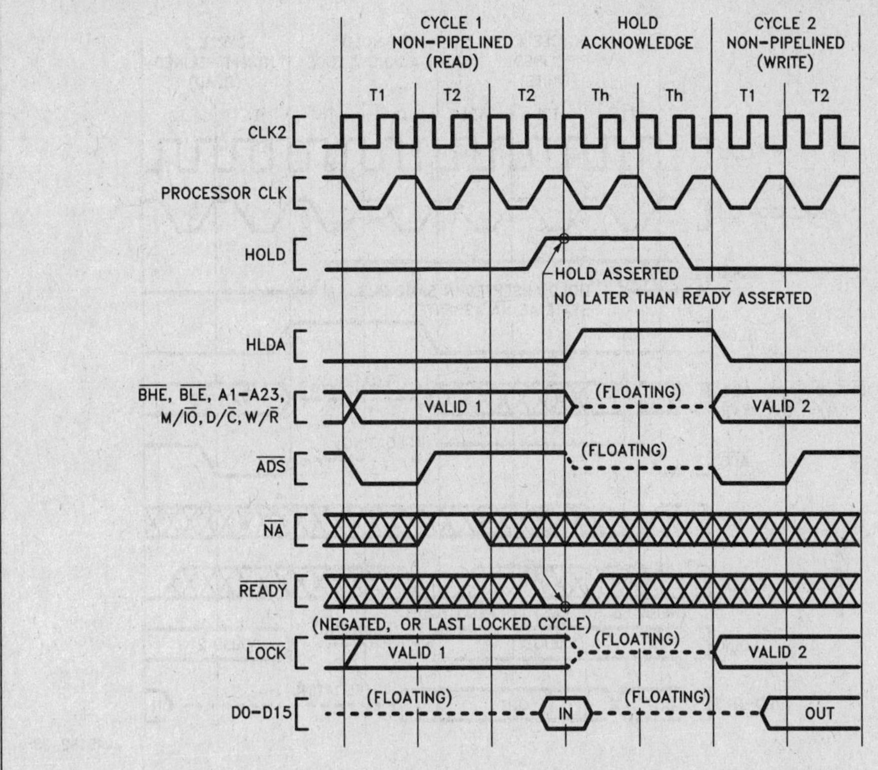

NOTE:
HOLD is a synchronous input and can be asserted at any CLK2 edge, provided setup and hold (t_{23} and t_{24}) requirements are met. This waveform is useful for determining Hold Acknowledge latency.

Figure 4.17. Requesting Hold from Active Bus ($\overline{\text{NA}}$ Inactive)

guaranteed to enter FLOAT in a valid state. After deactivating $\overline{\text{FLT}}$, the 80376 is not guaranteed to exit FLOAT mode in a valid state. This is not a problem as the $\overline{\text{FLT}}$ pin is meant to be used only during ONCE. After exiting FLOAT, the 80376 must be reset to return it to a valid state. Reset should be asserted before $\overline{\text{FLT}}$ is deasserted. This will ensure that the 80376 will exit float in a valid state.

$\overline{\text{FLT}}$ has an internal pull-up resistor, and if it is not used it should be unconnected.

BUS ACTIVITY DURING AND FOLLOWING RESET

RESET is the highest priority input signal, capable of interrupting any processor activity when it is asserted. A bus cycle in progress can be aborted at any stage, or idle states or bus hold acknowledge states discontinued so that the reset state is established.

RESET should remain asserted for at least 15 CLK2 periods to ensure it is recognized throughout the 80376, and at least 80 CLK2 periods if a 80376 self-test is going to be requested at the falling edge. RESET asserted pulses less than 15 CLK2 periods may not be recognized. RESET pulses less than 80 CLK2 periods followed by a self-test may cause the self-test to report a failure when no true failure exists.

Provided the RESET falling edge meets setup and hold times t_{25} and t_{26}, the internal processor clock phase is defined at that time as illustrated by Figure 4.19 and Figure 6.7.

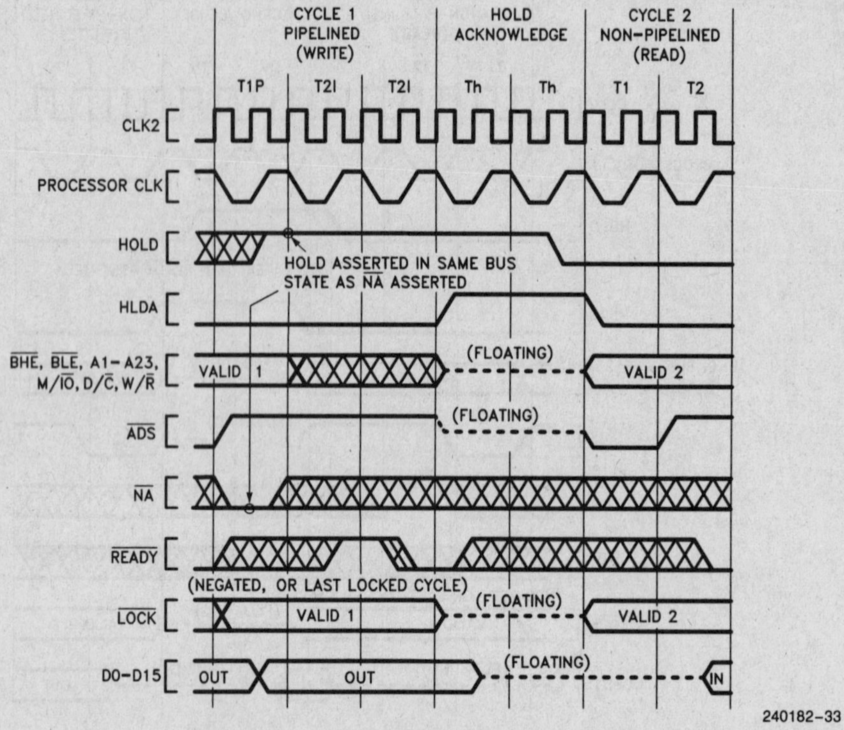

CYCLE 1 PIPELINED (WRITE) | HOLD ACKNOWLEDGE | CYCLE 2 NON-PIPELINED (READ)

T1P | T2I | T2I | Th | Th | T1 | T2

CLK2

PROCESSOR CLK

HOLD

HOLD ASSERTED IN SAME BUS STATE AS $\overline{NA}$ ASSERTED

HLDA

$\overline{BHE}$, $\overline{BLE}$, A1–A23, M/$\overline{IO}$, D/$\overline{C}$, W/$\overline{R}$ — VALID 1 — (FLOATING) — VALID 2

$\overline{ADS}$ — (FLOATING)

$\overline{NA}$

$\overline{READY}$

(NEGATED, OR LAST LOCKED CYCLE)

$\overline{LOCK}$ — VALID 1 — (FLOATING) — VALID 2

D0–D15 — OUT — OUT — (FLOATING) — IN

240182–33

NOTE:
HOLD is a synchronous input and can be asserted at any CLK2 edge, provided setup and hold (t_{23} and t_{24}) requirements are met. This waveform is useful for determining Hold Acknowledge latency.

Figure 4.18. Requesting Hold from Idle Bus ($\overline{NA}$ Active)

An 80376 self-test may be requested at the time RESET goes inactive by having the $\overline{BUSY}$ input at a LOW level as shown in Figure 4.19. The self-test requires (2^{20} + approximately 60) CLK2 periods to complete. The self-test duration is not affected by the test results. Even if the self-test indicates a problem, the 80376 attempts to proceed with the reset sequence afterwards.

After the RESET falling edge (and after the self-test if it was requested) the 80376 performs an internal initialization sequence for approximately 350 to 450 CLK2 periods.

RESET

≥15 CLK2 DURATION IF NOT GOING TO REQUEST SELF-TEST.

≥80 CLK2 DURATION BEFORE REQUESTING SELF-TEST.

INTERNAL INITIALIZATION

IF SELF-TEST IS PERFORMED, ADD (2^20)+60* TO THESE NUMBERS

CYCLE 1

NON-PIPELINED (READ)

T1 T2

1 2 3 17 18 19 395* 396* 397* 398*

CLK2

*APPROXIMATELY

RESET

φ2 | φ1 | φ2 | φ1 | φ2 | φ1 | φ2 | φ1 | φ2

CLK (INTERNAL)

PROCESSOR CLK

NO SELF-TEST

BUSY (NOTE 1)

LOW TO BEGIN SELF-TEST (NOTE 2)

ERROR

BHE, BLE, W/R, M/IO, HLDA — UP TO 30 CLK2 — LOW DURING RESET — VALID 1

A1–A23, D/C, LOCK — UP TO 30 CLK2 — HIGH DURING RESET — VALID 1

ADS — UP TO 30 CLK2 — HIGH DURING RESET

NA

READY

D0–D15 — (FLOATING)

240182–34

NOTES:

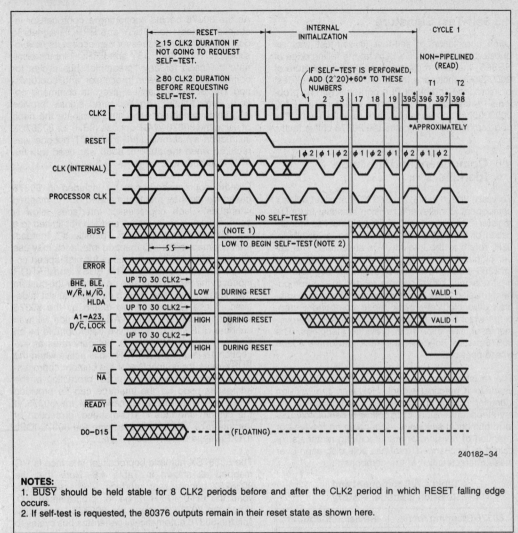

1. BUSY should be held stable for 8 CLK2 periods before and after the CLK2 period in which RESET falling edge occurs.
2. If self-test is requested, the 80376 outputs remain in their reset state as shown here.

Figure 4.19. Bus Activity from Reset until First Code Fetch

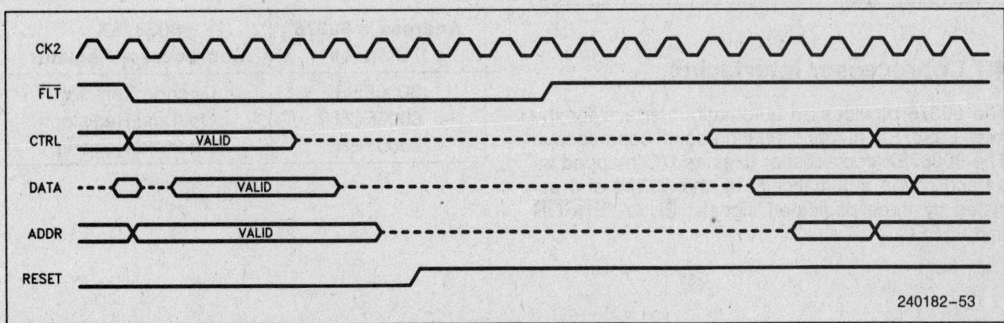

Figure 4.20. Entering and Exiting FLOAT

4.5 Self-Test Signature

Upon completion of self-test (if self-test was requested by driving BUSY LOW at the falling edge of RESET) the EAX register will contain a signature of 00000000H indicating the 80376 passed its self-test of microcode and major PLA contents with no problems detected. The passing signature in EAX, 00000000H, applies to all 80376 revision levels. Any non-zero signature indicates the 80376 unit is faulty.

4.6 Component and Revision Identifiers

To assist 80376 users, the 80376 after reset holds a component identifier and revision identifier in its DX register. The upper 8 bits of DX hold 33H as identification of the 80376 component. (The lower nibble, 03H, refers to the Intel386™ architecture. The upper nibble, 30H, refers to the third member of the Intel386 family). The lower 8 bits of DX hold an 8-bit unsigned binary number related to the component revision level. The revision identifier will, in general, chronologically track those component steppings which are intended to have certain improvements or distinction from previous steppings. The 80376 revision identifier will track that of the 80386 where possible.

The revision identifier is intended to assist 80376 users to a practical extent. However, the revision identifier value is not guaranteed to change with every stepping revision, or to follow a completely uniform numerical sequence, depending on the type or intention of revision, or manufacturing materials required to be changed. Intel has sole discretion over these characteristics of the component.

Table 4.7. Component and Revision Identifier History

80376 Stepping Name	Revision Identifier
A0	05H
B	00I I

4.7 Coprocessor Interfacing

The 80376 provides an automatic interface for the Intel 80387SX numeric floating-point coprocessor. The 80387SX coprocessor uses an I/O mapped interface driven automatically by the 80376 and assisted by three dedicated signals: BUSY, ERROR and PEREQ.

As the 80376 begins supporting a coprocessor instruction, it tests the BUSY and ERROR signals to determine if the coprocessor can accept its next instruction. Thus, the BUSY and ERROR inputs eliminate the need for any "preamble" bus cycles for communication between processor and coprocessor. The 80387SX can be given its command opcode immediately. The dedicated signals provide instruction synchronization, and eliminate the need of using the 80376 WAIT opcode (9BH) for 80387SX instruction synchronization (the WAIT opcode was required when the 8086 or 8088 was used with the 8087 coprocessor).

Custom coprocessors can be included in 80376 based systems by memory-mapped or I/O-mapped interfaces. Such coprocessor interfaces allow a completely custom protocol, and are not limited to a set of coprocessor protocol "primitives". Instead, memory-mapped or I/O-mapped interfaces may use all applicable 80376 instructions for high-speed coprocessor communication. The BUSY and ERROR inputs of the 80376 may also be used for the custom coprocessor interface, if such hardware assist is desired. These signals can be tested by the 80376 WAIT opcode (9BH). The WAIT instruction will wait until the BUSY input is inactive (interruptable by an NMI or enabled INTR input), but generates an exception 16 fault if the ERROR pin is active when the BUSY goes (or is) inactive. If the custom coprocessor interface is memory-mapped, protection of the addresses used for the interface can be provided with the segmentation mechanism of the 80376. If the custom interface is I/O-mapped, protection of the interface can be provided with the 80376 IOPL (I/O Privilege Level) mechanism.

The 80387SX numeric coprocessor interface is I/O mapped as shown in Table 4.8. Note that the 80387SX coprocessor interface addresses are beyond the 0H-0FFFFH range for programmed I/O. When the 80376 supports the 80387SX coprocessor, the 80376 automatically generates bus cycles to the coprocessor interface addresses.

Table 4.8 Numeric Coprocessor Port Addresses

Address in 80376 I/O Space	80387SX Coprocessor Register
8000F8H	Opcode Register
8000FCH	Operand Register
8000FEH	Operand Register

SOFTWARE TESTING FOR COPROCESSOR PRESENCE

When software is used to test coprocessor (80387SX) presence, it should use only the following coprocessor opcodes: FNINIT, FNSTCW and FNSTSW. To use other coprocessor opcodes when a coprocessor is known to be not present, first set EM = 1 in the 80376 CR0 register.

5.0 PACKAGE THERMAL SPECIFICATIONS

The Intel 80376 embedded processor is specified for operation when case temperature is within the range of 0°C–115°C for both the ceramic 88-pin PGA package and the plastic 100-pin PQFP package. The case temperature may be measured in any environment, to determine whether the 80376 is within specified operating range. The case temperature should be measured at the center of the top surface.

The ambient temperature is guaranteed as long as T_C is not violated. The ambient temperature can be calculated from the θ_{jc} and θ_{ja} from the following equations:

$$T_J = T_c + P^*\theta_{jc}$$

$$T_A = T_j - P^*\theta_{ja}$$

$$T_C = T_a + P^*[\theta_{ja} - \theta_{jc}]$$

Values for θ_{ja} and θ_{jc} are given in Table 5.1 for the 100-lead fine pitch. θ_{ja} is given at various airflows. Table 5.2 shows the maximum T_a allowable (without exceeding T_c) at various airflows. Note that T_a can be improved further by attaching "fins" or a "heat sink" to the package. P is calculated using the maximum ***cold*** I_{CC} of 305 mA and the maximum V_{CC} of 5.5V for both packages.

Table 5.1. 80376 Package Thermal Characteristics Thermal Resistances (°C/Watt) θ_{jc} and θ_{ja}

Package	θ_{jc}	θ_{ja} Versus Airflow-ft/min (m/sec)					
		0 (0)	200 (1.01)	400 (2.03)	600 (3.04)	800 (4.06)	1000 (5.07)
100-Lead Fine Pitch	7.5	34.5	29.5	25.5	22.5	21.5	21.0
88-Pin PGA	2.5	29.0	22.5	17.0	14.5	12.5	12.0

Table 5.2. 80376 Maximum Allowable Ambient Temperature at Various Airflows

Package	θ_{jc}	T_A(°C) vs Airflow-ft/min (m/sec)					
		0 (0)	200 (1.01)	400 (2.03)	600 (3.04)	800 (4.06)	1000 (5.07)
100-Lead Fine Pitch	7.5	70	78	85	90	92	93
88-Pin PGA	2.5	70	81	90	95	98	99

6.0 ELECTRICAL SPECIFICATIONS

The following sections describe recommended electrical connections for the 80376, and its electrical specifications.

6.1 Power and Grounding

The 80376 is implemented in CHMOS IV technology and has modest power requirements. However, its high clock frequency and 47 output buffers (address, data, control, and HLDA) can cause power surges as multiple output buffers drive new signal levels simultaneously. For clean on-chip power distribution at high frequency, 14 V_{CC} and 18 V_{SS} pins separately feed functional units of the 80376.

Power and ground connections must be made to all external V_{CC} and GND pins of the 80376. On the circuit board, all V_{CC} pins should be connected on a V_{CC} plane and all V_{SS} pins should be connected on a GND plane.

POWER DECOUPLING RECOMMENDATIONS

Liberal decoupling capacitors should be placed near the 80376. The 80376 driving its 24-bit address bus and 16-bit data bus at high frequencies can cause transient power surges, particularly when driving large capacitive loads. Low inductance capacitors and interconnects are recommended for best high frequency electrical performance. Inductance can be reduced by shortening circuit board traces between the 80376 and decoupling capacitors as much as possible.

RESISTOR RECOMMENDATIONS

The $\overline{ERROR}$, $\overline{FLT}$ and $\overline{BUSY}$ inputs have internal pull-up resistors of approximately 20 KΩ and the PEREQ input has an internal pull-down resistor of approximately 20 KΩ built into the 80376 to keep these signals inactive when the 80387SX is not present in the system (or temporarily removed from its socket).

In typical designs, the external pull-up resistors shown in Table 6.1 are recommended. However, a particular design may have reason to adjust the resistor values recommended here, or alter the use of pull-up resistors in other ways.

Table 6.1. Recommended Resistor Pull-Ups to V_{CC}

Pin	Signal	Pull-Up Value	Purpose
16	$\overline{ADS}$	20 KΩ ± 10%	Lightly Pull $\overline{ADS}$ Inactive during 80376 Hold Acknowledge States
26	$\overline{LOCK}$	20 KΩ ± 10%	Lightly Pull $\overline{LOCK}$ Inactive during 80376 Hold Acknowledge States

OTHER CONNECTION RECOMMENDATIONS

For reliable operation, always connect unused inputs to an appropriate signal level. N/C pins should always remain **unconnected. Connection of N/C pins to V_{CC} or V_{SS} will result in incompatibility with future steppings of the 80376.**

Particularly when not using interrupts or bus hold (as when first prototyping), prevent any chance of spurious activity by connecting these associated inputs to GND:

—INTR
—NMI
—HOLD

If not using address pipelining connect the $\overline{NA}$ pin to a pull-up resistor in the range of 20 KΩ to V_{CC}.

6.2 Absolute Maximum Ratings

Table 6.2. Maximum Ratings

Parameter	Maximum Rating
Storage Temperature	−65°C to +150°C
Case Temperature under Bias	−65°C to +120°C
Supply Voltage with Respect to V_{SS}	−0.5V to +6.5V
Voltage on Other Pins	−0.5V to (V_{CC} + 0.5)V

Table 6.2 gives a stress ratings only, and functional operation at the maximums is not guaranteed. Functional operating conditions are given in **Section 6.3, D.C. Specifications,** and **Section 6.4, A.C. Specifications.**

Extended exposure to the Maximum Ratings may affect device reliability. Furthermore, although the 80376 contains protective circuitry to resist damage from static electric discharge, always take precautions to avoid high static voltages or electric fields.

6.3 D.C. Specifications

ADVANCE INFORMATION SUBJECT TO CHANGE

Table 6.3: 80376 D.C. Characteristics

Functional Operating Range: V_{CC} = 5V ±10%; T_{CASE} = 0°C to 115°C for 88-pin PGA or 100-pin PQFP

Symbol	Parameter	Min	Max	Unit
V_{IL}	Input LOW Voltage	−0.3	+0.8	V(1)
V_{IH}	Input HIGH Voltage	2.0	V_{CC} +0.3	V(1)
V_{ILC}	CLK2 Input LOW Voltage	−0.3	+0.8	V(1)
V_{IHC}	CLK2 Input HIGH Voltage	V_{CC} − 0.8	V_{CC} + 0.3	V(1)
V_{OL}	Output LOW Voltage			
I_{OL} = 4 mA:	A_{23}–A_1, D_{15}–D_0		0.45	V(1)
I_{OL} = 5 mA:	$\overline{BHE}$, $\overline{BLE}$, W/$\overline{R}$, D/$\overline{C}$, M/$\overline{IO}$, $\overline{LOCK}$, $\overline{ADS}$, HLDA		0.45	V(1)
V_{OH}	Output High Voltage			
I_{OH} = −1 mA:	A_{23}–A_1, D_{15}–D_0	2.4		V(1)
I_{OH} = −0.2 mA:	A_{23}–A_1, D_{15}–D_0	V_{CC} − 0.5		V(1)
I_{OH} = −0.9 mA:	$\overline{BHE}$, $\overline{BLE}$, W/$\overline{R}$, D/$\overline{C}$, M/$\overline{IO}$, $\overline{LOCK}$, $\overline{ADS}$, HLDA	2.4		V(1)
I_{OH} = −0.18 mA:	$\overline{BHE}$, $\overline{BLE}$, W/$\overline{R}$, D/$\overline{C}$, M/$\overline{IO}$, $\overline{LOCK}$ $\overline{ADS}$, HLDA	V_{CC} − 0.5		V(1)
I_{LI}	Input Leakage Current (For All Pins except PEREQ, $\overline{BUSY}$, $\overline{FLT}$ and $\overline{ERROR}$)		±15	μA, 0V ≤ V_{IN} ≤ V_{CC}(1)
I_{IH}	Input Leakage Current (PEREQ Pin)		200	μA, V_{IH} = 2.4V(1, 2)
I_{IL}	Input Leakage Current ($\overline{BUSY}$ and $\overline{ERROR}$ Pins)		−400	μA, V_{IL} = 0.45V(3)
I_{LO}	Output Leakage Current		±15	μA, 0.45V ≤ V_{OUT} ≤ V_{CC}(1)
I_{CC}	Supply Current CLK2 = 32 MHz CLK2 = 40 MHz		 275 305	 mA, I_{CC} typ = 175 mA(4) mA, I_{CC} typ = 200 mA(4)
C_{IN}	Input Capacitance		10	pF, F_C = 1 MHz(5)
C_{OUT}	Output or I/O Capacitance		12	pF, F_C = 1 MHz(5)
C_{CLK}	CLK2 Capacitance		20	pF, F_C = 1 MHz(5)

NOTES:
1. Tested at the minimum operating frequency of the device.
2. PEREQ input has an internal pull-down resistor.
3. $\overline{BUSY}$, $\overline{FLT}$ and $\overline{ERROR}$ inputs each have an internal pull-up resistor.
4. I_{CC} max measurement at worse case load, V_{CC} and temperature (0°C).
5. Not 100% tested.

The A.C. specifications given in Table 6.4 consist of output delays, input setup requirements and input hold requirements. All A.C. specifications are relative to the CLK2 rising edge crossing the 2.0V level.

A.C. specification measurement is defined by Figure 6.1. Inputs must be driven to the voltage levels indicated by Figure 6.1 when A.C. specifications are measured. 80376 output delays are specified with minimum and maximum limits measured as shown. The minimum 80376 delay times are hold times provided to external circuitry. 80376 input setup and hold times are specified as minimums, defining the smallest acceptable sampling window. Within the sampling window, a synchronous input signal must be stable for correct 80376 processor operation.

Outputs $\overline{NA}$, W/$\overline{R}$, D/$\overline{C}$, M/$\overline{IO}$, $\overline{LOCK}$, $\overline{BHE}$, $\overline{BLE}$, A_{23}–A_1 and HLDA only change at the beginning of phase one. D_{15}–D_0 (write cycles) only change at the beginning of phase two. The $\overline{READY}$, HOLD, $\overline{BUSY}$, $\overline{ERROR}$, PEREQ and D_{15}–D_0 (read cycles) inputs are sampled at the beginning of phase one. The $\overline{NA}$, INTR and NMI inputs are sampled at the beginning of phase two.

LEGEND:
A—Maximum Output Delay Spec.
B—Minimum Output Delay Spec.
C—Minimum Input Setup Spec.
D—Minimum Input Hold Spec.

240182-35

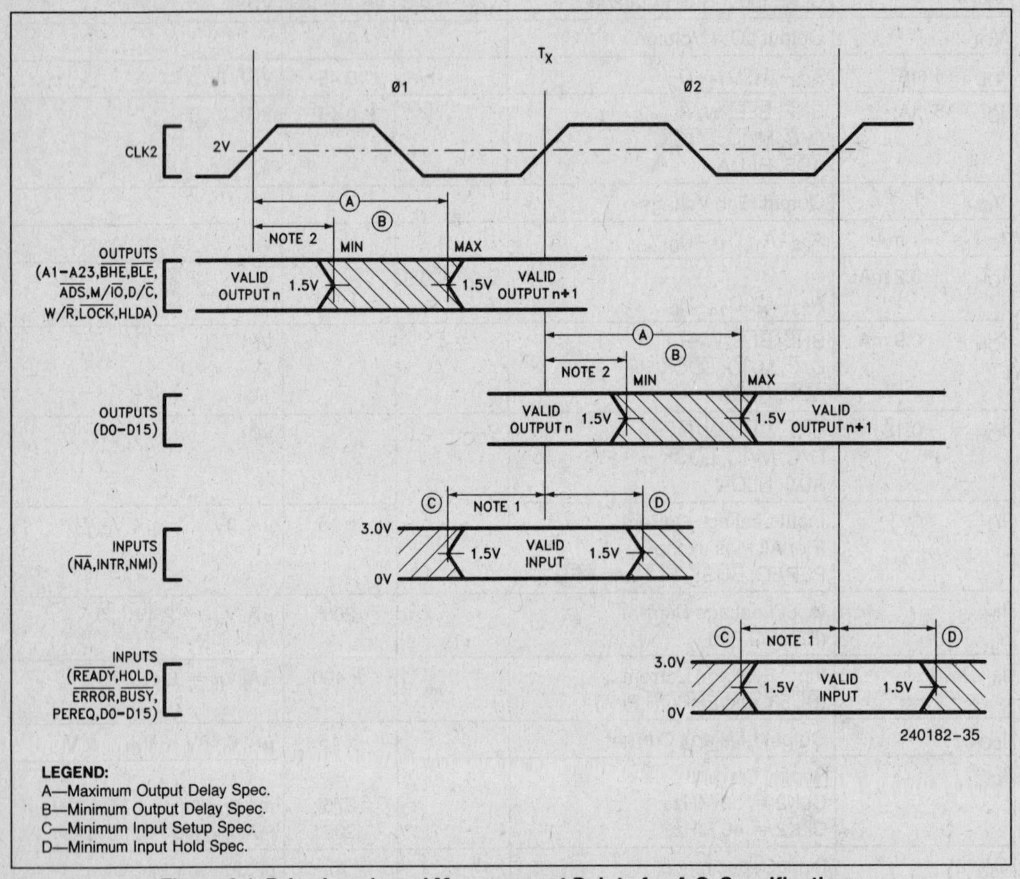

Figure 6.1. Drive Levels and Measurement Points for A.C. Specifications

6.4 A.C. Specifications

Table 6.4. 80376 A.C. Characteristics at 16 MHz

Functional Operating Range: V_{CC} = 5V ±10%; T_{CASE} = 0°C to 115°C for 88-pin PGA or 100-pin PQFP

Symbol	Parameter	Min	Max	Unit	Figure	Notes
	Operating Frequency	4	16	MHz		Half CLK2 Freq
t_1	CLK2 Period	31	125	ns	6.3	
t_{2a}	CLK2 HIGH Time	9		ns	6.3	At 2(3)
t_{2b}	CLK2 HIGH Time	5		ns	6.3	At (V_{CC} − 0.8)V(3)
t_{3a}	CLK2 LOW Time	9		ns	6.3	At 2V(3)
t_{3b}	CLK2 LOW Time	7		ns	6.3	At 0.8V(3)
t_4	CLK2 Fall Time		8	ns	6.3	(V_{CC}−0.8)V to 0.8V(3)
t_5	CLK2 Rise Time		8	ns	6.3	0.8V to (V_{CC}−0.8)(3)
t_6	A_{23}–A_1 Valid Delay	4	36	ns	6.5	C_L = 120 pF(4)
t_7	A_{23}–A_1 Float Delay	4	40	ns	6.6	(1)
t_8	$\overline{BHE}$, $\overline{BLE}$, $\overline{LOCK}$ Valid Delay	4	36	ns	6.5	C_L = 75 pF(4)
t_9	$\overline{BHE}$, $\overline{BLE}$, $\overline{LOCK}$ Float Delay	4	40	ns	6.6	(1)
t_{10}	W/$\overline{R}$, M/$\overline{IO}$, D/$\overline{C}$, $\overline{ADS}$ Valid Delay	6	33	ns	6.5	C_L = 75 pF(4)
t_{11}	W/$\overline{R}$, M/$\overline{IO}$, D/$\overline{C}$, $\overline{ADS}$ Float Delay	6	35	ns	6.6	(1)
t_{12}	D_{15}–D_0 Write Data Valid Delay	4	40	ns	6.5	C_L = 120 pF(4)
t_{13}	D_{15}–D_0 Write Data Float Delay	4	35	ns	6.6	(1)
t_{14}	HLDA Valid Delay	4	33	ns	6.6	C_L = 75 pF(4)
t_{15}	$\overline{NA}$ Setup Time	5		ns	6.4	
t_{16}	$\overline{NA}$ Hold Time	21		ns	6.6	
t_{19}	$\overline{READY}$ Setup Time	19		ns	6.4	
t_{20}	$\overline{READY}$ Hold Time	4		ns	6.4	
t_{21}	Setup Time D_{15}–D_0 Read Data	9		ns	6.4	
t_{22}	Hold Time D_{15}–D_0 Read Data	6		ns	6.4	
t_{23}	HOLD Setup Time	26		ns	6.4	
t_{24}	HOLD Hold Time	5		ns	6.4	
t_{25}	RESET Setup Time	13		ns	6.7	
t_{26}	RESET Hold Time	4		ns	6.7	

Table 6.4. 80376 A.C. Characteristics at 16 MHz (Continued)
Functional Operating Range: $V_{CC} = 5V \pm 10\%$; $T_{CASE} = 0°C$ to 115°C for 88-pin PGA or 100-pin PQFP

Symbol	Parameter	Min	Max	Unit	Figure	Notes
t_{27}	NMI, INTR Setup Time	16		ns	6.4	(2)
t_{28}	NMI, INTR Hold Time	16		ns	6.4	(2)
t_{29}	PEREQ, $\overline{ERROR}$, $\overline{BUSY}$, $\overline{FLT}$ Setup Time	16		ns	6.4	(2)
t_{30}	PEREQ, $\overline{ERROR}$, $\overline{BUSY}$, $\overline{FLT}$ Hold Time	5		ns	6.4	(2)

NOTES:
1. Float condition occurs when maximum output current becomes less than I_{LO} in magnitude. Float delay is not 100% tested.
2. These inputs are allowed to be asynchronous to CLK2. The setup and hold specifications are given for testing purposes, to assure recognition within a specific CLK2 period.
3. These are not tested. They are guaranteed by design characterization.
4. Tested with C_L set to 50 pF and derated to support the indicated distributed capacitive load. See Figures 6.8 through 6.10 for capacitive derating curves.
5. The 80376 does not have t_{17} or t_{18} timing specifications.

Table 6.5. 80376 A.C. Characteristics at 20 MHz
Functional Operating Range: $V_{CC} = 5V \pm 10\%$; $T_{CASE} = 0°C$ to 115°C for 88-pin PGA or 100-pin PQFP

Symbol	Parameter	Min	Max	Unit	Figure	Notes
	Operating Frequency	4	20	MHz		Half CLK2 Frequency
t_1	CLK2 Period	25	125	ns	6.3	
t_{2a}	CLK2 HIGH Time	8		ns	6.3	At 2V(3)
t_{2b}	CLK2 HIGH Time	5		ns	6.3	At $(V_{CC} - 0.8)V$(3)
t_{3a}	CLK2 LOW Time	8		ns	6.3	At 2V(3)
t_{3b}	CLK2 LOW Time	6		ns	6.3	At 0.8V(3)
t_4	CLK2 Fall Time		8	ns	6.3	$(V_{CC} - 0.8V)$ to 0.8V(3)
t_5	CLK2 Rise Time		8	ns	6.3	0.8V to $(V_{CC} - 0.8)$(3)
t_6	A_{23}–A_1 Valid Delay	4	30	ns	6.5	$C_L = 120$ pF(4)
t_7	A_{23}–A_1 Float Delay	4		ns	6.6	(1)
t_8	$\overline{BHE}$, $\overline{BLE}$, $\overline{LOCK}$ Valid Delay	4	30	ns	6.5	$C_L = 75$ pF(4)
t_9	$\overline{BHE}$, $\overline{BLE}$, $\overline{LOCK}$ Float Delay	4	32	ns	6.6	(1)
t_{10a}	M/$\overline{IO}$, D/$\overline{C}$ Valid Delay	6	28	ns	6.5	$C_L = 75$ pF(4)
t_{10b}	W/$\overline{R}$, $\overline{ADS}$ Valid Delay	6	26	ns	6.5	$C_L = 75$ pF(4)
t_{11}	W/$\overline{R}$, M/$\overline{IO}$, D/$\overline{C}$, $\overline{ADS}$ Float Delay	6	30	ns	6.6	(1)
t_{12}	D_{15}–D_0 Write Data Valid Delay	4	38	ns	6.5	$C_L = 120$ pF
t_{13}	D_{15}–D_0 Write Data Float Delay	4	27	ns	6.6	(1)

Table 6.5. 80376 A.C. Characteristics at 20 MHz (Continued)
Functional Operating Range: V_{CC} = 5V ±10%; T_{CASE} = 0°C to 115°C for 88-pin PGA or 100-pin PQFP

Symbol	Parameter	Min	Max	Unit	Figure	Notes
t_{14}	HLDA Valid Delay	4	28	ns	6.5	C_L = 75 pF(4)
t_{15}	$\overline{NA}$ Setup Time	5		ns	6.4	
t_{16}	$\overline{NA}$ Hold Time	12		ns	6.4	
t_{19}	$\overline{READY}$ Setup Time	12		ns	6.4	
t_{20}	$\overline{READY}$ Hold Time	4		ns	6.4	
t_{21}	D_{15}–D_0 Read Data Setup Time	9		ns	6.4	
t_{22}	D_{15}–D_0 Read Data Hold Time	6		ns	6.4	
t_{23}	HOLD Setup Time	17		ns	6.4	
t_{24}	HOLD Hold Time	5		ns	6.4	
t_{25}	RESET Setup Time	12		ns	6.7	
t_{26}	RESET Hold Time	4		ns	6.7	
t_{27}	NMI, INTR Setup Time	16		ns	6.4	(2)
t_{28}	NMI, INTR Hold Time	16		ns	6.4	(2)
t_{29}	PEREQ, $\overline{ERROR}$, $\overline{BUSY}$, $\overline{FLT}$ Setup Time	14		ns	6.4	(2)
t_{30}	PEREQ, $\overline{ERROR}$, $\overline{BUSY}$, $\overline{FLT}$ Hold Time	5		ns	6.4	(2)

NOTES:
1. Float condition occurs when maximum output current becomes less than I_{LO} in magnitude. Float delay is not 100% tested.
2. These inputs are allowed to be asynchronous to CLK2. The setup and hold specifications are given for testing purposes, to assure recognition within a specific CLK2 period.
3. These are not tested. They are guaranteed by design characterization.
4. Tested with C_L set to 50 pF and derated to support the indicated distributed capacitive load. See Figures 6.8 through 6.10 for capacitive derating curves.
5. The 80376 does not have t_{17} or t_{18} timing specifications.

A.C. TEST LOADS

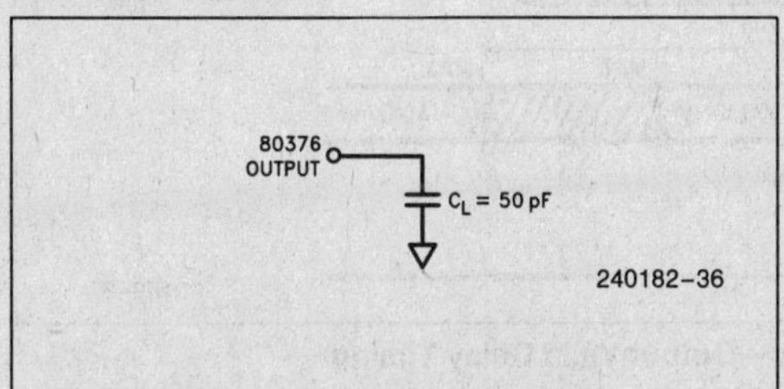

Figure 6.2. A.C. Test Loads

A.C. TIMING WAVEFORMS

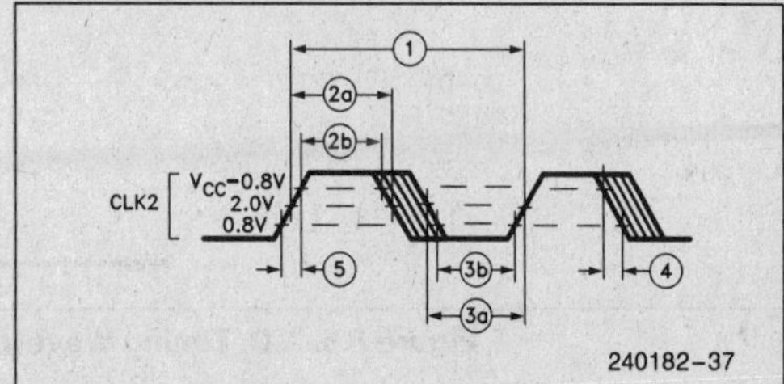

Figure 6.3. CLK2 Waveform

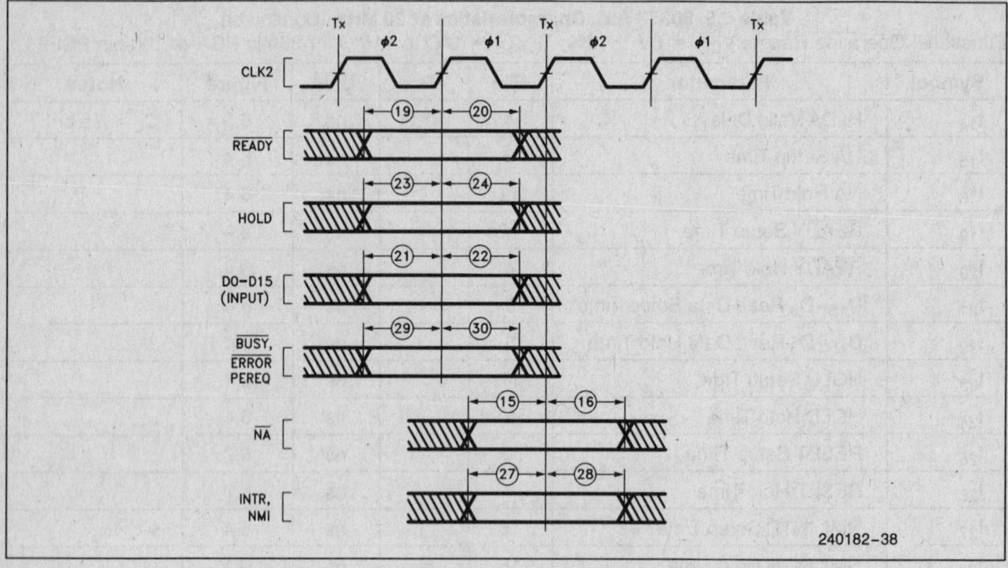

Figure 6.4. A.C. Timing Waveforms—Input Setup and Hold Timing

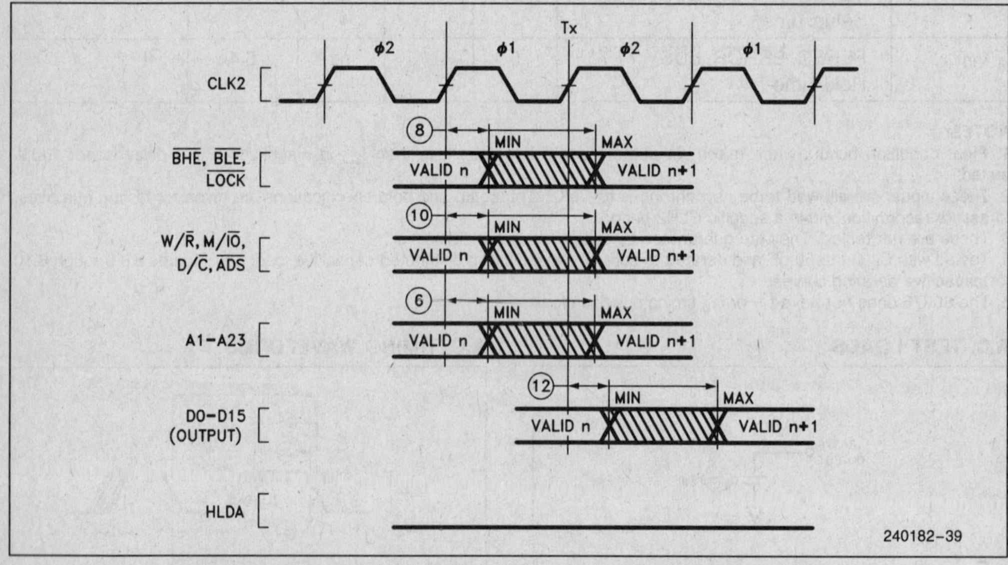

Figure 6.5. A.C. Timing Waveforms—Output Valid Delay Timing

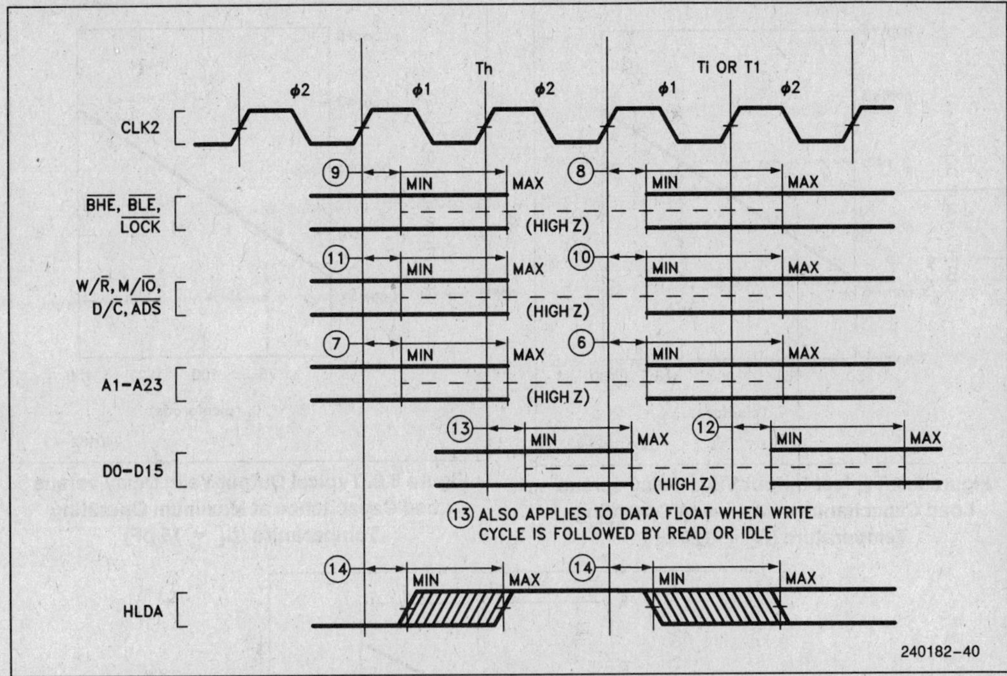

Figure 6.6. A.C. Timing Waveforms—Output Float Delay and HLDA Valid Delay Timing

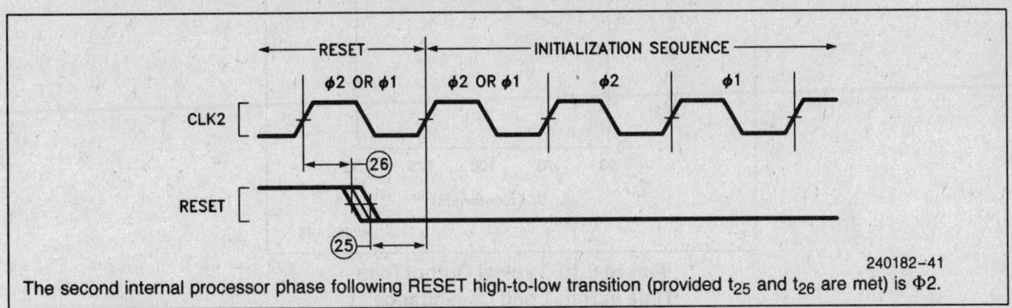

The second internal processor phase following RESET high-to-low transition (provided t_{25} and t_{26} are met) is $\Phi 2$.

Figure 6.7. A.C. Timing Waveforms—RESET Setup and Hold Timing, and Internal Phase

3

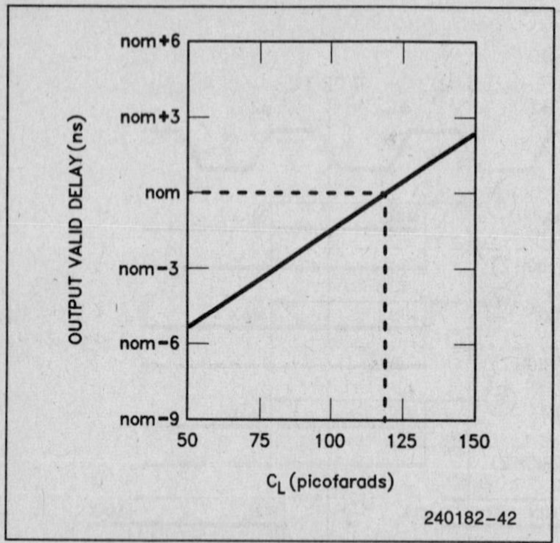

Figure 6.8. Typical Output Valid Delay versus Load Capacitance at Maximum Operating Temperature (C_L = 120 pF)

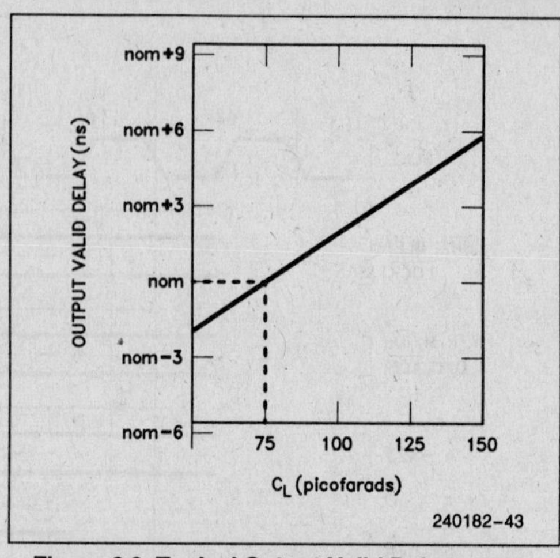

Figure 6.9. Typical Output Valid Delay versus Load Capacitance at Maximum Operating Temperature (C_L = 75 pF)

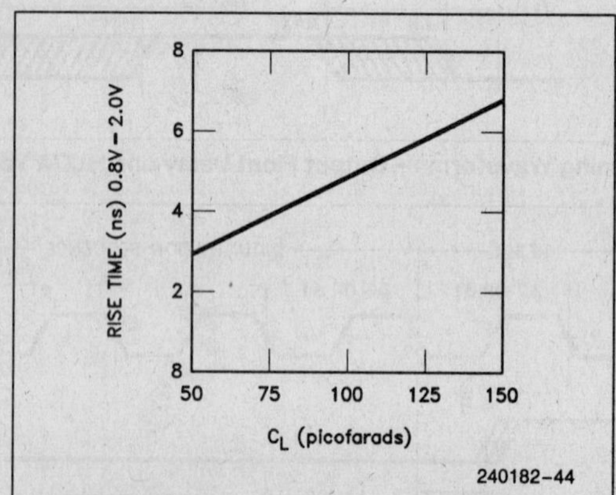

Figure 6.10. Typical Output Rise Time versus Load Capacitance at Maximum Operating Temperature

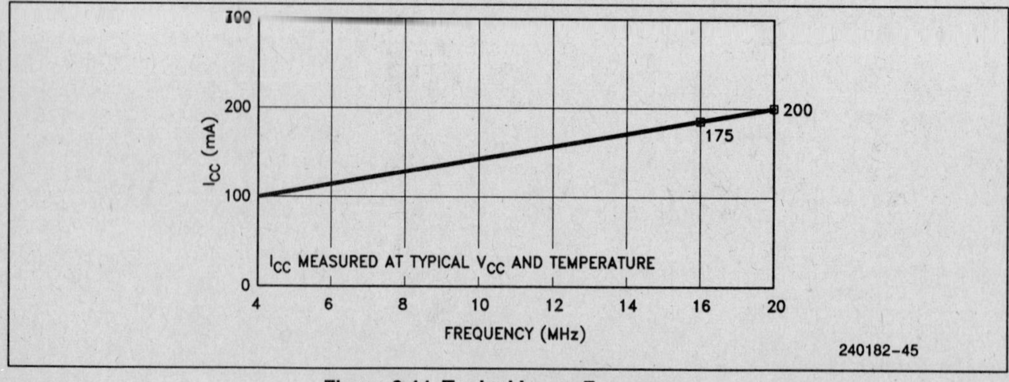

Figure 6.11. Typical I_{CC} vs Frequency

6.5 Designing for the ICE™-376 Emulator

The 376 embedded processor in-circuit emulator product is the ICE-376 emulator. Use of the emulator requires the target system to provide a socket that is compatible with the ICE-376 emulator. The 80376 offers two different probes for emulating user systems: an 88-pin PGA probe and a 100-pin fine pitch flat-pack probe. The 100-pin fine pitch flat-pack probe requires a socket, called the 100-pin PQFP, which is available from 3-M Textool (part number 2-0100-07243-000). The ICE-376 emulator probe attaches to the target system via an adapter which replaces the 80376 component in the target system. Because of the high operating frequency of 80376 systems and of the ICE-376 emulator, there is no buffering between the 80376 emulation processor in the ICE-376 emulator probe and the target system. A direct result of the non-buffered interconnect is that the ICE-376 emulator shares the address and data bus with the user's system, and the RESET signal is intercepted by the ICE emulator hardware. In order for the ICE-376 emulator to be functional in the user's system without the Optional Isolation Board (OIB) the designer must be aware of the following conditions:

1. The bus controller must only enable data transceivers onto the data bus during valid read cycles of the 80376, other local devices or other bus masters.
2. Before another bus master drives the local processor address bus, the other master must gain control of the address bus by asserting HOLD and receiving the HLDA response.
3. The emulation processor receives the RESET signal 2 or 4 CLK2 cycles later than an 80376 would, and responds to RESET later. Correct phase of the response is guaranteed.

In addition to the above considerations, the ICE-376 emulator processor module has several electrical and mechanical characteristics that should be taken into consideration when designing the 80376 system.

Capacitive Loading: ICE-376 adds up to 27 pF to each 80376 signal.

Drive Requirements: ICE-376 adds one FAST TTL load on the CLK2, control, address, and data lines. These loads are within the processor module and are driven by the 80376 emulation processor, which has standard drive and loading capability listed in Tables 6.3 and 6.4.

Power Requirements: For noise immunity and CMOS latch-up protection the ICE-376 emulator processor module is powered by the user system. The circuitry on the processor module draws up to 1.4A including the maximum 80376 I_{CC} from the user 80376 socket.

80376 Location and Orientation: The ICE-376 emulator processor module may require lateral clearance. Figure 6.12 shows the clearance requirements of the iMP adapter and Figure 6.13 shows the clearance requirements of the 88-pin PGA adapter. The

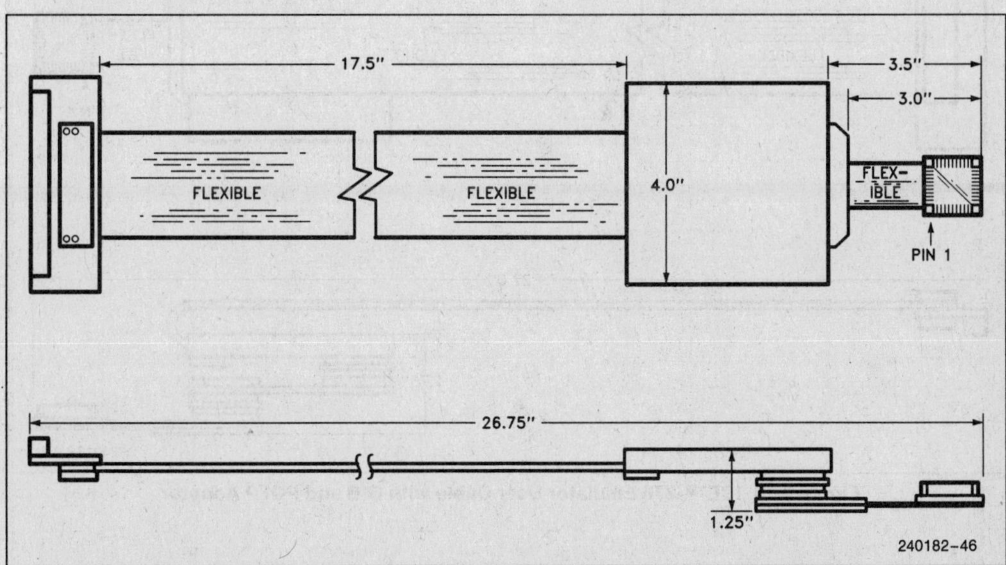

Figure 6.12. Preliminary ICE™-376 Emulator User Cable with PQFP Adapter

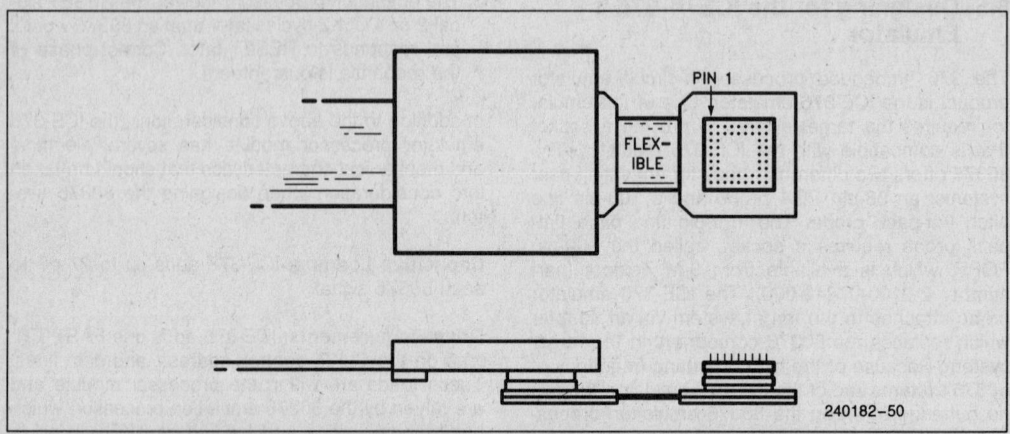

Figure 6.13. ICE™-376 Emulator User Cable with 88-Pin PGA Adapter

optional isolation board (OIB), which provides extra electrical buffering and has the same lateral clearance requirements as Figures 6.12 and 6.13, adds an additional 0.5 inches to the vertical clearance requirement. This is illustrated in Figure 6.14.

Optional Isolation Board (OIB) and the CLK2 speed reduction: Due to the unbuffered probe design, the ICE-376 emulator is susceptible to errors on the user's bus. The OIB allows the ICE-376 emulator to function in user systems with faults (shorted signals, etc.). After electrical verification the OIB may be removed. When the OIB is installed, the user system must have a maximum CLK2 frequency of 20 MHz.

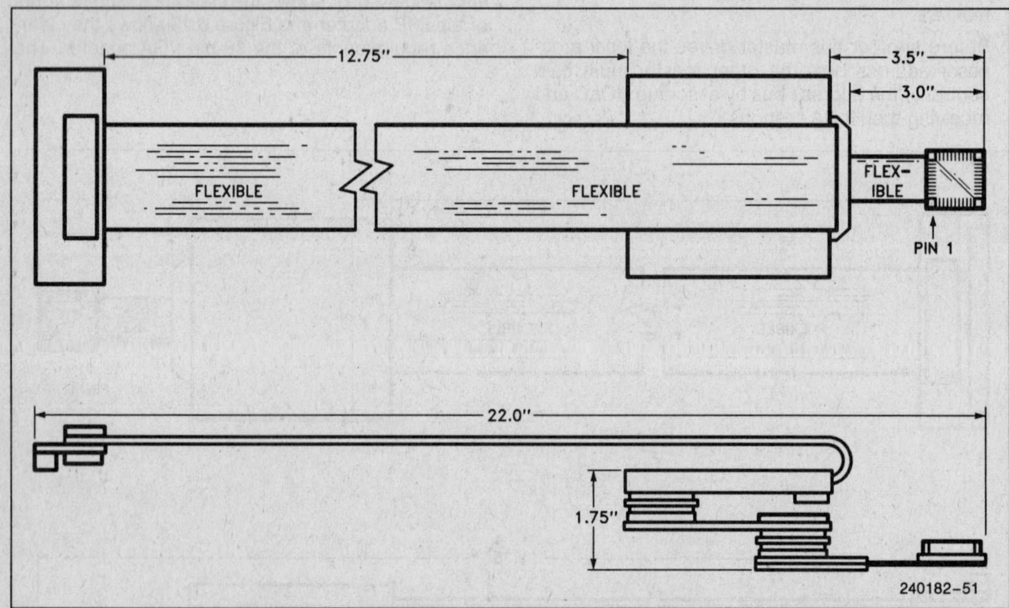

Figure 6.14. ICE™-376 Emulator User Cable with OIB and PQFP Adapter

7.0 DIFFERENCES BETWEEN THE 80376 AND THE 80386

The following are the major differences between the 80376 and the 80386.

1. The 80376 generates byte selects on $\overline{BHE}$ and $\overline{BLE}$ (like the 8086 and 80286 microprocessors) to distinguish the upper and lower bytes on its 16-bit data bus. The 80386 uses four-byte selects, $\overline{BE0}$–$\overline{BE3}$, to distinguish between the different bytes on its 32-bit bus.
2. The 80376 has no bus sizing option. The 80386 can select between either a 32-bit bus or a 16-bit bus by use of the $\overline{BS16}$ input. The 80376 has a 16-bit bus size.
3. The $\overline{NA}$ pin operation in the 80376 is identical to that of the $\overline{NA}$ pin on the 80386 with one exception: the $\overline{NA}$ pin of the 80386 cannot be activated on 16-bit bus cycles (where $\overline{BS16}$ is LOW in the 80386 case), whereas $\overline{NA}$ can be activated on any 80376 bus cycle.
4. The contents of all 80376 registers at reset are identical to the contents of the 80386 registers at reset, except the DX register. The DX register contains a component-stepping identifier at reset, i.e.

   in 80386, after reset DH = 03H indicates 80386
   DL = revision number;
   in 80376, after reset DH = 33H indicates 80376
   DL = revision number.

5. The 80386 uses A_{31} and M/$\overline{IO}$ as a select for numerics coprocessor. The 80376 uses the A_{23} and M/$\overline{IO}$ to select its numerics coprocessor.
6. The 80386 prefetch unit fetches code in four-byte units. The 80376 prefetch unit reads two bytes as one unit (like the 80286 microprocessor). In $\overline{BS16}$ mode, the 80386 takes two consecutive bus cycles to complete a prefetch request. If there is a data read or write request after the prefetch starts, the 80386 will fetch all four bytes before addressing the new request.
7. The 80376 has no paging mechanism.
8. The 80376 starts executing code in what corresponds to the 80386 protected mode. The 80386 starts execution in real mode, which is then used to enter protected mode.
9. The 80386 has a virtual-86 mode that allows the execution of a real mode 8086 program as a task in protected mode. The 80376 has no virtual-86 mode.
10. The 80386 maps a 48-bit logical address into a 32-bit physical address by segmentation and paging. The 80376 maps its 48-bit logical address into a 24-bit physical address by segmentation only.
11. The 80376 uses the 80387SX numerics coprocessor for floating point operations, while the 80386 uses the 80387 coprocessor.
12. The 80386 can execute from 16-bit code segments. The 80376 can **only** execute from 32-bit code Segments.
13. The 80376 has an input called $\overline{FLT}$ which three-states all bidirectional and output pins, including HLDA, when asserted. It is used with ON Circuit Emulation (ONCE).

3

8.0 INSTRUCTION SET

This section describes the 376 embedded processor instruction set. Table 8.1 lists all instructions along with instruction encoding diagrams and clock counts. Further details of the instruction encoding are then provided in the following sections, which completely describe the encoding structure and the definition of all fields occurring within 80376 instructions.

8.1 80376 Instruction Encoding and Clock Count Summary

To calculate elapsed time for an instruction, multiply the instruction clock count, as listed in Table 8.1 below, by the processor clock period (e.g. 50 ns for an 80376 operating at 20 MHz). The actual clock count of an 80376 program will average 10% more

than the calculated clock count due to instruction sequences which execute faster than they can be fetched from memory.

Instruction Clock Count Assumptions:

1. The instruction has been prefetched, decoded, and is ready for execution.
2. Bus cycles do not require wait states.
3. There are no local bus HOLD requests delaying processor acess to the bus.
4. No exceptions are detected during instruction execution.
5. If an effective address is calculated, it does not use two general register components. One register, scaling and displacement can be used within the clock counts showns. However, if the effective address calculation uses two general register components, add 1 clock to the clock count shown.
6. Memory reference instruction accesses byte or aligned 16-bit operands.

Instruction Clock Count Notation

— If two clock counts are given, the smaller refers to a register operand and the larger refers to a memory operand.

—n = number of times repeated.

—m = number of components in the next instruction executed, where the entire displacement (if any) counts as one component, the entire immediate data (if any) counts as one component, and all other bytes of the instruction and prefix(es) each count as one component.

Misaligned or 32-Bit Operand Accesses:

— If instructions accesses a misaligned 16-bit operand or 32-bit operand on even address add:

2* clocks for read or write.

4** clocks for read and write.

— If instructions accesses a 32-bit operand on odd address add:

4* clocks for read or write.

8** clocks for read and write.

Wait States:

Wait states add 1 clock per wait state to instruction execution for each data access.

Table 8.1. 80376 Instruction Set Clock Count Summary

Instruction	Format				Clock Counts	Number of Data Cycles	Notes
GENERAL DATA TRANSFER							
MOV = Move:							
Register to Register/Memory	1000100w	mod reg r/m			2/2*	0/1*	a
Register/Memory to Register	1000101w	mod reg r/m			2/4*	0/1*	a
Immediate to Register/Memory	1100011w	mod 000 r/m	immediate data		2/2*	0/1*	a
Immediate to Register (Short Form)	1011 w reg	immediate data			2	2	
Memory to Accumulator (Short Form)	1010000w	full displacement			4*	1*	a
Accumulator to Memory (Short Form)	1010001w	full displacement			2*	1*	a
Register/Memory to Segment Register	10001110	mod sreg3 r/m			22/23*	0/6*	a,b,c
Segment Register to Register/Memory	10001100	mod sreg3 r/m			2/2*	0/1*	a
MOVSX = Move with Sign Extension							
Register from Register/Memory	00001111	1011111w	mod reg r/m		3/6*	0/1*	a
MOVZX = Move with Zero Extension							
Register from Register/Memory	00001111	1011011w	mod reg r/m		3/6*	0/1*	a
PUSH = Push:							
Register/Memory	11111111	mod 110 r/m			7/9*	2/4*	a
Register (Short Form)	01010 reg				4	2	a
Segment Register (ES, CS, SS or DS)	000sreg2110				4	2	a
Segment Register (FS or GS)	00001111	10sreg3000			4	2	a
Immediate	011010s0	immediate data			4	2	a
PUSHA = Push All	01100000				34	16	a
POP = Pop							
Register/Memory	10001111	mod 000 r/m			7/9*	2/4*	a
Register (Short Form)	01011 reg				6	2	a
Segment Register (ES, SS or DS)	000 sreg 2111				25	6	a, b, c
Segment Register (FS or GS)	00001111	10 sreg 3001			25	6	a, b, c
POPA = Pop All	01100001				40	16	a
XCHG = Exchange							
Register/Memory with Register	1000011w	mod reg r/m			3/5**	0/2**	a, m
Register with Accumulator (Short Form)	10010 reg				3	0	
IN = Input from:							
Fixed Port	1110010w	port number			6*	1*	f,k
					26*	1*	f,l
Variable Port	1110110w				7*	1*	f,k
					27*	1*	f,l
OUT = Output to:							
Fixed Port	1110011w	port number			4*	1*	f,k
					24*	1*	f,l
Variable Port	1110111w				5*	1*	f,k
					26*	1*	f,l
LEA = Load EA to Register	10001101	mod reg r/m			2		

3

Table 8.1. 80376 Instruction Set Clock Count Summary (Continued)

Instruction	Format	Clock Counts	Number of Data Cycles	Notes
SEGMENT CONTROL				
LDS = Load Pointer to DS	11000101 mod reg r/m	26*	6*	a, b, c
LES = Load Pointer to ES	11000100 mod reg r/m	26*	6*	a, b, c
LFS = Load Pointer to FS	00001111 10110100 mod reg r/m	29*	6*	a, b, c
LGS = Load Pointer to GS	00001111 10110101 mod reg r/m	29*	6*	a, b, c
LSS = Load Pointer to SS	00001111 10110010 mod reg r/m	26*	6*	a, b, c
FLAG CONTROL				
CLC = Clear Carry Flag	11111000	2		
CLD = Clear Direction Flag	11111100	2		
CLI = Clear Interrupt Enable Flag	11111010	8		f
CLTS = Clear Task Switched Flag	00001111 00000110	5		e
CMC = Complement Carry Flag	11110101	2		
LAHF = Load AH into Flag	10011111	2		
POPF = Pop Flags	10011101	7		a, g
PUSHF = Push Flags	10011100	4		a
SAHF = Store AH into Flags	10011110	3		
STC = Set Carry Flag	11111001	2		
STD = Set Direction Flag	11111101	2		
STI = Set Interrupt Enable Flag	11111011	8		f
ARITHMETIC				
ADD = Add				
Register to Register	000000dw mod reg r/m	2		
Register to Memory	0000000w mod reg r/m	7**	2**	a
Memory to Register	0000001w mod reg r/m	6*	1*	a
Immediate to Register/Memory	100000sw mod 000 r/m immediate data	2/7**	0/2**	a
Immediate to Accumulator (Short Form)	0000010w immediate data	2		
ADC = Add with Carry				
Register to Register	000100dw mod reg r/m	2		
Register to Memory	0001000w mod reg r/m	7**	2**	a
Memory to Register	0001001w mod reg r/m	6*	1*	a
Immediate to Register/Memory	100000sw mod 010 r/m immediate data	2/7**	0/2**	a
Immediate to Accumulator (Short Form)	0001010w immediate data	2		
INC = Increment				
Register/Memory	1111111w mod 000 r/m	2/6**	0/2**	a
Register (Short Form)	01000 reg	2		
SUB = Subtract				
Register from Register	001010dw mod reg r/m	2		

Table 8.1. 80376 Instruction Set Clock Count Summary (Continued)

Instruction	Format	Clock Counts	Number Of Data Cycles	Notes
ARITHMETIC (Continued)				
Register from Memory	0010100w | mod reg r/m	7**	2**	a
Memory from Register	0010101w | mod reg r/m	6*	1	a
Immediate from Register/Memory	100000sw | mod 101 r/m | immediate data	2/7**	0/1**	a
Immediate from Accumulator (Short Form)	0010110w | immediate data	2		
SBB = Subtract with Borrow				
Register from Register	000110dw | mod reg r/m	2		
Register from Memory	0001100w | mod reg r/m	7**	2**	a
Memory from Register	0001101w | mod reg r/m	6*	1*	a
Immediate from Register/Memory	100000sw | mod 011 r/m | immediate data	2/7**	0/2**	a
Immediate from Accumulator (Short Form)	0001110w | immediate data	2		
DEC = Decrement				
Register/Memory	1111111w | reg 001 r/m	2/6**	0/2**	a
Register (Short Form)	01001 reg	2		
CMP = Compare				
Register with Register	001110dw | mod reg r/m	2		
Memory with Register	0011100w | mod reg r/m	5*	1*	a
Register with Memory	0011101w | mod reg r/m	6**	2**	a
Immediate with Register/Memory	100000sw | mod 111 r/m | immediate data	2/5*	0/1*	a
Immediate with Accumulator (Short Form)	0011110w | immediate data	2		
NEG = Change Sign	1111011w | mod 011 r/m	2/6*	0/2*	a
AAA = ASCII Adjust for Add	00110111	4		
AAS = ASCII Adjust for Subtract	00111111	4		
DAA = Decimal Adjust for Add	00100111	4		
DAS = Decimal Adjust for Subtract	00101111	4		
MUL = Multiply (Unsigned)				
Accumulator with Register/Memory	1111011w | mod 100 r/m			
Multiplier—Byte		12-17/15-20	0/1	a,n
—Word		12-25/15-28*	0/1*	a,n
—Doubleword		12-41/17-46*	0/2*	a,n
IMUL = Integer Multiply (Signed)				
Accumulator with Register/Memory	1111011w | mod 101 r/m			
Multiplier—Byte		12-17/15-20	0/1	a,n
—Word		12-25/15-28*	0/1*	a,n
—Doubleword		12-41/17-46*	0/2*	a,n
Register with Register/Memory	00001111 | 10101111 | mod reg r/m			
Multiplier—Byte		12-17/15-20	0/1	a,n
—Word		12-25/15-28*	0/1*	a,n
—Doubleword		12-41/17-46*	0/2*	a,n
Register/Memory with Immediate to Register	011010s1 | mod reg r/m | immediate data			
—Word		13-26/14-27*	0/1*	a,n
—Doubleword		13-42/16-45*	0/2*	a,n

3

Table 8.1. 80376 Instruction Set Clock Count Summary (Continued)

Instruction	Format	Clock Counts	Number Of Data Cycles	Notes
ARITHMETIC (Continued)				
DIV = Divide (Unsigned)				
Accumulator by Register/Memory	1111011w | mod 110 r/m			
Divisor—Byte		14/17	0/1	a, o
—Word		22/25*	0/1*	a, o
—Doubleword		38/43*	0/2*	a, o
IDIV = Integer Divide (Signed)				
Accumulator by Register/Memory	1111011w | mod 111 r/m			
Divisor—Byte		19/22	0/1	a, o
—Word		27/30*	0/1	a, o
—Doubleword		43/48*	0/2*	a, o
AAD = ASCII Adjust for Divide	11010101 | 00001010	19		
AAM = ASCII Adjust for Multiply	11010100 | 00001010	17		
CBW = Convert Byte to Word	10011000	3		
CWD = Convert Word to Double Word	10011001	2		
LOGIC				
Shift Rotate Instructions				
Not Through Carry **(ROL, ROR, SAL, SAR, SHL, and SHR)**				
Register/Memory by 1	1101000w | mod TTT r/m	3/7**	0/2**	a
Register/Memory by CL	1101001w | mod TTT r/m	3/7**	0/2**	a
Register/Memory by Immediate Count	1100000w | mod TTT r/m | immed 8-bit data	3/7**	0/2**	a
Through Carry **(RCL and RCR)**				
Register/Memory by 1	1101000w | mod TTT r/m	9/10**	0/2**	a
Register/Memory by CL	1101001w | mod TTT r/m	9/10**	10/2**	a
Register/Memory by Immediate Count	1100000w | mod TTT r/m | immed 8-bit data	9/10**	0/2**	a
	TTT Instruction 000 ROL 001 ROR 010 RCL 011 RCR 100 SHL/SAL 101 SHR 111 SAR			
SHLD = Shift Left Double				
Register/Memory by Immediate	00001111 | 10100100 | mod reg r/m | immed 8-bit data	3/7**	0/2**	
Register/Memory by CL	00001111 | 10100101 | mod reg r/m	3/7**	0/2**	
SHRD = Shift Right Double				
Register/Memory by Immediate	00001111 | 10101100 | mod reg r/m | immed 8-bit data	3/7**	0/2**	
Register/Memory by CL	00001111 | 10101101 | mod reg r/m	3/7**	0/2**	
AND = And				
Register to Register	001000dw | mod reg r/m	2		

Table 8.1. 80376 Instruction Set Clock Count Summary (Continued)

Instruction	Format			Clock Counts	Number of Data Cycles	Notes
LOGIC (Continued)						
Register to Memory	0010000w	mod reg r/m		7**	2**	a
Memory to Register	0010001w	mod reg r/m		6*	1*	a
Immediate to Register/Memory	1000000w	mod 100 r/m	immediate data	2/7**	0/2**	a
Immediate to Accumulator (Short Form)	0010010w	immediate data		2		
TEST = And Function to Flags, No Result						
Register/Memory and Register	1000010w	mod reg r/m		2/5*	0/1*	a
Immediate Data and Register/Memory	1111011w	mod 000 r/m	immediate data	2/5*	0/1*	a
Immediate Data and Accumulator (Short Form)	1010100w	immediate data		2		
OR = Or						
Register to Register	000010dw	mod reg r/m		2		
Register to Memory	0000100w	mod reg r/m		7**	2**	a
Memory to Register	0000101w	mod reg r/m		6*	1*	a
Immediate to Register/Memory	1000000w	mod 001 r/m	immediate data	2/7**	0/2**	a
Immediate to Accumulator (Short Form)	0000110w	immediate data		2		
XOR = Exclusive Or						
Register to Register	001100dw	mod reg r/m		2		
Register to Memory	0011000w	mod reg r/m		7**	2**	a
Memory to Register	0011001w	mod reg r/m		6*	1*	a
Immediate to Register/Memory	1000000w	mod 110 r/m	immediate data	2/7**	0/2**	a
Immediate to Accumulator (Short Form)	0011010w	immediate data		2		
NOT = Invert Register/Memory	1111011w	mod 010 r/m		2/6**	0/2**	a
STRING MANIPULATION						
CMPS = Compare Byte Word	1010011w			10*	2*	a
INS = Input Byte/Word from DX Port	0110110w			9** 29**	1** 1**	a,f,k a,f,l
LODS = Load Byte/Word to AL/AX/EAX	1010110w			5*	1*	a
MOVS = Move Byte Word	1010010w			7**	2**	a
OUTS = Output Byte/Word to DX Port	0110111w			8** 28**	1** 1**	a,f,k a,f,l
SCAS = Scan Byte Word	1010111w			7*	1*	a
STOS = Store Byte/Word from AL/AX/EX	1010101w			4*	1*	a
XLAT = Translate String	11010111			5*	1*	a
REPEATED STRING MANIPULATION Repeated by Count in CX or ECX						
REPE CMPS = Compare String (Find Non-Match)	11110011	1010011w		5 + 9n**	2n**	a

3

Table 8.1. 80376 Instruction Set Clock Count Summary (Continued)

Instruction	Format	Clock Counts	Number of Data Cycles	Notes
REPEATED STRING MANIPULATION (Continued)				
REPNE CMPS = Compare String				
(Find Match)	11110010 1010011w	$5 + 9n^{**}$	$2n^{**}$	a
REP INS = Input String	11110011 0110110w	$7 + 6n^{*}$ $27 + 6n^{*}$	$1n^{*}$ $1n^{*}$	a,f,k a,f,l
REP LODS = Load String	11110011 1010110w	$5 + 6n^{*}$	$1n^{*}$	a
REP MOVS = Move String	11110011 1010010w	$7 + 4n^{**}$	$2n^{**}$	a
REP OUTS = Output String	11110011 0110111w	$6 + 5n^{*}$ $26 + 5n^{*}$	$1n^{*}$ $1n^{*}$	a,f,k a,f,l
REPE SCAS = Scan String				
(Find Non-AL/AX/EAX)	11110011 1010111w	$5 + 8n^{*}$	$1n^{*}$	a
REPNE SCAS = Scan String				
(Find AL/AX/EAX)	11110010 1010111w	$5 + 8n^{*}$	$1n^{*}$	a
REP STOS = Store String	11110011 1010101w	$5 + 5n^{*}$	$1n^{*}$	a
BIT MANIPULATION				
BSF = Scan Bit Forward	00001111 10111100 mod reg r/m	$10 + 3n^{**}$	$2n^{**}$	a
BSR = Scan Bit Reverse	00001111 10111101 mod reg r/m	$10 + 3n^{**}$	$2n^{**}$	a
BT = Test Bit				
Register/Memory, Immediate	00001111 10111010 mod 100 r/m immed 8-bit data	3/6*	0/1*	a
Register/Memory, Register	00001111 10100011 mod reg r/m	3/12*	0/1*	a
BTC = Test Bit and Complement				
Register/Memory, Immediate	00001111 10111010 mod 111 r/m immed 8-bit data	6/8*	0/2*	a
Register/Memory, Register	00001111 10111011 mod reg r/m	6/13*	0/2*	a
BTR = Test Bit and Reset				
Register/Memory, Immediate	00001111 10111010 mod 110 r/m immed 8-bit data	6/8*	0/2*	a
Register/Memory, Register	00001111 10110011 mod reg r/m	6/13*	0/2*	a
BTS = Test Bit and Set				
Register/Memory, Immediate	00001111 10111010 mod 101 r/m immed 8-bit data	6/8*	0/2*	a
Register/Memory, Register	00001111 10101011 mod reg r/m	6/13*	0/2*	a
CONTROL TRANSFER				
CALL = Call				
Direct within Segment	11101000 full displacement	$9 + m^{*}$	2	j
Register/Memory				
Indirect within Segment	11111111 mod 010 r/m	9 + m/12 + m	2/3	a, j
Direct Intersegment	10011010 unsigned full offset, selector	42 + m	9	c, d, j

Table 8.1. 80376 Instruction Set Clock Count Summary (Continued)

Instruction	Format		Clock Counts	Number of Data Cycles	Notes
CONTROL TRANSFER (Continued)					
(Direct Intersegment)					
Via Call Gate to Same Privilege Level			64 + m	13	a,c,d,j
Via Call Gate to Different Privilege Level, (No Parameters)			98 + m	13	a,c,d,j
Via Call Gate to Different Privilege Level, (x Parameters)			106 + 8x + m	13 + 4x	a,c,d,j
From 386 Task to 386 TSS			392	124	a,c,d,j
Indirect Intersegment	11111111	mod 0 1 1 r/m	46 + m	10	a,c,d,j
Via Call Gate to Same Privilege Level			68 + m	14	a,c,d,j
Via Call Gate to Different Privilege Level, (No Parameters)			102 + m	14	a,c,d,j
Via Call Gate to Different Privilege Level, (x Parameters)			110 + 8x + m	14 + 4x	a,c,d,j
From 386 Task to 386 TSS			399	130	a,c,d,j
JMP = Unconditional Jump					
Short	11101011	8-bit displacement	7 + m		j
Direct within Segment	11101001	full displacement	7 + m		j
Register/Memory Indirect within Segment	11111111	mod 1 0 0 r/m	9 + m/14 + m	2/4	a,j
Direct Intersegment	11101010	unsigned full offset, selector	37 + m	5	c,d,j
Via Call Gate to Same Privilege Level			53 + m	9	a,c,d,j
From 386 Task to 386 TSS			395	124	a,c,d,j
Indirect Intersegment	11111111	mod 1 0 1 r/m	37 + m	9	a,c,d,j
Via Call Gate to Same Privilege Level			59 + m	13	a,c,d,j
From 386 Task to 386 TSS			401	124	a,c,d,j

3

Table 8.1. 80376 Instruction Set Clock Count Summary (Continued)

Instruction	Format	Clock Counts	Number of Data Cycles	Notes
CONTROL TRANSFER (Continued)				
RET = Return from CALL:				
Within Segment	11000011	12 + m	2	a,j,p
Within Segment Adding Immediate to SP	11000010 16-bit displ	12 + m	2	a,j,p
Intersegment	11001011	36 + m	4	a,c,d,j,p
Intersegment Adding Immediate to SP	11001010 16-bit displ	36 + m	4	a,c,d,j,p
to Different Privilege Level				
Intersegment		80	4	c,d,j,p
Intersegment Adding Immediate to SP		80	4	c,d,j,p
CONDITIONAL JUMPS				
NOTE: Times Are Jump "Taken or Not Taken"				
JO = Jump on Overflow				
8-Bit Displacement	01110000 8-bit displ	7 + m or 3		j
Full Displacement	00001111 10000000 full displacement	7 + m or 3		j
JNO = Jump on Not Overflow				
8-Bit Displacement	01110001 8-bit displ	7 + m or 3		j
Full Displacement	00001111 10000001 full displacement	7 + m or 3		j
JB/JNAE = Jump on Below/Not Above or Equal				
8-Bit Displacement	01110010 8-bit displ	7 + m or 3		j
Full Displacement	00001111 10000010 full displacement	7 + m or 3		j
JNB/JAE = Jump on Not Below/Above or Equal				
8-Bit Displacement	01110011 8-bit displ	7 + m or 3		j
Full Displacement	00001111 10000011 full displacement	7 + m or 3		j
JE/JZ = Jump on Equal/Zero				
8-Bit Displacement	01110100 8-bit displ	7 + m or 3		j
Full Displacement	00001111 10000100 full displacement	7 + m or 3		j
JNE/JNZ = Jump on Not Equal/Not Zero				
8-Bit Displacement	01110101 8-bit displ	7 + m or 3		j
Full Displacement	00001111 10000101 full displacement	7 + m or 3		j
JBE/JNA = Jump on Below or Equal/Not Above				
8-Bit Displacement	01110110 8-bit displ	7 + m or 3		j
Full Displacement	00001111 10000110 full displacement	7 + m or 3		j
JNBE/JA = Jump on Not Below or Equal/Above				
8-Bit Displacement	01110111 8-bit displ	7 + m or 3		j
Full Displacement	00001111 10000111 full displacement	7 + m or 3		j
JS = Jump on Sign				
8-Bit Displacement	01111000 8-bit displ	7 + m or 3		j
Full Displacement	00001111 10001000 full displacement	7 + m or 3		j

Table 8.1. 80376 Instruction Set Clock Count Summary (Continued)

Instruction	Format	Clock Counts	Number of Data Cycles	Notes
CONDITIONAL JUMPS (Continued)				
JNS = Jump on Not Sign				
8-Bit Displacement	01111001 | 8-bit displ	7 + m or 3		j
Full Displacement	00001111 | 10001001 | full displacement	7 + m or 3		j
JP/JPE = Jump on Parity/Parity Even				
8-Bit Displacement	01111010 | 8-bit displ	7 + m or 3		j
Full Displacement	00001111 | 10001010 | full displacement	7 + m or 3		j
JNP/JPO = Jump on Not Parity/Parity Odd				
8-Bit Displacement	01111011 | 8-bit displ	7 + m or 3		j
Full Displacement	00001111 | 10001011 | full displacement	7 + m or 3		j
JL/JNGE = Jump on Less/Not Greater or Equal				
8-Bit Displacement	01111100 | 8-bit displ	7 + m or 3		j
Full Displacement	00001111 | 10001100 | full displacement	7 + m or 3		j
JNL/JGE = Jump on Not Less/Greater or Equal				
8-Bit Displacement	01111101 | 8-bit displ	7 + m or 3		j
Full Displacement	00001111 | 10001101 | full displacement	7 + m or 3		j
JLE/JNG = Jump on Less or Equal/Not Greater				
8-Bit Displacement	01111110 | 8-bit displ	7 + m or 3		j
Full Displacement	00001111 | 10001110 | full displacement	7 + m or 3		j
JNLE/JG = Jump on Not Less or Equal/Greater				
8-Bit Displacement	01111111 | 8-bit displ	7 + m or 3		j
Full Displacement	00001111 | 10001111 | full displacement	7 + m or 3		j
JECXZ = Jump on ECX Zero	11100011 | 8-bit displ	9 + m or 5		j
(Address Size Prefix Differentiates JCXZ from JECXZ)				
LOOP = Loop ECX Times	11100010 | 8-bit displ	11 + m		j
LOOPZ/LOOPE = Loop with Zero/Equal	11100001 | 8-bit displ	11 + m		j
LOOPNZ/LOOPNE = Loop While Not Zero	11100000 | 8-bit displ	11 + m		j
CONDITIONAL BYTE SET				
NOTE: Times Are Register/Memory				
SETO = Set Byte on Overflow				
To Register/Memory	00001111 | 10010000 | mod 000 r/m	4/5*	0/1*	a
SETNO = Set Byte on Not Overflow				
To Register/Memory	00001111 | 10010001 | mod 000 r/m	4/5*	0/1*	a
SETB/SETNAE = Set Byte on Below/Not Above or Equal				
To Register/Memory	00001111 | 10010010 | mod 000 r/m	4/5*	0/1*	a

3

Table 8.1. 80376 Instruction Set Clock Count Summary (Continued)

Instruction	Format			Clock Counts	Number of Data Cycles	Notes
CONDITIONAL BYTE SET (Continued)						
SETNB = Set Byte on Not Below/Above or Equal						
To Register/Memory	00001111	10010011	mod 000 r/m	4/5*	0/1*	a
SETE/SETZ = Set Byte on Equal/Zero						
To Register/Memory	00001111	10010100	mod 000 r/m	4/5*	0/1*	a
SETNE/SETNZ = Set Byte on Not Equal/Not Zero						
To Register/Memory	00001111	10010101	mod 000 r/m	4/5*	0/1*	a
SETBE/SETNA = Set Byte on Below or Equal/Not Above						
To Register/Memory	00001111	10010110	mod 000 r/m	4/5*	0/1*	a
SETNBE/SETA = Set Byte on Not Below or Equal/Above						
To Register/Memory	00001111	10010111	mod 000 r/m	4/5*	0/1*	a
SETS = Set Byte on Sign						
To Register/Memory	00001111	10011000	mod 000 r/m	4/5*	0/1*	a
SETNS = Set Byte on Not Sign						
To Register/Memory	00001111	10011001	mod 000 r/m	4/5*	0/1*	a
SETP/SETPE = Set Byte on Parity/Parity Even						
To Register/Memory	00001111	10011010	mod 000 r/m	4/5*	0/1*	a
SETNP/SETPO = Set Byte on Not Parity/Parity Odd						
To Register/Memory	00001111	10011011	mod 000 r/m	4/5*	0/1*	a
SETL/SETNGE = Set Byte on Less/Not Greater or Equal						
To Register/Memory	00001111	10011100	mod 000 r/m	4/5*	0/1*	a
SETNL/SETGE = Set Byte on Not Less/Greater or Equal						
To Register/Memory	00001111	01111101	mod 000 r/m	4/5*	0/1*	a
SETLE/SETNG = Set Byte on Less or Equal/Not Greater						
To Register/Memory	00001111	10011110	mod 000 r/m	4/5*	0/1*	a
SETNLE/SETG = Set Byte on Not Less or Equal/Greater						
To Register/Memory	00001111	10011111	mod 000 r/m	4/5*	0/1*	a
ENTER = Enter Procedure	11001000	16-bit displacement, 8-bit level				
L = 0				10		a
L = 1				14	1	a
L > 1				17 + 8(n − 1)	4(n − 1)	a
LEAVE = Leave Procedure	11001001			6		a

Table 8.1. 80376 Instruction Set Clock Count Summary (Continued)

Instruction	Format	Clock Counts	Number of Data Cycles	Notes
INTERRUPT INSTRUCTIONS				
INT = Interrupt:				
Type Specified	11001101 | type			
Via Interrupt or Trap Gate to Same Privilege Level		71	14	c,d,j,p
Via Interrupt or Trap Gate to Different Privilege Level		111	14	c,d,j,p
From 386 Task to 386 TSS via Task Gate		467	140	c,d,j,p
Type 3	11001100			
Via Interrupt or Trap Gate to Same Privilege Level		71	14	c,d,j,p
Via Interrupt or Trap Gate to Different Privilege Level		111	14	c,d,j,p
From 386 Task to 386 TSS via Task Gate		308	138	c,d,j,p
INTO = Interrupt 4 if Overflow Flag Set	11001110			
If OF = 1:				
If OF = 0		3		
Via Interrupt or Trap Gate to Same Privilege Level		71	14	c,d,j,p
Via Interrupt or Trap Gate to Different Privilege Level		111	14	c,d,j,p
From 386 Task to 386 TSS via Task Gate		413	138	c,d,j,p

3

Table 8.1. 80376 Instruction Set Clock Count Summary (Continued)

Instruction	Format	Clock Counts	Number Of Data Cycles	Notes
INTERRUPT INSTRUCTIONS (Continued)				
Bound = Out of Range Interrupt 5 if Detect Value	01100010 | mod reg r/m			
If in Range		10	0	a,c,d,j,o,p
If Out of Range:				
Via Interrupt or Trap Gate to Same Privilege Level		71	14	c,d,j,p
Via Interrupt or Trap Gate to Different Privilege Level		111	14	c,d,j,p
From 386 Task to 386 TSS via Task Gate		398	138	c,d,j,p
INTERRUPT RETURN				
IRET = Interrupt Return	11001111			
To the Same Privilege Level (within Task)		42	5	a,c,d,j,p
To Different Privilege Level (within Task)		86	5	a,c,d,j,p
From 386 Task to 386 TSS		328	138	c,d,j,p
PROCESSOR CONTROL				
HLT = HALT	11110100	5		b
MOV = Move to and from Control/Debug/Test Registers				
CR0 from register	00001111 | 00100010 | 11 eee reg	10		b
Register from CR0	00001111 | 00100000 | 11 eee reg	6		b
DR0–3 from Register	00001111 | 00100011 | 11 eee reg	22		b
DR6–7 from Register	00001111 | 00100011 | 11 eee reg	16		b
Register from DR6–7	00001111 | 00100001 | 11 eee reg	14		b
Register from DR0–3	00001111 | 00100001 | 11 eee reg	22		b
NOP = No Operation	10010000	3		
WAIT = Wait until $\overline{\text{BUSY}}$ Pin is Negated	10011011	6		

Table 8.1. 80376 Instruction Set Clock Count Summary (Continued)

Instruction	Format	Clock Counts	Number of Data Cycles	Notes
PROCESSOR EXTENSION INSTRUCTIONS				
Processor Extension Escape	11011TTT | mod LLL r/m TTT and LLL bits are opcode information for coprocessor.	See 80387SX Data Sheet		a
PREFIX BYTES				
Address Size Prefix	01100111	0		
LOCK = Bus Lock Prefix	11110000	0		f
Operand Size Prefix	01100110	0		
Segment Override Prefix				
CS:	00101110	0		
DS:	00111110	0		
ES:	00100110	0		
FS:	01100100	0		
GS:	01100101	0		
SS:	00110110	0		
PROTECTION CONTROL				
ARPL = Adjust Requested Privilege Level				
From Register/Memory	01100011 | mod reg r/m	20/21**	2**	a
LAR = Load Access Rights				
From Register/Memory	00001111 | 00000010 | mod reg r/m	17/18*	1*	a,c,i,p
LGDT = Load Global Descriptor				
Table Register	00001111 | 00000001 | mod 010 r/m	13**	3*	a,e
LIDT = Load Interrupt Descriptor				
Table Register	00001111 | 00000001 | mod 011 r/m	13**	3*	a,e
LLDT = Load Local Descriptor				
Table Register to Register/Memory	00001111 | 00000000 | mod 010 r/m	24/28*	5*	a,c,e,p
LMSW = Load Machine Status Word				
From Register/Memory	00001111 | 00000001 | mod 110 r/m	10/13*	1*	a,e
LSL = Load Segment Limit				
From Register/Memory	00001111 | 00000011 | mod reg r/m			
Byte-Granular Limit		24/27*	2*	a,c,i,p
Page-Granular Limit		29/32*	2*	a,c,i,p
LTR = Load Task Register				
From Register/Memory	00001111 | 00000000 | mod 001 r/m	27/31*	4*	a,c,e,p
SGDT = Store Global Descriptor				
Table Register	00001111 | 00000001 | mod 000 r/m	11*	3*	a
SIDT = Store Interrupt Descriptor				
Table Register	00001111 | 00000001 | mod 001 r/m	11*	3*	a
SLDT = Store Local Descriptor Table Register				
To Register/Memory	00001111 | 00000000 | mod 000 r/m	2/2*	4*	a

3

Table 8.1. 80376 Instruction Set Clock Count Summary (Continued)

Instruction	Format			Clock Counts	Number of Data Cycles	Notes
PROTECTION CONTROL (Continued)						
SMSW = **Store Machine Status Word**	00001111	00000001	mod 100 r/m	2/2*	1*	a, c
STR = **Store Task Register**						
To Register/Memory	00001111	00000000	mod 001 r/m	2/2*	1*	a
VERR = **Verify Read Accesss**						
Register/Memory	00001111	00000000	mod 100 r/m	10/11**	2**	a,c,i,p
VERW = **Verify Write Accesss**	00001111	00000000	mod 101 r/m	15/16**	2**	a,c,i,p

NOTES:

a. Exception 13 fault (general violation) will occur if the memory operand in CS, DS, ES, FS or GS cannot be used due to either a segment limit violation or access rights violation. If a stack limit is violated, and exception 12 (stack segment limit violation or not present) occurs.

b. For segment load operations, the CPL, RPL and DPL must agree with the privilege rules to avoid an exception 13 fault (general protection violation). The segments's descriptor must indicate "present" or exception 11 (CS, DS, ES, FS, GS not present). If the SS register is loaded and a stack segment not present is detected, an exception 12 (stack segment limit violation or not present occurs).

c. All segment descriptor accesses in the GDT or LDT made by this instruction will automatically assert $\overline{\text{LOCK}}$ to maintain descriptor integrity in multiprocessor systems.

d. JMP, CALL, INT, RET and IRET instructions referring to another code segment will cause an exception 13 (general protection violation) if an applicable privilege rule is volated.

e. An exception 13 fault occurs if CPL is greater than 0.

f. An exception 13 fault occurs if CPL is greater than IOPL.

g. The IF bit of the flag register is not updated if CPL is greater than IOPL. The IOPL field of the flag register is updated only if CPL = 0.

h. Any violation of privelege rules as applied to the selector operand does not cause a protection exception; rather, the zero flag is cleared.

i. If the coprocessor's memory operand violates a segment limit or segment access rights, an exception 13 fault (general protection exception) will occur before the ESC instruction is executed. An exception 12 fault (stack segment limit violation or no present) will occur if the stack limit is violated by the operand's starting address.

j. The destination of a JMP, CALL, INT, RET or IRET must be in the defined limit of a code segment or an exception 13 fault (general protection violation) will occur.

k. If CPL ≤ IOPL

l. If CPL > IOPL

m. $\overline{\text{LOCK}}$ is automatically asserted, regardless of the presence or absence of the $\overline{\text{LOCK}}$ prefix.

n. The 80376 uses an early-out multiply algorithm. The actual number of clocks depends on the position of the most significant bit in the operand (multiplier). Clock counts given are minimum to maximum. To calculate actual clocks use the following formula:

Actual Clock = if m < > 0 then max ([$\log_2 |m|$], 3) + 9 clocks:
if m = 0 then 12 clocks (where m is the multiplier)

o. An exception may occur, depending on the value of the operand.

p. $\overline{\text{LOCK}}$ is asserted during descriptor table accesses.

8.2 INSTRUCTION ENCODING

Overview

All instruction encodings are subsets of the general instruction format shown in Figure 8.1. Instructions consist of one or two primary opcode bytes, possibly an address specifier consisting of the "mod r/m" byte and "scaled index" byte, a displacement if required, and an immediate data field if required.

Within the primary opcode or opcodes, smaller encoding fields may be defined. These fields vary according to the class of operation. The fields define such information as direction of the operation, size of the displacements, register encoding, or sign extension.

Almost all instructions referring to an operand in memory have an addressing mode byte following the primary opcode byte(s). This byte, the mod r/m byte, specifies the address mode to be used. Certain encodings of the mod r/m byte indicate a second addressing byte, the scale-index-base byte, follows the mod r/m byte to fully specify the addressing mode.

Addressing modes can include a displacement immediately following the mod r/m byte, or scaled index byte. If a displacement is present, the possible sizes are 8, 16 or 32 bits.

If the instruction specifies an immediate operand, the immediate operand follows any displacement bytes. The immediate operand, if specified, is always the last field of the instruction.

Figure 8.1 illustrates several of the fields that can appear in an instruction, such as the mod field and the r/m field, but the Figure does not show all fields. Several smaller fields also appear in certain instructions, sometimes within the opcode bytes themselves. Table 8.2 is a complete list of all fields appearing in the 80376 instruction set. Further ahead, following Table 8.2, are detailed tables for each field.

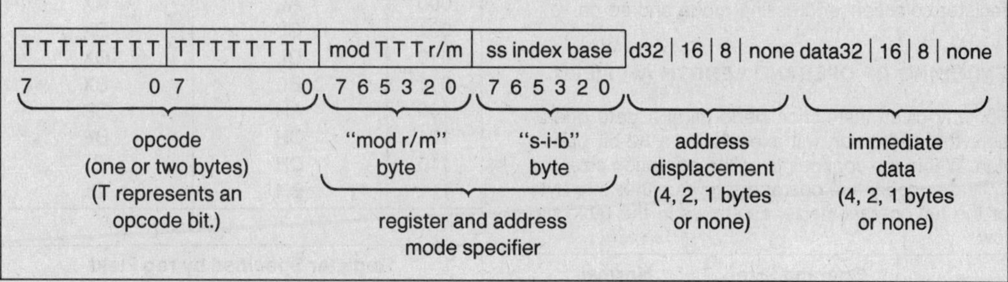

Figure 8.1. General Instruction Format

Table 8.2. Fields within 80376 Instructions

Field Name	Description	Number of Bits
w	Specifies if Data is Byte or Full Size (Full Size is either 16 or 32 Bits	1
d	Specifies Direction of Data Operation	1
s	Specifies if an Immediate Data Field Must be Sign-Extended	1
reg	General Register Specifier	3
mod r/m	Address Mode Specifier (Effective Address can be a General Register)	2 for mod; 3 for r/m
ss	Scale Factor for Scaled Index Address Mode	2
index	General Register to be used as Index Register	3
base	General Register to be used as Base Register	3
sreg2	Segment Register Specifier for CS, SS, DS, ES	2
sreg3	Segment Register Specifier for CS, SS, DS, ES, FS, GS	3
tttn	For Conditional Instructions, Specifies a Condition Asserted or a Condition Negated	4

Note: Table 8.1 shows encoding of individual instructions.

3

16-Bit Extensions of the Instruction Set

Two prefixes, the operand size prefix (66H) and the effective address size prefix (67H), allow overriding individually the default selection of operand size and effective address size. These prefixes may precede any opcode bytes and affect only the instruction they precede. If necessary, one or both of the prefixes may be placed before the opcode bytes. The presence of the operand size prefix (66H) and the effective address prefix will allow 16-bit data operation and 16-bit effective address calculations.

For instructions with more than one prefix, the order of prefixes is unimportant.

Unless specified otherwise, instructions with 8-bit and 16-bit operands do not affect the contents of the high-order bits of the extended registers.

Encoding of Instruction Fields

Within the instruction are several fields indicating register selection, addressing mode and so on.

ENCODING OF OPERAND LENGTH (w) FIELD

For any given instruction performing a data operation, the instruction will execute as a 32-bit operation. Within the constraints of the operation size, the w field encodes the operand size as either one byte or the full operation size, as shown in the table below.

w Field	Operand Size with 66H Prefix	Normal Operand Size
0	8 Bits	8 Bits
1	16 Bits	32 Bits

ENCODING OF THE GENERAL REGISTER (reg) FIELD

The general register is specified by the reg field, which may appear in the primary opcode bytes, or as the reg field of the "mod r/m" byte, or as the r/m field of the "mod r/m" byte.

Encoding of reg Field When w Field is not Present in Instruction

reg Field	Register Selected with 66H Prefix	Register Selected During 32-Bit Data Operations
000	AX	EAX
001	CX	ECX
010	DX	EDX
011	BX	EBX
100	SP	ESP
101	BP	EBP
110	SI	ESI
111	DI	EDI

Encoding of reg Field When w Field is Present in Instruction

Register Specified by reg Field with 66H Prefix		
reg	Function of w Field	
	(when w = 0)	(when w = 1)
000	AL	AX
001	CL	CX
010	DL	DX
011	BL	BX
100	AH	SP
101	CH	BP
110	DH	SI
111	BH	DI

Register Specified by reg Field without 66H Prefix		
reg	Function of w Field	
	(when w = 0)	(when w = 1)
000	AL	EAX
001	CL	ECX
010	DL	EDX
011	BL	EBX
100	AH	ESP
101	CH	EBP
110	DH	ESI
111	BH	EDI

PRELIMINARY

ENCODING OF THE SEGMENT REGISTER (sreg) FIELD

The sreg field in certain instructions is a 2-bit field allowing one of the CS, DS, ES or SS segment registers to be specified. The sreg field in other instructions is a 3-bit field, allowing the FS and GS segment registers to be specified also.

2-Bit sreg2 Field

2-Bit sreg2 Field	Segment Register Selected
00	ES
01	CS
10	SS
11	DS

3-Bit sreg3 Field

3-Bit sreg3 Field	Segment Register Selected
000	ES
001	CS
010	SS
011	DS
100	FS
101	GS
110	do not use
111	do not use

ENCODING OF ADDRESS MODE

Except for special instructions, such as PUSH or POP, where the addressing mode is pre-determined, the addressing mode for the current instruction is specified by addressing bytes following the primary opcode. The primary addressing byte is the "mod r/m" byte, and a second byte of addressing information, the "s-i-b" (scale-index-base) byte, can be specified.

The s-i-b byte (scale-index-base byte) is specified when using 32-bit addressing mode and the "mod r/m" byte has r/m = 100 and mod = 00, 01 or 10. When the sib byte is present, the 32-bit addressing mode is a function of the mod, ss, index, and base fields.

The primary addressing byte, the "mod r/m" byte, also contains three bits (shown as TTT in Figure 8.1) sometimes used as an extension of the primary opcode. The three bits, however, may also be used as a register field (reg).

When calculating an effective address, either 16-bit addressing or 32-bit addressing is used. 16-bit addressing uses 16-bit address components to calculate the effective address while 32-bit addressing uses 32-bit address components to calculate the effective address. When 16-bit addressing is used, the "mod r/m" byte is interpreted as a 16-bit addressing mode specifier. When 32-bit addressing is used, the "mod r/m" byte is interpreted as a 32-bit addressing mode specifier.

Tables on the following three pages define all encodings of all 16-bit addressing modes and 32-bit addressing modes.

Encoding of Normal Address Mode with "mod r/m" byte (no "s-i-b" byte present):

mod r/m	Effective Address
00 000	DS:[EAX]
00 001	DS:[ECX]
00 010	DS:[EDX]
00 011	DS:[EBX]
00 100	s-i-b is present
00 101	DS:d32
00 110	DS:[ESI]
00 111	DS:[EDI]
01 000	DS:[EAX+d8]
01 001	DS:[ECX+d8]
01 010	DS:[EDX+d8]
01 011	DS:[EBX+d8]
01 100	s-i-b is present
01 101	SS:[EBP+d8]
01 110	DS:[ESI+d8]
01 111	DS:[EDI+d8]

mod r/m	Effective Address
10 000	DS:[EAX+d32]
10 001	DS:[ECX+d32]
10 010	DS:[EDX+d32]
10 011	DS:[EBX+d32]
10 100	s-i-b is present
10 101	SS:[EBP+d32]
10 110	DS:[ESI+d32]
10 111	DS:[EDI+d32]
11 000	register—see below
11 001	register—see below
11 010	register—see below
11 011	register—see below
11 100	register—see below
11 101	register—see below
11 110	register—see below
11 111	register—see below

Register Specified by reg or r/m during Normal Data Operations:

mod r/m	function of w field	
	(when w=0)	(when w=1)
11 000	AL	EAX
11 001	CL	ECX
11 010	DL	EDX
11 011	BL	EBX
11 100	AH	ESP
11 101	CH	EBP
11 110	DH	ESI
11 111	BH	EDI

Register Specified by reg or r/m during 16-Bit Data Operations: (66H Prefix)

mod r/m	function of w field	
	(when w=0)	(when w=1)
11 000	AL	AX
11 001	CL	CX
11 010	DL	DX
11 011	BL	BX
11 100	AH	SP
11 101	CH	BP
11 110	DH	SI
11 111	BH	DI

Encoding of 16-bit Address Mode with "mod r/m" Byte Using 67H Prefix

mod r/m	Effective Address
00 000	DS:[BX+SI]
00 001	DS:[BX+DI]
00 010	SS:[BP+SI]
00 011	SS:[BP+DI]
00 100	DS:[SI]
00 101	DS:[DI]
00 110	DS:d16
00 111	DS:[BX]
01 000	DS:[BX+SI+d8]
01 001	DS:[BX+DI+d8]
01 010	SS:[BP+SI+d8]
01 011	SS:[BP+DI+d8]
01 100	DS:[SI+d8]
01 101	DS:[DI+d8]
01 110	SS:[BP+d8]
01 111	DS:[BX+d8]

mod r/m	Effective Address
10 000	DS:[BX+SI+d16]
10 001	DS:[BX+DI+d16]
10 010	SS:[BP+SI+d16]
10 011	SS:[BP+DI+d16]
10 100	DS:[SI+d16]
10 101	DS:[DI+d16]
10 110	SS:[BP+d16]
10 111	DS:[BX+d16]
11 000	register—see below
11 001	register—see below
11 010	register—see below
11 011	register—see below
11 100	register—see below
11 101	register—see below
11 110	register—see below
11 111	register—see below

3

Encoding of 32-bit Address Mode ("mod r/m" byte and "s-i-b" byte present):

mod base	Effective Address
00 000	DS:[EAX + (scaled index)]
00 001	DS:[ECX + (scaled index)]
00 010	DS:[EDX + (scaled index)]
00 011	DS:[EBX + (scaled index)]
00 100	SS:[ESP + (scaled index)]
00 101	DS:[d32 + (scaled index)]
00 110	DS:[ESI + (scaled index)]
00 111	DS:[EDI + (scaled index)]
01 000	DS:[EAX + (scaled index) + d8]
01 001	DS:[ECX + (scaled index) + d8]
01 010	DS:[EDX + (scaled index) + d8]
01 011	DS:[EBX + (scaled index) + d8]
01 100	SS:[ESP + (scaled index) + d8]
01 101	SS:[EBP + (scaled index) + d8]
01 110	DS:[ESI + (scaled index) + d8]
01 111	DS:[EDI + (scaled index) + d8]
10 000	DS:[EAX + (scaled index) + d32]
10 001	DS:[ECX + (scaled index) + d32]
10 010	DS:[EDX + (scaled index) + d32]
10 011	DS:[EBX + (scaled index) + d32]
10 100	SS:[ESP + (scaled index) + d32]
10 101	SS:[EBP + (scaled index) + d32]
10 110	DS:[ESI + (scaled index) + d32]
10 111	DS:[EDI + (scaled index) + d32]

NOTE:
Mod field in "mod r/m" byte; ss, index, base fields in "s-i-b" byte.

ss	Scale Factor
00	x1
01	x2
10	x4
11	x8

index	Index Register
000	EAX
001	ECX
010	EDX
011	EBX
100	no index reg**
101	EBP
110	ESI
111	EDI

****IMPORTANT NOTE:**
When index field is 100, indicating "no index register," then ss field MUST equal 00. If index is 100 and ss does not equal 00, the effective address is undefined.

ENCODING OF OPERATION DIRECTION (d) FIELD

In many two-operand instructions the d field is present to indicate which operand is considered the source and which is the destination.

d	Direction of Operation
0	Register/Memory <- - Register "reg" Field Indicates Source Operand; "mod r/m" or "mod ss index base" Indicates Destination Operand
1	Register <- - Register/Memory "reg" Field Indicates Destination Operand; "mod r/m" or "mod ss index base" Indicates Source Operand

ENCODING OF SIGN-EXTEND (s) FIELD

The s field occurs primarily to instructions with immediate data fields. The s field has an effect only if the size of the immediate data is 8 bits and is being placed in a 16-bit or 32-bit destination.

s	Effect on Immediate Data8	Effect on Immediate Data 16|32
0	None	None
1	Sign-Extend Data8 to Fill 16-Bit or 32-Bit Destination	None

ENCODING OF CONDITIONAL TEST (tttn) FIELD

For the conditional instructions (conditional jumps and set on condition), tttn is encoded with n indicating to use the condition (n = 0) or its negation (n = 1), and ttt giving the condition to test.

Mnemonic	Condition	tttn
O	Overflow	0000
NO	No Overflow	0001
B/NAE	Below/Not Above or Equal	0010
NB/AE	Not Below/Above or Equal	0011
E/Z	Equal/Zero	0100
NE/NZ	Not Equal/Not Zero	0101
BE/NA	Below or Equal/Not Above	0110
NBE/A	Not Below or Equal/Above	0111
S	Sign	1000
NS	Not Sign	1001
P/PE	Parity/Parity Even	1010
NP/PO	Not Parity/Parity Odd	1011
L/NGE	Less Than/Not Greater or Equal	1100
NL/GE	Not Less Than/Greater or Equal	1101
LE/NG	Less Than or Equal/Greater Than	1110
NLE/G	Not Less or Equal/Greater Than	1111

ENCODING OF CONTROL OR DEBUG REGISTER (eee) FIELD

For the loading and storing of the Control and Debug registers.

When Interpreted as Control Register Field

eee Code	Reg Name
000	CR0
010	Reserved
011	Reserved
Do not use any other encoding	

When Interpreted as Debug Register Field

eee Code	Reg Name
000	DR0
001	DR1
010	DR2
011	DR3
110	DR6
111	DR7
Do not use any other encoding	

9.0 REVISION HISTORY

The sections significantly revised since version -003 are:

Section 1.0	Added $\overline{\text{FLT}}$ pin.
Section 4.4	Added description of FLOAT operation and ONCE Mode. Figure 4.20 is new.
Section 4.6	Added revision identifier information for change to CHMOS IV manufacturing process.
Section 5.0	Both packages now specified for 0°C–115°C case temperature operation. Thermal resistance values changed.
Section 6.3	I_{CC} Max. specifications changed from 400 mA (cold) and 360 mA (hot) to 275 mA (cold, 16 MHz) and 305 mA (cold, 20 MHz).
Section 6.4	HLDA Valid Delay, t_{14}, min. changed from 6 ns to 4 ns. Added 20 MHz A.C. specifications in Table 6.5. Replaced Capacitive Derating Curves in Figures 6.8–6.10 to reflect new manufacturing process. Replaced I_{CC} vs. Frequency data (Figure 6.11) to reflect new specifications.

The sections significantly revised since version -002 are:

Section 1.0	Modified table 1.1. to list pins in alphabetical order.

The sections significantly revised since version -001 are:

Section 2.0	Figure 2.0 was updated to show the 16-bit registers SI, DI, BP and SP.
Section 2.1	Figure 2.2 was updated to show the correct bit polarity for bit 4 in the CR0 register.
Section 2.1	Tables 2.1 and 2.2 were updated to include additional information on the EFLAGs and CR0 registers.
Section 2.3	Figure 2.3 was updated to more accurately reflect the addressing mechanism of the 80376.
Section 2.6	In the subsection **Maskable Interrupt** a paragraph was added to describe the effect of interrupt gates on the IF EFLAGs bit.
Section 2.8	Table 2.7 was updated to reflect the correct power up condition of the CR0 register.
Section 2.10	Figure 2.6 was updated to show the correct bit positions of the BT, BS and BD bits in the DR6 register.
Section 3.0	Figure 3.1 was updated to clearly show the address calculation process.
Section 3.2	The subsection **DESCRIPTORS** was elaborated upon to clearly define the relationship between the linear address space and physical address space of the 80376.
Section 3.2	Figures 3.3 and 3.4 were updated to show the AVL bit field.
Section 3.3	The last sentence in the first paragraph of subsection **PROTECTION AND I/O PERMISSION BIT MAP** was deleted. This was an incorrect statement.
Section 4.1	In the Subsection **ADDRESS BUS ($\overline{\text{BHE}}$, $\overline{\text{BLE}}$, A_{23}–A_1** last sentence in the first paragraph was updated to reflect the numerics operand addresses as 8000FCH and 8000FEH. Because the 80376 sometimes does a double word I/O access a second access to 8000FEH can be seen.
Section 4.1	The Subsection **Hold Lantencies** was updated to describe how 32-bit and unaligned accesses are internally locked but do not assert the $\overline{\text{LOCK}}$ signal.
Section 4.2	Table 4.6 was updated to show the correct active data bits during a $\overline{\text{BLE}}$ assertion.

9.0 REVISION HISTORY (Continued)

Section 4.4	This section was updated to correctly reflect the pipelining of the address and status of the 80376 as opposed to "Address Pipelining" which occurs on processors such as the 80286.
Section 4.6	Table 4.7 was updated to show the correct Revision number, 05H.
Section 4.7	Table 4.8 was updated to show the numerics operand register 8000FEH. This address is seen when the 80376 does a DWORD operation to the port address 8000FCH.
Section 5.0	In the first paragraph the case temperatures were updated to reflect the 0°C–115°C for the ceramic package and 0°C–110°C for the plastic package.
Section 6.2	Table 6.2 was updated to reflect the Case Temperature under Bias specification of −65°C–120°C.
Section 6.4	Figure 6.8 vertical axis was updated to reflect "Output Valid Delay (ns)".
Section 6.4	Figure 6.11 was updated to show typical I_{CC} vs Frequency for the 80376.
Section 8.1	The clock counts and opcodes for various instructions were updated to their correct values.
Section 8.2	The section **INSTRUCTION ENCODING** was appended to the data sheet.

3

Intel387™ SX MATH COPROCESSOR

- **New Automatic Power Management**
  - **Low Power Consumption**
  - **Typically 100 mA in Dynamic Mode, and 4 mA in Idle Mode**
- **Socket Compatible with Intel387 Family of Math CoProcessors**
  - **Hardware and Software Compatible**
  - **Supported by Over 2100 Commercial Software Packages**
  - **10% to 15% Performance Increase on Whetstone and Livermore Benchmarks**
- **Compatible with the Intel386™ SX Microprocessor**
  - **Extends CPU Instruction Set to Include Trigonometric, Logarithmic, and Exponential**
- **High Performance 80-Bit Internal Architecture**
- **Implements ANSI/IEEE Standard 754-1985 for Binary Floating-Point Arithmetic**
- **Available in a 68-Pin PLCC Package**
  See Intel Packaging Specification, Order #231369

The Intel387™ SX Math CoProcessor is an extension to the Intel386™ SX microprocessor architecture. The combination of the Intel387™ SX with the Intel386™ SX microprocessor dramatically increases the processing speed of computer application software that utilizes high performance floating-point operations. An internal Power Management Unit enables the Intel387™ SX to perform these floating-point operations while maintaining very low power consumption for portable and desktop applications. The internal Power Management Unit effectively reduces power consumption by 95% when the device is idle.

The Intel387™ SX Math CoProcessor is available in a 68-pin PLCC package, and is manufactured on Intel's advanced 1.0 micron CHMOS IV technology.

240225–22

The complete document for this product is available on Intel's "Data-on-Demand" CD-ROM system and is in the 1994 Microprocessors Volume I handbook. To obtain a copy, contact your local Intel field sales office, Intel technical distributor or call 1-800-548-4725.

December 1992
Order Number: 240225-009

82355 BUS MASTER INTERFACE CONTROLLER (BMIC)

- **Designed for use in 32-Bit EISA Bus Master Expansion Board Designs**
  - **— Integrates Three Interfaces (EISA, Local CPU, and Transfer Buffer)**
- **Supports 16- and 32-Bit Burst Transfers**
  - **— 33 Mbytes/Sec Maximum Data Transfers**
- **Supports 32-Bit Non-Burst and Mismatched Data Size Transfers**
- **Supports 32-Bit EISA Addressability (4 Gigabyte)**
- **Two independent Data Transfer Channels with 24-Byte FIFOs**
  - **— Expansion Board Timing and EISA Timing Operate Asynchronously**
- **Supports Peek/Poke Operation with the Ability to Access Individual Locations in EISA Memory or I/O space**
- **Automatically Handles Misaligned Doubleword Data Transfers with No Performance Penalty**
- **Supports Automatic Handling of Complete EISA Bus Master Protocol**
  - **— EISA Arbitration/Preemption**
  - **— Cycle Timing and Execution**
  - **— Byte Alignment**
  - **— 1K Boundary Detection**
- **Supports Local Data Transfer Protocol Similar to Traditional DMA**
- **Supports a General Purpose Command and Status Interface**
  - **— Local and EISA System Interrupt Support**
  - **— General Purpose Information Transfers**
  - **— Set-and-Test-Functions in I/O Space (Semaphore Function)**
  - **— Supports the EISA Expansion Board ID Function**
- **Supports Decode of Slot Specific and General I/O Addresses**
- **132-Pin JEDEC PQFP Package**
  (See Packaging Specification Order #240800, Package Type NG)

82355 Internal Block Diagram

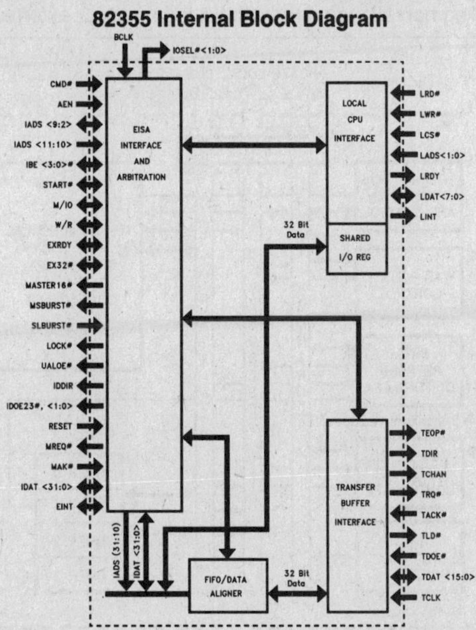

290255–1

The complete document for this product is available on Intel's "Data-on-Demand" CD-ROM system and is in the 1994 Peripherals handbook. To obtain a copy, contact your local Intel field sales office, Intel technical distributor or call 1-800-548-4725.

September 1993
Order Number: 290255-007

82370
INTEGRATED SYSTEM PERIPHERAL

- **High Performance 32-Bit DMA Controller for 16-Bit Bus**
  - **—16 MBytes/Sec Maximum Data Transfer Rate at 16 MHz**
  - **—8 Independently Programmable Channels**
- **20-Source Interrupt Controller**
  - **—Individually Programmable Interrupt Vectors**
  - **—15 External, 5 Internal Interrupts**
  - **—82C59A Superset**
- **Four 16-Bit Programmable Interval Timers**
  - **—82C54 Compatible**
- **Software Compatible to 82380**
- **Programmable Wait State Generator**
  - **—0 to 15 Wait States Pipelined**
  - **—1 to 16 Wait States Non-Pipelined**
- **DRAM Refresh Controller**
- **80376 Shutdown Detect and Reset Control**
  - **—Software/Hardware Reset**
- **High Speed CHMOS III Technology**
- **100-Pin Plastic Quad Flat-Pack Package and 132-Pin Pin Grid Array Package**
  (See Packaging Handbook Order #240800-001, Package Type NG or Package Type A)
- **Optimized for Use with the 80376 Microprocessor**
  - **—Resides on Local Bus for Maximum Bus Bandwidth**
  - **—16 MHz Clock**

The 82370 is a multi-function support peripheral that integrates system functions necessary in an 80376 environment. It has eight channels of high performance 32-bit DMA (32-bit internal, 16-bit external) with the most efficient transfer rates possible on the 80376 bus. System support peripherals integrated into the 82370 provide Interrupt Control, Timers, Wait State generation, DRAM Refresh Control, and System Reset logic.

The 82370's DMA Controller can transfer data between devices of different data path widths using a single channel. Each DMA channel operates independently in any of several modes. Each channel has a temporary data storage register for handling non-aligned data without the need for external alignment logic.

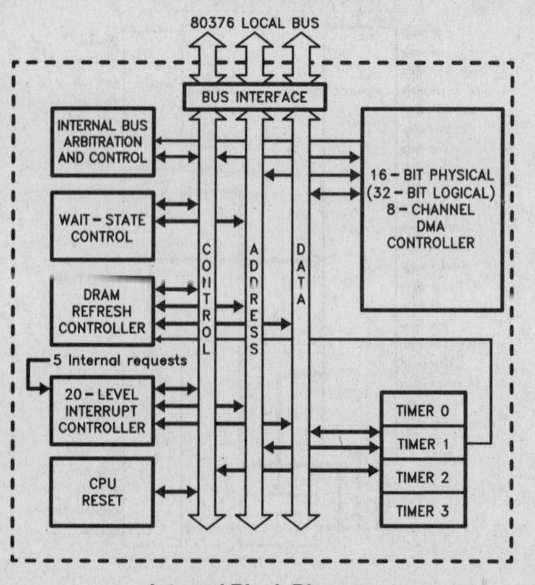

Internal Block Diagram

The complete document for this product is available on Intel's "Data-on-Demand" CD-ROM system. To obtain a copy, contact your local Intel field sales office, Intel technical distributor or call 1-800-548-4725.

November 1992
Order Number: 290164-005

82596DX AND 82596SX HIGH-PERFORMANCE 32-BIT LOCAL AREA NETWORK COPROCESSOR

- **Performs Complete CSMA/CD Medium Access Control (MAC) Functions— Independently of CPU**
  - **IEEE 802.3 (EOC) Frame Delimiting**
  - **HDLC Frame Delimiting**
- **Supports Industry Standard LANs**
  - **IEEE TYPE 10BASE-T (TPE), IEEE TYPE 10BASE5 (Ethernet*), IEEE TYPE 10BASE2 (Cheapernet), IEEE TYPE 1BASE5 (StarLAN), and the Proposed Standard TYPE 10BASE-F**
  - **Proprietary CSMA/CD Networks Up to 20 Mb/s**
- **On-Chip Memory Management**
  - **Automatic Buffer Chaining**
  - **Buffer Reclamation after Receipt of Bad Frames; Optional Save Bad Frames**
  - **32-Bit Segmented or Linear (Flat) Memory Addressing Formats**
- **82586 Software Compatible**
- **Optimized CPU Interface**
  - **82596DX Bus Interface Optimized to Intel's 32-Bit i386™DX**
  - **82596SX Bus Interface Optimized to Intel's 16-Bit i386™SX**
  - **Supports Big Endian and Little Endian Byte Ordering**
- **High-Performance 16-/32-Bit Bus Master Interface**
  - **66-MB/s Bus Bandwidth**
  - **33-MHz Clock, Two Clocks Per Transfer**
  - **Bus Throttle Timers**
  - **Transfers Data at 100% of Serial Bandwidth**
  - **128-Byte Receive FIFO, 64-Byte Transmit FIFO**
- **Network Management and Diagnostics**
  - **Monitor Mode**
  - **32-Bit Statistical Counters**
- **Self-Test Diagnostics**
- **Configurable Initialization Root for Data Structures**
- **High-Speed, 5-V, CHMOS** IV Technology**
- **132-Pin Plastic Quad Flat Pack (PQFP) and PGA Package**

(See Packaging Specifications Order Number: 240800-001, Package Type KU and A)

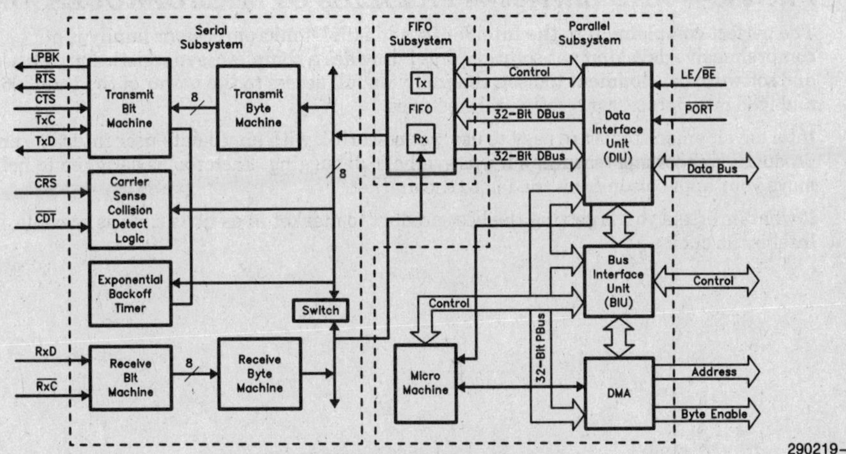

Figure 1. 82596DX/SX Block Diagram

The complete document for this product is available on Intel's "Data-on-Demand" CD-ROM system and is in the 1994 Networking handbook. To obtain a copy, contact your local Intel field sales office, Intel technical distributor or call 1-800-548-4725.

October 1993
Order Number: 290219-006

Intel386™ AND Intel486™ FAMILY DEVELOPMENT SUPPORT

280808-1

COMPREHENSIVE DEVELOPMENT SUPPORT FOR THE Intel386™ AND Intel486™ FAMILIES OF MICROPROCESSORS

The perfect complement to the Intel386™ and i486™ microprocessor family is a comprehensive development solution. Intel provides a complete, synergistic hardware and software development toolset, that delivers full access to the power of the Intel386 and i486 microprocessor family architectures.

Intel development tools are easy to use, yet powerful, with an up-date user interface and productivity boosting features such as symbolic debugging. Each tool is designed to help move your application from the lab to the market.

If what interests you is getting the best product to market in as little time as possible, Intel is the choice.

August 1992
Order Number: 280808-007

FEATURES

- Comprehensive support for the full 32 bit Intel386 and Intel486 microprocessor architectures—includes protected mode, 4 gigabyte physical memory addressing, and Intel486 microprocessor on-chip cache and numerics
- In-circuit emulators provide a standard windowed interface that is common across Intel debug tools and architectures
- Emulators also feature a source line display and symbolics to allow debugging in the context of the original program
- Intel high-level languages provide architectural extensions for manipulating hardware directly without assembly language routines
- Languages provide a common object code format (Intel OMF386) that supports symbolic debug and permits the intermixing of modules written in various languages
- ROM-able code is output directly from the language tools, significantly reducing the effort necessary to integrate software into the final target system
- Extensive support for the Intel family of math coprocessors
- Operation in DOS IBM PC AT and PS/2 Model 60 and 80, running DOS.

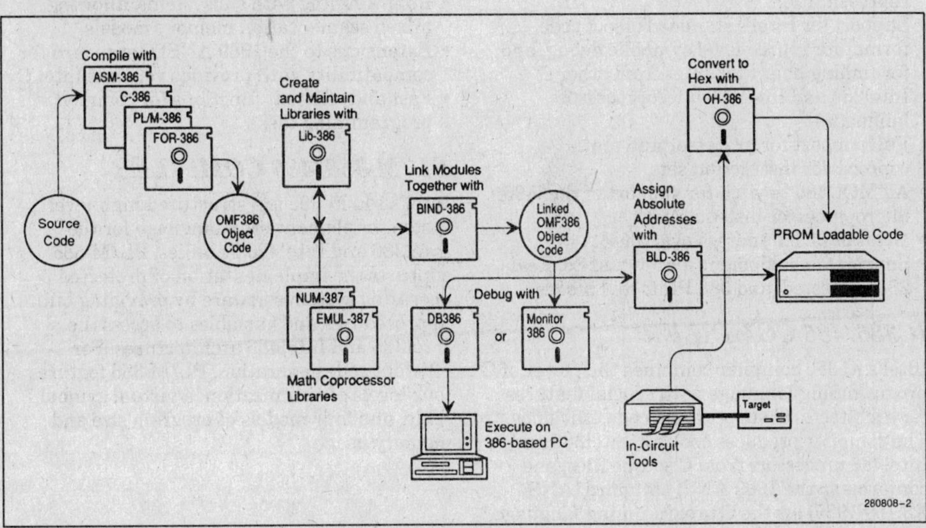

Figure 1: Intel Microprocessor Development Environment

FEATURES

ASM-386/486 MACRO ASSEMBLER

Intel's ASM 386 macro assembler for the Intel386 and Intel486 Families offers many features normally found only in high-level languages. The macro facility in ASM 386 saves development time by allowing common program sequences to be coded only once. The assembly language is strongly typed, performing extensive checks on the usage of variables and labels.

Other Intel ASM 386 features include:
- "High-level" assembler mnemonics to simplify the language
- Structures and records for data representation
- Support for Intel's standard object code format for source-level symbolic debug, and for linking object modules from other Intel386 and Intel486 microprocessor languages
- Full support for processor and math coprocessor instruction sets
- A "MOD486" switch for support of the i486 microprocessor instructions
- 16 bit or 32 bit address overrides
- Supports development for Virtual 86, Real, 286 Protected, and 386 Protected modes

iC386/486 COMPILER

Intel's iC-386 compiler combines the power of C programming language with special features for architectural support and code efficiency. The compiler produces code for Intel386 and Intel486 processors from C source files, and conforms to the 1989 ANSI standard (ANS X3.159-1989) for the C programming language.

Key Intel iC-386 features include:
- Controls to tailor the compilation for each step of your application development process
- In-line versions of many ANSI-standard library functions
- Expanded memory support (LIM Version 3.0 and higher) for large applications
- Object code (including supplied run-time libraries) suitable for ROM
- Three different levels of optimization
- A choice of three segmentation memory models (small, compact, and flat) to create compact and efficient code
- In-line processor-specific functions and time-saving macros that provide access to the special features of the Intel386 and Intel486 processors
- In-line floating-point instructions for the Intel387™ numerics coprocessor and Intel486 processor floating-point unit
- Time-saving macros and functions to help assembly language routines interface with Intel's high-level programming languages
- The standard C run-time library plus libraries for floating-point support and the iRMX® III C interface library
- An easy interface to Intel's non-C programming languages
- Support for source-level debugging
- Programming with subsystems, allowing mixed segmentation memory models
- Extensions to the 1989 ANSI C standard for compatibility with previous versions Intel C
- Fast and efficient functions for common programming tasks

PL/M-386/486 COMPILER

Intel's PL/M-386 is a structured high-level system implementation language for the Intel386 and Intel486 Families. PL/M-386 supports the implementation of protected operating system software by providing built-in procedures and variables to access the Intel386 and Intel486 architectures. For efficient code generation, PL/M-386 features four levels of optimization, a virtual symbol table, and four models of program size and memory usage.

FEATURES

Other Intel PL/M-386 features include:
- The ability to define a procedure as an interrupt handler as well as facilities for generating interrupts
- Direct support of input and output from microprocessor ports
- Upward compatibility with Intel PL/M-86 and PL/M-286 source code
- A "MOD486" compiler switch for Intel486 microprocessor instruction generation

PL/M-386 combines the benefits of a high-level language with the ability to access the Intel386 and Intel486 architectures. For the development of systems software, PL/M-386 is a costeffective alternative to assembly language programming.

FORTRAN-386/486 COMPILER

Intel's FORTRAN-386 compiler is a cross-compiler that supports the entire Intel386 family of components and Intel486 microprocessors (when operating in the 386 chip mode) microprocessors.

FORTRAN-386 features high-level support for floating-point calculations, transcendentals, interrupt procedures, and run-time exception handling. FORTRAN-386 meets the ANSI FORTRAN-77 language subset specification and supports extensions endorsed by the Department of Defense (DOD), extensions that support programs written for the ANSI FORTRAN 66 standard, and extensions that support the Intel386 microprocessor and related numerics coprocessors.

To aid in the development and debugging process, the compiler generates warning and error messages and an optional listing file. The listing file can include symbol cross-reference tables and a listing of the generated Intel386 microprocessor assembly-language instructions. Library routines are reentrant and ROMable.

Other Intel FORTRAN-386 compiler features include:
- Object code can be configured to reside in either RAM or ROM
- The program code can be optimized for execution speed or memory size
- Source-level debugging is supported via the rich symbolics provided in the object module format (Intel OMF386)
- Support for the proposed REALMATH IEEE floating point standard

RLL-386/486 RELOCATION, LINKAGE, AND LIBRARY TOOLS

The RLL 386 relocation, linkage, and library tools feature comprehensive support of the full Intel386 and Intel486 architectures. The tools link separate modules, build object libraries, link in Intel387 support, build tasks to execute under protected mode, or multitasking, memory protected software. RLL-386 supports loadable, linkable, and bootloadable Intel object module formats; and supports all segmentation models. RLL-386 consists of the following:

Binder — for linking multiple object modules into a single program and resolving references between modules.

Builder — for producing absolute object modules, assigning addresses, and creating protected mode data structures.

Librarian — for creating and maintaining libraries of object modules.

EMUL-387, NUM-387 NUMERICS SUPPORT LIBRARIES

Intel's EMUL-387 and NUM-387 Numerics Libraries fully support the Intel387™, Intel 387 DX, Intel 387 SX math coprocessors and the Intel486 internal numerics unit—whether an actual math coprocessor is used in the final system or not.

For Intel386 microprocessor based applications without a math coprocessor, EMUL-387, a numerics software emulator, will execute instructions as though the coprocessor were present. Its functionality is identical to that of the math coprocessor. It is ideal for prototyping and debugging floating-point application software independent of hardware. Further, this permits portability of application code regardless of the presence of math coprocessor hardware in target systems.

For applications with a math coprocessor, NUM-387 numerics support library provides Intel's ASM 386, C-386, PL/M-386, and FORTRAN-386 language users with enhanced numeric data processing capability. With the library, it is easy for programs to do floating point arithmetic. Programmers can bind in library modules to do trigonometric, logarithmic and other numeric functions.

FEATURES

The user is guaranteed accurate, reliable results for all appropriate inputs.

Intel's NUM-387 support library is a collection of four functionally distinct libraries:

- Common elementary function library routines perform algebraic, logarithmic, exponential, trigonometric, and hyperbolic operations on real and complex numbers, as well as real-to-integer conversions; the routines extend the ranges of the coprocessor instructions
- Initialization library routines set up the numerics processing environment for the Intel386 family of processors with an Intel387, DX, or SX or true software emulator
- Decimal conversion library routines convert floating-point numbers from one Intel387, DX, or SX binary storage format to another, or from ASCII decimal strings to Intel387, DX, or SX binary floating-point format and vice versa
- Exception handling library routines make writing numerics exception handlers easier

All support library modules are in Intel386 microprocessor object module format (Intel OMF-386) so they can be linked with the object output of any Intel language. All routines are reentrant and ROMable.

By using Intel's NUM-387, the user is guaranteed that the numeric software meets industry standard (ANSI/IEEE standard for binary floating point arithmetic, 754-1985) and is portable, thus maintaining software investment.

DB-386 Software Debugger

Intel's DB-386 is a PC-based software development environment with source-level symbolic debug capabilities for object modules produced by Intel's assembler and high-level language compilers. This software debug environment allows Intel386 microprocessor code to be executed and debugged directly on a Intel386 DX or Intel386 SX microprocessor based PC, without any additional target hardware required. With Intel's standard windowed human interface, users can focus their efforts on finding bugs rather than spending time learning and manipulating the debug environment.

Other Intel DB-386 features include:

- A run-time interface allows protected-mode Intel386 microprocessor programs to be executed directly on a Intel386 DX or Intel386 SX microprocessor based PC
- Drop-down menus make the tool easy to learn for new or casual users. A command line interface is also provided for more complex problems
- Watch windows (which display user-specified variables), trace points, and breakpoints (including fixed, temporary, and conditional) can be set and modified as needed
- The user can browse source and callstacks, observe processor registers, and access watch window variables by either pull down menus or by a single keystroke, using function keys
- The user need not know whether a variable is an unsigned integer, a real, or a structure—the debugger uses the wealth of typing information available in Intel languages to display program variables in their respective type formats
- DB-386 supports the Intel486 microprocessor when operated in the Intel386 microprocessor mode

Intel386 and Intel486 Family In-Circuit Tools

Intel in-circuit emulators are used in many different debug environments including the design and test of: PC BIOS software and motherboard hardware, Intel386 and Intel486 based single board computers, and application and operating system software for DOS-based, ROM-based, and UNIX-based systems.

The Intel386 and Intel486 In-Circuit Emulators (ICE™) take advantage of exclusive Intel technology to provide accurate emulation for Intel's 80386 SX, 80386 DX, 80376, and 80486 microprocessors. Special access to internal processor states provides information not available to emulators which simply monitor the external buses. Emulators which do not have access to the internal processor conditions cannot guarantee accurate display of instructions executed by the microprocessor. With an Intel In-circuit Emulator you can be certain that the emulator is displaying accurate execution history, even when executing code from the on-chip cache memory of the Intel486.

The DOS hosted Intel386 DX and Intel386 SX emulators feature a windowed, menu-driven, human interface which provides easy access to the powerful features of these emulators. This makes it easy for novice or infrequent users to get the most out of every debug session. This interface features multiple windows which

FEATURES

allow you to simultaneously view source code, assembly code, memory, trace, variables, and registers. This interface is fully symbolic when used with Intel languages.

All of the emulators feature a combination of powerful and flexible breakpoints. The products use a combination of software breakpoints, hardware breakpoints, and on-chip debug registers to provide a rich set of recognition logic. Flexible breakpoints make it possible to set breakpoints on instruction execution and/or any possible bus event.

Trace filtering provides the ability to select the information captured in the trace buffer. ICE-386 SX allows capture of solely bus cycle information or both bus cycle and execution information. In addition, the ICE-386 DX can filter wait-state information from the trace buffer. ICE-486 provides the most flexible trace collection by allowing capture of information by any combination of bus cycle type including filtering of wait states, by instructions only, or by both bus cycles and instructions.

Other features of Intel emulators include:

- Unparalleled support of the Intel386 and Intel486 architectures, notably the native protected mode
- Emulation at clock speeds to 33 MHz, and full featured trigger and trace capabilities
- The Intel386 family emulators are convertible using removable probes to support the 80386 DX and 80386 SX microprocessors. The Intel486 processor is also supported via a product upgrade.

Relocatable Expanded Memory

Designed to enhance your existing ICE-486 and the ICD-486 debugger (REM486 is included with ICE-486 and an option for ICD-486). This optional relocatable expansion memory board adds 2 Mbyte of memory which the ICE or ICD can use in place of memory on the user target board.

ONCE-386 and Transmuter Adapters

If you have a surface mount Intel386 SX microprocessor design using 100-pin PQFP parts, Intel ICE emulators have on-circuit emulation (ONCE) capability. With surface mounted components, the ICE-386 SX emulator cabling clamps over the part, tri-stating the component, and allowing the emulator to operate. This allows you to debug manufactured boards without resoldering. For early target load development, a transmuter adapter can be used. The transmuter provides a better connection technique for debugging systems where the adapter cable will have to be attached and removed many times (like in prototype development).

ICD-486 In-Circuit Debugger

The ICD-486 In-circuit Debugger provides a low-cost alternative for full speed in-target Intel486 development. ICD-486 implements a subset of ICE functionality including: symbolic debugging, debug of high-speed cached applications, software and debug register breakpoints, and in-circuit operation.

Worldwide Service, Support, and Training

To augment its developing tools, Intel offers field application engineering expertise, hotline technical support, and on-site service.

Intel also offers Software Support which includes technical software information, automatic distributions of software and documentation updates, *iCOMMENTS* publication, remote diagnostic software, and development tools troubleshooting guide.

Intel's 90-day Hardware Support package includes technical hardware information, telephone support, warranty on parts, labor, material, and on-site hardware support.

Intel Development Tools also offers a 30-day, money-back guarantee to customers who are not satisfied after purchasing any Intel development tool.

FEATURES

PRODUCT SUPPORT MATRIX

Product	Component			Host
	i486	386 DX	386 SX	DOS 3.x and 5.0
ASM-386 Macro Assembler	✔	✔	✔	✔
iC-386 Compiler	✔	✔	✔	✔
PL/M-386 Compiler	✔	✔	✔	✔
FORTRAN-386 Compiler	✔	✔	✔	✔
RLL-386 Relocation, Linkage, Library, Support Tools	✔	✔	✔	✔
NUM-387 Libraries	✔	✔	✔	✔
EMUL-387 Libraries	NA	✔	✔	✔
In-Circuit Emulators	✔	✔	✔	✔
In-Circuit Debugger	✔			✔
DB-386 Software Debugger	✔	✔	✔	✔

ORDERING INFORMATION

386/i486™ FAMILY DOS HOSTED DEVELOPMENT KIT ORDER CODES

Software Order Codes

All software supports 386 and 486 microprocessor families except where indicated.

DKIT386C — Compiler Software Development Kit (See following content list).

D86ASM386NL — ASM macro assembler for PC DOS systems.

D86C386NL — DOS resident, ANSI standard (ANS X3.159-1989) C compiler.

D86PLM386NL — DOS resident PL/M compiler.

D86FOR386NL — DOS resident Fortan Compiler.

D86RLL386NL — DOS resident software development package. Contains Binder (for linking separately compiled modules), a Builder (for configuring protected multi-tasking systems), a cross reference Mapper, and a Librarian. Use this tool in conjunction with Intel's 80386 compilers and macro assembler.

DB386 — DOS S/W debugger.

The Intel Basic Software Development Kit for the DOS hosted environment includes:

- iC386 compiler
- ASM386 assembler
- RLL386 relocation linker and locator
- NUM387 numerics library
- EMUL387 math coprocessor emulator library
- DB386 software debugger
- OMF386LOAD loader development object module format documentation

ORDERING INFORMATION

IN-CIRCUIT TOOL ORDER CODES

All In-circuit emulator codes include: control unit, power supply, processor module, Stand-Alone Self Test board, bus Isolation Board, and DOS host software and serial interface cable.

ICE386SX25V	ICE-386 SX In-circuit emulator for the Intel386 SX component to 25 MHz.
pICE386SX20D	ICE-386 SX In-circuit emulator for the 80386 SX component to 20 MHz.
pICE386DX25DZ	ICE-386 DX In-circuit emulator for the 80386 DX component to 25 MHz.
ICE386DX33D	ICE-386 DX In-circuit emulator for the 80386 DX component to 33 MHz.
ICD48650D	In-circuit debugger for the 80486 microprocessor to 50 MHz.
pICE48633DZ	ICE-486 In-circuit emulator for the 80486 component to 33 MHz.

ICE CONVERSION KITS

KBASECONC	Converts ICE-486 to ICE-376, ICE-386 SX, or ICE-386 DX.
KBASECONV	Converts ICE-386 SX or ICE-386 DX to ICE-486.
TOICE386SX20D	Converts ICE-386 DX to ICE-386 SX 20 MHz.
TOICE386DX25D	Converts ICE-386 SX to ICE-386 DX 20 MHz.
TOICE48633D	Converts ICE-386 SX or ICE-386 DX to ICE-486 33 MHz.

ADDITIONAL TOOL ORDER CODES

386SXONCE Kit	100 pin PQFP to 132 pin PGA adaptor kit.
REM486A	2 Mbyte relocatable expansion memory option for ICD-486 (included with ICE-486).

To order your Intel Development Tool product, for more information, or for the number of your nearest sales office or distributor, call 800-874-6835 (North America). For literature on other Intel products call 800-548-4725 (North America). Outside of North America, please contact your local Intel sales office or distributor for more information.

TRANS 186 → 376 ASSEMBLY CODE TRANSLATOR

270919-1

To Order TRANS 186 → 376 Software, contact your local Intel sales office

TRANS 186 → 376 PRESERVES YOUR PROGRAMMING INVESTMENT

When your embedded application outgrows the 80C186 family, TRANS 186 → 376 is ready to help you upgrade to the 376 Embedded Processor. TRANS 186 → 376 is a DOS-based tool to automate the translation of Intel ASM86 source code to ASM386 source code. This program can actually help protect the man-years of investment in your original 86 software.

TRANS 186 → 376 LOWERS THE 32-BIT BARRIER

TRANS 186 → 376 accepts 16-bit source code written for any member of the 8086/8088 and 80C186/80C188 families. The output source code, with its 32-bit offsets, is suitable for Protected Mode execution on the 376 Embedded Processor or any 386, 386SX, or 486 microprocessor. The time you save by recycling your software can be applied toward system enhancements.

You control TRANS 186 → 376 operation from either the DOS command line or a control file. Major control switches cover:

- Choice of FLAT model or LARGE16 memory environment
- Redefinition of segments
- Optional 32-bit data declaration

TRANS 186 → 376 translates your routines on a line-by-line basis, converting as much code as possible. Whenever the tool does not have enough information to make conversions, it highlights the code section with messages, alerting you to edit by hand. TRANS 186 → 376 can write the ASM86 source code as comments in the ASM386 source file for side-by-side comparison.

November 1990
Order Number: 270919-001

TRANS 186 → 376 ASSEMBLY CODE TRANSLATOR

TRANS 186 → 376 COMPLEMENTS OTHER DEVELOPMENT TOOLS

Upon request, TRANS 186 → 376 generates a build file for the Intel System Builder, BLD386. This allows you to get your software running with only minimal BLD386 experience. A 72-page manual accompanies the TRANS 186 → 376 tool. The manual coverage includes:

- Practical tips on the overall conversion process
- Initializing the CPU and generating Protected Mode data structures
- Producing code for emulators and debuggers

Your 80C186 experience can release the power of the 376 Embedded Processor with the TRANS 186 → 376 Assembly Language Translator as your partner.

System requirements: PC AT* or compatible computer with PC-DOS* or MS-DOS** operating system version 3.0 or later, hard disk, and 512K RAM.

Embedded Intel386™ Processors

4

Intel386™ CX EMBEDDED MICROPROCESSOR

- Static Intel386™ CPU Core
  - Low Power Consumption
  - Operating Power Supply 2.7V to 5.5V
  - Operating Frequency 12 MHz at 2.7V to 3.3V; 20 MHz at 3.0V to 3.6V; 25 MHz at 4.5V to 5.5V
- Transparent Power-Management System Architecture
  - Intel System Management Mode Architecture Extension for Truly Compatible Systems
  - Power Management Transparent to Operating Systems and Application Programs
  - Programmable Power-Management Modes
- Clock Freeze Mode Allows Clock Stopping at Any Time
- Full 32-Bit Internal Architecture
  - 8-, 16-, 32-Bit Data Types
  - 8 General Purpose 32-Bit Registers
- Runs Intel386 Architecture Software in a Cost Effective 16-Bit Hardware Environment
  - Runs Same Applications and Operating Systems as the Intel386 SX and Intel386 DX Processors
  - Object Code Compatible with 8086, 80186, 80286, and Intel386 Processors
- High Performance 16-Bit Data Bus
  - 12, 20, 25 MHz Clock
  - Two-Clock Bus Cycles
  - Address Pipelining Allows Use of Slower, Inexpensive Memories
- Integrated Memory Management Unit (MMU)
  - Virtual Memory Support
  - Optional On-Chip Paging
  - 4 Levels of Hardware-Enforced Protection
  - MMU Fully Compatible with Those of the 80286 and Intel386 DX Processors
- Virtual 8086 Mode Allows Execution of 8086 Software in a Protected and Paged System
- Large Uniform Address Space
  - 64 Megabyte Physical
  - 64 Terabyte Virtual
  - 4 Gigabyte Maximum Segment Size
- Numerics Support with Intel387™ SX and Intel387 SL Math Coprocessors
- On-Chip Debugging Support Including Breakpoint Registers
- Complete System Development Support
- High-Speed CHMOS Technology
- Two Package Types
  - 100-Pin Plastic Quad Flatpack
  - 100-Pin Shrink Quad Flatpack

4

The Intel386 CX embedded microprocessor is a 32-bit, fully static CPU with a 16-bit external data bus, a 26-bit external address bus, and Intel's System Management Mode (SMM). The Intel386 CX CPU brings the vast software library of the Intel386 architecture to embedded systems. It provides the performance benefits of 32-bit programming with the cost savings associated with 16-bit hardware systems.

September 1993
Order Number: 272418-001

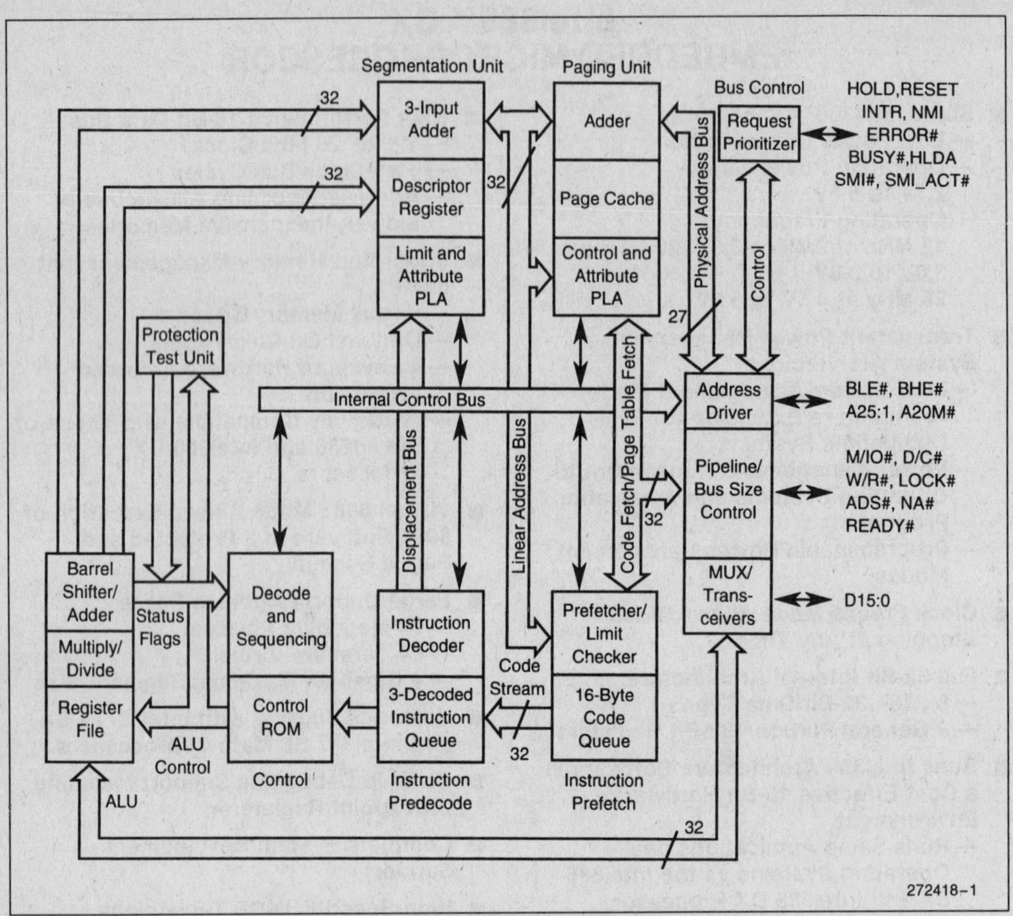

Segmentation Unit
Paging Unit
Bus Control
3-Input Adder
Descriptor Register
Limit and Attribute PLA
Adder
Page Cache
Control and Attribute PLA
Request Prioritizer
HOLD,RESET
INTR, NMI
ERROR#
BUSY#,HLDA
SMI#, SMI_ACT#
Physical Address Bus
Control
32
32
32
27
Protection Test Unit
Internal Control Bus
Address Driver
BLE#, BHE#
A25:1, A20M#
Displacement Bus
Linear Address Bus
Code Fetch/Page Table Fetch
Pipeline/ Bus Size Control
M/IO#, D/C#
W/R#, LOCK#
ADS#, NA#
READY#
32
Barrel Shifter/ Adder
Multiply/ Divide
Register File
Status Flags
ALU Control
ALU
Decode and Sequencing
Control ROM
Control
Instruction Decoder
3-Decoded Instruction Queue
Instruction Predecode
Code Stream
32
Prefetcher/ Limit Checker
16-Byte Code Queue
Instruction Prefetch
MUX/ Trans- ceivers
D15:0
32
272418–1

Figure 1. Intel386™ CX Microprocessor Block Diagram

1.0 PIN ASSIGNMENT

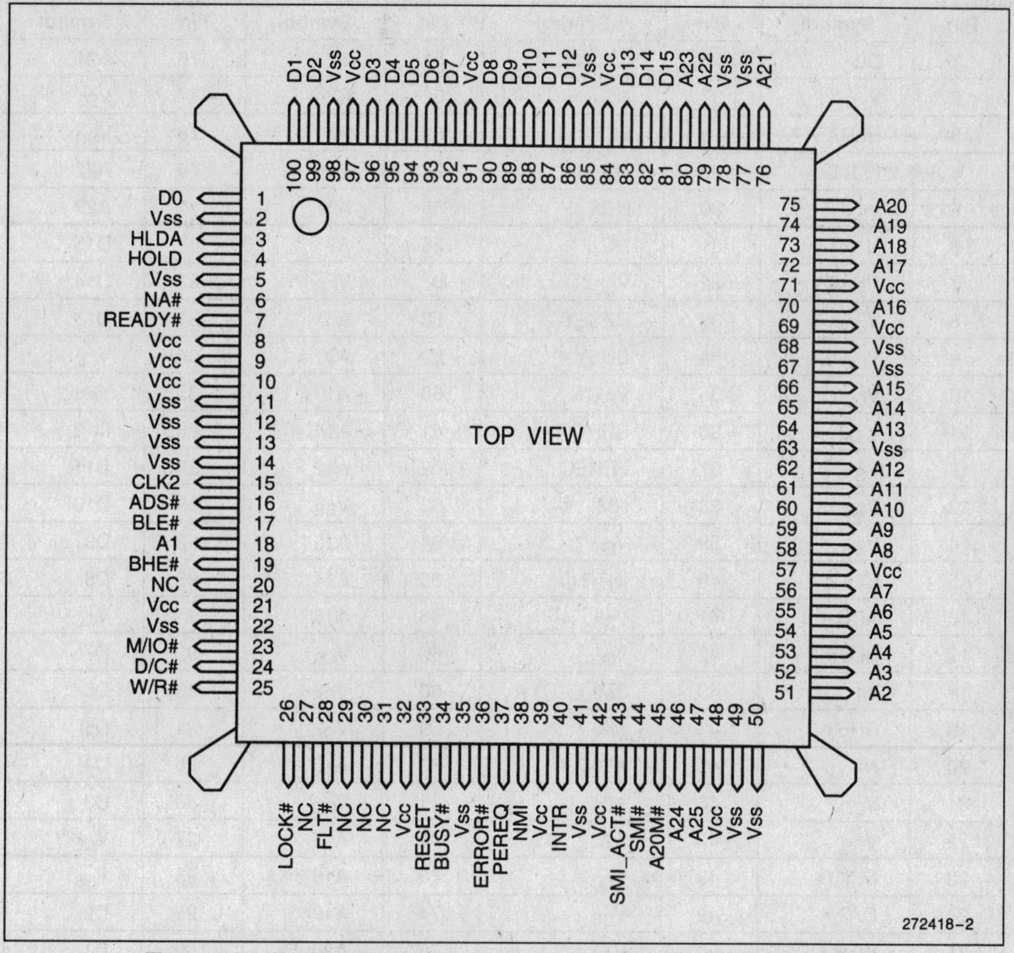

D1 100
D2 99
Vss 98
Vcc 97
D3 96
D4 95
D5 94
D6 93
D7 92
Vcc 91
D8 90
D9 89
D10 88
D11 87
D12 86
Vss 85
Vcc 84
D13 83
D14 82
D15 81
A23 80
A22 79
Vss 78
Vss 77
A21 76

D0 1
Vss 2
HLDA 3
HOLD 4
Vss 5
NA# 6
READY# 7
Vcc 8
Vcc 9
Vcc 10
Vss 11
Vss 12
Vss 13
Vss 14
CLK2 15
ADS# 16
BLE# 17
A1 18
BHE# 19
NC 20
Vcc 21
Vss 22
M/IO# 23
D/C# 24
W/R# 25

TOP VIEW

75 A20
74 A19
73 A18
72 A17
71 Vcc
70 A16
69 Vcc
68 Vss
67 Vss
66 A15
65 A14
64 A13
63 Vss
62 A12
61 A11
60 A10
59 A9
58 A8
57 Vcc
56 A7
55 A6
54 A5
53 A4
52 A3
51 A2

26 LOCK#
27 NC
28 FLT#
29 NC
30 NC
31 NC
32 Vcc
33 RESET
34 BUSY#
35 Vss
36 ERROR#
37 PEREQ
38 NMI
39 Vcc
40 INTR
41 Vss
42 Vcc
43 SMI_ACT#
44 SMI#
45 A20M#
46 A24
47 A25
48 Vcc
49 Vss
50 Vss

272418–2

Figure 2. Intel386™ CX Microprocessor Pin Assignment (PQFP and SQFP)

4

Table 1. Pin Assignment

Pin	Symbol	Pin	Symbol	Pin	Symbol	Pin	Symbol
1	D0	26	LOCK#	51	A2	76	A21
2	V_{SS}	27	NC	52	A3	77	V_{SS}
3	HLDA	28	FLT#	53	A4	78	V_{SS}
4	HOLD	29	NC	54	A5	79	A22
5	V_{SS}	30	NC	55	A6	80	A23
6	NA#	31	NC	56	A7	81	D15
7	READY#	32	V_{CC}	57	V_{CC}	82	D14
8	V_{CC}	33	RESET	58	A8	83	D13
9	V_{CC}	34	BUSY#	59	A9	84	V_{CC}
10	V_{CC}	35	V_{SS}	60	A10	85	V_{SS}
11	V_{SS}	36	ERROR#	61	A11	86	D12
12	V_{SS}	37	PEREQ	62	A12	87	D11
13	V_{SS}	38	NMI	63	V_{SS}	88	D10
14	V_{SS}	39	V_{CC}	64	A13	89	D9
15	CLK2	40	INTR	65	A14	90	D8
16	ADS#	41	V_{SS}	66	A15	91	V_{CC}
17	BLE#	42	V_{CC}	67	V_{SS}	92	D7
18	A1	43	SMI_ACT#	68	V_{SS}	93	D6
19	BHE#	44	SMI#	69	V_{CC}	94	D5
20	NC	45	A20M#	70	A16	95	D4
21	V_{CC}	46	A24	71	V_{CC}	96	D3
22	V_{SS}	47	A25	72	A17	97	V_{CC}
23	M/IO#	48	V_{CC}	73	A18	98	V_{SS}
24	D/C#	49	V_{SS}	74	A19	99	D2
25	W/R#	50	V_{SS}	75	A20	100	D1

2.0 PIN DESCRIPTIONS

Table 2 lists the Intel386 CX Microprocessor pin descriptions. The following definitions are used in the pin descriptions:

#	The named signal is active low.
I	Input signal.
O	Output signal.
I/O	Input and Output signal.
P	Power pin.
G	Ground pin.

Table 2. Pin Descriptions

Symbol	Type	Pin	Name and Function
A20M#(1)	I	45	**Address 20 Mask** controls the A20 address signal. When A20M# is low, the CPU masks off (forces low) the internal A20 physical address signal. This enables the CPU to run software that was developed using the 8086 address "wraparound" techniques. When A20M# is high, A20 is available on the address bus. While the bus is floating, A20M# has no effect on the A20 address signal. A20M# should be deasserted during SMM if the SMM handler accesses more than 1 Mbyte of memory.
A25:1(2)	O	47–46, 80–79, 76–72, 70, 66, 64, 62–58, 56–51, 18	**Address Bus** outputs physical memory or port I/O addresses.
ADS#	O	16	**Address Status** indicates that the processor is driving a valid bus-cycle definition and address onto its pins (W/R#, D/C#, M/IO#, BHE#, BLE#, and A25:1).
BHE#	O	19	**Byte High Enable** indicates that the processor is transferring a high data byte.
BLE#	O	17	**Byte Low Enable** indicates that the processor is transferring a low data byte.
BUSY#	I	34	**Busy** indicates that the math coprocessor is busy.
CLK2	I	15	**CLK2** provides the fundamental timing for the device.
D/C#	O	24	**Data/Control** indicates whether the current bus cycle is a data cycle (memory or I/O) or a control cycle (interrupt acknowledge, halt, or code fetch). When D/C# is high, the bus cycle is a data cycle; when D/C# is low, the bus cycle is a control cycle.

NOTES:
1. This pin supports the additional features of the Intel386 CX Microprocessor; it is not present on the Intel386 SX Microprocessor.
2. The A25:24 pins support the additional features of the Intel386 CX Microprocessor; they are not present on the Intel386 SX Microprocessor.

Table 2. Pin Descriptions (Continued)

Symbol	Type	Pin	Name and Function
D15:0	I/O	81–83, 86–90, 92–96, 99–100, 1	**Data Bus** inputs data during memory read, I/O read, and interrupt acknowledge cycles and outputs data during memory and I/O write cycles.
ERROR#	I	36	**Error** indicates that the math coprocessor has an error condition.
FLT#	I	28	**Float** forces all bidirectional and output signals, including HLDA, to a high-impedance state.
HLDA	O	3	**Bus Hold Acknowledge** indicates that the CPU has surrendered control of its local bus to another bus master.
HOLD	I	4	**Bus Hold Request** allows another bus master to request control of the local bus.
INTR	I	40	**Interrupt Request** is a maskable input that causes the CPU to suspend execution of the current program and then execute an interrupt acknowledge cycle.
LOCK#	O	26	**Bus Lock** prevents other system bus masters from gaining control of the system bus while it is active (low).
M/IO#	O	23	**Memory/IO** indicates whether the current bus cycle is a memory cycle or an input/output cycle. When M/IO# is high, the bus cycle is a memory cycle; when M/IO# is low, the bus cycle is an I/O cycle.
NA#	I	6	**Next Address** requests address pipelining.
NC		20, 27, 29–31	**No Connection** should always be left unconnected. Connecting a NC pin may cause the processor to malfunction or cause your application to be incompatible with future steppings of the device.
NMI	I	38	**Non-Maskable Interrupt Request** is a non-maskable input that causes the CPU to suspend execution of the current program and execute an interrupt acknowledge function.
PEREQ	I	37	**Processor Extension Request** indicates that the math coprocessor has data to transfer to the processor.
READY#	I	7	**Bus Ready** indicates that the current bus cycle is finished and the external device is ready to accept more data from the processor.

NOTES:
1. This pin supports the additional features of the Intel386 CX Microprocessor; it is not present on the Intel386 SX Microprocessor.
2. The A25:24 pins support the additional features of the Intel386 CX Microprocessor; they are not present on the Intel386 SX Microprocessor.

Table 2. Pin Descriptions (Continued)

Symbol	Type	Pin	Name and Function
RESET	I	33	**RESET** suspends any operation in progress and places the processor into a known reset state.
SMI# (1)	I	44	**System Management Interrupt** invokes System Management Mode (SMM). SMI# is the highest priority interrupt. It is latched on its falling edge and it forces the CPU into SMM upon completion of the current instruction. SMI# is recognized on an instruction boundary and at each iteration for repeat string instructions. SMI# cannot interrupt LOCKed bus cycles or a currently executing SMM. If the processor receives a second SMI# while it is in SMM, it will latch the second SMI# on the SMI# falling edge. However, the processor must exit SMM by executing a Resume instruction (RSM) before it can service the second SMI#.
SMI_ACT# (1)	O	43	**System Management Interrupt Active** indicates that the processor is operating in System Management Mode (SMM). It is asserted when the processor initiates an SMM sequence and remains asserted (low) until the processor executes the Resume instruction (RSM).
W/R#	O	25	**Write/Read** indicates whether the current bus cycle is a write cycle or a read cycle. When W/R# is high, the bus cycle is a write cycle; when W/R# is low, it is a read cycle.
V_{CC}	P	8–10, 21, 32, 39, 42, 48, 57, 69, 71, 84, 91, 97	**System Power** provides the nominal DC supply input.
V_{SS}	G	2, 5, 11–14, 22 35, 41, 49–50, 63, 67–68, 77–78, 85, 98	**System Ground** provides the 0V connection from which all inputs and outputs are measured.

NOTES:
1. This pin supports the additional features of the Intel386 CX Microprocessor; it is not present on the Intel386 SX Microprocessor.
2. The A25:24 pins support the additional features of the Intel386 CX Microprocessor; they are not present on the Intel386 SX Microprocessor.

4

3.0 DESIGN CONSIDERATIONS

This section describes the Intel386 CX Microprocessor's instruction set and its component and revision identifiers.

3.1 Instruction Set

The Intel386 CX Microprocessor uses the same instruction set as the Intel386 SX Microprocessor with the following exceptions.

The Intel386 CX Microprocessor has one new instruction (RSM). This Resume instruction causes the processor to exit System Management Mode (SMM). RSM requires 338 clocks per instruction (CPI).

The Intel386 CX Microprocessor requires more clock cycles than the Intel386 SX Microprocessor to execute some instructions. Table 3 lists these instructions and the Intel386 CX Microprocessor CPI. For the equivalent Intel386 SX Microprocessor CPI, refer to the "Instruction Set Clock Count Summary" table in the *Intel386™ SX Microprocessor* data sheet (order number 240187).

3.2 Component and Revision Identifiers

To assist users, the microprocessor holds a component identifier and revision identifier in its DX register after reset. The upper 8 bits of DX hold the component identifier, 23H. (The lower nibble, 03H, identifies the Intel386 Architecture, while the upper nibble, 02H, identifies the second member of the Intel386 Microprocessor family.)

The lower 8 bits of DX hold the revision level identifier. The revision identifier will, in general, chronologically track those component steppings that are intended to have certain improvements or distinction from previous steppings. The revision identifier will track that of the Intel386 CPU whenever possible. However, the revision identifier value is not guaranteed to change with every stepping revision or to follow a completely uniform numerical sequence, depending on the type or intent of the revision or the manufacturing materials required to be changed. Intel has sole discretion over these characteristics of the component. The initial revision identifier for the Intel386 CX Microprocessor is 09H.

Table 3. Intel386™ CX Microprocessor Clocks Per Instruction

Instruction	Clock Count		
	Virtual 8086 Mode(1)	Real Address Mode or Virtual 8086 Mode	Protected Virtual Address Mode(3)
POPA		28	35
IN:			
Fixed Port	27	14	7/29
Variable Port	28	15	8/29
OUT:			
Fixed Port	27	14	7/29
Variable Port	28	15	9/29
INS	30	17	9/32
OUTS	31	18	10/33
REP INS	31 + 6n(2)	17 + 6n(2)	10 + 6n/32 + 6n(2)
REP OUTS	30 + 8n(2)	16 + 8n(2)	10 + 8n/31 + 8n(2)
HLT		7	7
MOV C0, reg		10	10

NOTES:
1. The clock count values in this column apply if I/O permission allows I/O to the port in virtual 8086 mode. If the I/O bit map denies permission, exception fault 13 occurs; see clock counts for the INT 3 instruction in the "Instruction Set Clock Count Summary" table in the *Intel386™ SX Microprocessor* data sheet (order number 240187).
2. n = the number of times repeated.
3. When two clock counts are listed, the smaller value refers to a register operand and the larger value refers to a memory operand.

4

4.0 DC SPECIFICATIONS

ABSOLUTE MAXIMUM RATINGS*

Storage Temperature .... −65°C to +150°C

Case Temperature Under Bias... −65°C to +110°C

Supply Voltage with Respect to V_{SS}.. −0.5V to 6.5V

Voltage on Other Pins .... −0.5V to V_{CC} + 0.5V

OPERATING CONDITIONS*

Digital Supply Voltage (V_{CC}) ....2.7V to 5.5V

Case Temperature
  Under Bias (T_{CASE}) ....0°C to 100°C

Operating Frequency (F_{OSC}) .....0 MHz to 25 MHz

NOTICE: This document contains information on products in the design phase of development. Do not finalize a design with this information. Revised information will be published when the product is available. Verify with your local Intel Sales office that you have the latest data sheet before finalizing a design.

**WARNING: Stressing the device beyond the "Absolute Maximum Ratings" may cause permanent damage. These are stress ratings only. Operation beyond the "Operating Conditions" is not recommended and extended exposure beyond the "Operating Conditions" may affect device reliability.*

Table 4. DC Characteristics

Symbol	Parameter	Min	Max	Unit	Test Condition
V_{IL}	Input Low Voltage	−0.5	0.3 V_{CC}	V	
V_{IH}	Input High Voltage	0.7 V_{CC}	V_{CC} + 0.5	V	
V_{ILC}	CLK2 Input Low Voltage	−0.3	+0.8	V	
V_{IHC}	CLK2 Input High Voltage	V_{CC} − 0.6 V_{CC} − 0.8	V_{CC} + 0.3 V_{CC} + 0.3	V V	V_{CC} = 2.7V to 3.6V V_{CC} = 4.5V to 5.5V
V_{OL}	Output Low Voltage I_{OL} = 2 mA I_{OL} = 0.5 mA		 0.4 0.2	 V V	
V_{OH}	Output High Voltage I_{OH} = −0.5 mA I_{OH} = −0.1 mA	 V_{CC} − 0.4 V_{CC} − 0.2		 V V	 V_{CC} = 2.7V to 5.5V V_{CC} = 2.7V to 3.6V
I_{LI}	Input Leakage Current (for all pins except PEREQ, BUSY#, FLT#, ERROR#, A20M#, SMI#)		±15	μA	0 ≤ V_{IN} ≤ V_{CC}
I_{IH}	Input Leakage Current (PEREQ)		150 300	μA μA	V_{IH} = 2.2V, V_{CC} = 2.7V V_{IH} = 5.4V, V_{CC} = 5.5V(1)
I_{IL}	Input Leakage Current (BUSY#, FLT#, ERROR#, A20M#, and SMI#)		 −120 −130	 μA μA	(Note 2) V_{IL} = 0.45V, V_{CC} = 5.5V V_{IL} = 0.1V, V_{CC} = 5.5V

NOTES:
1. PEREQ input has an internal weak pull-down resistor.
2. BUSY#, FLT#, SMI#, A20M and ERROR# inputs each have an internal weak pull-up resistor.
3. I_{CC} max and I_{CCF} max measurement at worst-case frequency, V_{CC} and temperature, with 50 pF output load.
4. I_{CC} typ and I_{CCF} typ are measured at nominal V_{CC} and are not fully tested.
5. Not fully tested.

Table 4. DC Characteristics (Continued)

Symbol	Parameter	Min	Max	Unit	Test Conditions
I_{LO}	Output Leakage Current		±15	μA	$0.45V \leq V_{OUT} \leq V_{CC}$
I_{CC}	Supply Current				(Notes 3, 4)
	CLK2 = 50 MHz, CLK = 25 MHz		280	mA	typ = 210 mA
	CLK2 = 40 MHz, CLK = 20 MHz		160	mA	typ = 120 mA
	CLK2 = 24 MHz, CLK = 12 MHz		100	mA	typ = 70 mA
I_{CCF}	Standby Current (Freeze Mode)				(Notes 3, 4)
	CLK2 = 50 MHz, CLK = 25 MHz		TBD	μA	I_{CCF} typ = 20 μA, V_{CC} = 5V
	CLK2 = 40 MHz, CLK = 20 MHz		TBD	μA	I_{CCF} typ = 10 μA, V_{CC} = 3.3V
	CLK2 = 24 MHz, CLK = 12 MHz		TBD	μA	I_{CCF} typ = 10 μA, V_{CC} = 3V
C_{IN}	Input Capacitance		10	pF	F_C = 1 MHz[5]
C_{OUT}	Output or I/O Capacitance		12	pF	F_C = 1 MHz[5]
C_{CLK}	CLK2 Capacitance		20	pF	F_C = 1 MHz[5]

NOTES:
1. PEREQ input has an internal weak pull-down resistor.
2. BUSY#, FLT#, SMI#, A20M and ERROR# inputs each have an internal weak pull-up resistor.
3. I_{CC} max and I_{CCF} max measurement at worst-case frequency, V_{CC} and temperature, with 50 pF output load.
4. I_{CC} typ and I_{CCF} typ are measured at nominal V_{CC} and are not fully tested.
5. Not fully tested.

5.0 AC SPECIFICATIONS

Table 5 lists output delays, input setup requirements, and input hold requirements. All AC specifications are relative to the CLK2 rising edge crossing the $V_{CC}/2$ level.

Figure 3 shows the measurement points for AC specifications. Inputs must be driven to the indicated voltage levels when AC specifications are measured. Output delays are specified with minimum and maximum limits measured as shown. The minimum delay times are hold times provided to external circuitry. Input setup and hold times are specified as minimums, defining the smallest acceptable sampling window. Within the sampling window, a synchronous input signal must be stable for correct operation.

Outputs ADS#, W/R#, D/C#, MI/O#, LOCK#, BHE#, BLE#, A25:1, HLDA and SMI_ACT# change only at the beginning of phase one. D15:0 (write cycles) change only at the beginning of phase two.

The READY#, HOLD, BUSY#, ERROR#, PEREQ, FLT#, A20M# and D15:0 (read cycles) inputs are sampled at the beginning of phase one. The NA#, INTR, SMI# and NMI inputs are sampled at the beginning of phase two.

4

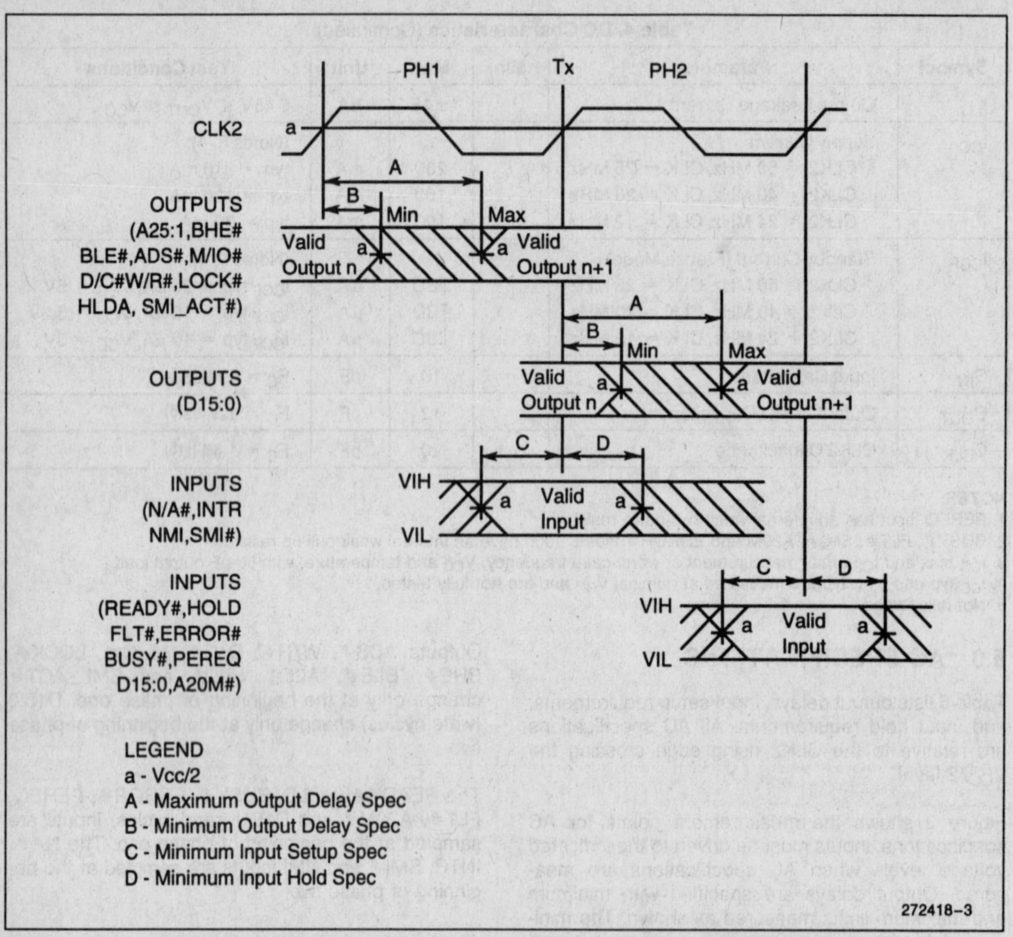

PH1 Tx PH2

CLK2 a

A
B
Min Max

OUTPUTS
(A25:1,BHE#
BLE#,ADS#,M/IO#
D/C#W/R#,LOCK#
HLDA, SMI_ACT#)

Valid Output n a a Valid Output n+1

A
B
Min Max

OUTPUTS
(D15:0)

Valid Output n a a Valid Output n+1

C D

INPUTS
(N/A#,INTR
NMI,SMI#)

VIH a Valid Input a
VIL

C D

INPUTS
(READY#,HOLD
FLT#,ERROR#
BUSY#,PEREQ
D15:0,A20M#)

VIH a Valid Input a
VIL

LEGEND
a - Vcc/2
A - Maximum Output Delay Spec
B - Minimum Output Delay Spec
C - Minimum Input Setup Spec
D - Minimum Input Hold Spec

272418–3

Figure 3. Drive Levels and Measurement Points for AC Specifications

Table 5. AC Characteristics

Symbol	Parameter	25 MHz 4.5V to 5.5V		20 MHz 3.0V to 3.6V		12 MHz 2.7V to 3.3V		Test Conditions(1)
		Min (ns)	Max (ns)	Min (ns)	Max (ns)	Min (ns)	Max (ns)	
	Operating Frequency	0	25	0	20	0	12.5	MHz(2)
t1	CLK2 Period	20		25		40		
t2a	CLK2 High Time	7		8		11		at $V_{CC}/2$(3)
t2b	CLK2 High Time	4		5		7		at $V_{CC} - 0.8V$ for HV, at $V_{CC} - 0.6V$ for LV(3)
t3a	CLK2 Low Time	7		8		11		at $V_{CC}/2$(3)
t3b	CLK2 Low Time	5		6		9		at 0.8V(3)
t4	CLK2 Fall Time		7		8		8	$V_{CC} - 0.8V$ to 0.8V for HV, $V_{CC} - 0.6V$ to 0.8V for LV(3)
t5	CLK2 Rise Time		7		8		8	0.8V to $V_{CC} - 0.8V$ for HV, 0.8V to $V_{CC} - 0.6V$ for LV(3)
t6	A25:1 Valid Delay	4	17	4	30	4	42	C_L = 50 pF(4)
t7	A25:1 Float Delay	4	30	4	32	4	45	(Note 5)

NOTES:

1. Throughout this table, HV refers to devices operating with V_{CC} = 4.5V to 5.5V. LV refers to devices operating with V_{CC} = 2.7V to 3.6V.
2. Tested at maximum operating frequency and guaranteed by design characterization at lower operating frequencies.
3. These are not tested. They are guaranteed by characterization.
4. Tested with C_L set at 50 pF. For the LV products, the t6 and t12 timings are guaranteed by design characterization with C_L set at 120 pF and all other Note 4 timings are guaranteed with C_L set at 75 pF.
5. Float condition occurs when maximum output current becomes less than I_{LO} in magnitude. Float delay is not fully tested.
6. These inputs may be asynchronous to CLK2. The setup and hold specifications are given for testing purposes to ensure recognition within a specific CLK2 period.

4

Table 5. AC Characteristics (Continued)

Symbol	Parameter	25 MHz 4.5V to 5.5V		20 MHz 3.0V to 3.6V		12 MHz 2.7V to 3.3V		Test Conditions(1)
		Min (ns)	Max (ns)	Min (ns)	Max (ns)	Min (ns)	Max (ns)	
t8	BHE#, BLE#, LOCK# Valid Delay	4	17	4	30	4	36	C_L = 50 pF(4)
t8a	SMI_ACT# Valid Delay	4	17	4	26	4	33	C_L = 50 pF(4)
t9	BHE#, BLE#, LOCK# Float Delay	4	30	4	32	4	40	(Note 5)
t10	W/R#, M/IO#, D/C#, ADS# Valid Delay	4	17	4	26	4	33	C_L = 50 pF(4)
t11	W/R#, M/IO#, D/C#, ADS# Float Delay	4	30	4	30	4	35	(Note 5)
t12	D15:0 Write Data Valid Delay	4	23	4	38	4	50	C_L = 50 pF(4)
t13	D15:0 Write Data Float Delay	4	22	4	27	4	35	(Note 5)
t14	HLDA Valid Delay	4	22	4	28	4	33	C_L = 50 pF(4)
t15	NA# Setup Time	5		5		7		
t16	NA# Hold Time	3		12		21		
t19	READY#, A20M# Setup Time	9		12		19		
t20	READY#, A20M# Hold Time	4		4		4		
t21	D15:0 Read Setup Time	7		9		9		

NOTES:
1. Throughout this table, HV refers to devices operating with V_{CC} = 4.5V to 5.5V. LV refers to devices operating with V_{CC} = 2.7V to 3.6V.
2. Tested at maximum operating frequency and guaranteed by design characterization at lower operating frequencies.
3. These are not tested. They are guaranteed by characterization.
4. Tested with C_L set at 50 pF. For the LV products, the t6 and t12 timings are guaranteed by design characterization with C_L set at 120 pF and all other Note 4 timings are guaranteed with C_L set at 75 pF.
5. Float condition occurs when maximum output current becomes less than I_{LO} in magnitude. Float delay is not fully tested.
6. These inputs may be asynchronous to CLK2. The setup and hold specifications are given for testing purposes to ensure recognition within a specific CLK2 period.

Table 5. AC Characteristics (Continued)

Symbol	Parameter	25 MHz 4.5V to 5.5V		20 MHz 3.0V to 3.6V		12 MHz 2.7V to 3.3V		Test Conditions(1)
		Min (ns)	Max (ns)	Min (ns)	Max (ns)	Min (ns)	Max (ns)	
t22	D15:0 Read Hold Time	5		6		6		
t23	HOLD Setup Time	9		17		26		
t24	HOLD Hold Time	3		5		7		
t25	RESET Setup Time	8		12		15		
t26	RESET Hold Time	3		4		6		
t27	NMI, INTR Setup Time	6		16		16		(Note 6)
t27a	SMI# Setup Time	6		16		16		(Note 6)
t28	NMI, INTR Hold Time	6		16		16		(Note 6)
t28a	SMI# Hold Time	6		16		16		(Note 6)
t29	PEREQ, ERROR#, BUSY#, FLT# Setup Time	6		14		16		(Note 6)
t30	PEREQ, ERROR#, BUSY#, FLT# Hold Time	5		5		5		(Note 6)

NOTES:

1. Throughout this table, HV refers to devices operating with V_{CC} = 4.5V to 5.5V. LV refers to devices operating with V_{CC} = 2.7V to 3.6V.
2. Tested at maximum operating frequency and guaranteed by design characterization at lower operating frequencies.
3. These are not tested. They are guaranteed by characterization.
4. Tested with C_L set at 50 pF. For the LV products, the t6 and t12 timings are guaranteed by design characterization with C_L set at 120 pF and all other Note 4 timings are guaranteed with C_L set at 75 pF.
5. Float condition occurs when maximum output current becomes less than I_{LO} in magnitude. Float delay is not fully tested.
6. These inputs may be asynchronous to CLK2. The setup and hold specifications are given for testing purposes to ensure recognition within a specific CLK2 period.

4

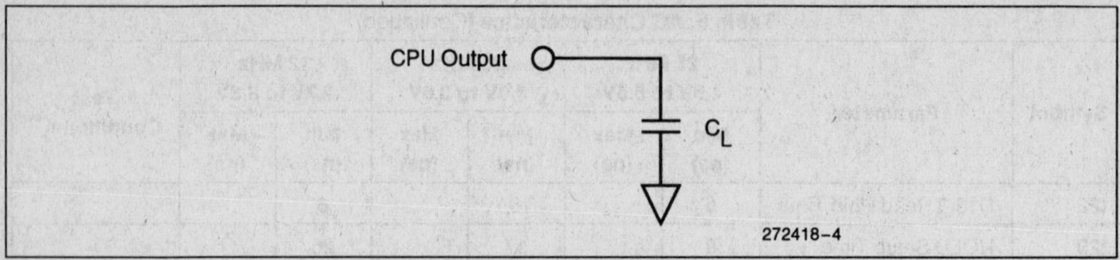

Figure 4. AC Test Loads

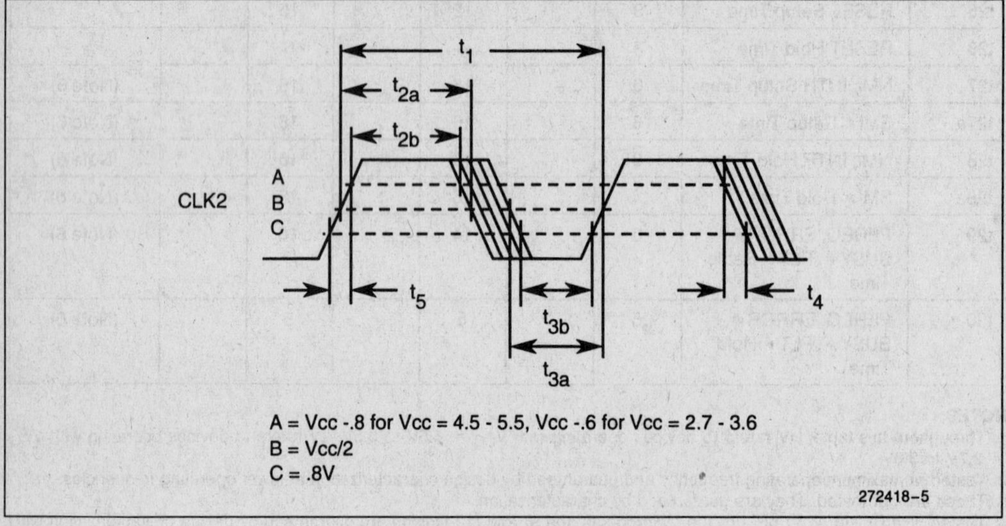

Figure 5. CLK2 Waveform

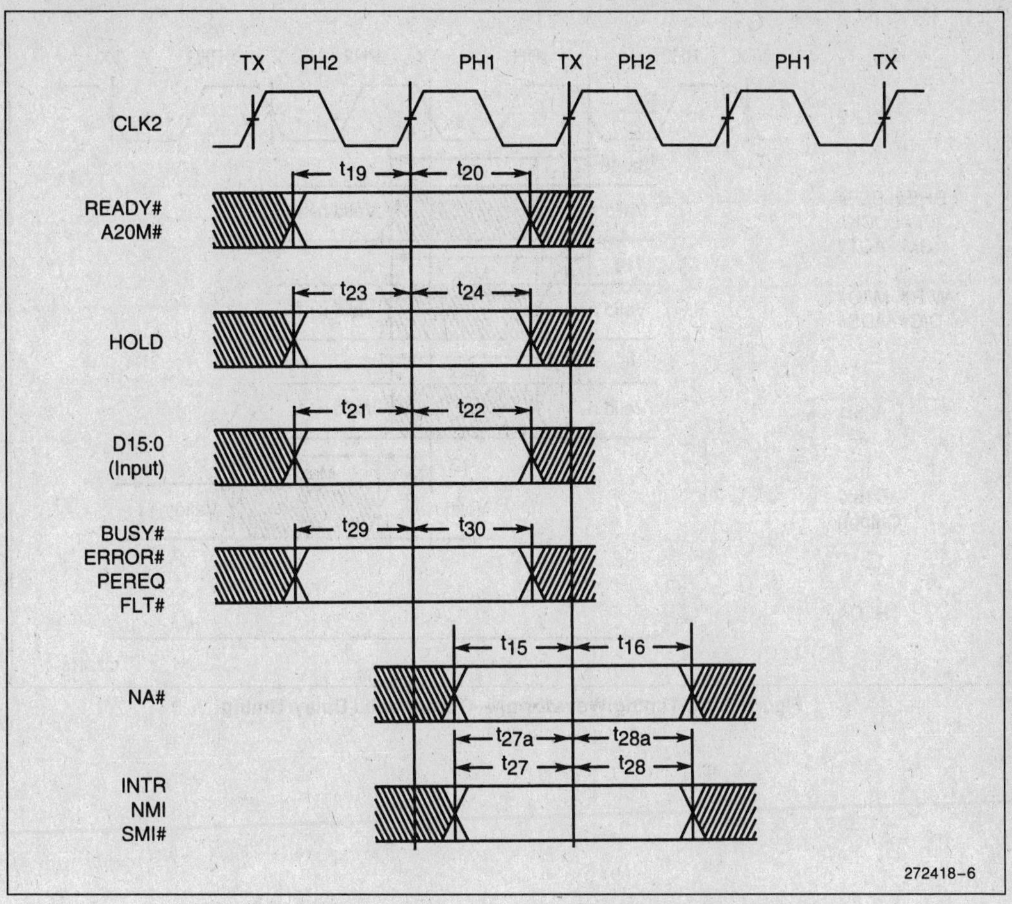

Figure 6. AC Timing Waveforms—Input Setup and Hold Timing

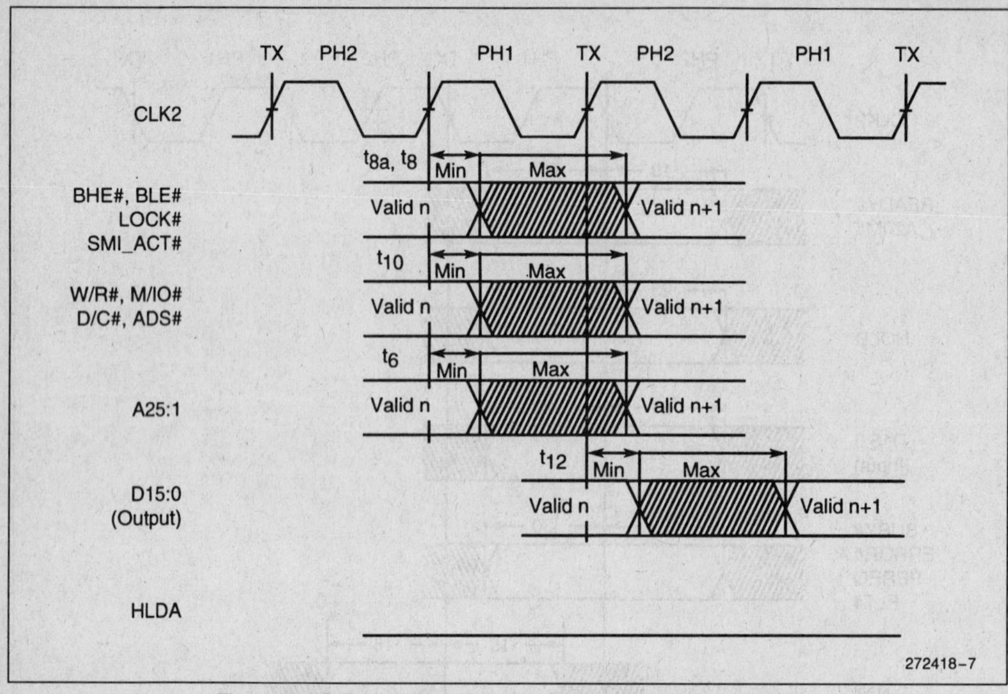

Figure 7. AC Timing Waveforms—Output Valid Delay Timing

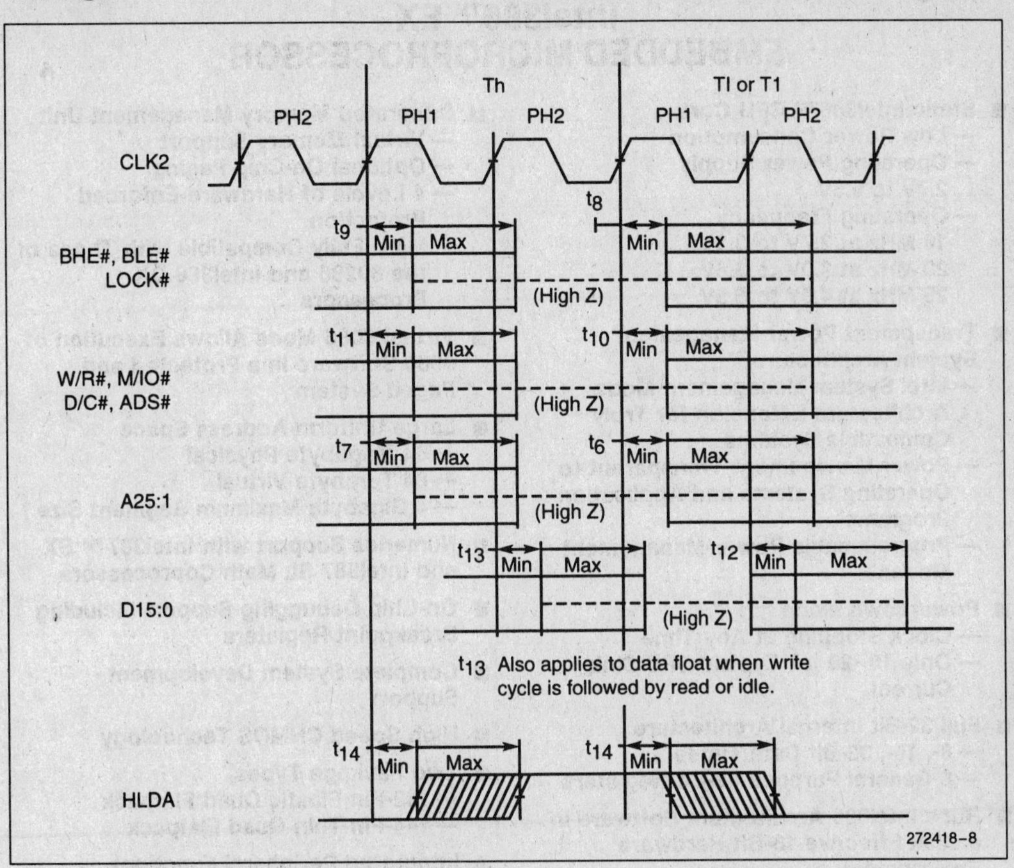

Th
Tl or T1
PH2 PH1 PH2 PH1 PH2
CLK2
t_8
t_9 Min Max
BHE#, BLE#
LOCK#
(High Z)
t_{11} Min Max
t_{10} Min Max
W/R#, M/IO#
D/C#, ADS#
(High Z)
t_7 Min Max
t_6 Min Max
A25:1
(High Z)
t_{13} Min Max
t_{12} Min Max
D15:0
(High Z)
t_{13} Also applies to data float when write cycle is followed by read or idle.
t_{14} Min Max
t_{14} Min Max
HLDA
272418–8

Figure 8. AC Timing Waveforms—Output Float Delay and HLDA Valid Delay Timing

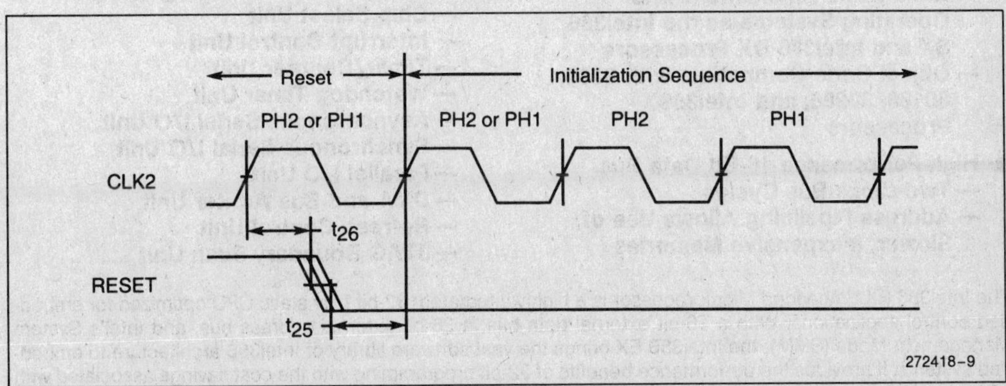

Figure 9. AC Timing Waveforms—RESET Setup and Hold Timing and Internal Phase

PRODUCT PREVIEW

Intel386™ EX EMBEDDED MICROPROCESSOR

- Static Intel386™ CPU Core
  - — Low Power Consumption
  - — Operating Power Supply 2.7V to 5.5V
  - — Operating Frequency 16 MHz at 2.7V to 3.3V; 20 MHz at 3.0V to 3.6V; 25 MHz at 4.5V to 5.5V
- Transparent Power-Management System Architecture
  - — Intel System Management Mode Architecture Extension for Truly Compatible Systems
  - — Power Management Transparent to Operating Systems and Application Programs
  - — Programmable Power-Management Modes
- Powerdown Mode
  - — Clock Stopping at Any Time
  - — Only 10–20 μA Typical CPU Sink Current
- Full 32-Bit Internal Architecture
  - — 8-, 16-, 32-Bit Data Types
  - — 8 General Purpose 32-Bit Registers
- Runs Intel386 Architecture Software in a Cost Effective 16-Bit Hardware Environment
  - — Runs Same Applications and Operating Systems as the Intel386 SX and Intel386 DX Processors
  - — Object Code Compatible with 8086, 80186, 80286, and Intel386 Processors
- High Performance 16-Bit Data Bus
  - — Two-Clock Bus Cycles
  - — Address Pipelining Allows Use of Slower, Inexpensive Memories
- Integrated Memory Management Unit
  - — Virtual Memory Support
  - — Optional On-Chip Paging
  - — 4 Levels of Hardware-Enforced Protection
  - — MMU Fully Compatible with Those of the 80286 and Intel386 DX Processors
- Virtual 8086 Mode Allows Execution of 8086 Software in a Protected and Paged System
- Large Uniform Address Space
  - — 64 Megabyte Physical
  - — 64 Terabyte Virtual
  - — 4 Gigabyte Maximum Segment Size
- Numerics Support with Intel387™ SX and Intel387 SL Math Coprocessors
- On-Chip Debugging Support Including Breakpoint Registers
- Complete System Development Support
- High Speed CHMOS Technology
- Two Package Types
  - — 132-Pin Plastic Quad Flatpack
  - — 144-Pin Thin Quad Flatpack
- Integrated Peripheral Functions
  - — Clock and Power Management Unit
  - — Chip Select Unit
  - — Interrupt Control Unit
  - — Timer/Counter Unit
  - — Watchdog Timer Unit
  - — Asynchronous Serial I/O Unit
  - — Synchronous Serial I/O Unit
  - — Parallel I/O Unit
  - — DMA and Bus Arbiter Unit
  - — Refresh Control Unit
  - — JTAG Boundary Scan Unit

The Intel386 EX Embedded Microprocessor is a highly integrated, 32-bit fully static CPU optimized for embedded control applications. With a 16-bit external data bus, a 26-bit external address bus, and Intel's System Management Mode (SMM), the Intel386 EX brings the vast software library of Intel386 architecture to embedded systems. It provides the performance benefits of 32-bit programming with the cost savings associated with 16-bit hardware systems.

October 1993
Order Number: 272420-001

Intel386™ EX Embedded Microprocessor

CONTENTS PAGE

1.0 PIN ASSIGNMENT 4-23

2.0 PIN DESCRIPTIONS 4-27

3.0 FUNCTIONAL DESCRIPTION 4-32

3.1 Clock Generation and Power Management Unit 4-32

3.2 Chip Select Unit 4-32

3.3 Interrupt Control Unit 4-32

3.4 Timer/Counter Unit 4-33

3.5 Watchdog Timer Unit 4-33

3.6 Asynchronous Serial I/O Unit 4-33

3.7 Synchronous Serial I/O Unit 4-33

3.8 Parallel I/O Unit 4-34

3.9 DMA and Bus Arbiter Unit 4-34

3.10 Refresh Control Unit 4-34

3.11 JTAG Boundary Scan Unit 4-35

4.0 DESIGN CONSIDERATIONS 4-35

4.1 Instruction Set 4-35

4.2 Component and Revision Identifiers 4-35

5.0 DC SPECIFICATIONS 4-37

6.0 AC SPECIFICATIONS 4-38

4

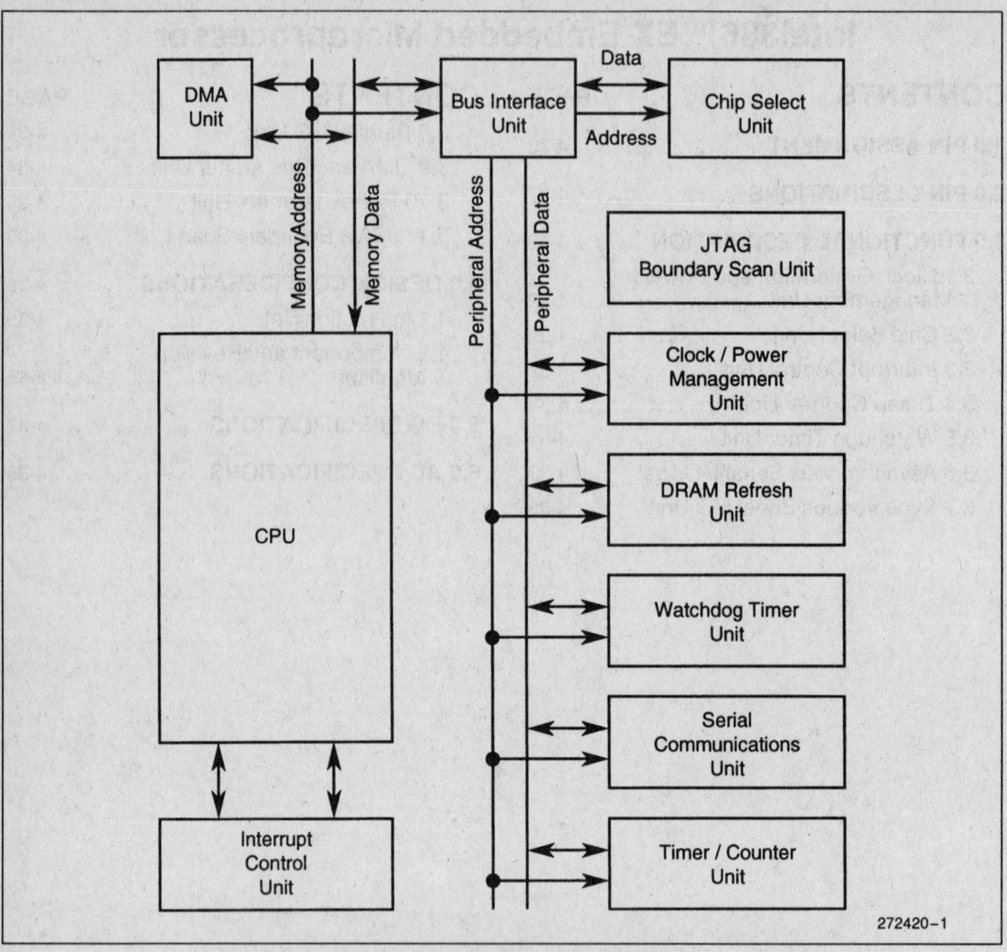

DMA Unit
Bus Interface Unit
Data
Address
Chip Select Unit
MemoryAddress
Memory Data
Peripheral Address
Peripheral Data
JTAG Boundary Scan Unit
CPU
Clock / Power Management Unit
DRAM Refresh Unit
Watchdog Timer Unit
Serial Communications Unit
Interrupt Control Unit
Timer / Counter Unit
272420–1

Figure 1. Intel386™ EX Microprocessor Block Diagram

1.0 PIN ASSIGNMENT

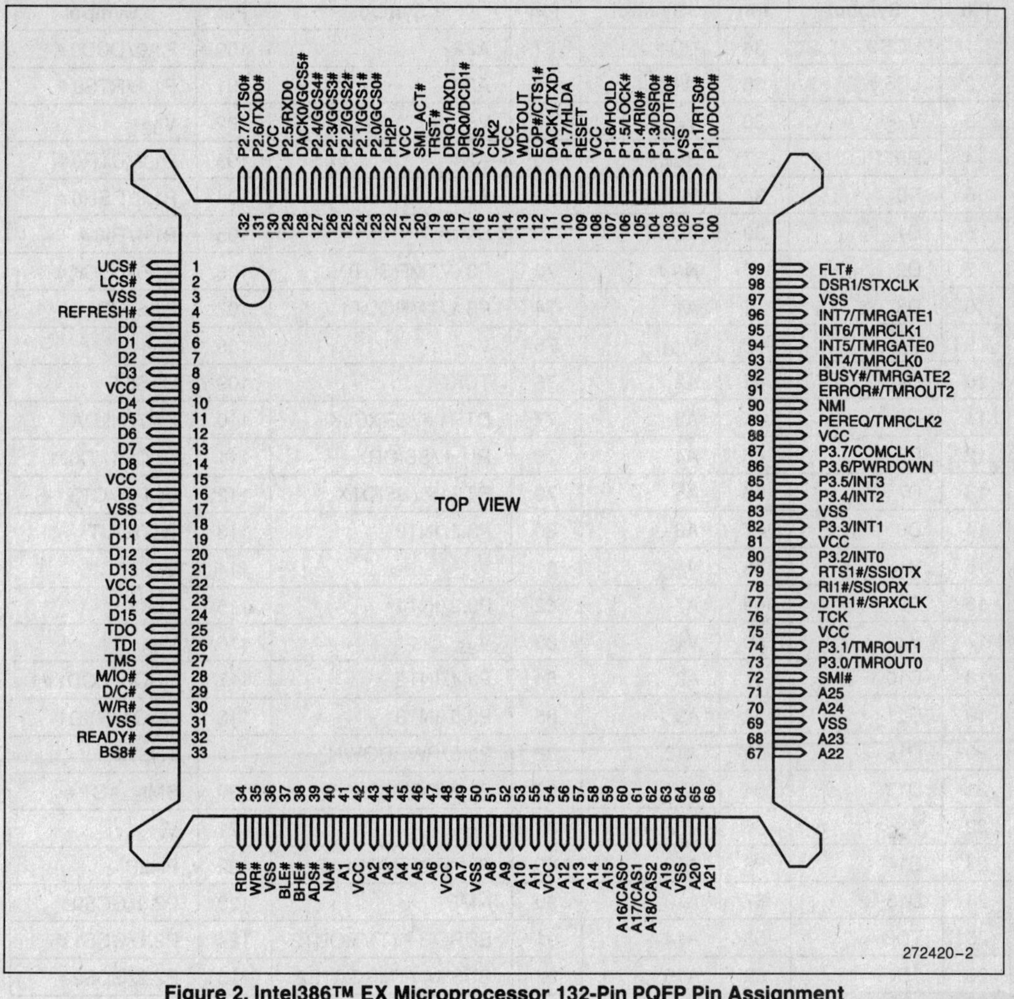

TOP VIEW

Pin	Name	Pin	Name	Pin	Name	Pin	Name
1	UCS#	34	RD#	67	A22	100	P1.0/DCD0#
2	LCS#	35	WR#	68	A23	101	P1.1/RTS0#
3	VSS	36	VSS	69	VSS	102	VSS
4	REFRESH#	37	BLE#	70	A24	103	P1.2/DTR0#
5	D0	38	BHE#	71	A25	104	P1.3/DSR0#
6	D1	39	ADS#	72	SMI#	105	P1.4/RI0#
7	D2	40	NA#	73	P3.0/TMROUT0	106	P1.5/LOCK#
8	D3	41	A1	74	P3.1/TMROUT1	107	P1.6/HOLD
9	VCC	42	VCC	75	VCC	108	VCC
10	D4	43	A2	76	TCK	109	RESET
11	D5	44	A3	77	DTR1#/SRXCLK	110	P1.7/HLDA
12	D6	45	A4	78	RI1#/SSIORX	111	DACK1/TXD1
13	D7	46	A5	79	RTS1#/SSIOTX	112	EOP#/CTS1#
14	D8	47	A6	80	P3.2/INT0	113	WDTOUT
15	VCC	48	VCC	81	VCC	114	VCC
16	D9	49	A7	82	P3.3/INT1	115	CLK2
17	VSS	50	VSS	83	VSS	116	VSS
18	D10	51	A8	84	P3.4/INT2	117	DRQ0/DCD1#
19	D11	52	A9	85	P3.5/INT3	118	DRQ1/RXD1
20	D12	53	A10	86	P3.6/PWRDOWN	119	TRST#
21	D13	54	A11	87	P3.7/COMCLK	120	SMI_ACT#
22	VCC	55	VCC	88	VCC	121	VCC
23	D14	56	A12	89	PEREQ/TMRCLK2	122	PH2P
24	D15	57	A13	90	NMI	123	P2.0/GCS0#
25	TDO	58	A14	91	ERROR#/TMROUT2	124	P2.1/GCS1#
26	TDI	59	A15	92	BUSY#/TMRGATE2	125	P2.2/GCS2#
27	TMS	60	A16/CAS0	93	INT4/TMRCLK0	126	P2.3/GCS3#
28	M/IO#	61	A17/CAS1	94	INT5/TMRGATE0	127	P2.4/GCS4#
29	D/C#	62	A18/CAS2	95	INT6/TMRCLK1	128	DACK0/GCS5#
30	W/R#	63	A19	96	INT7/TMRGATE1	129	P2.5/RXD0
31	VSS	64	VSS	97	VSS	130	VCC
32	READY#	65	A20	98	DSR1/STXCLK	131	P2.6/TXD0#
33	BS8#	66	A21	99	FLT#	132	P2.7/CTS0#

272420–2

Figure 2. Intel386™ EX Microprocessor 132-Pin PQFP Pin Assignment

4

Table 1. 132-Pin PQFP Pin Assignment

Pin	Symbol	Pin	Symbol	Pin	Symbol	Pin	Symbol
1	UCS#	34	RD#	67	A22	100	P1.0/DCD0#
2	LCS#	35	WR#	68	A23	101	P1.1/RTS0#
3	V_{SS}	36	V_{SS}	69	V_{SS}	102	V_{SS}
4	REFRESH#	37	BLE#	70	A24	103	P1.2/DTR0#
5	D0	38	BHE#	71	A25	104	P1.3/DSR0#
6	D1	39	ADS#	72	SMI#	105	P1.4/RI0#
7	D2	40	NA#	73	P3.0/TMROUT0	106	P1.5/LOCK#
8	D3	41	A1	74	P3.1/TMROUT1	107	P1.6/HOLD
9	V_{CC}	42	V_{CC}	75	V_{CC}	108	V_{CC}
10	D4	43	A2	76	TCK	109	RESET
11	D5	44	A3	77	DTR1#/SRXCLK	110	P1.7/HLDA
12	D6	45	A4	78	RI1#/SSIORX	111	DACK1/TXD1
13	D7	46	A5	79	RTS1#/SSIOTX	112	EOP#/CTS1#
14	D8	47	A6	80	P3.2/INT0	113	WDTOUT
15	V_{CC}	48	V_{CC}	81	V_{CC}	114	V_{CC}
16	D9	49	A7	82	P3.3/INT1	115	CLK2
17	V_{SS}	50	V_{SS}	83	V_{SS}	116	V_{SS}
18	D10	51	A8	84	P3.4/INT2	117	DRQ0/DCD1#
19	D11	52	A9	85	P3.5/INT3	118	DRQ1/RXD1
20	D12	53	A10	86	P3.6/PWRDOWN	119	TRST#
21	D13	54	A11	87	P3.7/COMCLK	120	SMI_ACT#
22	V_{CC}	55	V_{CC}	88	V_{CC}	121	V_{CC}
23	D14	56	A12	89	PEREQ/TMRCLK2	122	PH2P
24	D15	57	A13	90	NMI	123	P2.0/GCS0#
25	TDO	58	A14	91	ERROR#/TMROUT2	124	P2.1/GCS1#
26	TDI	59	A15	92	BUSY#/TMRGATE2	125	P2.2/GCS2#
27	TMS	60	A16/CAS0	93	INT4/TMRCLK0	126	P2.3/GCS3#
28	M/IO#	61	A17/CAS1	94	INT5/TMRGATE0	127	P2.4/GCS4#
29	D/C#	62	A18/CAS2	95	INT6/TMRCLK1	128	DACK0/GCS5#
30	W/R#	63	A19	96	INT7/TMRGATE1	129	P2.5/RXD0
31	V_{SS}	64	V_{SS}	97	V_{SS}	130	V_{SS}
32	READY#	65	A20	98	DSR1/STXCLK	131	P2.6/TXD0#
33	BS8#			99	FLT#	132	P2.7/CTS0#

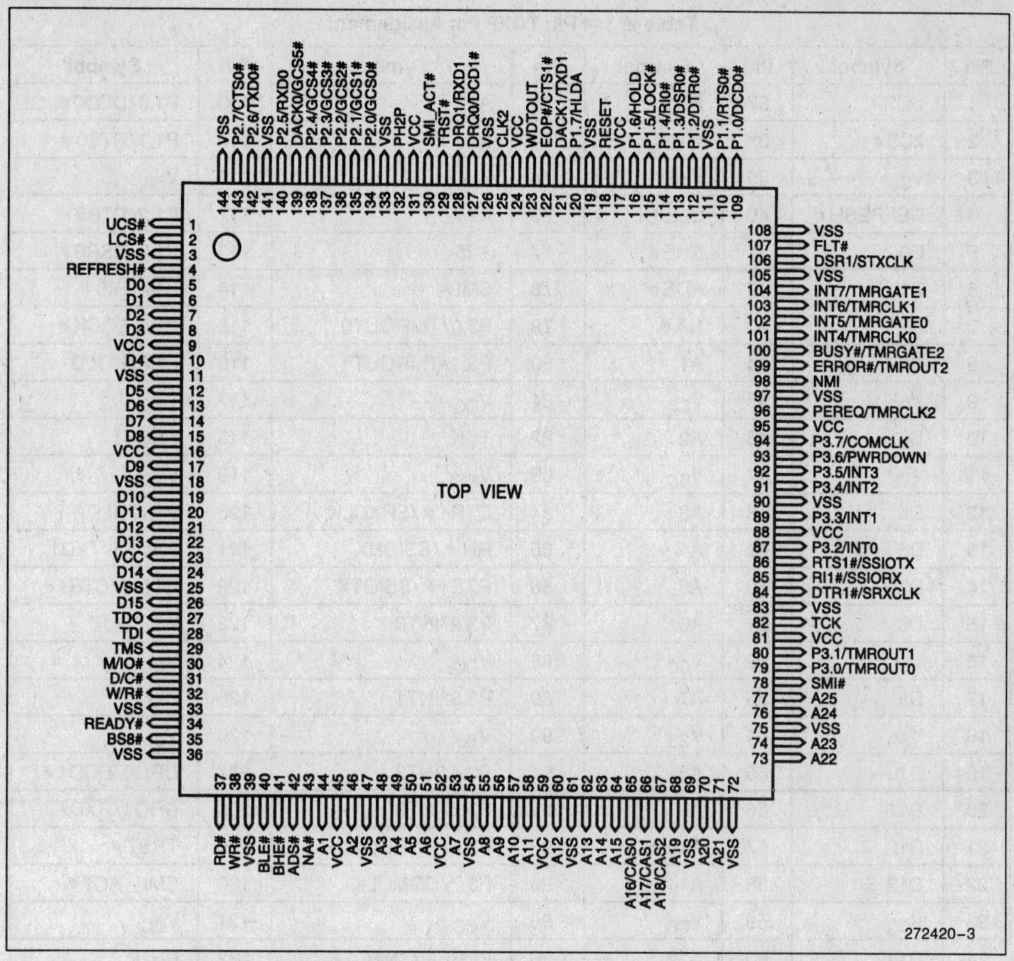

TOP VIEW

1 UCS#
2 LCS#
3 VSS
4 REFRESH#
5 D0
6 D1
7 D2
8 D3
9 VCC
10 D4
11 VSS
12 D5
13 D6
14 D7
15 D8
16 VCC
17 D9
18 VSS
19 D10
20 D11
21 D12
22 D13
23 VCC
24 D14
25 VSS
26 D15
27 TDO
28 TDI
29 TMS
30 M/IO#
31 D/C#
32 W/R#
33 VSS
34 READY#
35 BS8#
36 VSS

37 RD#
38 WR#
39 VSS
40 BLE#
41 BHE#
42 ADS#
43 NA#
44 A1
45 VCC
46 A2
47 VSS
48 A3
49 A4
50 A5
51 A6
52 VCC
53 A7
54 VSS
55 A8
56 A9
57 A10
58 A11
59 VCC
60 A12
61 VSS
62 A13
63 A14
64 A15
65 A16/CAS0
66 A17/CAS1
67 A18/CAS2
68 A19
69 VSS
70 A20
71 A21
72 VSS

73 A22
74 A23
75 VSS
76 A24
77 A25
78 SMI#
79 P3.0/TMROUT0
80 P3.1/TMROUT1
81 VCC
82 TCK
83 VSS
84 DTR1#/SRXCLK
85 RI1#/SSIORX
86 RTS1#/SSIOTX
87 P3.2/INT0
88 VCC
89 P3.3/INT1
90 VSS
91 P3.4/INT2
92 P3.5/INT3
93 P3.6/PWRDOWN
94 P3.7/COMCLK
95 VCC
96 PEREQ/TMRCLK2
97 VSS
98 NMI
99 ERROR#/TMROUT2
100 BUSY#/TMRGATE2
101 INT4/TMRCLK0
102 INT5/TMRGATE0
103 INT6/TMRCLK1
104 INT7/TMRGATE1
105 VSS
106 DSR1/STXCLK
107 FLT#
108 VSS

109 P1.0/DCD0#
110 P1.1/RTS0#
111 VSS
112 P1.2/DTR0#
113 P1.3/DSR0#
114 P1.4/RI0#
115 P1.5/LOCK#
116 P1.6/HOLD
117 VCC
118 RESET
119 VSS
120 P1.7/HLDA
121 DACK1/TXD1
122 EOP#/CTS1#
123 WDTOUT
124 VCC
125 CLK2
126 VSS
127 DRQ0/DCD1#
128 DRQ1/RXD1
129 TRST#
130 SMI_ACT#
131 VCC
132 PH2P
133 VSS
134 P2.0/GCS0#
135 P2.1/GCS1#
136 P2.2/GCS2#
137 P2.3/GCS3#
138 P2.4/GCS4#
139 DACK0/GCS5#
140 P2.5/RXD0
141 VSS
142 P2.6/TXD0#
143 P2.7/CTS0#
144 VSS

272420-3

Figure 3. Intel386™ EX Microprocessor 144-Pin TQFP Pin Assignment

4

Table 2. 144 Pin TQFP Pin Assignment

Pin	Symbol	Pin	Symbol	Pin	Symbol	Pin	Symbol
1	UCS#	37	RD#	73	A22	109	P1.0/DCD0#
2	LCS#	38	WR#	74	A23	110	P1.1/RTS0#
3	V_{SS}	39	V_{SS}	75	V_{SS}	111	V_{SS}
4	REFRESH#	40	BLE#	76	A24	112	P1.2/DTR0#
5	D0	41	BHE#	77	A25	113	P1.3/DSR0#
6	D1	42	ADS#	78	SMI#	114	P1.4/RI0#
7	D2	43	NA#	79	P3.0/TMROUT0	115	P1.5/LOCK#
8	D3	44	A1	80	P3.1/TMROUT1	116	P1.6/HOLD
9	V_{CC}	45	V_{CC}	81	V_{CC}	117	V_{CC}
10	D4	46	A2	82	TCK	118	RESET
11	V_{SS}	47	V_{SS}	83	V_{SS}	119	V_{SS}
12	D5	48	A3	84	DTR1#/SRXCLK	120	P1.7/HLDA
13	D6	49	A4	85	RI1#/SSIORX	121	DACK1/TXD1
14	D7	50	A5	86	RTS1#/SSIOTX	122	EOP#/CTS1#
15	D8	51	A6	87	P3.2/INT0	123	WDTOUT
16	V_{CC}	52	V_{CC}	88	V_{CC}	124	V_{CC}
17	D9	53	A7	89	P3.3/INT1	125	CLK2
18	V_{SS}	54	V_{SS}	90	V_{SS}	126	V_{SS}
19	D10	55	A8	91	P3.4/INT2	127	DRQ0/DCD1#
20	D11	56	A9	92	P3.5/INT3	128	DRQ1/RXD1
21	D12	57	A10	93	P3.6/PWRDOWN	129	TRST#
22	D13	58	A11	94	P3.7/COMCLK	130	SMI_ACT#
23	V_{CC}	59	V_{CC}	95	V_{CC}	131	V_{CC}
24	D14	60	A12	96	PEREQ/TMRCLK2	132	PH2P
25	V_{SS}	61	V_{SS}	97	V_{SS}	133	V_{SS}
26	D15	62	A13	98	NMI	134	P2.0/GCS0#
27	TDO	63	A14	99	ERROR#/TMROUT2	135	P2.1/GCS1#
28	TDI	64	A15	100	BUSY#/TMRGATE2	136	P2.2/GCS2#
29	TMS	65	A16/CAS0	101	INT4/TMRCLK0	137	P2.3/GCS3#
30	M/IO#	66	A17/CAS1	102	INT5/TMRGATE0	138	P2.4/GCS4#
31	D/C#	67	A18/CAS2	103	INT6/TMRCLK1	139	DACK0/GCS5#
32	W/R#	68	A19	104	INT7/TMRGATE1	140	P2.5/RXD0
33	V_{SS}	69	V_{SS}	105	V_{SS}	141	V_{SS}
34	READY#	70	A20	106	DSR1/STXCLK	142	P2.6/TXD0#
35	BS8#	71	A21	107	FLT#	143	P2.7/CTS0#
36	V_{SS}	72	V_{SS}	108	V_{SS}	144	V_{SS}

2.0 PIN DESCRIPTIONS

Table 3 lists the Intel386 EX microprocessor pin descriptions. The following definitions are used in the pin descriptions:

#	The named signal is active low.
I	Standard CMOS Input signal.
O	Standard CMOS Output signal.
I/O	Input and Output signal.
I/OD	Input and Open-Drain Output signal.
ST	Schmitt-Triggered Input signal.
P	Power pin.
G	Ground pin.

Table 3. Intel386™ EX Microprocessor Pin Descriptions

Symbol	Type	Name and Function
A25:1	O	**Address Bus** outputs physical memory or port I/O addresses. These signals are valid when ADS# is active and remain valid until the next T1, T2P, or Ti. During HOLD cycles they are driven to a high-impedance state. A18:16 are multiplexed with CAS2:0.
ADS#	O	**Address Status** indicates that the processor is driving a valid bus-cycle definition and address (W/R#, D/C#, M/IO#, A25:1, BHE#, BLE#) onto its pins.
BHE#	O	**Byte High Enable** indicates that the processor is transferring a high data byte.
BLE#	O	**Byte Low Enable** indicates that the processor is transferring a low data byte.
BS8#	I	**Bus Size** indicates that an 8-bit device is currently being addressed.
BUSY#	I	**Busy** indicates that the math coprocessor is busy. If BUSY# is sampled low at the falling edge of RESET, the processor performs an internal self test. BUSY# is multiplexed with TMRGATE2.
CAS2:0	O	**Cascade Address** carries the slave address information from the 8259A master interrupt module during interrupt acknowledge bus cycles. CAS2:0 are multiplexed with A18:16.
CLK2	ST	**Clock Input** is connected to an external clock that provides the fundamental timing for the device.
COMCLK	I	**Serial Communications Baud Clock** is an alternate clock source for the asynchronous serial port. COMCLK is multiplexed with P3.7.
CTS1:0#	I	**Clear to Send 1 and 0** prevent the transmission of data to the asynchronous serial port's RXD1 and RXD0 pin, respectively. CTS1# is multiplexed with EOP#, and CTS0# is multiplexed with P2.7. CTS1# requires an external pull-up resistor.

4

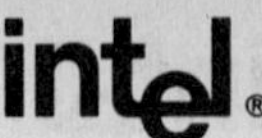

Table 3. Intel386™ EX Microprocessor Pin Descriptions (Continued)

Symbol	Type	Name and Function
D15:0	I/O	**Data Bus** inputs data during memory read, I/O read, and interrupt acknowledge cycles and outputs data during memory and I/O write cycles. During writes, this bus is driven during phase 2 of T1 and remains active until phase 2 of the next T1, T1P, or Ti. During reads, data is latched on the falling edge of phase 2.
DACK1:0	O	**DMA Acknowledge 1 and 0** signal to an external device that the processor has acknowledged the corresponding DMA request and is relinquishing the bus. DACK1 is multiplexed with TXD1, and DACK0 is multiplexed with GCS5#.
D/C#	O	**Data/Control** indicates whether the current bus cycle is a data cycle (memory or I/O read or write) or a control cycle (interrupt acknowledge, halt, or code fetch).
DCD1:0#	I	**Data Carrier Detect SIO1 and SIO0** indicate that the modem or data set has detected the corresponding asynchronous serial channel's data carrier. DCD1# is multiplexed with DRQ0, and DCD0# is multiplexed with P1.0.
DRQ1:0	I	**DMA External Request 1 and 0** indicate that a peripheral requires DMA service. DRQ1 is multiplexed with RXD1, and DRQ0 is multiplexed with DCD1#.
DSR1:0#	I	**Data Set Ready SIO1 and SIO0** indicate that the modem or data set is ready to establish a communication link with the corresponding asynchronous serial channel. DSR1# is not multiplexed; DSR0# is multiplexed with P1.3.
DTR1:0#	O	**Data Terminal Ready SIO1 and SIO0** indicate that the corresponding asynchronous serial channel is ready to establish a communication link with the modem or data set. DTR1# is multiplexed with SRXCLK, and DTR0# is multiplexed with P1.2.
EOP#	I/OD	**End of Process** indicates that the processor has reached terminal count during a DMA transfer. An external device can also pull this pin low. EOP# is multiplexed with CTS1#.
ERROR#	I	**Error** indicates that the math coprocessor has an error condition. ERROR# is multiplexed with TMROUT2.
FLT#	I	**Float** forces all bidirectional and output signals, including HLDA, to a high-impedance state.
GCS5:0#	O	**General Chip Selects** are activated when the address of a memory or I/O bus cycle is within the address region programmed by the user. GCS5# is multiplexed with DACK0, and GCS4:0# are multiplexed with P2.4:0.
HLDA	O	**Bus Hold Acknowledge** indicates that the processor has surrendered control of its local bus to another bus master. HLDA remains active until HOLD is deasserted. HLDA is multiplexed with P1.7.
HOLD	I	**Bus Hold Request** allows another bus master to request control of the local bus HLDA active indicates that bus control has been granted. HOLD is multiplexed with P1.6.

Table 3. Intel386™ EX Microprocessor Pin Descriptions (Continued)

Symbol	Type	Name and Function
INT7:0	I	**Interrupt Requests** are maskable inputs that cause the CPU to suspend execution of the current program and then execute an interrupt acknowledge cycle. They are multiplexed as follows: INT7 with TMRGATE1, INT6 with TMRCLK1, INT5 with TMRGATE0, INT4 with TMRCLK0, and INT3:0 with P3.5:2.
LCS#	O	**Lower Chip Select** is activated when the address of a memory or I/O bus cycle is within the address region programmed by the user. LCS# is inactive after reset.
LOCK#	O	**Bus Lock** prevents other bus masters from gaining control of the system bus. LOCK# is multiplexed with P1.5.
M/IO#	O	**Memory/IO** Indicates whether the current bus cycle is a memory cycle or an I/O cycle. When M/IO# is high, the bus cycle is a memory cycle; when M/IO# is low, the bus cycle is an I/O cycle.
NA#	I	**Next Address** requests address pipelining.
NMI	ST	**Non-Maskable Interrupt Request** is a non-maskable input that causes the CPU to suspend execution of the current program and execute an interrupt acknowledge cycle.
PEREQ	I	**Processor Extension Request** indicates that the math coprocessor has data to transfer to the processor. PEREQ is multiplexed with TMRCLK2.
PHCLK	O	**Peripheral Clock** represents the processor's internal operating frequency. The PHCLK frequency decreases when the processor is in power save mode.
P1.7:0	I/O	**Port 1, Pins 7:0** are multipurpose bidirectional port pins. They are multiplexed as follows: P1.7 with HLDA, P1.6 with HOLD, P1.5 with LOCK#, P1.4 with RI0#, P1.3 with DSR0#, P1.2 with DTR0#, P1.1 with RTS0#, and P1.0 with DCD0#.
P2.7:0	I/O	**Port 2, Pins 7:0** are multipurpose bidirectional port pins. They are multiplexed as follows: P2.7 with CTS0#, P2.6 with TXD0, P2.5 with RXD0, and P2.4:0 with GCS4:0#.
P3.7:0	I/O	**Port 3, Pins 7:0** are multipurpose bidirectional port pins. They are multiplexed as follows: P3.7 with COMCLK, P3.6 with PWRDOWN, P3.5:2 with INT3:0, and P3.1:0 with TMROUT1:0.
PWRDOWN	O	**Powerdown** indicates that the processor is in powerdown mode. PWRDOWN is multiplexed with P3.6.
RD#	O	**Read Enable** indicates that the current bus cycle is a read cycle.
READY#	I/OD	**Ready** indicates that the current bus transaction has completed. An external device or an internal signal can drive READY#. Internally, the chip-select wait-state logic can generate the ready signal and drive the READY# pin active.

4

Table 3. Intel386™ EX Microprocessor Pin Descriptions (Continued)

Symbol	Type	Name and Function
RESET	ST	**Reset** suspends any operation in progress and places the processor into a known reset state.
RFSH#	O	**Refresh** indicates that the current bus cycle is a refresh cycle.
RI1:0#	I	**Ring Indicator SIO1 and SIO0** indicate that the modem or data set has received a telephone ringing signal. RI1# is multiplexed with SSIORX, and RI0# is multiplexed with P1.4.
RTS1:0#	O	**Request-to-Send SIO1 and SIO0** indicate that corresponding asynchronous serial channel is ready to exchange data with the modem or data set. RTS1# is multiplexed with SSIOTX, and RTS0# is multiplexed with P1.1.
RXD1:0	I	**Receive Data SIO1 and SIO0** accept serial data from the modem or data set to the corresponding asynchronous serial channel. RXD1 is multiplexed with DRQ1, and RXD0 is multiplexed with P2.5.
SMI#	ST	**System Management Interrupt** invokes System Management Mode (SMM). SMI# is the highest priority interrupt. It is latched on its falling edge and it forces the CPU into SMM upon completion of the current instruction. SMI# is recognized on an instruction boundary and at each iteration for repeat string instructions. SMI# cannot interrupt LOCKed bus cycles or a currently executing SMM. If the processor receives a second SMI# while it is in SMM, it will latch the second SMI# on the SMI# falling edge. However, the processor must exit SMM by executing a Resume instruction (RSM) before it can service the second SMI#.
SMI_ACT#	O	**System Management Interrupt Active** indicates that the processor is operating in System Management Mode (SMM). It is asserted when the processor initiates an SMM sequence and remains asserted (low) until the processor executes the Resume instruction (RSM).
SRXCLK	I/O	**SSIO Receive Clock** synchronizes data being accepted by the synchronous serial port. SSIORX is multiplexed with DTR1#.
STXCLK	I/O	**SSIO Transmit Clock** synchronizes data being sent by the synchronous serial port. STXCLK is multiplexed with DSR#1.
SSIORX	I	**SSIO Receive Serial Data** accepts serial data (most-significant bit first) being sent to the synchronous serial port. SSIORX is multiplexed with RI1#.
SSIOTX	O	**SSIO Transmit Serial Data** sends serial data (most-significant bit first) from the synchronous serial port. SSIOTX is multiplexed with RTS1#.
TCK	I	**JTAG TAP (Test Access Port) Controller Clock** provides the clock input for the JTAG logic.
TDI	I	**JTAG TAP (Test Access Port) Controller Data Input** is the serial input for test instructions and data.

Table 3. Intel386™ EX Microprocessor Pin Descriptions (Continued)

Symbol	Type	Name and Function
TDO	O	**JTAG TAP (Test Access Port) Controller Data Output** is the serial output for test instructions and data.
TMRCLK2:0	I	**Timer/Counter Clock Inputs** can serve as external clock inputs for the corresponding timer/counters. (The timer/counters can also be clocked internally.) TMRCLK2 is multiplexed with PEREQ; TMRCLK1, with INT6; and TMRCLK0, with INT4.
TMRGATE2:0	I	**Timer/Counter Gate Inputs** can control the corresponding timer/counter's counting (enable, disable, or trigger, depending on the programmed mode). (Alternatively, a V_{CC} pin can serve this function.) TMRGATE2 is multiplexed with BUSY#; TMRGATE1, with INT7; and TMRGATE0, with INT5.
TMROUT2:0	O	**Timer/Counter Outputs** provide the output of the corresponding timer/counter. The form of the output depends on the programmed mode. TMROUT2 is multiplexed with ERROR#; TMROUT1, with P3.1; and TMROUT0, with P3.0.
TMS	I	**JTAG TAP (Test Access Port) Controller Mode Select** controls the sequence of the TAP controller's states.
TRST#	ST	**JTAG TAP (Test Access Port) Controller Reset** resets the TAP controller at power-up.
TXD1:0	O	**Transmit Data SSIO1/SSIO0** transmits serial data from the individual serial channel. TXD1 is multiplexed with DACK1 and TXD0 is multiplexed with P2.6.
UCS#	O	**Upper Chip Select** is activated when the address of a memory or I/O bus cycle is within the address region programmed by the user.
V_{CC}	P	**System Power** provides the nominal DC supply input. Connected externally to a V_{CC} board plane.
V_{SS}	G	**System Ground** provides the 0V connection from which all inputs and outputs are measured. Connected externally to a ground board plane.
WDTOUT	O	**Watchdog Timer Output** indicates that the watchdog timer has expired.
W/R#	O	**Write/Read** indicates whether the current bus cycle is a write cycle or a read cycle. When W/R# is high, the bus cycle is a write cycle; when W/R# is low, the bus cycle is a read cycle.
WR#	O	**Write Enable** indicates that the current bus cycle is a write cycle.

3.0 FUNCTIONAL DESCRIPTION

The Intel386 EX microprocessor is a fully static, 32-bit processor optimized for embedded applications. It features low power and low voltage capabilities, integration of many commonly used DOS-type peripherals, and a 32-bit programming architecture compatible with the large software base of Intel386 processors. The following sections provide an overview of the integrated peripherals.

3.1 Clock Generation and Power Management Unit

The clock generation circuit includes a divide-by-two counter, a programmable divider for generating a prescaled clock (PSCLK), a divide-by-three counter for generating baud rate clock inputs, a power-save clock divider circuit, and Reset circuitry. The CLK2 input provides the fundamental timing for the chip. It is divided by two internally to generate a 50% duty cycle Phase1 (PH1) and Phase 2 (PH2) for the core and integrated peripherals. For power management, separate clocks are routed to the core (PH1C/PH2C) and the peripheral modules (PH1P/PH2P).

Three Power Management modes are provided for flexible power-saving options. During Idle mode, the clocks to the CPU core are frozen in a known state (PH1C low and PH2C high), while the clocks to the peripherals continue to toggle. In Powerdown mode, the clocks to both core and peripherals are frozen in a known state (PH1C low and PH2C high). The Bus Interface Unit will not honor any DMA, DRAM refresh, or HOLD requests in Powerdown mode because the clocks to the entire device are frozen. In Power-save mode, a programmable divider decreases the frequency of the incoming CLK2 signal. Allowable clock division settings are 1, 2, 4, 8, 16, 32, and 64 (divide-by-1 has no effect). Once Power-save is enabled, the core and peripherals continue to run at the divided clock rate. The prescaled clock (PSCLK) and the baud input clock do not change frequency in Power-save mode.

3.2 Chip Select Unit

The Chip Select Unit (CSU) decodes bus cycle address and status information and enables the appropriate chip-selects. The individual chip-selects become valid in the same bus state as the address and become inactive when either a new address is selected or the current bus cycle is complete.

The CSU is divided into eight separate chip-select regions, each of which can enable one of the eight chip-select pins. Each chip-select region can be mapped into memory or I/O space. A memory-mapped chip-select region can start on any 2^n Kbyte address location (where n = 0–22, depending upon the mask register). An I/O-mapped chip-select region can start on any 2^n word address location (where n = 0–15, depending upon the mask register). The size of the region is also dependent upon the mask used.

3.3 Interrupt Control Unit

The Intel386 EX microprocessor's Interrupt Control Unit (ICU) contains two 8259A modules connected in a cascade mode. The 8259A modules make up the heart of the ICU. These modules are similar to the industry-standard 8259A architecture.

The Interrupt Control Unit directly supports up to eight external (INT7:0) and up to eight internal (IR7:0) interrupt request signals. Pending interrupt requests are posted in the Interrupt Request Register, which contains one bit for each interrupt request signal. When an interrupt request is asserted, the corresponding Interrupt Request Register bit is set. The 8259A module can be programmed to recognize either an active-high level or a positive transition on the interrupt request lines. An internal Priority Resolver decides which pending interrupt request (if more than one exists) is the highest priority, based on the programmed operating mode. The Priority Resolver controls the single interrupt request line to the CPU. The Priority Resolver's default priority scheme places IR0 as the highest priority and IR7 as the lowest. The priority can be modified through software.

Besides the eight interrupt request inputs available to the Intel386 EX microprocessor, additional interrupts can be supported by cascaded external 8259A modules. Up to four external 8259A units can be cascaded to the master through connections to the INT3:0 pins. In this configuration, the interrupt acknowledge (INTA#) signal can be decoded externally using the ADS#, D/C#, R/W#, and M/IO# signals.

3.4 Timer/Counter Unit

The Timer/Counter unit on the Intel386 EX microprocessor has the same basic functionality as the industry-standard 82C54 counter/timer. It provides three independent 16-bit counters, each capable of handling clock inputs up to 8 MHz. This maximum frequency must be considered when programming the input clocks for the counters. Six programmable timer modes allow the timers to be used as event counters, elapsed-time indicators, programmable one-shots, and in many other applications. All modes are software programmable.

3.5 Watchdog Timer Unit

The Watchdog Timer (WDT) unit consists of a 32-bit down-counter that decrements every PH1P cycle, allowing up to 4.3 billion count intervals. The WDTOUT pin is driven high for sixteen CLK2 cycles when the down-counter reaches zero (the WDT times out). The WDTOUT signal can be used to reset the chip, to request an interrupt, or to indicate to the user that a ready-hang situation has occurred. The down-counter can also be updated with a user-defined 32-bit reload value under certain conditions. Alternatively, the WDT unit can be used as a bus monitor or as a general-purpose timer.

3.6 Asynchronous Serial I/O Unit

The Intel386 EX microprocessor's asynchronous serial I/O (SIO) unit is a Universal Asynchronous Receiver/ Transmitter (UART). Functionally, it is equivalent to the National Semiconductor NS16450 and INS8250. The Intel386 EX microprocessor contains two asynchronous serial channels.

The SIO unit converts serial data characters received from a peripheral device or modem to parallel data and converts parallel data characters received from the CPU to serial data. The CPU can read the status of the serial port at any time during its operation. The status information includes the type and condition of the transfer operations being performed and any errors (parity, framing, overrun, or break interrupt).

Each asynchronous serial channel includes full modem control support (CTS#, RTS#, DSR#, DTR#, RI#, and DCD#) and is completely programmable. The programmable options include character length (5, 6, 7, or 8 bits), stop bits (1, 1.5, or 2), and parity (even, odd, forced, or none). In addition, it contains a programmable baud rate generator capable of DC to 512 Kbaud.

3.7 Synchronous Serial I/O Unit

The Synchronous Serial I/O (SSIO) unit provides for simultaneous, bidirectional communications. It consists of a transmit channel, a receive channel, and a dedicated baud rate generator. It is compatible with several popular synchronous protocols. The transmit and receive channels can be operated independently (with different clocks) to provide non-lockstep, full-duplex communications; either channel can originate the clocking signal (Master Mode) or receive an externally generated clocking signal (Slave Mode).

The SSIO provides numerous features for ease and flexibility of operation. With a maximum clock input of 20 MHz to the baud rate generator, the SSIO can deliver a baud rate of 5 Mbits per second. Each channel is double buffered. The two channels share the baud rate generator and a multiply-by-four transmit and receive clock. The SSIO supports 16-bit serial communications with independently enabled transmit and receive functions and gated interrupt outputs to the interrupt controller.

3.8 Parallel I/O Unit

The Intel386 EX microprocessor has three 8-bit, general-purpose I/O ports. All port pins are bidirectional, with CMOS-level input and outputs. All pins have both a standard operating mode and a peripheral mode (a multiplexed function), and all have similar sets of control registers located in I/O address space. Ports 1 and 2 provide 8 mA of drive capability, while port 3 provides 16 mA.

3.9 DMA and Bus Arbiter Unit

The Intel386 EX microprocessor's DMA controller is a two-channel DMA; each channel operates independently of the other. Within the operation of the individual channels, several different data transfer modes are available. These modes can be combined in various configurations to provide a very versatile DMA controller. Its feature set has enhancements beyond the 8237 DMA family; however, it can be configured such that it can be used in an 8237-like mode. Each channel can transfer data between any combination of memory and I/O with any combination (8 or 16 bits) of data path widths. An internal temporary register that can disassemble or assemble data to or from either an aligned or a nonaligned destination or source optimizes bus bandwidth.

The bus arbiter, a part of the DMA controller, works much like the priority resolving circuitry of a DMA. It receives service requests from the two DMA channels, the external bus master, and the DRAM Refresh controller. The bus arbiter requests bus ownership from the core and resolves priority issues among all active requests when bus mastership is granted.

Each DMA channel consists of three major components: the Requestor, the Target, and the Byte Count. These components are identified by the contents of programmable registers that define the memory or I/O device being serviced by the DMA. The Requestor is the device that requires and requests service from the DMA controller. Only the Requestor is considered capable of initializing or terminating a DMA process. The Target is the device with which the Requestor wishes to communicate. The DMA process considers the Target a slave that is incapable of controlling the process. The Byte Count dictates the amount of data that must be transferred.

3.10 Refresh Control Unit

The Refresh Control Unit (RCU) simplifies dynamic memory controller design with its integrated address and clock counters. Integrating the RCU into the processor allows an external DRAM controller to use chip-selects, wait state logic, and status lines.

The Intel386 EX microprocessor's RCU consists of four basic functions. First, it provides a programmable-interval timer that keeps track of time. Second, it provides the bus arbitration logic to gain control of the bus to run refresh cycles. Third, it contains the logic to generate row addresses to refresh DRAM rows individually. And fourth, it contains the logic to signal the start of a refresh cycle.

Additionally, it contains a 13-bit address counter that forms the refresh address, supporting DRAMs with up to 13 rows of memory cells (13 refresh address bits). This includes all practical DRAM sizes for the Intel386 microprocessor's 64 Mbyte address space.

3.11 JTAG Boundary Scan Unit

The JTAG Boundary Scan Unit provides access to the device pins and to a number of other testable areas on the device. It is fully compliant with the IEEE 1149.1 standard and thus interfaces with five JTAG-dedicated pins: TRST#, TCK, TMS, TDI, and TDO. It contains the Test Access Port (TAP) finite-state machine, a 4-bit instruction register, a 32-bit identification register, a single-bit bypass register, and an 8-bit test mode register. The JTAG unit also contains the necessary logic to generate clock and control signals for the chains that reside outside the JTAG unit itself: the SCANOUT and Boundary Scan chains.

Since the JTAG unit has its own clock and reset signals, it can operate autonomously. Thus, while the rest of the microprocessor is in Reset or Powerdown, the JTAG unit can read or write various register chains. This feature can be used, for example, to write to the test mode register while the rest of the chip is in Reset or Powerdown. Then when the microprocessor exits Reset or Powerdown, it will enter the specified test mode.

4.0 DESIGN CONSIDERATIONS

This section describes the Intel386 EX microprocessor's instruction set and its component and revision identifiers.

4.1 Instruction Set

The Intel386 EX microprocessor uses the same instruction set as the Intel386 SX microprocessor with the following exceptions.

The Intel386 EX microprocessor has one new instruction (RSM). This Resume instruction causes the processor to exit System Management Mode (SMM). RSM requires 338 clocks per instruction (CPI).

The Intel386 EX microprocessor requires more clock cycles than the Intel386 SX microprocessor to execute some instructions. Table 4 lists these instructions and the Intel386 EX microprocessor CPI. For the equivalent Intel386 SX microprocessor CPI, refer to the "Instruction Set Clock Count Summary" table in the *Intel386™ SX Microprocessor* data sheet (order number 240187).

4.2 Component and Revision Identifiers

To assist users, the microprocessor holds a component identifier and revision identifier in its DX register after reset. The upper 8 bits of DX hold the component identifier, 23H. (The lower nibble, 03H, identifies the Intel386 architecture, while the upper nibble, 02H, identifies the second member of the Intel386 microprocessor family.)

The lower 8 bits of DX hold the revision level identifier. The revision identifier will, in general, chronologically track those component steppings that are intended to have certain improvements or distinction from previous steppings. The revision identifier will track that of the Intel386 CPU whenever possible. However, the revision identifier value is not guaranteed to change with every stepping revision or to follow a completely uniform numerical sequence, depending on the type or intent of the revision or the manufacturing materials required to be changed. Intel has sole discretion over these characteristics of the component. The initial revision identifier for the Intel386 EX microprocessor is 09H.

Table 4. Intel386™ CX Microprocessor Clocks Per Instruction

Instruction	Clock Count		
	Virtual 8086 Mode(1)	Real Address Mode or Virtual 8086 Mode	Protected Virtual Address Mode(3)
POPA		28	35
IN: Fixed Port Variable Port	 27 28	 14 15	 7/29 8/29
OUT: Fixed Port Variable Port	 27 28	 14 15	 7/29 9/29
INS	30	17	9/32
OUTS	31	18	10/33
REP INS	31 + 6n(2)	17 + 6n(2)	10 + 6n/32 + 6n(2)
REP OUTS	30 + 8n(2)	16 + 8n(2)	10 + 8n/31 + 8n(2)
HLT		7	7
MOV C0, reg		10	10

NOTES:
1. The clock count values in this column apply if I/O permission allows I/O to the port in virtual 8086 mode. If the I/O bit map denies permission, exception fault 13 occurs; see clock counts for the INT 3 instruction in the "Instruction Set Clock Count Summary" table in the *Intel386™ SX Microprocessor* data sheet (order number 240187).
2. n = the number of times repeated.
3. When two clock counts are listed, the smaller value refers to a register operand and the larger value refers to a memory operand.

5.0 DC SPECIFICATIONS

ABSOLUTE MAXIMUM RATINGS*

Storage Temperature .... −65°C to +150°C

Case Temperature Under Bias... −65°C to +110°C

Supply Voltage with Respect to V_{SS}.. −0.5V to 6.5V

Voltage on Other Pins .... −0.5V to V_{CC} + 0.5V

OPERATING CONDITIONS*

V_{CC} (Digital Supply Voltage) ....2.7V to 5.5V

T_{CASE} (Case Temperature Under Bias) 0°C to 100°C

F_{OSC} (Operating Frequency) .....0 MHz to 25 MHz

NOTICE: This document contains information on products in the design phase of development. Do not finalize a design with this information. Revised information will be published when the product is available. Verify with your local Intel Sales office that you have the latest data sheet before finalizing a design.

**WARNING: Stressing the device beyond the "Absolute Maximum Ratings" may cause permanent damage. These are stress ratings only. Operation beyond the "Operating Conditions" is not recommended and extended exposure beyond the "Operating Conditions" may affect device reliability.*

Table 5. DC Characteristics

Symbol	Parameter	Min.	Max.	Unit	Test Condition
V_{IL}	Input Low Voltage (for all pins except CLK2, RESET, NMI, TRST#, and SMI#)	−0.5	0.3 V_{CC}	V	
V_{IL1}	Input Low Voltage (CLK2, RESET, NMI, TRST#, and SMI#)	−0.5	0.35 V_{CC}	V	
V_{IH}	Input High Voltage (for all pins except CLK2, RESET, NMI, TRST#, and SMI#)	0.7 V_{CC}	V_{CC} + 0.5	V	
V_{IH1}	Input High Voltage (CLK2, RESET, NMI, TRST#, and SMI#)	0.65 V_{CC}	V_{CC} + 0.5	V	
V_{OL}	Output Low Voltage All pins except Port 3 Port 3		 0.40 0.40	 V V	V_{CC} = 4.5V to 5.5V I_{OL} = 8 mA I_{OL} = 16 mA
V_{OL1}	Output Low Voltage All pins except Port 3 Port 3		 0.40 0.40	 V V	V_{CC} = 2.7V to 3.6V I_{OL} = 4 mA I_{OL} = 8 mA
V_{OH}	Output High Voltage All pins except Port 3 Port 3	 V_{CC} −0.8 V_{CC} − 0.8		 V V	V_{CC} = 4.5V to 5.5V I_{OH} = −8 mA I_{OH} = −16 mA
V_{OH1}	Output High Voltage All pins except Port 3 Port 3	 V_{CC} − 0.6 V_{CC} − 0.6		 V V	V_{CC} = 2.7V to 3.6V I_{OH} = −4 mA I_{OH} = −8 mA

Table 5. DC Characteristics (Continued)

Symbol	Parameter	Min.	Max.	Unit	Test Condition
I_{LI}	Input Leakage Current		±15	μA	$0 \le V_{IN} \le V_{CC}$
I_{LO}	Output Leakage Current		±15	μA	$0.45V \le V_{OUT} \le V_{CC}$
I_{CC}	Supply Current		140 200 420	mA mA mA	16 MHz, 3.0V 20 MHz, 3.3V 25 MHz, 5.0V
I_{IDLE}	Idle Mode Current		TBD	mA	
I_{PSV}	Power-save Current		TBD TBD TBD TBD TBD TBD TBD	μA μA μA μA μA μA μA	divide by 1 clock divide by 2 clock divide by 4 clock divide by 8 clock divide by 16 clock divide by 32 clock divide by 64 clock
I_{PD}	Powerdown Current		TBD	μA	
C_S	Pin Capacitance (any pin to V_{SS})		TBD	pF	

6.0 AC SPECIFICATIONS

Table 6 lists output delays, input setup requirements, and input hold requirements. All AC specifications are relative to the CLK2 rising edge crossing the $V_{CC}/2$ level.

Figure 4 shows the measurement points for AC specifications. Inputs must be driven to the indicated voltage levels when AC specifications are measured. Output delays are specified with minimum and maximum limits measured as shown. The minimum delay times are hold times provided to external circuitry. Input setup and hold times are specified as minimums, defining the smallest acceptable sampling window. Within the sampling window, a synchronous input signal must be stable for correct operation.

Outputs ADS#, W/R#, D/C#, MI/O#, LOCK#, BHE#, BLE#, A25:1, HLDA and SMI_ACT# change only at the beginning of phase one. D15:0 (write cycles) change only at the beginning of phase two.

The READY#, HOLD, BUSY#, ERROR#, PEREQ, FLT#, A20M# and D15:0 (read cycles) inputs are sampled at the beginning of phase one. The NA#, INTR, SMI# and NMI inputs are sampled at the beginning of phase two.

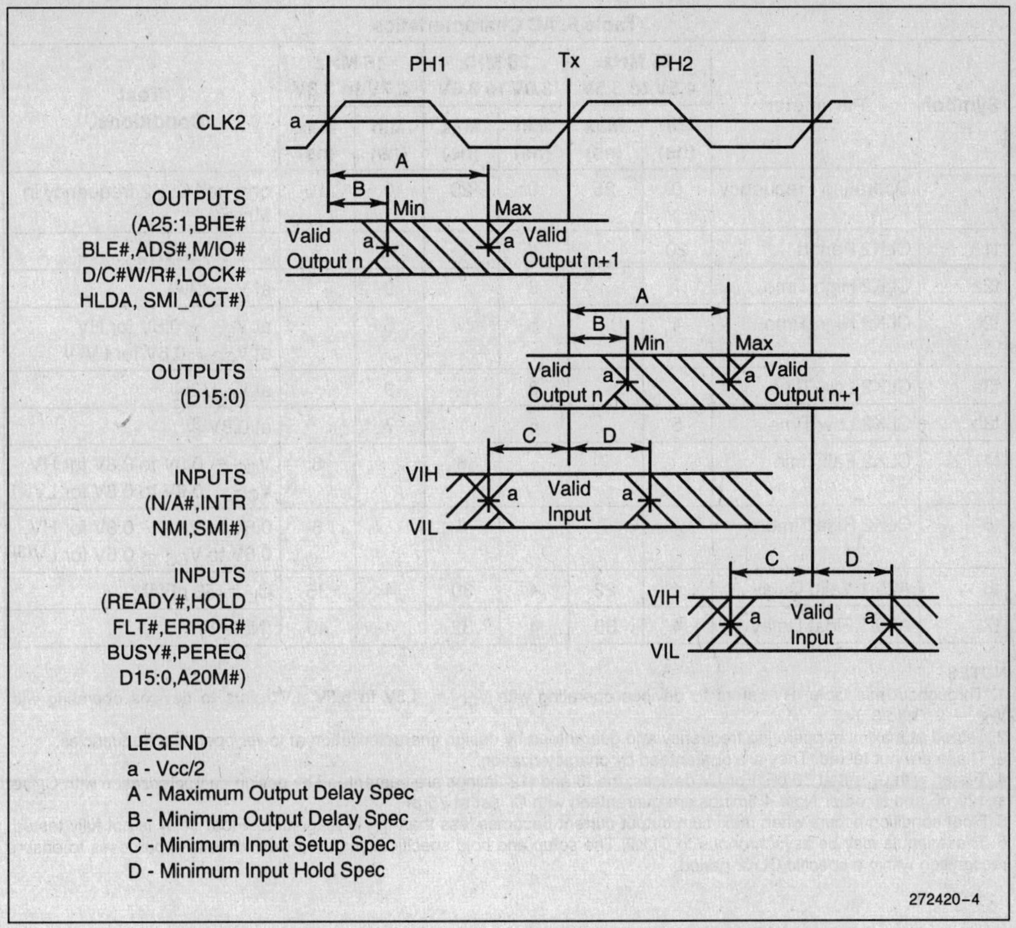

Figure 4. Drive Levels and Measurement Points for AC Specifications

4

Table 6. AC Characteristics

Symbol	Parameter	25 MHz 4.5V to 5.5V		20 MHz 3.0V to 3.6V		16 MHz 2.7V to 3.3V		Test Conditions(1)
		Min (ns)	Max (ns)	Min (ns)	Max (ns)	Min (ns)	Max (ns)	
	Operating Frequency	0	25	0	20	0	16	one-half CLK2 frequency in MHz(2)
t1	CLK2 Period	20		25		31		
t2a	CLK2 High Time	7		8		9		at $V_{CC}/2$(3)
t2b	CLK2 High Time	4		5		5		at V_{CC} − 0.8V for HV, at V_{CC} −0.6V for LV(3)
t3a	CLK2 Low Time	7		8		9		at $V_{CC}/2$(3)
t3b	CLK2 Low Time	5		6		7		at 0.8V(3)
t4	CLK2 Fall Time		7		8		8	V_{CC} − 0.8V to 0.8V for HV, V_{CC} − 0.6V to 0.8V for LV(3)
t5	CLK2 Rise Time		7		8		8	0.8V to V_{CC} − 0.8V for HV, 0.8V to V_{CC} − 0.6V for LV(3)
t6	A25:1 Valid Delay	4	22	4	30	4	36	C_L = 50 pF(4)
t7	A25:1 Float Delay	4	30	4	32	4	40	(Note 5)

NOTES:
1. Throughout this table, HV refers to devices operating with V_{CC} = 4.5V to 5.5V. LV refers to devices operating with V_{CC} = 2.7V to 3.6V.
2. Tested at maximum operating frequency and guaranteed by design characterization at lower operating frequencies.
3. These are not tested. They are guaranteed by characterization.
4. Tested with C_L set at 50 pF. For LV devices, the t6 and t12 timings are guaranteed by design characterization with C_L set at 120 pF and all other Note 4 timings are guaranteed with C_L set at 75 pF.
5. Float condition occurs when maximum output current becomes less than I_{LO} in magnitude. Float delay is not fully tested.
6. These inputs may be asynchronous to CLK2. The setup and hold specifications are given for testing purposes to ensure recognition within a specific CLK2 period.

Table 6. AC Characteristics (Continued)

Symbol	Parameter	25 MHz 4.5V to 5.5V		20 MHz 3.0V to 3.6V		16 MHz 2.7V to 3.3V		Test Conditions(1)
		Min (ns)	Max (ns)	Min (ns)	Max (ns)	Min (ns)	Max (ns)	
t8	BHE#, BLE#, LOCK# Valid Delay	4	19	4	30	4	36	C_L = 50 pF(4)
t8a	SMI_ACT# Valid Delay	4	19	4	26	4	33	C_L = 50 pF(4)
t9	BHE#, BLE#, LOCK# Float Delay	4	30	4	32	4	40	(Note 5)
t10a	M/IO#, D/C# Valid Delay	4	19	4	28	4	33	C_L = 50 pF(4)
t10b	W/R#, RD#, WR#, ADS# Valid Delay	4	19	4	16	4	33	C_L = 50 pF(4)
t11	W/R#, M/IO#, D/C#, RD#, WR#, ADS# Float Delay	4	30	4	30	4	35	(Note 5)
t12	D15:0 Write Data Valid Delay	4	28	4	38	4	40	C_L = 50 pF(4)
t13	D15:0 Write DataD15:0 Write Data Float delay	4	22	4	27	4	35	(Note 5)
t14	HLDA Valid Delay	4	22	4	28	4	33	C_L = 50 pF(4)
t15	NA# Setup Time	5		5		5		
t16	NA# Hold Time	3		12		21		
t19	READY#, A20M# Setup Time	9		12		19		
t20	READY#, A20M# Hold Time	4		4		4		

NOTES:

1. Throughout this table, HV refers to devices operating with V_{CC} = 4.5V to 5.5V. LV refers to devices operating with V_{CC} = 2.7V to 3.6V.
2. Tested at maximum operating frequency and guaranteed by design characterization at lower operating frequencies.
3. These are not tested. They are guaranteed by characterization.
4. Tested with C_L set at 50 pF. For LV devices, the t6 and t12 timings are guaranteed by design characterization with C_L set at 120 pF and all other Note 4 timings are guaranteed with C_L set at 75 pF.
5. Float condition occurs when maximum output current becomes less than I_{LO} in magnitude. Float delay is not fully tested.
6. These inputs may be asynchronous to CLK2. The setup and hold specifications are given for testing purposes to ensure recognition within a specific CLK2 period.

Table 6. AC Characteristics (Continued)

Symbol	Parameter	25 MHz 4.5V to 5.5V		20 MHz 3.0V to 3.6V		16 MHz 2.7V to 3.3V		Test Conditions(1)
		Min (ns)	Max (ns)	Min (ns)	Max (ns)	Min (ns)	Max (ns)	
t21	D15:0 Read Setup Time	7		9		9		
t22	D15:0 Read Hold Time	5		6		6		
t23	HOLD Setup Time	9		17		26		
t24	HOLD Hold Time	3		5		5		
t25	RESET Setup Time	8		12		13		
t26	RESET Hold Time	3		4		4		
t27	NMI, INTR Setup Time	6		16		16		(Note 6)
t27a	SMI# Setup Time	6		16		16		(Note 6)
t28	NMI, INTR Hold Time	6		16		16		(Note 6)
t28a	SMI# Hold Time	6		16		16		(Note 6)
t29	PEREQ, ERROR#, BUSY#, FLT# Setup Time	6		14		16		(Note 6)
t30	PEREQ, ERROR#, BUSY#, FLT# Hold Time	5		5		5		(Note 6)

NOTES:

1. Throughout this table, HV refers to devices operating with V_{CC} = 4.5V to 5.5V. LV refers to devices operating with V_{CC} = 2.7V to 3.6V.
2. Tested at maximum operating frequency and guaranteed by design characterization at lower operating frequencies.
3. These are not tested. They are guaranteed by characterization.
4. Tested with C_L set at 50 pF. For LV devices, the t6 and t12 timings are guaranteed by design characterization with C_L set at 120 pF and all other Note 4 timings are guaranteed with C_L set at 75 pF.
5. Float condition occurs when maximum output current becomes less than I_{LO} in magnitude. Float delay is not fully tested.
6. These inputs may be asynchronous to CLK2. The setup and hold specifications are given for testing purposes to ensure recognition within a specific CLK2 period.

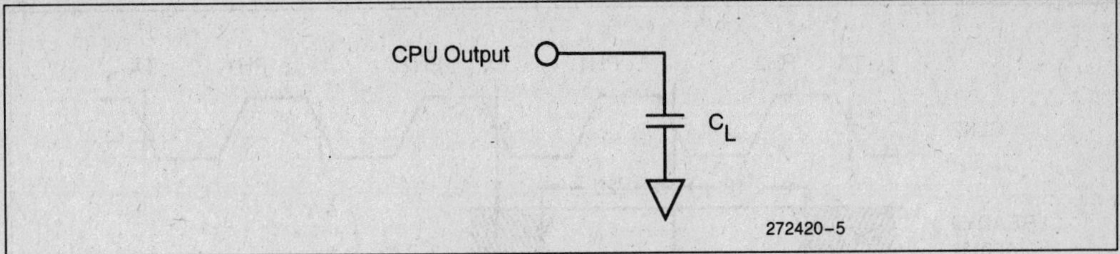

Figure 5. AC Test Loads

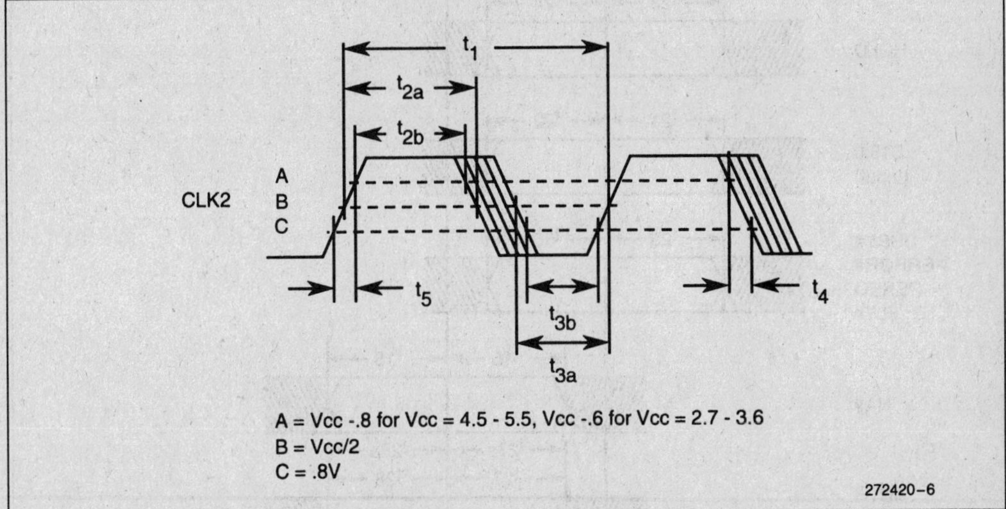

Figure 6. CLK2 Waveform

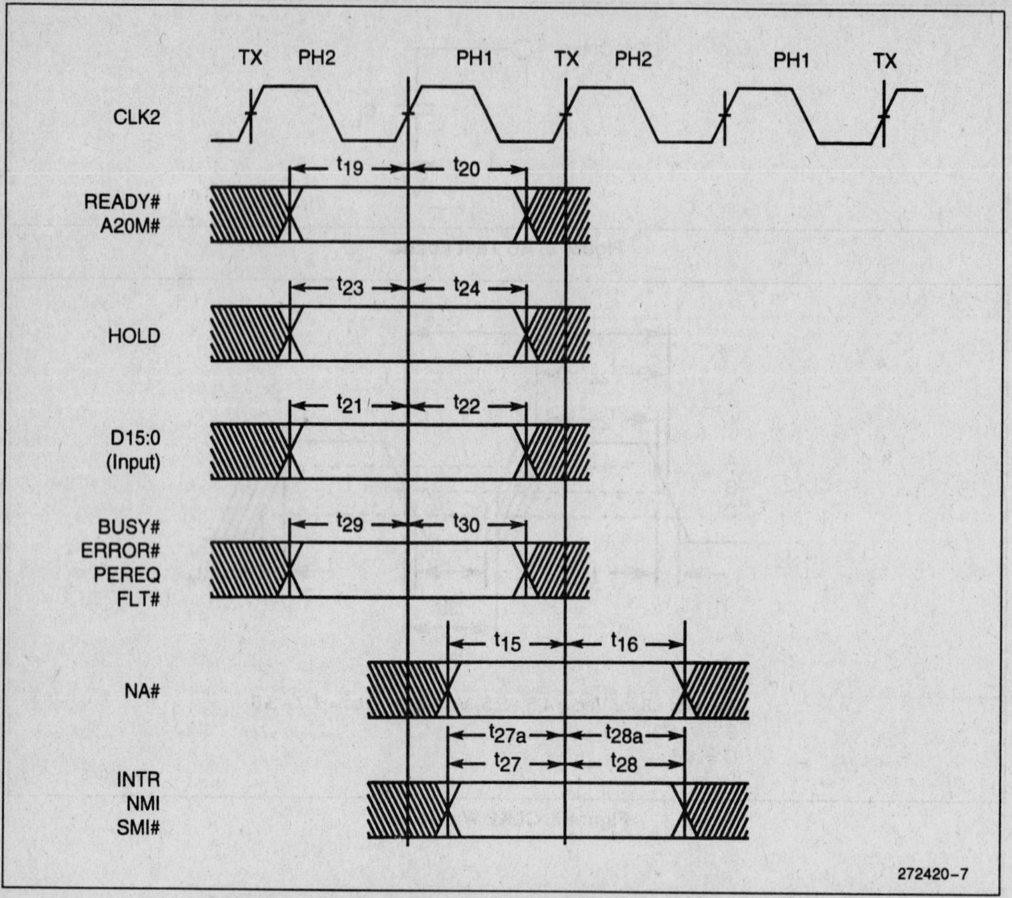

272420–7

Figure 7. AC Timing Waveforms—Input Setup and Hold Timing

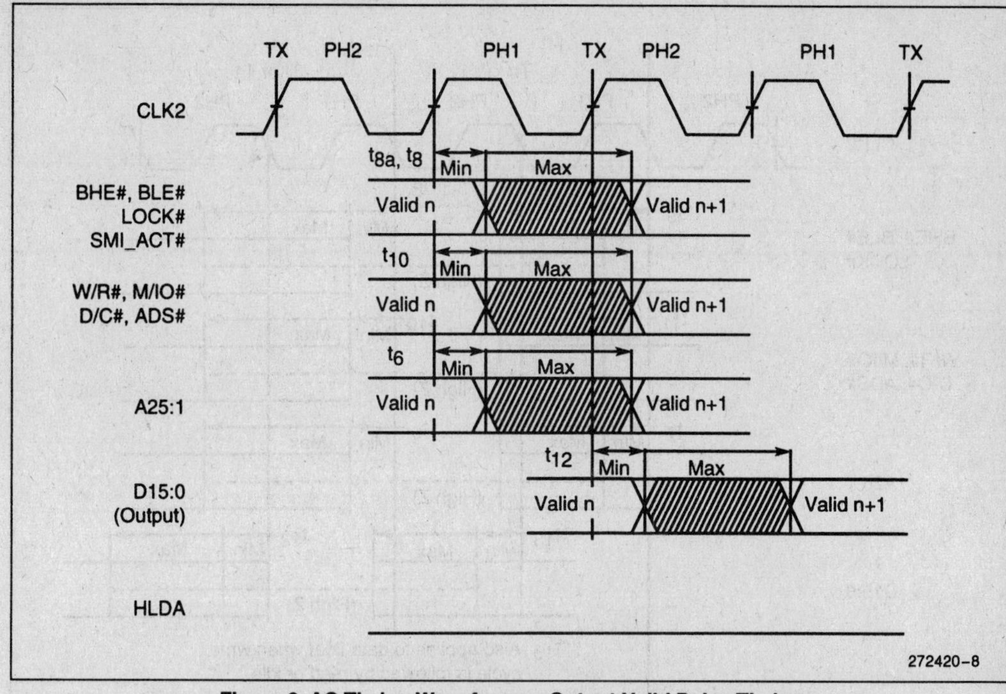

Figure 8. AC Timing Waveforms—Output Valid Delay Timing

4

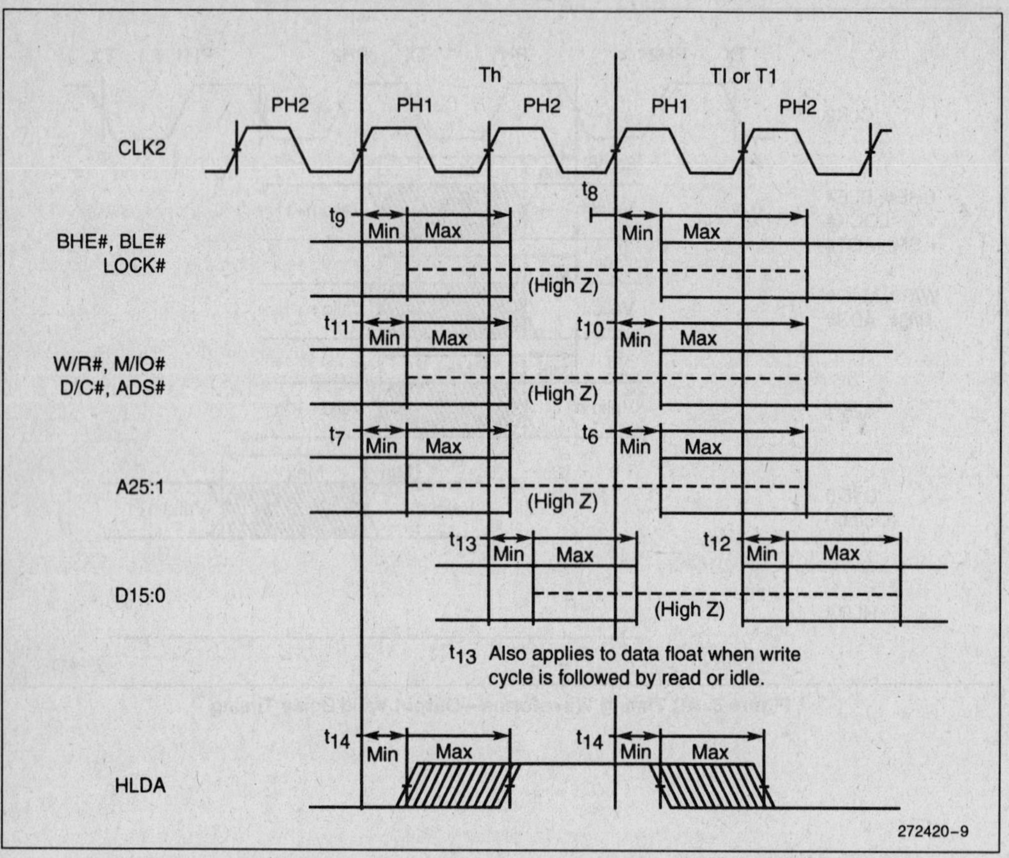

272420-9

Figure 9. AC Timing Waveforms—Output Float Delay and HLDA Valid Delay Timing

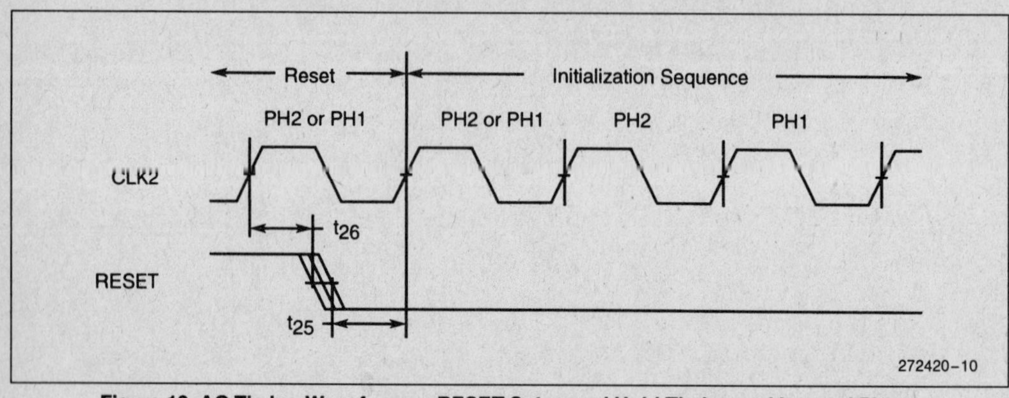

Figure 10. AC Timing Waveforms—RESET Setup and Hold Timing and Internal Phase

STATIC Intel386™ SX EMBEDDED MICROPROCESSOR

- **Static Intel386™ CPU Core**
  - **Low Power Consumption**
  - **Operating Frequency 25 MHz at 4.5V to 5.5V**
- **Clock Freeze Mode Allows Clock Stopping at Any Time**
- **Full 32-Bit Internal Architecture**
  - **8-, 16-, 32-Bit Data Types**
  - **8 General Purpose 32-Bit Registers**
- **Runs Intel386 Architecture Software in a Cost Effective 16-Bit Hardware Environment**
  - **Runs Same Applications and Operating Systems as the Intel386 SX and Intel386 DX Processors**
  - **Object Code Compatible with 8086, 80186, 80286, and Intel386 Processors**
- **TTL-Compatible Inputs**
- **High Performance 16-Bit Data Bus**
  - **25 MHz Clock**
  - **Two-Clock Bus Cycles**
  - **Address Pipelining Allows Use of Slower, Inexpensive Memories**
- **Integrated Memory Management Unit (MMU)**
  - **Virtual Memory Support**
  - **Optional On-Chip Paging**
  - **4 Levels of Hardware-Enforced Protection**
  - **MMU Fully Compatible with Those of the 80286 and Intel386 DX Processors**
- **Virtual 8086 Mode Allows Execution of 8086 Software in a Protected and Paged System**
- **Large Uniform Address Space**
  - **16 Megabyte Physical**
  - **64 Terabyte Virtual**
  - **4 Gigabyte Maximum Segment Size**
- **Numerics Support with Intel387™ SX and Intel387 SL Math Coprocessors**
- **On-Chip Debugging Support Including Breakpoint Registers**
- **Complete System Development Support**
- **High-Speed CHMOS Technology**
- **100-Pin Plastic Quad Flatpack Package**

The Intel386 SX Embedded Microprocessor is a 32-bit, fully static CPU with a 16-bit external data bus and a 24-bit external address bus. The Intel386 SX CPU brings the vast software library of the Intel386 architecture to embedded systems. It provides the performance benefits of 32-bit programming with the cost savings associated with 16-bit hardware systems.

4

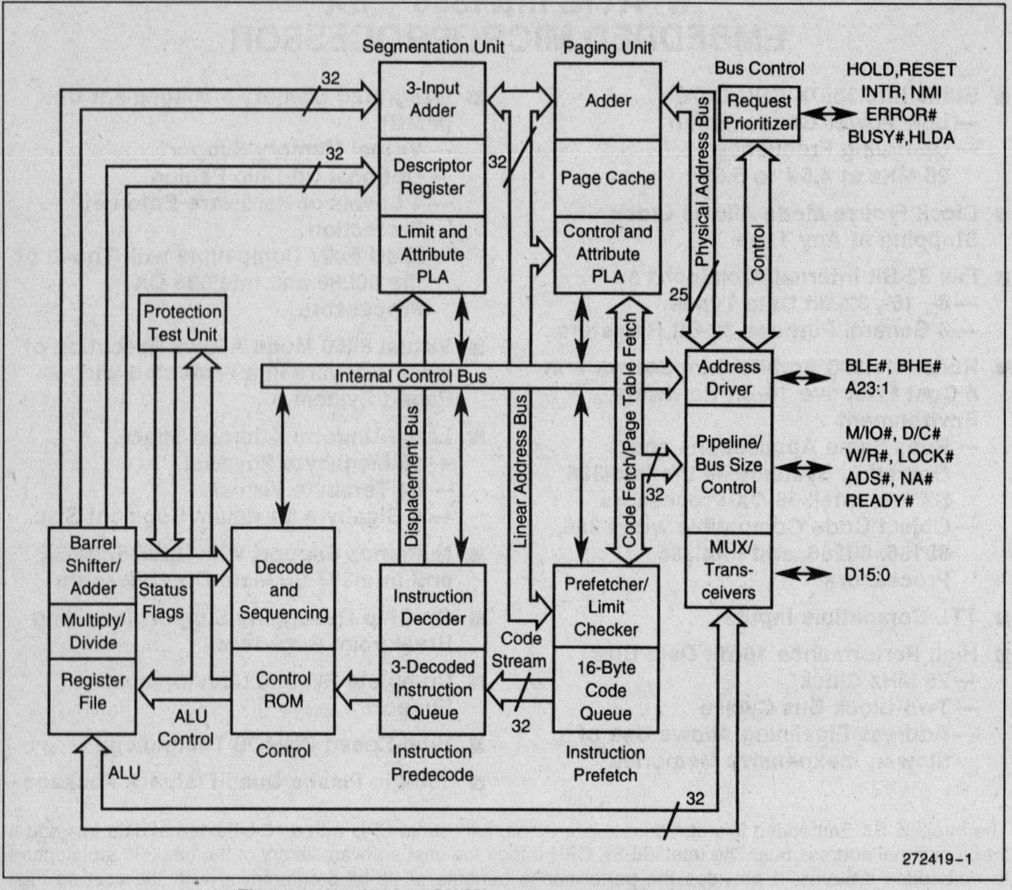

Figure 1. Intel386™ SX Microprocessor Block Diagram

1.0 PIN ASSIGNMENT

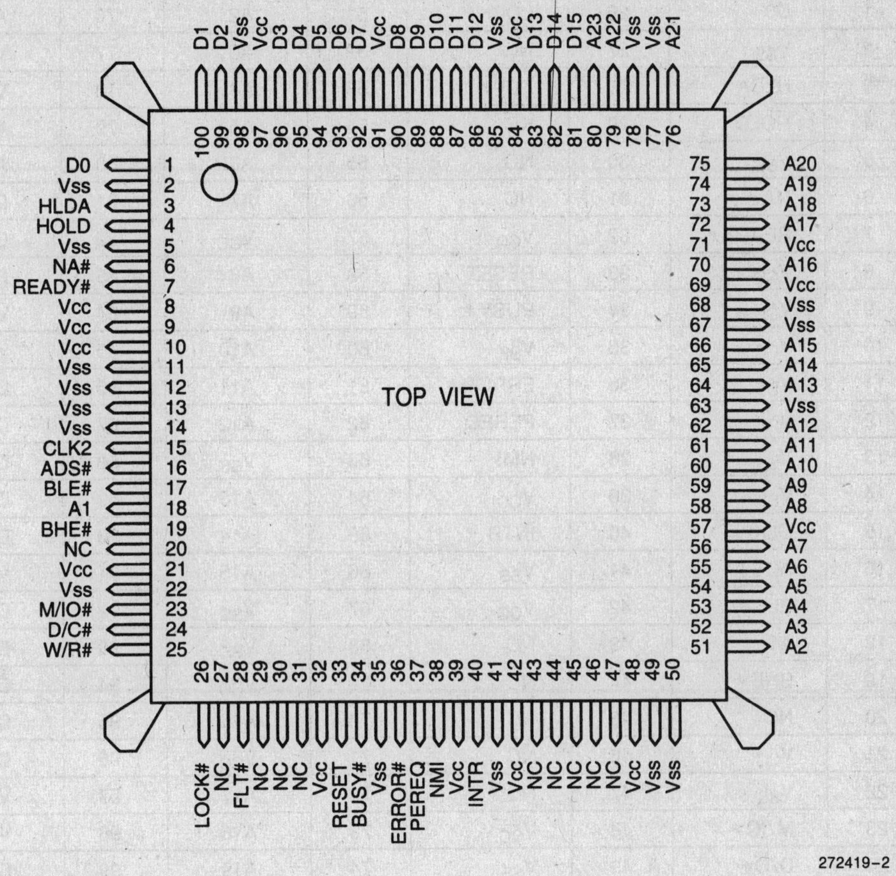

NOTE:
NC = No Connection

Figure 2. Intel386™ SX Microprocessor Pin Assignment (PQFP)

4

Table 1. Pin Assignment

Pin	Symbol	Pin	Symbol	Pin	Symbol	Pin	Symbol
1	D0	26	LOCK#	51	A2	76	A21
2	V_{SS}	27	NC	52	A3	77	V_{SS}
3	HLDA	28	FLT#	53	A4	78	V_{SS}
4	HOLD	29	NC	54	A5	79	A22
5	V_{SS}	30	NC	55	A6	80	A23
6	NA#	31	NC	56	A7	81	D15
7	READY#	32	V_{CC}	57	V_{CC}	82	D14
8	V_{CC}	33	RESET	58	A8	83	D13
9	V_{CC}	34	BUSY#	59	A9	84	V_{CC}
10	V_{CC}	35	V_{SS}	60	A10	85	V_{SS}
11	V_{SS}	36	ERROR#	61	A11	86	D12
12	V_{SS}	37	PEREQ	62	A12	87	D11
13	V_{SS}	38	NMI	63	V_{SS}	88	D10
14	V_{SS}	39	V_{CC}	64	A13	89	D9
15	CLK2	40	INTR	65	A14	90	D8
16	ADS#	41	V_{SS}	66	A15	91	V_{CC}
17	BLE#	42	V_{CC}	67	V_{SS}	92	D7
18	A1	43	NC	68	V_{SS}	93	D6
19	BHE#	44	NC	69	V_{CC}	94	D5
20	NC	45	NC	70	A16	95	D4
21	V_{CC}	46	NC	71	V_{CC}	96	D3
22	V_{SS}	47	NC	72	A17	97	V_{CC}
23	M/IO#	48	V_{CC}	73	A18	98	V_{SS}
24	D/C#	49	V_{SS}	74	A19	99	D2
25	W/R#	50	V_{SS}	75	A20	100	D1

2.0 PIN DESCRIPTIONS

Table 2 lists the Intel386 SX Microprocessor pin descriptions. The following definitions are used in the pin descriptions:

- # The named signal is active low.
- I Input signal.
- O Output signal.
- I/O Input and Output signal.
- P Power pin.
- G Ground pin.

Table 2. Pin Descriptions

Symbol	Type	Pin	Name and Function
A23:1	O	80–79, 76–72, 70, 66, 64, 62–58, 56–51, 18	**Address Bus** outputs physical memory or port I/O addresses.
ADS#	O	16	**Address Status** indicates that the processor is driving a valid bus-cycle definition and address onto its pins (W/R#, D/C#, M/IO#, BHE#, BLE#, and A23:1).
BHE#	O	19	**Byte High Enable** indicates that the processor is transferring a high data byte.
BLE#	O	17	**Byte Low Enable** indicates that the processor is transferring a low data byte.
BUSY#	I	34	**Busy** indicates that the math coprocessor is busy.
CLK2	I	15	**CLK2** provides the fundamental timing for the device.
D/C#	O	24	**Data/Control** indicates whether the current bus cycle is a data cycle (memory or I/O) or a control cycle (interrupt acknowledge, halt, or code fetch). When D/C# is high, the bus cycle is a data cycle; when D/C# is low, the bus cycle is a control cycle.
D15:0	I/O	81–83, 86–90, 92–96, 99–100, 1	**Data Bus** inputs data during memory read, I/O read, and interrupt acknowledge cycles and outputs data during memory and I/O write cycles.
ERROR#	I	36	**Error** indicates that the math coprocessor has an error condition.
FLT#	I	28	**Float** forces all bidirectional and output signals, including HLDA, to a high-impedance state.
HLDA	O	3	**Bus Hold Acknowledge** indicates that the CPU has surrendered control of its local bus to another bus master.

4

Table 2. Pin Descriptions (Continued)

Symbol	Type	Pin	Name and Function
HOLD	I	4	**Bus Hold Request** allows another bus master to request control of the local bus.
INTR	I	40	**Interrupt Request** is a maskable input that causes the CPU to suspend execution of the current program and then execute an interrupt acknowledge cycle.
LOCK#	O	26	**Bus Lock** prevents other system bus masters from gaining control of the system bus while it is active (low).
M/IO#	O	23	**Memory/IO** indicates whether the current bus cycle is a memory cycle or an input/output cycle. When M/IO# is high, the bus cycle is a memory cycle; when M/IO# is low, the bus cycle is an I/O cycle.
NA#	I	6	**Next Address** requests address pipelining.
NC		20, 27, 29–31, 43–47	**No Connection** should always be left unconnected. Connecting a NC pin may cause the processor to malfunction or cause your application to be incompatible with future steppings of the device.
NMI	I	38	**Non-Maskable Interrupt Request** is a non-maskable input that causes the CPU to suspend execution of the current program and execute an interrupt acknowledge function.
PEREQ	I	37	**Processor Extension Request** indicates that the math coprocessor has data to transfer to the processor.
READY#	I	7	**Bus Ready** indicates that the current bus cycle is finished and the external device is ready to accept more data from the processor.
RESET	I	33	**RESET** suspends any operation in progress and places the processor into a known reset state.
W/R#	O	25	**Write/Read** indicates whether the current bus cycle is a write cycle or a read cycle. When W/R# is high, the bus cycle is a write cycle; when W/R# is low, it is a read cycle.
V_{CC}	P	8–10, 21, 32, 39, 42, 48, 57, 69, 71, 84, 91, 97	**System Power** provides the nominal DC supply input.
V_{SS}	G	2, 5, 11–14, 22 35, 41, 49–50, 63, 67–68, 77–78, 85, 98	**System Ground** provides the 0V connection from which all inputs and outputs are measured.

3.0 DESIGN CONSIDERATIONS

This section describes the Static Intel386 SX Microprocessor's Instruction Set and its component and revision identifiers.

3.1 Instruction Set

The Static Intel386 SX Microprocessor uses the same instruction set as the dynamic Intel386 SX Microprocessor. However, the Static Intel386 SX Microprocessor requires more clock cycles than the dynamic Intel386 SX Microprocessor to execute some instructions. Table 3 lists these instructions and the Static Intel386 SX Microprocessor CPI. For the equivalent dynamic Intel386 SX Microprocessor CPI, refer to the "Instruction Set Clock Count Summary" table in the *Intel386 SX Microprocessor* data sheet (order number 240187).

3.2 Component and Revision Identifiers

To assist users, the microprocessor holds a component identifier and revision identifier in its DX register after reset. The upper 8 bits of DX hold the component identifier, 23H. (The lower nibble, 03H, identifies the Intel386 Architecture, while the upper nibble, 02H, identifies the second member of the Intel386 Microprocessor family.)

The lower 8 bits of DX hold the revision level identifier. The revision identifier will, in general, chronologically track those component steppings that are intended to have certain improvements or distinction from previous steppings. The revision identifier will track that of the Intel386 CPU whenever possible. However, the revision identifier value is not guaranteed to change with every stepping revision or to follow a completely uniform numerical sequence, depending on the type or intent of the revision or the manufacturing materials required to be changed. Intel has sole discretion over these characteristics of the component. The initial revision identifier for the Static Intel386 SX Microprocessor is 09H.

Table 3. Intel386™ SX Microprocessor Clocks Per Instruction

Instruction	Clock Count		
	Virtual 8086 Mode(1)	Real Address Mode or Virtual 8086 Mode	Protected Virtual Address Mode(3)
POPA		28	35
IN: Fixed Port Variable Port	 27 28	 14 15	 7/29 8/29
OUT: Fixed Port Variable Port	 27 28	 14 15	 7/29 9/29
INS	30	17	9/32
OUTS	31	18	10/33
REP INS	31 + 6n(2)	17 + 6n(2)	10 + 6n/32 + 6n(2)
REP OUTS	30 + 8n(2)	16 + 8n(2)	10 + 8n/31 + 8n(2)
HLT		7	7
MOV C0, reg		10	10

NOTES:
1. The clock count values in this column apply if I/O permission allows I/O to the port in virtual 8086 mode. If the I/O bit map denies permission, exception fault 13 occurs; see clock counts for the INT 3 instruction in the "Instruction Set Clock Count Summary" table in the *Intel386 SX Microprocessor* data sheet (order number 240187).
2. n = the number of times repeated.
3. When two clock counts are listed, the smaller value refers to a register operand and the larger value refers to a memory operand.

4.0 DC SPECIFICATIONS

ABSOLUTE MAXIMUM RATINGS*

Storage Temperature .... −65°C to +150°C

Case Temperature Under Bias... −65°C to +110°C

Supply Voltage with Respect to V_{SS}.. −0.5V to 6.5V

Voltage on Other Pins .... −0.5V to V_{CC} + 0.5V

OPERATING CONDITIONS*

Digital Supply Voltage (V_{CC}) ....4.5V to 5.5V

Case Temperature Under Bias (T_{CASE}) 0°C to 100°C

Operating Frequency (F_{OSC}) .....0 MHz to 25 MHz

NOTICE: This document contains information on products in the design phase of development. Do not finalize a design with this information. Revised information will be published when the product is available. Verify with your local Intel Sales office that you have the latest data sheet before finalizing a design.

**WARNING: Stressing the device beyond the "Absolute Maximum Ratings" may cause permanent damage. These are stress ratings only. Operation beyond the "Operating Conditions" is not recommended and extended exposure beyond the "Operating Conditions" may affect device reliability.*

Table 4. DC Characteristics

Symbol	Parameter	Min	Max	Unit	Test Conditions(1)
V_{IL}	Input Low Voltage	−0.3	+0.8	V	
V_{IH}	Input High Voltage	2.0	V_{CC} + 0.3	V	
V_{ILC}	CLK2 Input Low Voltage	−0.3	+0.8	V	
V_{IHC}	CLK2 Input High Voltage	V_{CC} − 0.8	V_{CC} + 0.3	V	
V_{OL}	Output Low Voltage		0.45	V	I_{OL} = 5 mA
V_{OH}	Output High Voltage	2.4 V_{CC} − 0.5		V V	I_{OH} = −1 mA I_{OH} = −0.2 mA
I_{LI}	Input Leakage Current (for all pins except PEREQ, BUSY#, FLT#, ERROR#)		±15	μA	0 ≤ VIN ≤ V_{CC}
I_{IH}	Input Leakage Current (PEREQ)		150	μA	V_{IH} = 2.4V(2)
I_{IL}	Input Leakage Current (BUSY#, FLT#, ERROR#)		−120	μA	V_{IL} = 0.45V(3)
I_{LO}	Output Leakage Current		±15	μA	0.45V ≤ V_{OUT} ≤ V_{CC}

NOTES:
1. All values except I_{CC} tested at 25 MHz operating frequency (CLK = 25 MHz, CLK2 = 50 MHz).
2. PEREQ input has an internal weak pull-down resistor.
3. BUSY#, FLT# and ERROR# inputs each have an internal weak pull-up resistor.
4. I_{CC} max and I_{CCF} max measurement at worst-case frequency, V_{CC} and temperature, with 50 pF output load.
5. I_{CC} typ and I_{CCF} typ are measured at nominal V_{CC} and are not fully tested.
6. Not fully tested.

Table 4. DC Characteristics (Continued)

Symbol	Parameter	Min	Max	Unit	Test Conditions(1)
I_{CC}	Supply Current CLK2 = 50 MHz, CLK = 25 MHz		280	mA	(Notes 4, 5) typ = 210 mA
I_{CCF}	Standby Current (Freeze Mode)		TBD	μA	I_{CCF} typ = 20 μA(5)
C_{IN}	Input Capacitance		10	pF	F_C = 1 MHz(6)
C_{OUT}	Output or I/O Capacitance		12	pF	F_C = 1 MHz(6)
C_{CLK}	CLK2 Capacitance		20	pF	F_C = 1 MHz(5)

NOTES:
1. All values except I_{CC} tested at 25 MHz operating frequency (CLK = 25 MHz, CLK2 = 50 MHz).
2. PEREQ input has an internal weak pull-down resistor.
3. BUSY#, FLT# and ERROR# inputs each have an internal weak pull-up resistor.
4. I_{CC} max and I_{CCF} max measurement at worst-case frequency, V_{CC} and temperature, with 50 pF output load.
5. I_{CC} typ and I_{CCF} typ are measured at nominal V_{CC} and are not fully tested.
6. Not fully tested.

5.0 AC SPECIFICATIONS

Table 5 lists output delays, input setup requirements, and input hold requirements. All AC specifications are relative to the CLK2 rising edge crossing the 2.0V level.

Figure 3 shows the measurement points for AC specifications. Inputs must be driven to the indicated voltage levels when AC specifications are measured. Output delays are specified with minimum and maximum limits measured as shown. The minimum delay times are hold times provided to external circuitry. Input setup and hold times are specified as minimums, defining the smallest acceptable sampling window. Within the sampling window, a synchronous input signal must be stable for correct operation.

Outputs ADS#, W/R#, D/C#, MI/O#, LOCK#, BHE#, BLE#, A23:1, and HLDA change only at the beginning of phase one. D15:0 (write cycles) change only at the beginning of phase two.

The READY#, HOLD, BUSY#, ERROR#, PEREQ, FLT# and D15:0 (read cycles) inputs are sampled at the beginning of phase one. The NA#, INTR and NMI inputs are sampled at the beginning of phase two.

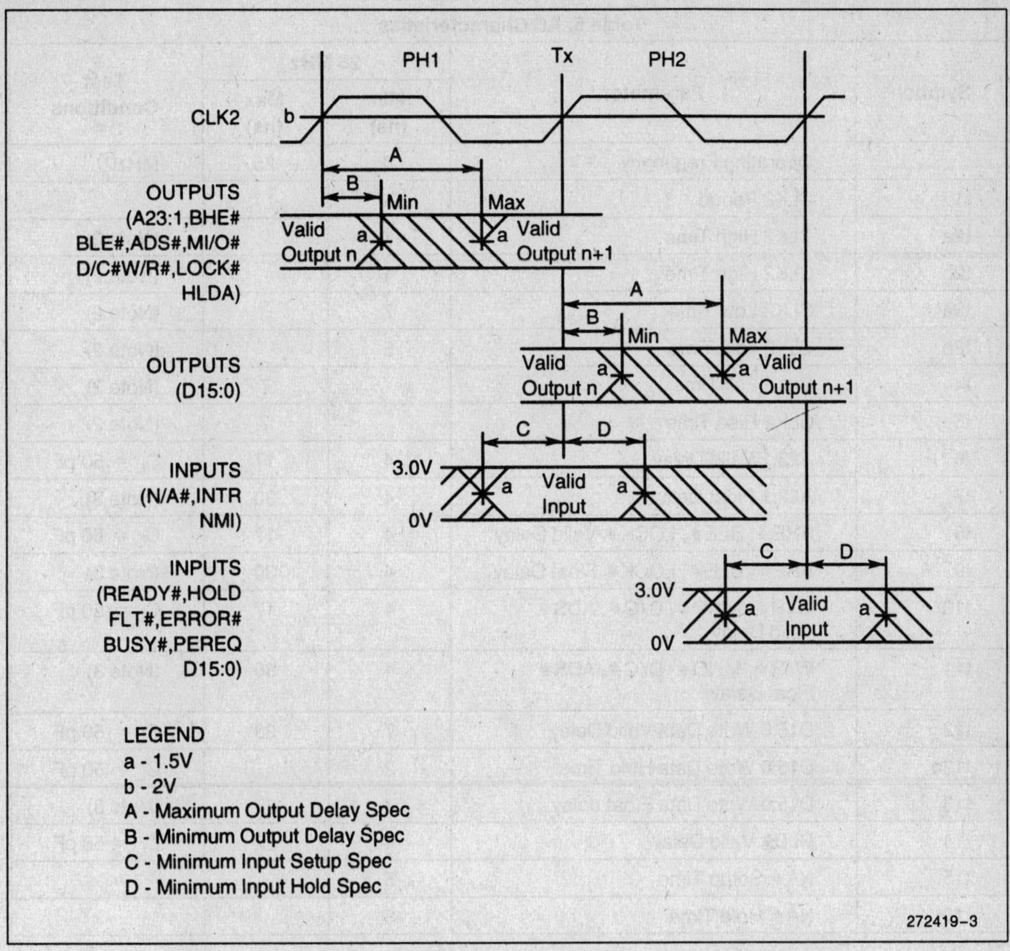

PH1 Tx PH2

CLK2 b

OUTPUTS (A23:1,BHE# BLE#,ADS#,MI/O# D/C#W/R#,LOCK# HLDA)

A B Min Max Valid Output n a a Valid Output n+1

OUTPUTS (D15:0)

A B Min Max Valid Output n a a Valid Output n+1

INPUTS (N/A#,INTR NMI)

C D 3.0V 0V a Valid Input a

INPUTS (READY#,HOLD FLT#,ERROR# BUSY#,PEREQ D15:0)

C D 3.0V 0V a Valid Input a

LEGEND
a - 1.5V
b - 2V
A - Maximum Output Delay Spec
B - Minimum Output Delay Spec
C - Minimum Input Setup Spec
D - Minimum Input Hold Spec

272419–3

Figure 3. Drive Levels and Measurement Points for AC Specifications

4

Table 5. AC Characteristics

Symbol	Parameter	25 MHz		Test Conditions
		Min (ns)	Max (ns)	
	Operating Frequency	0	25	MHz[1]
t1	CLK2 Period	20		
t2a	CLK2 High Time	7		(Note 2)
t2b	CLK2 High Time	4		(Note 2)
t3a	CLK2 Low Time	7		(Note 2)
t3b	CLK2 Low Time	5		(Note 2)
t4	CLK2 Fall Time		7	(Note 2)
t5	CLK2 Rise Time		7	(Note 2)
t6	A23:1 Valid Delay	4	17	C_L = 50 pF
t7	A23:1 Float Delay	4	30	(Note 3)
t8	BHE#, BLE#, LOCK# Valid Delay	4	17	C_L = 50 pF
t9	BHE#, BLE#, LOCK# Float Delay	4	30	(Note 3)
t10	W/R#, M/IO#, D/C#, ADS# Valid Delay	4	17	C_L = 50 pF
t11	W/R#, M/IO#, D/C#, ADS# Float Delay	4	30	(Note 3)
t12	D15:0 Write Data Valid Delay	7	23	C_L = 50 pF
t12a	D15:0 Write Data Hold Time	2		C_L = 50 pF
t13	D15:0 Write Data Float delay	4	22	(Note 3)
t14	HLDA Valid Delay	4	22	C_L = 50 pF
t15	NA# Setup Time	5		
t16	NA# Hold Time	3		

NOTES:
1. Tested at maximum operating frequency and guaranteed by design characterization at lower operating frequencies.
2. These are not tested. They are guaranteed by characterization.
3. Float condition occurs when maximum output current becomes less than I_{LO} in magnitude. Float delay is not fully tested.
4. These inputs may be asynchronous to CLK2. The setup and hold specifications are given for testing purposes to ensure recognition within a specific CLK2 period.

Table 5. AC Characteristics (Continued)

Symbol	Parameter	25 MHz		Test Conditions
		Min (ns)	Max (ns)	
t19	READY# Setup Time	9		
t20	READY# Hold Time	4		
t21	D15:0 Read Setup Time	7		
t22	D15:0 Read Hold Time	5		
t23	HOLD Setup Time	9		
t24	HOLD Hold Time	3		
t25	RESET Setup Time	8		
t26	RESET Hold Time	3		
t27	NMI, INTR Setup Time	6		(Note 4)
t28	NMI, INTR Hold Time	6		(Note 4)
t29	PEREQ, ERROR#, BUSY#, FLT# Setup Time	6		(Note 4)
t30	PEREQ, ERROR#, BUSY#, FLT# Hold Time	5		(Note 4)

NOTES:
1. Tested at maximum operating frequency and guaranteed by design characterization at lower operating frequencies.
2. These are not tested. They are guaranteed by characterization.
3. Float condition occurs when maximum output current becomes less than I_{LO} in magnitude. Float delay is not fully tested.
4. These inputs may be asynchronous to CLK2. The setup and hold specifications are given for testing purposes to ensure recognition within a specific CLK2 period.

4

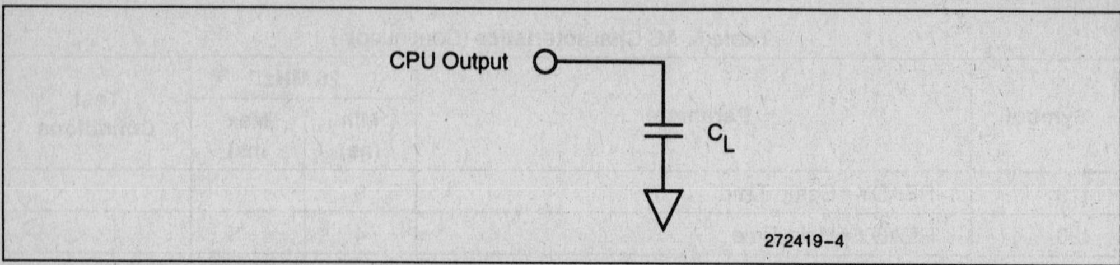

Figure 4. AC Test Loads

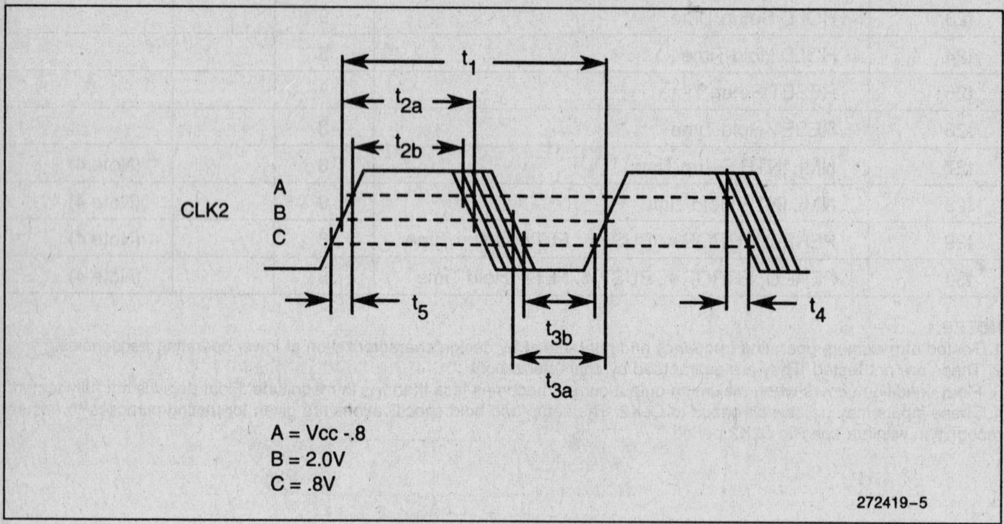

Figure 5. CLK2 Waveform

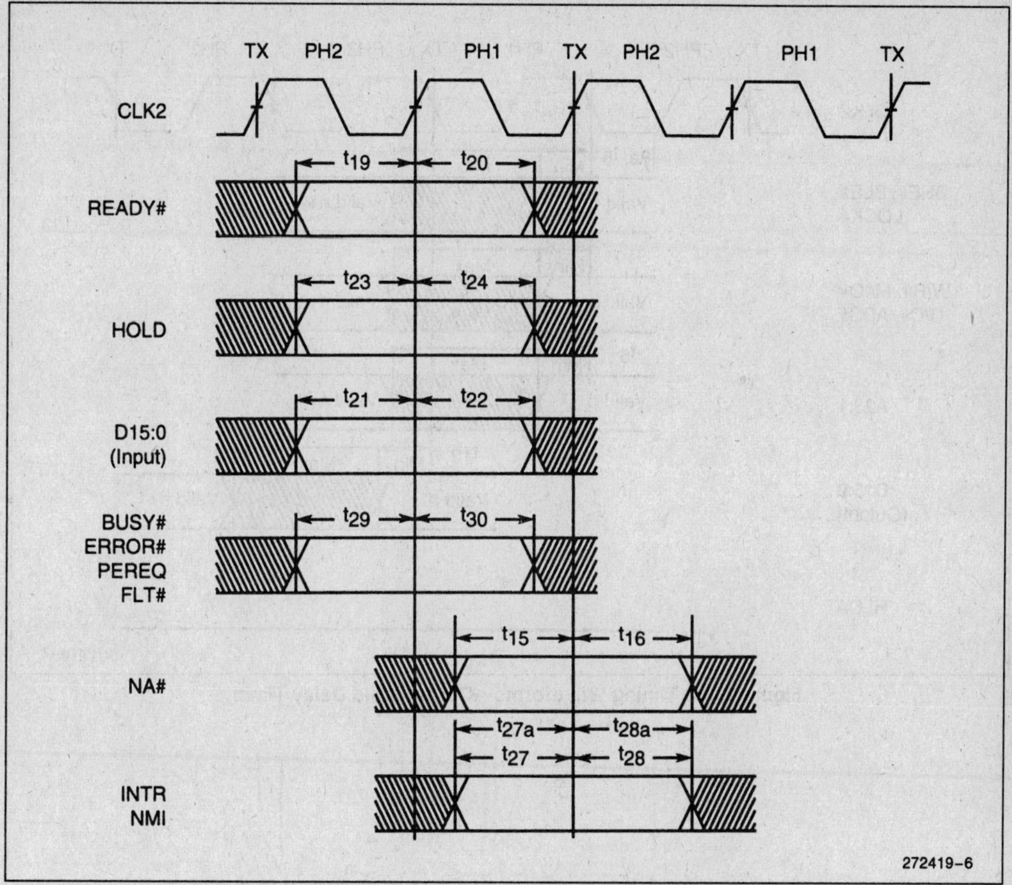

Figure 6. AC Timing Waveforms—Input Setup and Hold Timing

4

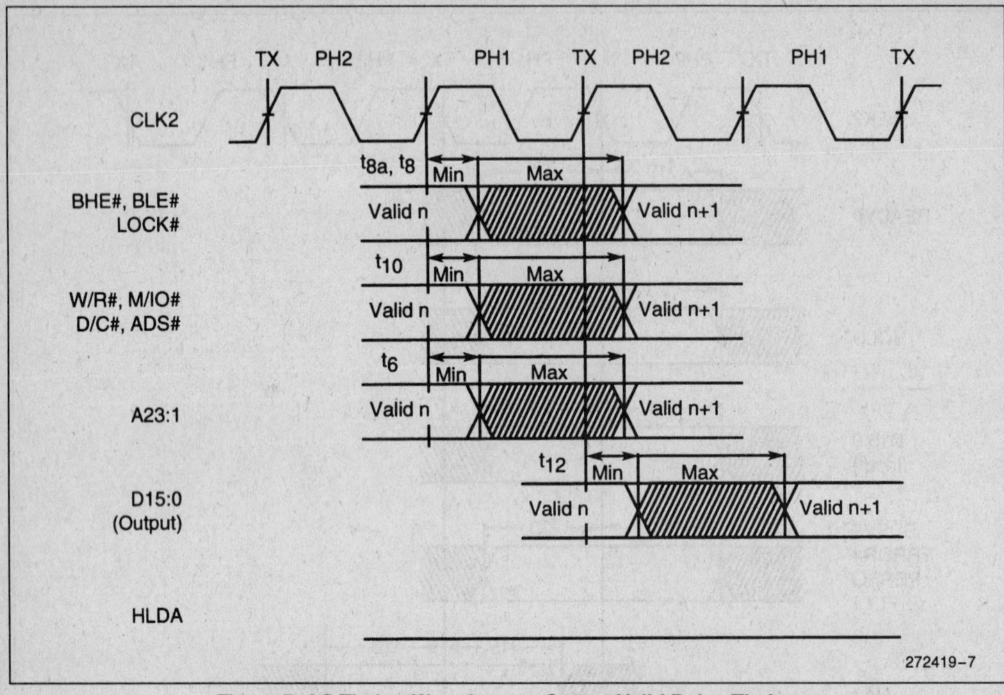

Figure 7. AC Timing Waveforms—Output Valid Delay Timing

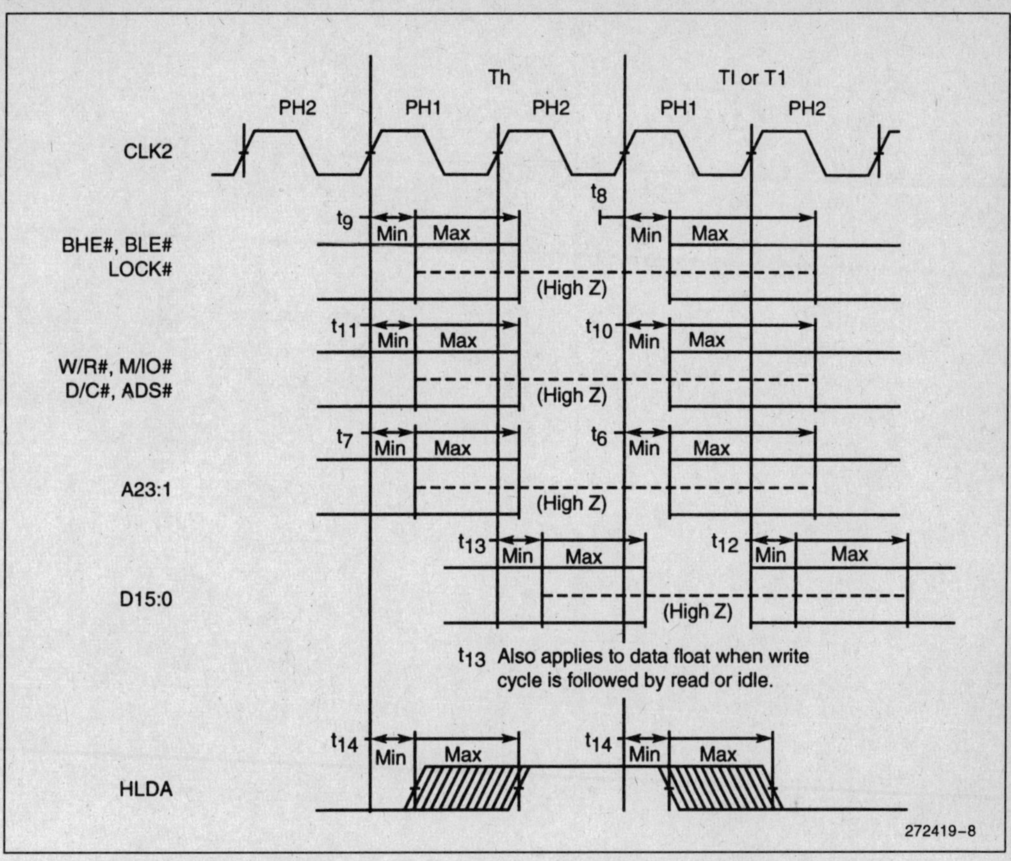

Th
TI or T1
PH2
PH1
PH2
PH1
PH2
CLK2
t_8
t_9
Min
Max
Min
Max
BHE#, BLE#
LOCK#
(High Z)
t_{11}
Min
Max
t_{10}
Min
Max
W/R#, M/IO#
D/C#, ADS#
(High Z)
t_7
Min
Max
t_6
Min
Max
A23:1
(High Z)
t_{13}
Min
Max
t_{12}
Min
Max
D15:0
(High Z)
t_{13} Also applies to data float when write cycle is followed by read or idle.
t_{14}
Min
Max
t_{14}
Min
Max
HLDA
272419–8

Figure 8. AC Timing Waveforms—Output Float Delay and HLDA Valid Delay Timing

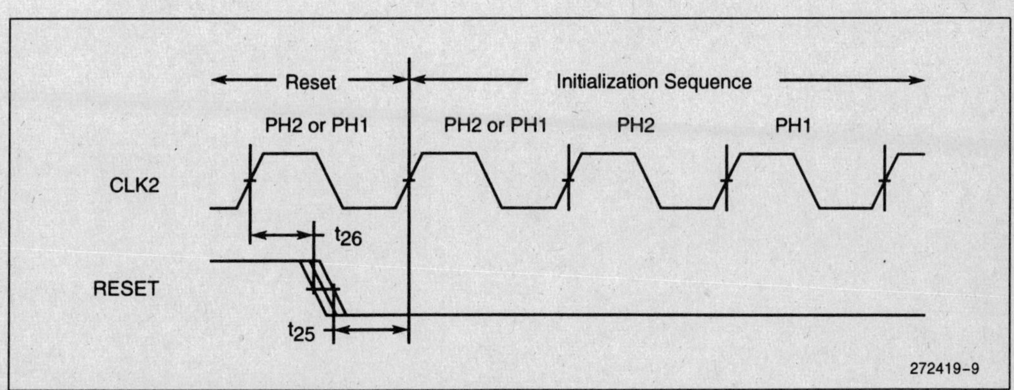

Figure 9. AC Timing Waveforms—RESET Setup and Hold Timing and Internal Phase

NORTH AMERICAN SALES OFFICES

ALABAMA

Intel Corp.
600 Boulevard South
Suite 104-I
Huntsville 35802
Tel: (800) 628-8686
FAX: (205) 883-3511

ARIZONA

†Intel Corp.
410 North 44th Street
Suite 500
Phoenix 85008
Tel: (800) 628-8686
FAX: (602) 244-0446

CALIFORNIA

Intel Corp.
3550 Watt Avenue
Suite 140
Sacramento 95821
Tel: (800) 628-8686
FAX: (916) 488-1473

†Intel Corp.
9655 Granite Ridge Dr.
3rd Floor, Suite 4A
San Diego 92123
Tel: (800) 628-8686
FAX: (619) 467-2460

Intel Corp.
1781 Fox Drive
San Jose 95131
Tel: (800) 628-8686
FAX: (408) 441-9540

*†Intel Corp.
1551 N. Tustin Avenue
Suite 800
Santa Ana 92701
Tel: (800) 628-8686
TWX: 910-595-1114
FAX: (714) 541-9157

†Intel Corp.
15260 Ventura Boulevard
Suite 360
Sherman Oaks 91403
Tel: (800) 628-8686
FAX: (818) 995-6624

COLORADO

*†Intel Corp.
600 S. Cherry St.
Suite 700
Denver 80222
Tel: (800) 628-8686
TWX: 910-931-2289
FAX: (303) 322-8670

CONNECTICUT

†Intel Corp.
103 Mill Plain Road
Danbury 06811
Tel: (800) 628-8686
FAX: (203) 794-0339

FLORIDA

†Intel Corp.
800 Fairway Drive
Suite 160
Deerfield Beach 33441
Tel: (800) 628-8686
FAX: (305) 421-2444

Intel Corp.
2250 Lucien Way
Suite 100, Room 8
Maitland 32751
Tel: (800) 628-8686
FAX: (407) 660-1283

GEORGIA

†Intel Corp.
20 Technology Parkway
Suite 150
Norcross 30092
Tel: (800) 628-8686
FAX: (404) 605-9762

IDAHO

Intel Corp.
9456 Fairview Ave., Suite C
Boise 83704
Tel: (800) 628-8686
FAX: (208) 377-1052

ILLINOIS

*†Intel Corp.
Woodfield Corp. Center III
300 N. Martingale Road
Suite 400
Schaumburg 60173
Tel: (800) 628-8686
FAX: (708) 706-9762

INDIANA

†Intel Corp.
8910 Purdue Road
Suite 350
Indianapolis 46268
Tel: (800) 628-8686
FAX: (317) 875-8938

MARYLAND

*†Intel Corp.
10010 Junction Dr.
Suite 200
Annapolis Junction 20701
Tel: (800) 628-8686
FAX: (410) 206-3678

MASSACHUSETTS

*†Intel Corp.
Westford Corp. Center
5 Carlisle Road
2nd Floor
Westford 01886
Tel: (800) 628-8686
TWX: 710-343-6333
FAX: (508) 692-7867

MICHIGAN

†Intel Corp.
7071 Orchard Lake Road
Suite 100
West Bloomfield 48322
Tel: (800) 628-8686
FAX: (313) 851-8770

MINNESOTA

†Intel Corp.
3500 W. 80th St.
Suite 360
Bloomington 55431
Tel: (800) 628-8686
TWX: 910-576-2867
FAX: (612) 831-6497

NEW JERSEY

Intel Corp.
2001 Route 46, Suite 310
Parsippany 07054-1315
Tel: (800) 628-8686
FAX: (201) 402-4893

*†Intel Corp.
Lincroft Office Center
125 Half Mile Road
Red Bank 07701
Tel: (800) 628-8686
FAX: (908) 747-0983

NEW YORK

*Intel Corp.
850 Crosskeys Office Park
Fairport 14450
Tel: (800) 628-8686
TWX: 510-253-7391
FAX: (716) 223-2561

†Intel Corp.
300 Westage Business Center
Suite 230
Fishkill 12524
Tel: (800) 628-8686
FAX: (914) 897-3125

*†Intel Corp.
2950 Express Dr., South
Suite 130
Islandia 11722
Tel: (800) 628-8686
TWX: 510-227-6236
FAX: (516) 348-7939

OHIO

*Intel Corp.
56 Milford Dr., Suite 205
Hudson 44236
Tel: (800) 628-8686
FAX: (216) 528-1026

*†Intel Corp.
3401 Park Center Drive
Suite 220
Dayton 45414
Tel: (800) 628-8686
TWX: 810-450-2528
FAX: (513) 890-8658

OKLAHOMA

Intel Corp.
6801 N. Broadway
Suite 115
Oklahoma City 73162
Tel: (800) 628-8686
FAX: (405) 840-9819

OREGON

†Intel Corp.
15254 N.W. Greenbrier Pkwy.
Building B
Beaverton 97006
Tel: (800) 628-8686
TWX: 910-467-8741
FAX: (503) 645-8181

PENNSYLVANIA

*†Intel Corp.
925 Harvest Drive
Suite 200
Blue Bell 19422
Tel: (800) 628-8686
FAX: (215) 641-0785

SOUTH CAROLINA

Intel Corp.
7403 Parklane Rd., Suite 3
Columbia 29223
Tel: (800) 628-8686
FAX: (803) 788-7999

Intel Corp.
100 Executive Center Drive
Suite 109, B183
Greenville 29615
Tel: (800) 628-8686
FAX: (803) 297-3401

TEXAS

†Intel Corp.
8911 N. Capital of Texas Hwy.
Suite 4230
Austin 78759
Tel: (800) 628-8686
FAX: (512) 338-9335

*†Intel Corp.
5000 Quorum Drive
Suite 750
Dallas 75240
Tel: (800) 628-8686

*†Intel Corp.
20515 SH 249
Suite 401
Houston 77070
Tel: (800) 628-8686
TWX: 910-881-2490
FAX: (713) 988-3660

UTAH

†Intel Corp.
428 East 6400 South
Suite 135
Murray 84107
Tel: (800) 628-8686
FAX: (801) 268-1457

WASHINGTON

†Intel Corp.
2800 156th Avenue S.E.
Suite 105
Bellevue 98007
Tel: (800) 628-8686
FAX: (206) 746-4495

WISCONSIN

Intel Corp.
400 N. Executive Dr.
Suite 401
Brookfield 53005
Tel: (800) 628-8686
FAX: (414) 789-2746

CANADA

BRITISH COLUMBIA

Intel Semiconductor of Canada, Ltd.
999 Canada Place
Suite 404, #11
Vancouver V6C 3E2
Tel: (800) 628-8686
FAX: (604) 844-2813

ONTARIO

†Intel Semiconductor of Canada, Ltd.
2650 Queensview Drive
Suite 250
Ottawa K2B 8H6
Tel: (800) 628-8686
FAX: (613) 820-5936

†Intel Semiconductor of Canada, Ltd.
190 Attwell Drive
Suite 500
Rexdale M9W 6H8
Tel: (800) 628-8686
FAX: (416) 675-2438

QUEBEC

†Intel Semiconductor of Canada, Ltd.
1 Rue Holiday
Suite 320
Tour East
Pt. Claire H9R 5N3
Tel: (800) 628-8686
FAX: 514-694-0064

†Sales and Service Office
*Field Application Location

NORTH AMERICAN DISTRIBUTORS

ALABAMA

Arrow/Schweber Electronics
1015 Henderson Road
Huntsville 35806
Tel: (205) 837-6955
FAX: (205) 721-1581

Hamilton Hallmark
4890 University Square, #1
Huntsville 35816
Tel: (205) 837-8700
FAX: (205) 830-2565

MTI Systems
4950 Corporate Dr., #120
Huntsville 35805
Tel: (205) 830-9526
FAX: (205) 830-9557

Pioneer Technologies Group
4835 University Square, #5
Huntsville 35805
Tel: (205) 837-9300
FAX: (205) 837-9358

Wyle Laboratories
7800 Governers Drive
Tower Building, 2nd Floor
Huntsville 35806
Tel: (205) 830-1119
FAX: (205) 830-1520

ARIZONA

Anthem Electronics
1555 W. 10th Place, #101
Tempe 85281
Tel: (602) 966-6600
FAX: (602) 966-4826

Arrow/Schweber Electronics
2415 W. Erie Drive
Tempe 85282
Tel: (602) 431-0030
FAX: (602) 252-9109

Avnet Computer
1626 S. Edwards Drive
Tempe 85281
Tel: (602) 902-4600
FAX: (602) 902-4640

Hamilton Hallmark
4637 S. 36th Place
Phoenix 85040
Tel: (602) 437-1200
FAX: (602) 437-2348

Wyle Laboratories
4141 E. Raymond
Phoenix 85040
Tel: (602) 437-2088
FAX: (602) 437-2124

CALIFORNIA

Anthem Electronics
9131 Oakdale Ave.
Chatsworth 91311
Tel: (818) 775-1333
FAX: (818) 775-1302

Anthem Electronics
1 Oldfield Drive
Irvine 92718-2809
Tel: (714) 768-4444
FAX: (714) 768-6456

Anthem Electronics
580 Menlo Drive, #8
[illegible]
Tel: (916) 624-9744
FAX: (916) 624-9750

Anthem Electronics
9369 Carroll Park Drive
San Diego 92121
Tel: (619) 453-9005
FAX: (619) 546-7893

Anthem Electronics
1160 Ridder Park Drive
San Jose 95131
Tel: (408) 452-2219
FAX: (408) 441-4504

Arrow Commercial Systems Group
1502 Crocker Avenue
Hayward 94544
Tel: (510) 489-5371
FAX: (510) 489-9393

Arrow Commercial Systems Group
14242 Chambers Road
Tustin 92680
Tel: (714) 544-0200
FAX: (714) 731-8438

Arrow/Schweber Electronics
26707 W. Agoura Road
Calabasas 91302
Tel: (818) 880-9686
FAX: (818) 772-8930

Arrow/Schweber Electronics
48834 Kato Road, Suite 103
Fremont 94538
Tel: (510) 490-9477

Arrow/Schweber Electronics
6 Cromwell #100
Irvine 92718
Tel: (714) 838-5422
FAX: (714) 454-4206

Arrow/Schweber Electronics
9511 Ridgehaven Court
San Diego 92123
Tel: (619) 565-4800
FAX: (619) 279-8062

Arrow/Schweber Electronics
1180 Murphy Avenue
San Jose 95131
Tel: (408) 441-9700
FAX: (408) 453-4810

Avnet Computer
3170 Pullman Street
Costa Mesa 92626
Tel: (714) 641-4150
FAX: (714) 641-4170

Avnet Computer
1361B West 190th Street
Gardena 90248
Tel: (800) 426-7999
FAX: (310) 327-5389

Avnet Computer
755 Sunrise Boulevard, #150
Roseville 95661
Tel: (916) 781-2521
FAX: (916) 781-3819

Avnet Computer
1175 Bordeaux Drive, #A
Sunnyvale 94089
Tel: (408) 743-3454
FAX: (408) 743-3348

Avnet Computer
21150 Califa Street
Woodland Hills 91376
Tel: (818) 594-8301
FAX: (818) 594-8333

Hamilton Hallmark
3170 Pullman Street
Costa Mesa 92626
Tel: (714) 641-4100
FAX: (714) 641-4122

Hamilton Hallmark
1175 Bordeaux Drive, #A
Sunnyvale 94089
Tel: (408) 435-3500
FAX: (408) 745-6679

Hamilton Hallmark
4545 Viewridge Avenue
San Diego 92123
Tel: (619) 571-7540
FAX: (619) 277-6136

Hamilton Hallmark
21150 Califa St.
Woodland Hills 91367
Tel: (818) 594-0404
FAX: (818) 594-8234

Hamilton Hallmark
580 Menlo Drive, #2
Rocklin 95762
Tel: (916) 624-9781
FAX: (916) 961-0922

Pioneer Standard
5850 Canoga Blvd., #400
Woodland Hills 91367
Tel: (818) 883-4640

Pioneer Standard
217 Technology Dr., #110
Irvine 92718
Tel: (714) 753-5090

Pioneer Technologies Group
134 Rio Robles
San Jose 95134
Tel: (408) 954-9100
FAX: (408) 954-9113

Wyle Laboratories
15370 Barranca Pkwy.
Irvine 92713
Tel: (714) 753-9953
FAX: (714) 753-9877

Wyle Laboratories
15360 Barranca Pkwy., #200
Irvine 92713
Tel: (714) 753-9953
FAX: (714) 753-9877

Wyle Laboratories
2951 Sunrise Blvd., #175
Rancho Cordova 95742
Tel: (916) 638-5282
FAX: (916) 638-1491

Wyle Laboratories
9525 Chesapeake Drive
San Diego 92123
Tel: (619) 565-9171
FAX: (619) 365-0512

Wyle Laboratories
3000 Bowers Avenue
Santa Clara 95051
Tel: (408) 727-2500
FAX: (408) 727-5896

Wyle Laboratories
17872 Cowan Avenue
Irvine 92714
Tel: (714) 863-9953
FAX: (714) 263-0473

Wyle Laboratories
26010 Mureau Road, #150
Calabasas 91302
Tel: (818) 880-9000
FAX: (818) 880-5510

Zeus Arrow Electronics
6276 San Ignacio Ave., #E
San Jose 95119
Tel: (408) 629-4789
FAX: (408) 629-4792

Zeus Arrow Electronics
22700 Savi Ranch Pkwy.
Yorba Linda 92687-4613
Tel: (714) 921-9000
FAX: (714) 921-2715

COLORADO

Anthem Electronics
373 Inverness Drive South
Englewood 80112
Tel: (303) 790-4500
FAX: (303) 790-4532

Arrow/Schweber Electronics
61 Inverness Dr. East, #105
Englewood 80112
Tel: (303) 799-0258
FAX: (303) 373-5760

Hamilton Hallmark
12503 E. Euclid Drive, #20
Englewood 80111
Tel: (303) 790-1662
FAX: (303) 790-4991

Hamilton Hallmark
710 Wooten Road, #102
Colorado Springs 80915
Tel: (719) 637-0055
FAX: (719) 637-0088

Wyle Laboratories
451 E. 124th Avenue
Thornton 80241
Tel: (303) 457-9953
FAX: (303) 457-4831

CONNECTICUT

Anthem Electronics
61 Mattatuck Heights Road
Waterburg 06705
Tel: (203) 575-1575
FAX: (203) 596-3232

Arrow/Schweber Electronics
12 Beaumont Road
Wallingford 06492
Tel: (203) 265-7741
FAX: (203) 265-7988

Avnet Computer
55 Federal Road, #103
Danbury 06810
Tel: (203) 797-2880
FAX: (203) 791-9050

Hamilton Hallmark
125 Commerce Court, Unit 6
Cheshire 06410
Tel: (203) 271-2844
FAX: (203) 272-1704

Pioneer Standard
2 Trap Falls Road
Shelton 06484
Tel: (203) 929-5600

FLORIDA

Anthem Electronics
598 South Northlake Blvd., #1024
Altamonte Springs 32701
Tel: (813) 797-2900
FAX: (813) 796-4880

Arrow/Schweber Electronics
400 Fairway Drive, #102
Deerfield Beach 33441
Tel: (305) 429-8200
FAX: (305) 428-3991

Arrow/Schweber Electronics
37 Skyline Drive, #3101
Lake Mary 32746
Tel: (407) 333-9300
FAX: (407) 333-9320

Avnet Computer
3343 W. Commercial Boulevard
Bldg. C/D, Suite 107
Ft. Lauderdale 33309
Tel: (305) 730-9110
FAX: (305) 730-0368

Avnet Computer
3247 Tech Drive North
St. Petersburg 33716
Tel: (813) 573-5524
FAX: (813) 572-4324

Hamilton Hallmark
3350 N.W. 53rd St., #105-107
Ft. Lauderdale 33309
Tel: (305) 484-5482
FAX: (305) 484-2995

Hamilton Hallmark
10491 72nd St. North
Largo 34647
Tel: (813) 541-7440
FAX: (813) 544-4394

Hamilton Hallmark
7079 University Boulevard
Winter Park 32792
Tel: (407) 657-3300
FAX: (407) 678-4414

Pioneer Technologies Group
337 Northlake Blvd., #1000
Alta Monte Springs 32701
Tel: (407) 834-9090
FAX: (407) 834-0865

Pioneer Technologies Group
674 S. Military Trail
Deerfield Beach 33442
Tel: (305) 428-8877
FAX: (305) 481-2950

Pioneer Technologies Group
8031-2 Phillips Highway
Jacksonville 32256
Tel: (904) 730-0065

Wyle Laboratories
1000 112 Circle North
St. Petersburg 33716
Tel: (813) 530-3400
FAX: (813) 579-1518

GEORGIA

Arrow Commercial Systems Group
3400 C. Corporate Way
Duluth 30136
Tel: (404) 623-8825
FAX: (404) 623-8802

Arrow/Schweber Electronics
4250 E. Rivergreen Pkwy.,
Duluth 30136
Tel: (404) 497-1300
FAX: (404) 476-1493

Avnet Computer
3425 Corporate Way, #G
Duluth 30136
Tel: (404) 623-5452
FAX: (404) 476-0125

Hamilton Hallmark
3425 Corporate Way, #G &
Duluth 30136
Tel: (404) 623-5475
FAX: (404) 623-5490

Pioneer Technologies Grou
4250 C. Rivergreen Parkwa
Duluth 30136
Tel: (404) 623-1003
FAX: (404) 623-0665

Wyle Laboratories
6025 The Corners Pkwy., #
Norcross 30092
Tel: (404) 441-9045
FAX: (404) 441-9086

ILLINOIS

Anthem Electronics
1300 Remington Road, Sui
Schaumberg 60173
Tel: (708) 884-0200
FAX: (708) 885-0480

Arrow/Schweber Electronics
1140 W. Thorndale Rd.
Itasca 60143
Tel: (708) 250-0500

Avnet Computer
1124 Thorndale Avenue
Bensenville 60106
Tel: (708) 860-8572
FAX: (708) 773-7976

Hamilton Hallmark
1130 Thorndale Avenue
Bensenville 60106
Tel: (708) 860-7780
FAX: (708) 860-8530

MTI Systems
1140 W. Thorndale Avenue
Itasca 60143
Tel: (708) 250-8222
FAX: (708) 250-8275

Pioneer Standard
2171 Executive Dr., #200
Addison 60101
Tel: (708) 495-9680
FAX: (708) 495-9831

Wyle Laboratories
2055 Army Trail Road, #14
Addison 60101
Tel: (800) 853-9953
FAX: (708) 620-1610

INDIANA

Arrow/Schweber Electronics
7108 Lakeview Parkway We
Indianapolis 46268
Tel: (317) 299-2071
FAX: (317) 299-2379

Avnet Computer
485 Gradle Drive
Carmel 46032
Tel: (317) 575-8029
FAX: (317) 844-4964

Hamilton Hallmark
4275 W. 96th
Indianapolis 46268
Tel: (317) 872-8875
FAX: (317) 876-7165

Pioneer Standard
9350 Priority Way West Dr.
Indianapolis 46250
Tel: (317) 573-0880
FAX: (317) 573-0979

NORTH AMERICAN DISTRIBUTORS (Contd.)

KANSAS

Arrow/Schweber Electronics
9801 Legler Road
Lenexa 66219
Tel: (913) 541-9542
FAX: (913) 541-0328

Avnet Computer
15313 W. 95th Street
Lenexa 61219
Tel: (913) 541-7989
FAX: (913) 541-7904

Hamilton Hallmark
10809 Lakeview Avenue
Lenexa 66215
Tel: (913) 888-4747
FAX: (913) 888-0523

KENTUCKY

Hamilton Hallmark
1847 Mercer Road, #G
Lexington 40511
Tel: (800) 235-6039
FAX: (606) 288-4936

MARYLAND

Anthem Electronics
7168A Columbia Gateway Drive
Columbia 21046
Tel: (410) 995-6640
FAX: (410) 290-9862

Arrow Commercial Systems Group
200 Perry Parkway
Gaithersburg 20877
Tel: (301) 670-1600
FAX: (301) 670-0188

Arrow/Schweber Electronics
9800J Patuxent Woods Dr.
Columbia 21046
Tel: (301) 596-7800
FAX: (301) 995-6201

Avnet Computer
7172 Columbia Gateway Dr., #G
Columbia 21045
Tel: (301) 995-3571
FAX: (301) 995-3515

Hamilton Hallmark
10240 Old Columbia Road
Columbia 21046
Tel: (410) 988-9800
FAX: (410) 381-2036

North Atlantic Industries
Systems Division
7125 River Wood Dr.
Columbia 21046
Tel: (301) 312-5800
FAX: (301) 312-5850

Pioneer Technologies Group
15810 Gaither Road
Gaithersburg 20877
Tel: (301) 921-0660
FAX: (301) 670-6746

Wyle Laboratories
7180 Columbia Gateway Dr.
Columbia 21046
Tel: (410) 312-4844
FAX: (410) 312-4953

MASSACHUSETTS

Anthem Electronics
36 Jonspin Road
Wilmington 01887
Tel: (508) 657-5170
FAX: (508) 657-6008

Arrow/Schweber Electronics
25 Upton Dr.
Wilmington 01887
Tel: (508) 658-0900
FAX: (508) 694-1754

Avnet Computer
10 D Centennial Drive
Peabody 01960
Tel: (508) 532-9886
FAX: (508) 532-9660

Hamilton Hallmark
10 D Centennial Drive
Peabody 01960
Tel: (508) 531-7430
FAX: (508) 532-9802

Pioneer Standard
44 Hartwell Avenue
Lexington 02173
Tel: (617) 861-9200
FAX: (617) 863-1547

Wyle Laboratories
15 Third Avenue
Burlington 01803
Tel: (617) 272-7300
FAX: (617) 272-6809

MICHIGAN

Arrow/Schweber Electronics
19880 Haggerty Road
Livonia 48152
Tel: (800) 231-7902
FAX: (313) 462-2686

Avnet Computer
2876 28th Street, S.W., #5
Grandville 49418
Tel: (616) 531-9607
FAX: (616) 531-0059

Avnet Computer
41650 Garden Brook Rd. #120
Novi 48375
Tel: (313) 347-1820
FAX: (313) 347-4067

Hamilton Hallmark
44191 Plymouth Oaks Blvd., #1300
Plymouth 48170
Tel: (313) 416-5800
FAX: (313) 416-5811

Hamilton Hallmark
41650 Garden Brook Rd., #100
Novi 49418
Tel: (313) 347-4271
FAX: (313) 347-4021

Pioneer Standard
4505 Broadmoor S.E.
Grand Rapids 49512
Tel: (616) 698-1800
FAX: (616) 698-1831

Pioneer Standard
13485 Stamford
Livonia 48150
Tel: (313) 525-1800
FAX: (313) 427-3720

MINNESOTA

Anthem Electronics
7646 Golden Triangle Drive
Eden Prairie 55344
Tel: (612) 944-5454
FAX: (612) 944-3045

Arrow/Schweber Electronics
10100 Viking Drive, #100
Eden Prairie 55344
Tel: (612) 941-5280
FAX: (612) 942-7803

Avnet Computer
10000 West 76th Street
Eden Prairie 55344
Tel: (612) 829-0025
FAX: (612) 944-2781

Hamilton Hallmark
9401 James Ave South, #140
Bloomington 55431
Tel: (612) 881-2600
FAX: (612) 881-9461

Pioneer Standard
7625 Golden Triange Dr., #G
Eden Prairie 55344
Tel: (612) 944-3355
FAX: (612) 944-3794

Wyle Laboratories
1325 E. 79th Street, #1
Bloomington 55425
Tel: (612) 853-2280
FAX: (612) 853-2298

MISSOURI

Arrow/Schweber Electronics
2380 Schuetz Road
St. Louis 63141
Tel: (314) 567-6888
FAX: (314) 567-1164

Avnet Computer
741 Goddard Avenue
Chesterfield 63005
Tel: (314) 537-2725
FAX: (314) 537-4248

Hamilton Hallmark
3783 Rider Trail South
Earth City 63045
Tel: (314) 291-5350
FAX: (314) 291-0362

NEW HAMPSHIRE

Avnet Computer
2 Executive Park Drive
Bedford 03102
Tel: (800) 442-8638
FAX: (603) 624-2402

NEW JERSEY

Anthem Electronics
26 Chapin Road, Unit K
Pine Brook 07058
Tel: (201) 227-7960
FAX: (201) 227-9246

Arrow/Schweber Electronics
4 East Stow Rd., Unit 11
Marlton 08053
Tel: (609) 596-8000
FAX: (609) 596-9632

Arrow/Schweber Electronics
43 Route 46 East
Pine Brook 07058
Tel: (201) 227-7880
FAX: (201) 538-4962

Avnet Computer
1-B Keystone Ave., Bldg. 36
Cherry Hill 08003
Tel: (609) 424-8961
FAX: (609) 751-2502

Hamilton Hallmark
1 Keystone Ave., Bldg. 36
Cherry Hill 08003
Tel: (609) 424-0110
FAX: (609) 751-2552

Hamilton Hallmark
10 Lanidex Plaza West
Parsippani 07054
Tel: (201) 515-5300
FAX: (201) 515-1601

MTI Systems
43 Route 46 East
Pinebrook 07058
Tel: (201) 882-8780
FAX: (201) 539-6430

Pioneer Standard
14-A Madison Rd.
Fairfield 07006
Tel: (201) 575-3510
FAX: (201) 575-3454

Wyle Laboratories
20 Chapin Road, Bldg. 10-13
Pinebrook 07058
Tel: (201) 882-8358
FAX: (201) 882-9109

NEW MEXICO

Alliance Electronics, Inc.
10510 Research Ave.
Albuquerque 87123
Tel: (505) 292-3360
FAX: (505) 275-6392

Avnet Computer
7801 Academy Rd.
Bldg. 1, Suite 204
Albuquerque 87109
Tel: (505) 828-9725
FAX: (505) 828-0360

NEW YORK

Anthem Electronics
47 Mall Drive
Commack 11725
Tel: (516) 864-6600
FAX: (516) 493-2244

Arrow/Schweber Electronics
3375 Brighton Henrietta
Townline Rd.
Rochester 14623
Tel: (716) 427-0300
FAX: (716) 427-0735

Arrow/Schweber Electronics
20 Oser Avenue
Hauppauge 11788
Tel: (516) 231-1000
FAX: (516) 231-1072

Avnet Computer
933 Motor Parkway
Hauppauge 11788
Tel: (516) 434-7443
FAX: (516) 434-7426

Avnet Computer
2060 Townline Rd.
Rochester 14623
Tel: (716) 272-9110
FAX: (716) 272-9685

Hamilton Hallmark
933 Motor Parkway
Hauppauge 11788
Tel: (516) 434-7470
FAX: (516) 434-7491

Hamilton Hallmark
1057 E. Henrietta Road
Rochester 14623
Tel: (716) 475-9130
FAX: (716) 475-9119

Hamilton Hallmark
3075 Veterans Memorial Hwy.
Ronkonkoma 11779
Tel: (516) 737-0600
FAX: (516) 737-0838

MTI Systems
1 Penn Plaza
250 W. 34th Street
New York 10119
Tel: (212) 643-1280
FAX: (212) 643-1288

Pioneer Standard
68 Corporate Drive
Binghamton 13904
Tel: (607) 722-9300
FAX: (607) 722-9562

Pioneer Standard
60 Crossway Park West
Woodbury, Long Island 11797
Tel: (516) 921-8700
FAX: (516) 921-2143

Pioneer Standard
840 Fairport Park
Fairport 14450
Tel: (716) 381-7070
FAX: (716) 381-5955

Zeus Arrow Electronics
100 Midland Avenue
Port Chester 10573
Tel: (914) 937-7400
FAX: (914) 937-2553

NORTH CAROLINA

Arrow/Schweber Electronics
5240 Greensdairy Road
Raleigh 27604
Tel: (919) 876-3132
FAX: (919) 878-9517

Avnet Computer
2725 Millbrook Rd., #123
Raleigh 27604
Tel: (919) 790-1735
FAX: (919) 872-4972

Hamilton Hallmark
5234 Greens Dairy Road
Raleigh 27604
Tel: (919) 878-0819
FAX: (919) 878-8729

Pioneer Technologies Group
2200 Gateway Ctr. Blvd, #215
Morrisville 27560
Tel: (919) 460-1530
FAX: (919) 460-1540

OHIO

Arrow Commercial Systems Group
284 Cramer Creek Court
Dublin 43017
Tel: (614) 889-9347
FAX: (614) 889-9680

Arrow/Schweber Electronics
6573 Cochran Road, #E
Solon 44139
Tel: (216) 248-3990
FAX: (216) 248-1106

Arrow/Schweber Electronics
8200 Washington Village Dr.
Centerville 45458
Tel: (513) 435-5563
FAX: (513) 435-2049

Avnet Computer
7764 Washington Village Dr.
Dayton 45459
Tel: (513) 439-6756
FAX: (513) 439-6719

Avnet Computer
30325 Bainbridge Rd., Bldg. A
Solon 44139
Tel: (216) 349-2505
FAX: (216) 349-1894

Hamilton Hallmark
7760 Washington Village Dr.
Dayton 45459
Tel: (513) 439-6735
FAX: (513) 439-6711

Hamilton Hallmark
5821 Harper Road
Solon 44139
Tel: (216) 498-1100
FAX: (216) 248-4803

Hamilton Hallmark
777 Dearborn Park Lane, #L
Worthington 43085
Tel: (614) 888-3313
FAX: (614) 888-0767

MTI Systems
23404 Commerce Park Rd.
Beachwood 44122
Tel: (216) 464-6688
FAX: (216) 464-3564

Pioneer Standard
4433 Interpoint Boulevard
Dayton 45424
Tel: (513) 236-9900
FAX: (513) 236-8133

Pioneer Standard
4800 E. 131st Street
Cleveland 44105
Tel: (216) 587-3600
FAX: (216) 663-1004

OKLAHOMA

Arrow/Schweber Electronics
12101 E. 51st Street, #106
Tulsa 74146
Tel: (918) 252-7537
FAX: (918) 254-0917

Hamilton Hallmark
5411 S. 125th E. Ave., #305
Tulsa 74146
Tel: (918) 254-6110
FAX: (918) 254-6207

Pioneer Standard
9717 E. 42nd St., #105
Tulsa 74146
Tel: (918) 665-7840
FAX: (918) 665-1891

NORTH AMERICAN DISTRIBUTORS (Contd.)

OREGON

Almac Arrow Electronics
1885 N.W. 169th Place
Beaverton 97006
Tel: (503) 629-8090
FAX: (503) 645-0611

Anthem Electronics
9090 S.W. Gemini Drive
Beaverton 97005
Tel: (503) 643-1114
FAX: (503) 626-7928

Avnet Computer
9750 Southwest Nimbus Ave.
Beaverton 97005
Tel: (503) 627-0900
FAX: (502) 526-6242

Hamilton Hallmark
9750 S.W. Nimbus Ave.
Beaverton 97005
Tel: (503) 526-6200
FAX: (503) 641-5939

Wyle Laboratories
9640 Sunshine Court
Bldg. G, Suite 200
Beaverton 97005
Tel: (503) 643-7900
FAX: (503) 646-5466

PENNSYLVANIA

Anthem Electronics
355 Business Center Dr.
Horsham 19044
Tel: (215) 443-5150
FAX: (215) 675-9875

Avnet Computer
213 Executive Drive, #320
Mars 16046
Tel: (412) 772-1888
FAX: (412) 772-1890

Pioneer Technologies Group
259 Kappa Drive
Pittsburgh 15238
Tel: (412) 782-2300
FAX: (412) 963-8255

Pioneer Technologies Group
500 Enterprise Road
Keith Valley Business Center
Horsham 19044
Tel: (713) 530-4700

Wyle Laboratories
1 Eves Drive, #111
Marlton 08053-3185
Tel: (609) 985-7953
FAX: (609) 985-8757

TEXAS

Anthem Electronics
651 N. Plano Road, #401
Richardson 75081
Tel: (214) 238-7100
FAX: (214) 238-0237

Arrow/Schweber Electronics
11500 Metric Blvd., #160
Austin 78758
Tel: (512) 835-4180
FAX: (512) 832-5921

Arrow/Schweber Electronics
3220 Commander Dr.
Carrollton 75006
Tel: (214) 380-6464
FAX: (214) 248-7208

Arrow/Schweber Electronics
10899 Kinghurst Dr., #100
Houston 77099
Tel: (713) 530-4700

Avnet Computer
4004 Beltline, Suite 200
Dallas 75244
Tel: (214) 308-8181
FAX: (214) 308-8129

Avnet Computer
1235 North Loop West, #525
Houston 77008
Tel: (713) 867-8572
FAX: (713) 861-6851

Hamilton Hallmark
12211 Technology Blvd.
Austin 78727
Tel: (512) 258-8848
FAX: (512) 258-3777

Hamilton Hallmark
11420 Page Mill Road
Dallas 75243
Tel: (214) 553-4300
FAX: (214) 553-4395

Hamilton Hallmark
8000 Westglen
Houston 77063
Tel: (713) 781-6100
FAX: (713) 953-8420

Pioneer Standard
1826-D Kramer Lane
Austin 78758
Tel: (512) 835-4000
FAX: (512) 835-9829

Pioneer Standard
13765 Beta Road
Dallas 75244
Tel: (214) 263-3168
FAX: (214) 490-6419

Pioneer Standard
10530 Rockley Road, #100
Houston 77099
Tel: (713) 495-4700
FAX: (713) 495-5642

Wyle Laboratories
1810 Greenville Avenue
Richardson 75081
Tel: (214) 235-9953
FAX: (214) 644-5064

Wyle Laboratories
4030 West Braker Lane, #330
Austin 78758
Tel: (512) 345-8853
FAX: (512) 345-9330

Wyle Laboratories
11001 South Wilcrest, #100
Houston 77099
Tel: (713) 879-9953
FAX: (713) 879-6540

UTAH

Anthem Electronics
1279 West 2200 South
Salt Lake City 84119
Tel: (801) 973-8555
FAX: (801) 973-8909

Arrow/Schweber Electronics
1946 W. Parkway Blvd.
Salt Lake City 84119
Tel: (801) 973-6913
FAX: (801) 972-0200

Avnet Computer
1100 E. 6600 South, #150
Salt Lake City 84121
Tel: (801) 266-1115
FAX: (801) 266-0362

Hamilton Hallmark
1100 East 6600 South, #120
Salt Lake City 84121
Tel: (801) 266-2022
FAX: (801) 263-0104

Wyle Laboratories
1325 West 2200 South, #E
West Valley 84119
Tel: (801) 974-9953
FAX: (801) 972-2524

WASHINGTON

Almac Arrow Electronics
14360 S.E. Eastgate Way
Bellevue 98007
Tel: (206) 643-9992
FAX: (206) 643-9709

Anthem Electronics
19017 - 120th Ave., N.E. #102
Bothell 98011
Tel: (206) 483-1700
FAX: (206) 486-0571

Avnet Computer
17761 N.E. 78th Place
Redmond 98052
Tel: (206) 867-0160
FAX: (206) 867-0161

Hamilton Hallmark
8630 154th Avenue
Redmond 98052
Tel: (206) 881-6697
FAX: (206) 867-0159

Wyle Laboratories
15385 N.E. 90th Street
Redmond 98052
Tel: (206) 881-1150
FAX: (206) 881-1567

WISCONSIN

Arrow/Schweber Electronics
200 N. Patrick, #100
Brookfield 53045
Tel: (414) 792-0150
FAX: (414) 792-0156

Avnet Computer
20875 Crossroads Circle, #400
Waukesha 53186
Tel: (414) 784-8205
FAX: (414) 784-6006

Hamilton Hallmark
2440 S. 179th Street
New Berlin 53146
Tel: (414) 797-7844
FAX: (414) 797-9259

Pioneer Standard
120 Bishop Way #163
Brookfield 53005
Tel: (414) 784-3480
FAX: (414) 780-3613

Wyle Laboratories
W226 N555 Eastmound Drive
Waukesha 53186
Tel: (414) 521-9333
FAX: (414) 521-9498

ALASKA

Avnet Computer
1400 West Benson Blvd., #400
Anchorage 99503
Tel: (907) 274-9899
FAX: (907) 277-2639

CANADA

ALBERTA

Avnet Computer
2816 21st Street Northeast
Calgary T2E 6Z2
Tel: (403) 291-3284
FAX: (403) 250-1591

Zentronics
6815 8th Street N.E., #100
Calgary T2E 7H
Tel: (403) 295-8838
FAX: (403) 295-8714

BRITISH COLUMBIA

Almac Arrow Electronics
8544 Baxter Place
Burnaby V5A 4T8
Tel: (604) 421-2333
FAX: (604) 421-5030

Hamilton Hallmark
8610 Commerce Court
Burnaby V5A 4N6
Tel: (604) 420-4101
FAX: (604) 420-5376

Zentronics
11400 Bridgeport Rd., #108
Richmond V6X 1T2
Tel: (604) 273-5575
FAX: (604) 273-2413

ONTARIO

Arrow/Schweber Electronics
1093 Meyerside, Unit 2
Mississauga L5T 1M4
Tel: (416) 670-7769
FAX: (416) 670-7781

Arrow/Schweber Electronics
36 Antares Dr., Unit 100
Nepean K2E 7W5
Tel: (613) 226-6903
FAX: (613) 723-2018

Avnet Computer
Canada System Engineering
151 Superior Blvd.
Mississuaga L5T 2L1
Tel: (416) 795-3835
FAX: (416) 677-5091

Avnet Computer
190 Colonade Road
Nepean K2E 7J5
Tel: (613) 727-2000
FAX: (613) 226-1184

Hamilton Hallmark
151 Superior Blvd., Unit 1-6
Mississauga L5T 2L1
Tel: (416) 564-6060
FAX: (416) 564-6033

Hamilton Hallmark
190 Colonade Road
Nepean K2E 7J5
Tel: (613) 226-1700
FAX: (613) 226-1184

Zentronics
5600 Keaton Crescent, #1
Mississauga L5R 3S5
Tel: (416) 507-2600
FAX: (416) 507-2831

Zentronics
155 Colonnade Rd., South
#17
Nepean K2E 7K1
Tel: (613) 226-8840
FAX: (613) 226-6352

QUEBEC

Arrow/Schweber Electronics
1100 St. Regis Blvd.
Dorval H9P 2T5
Tel: (514) 421-7411
FAX: (514) 421-7430

Arrow/Schweber Electronics
500 Boul. St.-Jean-Baptiste A
Quebec H2E 5R9
Tel: (418) 871-7500
FAX: (418) 871-6816

Avnet Computer
2795 Reu Halpern
St. Laurent H4S 1P8
Tel: (514) 335-2483
FAX: (514) 335-2481

Hamilton Hallmark
7575 Transcanada Highway
#600
St. Laurent H4T 2V6
Tel: (514) 335-1000
FAX: (514) 335-2481

Zentronics
520 McCaffrey
St. Laurent H4T 1N3
Tel: (514) 737-9700
FAX: (514) 737-5212